W0245897

Summary of Contents

Flash MX ActionScript Designer's Reference

Sham Bhangal
John Davey
Jen deHaan
Scott Mebberson
Tim Parker
Glen Rhodes

Flash MX ActionScript Designer's Reference

© 2002 Apress

Originally published by friends of ED in 2002

All rights reserved. No part of this book may be reproduced, stored in a retrieval system or transmitted in any form or by any means, without the prior written permission of the publisher, except in the case of brief quotations embodied in critical articles or reviews.

The authors and publisher have made every effort in the preparation of this book to ensure the accuracy of the information. However, the information contained in this book is sold without warranty, either express or implied. Neither the authors, APress Media, LLC nor its dealers or distributors will be held liable for any damages caused or alleged to be caused either directly or indirectly by this book.

First Printed August 2002
First Reprint November 2002

Trademark Acknowledgements

APress Media, LLC has endeavored to provide trademark information about all the companies and products mentioned in this book by the appropriate use of capitals. However, APress Media, LLC cannot guarantee the accuracy of this information.

Additional material to this book can be downloaded from http://extras.springer.com

ISBN 978-1-59059-165-9   ISBN 978-1-4302-5147-7 (eBook)
DOI 10.1007/978-1-4302-5147-7

Flash MX ActionScript Designer's Reference

Authors
Sham Bhangal
John Davey
Jen deHann
Scott Mebberson
Tim Parker
Glen Rhodes

Reviewers
Chris Crane
Leon Cych
Brandon Houston
Minty Hunter
Todd Marks
Steve McCormick
Mike Pearce
George Shaw
Jon Steer
Eng Wei Chua
Steve Williams

Managing Editor
Sonia Mullineux

Project Manager
Vicky Idiens

Author Agent
Gaynor Riopedre

Commissioning Editor
Andy Corsham

Technical Editors
Dan Britton
Phillip Jackson
Jake Manning
Steve Rycroft
Gavin Wray

Graphic Editors
Ty Bhogal
Matt Clark
Fiona Murray
Rob Sharp

Indexer
Fiona Murray

Cover Design
Katy Freer

CD Design
Pete Aylward

CD Content
Dan Britton
Phillip Jackson

Proofing
Victoria Blackburn
Simon Collins
Chris Matterface

Jen is a fresh young Flash designer/developer in Canada. She has high ambitions, a die-hard mentality, a BFA in Art/Eduation and certification in New Media. She lives for compression, and loves Cleaner and After Effects about as much as coffee but not as much as Flash. She has enjoyed writing for and editing many books on Flash and ColdFusion with her husband Peter. Jen has two cats, and likes to think she is friendly. Her homes on the web are www.ejepo.com and www.flash-mx.com.

Before getting into Flash and Actionscript, John Davey tried everything from working overseas as a ski guide to stand-up comedy. John now works for Develop, www.developette.com, and he's lucky enough to have clients like the BBC, Disney, Robbie Williams, the Science Museum, Asda, Kellogg's, and more. He's grateful to a lot of people for their help, in particular Gaynor and Andy at friends of ED for their unfaltering support, and a few rogues disguised as developers: Barr-Watson, Beaumont, and Dawes. Most of all, he thanks his wife Jo and daughter Amy for helping him to realize that there's more to life than Flash!

Glen Rhodes started his mind going early in life, when he was about 4 years old. At that age, he began playing the piano, which was sitting unused in his house. He's been playing ever since then. Later, in 1997, he co-wrote a full-length musical called Chrystanthia. Somewhere along the way, he picked up game programming as a hobby, and eventually ended up making games professionally for home console systems. Then, in 1998, he learned how to take all of his experiences and combine them when he discovered Flash. The rest is history. Glen shares his ideas at, www.glenrhodes.com.

Author Biographies

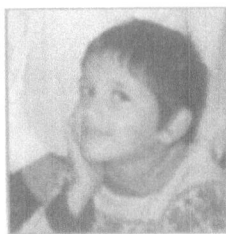

Sham Bhangal originally started out as an engineer, specializing in industrial computer based display and control systems. His spare time was partly taken up by freelance web design, something that slowly took up more and more of his time until the engineering had to go. He is now also writing for friends of ED, something that is taking more and more time away from web design—funny how life repeats itself! Sham lives in Devon, England, with his partner Karen.

From Adelaide, Australia, Scott Mebberson collaborates with developers, artists, and writers all around the world. His daily life includes writing books on Flash, and for various columns, creating experimental art, and teaching and preaching Flash to the masses. An active member of the Flash community, Scott communicates to the world via www.pixelogic.org. Scott tries to make a living from freelancing, the world over. You can reach him almost 24 hours a day at the office, www.scottmebberson.com, and he's always interested in collaboration – don't be shy, make contact! He wants to thank everyone who has helped him, most importantly, his partner Kate – she kicks arse!

Dr. Tim Parker has been working with and writing about computers for 25 years. He's written 60 books and 3,500 magazine articles. He's worked with Flash since its first release, and continues to develop Flash movies for clients around the world. Dr. Parker can be reached at tparker@tpci.com.

Flash MX Designer's ActionScript Reference

14   Feedback and Debugging   314

15   Modular Programming Techniques   340

16   Object Oriented Programming Techniques   384

Introduction

Welcome to *Flash MX Designer's ActionScript Reference.*

This book/CD package combines *the* comprehensive reference resource for Flash MX ActionScript with a rich tutorial guide to getting the best out of ActionScript in your Flash movies. We've set out to give you the most in-depth reference coverage of the language *and* a designer-oriented guide to help you use it. Our aim has been to make this book the best Flash MX ActionScript resource – the book that you'll keep on your desk and never exhaust.

What's in the Package

This package consists of two complementary elements – the printed book, and the accompanying CD.

The Book

This book has two sections:

- **A series of detailed tutorials** that place Flash MX ActionScript in the *design context*. These tutorial chapters – the first half of the book – show how to use the language practically to build the kind of Flash movies that you want to make. The initial tranche of chapters (Chapters 1 through 13) focus on the core ActionScript skills and techniques that you need to make your motion graphics really sing, while the next sequence (Chapters 14 through 17) concentrate on the programming principles that will help you make your movies and applications more robust and economical. All the chapters come with a set of illustrative FLAs, SWFs, and source code (on the CD – see below).
- **A comprehensive reference section – the Dictionary**. This comprises the second half of the book, and contains entries for *every* action, object, method, property, and function in the ActionScript language. These printed entries encapsulate the *essential* reference material that you reach for all the time when you're coding ActionScript: syntax, compatibility information, a detailed description of the element, information on when you might use it, and a quick reference table summarizing code examples/usage. There's an expanded version of this reference information on the CD.

The CD

The CD contains:

- **Three bonus tutorial chapters** (Chapters 18 through 20, in PDF format), which cover how to use Flash MX in conjunction with XML.

- **All the FLAs (plus other assorted code files and SWFs) for the tutorial chapters**.

- **A significantly expanded version of the printed Dictionary**. This is the most comprehensive and up to date ActionScript dictionary, covering all the actions, objects, methods, properties, and functions, in even more detail than the printed entries. The CD-based Dictionary provides a full and informative description, code example (also showing common mistakes), usage examples, and tips from our author team of professional Flash designers. Hundreds of these entries also have a dedicated FLA (and SWF), launchable from the Dictionary window, showing the relevant ActionScript in design-oriented use, and many also have useful images and diagrams to illustrate them further.

The Dictionary's CD interface is clean and simple: there's an A-Z listing across the top, and clicking on a letter brings up all that letter's entries in the left hand pane. Clicking on an entry there displays that entry's details in the right hand pane:

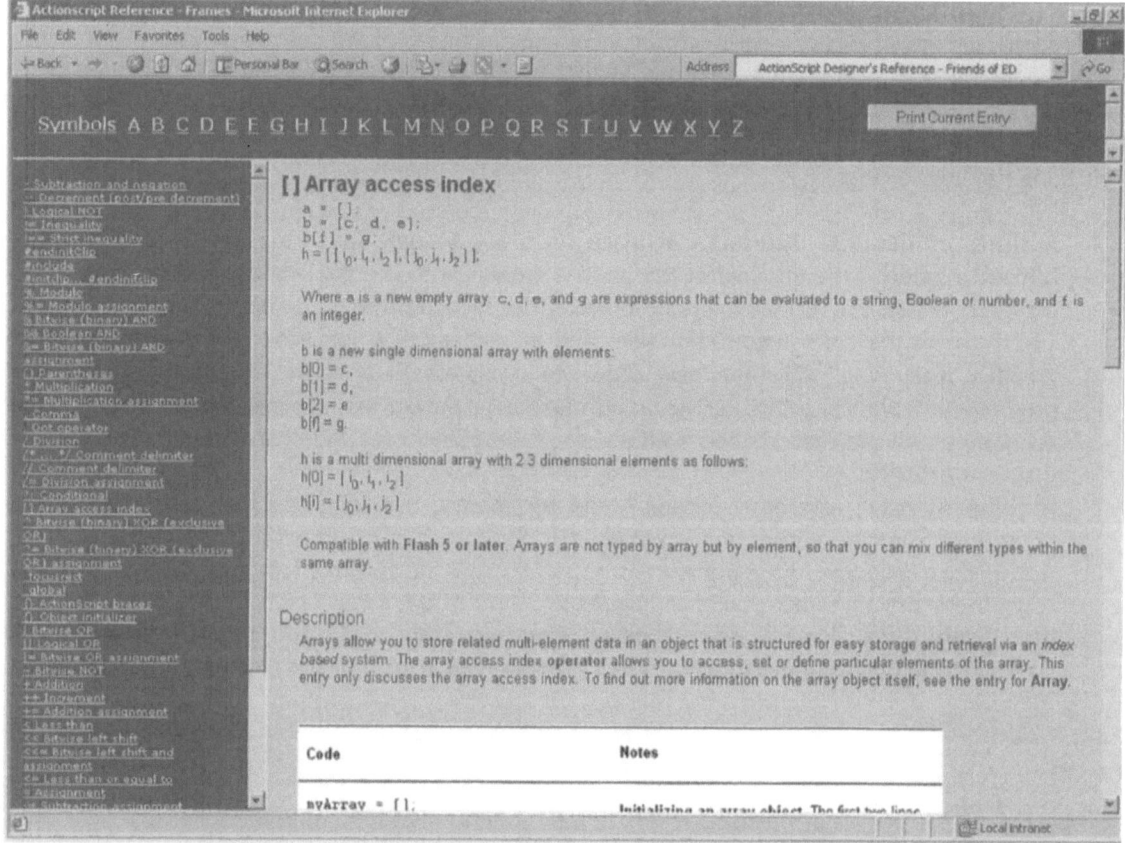

Where an entry has a supporting FLA/SWF, you can launch them from within the Dictionary interface:

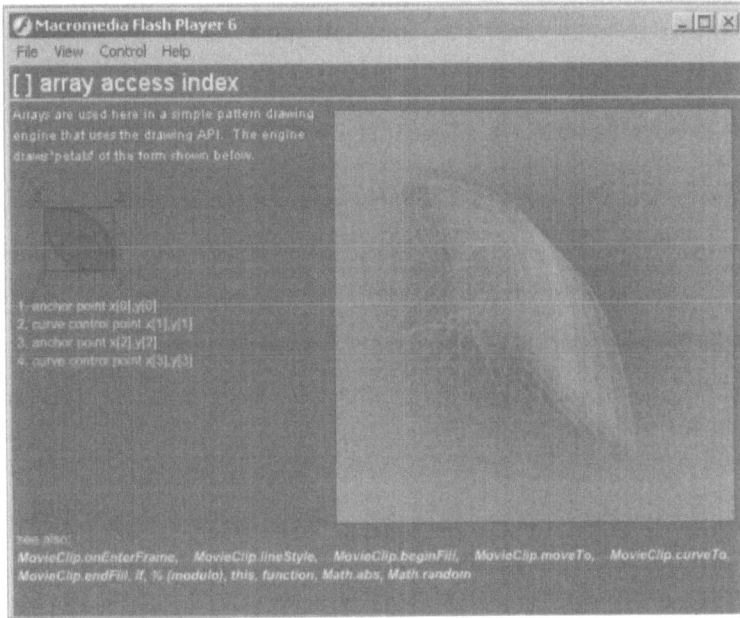

Enjoy!

Styles Used in this Book

We use some simple layout conventions to make things clearer throughout the book:

We'll use **this style** to introduce **new terms**, and to stress **important things** in the text.

We use `this style` for code that appears in text.

```
Blocks of code
Will appear in this style,
And we'll also use
This style to highlight new code,
Or code that deserves your attention
```

> When we want to draw your attention to something really important,
> we'll put it in a bubble like this.

File names will appear in this style: `object.property.swf`.

Where we're indicating that you need to input text, you'll see this style: "type monkeyBoy into the Var field".

URLs will be shown in this style: www.friendsofed.com

Menu path descriptions will appear like this: File>Open>Monkey>Banana.

Keyboard stroke sequences will be displayed in this style: F4 *and* CTRL+ALT+DEL.

Support at Friends of ED

This Friends of ED book is fully supported at www.friendsofed.com, and you can also visit our support forums for help, inspiration or just to chat.

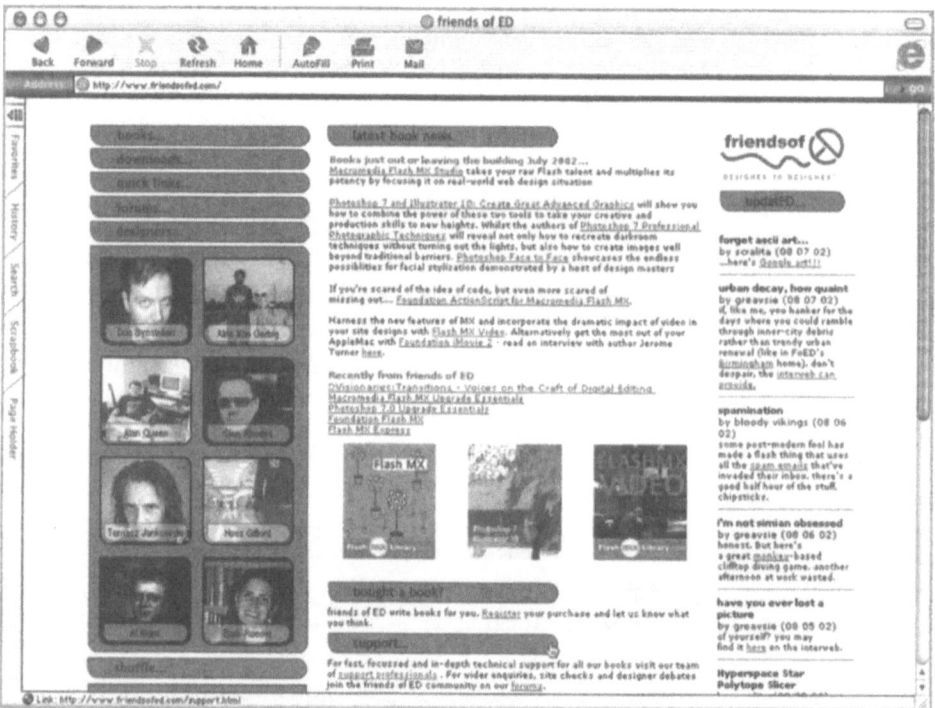

However, if you do run into trouble, and maybe have a problem with a certain file or tutorial or just get plain muddled, we're right here for you. Leave a message on the forum, use the online feedback form or drop a mail to support@friendsofed.com – we'll get you sorted in no time.

And even if you don't have problems, let us know what you think. E-mail feedback@friendsofed.com or fill out the reply card at the back of the book – that's what it's there for, and we'd love to hear from you!

MACROMEDIA

Flash MX ActionScript Designer's Reference

Sham Bhangal
John Davey
Jen deHaan
Scott Mebberson
Tim Parker
Glen Rhodes

Objectives

- Simple animation in Flash MX

- The movie clip as the foundation for ActionScript-based animation

- Integrating graphics with ActionScript

- Animating with ActionScript and the various motion-scripting properties

- Combining *manual* animation with script-based dynamics:

  - Cyclic animation

  - Duplicating and attaching movie clips at runtime

  - Kinetic effects

- Dynamic masking

- User interactions with the mouse and keyboard

Animation basics

Even newcomers to Flash are familiar with the concept of frame-based animation. With this technique, we create a graphical object of any sort on a specific frame. We can then make subtle changes to the graphics, either its shape or its position, by adding a new **keyframe** in each subsequent frame along the timeline – this is known as *frame-by-frame* animation. Alternatively, we can insert some blank frames after our initial content, move our object to a new location in a keyframe, and then **tween** the two objects into a single motion, producing a quick and easy animation of our object moving across the screen.

Take a look at `simple_tween.fla` from this chapter's source code folder – this is a very simple frame-based animation of a circle moving horizontally across the screen:

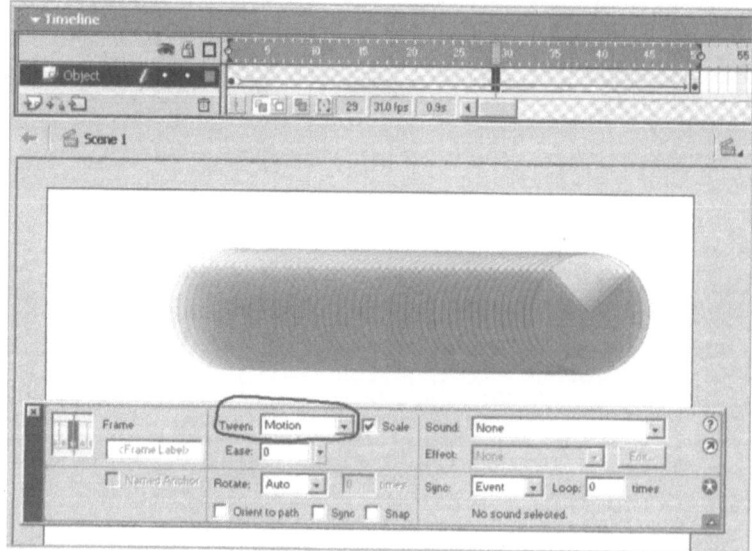

This movie is 50 frames long, and consists of a keyframe on frame 1 where the circle begins, and a second keyframe on frame 50, where the circle ends up. When we test this movie (select Control>Test Movie, or just use the keyboard shortcut by pressing CTRL+ENTER), we can see the ball takes less than a second to move from starting to ending position. Note that this animation has been achieved by using the Motion selection from the Tween drop-down menu in the Property inspector, as shown above.

Frame-based animation has both advantages and disadvantages. One of the key problems is that once the animation is made, there's very little room for variation without reanimating it, or creating several hundred different animations. What if we wanted our circle to move in a similar fashion, yet also move down a fraction every frame? Well, we could either go back and move it's position in the final keyframe down slightly, or we could simply animate the whole movie using the concept of **scripted motion**. With scripted motion, our entire movie only really has to be one frame long, and we use ActionScript code to define the details of the motion of our objects. The objects in question are called **movie clips**. Movie clips are fundamental to the use of scripted motion. Indeed, everything that we may want to do with scripted motion is applied to movie clips.

Creating a simple movie clip

Let's have a quick reminder of how movie clips are created, so that we're all speaking the same language from here on in. Open a new movie in Flash MX and, using the various drawing tools, create a simple image of your choice. After you've drawn your image, use the Arrow selection tool to select the entire graphic (or better yet, just hit CTRL+A *to select everything on the stage*). Here's my image, a smiley face in a box:

Next, go to Insert>Convert To Symbol..., or simply press F8. The Convert to Symbol dialog box will now appear. In the Name field, enter a unique name that you want to give to this movie clip. Make sure that the Movie Clip behavior radio button is selected, and your registration point is centered, then press OK:

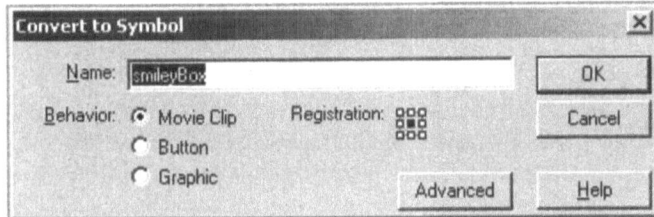

It's as easy as that! We now have a movie clip on the stage called smileyBox and, if you select Window>Library (F11 or CTRL+L), you'll see that this movie clip has even been added to the Library of your FLA:

Instance names

We're now able to make multiple copies of this movie clip, so we need a way of uniquely identifying them from each other so that we can reference them in our ActionScript code. On our stage right now, we should see only one movie clip. If we want, we can add another **instance** of the same movie clip on to the stage – just drag it from the Library and drop it on the stage (alternatively, you could copy and paste the instance that is already on the stage).

Now that we have two instances of the same movie clip on the stage, it's important to give each one its own **instance name**. Click on one of the movie clips to select it, and open up the Property inspector, if it's not already open (CTRL+F3). It is here where we must name our movie clip instances – give each box a unique and preferably simple name like box1 and box2 (take a look at smileyBoxMovieClip.fla to see this in more detail):

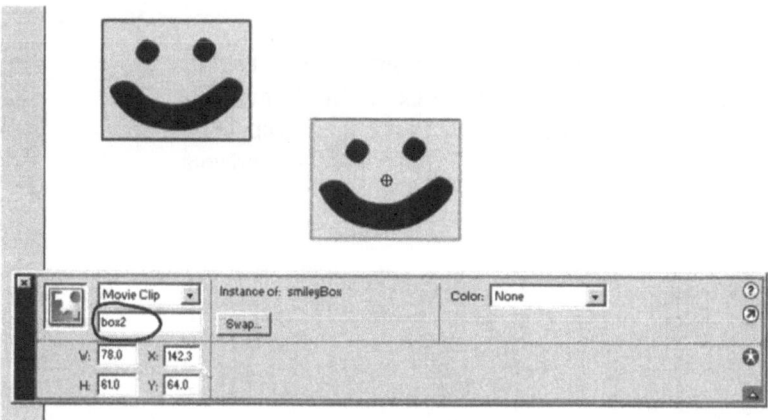

Design potential of script-based animation

Now that we know how to give our movie clips instance names, we're ready to start applying scripted motion to them. We'll get to some samples in a moment, but first let's look at a few of the possibilities and benefits of ActionScript-based motion.

We can remotely change all of the following fundamental properties of a movie clip using the appropriate ActionScript commands:

- Position

- Rotation

- Horizontal and vertical scale (to effectively stretch and squash our graphics)

- Opacity (alpha)

- Absolute visibility (on or off)

- Current frame (if the movie clip has an animated timeline of its own, we can *jump* to any frame within that timeline)

These properties represent the very basics of scripted motion and animation. So, for example, we can easily make an object that zooms around the screen, rotating and fading out, all with ActionScript code. But using ActionScript code to make visual changes on the screen is just the tip of the iceberg as far as the possibilities are concerned – as we shall soon see, our imagination is really the only limit!

That said, when first creating a design, it's worth keeping in mind that while we can move, rotate, scale, and fade any movie clip with ActionScript, we cannot control the specific shapes within a movie clip unless they themselves are also movie clips nested within the original. It's important to understand that any shape tweening animations that are within movie clips cannot be adjusted with ActionScript. A shape tween is a fixed, pre-rendered animation and the complexity of it means that it is beyond the scope of using pure ActionScript to control. Later on in this book, when we look at the drawing API of Flash MX in **Chapter 3**, we'll see how to use ActionScript to draw lines and shapes at runtime.

To animate a movie clip remotely via ActionScript we must either attach the relevant code to the specific instance of the movie clip, or call the movie clip remotely from a different timeline. Both techniques have their own advantages – by attaching code to movie clips, literally by selecting the movie clip, opening up the Actions panel, and entering our code, we are actually using the movie clip objects themselves to control their own motion. Alternatively, calling the movie clips remotely using an appropriate path description allows us to keep all of our code in one centralized place – usually the first frame in the main (or **root**) timeline. This latter method is the preferred coding practice in Flash MX; it gives us a robust, object oriented approach, forming a solid basis for all Flash scripted motion.

These concepts may seem rather vague at the moment, but everything will become clear after we go through a few examples. We'll be getting our hands dirty shortly, but first we should cover some important considerations when using ActionScript to talk to your graphical objects.

Integrating graphical elements with ActionScript

In Flash MX we'll be using the object oriented approach of building all our code on frame 1 of the main timeline, and specifying within that code the movie clip instances that we will control.

In order to 'connect' a piece of code to a movie clip, we must first specify what is known as an **event** that will trigger the code. For example, when the mouse is moved, an onMouseMove event is issued by Flash, and our movie clip can be triggered to run its motion code when this event takes place. Likewise, we might choose to use the onMouseDown event, which is triggered when the mouse button is pressed down.

The most common event is known as the onEnterFrame event, and this is where we'll be controlling most of our motion. The onEnterFrame event is triggered every time that our main timeline enters a new frame. So, if we have a movie running at 30 frames per second, then the onEnterFrame event is also triggered 30 times per second, and therefore any code linked to movie clips and triggered by the onEnterFrame event will run 30 times per second too.

With ActionScript, it's crucial to explicitly associate each command with the necessary movie clip. If, for example, we have a movie clip with the instance name myMovieClip, and it contains a multi-framed animation on its own timeline, then we can navigate through its animation with the use of some simple ActionScript commands, which move the playhead around. As a teaser of what's to come, let's take a look at how we'd link up some of the more common actions to our movie clip:

- **stop**() – myMovieClip.stop() tells myMovieClip to stop playing, wherever it is in its timeline. If we have this code at the very beginning of our movie, then when our movie clip begins it will immediately stop on frame 1.

- **gotoAndStop**() – myMovieClip.gotoAndStop(5) tells myMovieClip to jump to frame 5 of its timeline, and then stop playing.

- **gotoAndPlay**() – myMovieClip.gotoAndPlay(5) tells myMovieClip to jump to frame 5 of its timeline, and then continue playing along.

- **nextFrame**() – myMovieClip.nextFrame() tells myMovieClip to move to the next frame in its timeline and stop there.

- **prevFrame**() – myMovieClip.prevFrame() tells myMovieClip to move to the previous frame in its timeline and stop there.

If we were to use any of these actions from frame 1 of the root timeline without a defined path using the dot notation prefix and a target object (usually a movie clip), then we'd be referring to the timeline of our main movie. This dot notation introduces the notion of **scope** to our Flash MX scripting.

Scope and the global level

One of the most important concepts to remember when working with Flash MX ActionScript is the scope of your functions and variables. Exactly where we put the ActionScript in our programs determines just how many objects within our movie can *see*, or access, that code without having to specify where to look.

In a typical movie, we will enter our ActionScript code into frame 1 of the root timeline. This code is said to exist on the root timeline. For example, if we have the following code attached to frame 1 of the root timeline:

```
a = 11;
b = 23;
username = "bob";
```

then these variables could be accessed anywhere from within our movie by specifying a, b, and username. We use dot notation to refer to our variables from other locations, with the formula location-dot-item. For instance, _root refers to the root timeline where the variable is located, and username is the item where talking about (a variable in this case, but it can also be a function, as we'll see later).

Scope comes into play when we consider *where* the variables are being called from. If we had code that was within the root timeline, and it was referring to a variable within myMovieClip, say varName, then we would be required to include the movie clip's name in the dot notation path and write `myMovieClip.varName`.

On the other hand, if we were accessing variables defined in `myMovieClip` from within the `myMovieClip` code, we would only be required to write the variable name itself. It is, however, good practice to use the word `this` when referring to an object's own variables from within that object. This will be easier to understand when we start to use functions and events – in fact, the scope of a function is such that we *must* use `this` in order to make them work properly.

There is another important level of scope called **global**. When an object or variable is declared within the _global scope then it can be accessed from *anywhere* in our movie without needing any dot notation precursor.

If, for example, we declared the following global variable on frame 1 of the root timeline:

```
_global.gUsername = "Administrator1";
```

then we can simply write `gUsername` anywhere in our movie's code and, no matter which timeline we're in, it will always return `Administrator1` as the value. Note that when declaring global variables it is very good practice to give them a prefix ('g', for example) to distinguish them from normal variables. Similarly, if we had the following declaration on frame 1 of `myMovieClip`:

```
_global.gMyMovieClipUserName = "Administrator2";
```

then `gMyMovieClipUserName` could be used anywhere in our movie, even on the root timeline, to return `Administrator2`. The global definition is useful if we want to create a variable or function, and then just forget about its scope.

The table below summarizes the most important rules regarding the scope of a variable:

Variable name	Location of declaration	Referenced from root timeline	Referenced from `myMovieClip`
`myVariable`	Root timeline	`myVariable`	`_root.myVariable`
`myVariable`	`myMovieClip`	`myMovieClip.myVariable`	`this.myVariable`
`gMyVariable`	Anywhere (global)	`gMyVariable`	`gMyVariable`

High level properties

Earlier, we mentioned the main movie clip properties that affect motion. Before we start looking at examples of these properties, let's examine what are known as high level scripting properties. These are special properties that we can use to determine and globally set details of our movie.

_quality

The `_quality` property is something we can use to force our movies to switch to a certain mode of graphics quality. Depending upon the quality of the graphics, some movies can have trouble performing properly due to the speed of the computer and the complexity of the images. In such cases it can be helpful to switch the rendering quality to a lower setting. By default, when we test our movies in Flash, graphics are rendered at high quality, but there are a few other settings possible, as described in the following table. Simply placing this code anywhere in a movie will have the global effect of changing the quality setting for the entire movie.

Variable name	Description
`_quality = "BEST";`	The highest quality mode - includes optimum quality anti-aliasing on all graphics, except device fonts, which are rendered as aliased images. Bitmaps are always smoothed.
`_quality = "HIGH";`	Graphics are anti-aliased, and static bitmaps are smoothed.
`_quality = "MEDIUM";`	Graphics are anti-aliased with a lower quality, faster anti-aliasing method, and bitmaps are not smoothed.
`_quality = "LOW";`	Graphics are not anti-aliased, and bitmaps are not smoothed.

_framesloaded and _totalframes

These two properties can be used to determine how many frames of a particular movie, or movie clip, have been loaded or streamed from the server. If we write:

```
_root._framesloaded;
```

then we're looking at the number of frames that have been loaded from the main timeline. Alternatively, if we state:

```
myMovieClip._framesloaded;
```

then we're concerned with the number of frames that have been loaded of a particular movie clip (in this case, myMovieClip).

The `_totalframes` property is used in a similar fashion to `_framesloaded`, except instead of returning the number of frames that have been loaded, we're given the total number of frames in the entire object. So, `_root._totalframes` will return the number of frames in the root timeline, while `myMovieClip._totalframes` tells us the number of frames in the timeline myMovieClip.

Note that since Flash can begin to play movies while they are still downloading, that is, it can *stream* the movies, `_totalframes` and `_framesloaded` may not always match. They will match only when the particular object or movie has completely loaded. This is worth noting since streaming is such an important concept when dealing with web-based technologies.

_soundbuftime

When a movie contains streaming sound, then this value is used to determine how many seconds of that sound should be loaded before the sound itself begins to play. Since networks can sometimes be unstable, delivering content at fluctuating rates, it is important to preload, or *buffer*, some of the material, so that there's a fallback in case the network slows its transfer of the file (this works somewhat like the anti-skip feature on most CD players). The default value for this is 5, corresponding to 5 seconds of buffer material. So if we wanted to extend this to a 10 second buffer, we would write `_soundbuftime = 10`.

_url

This global property returns the URL address of the SWF file itself. For example, if a SWF file called `flashmovie.swf` was residing at `www.mywebsite.com`, `_url` would refer to the property `http://www.mywebsite.com/flashmovie.swf`. Note that this is a read-only property, meaning that it cannot be set or changed at runtime.

getBytesLoaded and getBytesTotal

These two methods are again quite similar to `_framesloaded` and `_totalframes`, except that they return the total number of bytes that have been loaded, and they are actually methods rather than properties. In fact, `getBytesLoaded` offers a much more accurate form of measurement than `_framesloaded` because it tells us exactly how much of the movie has been downloaded, whereas `_framesloaded` lacks detail – remember, some frames may use up more bytes than others.

We can look at the total number of bytes loaded of the main movie:

```
myLoaded = _root.getBytesLoaded();
```

This will check how many bytes have been loaded overall, and store the result in the variable `myLoaded`.

Additionally, we can determine the number of bytes loaded of a specific movie clip (`myMovieClip`, for example) with the following line:

```
myLoaded = myMovieClip.getBytesLoaded();
```

Once we know how many bytes are loaded, we can also look at how many total bytes there are in a movie or movie clip:

```
myTotal = _root.getBytesTotal();
```

And:

```
myTotal = myMovieClip.getBytesTotal();
```

Ultimately, we could then determine what percentage of the movie has been loaded:

```
perc = (myLoaded/myTotal)*100;
```

With this technique, `perc` will correspond nicely to the percentage of the total bytes loaded. This technique is often used in order to create a preloader, where perhaps the value of `perc` is used to set the `_width` of a load bar movie clip.

The Flash coordinate system

Since most motion graphics involve moving objects around the screen, it's important to understand the Flash coordinate system. In Flash, the screen is divided into units of measurement that, at a scale of 100%, correspond to screen pixels. When we set the resolution of our movie, we're specifying exactly how many of these units there are going to be horizontally and vertically.

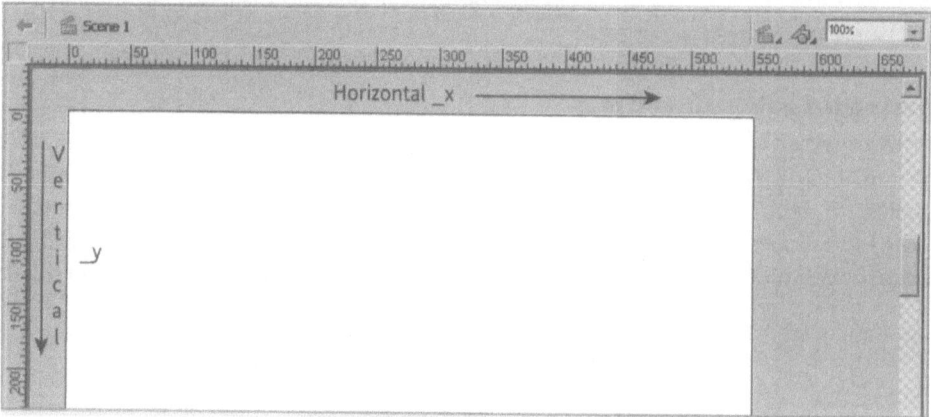

In this image, we're looking at the stage of a movie with dimensions 550 x 400. Notice the rulers on the top and the left hand side – select View>Rulers (CTRL+ALT+SHIFT+R) to bring up your rulers as and when required. Along the top (`_x`) we have a width of 550, and along the side (`_y`) we have a height of 400. Note that `_x` increases from left to right, and `_y` increases from top to bottom (contrary to the usual Cartesian geometry that we learn at school). These are the coordinates of the main stage.

So, in order to make something move right, we must increase its x-coordinate, and to move left we must decrease this x-coordinate. Likewise, to move something down and up, we must increase and decrease its y-coordinate, respectively.

However, things become more complicated when we have a movie clip within our movie. This is because the movie clip has its own *local* coordinates. Whenever we create a movie clip, we define its registration point in the Convert to Symbol window. The small plus + symbol in the center of this movie clip denotes that its registration point is in the center:

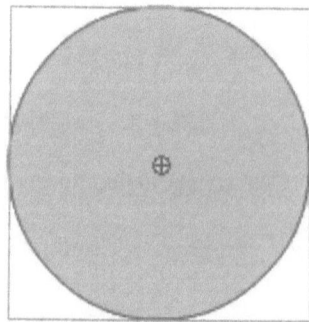

This is the point from which all local coordinates are measured within that movie clip. That point is known as (0, 0). If we place this movie clip in the center of our stage, it will have an _x and _y coordinate of (275, 200). However, if we place an object *within* the movie clip's timeline, at the registration point of the movie clip, that object's _x and _y coordinates will both be 0, even though it may actually appear to be in the center of our stage:

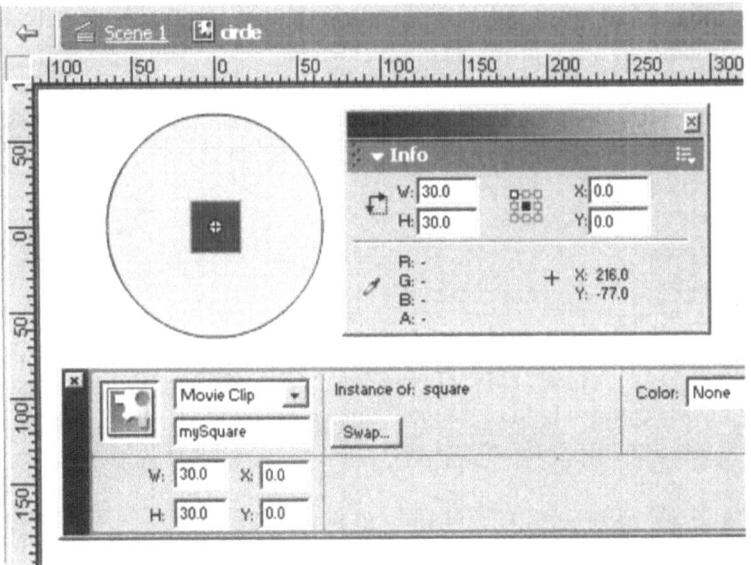

Note that we can use both the Property inspector and the Info panel (CTRL+I) to read and write the _x and _y positions.

It's important to realize that all coordinates are relative to the movie clip that encompasses them. For example, if we were to move the instance of the square movie clip within the circle, like this:

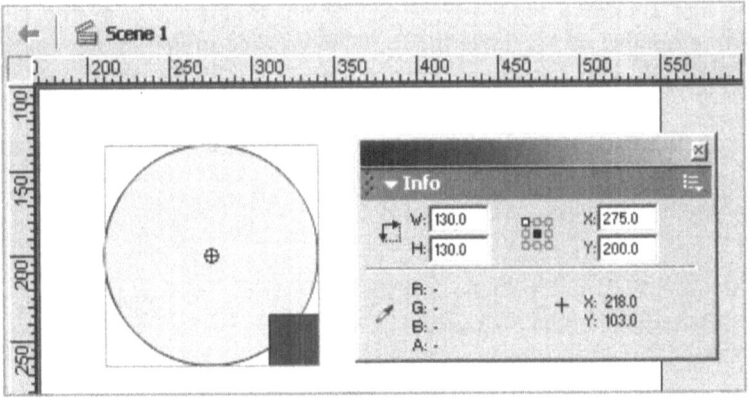

The coordinates of the objects would be as follows:

circle: (275, 200) – relative to the upper-left corner of the stage
square: (50, 50) – relative to the registration point of the circle

This essentially means that we don't immediately know the *global* position of the square movie clip relative to the stage. Well, not without a little bit of code – the globalToLocal() and localToGlobal() commands will prove themselves useful here.

Take a look at the example flashCoords.fla for a demonstration of these methods. Within frame 1 of the circle's timeline, we have the following script:

```
pt = new Object();
pt.x = mySquare._x;
pt.y = mySquare._y;
localToGlobal(pt);
```

Don't worry about the new Object() declaration for the moment – we'll cover that later in the book. What we're doing here is converting the local coordinates of the small square (called mySquare here) to global coordinates, measured from the main stage.

We can, of course, go the other way, where we have global coordinates that we want brought into the local coordinate space of a movie clip. Take a look at the code attached to the root timeline of flashCoords.fla:

```
gPt = new Object();
gPt.x = myCircle._x;
gPt.y = myCircle._y;
myCircle.globalToLocal(gPt);
```

Again, this code first creates a point object called gPt that consists of the global coordinates of myCircle. When we run this, gPt is converted to the internal coordinate system of the circle. This should obviously result in (0, 0) – the registration point of the circle movie clip.

Once the localToGlobal() and globalToLocal() commands have been issued, we can view the contents of pt and gPt using the appropriately modified trace() operation (see flashCoords.fla, and **Chapter 16** for more details):

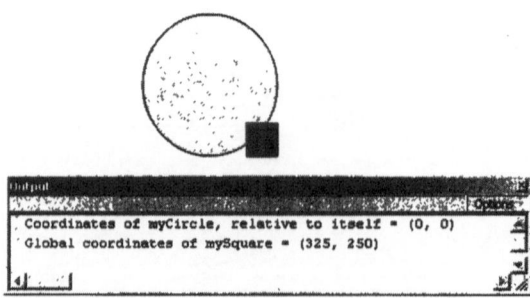

```
Output
  Coordinates of myCircle, relative to itself = (0, 0)
  Global coordinates of mySquare = (325, 250)
```

Animating with ActionScript

OK, enough background details - let's now cover the essentials of script-based animation in Flash MX. So far we've mentioned briefly that we need to *connect* the actions in our code to the relevant movie clips using dot notation. In this section we'll start to get our hands dirty and demonstrate exactly how this is achieved.

Let's look at an example – open `smileyBox_scriptedMotion.fla`. This file is essentially the same as the movie clip example that we saw earlier, `smileyBoxMovieClip.fla`. Notice, however, that there's a new layer on the main timeline, called actions:

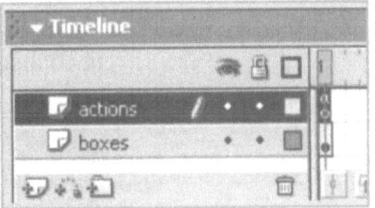

Although this layer contains no actual graphics, we can tell by the small 'a' in frame 1 that it actually contains some ActionScript. It is a good standard practice to always keep your code somewhere easily accessible and obvious, separate from your graphical objects, in an appropriately named layer.

OK, so what code is attached to this frame? Select frame 1 of the actions layer and open up the Actions panel by pressing F9:

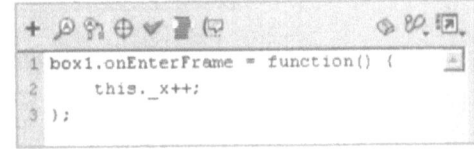

Note that in this book we're going to be using Expert Mode to enter ActionScript. Make sure that Expert Mode is selected, via the Actions panel menu in the top right corner, or by pressing CTRL+SHIFT+E:

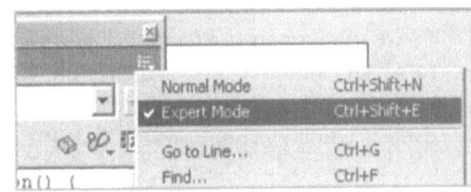

Back to the code on frame 1 of the actions layer – what exactly does it do? Well, try testing the movie and see what happens (just press CTRL+ENTER):

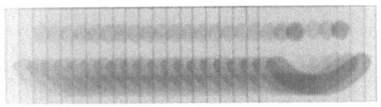

As you can see, the instance of the `smileyBox` movie clip named `box1` now slowly moves horizontally across the screen, reminiscent of the keyframe animation that we saw earlier in `simple_tween.fla`. However, this time we only have one frame in our timeline, and there is no frame-based animation anywhere to be found! The animation is completely defined by the ActionScript and generated at runtime.

Now that we've seen the effect, let's examine the three lines of code in detail:

```
box1.onEnterFrame = function() {
```

First, by writing `box1.onEnterFrame` we're telling Flash MX to attach the code that follows to the `onEnterFrame` event connected to the movie clip instance `box1`. Next we're saying that a **function** is to follow.

> *A function is a fixed block of code that can be re-used anywhere in a movie, and it is defined within the opening and closing braces. The opening brace '{' says to Flash, "our* `onEnterFrame` *code begins now".*

Next we have the code that actually produces the motion:

```
        this._x++;
    };
```

As we mentioned briefly earlier, the word `this` means "apply the following command to the movie clip to which I am attached". So, since our function was defined with `box1.onEnterFrame`, then `box1` is what we mean when we use the word `this`, inside the function. This scope is required because the function itself is being written in frame 1 of the root timeline, which inherently has a scope of `_root`.

> *It's important to note that if we didn't write this inside the function, then Flash would assume we were referring to variables of the* `_root` *scope.*

After the `this` scope declaration, we have `_x++`, connected to `this` with the usual dot notation. This is a small but powerful operator responsible for moving the movie clip. For clarity, we'll first look at `_x`, and then at `++`.

We mentioned earlier the different types of motion scripting we can perform on a movie clip, position being an important one. The position of a movie clip is changed via the `_x` and `_y` properties of the movie clip, which correspond to the horizontal and vertical positions, respectively. So the `_x` and `_y` properties refer to an actual location on the stage. If, for example, we had written `this._x = 200` instead of the existing line, the code would simply move our `box1` instance to the center of the screen.

The ++ is an incremental operator which, when connected to the _x position property like _x++, means "increase the x position by 1". So, in the context of our onEnterFrame function, the horizontal position of box1 is increased by 1 with every new frame. This is reflected on screen by the movie clip moving horizontally to the right.

Note that we signal the line is complete with a semicolon ';'. It's worthwhile getting into the habit of putting a semicolon at the end of every statement of code (except after an open brace, obviously). Finally, the closing brace and semicolon '};' indicates the end of the box1.onEnterFrame function code.

Motion scripting properties

The main motion scripting properties of movie clips are shown in the table below:

ActionScript property name	Description
_x	The x, or horizontal, position of the movie clip.
_y	The y, or vertical, position of the movie clip
_rotation	The rotation of the movie clip in degrees, based on a 360 degree circle.
_xscale	The percentage of horizontal scaling to apply along the x-axis. 100 is unchanged, 50 is half width, 200 is double width, and so on.
_yscale	The percentage of vertical scaling to apply along the y-axis.
_alpha	The percentage of opacity that the movie clip should have. 100 is completely solid, 50 is half visible, half transparent, and 0 is completely transparent (invisible).
_visible	A property, which determines whether or not to draw the movie clip at all. Can be set to either true or false.

With the previous table in mind, in the following subsections we'll be adding code to the previous example to demonstrate a few more of the properties for motion scripting.

Rotation

In smileyBox_rotation.fla we have added the following code to the actions frame (beneath the onEnterFrame function discussed above):

```
box2.onEnterFrame = function() {
    this._rotation++;
};
```

So our Actions panel now looks like this:

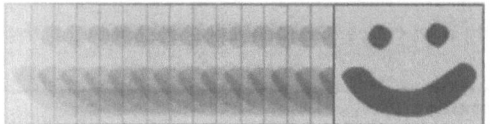

```
1 box1.onEnterFrame = function() {
2     this._x++;
3 );
4 box2.onEnterFrame = function() {
5     this._rotation++;
6 );
7
```

Test the movie with CTRL+ENTER, as usual, and you'll see box1 moving horizontally as before, and box2 will now spring into life and start spinning around:

They're both alive! Well, sort of... one of them is moving blindly off the screen into oblivion, and the other is spinning around and around like a one-legged duck. With the newly added code, we're attaching an onEnterFrame event to the other instance of the smileyBox movie clip on the stage, box2. This time we utilize the _rotation property combined with the incremental operator ++ to cause box2 to rotate by 1 degree on every new frame. The finished effect is the spinning movie clip that we have just seen. Easy, huh?

Alpha and scale

Let's see what else we can do. We'll move on with our ActionScript now, and make use of concepts like variables, loops, and logic. Open up smileyBox_alphaScale.fla in which we've altered the code in frame 1 of the actions layer to look like this:

```
box1.onEnterFrame = function() {
     this._x += 2;
     this._y += 2;
};
box2.onEnterFrame = function() {
     this._alpha -= 0.5;
     this._xscale += 2;
     this._yscale += 2;
     if (this._alpha<=0) {
```

```
        this._alpha = 100;
    }
};
```

When we run this, we'll see box1 move diagonally down and to the
right. This time we've used the addition assignment operator += to
increment both the _x and _y properties by 2 on each new frame.
Remember, the increment operator ++ only increments by 1 at a
time, so for anything else we must use +=. The other movie clip
instance, box2, appears to be coming towards us while fading out
at the same time.

Note, however, that once box2 has completely faded out, it will suddenly become 100% solid again, and
the fade cycle will repeat continuously, until box1 heads off to nowhere, and box2 takes over the whole
screen:

The inclusion of a 'continuous cycle' of motion within your scripted animation is an important and useful
coding trick. Accordingly, let's take a closer look at the motion script that we have defined within the
onEnterFrame function of box2. First, we set up the _alpha and _xscale/_yscale properties with
subtraction and addition assignment operators, respectively:

```
        this._alpha -= 0.5;
        this._xscale += 2;
        this._yscale += 2;
```

This has the effect of causing box2 to slowly fade away and simultaneously grow in size. The _xscale and _yscale are wonderful for simulating perspective motion, where objects appear larger when they're nearer and smaller as they get farther away.

Then comes the clever part:

```
if (this._alpha<=0) {
        this._alpha = 100;
}
```

This is what is known as an if loop; here it checks to see if the _alpha has reached 0 (completely invisible) on each frame and, if so, resets it to 100% solid again. Neat!

Cross fade

Let's look at another useful effect – in the file crossFade.fla we perform a cross fade between two movie clips. With a cross fade, as one image fades out, it is replaced by another image that is simultaneously fading in. In this movie, we have two movie clips of the same size, in the exact same position. Look on the stage and you'll immediately see our familiar smiley face image:

But wait a minute! The layer structure in the timeline suggests something strange is going on. Use the show/hide dot icon (beneath the 'eye' icon) to hide everything on the layer named image1 – you'll soon see that something sinister is afoot!

There's another image lurking below the first – these two images represent two different movie clips, and they have instance names image1 and image2. Test the movie to see what happens:

The images fade in and out in a cycle. Now to find out how it works – the effect is accomplished with the following code, attached to frame 1 of the actions layer:

```
image2.onEnterFrame = function() {
    this._alpha = 100-_root.image1._alpha;
};
image1.dir = -1;
image1.onEnterFrame = function() {
    this._alpha += this.dir;
    if (this._alpha<=0) {
        this.dir = 1;
    }
    if (this._alpha>=100) {
        this.dir = -1;
    }
};
```

In this code, the first function sets the alpha value of image2 to 100 minus the alpha of image1. So, for instance, when image1 has an alpha of 20, then image2 will have an alpha of 80.

Next we take care of image1. First, we declare the variable dir (this stands for 'direction') to be -1. Note that by declaring it as we have done, image1.dir = -1, directly connecting to the image1 movie clip, the dir variable is always a *member* of this movie clip. This means that whenever we want to access this variable, we must refer to it specifically as image1.dir or, if the code is within a function linked to image1, then as this.dir. As we shall see, image1.dir will be either 1 or -1, depending on whether it is fading in or out.

Finally, in the onEnterFrame event function attached to image1, we have the following if loops:

```
this._alpha += this.dir;
if (this._alpha<=0) {
    this.dir = 1;
}
```

continues overleaf

```
if (this._alpha>=100) {
      this.dir = -1;
}
```

Very simply, we're increasing the alpha value of `image1` by the value of `dir` (which starts off as `-1`, so it will begin by decreasing the alpha by 1 every frame). Once the alpha reaches 0, then `dir` is flipped to 1, with the result is that the alpha will start increasing. Once it reaches an alpha of 100, then it will reverse direction again, and begin fading out.

All the while, `image2` is dependent upon this code in order to determine its own alpha value because of first line of code in the first function.

An interesting point to note is that we don't actually have to fade `image2` at all. We can completely remove the `image2.onEnterFrame` code – try it out yourself. Technically, because the images lie happily on top of each other on the stage, only the topmost image needs to fade out and in, giving the impression that bottom image is fading in or out. But it was nice to demonstrate how you might go about scripting one movie clip's properties dependent on another.

Combining timeline- and script-based animation

Earlier we touched upon the fact that tweened animation couldn't be controlled with ActionScript as it is pre-rendered. We can, however, do some interesting things in the timeline of a tweened animation. Look at `script_controlled_tween.fla` – here we have a movie clip called `tweener`. If we look at the timeline of the movie clip, just double-click on it to dig inside it, we can see that it consists of a 40-frame cartoon that shape tweens from a red circle to a blue circle with some notches in its side:

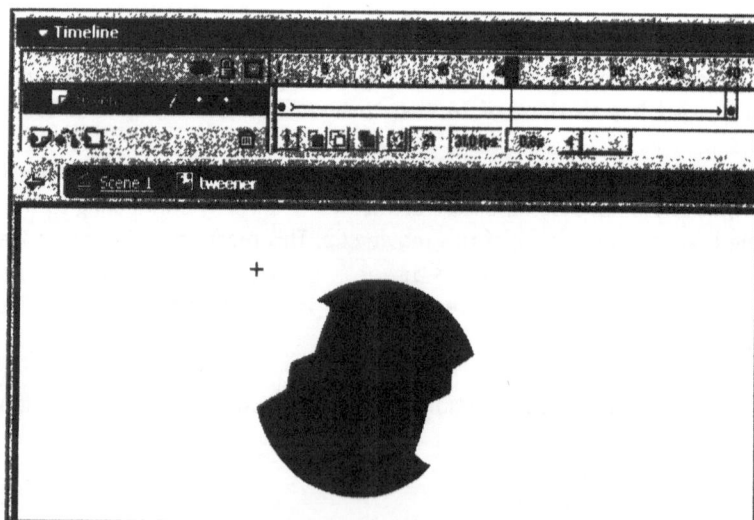

Back on the root timeline, in frame 1 of the actions layer, we find the following lines of code:

```
tweener.stop();
tweener.onEnterFrame = function() {
     this.gotoAndStop(Math.floor(_root._xmouse/14));
};
```

The first thing we're doing, is telling the tweener movie clip not to play. This is not as foolish as it sounds because we want to control the playhead of the movie clip with the script that follows, so we don't want Flash to begin with it playing.

Next up we've got an onEnterFrame function attached to tweener with some rather interesting looking code in it. This line effectively tells Flash to go to a specific frame relating directly to the mouse's x-position. The effect? Go ahead and test the movie to find out.

Notice that as we move the mouse left and right, the shape appears to tween back and forth depending upon the mouse movement. This movie has a dependency upon the mouse position, so the code *appears* to control the shape tweening.

We're using the line:

```
this.gotoAndStop(Math.floor(_root._xmouse/14));
```

This tells Flash to 'go to and stop' on a frame of tweener defined by taking the mouse's x-position and dividing it by 14. The mouse's x-position is found using the property _root._xmouse, and we divide it by 14 because our movie is 560 pixels wide, meaning that the frame number will be from 0 to 40 – which happens to correlate nicely to the total number of frames on the timeline of tweener. Note that we use the math function Math.floor to force the result to be a whole number rather than a decimal fraction (obviously we can't go to frame 22.79 – it must be 'floored', or rounded down, to 22.

Cyclic animation

In the previous example, we saw how the timeline of a movie clip can be independent of any code that is actually controlling it. Another great use for this technique is moving a movie clip on screen, which has a cycled animation, thus giving the impression of complex animated motion – this is a classic trick that's been used in cartoons for years.

1   Flash MX Designer's ActionScript Reference

On the stage in `inchworm_cycle.fla` you'll see a cute little `inchworm` movie clip lying on a branch:

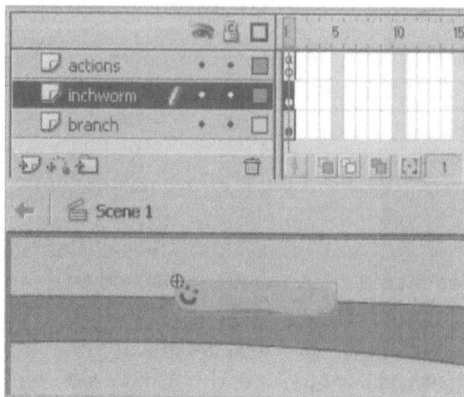

You'll also notice that the following code has been added to frame 1 of the actions layer:

```
inchworm.onEnterFrame = function() {
     this._x -= 2;
};
```

We've seen code like this before – it's just going to move the worm to the left at a constant rate of 2 pixels per frame, right? Test the movie to see what happens:

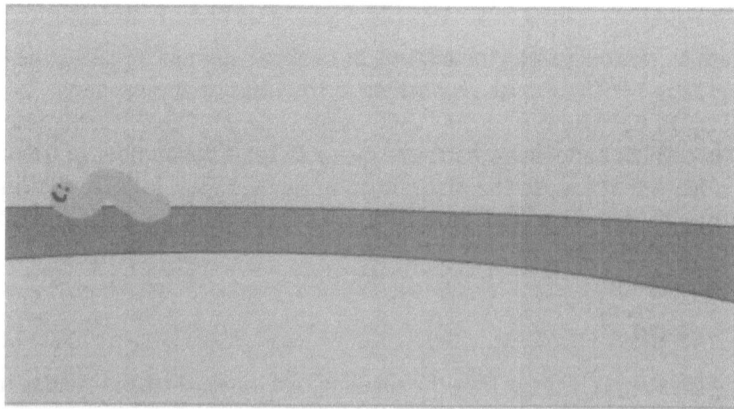

Whoa! The little critter is actually crawling! Clearly, we've missed a sneaky trick somewhere along the way. Yep, you've probably guessed it by now, the `inchworm` movie clip itself is also animated.

Go back to the main stage of `inchworm_cycle.fla` and double click on the `inchworm` instance:

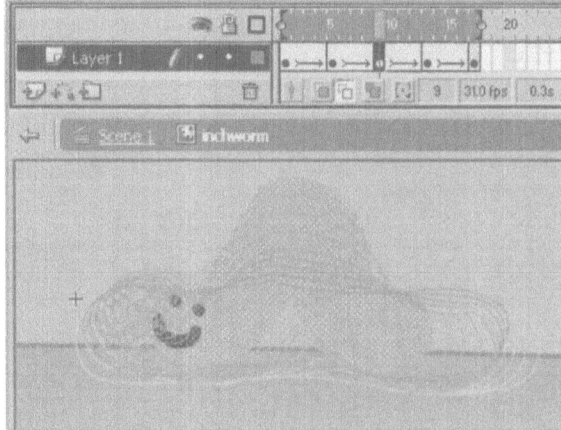

So when we play the movie, not only does our script-based motion run, but the tweened motion within the `inchworm` movie clip plays too. The combined result is that our inchworm happily crawls along the branch, until he disappears off screen.

The key point to remember when using cyclic animations is that the secondary animation (the 'wriggle' of the inchworm in our case) must actually be a cycle – it must begin and end in approximately the same state to avoid any jerky movements when the movie clip is repeated:

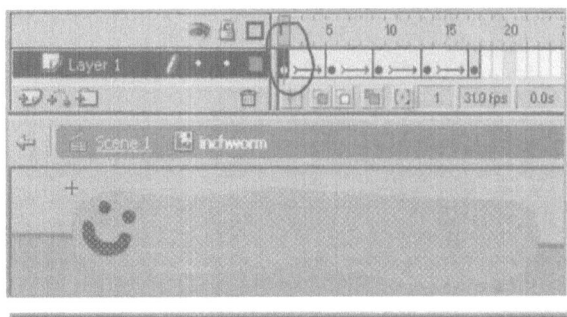

Duplicating movie clips

What if we want an army of inchworms instead of just one – can we do this with ActionScript alone? Of course we can, thanks to the wonders of the `duplicateMovieClip()` method. Load up `inchworm_invasion.fla`:

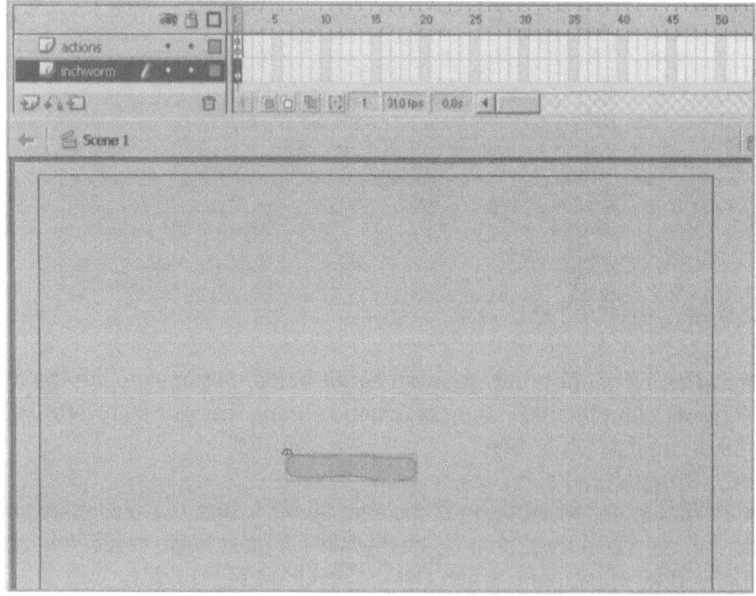

You'll immediately see the one lonely little inchworm, lying innocently in the middle of the stage. Now test the movie:

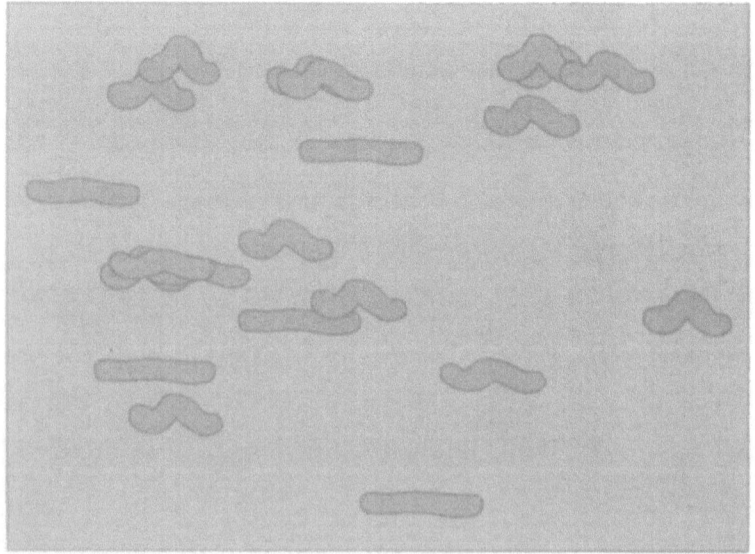

Wow! Now we've got lots of inchworms crawling all over the place. Let's examine the code that produces this effect – we'll soon see that what is known as a `for` loop enables the multiplication of our movie clip.

> *The `for` loop is an essential building block of all programming. It can be used to perform a section of code a certain number of times. When looping, the current loop number is kept track of by a variable known as the loop counter, which is usually denoted as* `i`. *For example, consider the following line:*
>
> `for (i=0; i<20; i++)`
>
> *First we state* `i = 0`, *which is the value that we want the loop counter to start at. Next, we say* `i < 20`, *which is a way of saying when to end the loop, that is, "loop as long as* `i` *is less than 20". Finally, we have* `i++`, *which defines what we want the counter to do with each iteration of the loop – this incremental operator increases the loop counter by one after each iteration, effectively counting each loop.*

Now back to the current example – take a look at frame 1 of the actions layer of `inchworm_invasion.fla` and you'll find the following ActionScript:

```
moveMe = function () {
      this._x -= this.speed;
      if (this._x<0) {
            this._x = 550;
      }
      if (this._x>550) {
            this._x = 0;
      }
};
for (i=0; i<20; i++) {
      nm = "worm"+i;
      inchworm.duplicateMovieClip(nm, i);
      d = Math.random()*2;
      if (d<1) {
            _root[nm].speed = -3;
      } else {
            _root[nm].speed = 3;
```

```
        }
        _root[nm].onEnterFrame = moveMe;
        _root[nm].gotoAndPlay(random(17));
        _root[nm]._x = Math.random()*550;
        _root[nm]._y = Math.random()*400;
    }
```

First, we create some code that will be the function used to move each inchworm. We've talked about creating functions before, specifically with the onEnterFrame event, but now we're going to do things a little bit differently. We're initially defining a function, called moveMe, which we will not actually use until later in the script – this demonstrates the modular nature of ActionScript. Here's a reminder of what the function looks like:

```
moveMe = function () {
    this._x -= this.speed;
    if (this._x<0) {
        this._x = 550;
    }
    if (this._x>550) {
        this._x = 0;
    }
};
```

So, we're moving the inchworm in increments defined by a variable called this.speed (which will be either -3 or 3, as declared later). Next, we check to see if the worm has moved off screen, where x is less than 0, or greater than 550. If it does, we wrap it back around to the other side of the screen. This means that our inchworms will always walk off screen, and then reappear at the other edge.

Next, we start a for loop, which creates 20 copies of the inchworm. Note that this code is not within an onEnterFrame event, so it only runs once, when our movie first loads up:

```
for (i=0; i<20; i++) {
    nm = "worm"+i;
    inchworm.duplicateMovieClip(nm, i);
```

This for loop relies on the variable i, which will loop from 0 to 19. The variable nm is used to store the name of the new instance we're creating – this will be the word worm followed by the value of i (that is, worm0, worm1, worm2, all the way up to worm19. The duplicateMovieClip method of our inchworm movie clip is then used to make copies of the original inchworm.

The duplicateMovieClip method takes a couple of parameters here. First, it wants to know the name of the new instance. In this case, we're giving it the variable nm, which we have preset to be the name of our new worm, as discussed above. The next parameter is depth level (or stacking order) of the new movie clip. In this case the depth level will relate directly to the number of the duplicated movie clip (that is 0, 1, 2, etc., up to 19). The stacking order determines the order in which the worms will be drawn at runtime before being displayed; the lower the depth level, the earlier it will be drawn.

> *Depth level is a very important concept, and it's important to note that Flash will only allow one movie clip per depth level. If you created a worm on level 5, and then attempted to duplicate another movie clip also into level 5, the first worm would be erased. This is why, in our worm example, we use i as the unique value of our level so that no two worms will attempt to occupy the same level. We'll look at the depth level of movie clips in more detail in the next section.*

Back to our study of the code in `inchworm_invasion.fla`:

```
for (i=0; i<20; i++) {
    nm = "worm"+i;
    inchworm.duplicateMovieClip(nm, i);
    d = Math.random()*2;
    if (d<1) {
        _root[nm].speed = -3;
    } else {
        _root[nm].speed = 3;
    }
    _root[nm].onEnterFrame = moveMe;
    _root[nm].gotoAndPlay(random(17));
    _root[nm]._x = Math.random()*550;
    _root[nm]._y = Math.random()*400;
}
```

We continue by setting some properties of the newly created inchworm. First, we're using a random number from the Math object to set the `speed` variable to either 3 or -3. Then we tell the new instance to set its `onEnterFrame` event to equate to the function `moveMe`, which we defined at the start of the code. Next, we tell each worm to go to a random frame in its cycle between 0 and 17 so that it appears that all the worms are moving independently of each other. Finally, we move the new worm to a random position on screen. Because of the `for` loop, this process is repeated 20 times, creating our army of inchworms.

Stacking order of movie clips

It's worth our while taking a more detailed look at the concept of the stacking order (or depth level) of movie clips. Open up `inchworm_stacking.fla`, which you'll find to be very similar to the previous example with only a couple of subtle changes. Test the movie to see the difference:

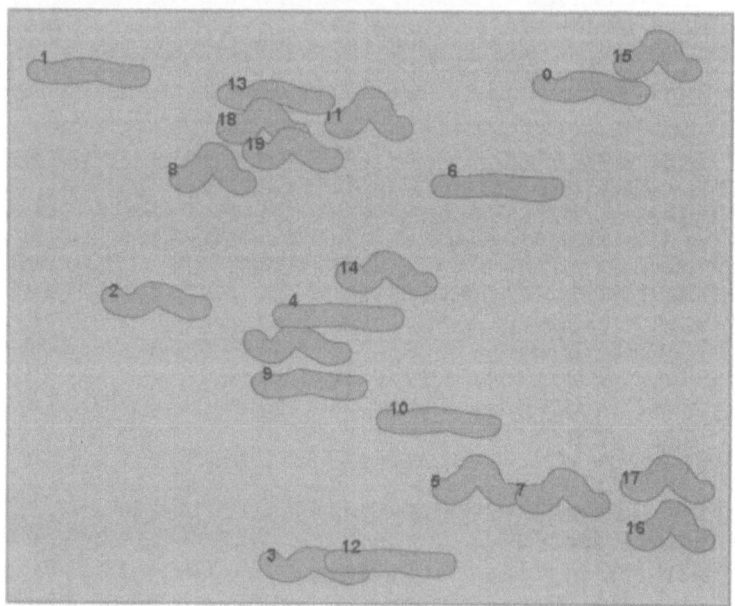

This time, we are printing the depth level above each worm. Take a close look – notice that higher depths are drawn above lower depths. For example, `worm19` lies above `worm18`, which in turn lies on top of `worm13`:

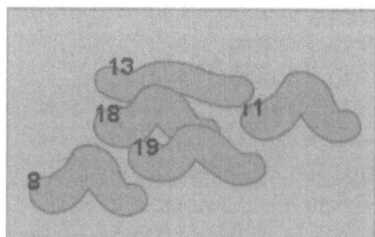

This is how the depth level relates specifically to the stacking order of a movie clip. The code to show this effect was exactly as in the previous example, except for a single new line at the end of the `for` loop in our script:

```
_root[nm].mydep = i;
```

Additionally, we've inserted a dynamic text field inside our `inchworm` movie clip, and given it the variable name `mydep`:

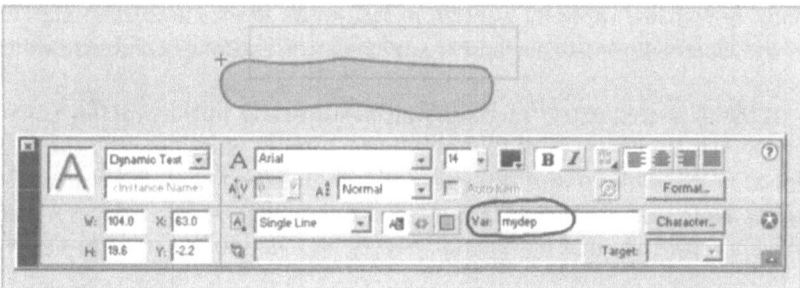

So, our new line of code simply attaches the loop counter and depth level variable `i` to this dynamic text field and thus prints the depth level of each instance of `inchworm` on the screen.

Now, what if we wanted to move a movie clip to a new depth level for some reason? Well, we would simply use the `swapDepths()` method of any movie clip. Consider `worm0`, for example – let's say we wanted this poor buried worm to be thrust to the top of the stack – to be drawn last so that he's always on top of everyone else. We could write something like this:

```
worm0.swapDepths(1000);
```

Here, we're moving `worm0` to depth level 1000, which is quite far above everyone else. Notice that, once we add this code, `worm0` is above the rest of the pack:

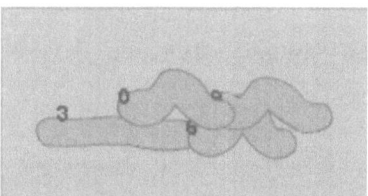

As a side note, the reason this method is referred to as **swap**Depths(), rather than something like 'move' depths or 'set' depths is because, as we stated earlier, no two movie clips can occupy the same depth layer, so in order to put a movie clip on a particular depth level, `swapDepths()` must actually *swap* the contents of the original layer and the destination layer. In the example above, whatever was on layer 1000 will be moved to layer 0, and the worm on layer 0 will be moved to layer 1000. In this case, we know that there's nothing on layer 1000, so there's nothing to swap. However, if we were to issue `worm2.swapDepths(7)`, we'd actually have the effect of swapping the depth layers of `worm2` and `worm7`.

Attaching movie clips

In the previous example we created our inchworm army from a copy of one sitting on the stage. That's all fine and dandy, but what if we don't want an inchworm on the stage to start with. Could we not just pull one out of the Library automatically and create copies of that one? Of course we can!

Flash MX gives us the `attachMovie()` method, which allows us to take a properly configured movie clip from the Library and create instances of it in our movie, without having one on the stage to begin with. This is much more in line with good programming techniques, where resources can be allocated (and deleted) on the fly. Note that we also have a method called `removeMovieClip()`, but remember that we cannot remove a movie clip that has been *physically* attached to the stage to begin with.

Let's look at an example – open up `inchworm_attach.fla`. Notice that the stage is completely empty. However, run the movie, and we'll see 20 inchworms moving around the screen, as we did in the previous example. Look at the code on frame 1 of the actions layer. Everything is identical to the previous example, except for a couple of highlighted differences:

```
moveMe = function () {
        this._x -= this.speed;
        if (this._x<0) {
                this._x = 550;
        }
        if (this._x>550) {
                this._x = 0;
        }
};
for (i=0; i<20; i++) {
        nm = "worm" add i;
        _root.attachMovie("inchwormID", nm, i);
        d = Math.random()*2;
        if (d<1) {
                _root[nm].speed = -3;
        } else {
                _root[nm].speed = 3;
        }
        _root[nm].onEnterFrame = moveMe;
        _root[nm].gotoAndPlay(random(17));
        _root[nm]._x = Math.random()*550;
        _root[nm]._y = Math.random()*400;
}
_root.onMouseDown = function() {
        for (i=0; i<20; i++) {
                nm = "worm" add i;
                removeMovieClip(nm);
        }
};
```

This time, we're using the `attachMovie()` method to create our instances. The code is pretty straightforward:

```
_root.attachMovie("inchwormID", nm, i);
```

Here we have three parameters to enter – a linkage ID name, followed by the new name and depth level of the new movie clip. We saw the latter two of these parameters in the previous example, but the ID name is new. In this case we've used `inchwormID` as the linkage ID. Open the Library by pressing F11, right click on the `inchworm` movie clip (the only item in the Library), and then choose Linkage... from the menu that comes up:

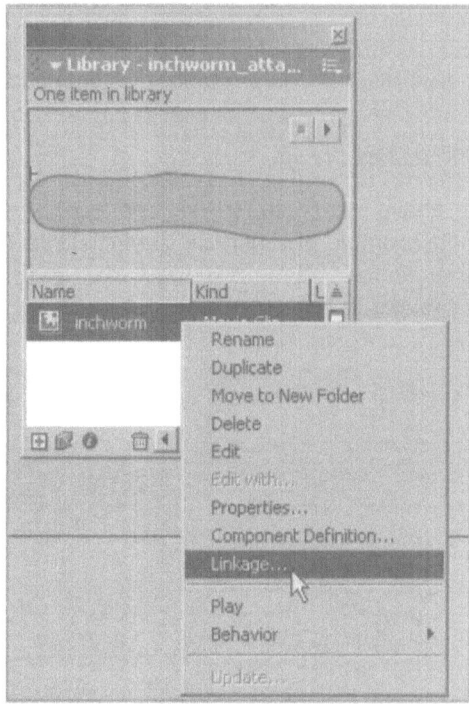

In the Linkage Properties box that opens up, notice that the Identifier is also set to `inchwormID`, and that the Linkage is set to Export for ActionScript and Export in first frame:

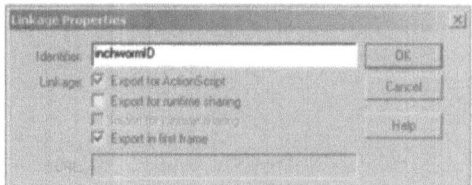

By doing this, we've set the movie clip to be exported in such a way that we can now use `attachMovie()` to create an entirely new instance on the stage, referenced through the linkage ID `inchwormID`.

One more thing: you may have noticed when testing the movie that if you press the mouse button down, all the worms will vanish! We're making use of the `removeMovieClip()` method in the latter part of the script – you can use it to erase movie clip instances that have been created with `duplicateMovieClip()` or `attachMovie()`:

```
_root.onMouseDown = function() {
    for (i=0; i<20; i++) {
        nm = "worm" add i;
        removeMovieClip(nm);
    }
}
```

So, using the `onMouseDown` event means that we use the mouse button as a trigger. Again, we loop through all 20 worms and issue the `removeMovieClip()` command on each one.

Kinetic effects with particles

In the inchworm examples above, we create several copies of a movie clip which all obey the same motion rules. This is a simple example of a particle system. However, inchworms aren't really what we might consider to be particles, so have a look at `kineticParticles.fla` to see how a better example of a dynamic particle system might look:

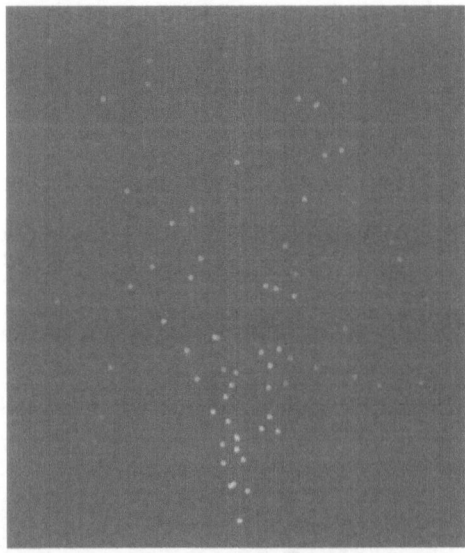

Test the movie and you'll see what is effectively a spray of particles – we have 120 particles (or *stars*), which begin their lives at the same point, and then shoot off at different trajectories, following an arc that is influenced by a gravity effect. As they fly, they're also fading out, creating a nice effect kind of like fireworks. The code is, as usual, quite simple:

```
moveMe = function () {
        this._x += this.dx;
        this._y += this.dy;
        this.dy += .5;
        this._alpha -= 2;
        if (this._y>400) {
                this.dx = Math.random()*10-5;
                this.dy = Math.random()*-10-10;
                this._alpha = 100;
                this._x = 275;
                this._y = 390;
        }
};
for (i=0; i<120; i++) {
        nm = "star" add i;
        mainstar.duplicateMovieClip(nm, i);
        _root[nm].dx = Math.random()*10-5;
        _root[nm].dy = Math.random()*-10-10;
        _root[nm].onEnterFrame = moveMe;
        _root[nm]._x = 275;
        _root[nm]._y = 390;
}
mainstar.onEnterFrame = moveMe;
```

First we create a function called moveMe, as before, but this time we're moving the _x and _y properties by two variables: dx and dy. These are initially set to random values, making each particle move at a random speed. However, on each frame the dy value will be increased by 0.5 – the effect is that the particle's speed will slowly increase in the positive vertical direction. In other words, the particle will begin to fall as it would under the influence of gravity. As it falls, we're also fading the _alpha of the particle by 2% each frame.

When the particle reaches the bottom of the screen then we give the appearance that a new particle has been released by moving it back to the origin point (275, 390), giving it a new random speed, and resetting its _alpha to 100. This creates the continuous spray effect.

Note the following important lines:

```
this.dx = Math.random()*10-5;
this.dy = Math.random()*-10-10;
```

Here, the dx speed will start out as a number from -5 to 5. If the number is negative, the particle flies to the left, and if it is positive then the particle flies to the right. The larger the number, the faster the particle moves. We then set the dy value as a number from -10 to -20. This way, it will always start out by moving up, but the speed at which it ascends will vary.

Next comes the `for` loop in which we create our 120 particles (much like we created our 20 inchworms earlier):

```
for (i=0; i<120; i++) {
        nm = "star" add i;
        mainstar.duplicateMovieClip(nm, i);
        _root[nm].dx = Math.random()*10-5;
        _root[nm].dy = Math.random()*-10-10;
        _root[nm].onEnterFrame = moveMe;
        _root[nm]._x = 275;
        _root[nm]._y = 390;
}
```

We're creating the stars, setting their position and speed, and then setting their `onEnterFrame` event to trigger the `moveMe` function defined at the start of the code.

Finally, we need to activate the star that is on the stage (remember that we're using the `duplicateMovieClip()` method here rather than `attachMovie()`). Otherwise it would just sit there motionless – this is our master star movie clip called `mainstar`, the source movie clip from which all of our copies were duplicated. We have one line of code to do this:

```
mainstar.onEnterFrame = moveMe;
```

That's it! Test the movie and watch the fireworks show again.

Dynamic masking

Arguably one of the coolest features of Flash MX is the ability to create dynamic, animated mask effects. We can actually use movie clips as masks, and they can include all the standard features, like animation, motion tween, shape tween, and script-based motion, as part of the mask.

As usual, an example is needed to demonstrate – take a look at `dynamicMask.fla` to see dynamic masking in action. First, test the movie and see what happens when the mouse is moved around:

We can see a green background and a dynamic mask that consists of spinning stars, and a shape tweening movie made up of the numbers 1 to 5 sequentially morphing into each other, and then cycling back through 1. Through the mask, we can see a nice colorful gradient with text in white on black. When the mouse is moved around, the mask follows. Pretty cool!

Starting with a look at the movie layout, we'll now examine how these effects were accomplished. Look at the stage – the mask is on the top layer, it's the movie clip consisting of a black number 1 with 5 stars next to it. Looking at the layer structure of the timeline, you'll see that the background to be masked is on the next layer down. Underneath that is the green background (which is actually the foreground in the movie):

There's also an actions layer with some ActionScript attached to it – let's look at that code:

```
masker.onEnterFrame = function() {
    this._rotation--;
    this._x = _root._xmouse;
    this._y = _root._ymouse;
};
crazybackground.setMask(masker);
```

The movie clip we're going to be using as the mask on the stage has an instance name of masker, while the movie clip that we're going to be masking has an instance name crazybackground. The first thing we do is create an onEnterFrame function for the masker that simply uses the _rotation property to rotate it counter-clockwise every frame, and sets its _x and _y coordinates to be the same as the mouse (we'll learn more about user interaction via the mouse and the keyboard shortly).

On the last line of code we use the setMask() method. This extremely useful command tells Flash to use masker as a mask for the movie clip crazybackground. This means that masker will continue to run as a normal movie clip, rotating counter-clockwise and following the mouse, except now it will behave in such a way that any solid portions of masker will instead show `crazybackground`. As for `crazybackground` itself, the parts that aren't directly under solid pixels from `masker` will be invisible, and our main green background will show through.

If we wanted to disable the mask, we need only pass `null` as the parameter in the `setMask()` method, like so:

```
crazybackground.setMask(null);
```

This would make `crazybackground` become completely visible again, and `masker` would play as a normal movie clip.

OK, so that explains how the actual masking effect is taking place – but what about the morphing image and the fact that the stars are orbiting in a circle? For this, we must delve deeper into the `masker` movie clip. Right-click on it and select Edit to see what's going on within it :

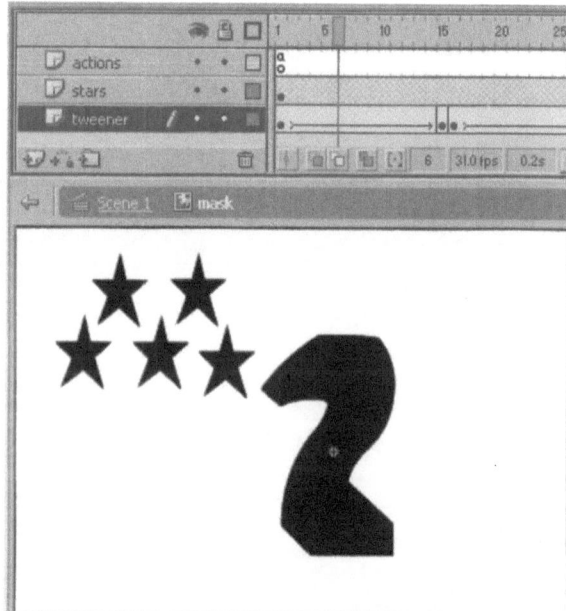

Looking closely, we can see that there are three layers: actions, stars, and tweener. The bottom layer, tweener, is a traditional shape tween animation, with a keyframe every 15 frames and shape tweens that morph the numbers together – click on the playhead and run it along the top of the timeline to see the finished effect.

Note also that the stars in the layer of the same name are instances of the star movie clip, and each have sequentially numbered instance names: star1, star2, star3, star4, and star5:

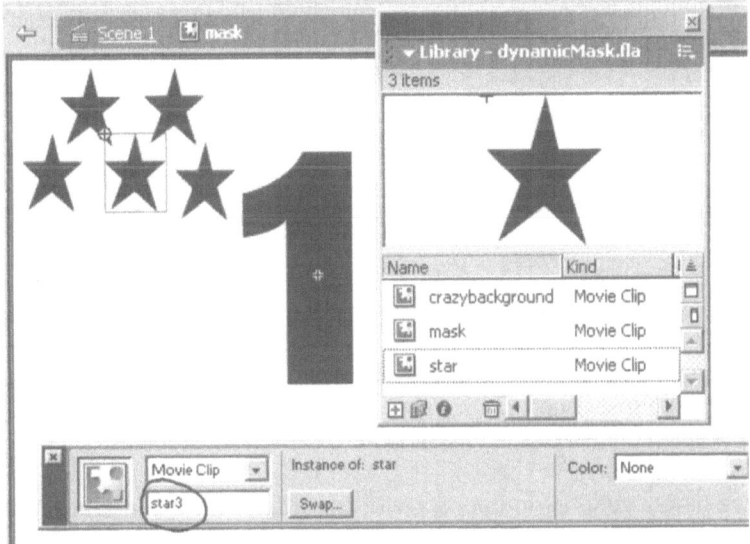

On the actions layer in frame 1, there is some code that is local to the scope of the masker movie clip:

```
movestar = function () {
    this._x = Math.cos(this.ang)*60;
    this._y = Math.sin(this.ang)*60;
    this.ang += 0.1;
};
star1.ang = 1;
star1.onEnterFrame = movestar;
star2.ang = 2;
star2.onEnterFrame = movestar;
star3.ang = 3;
star3.onEnterFrame = movestar;
star4.ang = 4;
star4.onEnterFrame = movestar;
star5.ang = 5;
star5.onEnterFrame = movestar;
```

This script is really quite simple – we create a function called movestar, which is responsible for moving the star in a circle around the registration point of the masker movie clip. The code is rather mathematical, but what we're basically doing is using the sine and cosine functions to move the star around the circumference of a circle. Each star instance has a local variable called ang, and it corresponds to the current angle that the star is at, in its circular path. Since we don't want all 5 stars to be exactly on top of each other, we set the starting ang of each star to 1, 2, 3, 4, and 5 for each respective star. Then we assign each star's onEnterFrame event to trigger the movestar function.

There we have it: multiple levels of ActionScript, animation, and masking. The effects are limitless – think of all the cool transitions that can be made with dynamic masks.

Interacting with the user

We'll finish up this introduction to scripted motion techniques in Flash MX by learning how to incorporate user interaction in our designs – this is the next great step in adding ActionScript-based animation to our movies.

The mouse

Earlier, we looked briefly at using code to respond to the mouse position to determine which frame in a tweened movie clip to display (see script_controlled_tween.fla). This is, in effect, user interactivity. Now we'll see the full potential of the mouse interaction – take a look at interaction_mouse.fla.

In this movie, we have a gold bar in the center of the stage, with the instance name goldbar. Test the movie, and we'll see that the gold bar seems to move in opposite directions to our mouse – like a mirror image. Additionally, when we press the mouse button down, the gold bar grows to five times its normal width, and when the mouse button is released, the gold bar returns to its normal width:

The code attached to the main timeline is simple, as ever:

```
goldbar.onMouseMove = function() {
    this._x = 550-_root._xmouse;
    this._y = 400-_root._ymouse;
};
goldbar.onMouseDown = function() {
    this._xscale = 500;
};
goldbar.onMouseUp = function() {
    this._xscale = 100;
};
```

We're not using the onEnterFrame event here because we don't need that much detail – we only need to respond to mouse actions. Hence, we use the onMouseMove event, which is triggered whenever the mouse is moved, onMouseDown, which is triggered when the mouse button is pressed, and finally onMouseUp, which is triggered when the mouse button is released.

We set the _x position of goldbar to be 550-_root._xmouse, which is directly opposite the position of the mouse cursor on the screen, and similarly, the _y position of goldbar to be 400-_root._ymouse, also the mirror position (remember, our screen size is 550 x 400 pixels).

Finally, when the mouse button is pressed, we set the _xscale of the goldbar to 500, which means 500% of normal, and when the button is released we reset the _xscale to 100.

The keyboard

Keyboard interaction is created similarly to the mouse interaction, except we will use an onEnterFrame function to look at the current state of several keys to determine our course of action.

Look at interaction_keyboard.fla. In this example we can use the arrow keys to move the gold bar from the previous example around the screen in response to our key presses. The ActionScript code to achieve this is attached to frame 1 of the actions layer:

```
goldbar.onEnterFrame = function() {
    if (Key.isDown(Key.RIGHT)) {
        this._x += 4;
    }
    if (Key.isDown(Key.LEFT)) {
        this._x -= 4;
    }
    if (Key.isDown(Key.DOWN)) {
        this._y += 4;
    }
    if (Key.isDown(Key.UP)) {
        this._y -= 4;
    }
};
```

Very simply, we're moving by adjusting the _x and _y properties, depending upon the state of the cursor keys. We use the isDown() method of the Key object, linked by dot notation, to determine the state of the key. The keys are Key.RIGHT, Key.LEFT, Key.UP, and Key.DOWN, corresponding to the right, left, up, and down arrow keys. If a particular key is being held down, then we adjust the corresponding position property, by increasing or decreasing the _x and _y position by 4. This moves the gold bar at a reasonable speed in response to our key presses.

This is a very simple introduction to keyboard interactivity – there are actually several other methods of keyboard detection, not the least of which is the *listener*, which we'll look at in a moment. Refer to the movie clip key events, and the Key object properties in the reference section of this book for more details.

Advanced animation with listeners

If we want ActionScript to be triggered by pressing and releasing keys, one of the techniques we can now use relies on what are known as **listeners**. A listener is an object that contains code, and it is tied to certain Flash objects that will generate an appropriate event when the user takes certain actions. Prime examples are the 'key down' and 'key up' actions. Let's see how it's done – check out `listeners.fla`:

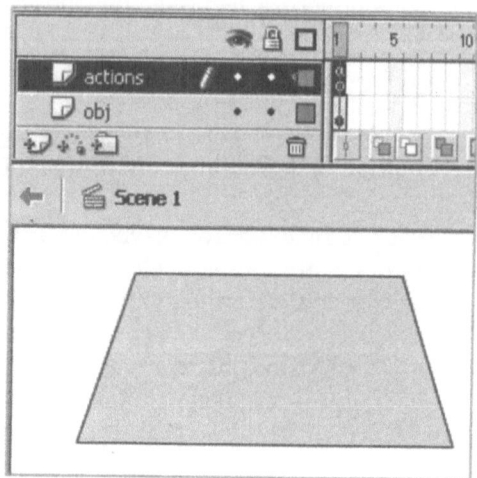

On the stage we have a simple movie clip with the instance name keyprofile (it represents the side profile of a key on your keyboard). The following script is attached to frame 1 of the actions layer:

```
listenerObject = new Object();
listenerObject.onKeyUp = function() {
      keyprofile._yscale = 100;
};
listenerObject.onKeyDown = function() {
      keyprofile._yscale = 40;
};
Key.addListener(listenerObject);
```

This code creates a new listener object called listenerObject, and then attaches two functions to this object: onKeyUp and onKeyDown. In the onKeyDown function, we set the _yscale of keyprofile to 40, which means it will shrink to 40% in height when a key is pressed. The onKeyUp function restores the _yscale of keyprofile back to 100. Finally, and importantly, the last line of code *assigns* the listener object to be an active listener of the Key object. We'll get into more details of this later in the book, but this example serves well as an introduction to the concept of listeners and the events that they can trigger. There are actually several other listener events and objects that respond to listeners, including the Mouse and the Textfield object – more details about these in **Chapter 10**.

When we test this movie, a key listener is indeed created – press any key and the keyprofile shrinks in height, giving the appearance that it has been pressed. When we release the key, the keyprofile returns to 100% height:

On key down

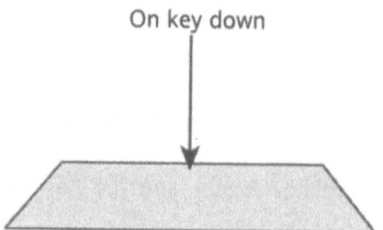

Objectives

- Simple animation in Flash MX

- The movie clip as the foundation for ActionScript-based animation

- Integrating graphics with ActionScript

- Animating with ActionScript and the various motion-scripting properties

- Combining *manual* animation with script-based dynamics:

  - Cyclic animation

  - Duplicating and attaching movie clips at runtime

  - Kinetic effects

- Dynamic masking

- User interactions with the mouse and keyboard

Objectives

- Using movie clips and buttons in your user interface

- Creating draggable UI elements:

    - Drag-and-drop control

    - Collision detection

    - Creating sliders

- Controlling and detecting the mouse

- Flash MX UI components:

    - Updating smart clips

    - Using UI components

    - Customizing and creating components

Introduction

Using ActionScript to control the user interface (UI) of our Flash sites and applications is integral to creating successful and usable designs. Adding script-based functionality to a movie can be a little daunting at first – but once you learn some of the fundamental aspects of using code for interactive interface elements, you'll see how easy it can be.

Creating a movie in which a user can interact with objects, the timeline, a database, or even a server is common with script-enhanced Flash design and development. Using buttons, movie clips, components, and advanced mouse control is central to making this interaction happen.

More complicated interfaces may include draggable elements, custom-built sliders and toggles, collision detection, and so on. You might add elements with a *drag-and-drop* feature to allow users to manipulate and personalize your site/application's UI. Of course, this is simple to achieve by adding just a small amount of ActionScript to your movies.

No matter how creative you are, sometimes all a project requires is a simple, and highly intuitive interface for a diverse audience. This is readily achievable by using the default set of UI components that ships with Macromedia Flash MX. The use of components in Flash MX greatly simplifies UI design and puts the emphasis on producing highly *usable* designs. The Flash components were all designed to include the full functionality of a traditional UI element (like a scroll bar). It's even possible to spice them up and customize them to suit your needs with a little ActionScript.

We'll look at all these elements of interactive UI design in this chapter, but let's begin with a look at some of the more basic interactive elements that we can use – buttons and movie clips.

Buttons and movie clips

Buttons, movie clips, text, and graphics are four of the main elements you will find in Flash movies. Of these, buttons and movie clips are the two primary methods used for controlling the timeline and for enabling user interaction within an interface.

Creating and using basic buttons

Basic buttons are used in Flash for navigation and user interaction. In Flash MX, the button is actually an *object*, so it can use ActionScript events and properties to manipulate and control its instances, just like movie clips can. In fact, buttons are quite similar to movie clips and the ability to name and remotely reference them means that we can centralize all of our ActionScript. Indeed, code can be either directly attached to the button instance itself (but this is now a rather outdated practice), or it can be connected to the button's name via dot notation called from the root timeline.

Of course, it's beneficial to keep our ActionScript in one place, and the root timeline is the obvious location. This makes editing, updating, debugging, and manipulating your code much easier (for instance, you can search and replace code that is all in one place), and is especially useful when you're working in a team of developers. If you've ever had to scan through a load of source files in attempt to figure out what someone else has done, you'll realize how frustrating decentralized code can be.

The process involved in creating a button symbol is very simple in Flash MX – open a new FLA file and choose Insert>New Symbol... (or just press CTRL+F8):

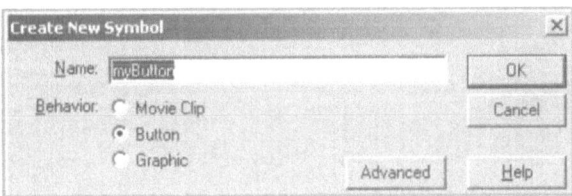

Select the Button option in the Create New Symbol window, and give your button a name. This will open the button editing environment, which provides a place for you to insert graphics (or even movie clips) into the Up, Over, Down, and Hit states:

As these names imply, each button state is related to the current mouse position. If the mouse is not interacting with the button, it is in the Up state. If the mouse is hovering over the button, the Over state is visible. When the user clicks on the button, the Down state is visible. The Hit state is never seen in your final movie, as it refers only to the *hotspot* area of the button; the area where the user can click, and any ActionScript applied to the button will execute. The hit area will only apply to the solid areas of your button graphics, so if you're using text as your button, it's very important to make sure you have filled in a solid hit area surrounding the letters, otherwise users will have a difficult time clicking on your text buttons.

Once you've added graphics to your button and have closed its editing environment, drag an instance of the new button from your Library (hit F11) onto the stage. You're now ready to use this button with ActionScript – be sure to select the button instance on the stage and give it an instance name (myButton, for example). You can then call and use your named button remotely from any other timeline. For example, we could add the following code to the Actions panel in the root timeline:

```
1 myButton.onPress = function() {
2     _root.getURL("http://www.macromedia.com");
3 };
4
```

This simple getURL() action will execute when the button named myButton is pressed. As we'll see in this section, you can use other events with buttons, such as rollover, release, dragOut, or even a key press.

Using buttons with ActionScript

Let's look more closely at how we can use ActionScript functions with button instances. As we have seen above, if we want to control our button instances with code on the main timeline, it's vital to give each button an instance name. This name is given in the Property inspector when the button is selected on the stage:

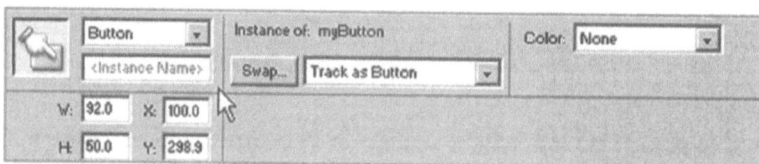

ActionScript can manipulate a movie clip by referencing its given instance name. We can use events, such as onMouseDown or onMouseUp, to change the properties of the button, as we'll see later on in this chapter. Another advantage of having instance names is that we can control the tabbing order of our buttons – this is useful when producing a highly usable web interface, which we'll examine shortly.

When we select our button instance on the stage, we have an additional option in a drop-down box in the Property inspector that allows us to set buttons to either Track as Button or Track as Menu Item:

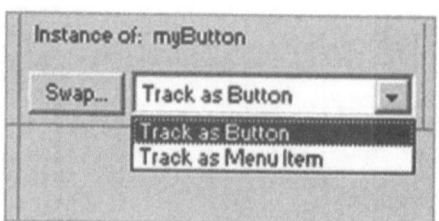

The difference between these two is simple to see. Let's demonstrate by dragging several instances of buttons onto the stage – grab some from the Window>Common Libraries>Buttons Library . Line up a few instances, and make sure they are all set to the default Track as Button setting. Click on the first button, and keep the mouse depressed. Then roll over the other buttons, and you'll notice that the Over state of the first instance remains triggered. If you were to release the mouse over any of the other buttons, the first button's action would still be triggered. As you can imagine, this would be no use at all if you were constructing a menu of selectable options.

Now change your buttons to Track as Menu Item and repeat the process:

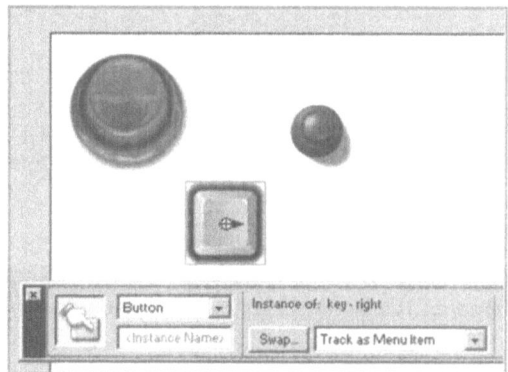

This time you'll see that once the mouse is depressed, any button instance you roll over will change to an Over state. If these buttons had functions applied to them, the function attached to the button that you release the mouse over is the one that would be called. If you had fashioned a drop-down menu, this would obviously be the kind of functionality you would require your buttons to have.

Attaching functions to buttons

Now let's see an example of how we can efficiently centralize our ActionScript and attach functions to buttons remotely, from the root timeline. In the following example, some buttons are placed within a movie clip, and others are on the root timeline. Open up the file button_script.fla from the CD – on the stage you'll immediately notice four buttons. First, on the left-hand side, we have button1 and button2. On the right-hand side, there's a movie clip called myMC that contains the two other buttons, with instance names button3 and button4.

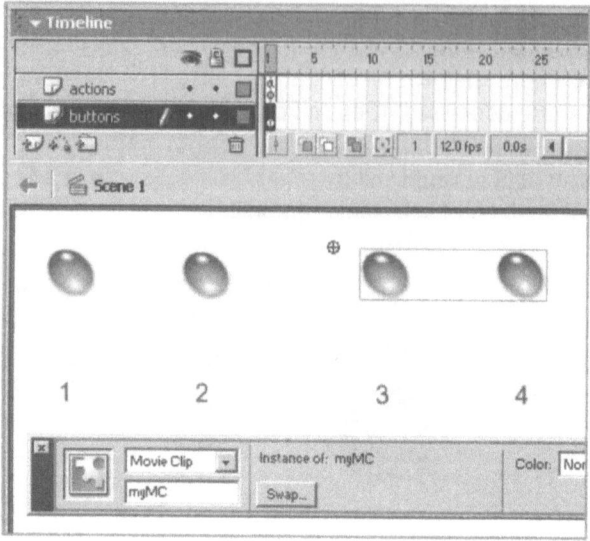

Now look on frame 1 of the actions layer and note that we've added some functions and event handlers to our button instances. Open up the Actions panel (F9) to see what this code looks like:

```
button1.onPress = function() {
    button2.useHandCursor = false;
    myMC.button3._alpha = 50;
    myMC.button4._visible = false;
};
button2.onRelease = function() {
    this._height = 10;
    this._width = 10;
    button1._x = 400;
    button1._y = 200;
    myMC.button3._xscale = 20;
    myMC.button4._yscale = 20;
};
myMC.button3.onPress = function() {
    myMC._parent.button1._alpha = 50;
    myMC.button4._width = 200;
};
myMC.button4.onRollOver = function() {
    this._rotation = 45;
};
```

This code attaches various actions to the buttons that will fire whenever each button is either pressed (onPress), pressed then released (onRelease), or rolled over by the mouse (onRollOver). Test the code by pressing CTRL+ENTER, and press the buttons to see what the ActionScript attached to each one does. Although you would never manipulate buttons in this particular fashion, this example at least gives an idea of some of the properties of buttons that you can change.

The most important point to note here, however, is the way in which we accessed the buttons nested within the myMC movie clip. Consider the first function definition:

```
button1.onPress = function() {
    button2.useHandCursor = false;
    myMC.button3._alpha = 50;
    myMC.button4._visible = false;
};
```

This chunk of code causes three things to happen when button1 is pressed:

- The hand icon of the cursor is deactivated on button2
- The alpha of button3 is set to 50%
- button4 is made invisible

These actions are achieved by taking note of the location and *scope* of each button. For example, because button2 lies directly on the root timeline, it may be referred to here simply as button2. On the other hand, button3 and button4 are located within the myMC movie clip and must therefore be referenced as myMC.button3 and myMC.button4.

Buttons and scope

When writing ActionScript to control your buttons, determining the proper scope of the instance is the first thing you'll want to do. As we've seen above, applying scope in your code is essential when you're working with multiple timelines, such as buttons within a movie clip, or in a dynamically loaded SWF file.

For reference, let's look at three different scenarios in which the scope of a button, with the instance name myButton, is important:

- If we have a movie clip called myMC on the stage that we want to go to frame 5 when we press the button, we could enter the following code, to frame 1 of the Actions layer, on the root timeline:

```
myButton.onPress = function() {
   myMC.gotoAndStop(5);
};
```

- If we want to target a SWF file loaded into level 1, the scope is slightly different:

```
myButton.onPress = function() {
   _level1.gotoAndStop(5);
};
```

- If we have a button *inside* the movie clip myMC that we want to press and have the root timeline advance to frame 5, we'd apply the following code on the root timeline:

```
myMC.myButton.onPress = function() {
    _parent.gotoAndStop(5);
};
```

When you're working with loaded movies, or are planning to load the current movie into another SWF file, it's recommended that you use _parent or this instead of _root whenever possible, because _root will scope to the main timeline of the movie loading the SWFs, which could potentially cause some scoping problems. If you ever have a problem determining the scope of an instance, just select it, open the Actions panel, and press the Insert a target path button:

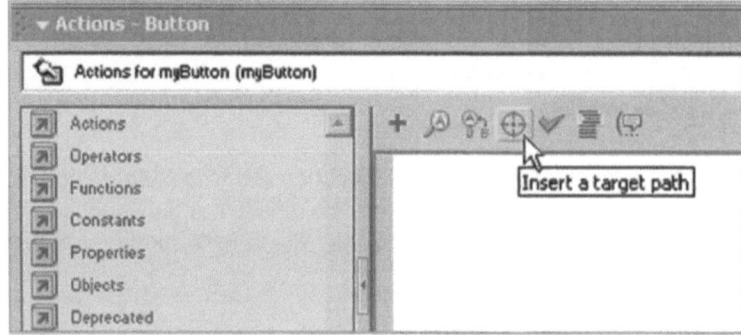

This will automatically insert the scope chain into your ActionScript.

Invisible buttons

Invisible buttons are often used to hide additional interface interaction on a page. With an invisible button, you can define a hit area without actually adding button graphics. This is useful when you need to define an active area to interact with the mouse – you might, for example, want to add a hotspot to your interface that, when rolled over with the mouse cursor, plays an animation. Let's look at how we'd achieve this through a basic invisible button – open up invisibleButton.fla:

You'll find two items on the graphics layer of the stage – there's an instance of the `invisible_button` button called `button1` on the right hand side, and there's an innocent-looking cartoon image of a cat on the left-hand side. Before moving on, test the movie (CTRL+ENTER) to see what it does; notice that when you mouse over where the button should be (it's now invisible!), the tail of our cat wags – it's actually an animation! When you roll off the invisible button, the animation will stop:

Return to the Flash authoring environment, select the `cat_mc` movie clip on the stage (it has an instance name of `cat`), and open it up to see what its timeline consists of. As you'll see, it's a short looping animation with a `stop` action on frame 1, and a `gotoAndPlay(2)` action on the last frame:

Next, go back to the root timeline and open up the instance of the invisible_button movie clip – note that this button has *no* graphics for its Up, Over, and Down states (hence its invisibility), and its Hit state take the form of a simple rectangle:

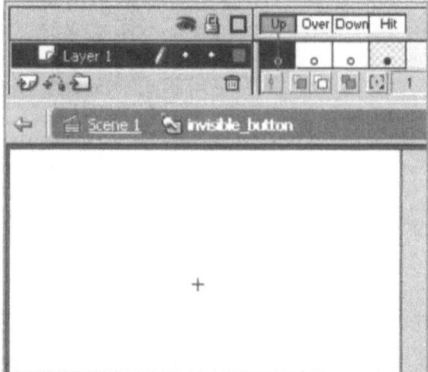

Time to see how it all fits together – return to the main timeline, select frame 1 of the actions layer, and bring up the Actions panel (F9), where you'll see the following ActionScript:

```
_root.button1.onRollOver = function() {
    _root.cat.gotoAndPlay(2);
    this.useHandCursor = false;
};
_root.button1.onRollOut = function() {
    _root.cat.gotoAndStop(1);
};
```

In our first function definition, we essentially state that every time the mouse cursor rolls over `button1` we will play our cat animation from frame 2 (so the animation will keep looping if our cursor remains over the button's hit area) and disable the hand icon of the mouse cursor to ensure the invisibility of the button. In the second function, we simply stop the animation whenever the mouse cursor rolls out of the hit area of our button. Simple and sneaky!

> *Even though using an invisible button is extremely useful in many situations, it is not recommended you use them when designing an interface that has universal accessibility as its motivation (aimed at users with a visual disability, for instance). Invisible buttons will not be accessible to a screen reader, which will only recognize buttons with content, so when the hit state calls a function, the screen reader will not be able to describe what is happening.*

Creating movie clips for the UI

Using movie clips in your user interface for navigation presents a powerful way of controlling your Flash movies. Furthermore, movie clip buttons are commonly used by designers because they give us plenty of room for creative animations and cool effects; a movie clip button can have all the functionality of a standard Flash button, except it has a timeline that you can work with too. In many cases it is preferable to using buttons themselves, since all the behaviors of a button can be added to a movie clip.

Building a movie clip button

Using movie clip buttons is great when you need a timeline for animation with your button, or for the extra power that the methods and properties of the movie clip object can offer you. For the reasons we've mentioned above, you have a lot more flexibility during production, and also more room for your design to expand and evolve if you decide to update or edit a movie later on. Another major bonus is that a standard button can only have three graphic states associated with it: up, over, and down, whereas a movie clip can have many more – as many as you like really!

Let's go through the general steps necessary to create a basic movie clip button (note that the finished version of this example can be found on the CD in the file `mcButton.fla`):

1.   Open a new FLA file, and then create a new movie clip (CTRL+F8) – name it `button_mc`. Add four new layers to `button_mc`: graphics, hitArea, labels, and actions. Add a keyframe (F6) to frames 10 and 20 of each layer, and add several new frames (F5) after the final keyframe on each layer:

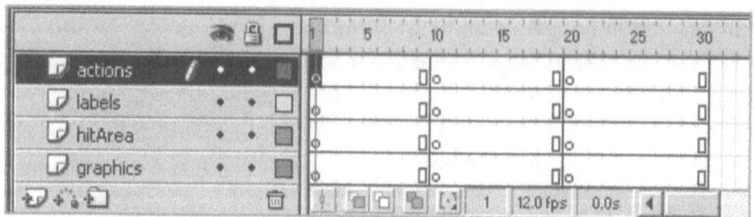

2.   Next, go to the labels layer and give each state a label – select the keyframes on frames 1, 10, and 20, and enter the label name in the Property inspector as _up, _over, and _down, respectively.

3.   On the graphics layer we'll need to create these three different button states. Select frame 1, and create a graphic or some text on the stage. This will be the _up state. If you're going to be reusing the same image or text, it's worth converting it to a graphic (F8) – then you can copy it (CTRL+C) and use Edit>Paste in Place (CTRL+SHIFT+V) to put the same image on the _over and _down keyframes. Finally, change the color of each instance of the graphic to reflect the differences in the button's state:

4.   Now we need to define a hit area – this is the hotspot where the mouse cursor changes and your movie clip button can be clicked. We should make sure that each graphic has a hit area fully covering the instance below. On frame 1 of the hitArea layer, draw a solid shape (without a stroke) covering your graphic for the _up state. Press F8 to change this graphic into a movie clip (as usual, name it clearly – we've chosen hitArea_mc), and change the opacity to about 50%, so you're able to see your button text/graphics underneath, and can resize the hit area as needed:

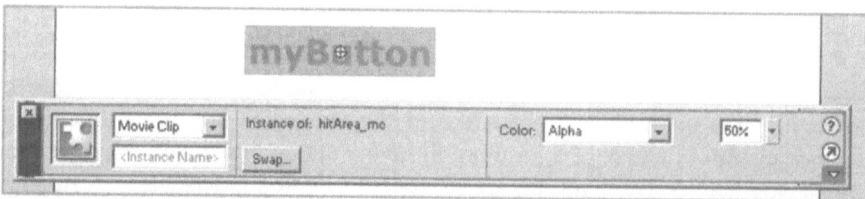

5.   Give it an instance name of hitArea, and add this hit area to the other two states (you can use Paste in Place again).

6.   Now we need to add some ActionScript so that our button works. Create a new layer called actions inside the hitArea_mc movie clip and enter the following code:

```
_parent.hitArea = this;
this._visible = false;
```

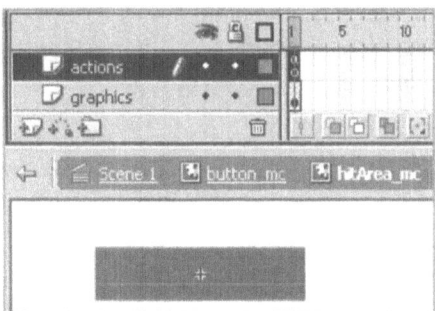

7. If you now click the back button on the navigation bar to go back to button_mc and check each keyframe containing hitArea, you'll find your code is applied to each instance already, since we were editing the movie clip itself. The first line of code defines the movie clip hitArea as the hit area of our movie clip button. The second line of code will make our hit area invisible at runtime. Of course, we'll have to live with it when we're editing our movie in the authoring environment – but we'll soon see the final result when we test our movie.

8. We need some final pieces of ActionScript in myButton_mc for our movie clip button to function as we wish. Select frame 1 of the actions layer and enter the following code into the script pane of the Actions panel:

```
onRollOver = function () {
    this.gotoAndPlay("_over");
};
onRollOut = function () {
    this.gotoAndPlay("_up");
};
onPress = function () {
    this.gotoAndStop("_down");
    _parent.getURL("http://www.flashmxlibrary.com/");
};
```

With this code, we're creating functions for each state of the button that are called when the associated mouse event occurs. This code makes our movie clip mimic the functionality of a button. Each function simply tells Flash that when the event happens (onRollOver, onRollOut, or onPress), go to a specified frame and play, via a gotoAndPlay() command. The usage of this in our code means that we are referencing the object itself. Obviously, you can add further statements within each function if you want other events to occur as well.

In the final function, we want the button to go to a web site. We have to change the scope of the getURL() action to _parent (or _root) so it doesn't open multiple browser windows.

9. Now, to stop our movie clip button continuously looping around its states we need to add a little bit of script on or before each new state. So on frame 9 of the actions layer, insert a new keyframe and add the following line:

```
gotoAndPlay("_up");
```

Likewise, on frame 19 insert a keyframe with this line of code:

```
gotoAndPlay("_over");
```

And finally, just add a `stop()` command on frame 20. (Note that if you have an animated movie clip button, you'll have to change your `gotoAndStop()` actions to `gotoAndPlay()`. You'll also have to loop each state.)

10. The timeline of `button_mc` should now look rather busy:

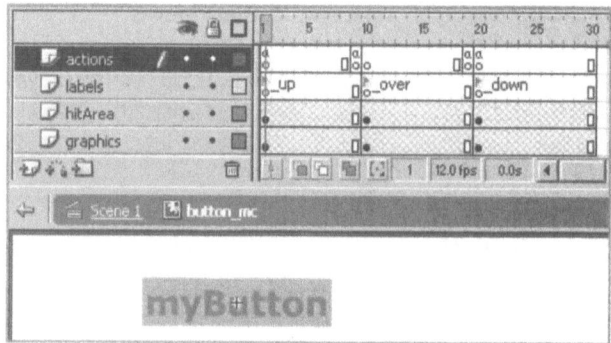

The last thing to do is return to the root timeline and drag an instance of `button_mc` from the Library onto the stage. And that's it! Test your movie and you'll have a movie clip button that functions as a regular instance of the button object. Click on the button, and your web browser should open up the site specified:

Adding custom button graphic states

But why not just use a button? Well, the advantage of using a movie clip is that you can now make an animated button and add additional states to your button. The option of creating different graphic states brings clear benefits to our designs. Just like an HTML page, we could use a different color to show a link has been visited. In addition to this, we could disable our buttons setting the `MovieClip.enabled` or `Button.enabled` properties to `false`. With movie clips you can add effects to each state by adding and labeling more states in your movie clip buttons. You may also want to add more states for `onDragOut`, or any other event that you want your interface to recognize.

For a simple demonstration of how we might animate our movie clip buttons, open up mcButton_anim.fla – in this FLA file, we've simply extended the previous example by adding some simple color tweens to the _up and _over states of the graphics layer:

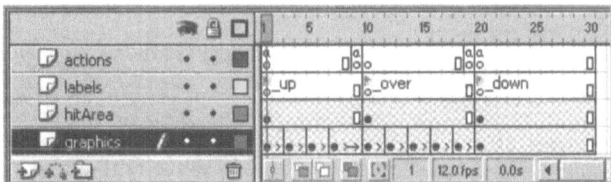

When you test this movie, you'll see that our button now looks animated, and the animation changes when we move the mouse cursor over it. Simple!

Another feature of button movie clips in Flash MX is the ability to disable a button's state. This is particularly useful when you don't want your user to be able to click on the button instance on certain pages. It's also a nice interface feature when you want to remind the user that they have reached, or gone past, a particular point in your movie. Disabling a button or movie clip button can also prevent a movie reloading once it has already been loaded.

Open mcButton_disable.fla and note that we've added a new _disabled button state on the movie clip button's timeline:

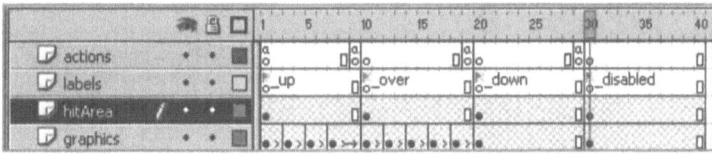

Additionally, on frame 1 of the actions layer, we've added another button function:

```
onRelease = function () {
    this.gotoAndStop("_disabled");
    this.enabled = false;
};
```

Adding this code means that after the getURL() action is called, the button state will change to _disabled, and the button will become unclickable – test the movie to see for yourself.

Controlling your UI

There are several different ways in which you can control a Flash movie using ActionScript; it's worth our while taking a moment to look at the three main techniques that we can use to control buttons and movie clips:

- Controlling the root timeline

- Property-based control

- Timeline-based control

Controlling the root timeline

The root timeline is commonly used to navigate through content in a movie. It can be controlled either by user input, or by actions on the frame itself. For example, if a playhead is moving along the timeline and encounters a frame action of gotoAndPlay("page8"), it will automatically jump to the frame labeled page8. This movement is linear in fashion, and does not involve the user. However, by adding code to buttons and movie clips, adding listeners for key press or mouse movements, or calling functions based on a combination of events, the user can gain efficient control of the main timeline.

Taking this idea a step further, our root timeline may contain a series of *pages*, similar to a succession of scenes. Moving amongst them will advance the user to new content and, since the user controls which page is seen first, this movement does not need to be linear.

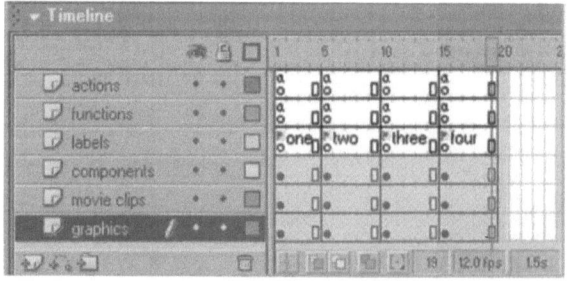

The actions used to control this kind of navigation are typically very simple. For example, gotoAndPlay(), gotoAndStop(), stop(), play(), nextFrame(), and prevFrame() can all be used on buttons or button functions to navigate your interface.

Property-based control

Controlling different properties is also easily accomplished using simple ActionScript. As described in **Chapter 1**, making changes in x and y coordinates, scale, width, height, alpha, and RGB colors can be accomplished using fundamental ActionScript properties. These properties can be changed in frame actions or when functions are called based on user input. You can even change properties based on events, and by using listeners. For example, you can *listen* to the _xmouse and _ymouse positions of a mouse, and change scale or alpha depending on where they are on your interface. Changing properties of instances on the stage can create some interesting designs and allows for a highly interactive environment.

Timeline-based control

One of the most important things to understand about Flash MX is the use of multiple timelines. Movie clips have their own timelines, which run independently from the main one. If, for instance, you load a SWF into the movie at runtime using `loadMovie()`, it too will function in its own timeline on a different level. This may seem confusing (indeed it can get very confusing at times!), but it's definitely an advantage to you as a designer. For example, having one movie continually loop in its own timeline is very useful for animation purposes. Separate timelines also allow us to create new movies on the fly, and have them run independently from our main timeline. You can control these timelines using code on another timeline through an appropriately scoped dot notation chain to reference the correct instance timeline.

Using a separate timeline is also useful when you need an action to repeatedly call and update values. For example, if you need an instance to follow a mouse, you'll need to continually retrieve the x and y coordinates of the mouse. In older versions of Flash, we used to create a *dummy* clip, which was essentially a movie clip into which ActionScript is placed, and then this clip was placed somewhere off-stage, or disguised on the stage. Now, with Flash MX, we can create an empty movie clip and give it an instance name on the fly using `MovieClip.createEmptyMovieClip()` method. Once you've done this, you can add your code to this new movie clip instance, all from the main timeline frame action. We'll see an example of this type of timeline control shortly.

Draggable interface elements

You may have noticed Flash interfaces containing instances that you can drag around within the user interface. Some of these interfaces may even include draggable instances as part of their navigation, or an interactive game. Dragging, dropping, sliding, and colliding use some of the same ActionScript methods and events to achieve their effects. In this section we'll look at how these effects are constructed.

Drag-and-drop control

The movie clip methods `startDrag()` and `stopDrag()` are used to drag an instance around the stage. The `startDrag()` method uses the following format:

```
MovieClip.startDrag(lock, left, top, right, bottom);
```

You need to enter a Boolean value (`true` or `false`) for `lock` – if `true`, this will set the cursor position to the center of the mouse, whereas `false` will lock it to the point where the mouse clicked. `left`, `top`, `right`, and `bottom` all refer to the bounding co-ordinates of a rectangle (note that these values are relative to the co-ordinates of the parent movie clip). The instance is only draggable within this area.

As we'll see, these methods are commonly used when you work with `_droptarget` and custom cursors.

Using startDrag() and stopDrag()

Open up dragMe.fla – here we have a movie clip on the stage. Inside this movie clip are two more movie clip instances. We want the instance of the drag_bar movie clip on the top of the photo_gallery movie clip to be draggable when a user presses on it, and we want the panel_bottom instance on the bottom to be clickable, and fetch a URL. But we also want these two instances to be connected and follow each other.

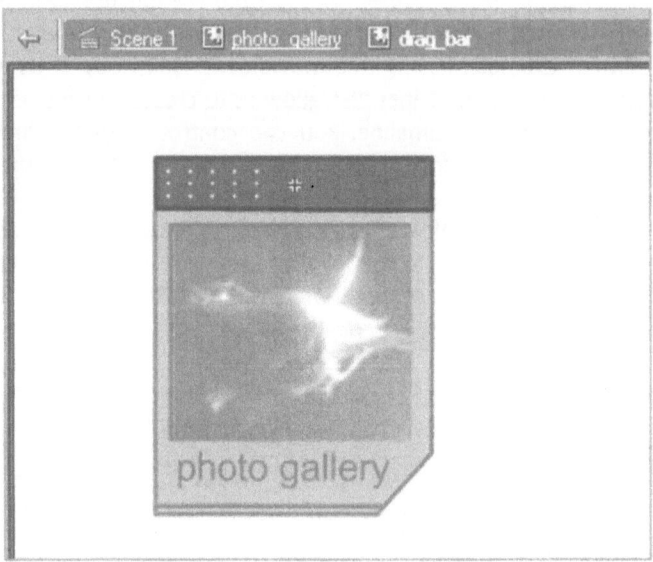

To achieve this, we can add the following code to the timeline of the drag_bar movie clip:

```
this.onPress = function() {
    this.startDrag(true, 550, 280, 0, 15);
    _parent.startDrag(true, 550, 280, 0, 15);
};
this.onMouseUp = function() {
    this.stopDrag();
    _parent.stopDrag();
};
```

Here we are enabling the mouse to drag both the drag_bar movie clip *and* its _parent, the photo_gallery movie clip, together. Try changing the first parameter of the startDrag() method to false and notice the subtle difference that it has when you run the code. Additionally, we can attach an onPress function to the panel_bottom movie clip so that it reacts to a click:

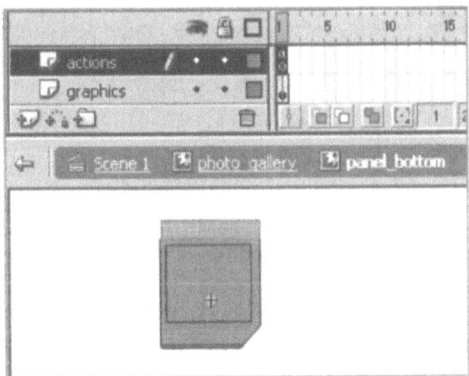

In this case, we've added the following ActionScript, which will open up the specified web page:

```
onPress = function () {
    _root.getURL("http://www.flash-mx.com");
};
```

Test the movie by pressing CTRL+ENTER to see the result.

Using _droptarget

The `_droptarget` command can also be useful for achieving certain effects – take a look at `dropTarget.fla` from the CD for a demonstration. Test this movie, and notice that you can drag and drop the piece of paper into the trashcan:

Let's now learn exactly how this was accomplished; first, take a look at the code on frame 1 of the actions layer:

```
stop();
_root.thepaper.onPress = function() {
    this.startDrag(false);
};
_root.thepaper.onRelease = function() {
    this.stopDrag();
    if (this._droptarget == "/thetrash") {
        _root.gotoAndStop("end");
    }
};
```

We make the piece of paper (which is actually a movie clip with instance name thepaper) draggable when the mouse cursor is clicked on it. When the paper is released, if its position coincides with the top of the trashcan (this is another movie clip, with instance name thetrash), we move the playhead to the frame on the root timeline labeled end. This code relies on the MovieClip._droptarget property to identify the final target position of the thepaper movie clip.

Creating sliders

Sliders are extremely useful interface elements for controlling sound, inputting values, or for allowing a user to adjust their interface. In this section, we'll look at how we'd go about constructing a simple slider using startDrag() and stopDrag() methods.

The source file for this example is called slider.fla – here we're using several movie clips to construct a very simple slider that toggles the size of another couple of movie clip instances. Test this movie, and play around with the slider – moving it to the left shrinks the circles, and moving it right makes them grow larger:

Before we get into the ActionScript that makes our slider possible, let's briefly study how we constructed the slider movie clip. First, we drew a line (ours is 100 pixels long – note that the Info panel is useful for controlling the length, just press CTRL+I to open it up), and then converted this line into a graphic symbol by selecting it and hitting F8. Next we added a slider toggle – we simply created a small square and changed it into a movie clip with the instance name toggle. We placed the toggle movie clip in the middle of the slider bar graphic, checking that its x coordinate was half the length of the line in the Info panel:

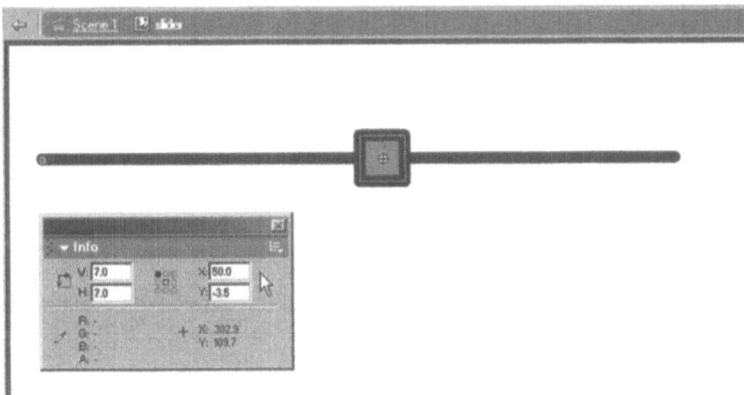

Finally, we selected both the line graphic and the `toggle` movie clip and hit F8 again to change it into the `slider` movie clip symbol. Additionally, we've added a couple of instances of a circle movie clip onto the stage and named them `ball1` and `ball2`.

Now let's get to grips with the code – on frame 1 of the actions layer on the root timeline of `slider.fla` you'll find the following script:

```
_root.slider.toggle.onMouseDown = function() {
      this.startDrag(true, 0, 0, 100, 0);
};
_root.slider.toggle.onMouseUp = function() {
      this.stopDrag();
};
```

These functions will allow the slider toggle to be dragged within the constraints of our slider bar (note that the left and right limits are 0 and 100 respectively) during the onMouseDown event. When onMouseUp occurs, the slider toggle will stop dragging.

Our script continues like this:

```
this.createEmptyMovieClip("checkme", 2);
_root.checkme.onEnterFrame = function() {
      _root.ball1._xscale = _root.slider.toggle._x;
      _root.ball1._yscale = _root.slider.toggle._x;
      _root.ball2._yscale = _root.slider.toggle._x;
};
```

Now we create a movie clip, called checkme, that will continually check for the value of the x coordinate of the slider toggle, and apply it to the _xscale or _yscale of the ball instances.

In fact, another option when creating sliders is to simply use the ScrollBar component – we'll look at this a little later in this chapter.

Collision testing

Testing for collisions between movie clips is very common when you're creating games in Flash. It's also useful when you need to limit where an instance is able to move, particularly if that shape is not a square or rectangle and the co-ordinates are therefore difficult to specify. The `MovieClip.hitTest()` method can hit test either a target instance, or co-ordinates on the stage. Let's look at a couple of examples of these different uses.

First, we can apply a `hitTest()` to a movie clip instance by specifying the target movie clip as the single parameter. So if we have a circle clip, we can check when it hits a wall clip like this:

```
if (myCircle.hitTest(_root.myWall)) {
        trace("You've hit the wall!");
}
```

Open up `hitTest1.fla` to see this in action with a draggable circle:

The second `hitTest()` technique works somewhat differently; this time we have three parameters to specify:

```
MovieClip.hitTest(X, Y, shapeFlag)
```

Here, X and Y refer to the x and y co-ordinates of our hit area on the stage, while `shapeFlag` takes the form of a Boolean value indicating whether to evaluate just the shape of the attached movie clip (in which case we'd enter `true`), or the shape defined by its bounding box (`false`).

An example is necessary to clarify the use of the `shapeFlag` parameter – open up `hitTest2.fla`. Here we have two circles on the stage: `circle1` and `circle2`, and we use `hitTest()` on the location of our mouse compared to each circle using this code:

```
_root.circle1.onMouseMove = function() {
    if (this.hitTest(_root._xmouse, _root._ymouse, true)) {
        trace("Hitting circle1!");
    }
};
_root.circle2.onMouseMove = function() {
    if (this.hitTest(_root._xmouse, _root._ymouse, false)) {
        trace("Hitting circle2!");
    }
};
```

Test the movie and notice the difference that the two shapeFlag value makes: circle1 has this parameter set to true so the output message will only be seen if the mouse cursor touches the red circle. With circle2 the shapeFlag parameter is set to false and therefore the bounding box of the instance defines the shape to hit test:

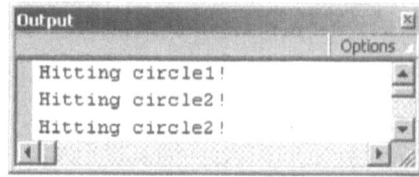

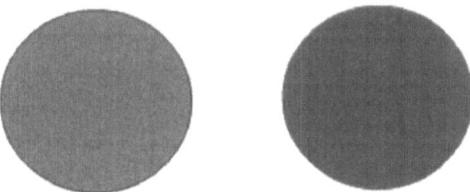

Advanced mouse control

Detecting where the mouse is and using its location to control elements within a movie can add some exciting new interactivity to your UI. Imagine having a movie clip on the stage that essentially *listens* to where the mouse moves to, and then acts according to where it is – as we shall see, this is simple in Flash MX.

Customizing the mouse cursor

Making a custom cursor is rather similar to making a movie clip button. For example, you can add different states like up, down, and over to the movie clip you use with your mouse. In this example we'll discover how to customize our mouse cursor into a movie clip graphic with a couple of different states – open up customCursor.fla. At first you'll see an innocent-looking arrow movie clip on the stage; now test the movie with CTRL+ENTER.

Woah! The blue arrow now acts like our cursor in the Flash movie and when we press down on the mouse button, the graphic changes subtly and pulsates – it's animated! Pretty cool, huh? Let's see how this was achieved.

Return to the Flash MX authoring environment and double-click on the arrow movie clip to see how it's constructed:

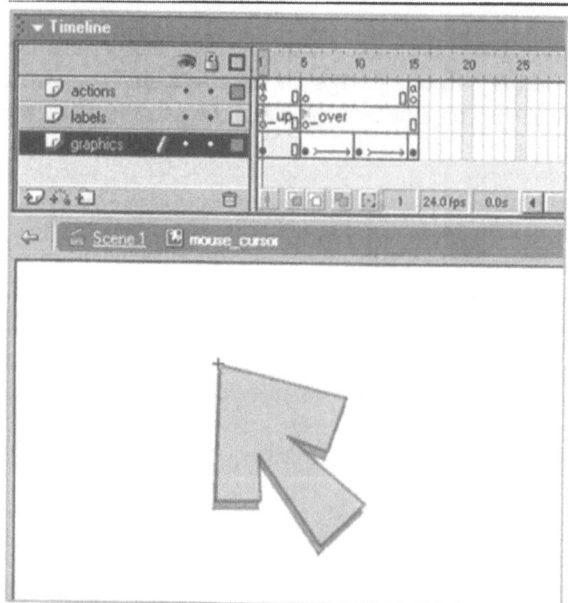

Inside the movie clip you'll see three layers on the timeline: graphics, labels, and actions. Note also that there are two different labeled states: _up and _over, similar to our movie clip button. Now drag the playhead to the _over frames and notice how the arrow changes its color and characteristics – obviously we must have some ActionScript to change our standard cursor into this movie clip.

In frame 1 of the actions layer, as usual, you'll find the code in question. Let's look at the most important commands:

```
Mouse.hide();
this.onMouseMove = function() {
    this._x = _root._xmouse;
    this._y = _root._ymouse;
    updateAfterEvent();
};
this.onMouseDown = function() {
    gotoAndPlay("_over");
```

```
    };
    this.onMouseUp = function() {
        gotoAndPlay("_up");
    };
```

With this code the mouse is initially hidden, and then essentially swapped for this instance of our mouse_cursor movie clip (as referenced with this) by keeping track of its x and y co-ordinates and constantly updating the position of the movie clip. Then, the onMouseDown and onMouseUp events are linked to our movie clip so it goes into the _over state when the mouse is clicked (admittedly, linking an onMouseDown event to an _over state isn't very good design practice, so we'll look at a better technique shortly).

In an actual interface, using this approach alone is not terribly useful; we can end up with all of our code attached to individual movie clips, which makes debugging or file-sharing a bit of a nightmare! So, let's look at a better way of activating our custom cursor – remotely from the root timeline.

Open up mcButton_customCursor.fla. In this example we're combining our movie clip button from earlier in the chapter with the customized cursor – and placing the bulk of our ActionScript on the root timeline so that we know exactly what is going on. Check out the code on frame 1 of the actions layer:

```
    button1.onRollOver = function() {
        button1.gotoAndPlay("_over");
        _root.cursor.gotoAndPlay("_over");
    };
    button1.onRollOut = function() {
        button1.gotoAndPlay("_up");
        _root.cursor.gotoAndStop("_up");
    };
    button1.onPress = function() {
        button1.gotoAndStop("_down");
        _root.getURL("http://www.friendsofed.com/");
    };
```

Here we're essentially stating our button code at the same time as our cursor code; we set the _over and _up states of our cursor and button movie clips within the same onRollOver and onRollOut functions. In fact, this technique can be applied to any more buttons or movie clip instances that you add. Everything is now kept neatly on frame 1 of the main timeline, so it's easy to edit if the need arises..

To finish with, let's remind ourselves of a couple of important points that are well worth keeping in mind when we are customizing our cursor:

- Make sure that the part of the graphic you want to be the tip of the pointer is located at the (0, 0) co-ordinate of the movie clip.

- Put the movie clip on the top most layer so it doesn't pass underneath instances on the stage.

Mouse detection and listeners

In Flash MX we can have instances on the stage registered to *listen* to what the mouse is doing – essentially, they detect and act on the mouse's properties. This opens a lot of doors for us in the context of UI design and interactivity within our movies.

In the following example, we're going to use the drawing API of Flash MX with a mouse listener. We'll create a small drawing application where you can draw boxes using the mouse. Don't worry about the details of how we use drawing API commands here, we're really only interested in how the listeners work anyway – all will be revealed about the drawing API in **Chapter 3**. For the moment, this will at least serve as a nice teaser of what's to come in the next chapter.

The code for this example is found in mouse_listener.fla on the CD. Open up this FLA file, and notice that the only thing we've added to the stage is a dynamic text box called mousecoords in the top left corner. Now test the movie – we've got the early stages of an online drawing application here. You can click and drag a box out to any size, and lay boxes over each other:

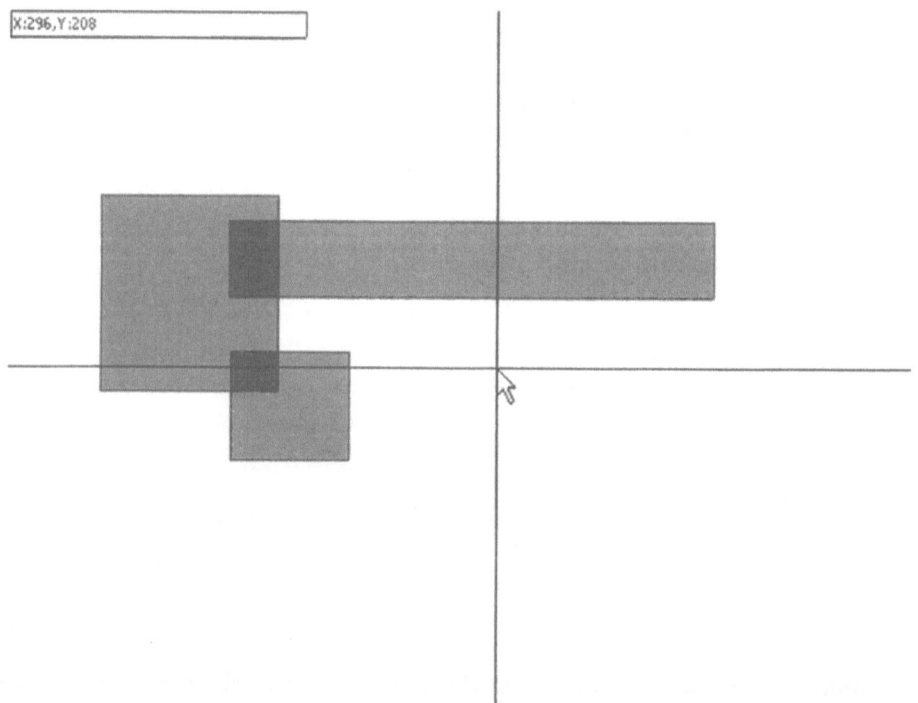

Now let's look at the ActionScript on frame 1 of the actions layer (printed here for completeness, but don't panic – an explanation will follow!):

```
obj = new Object();
obj.onMouseMove = function() {
     var thisX = Math.round(_xmouse);
     var thisY = Math.round(_ymouse);
     _root.mousecoords.text = "X:"+thisX+",Y:"+thisY;
     _root.createEmptyMovieClip("xline", -1);
     with (_root["xline"]) {
            lineStyle(1, 0x000000, 100);
            moveTo(thisX, 0);
            lineTo(thisX, Stage.height);
     }
     _root.createEmptyMovieClip("yline", -2);
     with (_root["yline"]) {
            lineStyle(1, 0x000000, 100);
            moveTo(0, thisY);
            lineTo(Stage.width, thisY);
     }
};


// Listen to where the mouse is depressed and
// released in order to draw boxes.
obj.onMouseDown = function() {
     _root.pressX = _xmouse;
     _root.pressY = _ymouse;
};
obj.onMouseUp = function() {
     _root.releaseX = _xmouse;
     _root.releaseY = _ymouse;

     // Draw boxes
     _root.createEmptyMovieClip("box", _root.numBoxes);
     with (_root.box) {
            beginFill(0x0000FF, 50);
            lineStyle(1, 0x0000FF, 100);
            moveTo(pressX, pressY);
            lineTo(releaseX, pressY);
            lineTo(releaseX, releaseY);
            lineTo(pressX, releaseY);
            lineTo(pressX, pressY);
            endFill();
     }

     // Increments current level value so that
     // boxes are not overwritten
     _root.numBoxes++;
```

continues overleaf

```
};

// Register a listener to obj
Mouse.addListener(obj);

// Intialize numBox variable
_root.numBoxes = 1;
```

First of all, we create a new object called obj. This object will listen to the movement of the mouse by first associating an onMouseMove event to it, and ultimately registering obj as a listener. Next, within the onMouseMove function we connect the mouse coordinates (_xmouse, _ymouse) to our mousecoords dynamic text field so that it is constantly reading and printing the position of the mouse:

```
obj = new Object();
obj.onMouseMove = function() {
     var thisX = Math.round(_xmouse);
     var thisY = Math.round(_ymouse);
     _root.mousecoords.text = "X:"+thisX+",Y:"+thisY;
```

Next up we create two empty movie clips called xline and yline – these use drawing API methods to draw horizontal and vertical lines over the entire width and height of the stage (Stage.width and Stage.height) while listening to the x and y co-ordinates of the mouse position:

```
     _root.createEmptyMovieClip("xline", -1);
     with (_root["xline"]) {
          lineStyle(1, 0x000000, 100);
          moveTo(thisX, 0);
          lineTo(thisX, Stage.height);
     }
     _root.createEmptyMovieClip("yline", -2);
     with (_root["yline"]) {
          lineStyle(1, 0x000000, 100);
          moveTo(0, thisY);
          lineTo(Stage.width, thisY);
     }
};
```

In the next chunks of code, we rely on the onMouseDown and onMouseUp events to gather the x and y co-ordinates each time the mouse is pressed and then released:

```
obj.onMouseDown = function() {
     _root.pressX = _xmouse;
     _root.pressY = _ymouse;
};
obj.onMouseUp = function() {
```

```
_root.releaseX = _xmouse;
_root.releaseY = _ymouse;
```

We then create another empty movie clip, this time called box, which takes the new co-ordinates (pressX, pressY) and (releaseX, releaseY) to form the shape of a box. With the drawing API we can move to (moveTo()) the point where the onMouseDown event was registered, and then draw a box to where the onMouseUp event took place:

```
_root.createEmptyMovieClip("box", _root.numBoxes);
with (_root.box) {
        beginFill(0x0000FF, 50);
        lineStyle(1, 0x0000FF, 100);
        moveTo(pressX, pressY);
        lineTo(releaseX, pressY);
        lineTo(releaseX, releaseY);
        lineTo(pressX, releaseY);
        lincTo(pressX, pressY);
        endFill();
}
```

Finally, we need to increment. the current level value so that boxes are not overwritten (note that the level of the box movie clip was set to the variable numBoxes in the previous code segment). Then, importantly, we must register a listener to the obj object, and remember to initialize the numBoxes variable to 1:

```
        _root.numBoxes++;
};
Mouse.addListener(obj);
_root.numBoxes = 1;
```

Pretty cool! Of course, to truly understand this program, it's worth becoming familiar with the Flash MX drawing API – see **Chapter 3**. Additionally, we'll discuss the use of listeners in depth in **Chapter 10**.

Flash MX UI components

The addition of standardized *off-the-shelf* UI components with the release of Flash MX marks a huge enrichment of the design possibilities of Flash. Enhancing UI design was the major reason for the inclusion of a set of scroll bars, buttons, list boxes, and so on, in the Flash authoring environment. Using standardized user interface elements is a huge plus when it comes to usability. When you're aiming for an easy to understand design targeted at a wide, diverse audience, using elements of consistent functionality is ideal.

This of course is only one of the benefits of components in general. Components themselves are instantly beneficial to busy designers who want to reuse and re-purpose as much of their design elements as possible. Similarly, the components shipping with Flash MX are great for quick mock-ups and proof-of-concept experiments.

Also, we can make custom components of our own design, and build up a comprehensive set of component functionality that we can ultimately distribute (share, trade, or sell...) to other designers.

From smart clips to components

If you needed to create reusable UI elements in Flash 5, the answer was to use what was known as a *smart clip*. Smart clips helped you reuse the same piece of code, with the added option of being easily able to modify the parameters of your code. Smart clips were basically movie clips with an edge, which were added to your Library and utilized as you wished.

In Flash MX, smart clips have been completely replaced by components. So, if you're already familiar with building smart clips then you're a step ahead when it comes to building custom components (if not, then don't worry about it – just skip ahead to the next section where we'll learn about using the Flash MX UI components). But how is a component different from a smart clip?

Components are much more robust than smart clips ever were – they can handle extended tasks, and can even be animated in the authoring environment via a *live preview* option. Also, it's possible for a component to consist only of code, which then attaches itself onto the designated movie clip. So components are not simply UI elements, they add custom methods and properties to the movie too.

When switching from smart clips to components, you should note that:

- You can't just double-click your component on the stage to edit its parameters, you can only edit it through the Library options.

- You can make components in Flash MX and save them as a Flash 5 document, and you'll find that most (but not all!) Flash 5 players will support the component!

Now you must be wondering how to convert your old smart clips into components. Well it's pretty simple – you can actually take your old libraries of smart clips and add them right into the Components panel in Flash MX. Remember, the Flash MX default set of components is essentially just a set of FLA files. So, group all of your related smart clips into one FLA, give it an appropriate name, and save this file as a Flash 5 document. Open it in Flash MX, and you'll find all of your smart clips sitting happily in the Library. At this point, you can rename the clips in the Library to whatever you want them to be named in the component panel.

The next step is to right click on the smart clips and select Component Definition... from the contextual menu (the panel that opens up is actually very similar to the Define Clip Parameters window from Flash 5). Near the bottom of this window is a check box called Display in Components panel – obviously, this is what you need to select to have your components show up in the panel. Tool tips and icons can also be set and imported from this window if you would like to include these features with your smart clips:

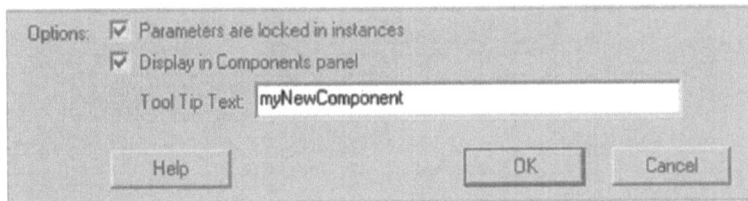

Finally, it's a good idea to set the Linkage… with your smart clips, and make sure Export for ActionScript and Export in first frame are both selected. It's standard for Flash components to export on the first frame at runtime:

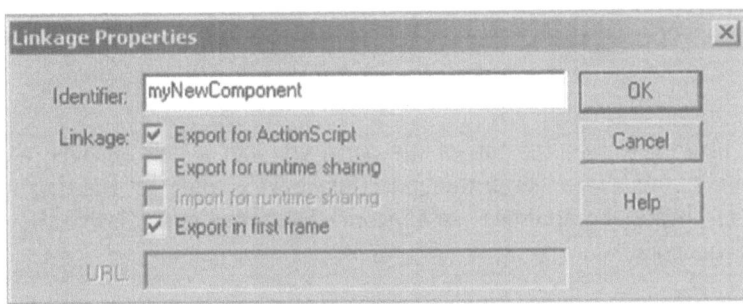

This process should be repeated for each of your smart clips, and then the FLA file saved as a Flash MX document with the other component FLA files on your system. If you search for the `FlashUIComponents.fla` that came with your copy of Macromedia Flash MX, you'll find the correct directory for your new FLA file. For instance, on a Windows 2000 system the default location of this file is `C:\Program Files\Macromedia\Flash MX\First Run\Components`.

So now that we're all familiar with reusing Flash 5 smart clips, let's take a detailed look at the powerful set of default components in Flash MX.

Using the default UI components set

Before looking at using each of the default Macromedia Flash UI components, let's take a look at where components live in the authoring environment. Select Window>Components (CTRL+F7) to open the Components panel; here is where you'll find the default Flash MX components (and any additional sets you install):

With the pull-down box near the top of the panel you can switch between each set of components installed in your system. Note that in the above image we've only got the default Flash UI set, but you can download more component sets from Macromedia's Flash MX resource center at www.macromedia.com.

From the Components panel, it's a simple matter of dragging and dropping the required component onto the stage. After you drag an instance onto the stage, you can access and change the parameters of the component in the Property inspector (CTRL+F3). Using the Properties tab, you can change basic properties such as tint and alpha. In the Parameters tab, you can assign a Change Handler, set Labels, add Data, and any other parameter significant to the individual component. Other labels and values are added in the Values window, which pops up after the magnifying glass icon is pressed for certain parameters:

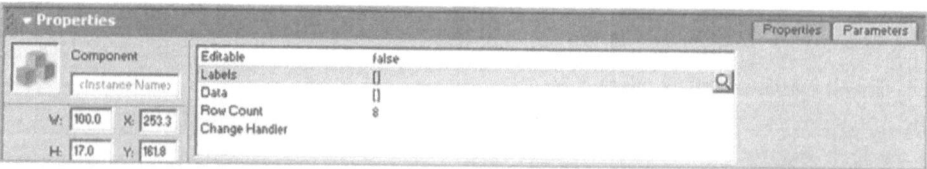

After an instance of a component is on the stage, open the Library (F11) and you'll find that many new elements have been added within a folder. This folder contains all the movie clips, ActionScript, and graphics that make up the component. In fact, some of the components in the default UI components set share certain elements, such as the scroll bar. If we were to use *all* of the Flash UI components in a design, our Library would look something like this:

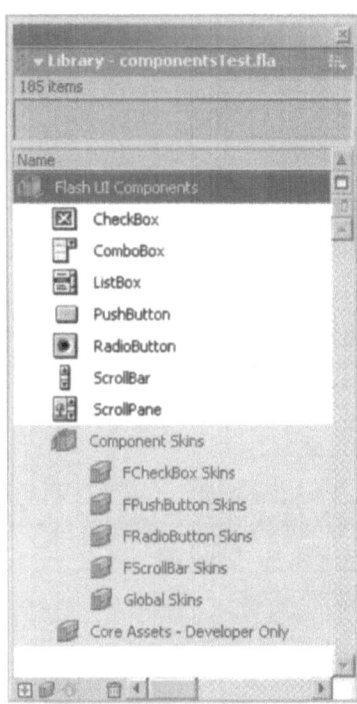

As we'll see when we study each component individually, it's important to realize that functions aimed at components must be linked to **the component's timeline**.

Now that we know where to find components in the authoring environment, it's time to put them to work. In the following subsections, for quick and easy reference, we'll present tutorial-style instructions for setting up each component in the Flash UI default set.

Using the CheckBox

The CheckBox component is used when you need to collect a number of set values from a user. CheckBox instances return a `true` or `false` Boolean value to Flash, depending on whether or not the box is selected. A CheckBox is typically used when multiple values from a set need to be returned. This is in contrast to RadioButtons, which are used when only one value from a group should be selected.

After dragging an instance of a CheckBox to the stage, select the Parameters tab in the Property inspector (as described earlier):

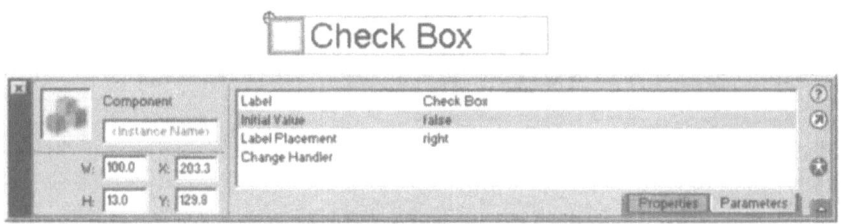

These parameters are described in the following table:

Checkbox parameters	Description
Label	Used to change the text associated with each instance of the CheckBox component
Initial Value	Can be set to initially show a check mark when the movie plays, the default value being false (no check mark)
Label Placement	Refers to whether or not the text is placed to the left or to the right of the component
Change Handler	Where you can enter the name of a function. The function will be called when the check box is selected or deselected

Note that the hit area of the CheckBox component covers both the CheckBox itself, as well as the text label accompanying it. You can change the width of a CheckBox component so longer text can be made visible by using either the Free Transform tool or the FCheckBox.setSize() method.

> A CheckBox component is typically used to turn something on and off –
> such as sound or video. They are also sometimes used as polling or
> questionnaire elements.

One of the most important things we should learn is how to manipulate the **Change Handler** parameter and use the getValue() methods with the CheckBox. Let's look at how this is done (checkbox.fla is provided on the CD for reference).

1. Drag an instance of the CheckBox component onto the stage, open the Property inspector (CTRL+F3) and set the value of the Change Handler to checkIt.

2. Now select frame 1 of the actions layer, and add the following function:

```
function checkIt(check1) {
    myCheck = check1.getValue();
    if (myCheck) {
        music.start();
    } else {
        music.stop();
    }
}
```

This code will get the true or false value being passed by the CheckBox. If you then initialize a sound object with the instance name music, the song will start when the value returned is true, that is, when the CheckBox is *checked*. If the value is `false`, the song will not play. The component is initialized in the second line when `myCheck` is set to the value of `true` or `false` (depending on what the component returns). Take a look at `checkbox.fla` to see this example in full.

Using the ComboBox

The ComboBox presents a drop-down list, typically used to offer one selection from several options, while occupying very little of the stage. The ComboBox can be manipulated with the END, HOME, PAGE UP, and PAGE DOWN key presses.

Let's take a look at parameters for this component, found in the Property inspector:

ComboBox parameters	Description
Editable	Means the box on the stage can receive textual input. The default value of this parameter is false (not editable). The data entered in the input field can be passed through the getValue() method.
Labels	Can be used to enter the text that is seen in the ComboBox drop-down. After selecting this parameter, press the magnifying glass icon to open the Values window. This is where you make your entries.
Data	Represents the elements of the Labels parameter. Row Count controls how many labels are seen in the drop down before a scrollbar appears (takes integer values).
Change Handler	A text string specifying a function located on the same timeline. This function is called when the user selects a drop down value, or presses the ENTER key after entering a string into an editable instance.

You might use a ComboBox selection to allow your user to navigate to a different point on the timeline. In the following example, `combobox.fla`, we'll use a ComboBox to navigate the timeline to three different labeled frames.

1. Open a new FLA, add a graphics layer, add keyframes at frames 2, 5, and 10, and put some simple artwork on each one. It's important that your first content page is on frame 2 – we'll see why shortly.

2. Add a new layer called labels, and label your three pages `page1`, `page2`, and `page3`. Then add a component layer, and drag an instance of the ComboBox to the stage. Give it the instance name `combo1`. Select `combo1`, and open the Parameters tab in the Property inspector. The parameter we want to change is the Change Handler. Add the name `changepage` as a parameter:

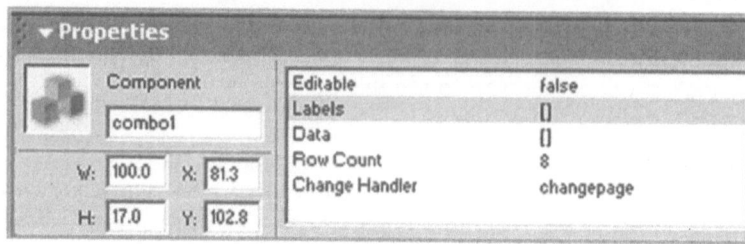

3. Now go back to the main timeline, add a new actions layer, and type the following ActionScript into the script pane for frame 1:

```
gotoAndStop(2);
combo1.addItem("cat", "page1");
combo1.addItem("dog", "page2");
combo1.addItem("hamster", "page3");
```

With this ActionScript, we're just adding Labels and Values to our ComboBox using code. An issue with using this method is that each time the playhead returns to the frame the code is situated on, the same items will be added to the end of the list. Our workaround for this problem is that our pages start on frame 2, so our Combo Box does not get bigger each time frame 1 is revisited. A pretty easy solution!

> *Instead of using ActionScript, you may want to simply go to the Property inspector and add these values. To do this, select the Labels parameter and then press the magnifying glass icon. In the Value panel, press the + button, and enter values of cat, dog, and hamster. Close the Value panel. Repeat this step for the Data parameter, and enter the values "page1", "page2" and "page3" into the Value panel. Remember to add the quotation marks, because these values are our frame labels.*

4. The next step is to add the following code after our addItem list:

```
function changepage() {
     gotoAndStop(_root.combo1.getValue());
}
```

This function is called from the changepage Change Handler we gave our combo1 instance. _root.combo1.getValue() will return the frame label, which we set as our value, and will then be applied to the gotoAndStop() action.

5. Test your movie (CTRL+ENTER) and try out your ComboBox. The page of your movie will automatically change when you select a label in the ComboBox. The completed example of this exercise can be found on the CD as combobox.fla.

Using the PushButton

The PushButton component is a quick and easy way to add button functionality to an interface. This component is great for mock-ups, and even esthetic presentations when it's skinned. The button has all four usual states, and the option of calling a function when pressed.

Let's take a look at the two parameters for the PushButton:

PushButton parameters	Description
Label	The visible text on the PushButton instance.
Click Handler	Where you enter the name of a function to be called when the button instance is pressed.

An instance of the PushButton component will call a defined Click Handler when the button is pressed. The Click Handler is the same as a Change Handler in that a function is called when the button is selected (in this case, pressed). You can control and perform any number of actions using a simple PushButton instance.

For example, if you wanted to load a movie when a button is pressed, you could use a PushButton in the following way:

1. Give your button a Click Handler name of `loadVideo`. Then, on frame 1 of the main timeline, enter the following code:

```
function loadVideo() {
    loadMovie("myVideo.swf", "myPlaceholder");
}
```

2. You may want to disable PushButton instances at certain points of your movie, by using the `FPushButton.setEnabled()` method. This is particularly useful for situations where, for example, your movie has already been loaded and you don't need the button to be pressed. After you've given your button an instance name `button1`, your function would look like this:

```
function loadVideo() {
    loadMovie("myVideo.swf", "myPlaceholder");
    button1.setEnabled(false);
}
```

We'll also see PushButtons in action as part of the next example.

Using the ListBox

The ListBox can be a very powerful component when you realize its full potential. It's similar to the ComboBox in what it can be used for; however, it offers the additional possibility of adding graphics and large amounts of information into each entry.

The parameters for the ListBox are as follows:

ListBox parameters	Description
Label	Refers to the visible labeling of the ListBox instance.
Data	An array of data directly related to the Labels entries.
Select Multiple	A unique parameter that can be set either to true or false. A setting of true allows multiple values to be selected at once by depressing the CTRL (or COMMAND) key. The default setting of false means only one selection can be made at a time.
Change Handler	Calls a function when a selection is made.

1. Open a new FLA file, and create layers for components and actions. In the components layer, drag one instance of the ListBox, and three PushButtons onto the stage. Give the ListBox an instance name of `list1`, and the PushButtons instance names of `button1`, `button2`, and `button3`, and labels of `Add Entry`, `Get Age`, and `remove`, respectively. All of these changes can be made in the Property inspector.

2. Create two input text fields on the stage, with the instance names `myname` and `myage`, and label them appropriately with static text boxes. Then create one dynamic text field with the instance name `agebox`. Your stage should now look something like this:

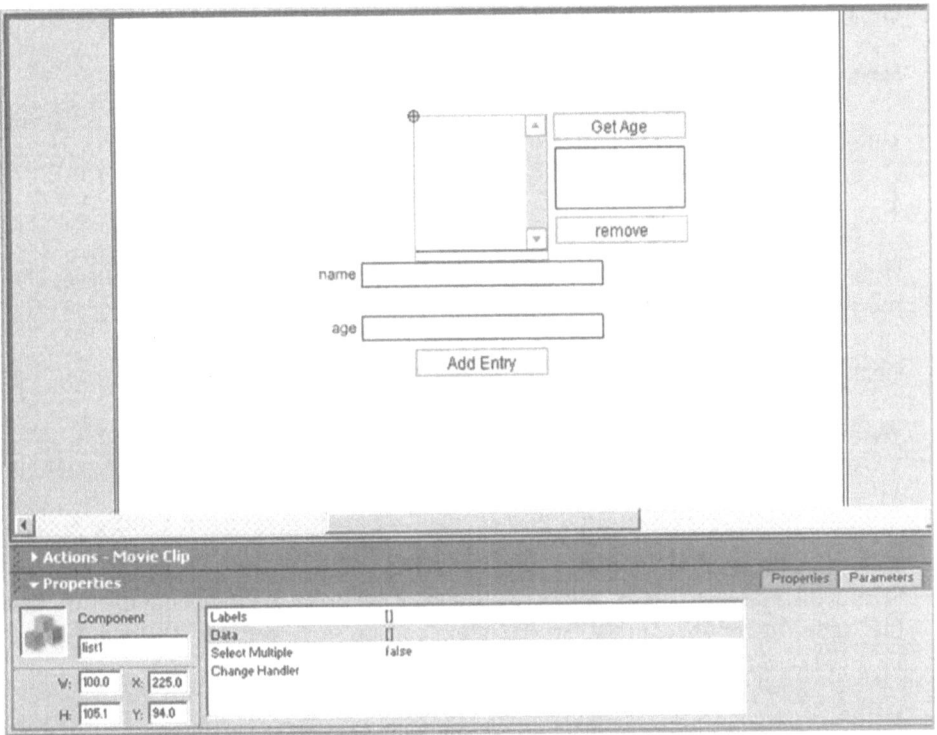

3. Before we add the code, we have to add Click Handlers to each of our button instances. Select `button1` (Add Entry), and open the Property inspector (CTRL+F3). In the Click Handler field, enter the handler `addIt`. For `button2` (Get Age), enter a handler of `theAge`. Finally, for `button3` (remove), provide a handler name of `removeMe`. Now we're ready to add some ActionScript!

4. Go to frame 1 of the actions layer, and enter the following code:

```
list1.setSelectMultiple(false);
```

This line means that multiple simultaneous selections cannot be made (note that we could also change this setting via the Property inspector).

5.   Now add the following function definition:

```
function addIt() {
      list1.addItem(_root.myname.text, _root.myage.text);
      _root.myname.text = "";
      _root.myage.text = "";
}
```

This first function adds the text input made in the text fields myname and myage. When the function is called, it adds myname to the bottom of the ListBox entries, and sets myage as the value for that entry. Then, it clears the text from the input text fields.

6.   Next, add the following code into the script pane:

```
function theAge() {
      _root.agebox.text = _root.list1.getValue();
}
```

When you click on the Get Age button, this function will be called. It retrieves the data value for the selected item.

7.   Finally, add this code:

```
function removeMe() {
      list1.removeItemAt(list1.getSelectedIndex());
}
```

This function will remove the selected item. The method for this action is FListBox.removeItemAt(index). Since we cannot set the index number, we have to substitute the code FListBox.getSelectedIndex(). This will retrieve the number and pass it to removeItemAt.

Test this example – you can dynamically populate the ListBox with data from the input text boxes, via the Add Entry PushButton, then retrieve and delete data from the ListBox using the other PushButtons:

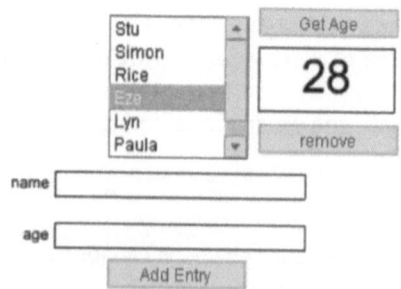

Using the ScrollBar

The most typical use of a ScrollBar is to scroll the contents of a dynamic text field. The ScrollBar can also be used as a slider of any kind, such as for volume control, panning sound, or scaling an image (as we saw earlier in this chapter when looking at draggable UI elements). Note that the ScrollBar works with dynamic or input text fields, but not with static text.

There only two parameters for this component:

ScrollBar parameters	Description
Target Textfield	The instance name of the text field attached to the ScrollBar component.
Horizontal	Can be set to either true or false. true will make the ScrollBar instance function horizontally, and a false will set the instance as a vertical scroll bar. Remember that if you set it to true, you also need to set your text field to Multiline no wrap in the Property inspector.

1. Let's start by adding a ScrollBar to a text input field. Open a new FLA file, and create a new text input field that's at least a couple of lines in height. Open the Property inspector, and give the text field the instance name myField.. Also set it to Multiline, and make sure your text is a different color from your stage:

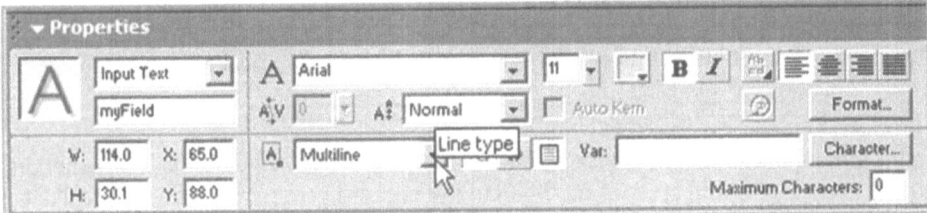

2. Open the Components panel (CTRL+F7), and drag an instance of the ScrollBar on to the stage. Drag it over the text field instance you created, and it should automatically snap to the input field while resizing to fit its height. If it doesn't snap, make sure that View>Snap to Objects is enabled. If you still have difficulty snapping the component to the text field, try dragging it from left to right over the text field, and letting go directly over the text field.

3. Test your movie, and type into the text field. Once there is sufficient text, your Scroll Bar will activate. One of the nice features built into the Scroll Bar is that it remains in a disabled state until there is enough text to scroll. You can manually set a Scroll Bar instance (named, for example, myScrollbar) to be enabled using the following ActionScript:

```
myScrollbar.enabled(true);
```

Obviously, a false value will disable the Scroll Bar instance.

Using the RadioButton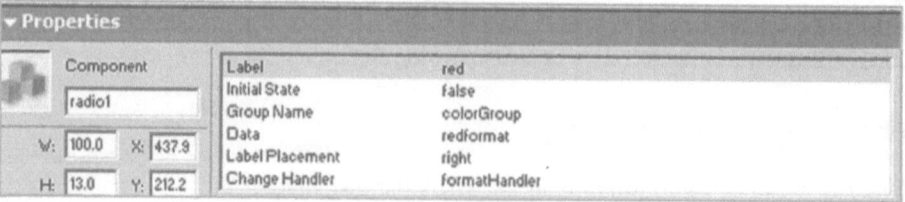

The RadioButton component is typically used in a group of RadioButton instances when you need to allow a user to select one value from many possible choices. RadioButtons are therefore a great way to retrieve multiple values from a set. This is in contrast to CheckBoxes, where many values from a set can be selected. A RadioButton returns a true or false Boolean value to Flash, depending on whether or not the button is selected.

The RadioButton component uses the following parameters:

RadioButton parameters	Description
Label	Used to change the text associated with each instance of the RadioButton component.
Initial State	Used to set whether or not a RadioButton is true or false when the movie starts, the default value being false (no RadioButton selected). In a group of RadioButtons, only one button can be selected - if more than one instance is set to true, only the first instance will actually be made true and the other instances will be false. Accordingly, it's a good idea to have at least one RadioButton in a group set to true at runtime.
Group	The same name can be applied to several instances on the stage. When instances belong to a group, only one of the instances sharing the name can be selected at one time.
Data	The value associated with the **Label** entry.
Label Placement	Refers to whether or not the text is placed to the left or to the right of the instance.
Change Handler	The name of the function that will be called when the RadioButton is selected or deselected.

RadioButtons are unique among the UI components because they can be set up and named in groups. In this example, called radiobutton.fla on the CD, we'll create a group of buttons that call a custom style format, which will color the component instances on the stage. Let's get started!

1. In a new FLA file, add a ScrollBar and ListBox (with associated text box) onto the stage, giving them instance names scroll1 and list1. Then add a set of three RadioButton instances on the stage called radio1, radio2, and radio3.

2. Open the Property inspector with radio1 selected. Give it a Label of red, Group Name of colorGroup, Data of redformat, and Change Handler of formatHandler:

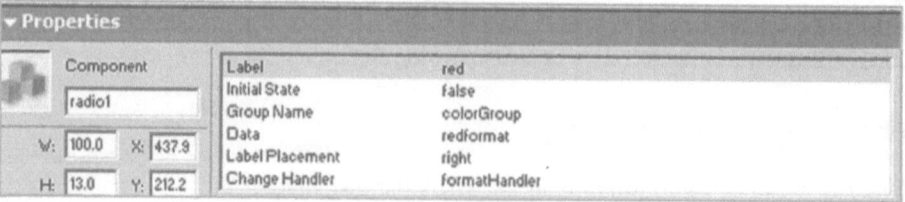

Repeat this step for radio2 and radio3, but give radio2 a Label of purple, and Data of purpleformat. Give radio3 the Label blue, and Data of blueformat:

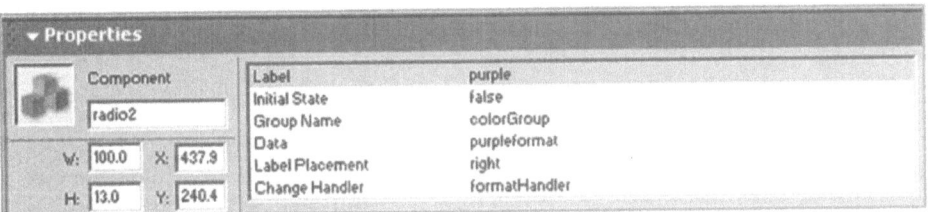

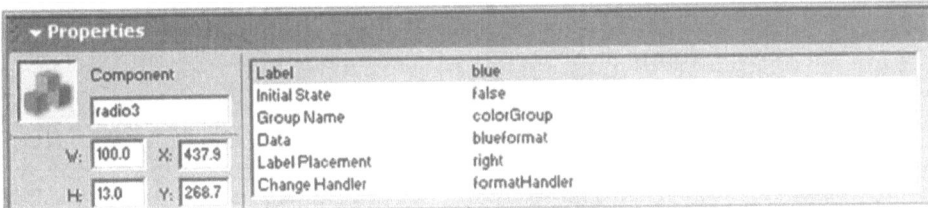

3. Now that our stage is set, we need to add color style formats for each instance (more on this shortly when we look at customizing components), so add a layer for actions, and a layer for style formats. Each style format (for red, purple, and blue) is constructed in exactly the same way, with modifications only made in the format name and colors. An example of the red style format is as follows:

```
redformat = new FStyleFormat({textColor:0x8D0101, highlight:0xD30101,
➥highlight3D:0xFE8585, shadow:0x8D0101, background:0xFE8585,
➥face:0xFE5050});
redformat.applyChanges();
```

4. Refer to frame 1 of the style formats layer in the example file radiobutton.fla for the complete sets of color style format. Alternatively, modify the styles, or create your own using the properties within the FStyleFormat object constructor. Add a redformat, purpleformat, and blueformat custom style format to frame 1 of the style format layer.

5. Now let's add some code for our RadioButtons onto frame 1 of the actions layer. First of all, we want to set our first radio button instance to true, which can be done using the line:

```
_root.radio1.setState(true);
```

6. Then, add the following function:

```
function formatHandler() {
    _root[_root.colorGroup.getData()].addListener(list1, scroll1,
➥colorGroup);
}
```

The `formatHandler` function gets called whenever the Change Handler on our instances is called. The code `_root.colorGroup.getData()` will return the color format being called (`redformat`, `blueformat`, or `purpleformat`). Then listeners are added for each component instance on the stage. Each time the function is called, the style format will change:

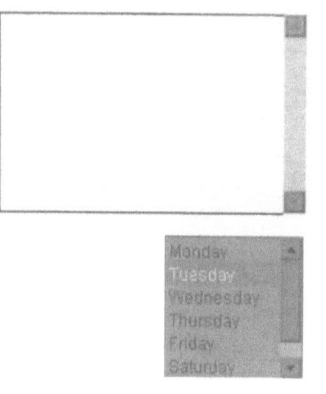

Using the ScrollPane

The ScrollPane component is very similar to the ScrollBar, except that it can scroll more than just text fields – it can scroll movie clips, or external JPG and SWF files loaded at runtime into the ScrollPane. You can set your content to be a movie clip from your Library, or you can use ActionScript to dynamically load the SWF and JPG files. The ScrollPane component is useful when you need to display a large amount of content, but have limited stage space. It's also an ideal tool for when you don't know the width and height of the file you're loading, but have a fixed stage area to display the content in.

The ScrollPane has four different parameters to set in the Property inspector:

ScrollPane parameters	Description
Scroll Content	Holds a text string that is the Linkage ID of the movie clip you want to appear in the ScrollPane instance.
Horizontal Scroll	Has three possible settings: `true`, `false`, or `auto`. `true` will always leave the ScrollBar visible, and `false` will turn the ScrollBar off. `auto` means a horizontal scroll bar will display if necessary.
Vertical Scroll	`true`, `false`, or `auto`, as above.
Drag Content	Can be set to `true` or `false`. A setting of `true` means the users can drag the scroll content in the pane. A setting of `false` means the content can only be scrolled using the scroll bars. If you're loading a SWF with buttons or draggable content, make sure this setting is set to `false`.

1. Create a new FLA file, and drag a ScrollPane instance onto the stage. In the Property inspector, give this ScrollPane an instance name of `panel`.

2. Create a large graphic on the stage, and press F8 to change it into a movie clip. Make sure that the graphic is larger than the ScrollPane instance on the stage (so we can scroll the content!). Now delete the instance from the stage (it'll still be in the Library).

3. Open your Library (F11) and right-click on the movie clip you've just created. Select Linkage... from the contextual menu. In the Linkage Properties window, select the Export for ActionScript and Export in First Frame check boxes. Enter myImage into the Identifier input field, and click OK:

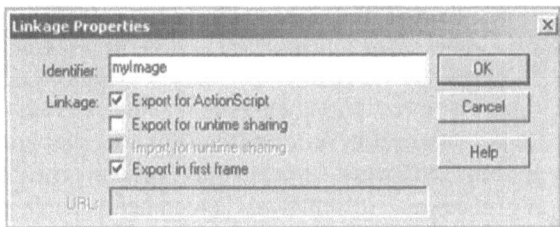

4. Return to the stage, select panel and open the Property inspector. Enter the linkage Identifier ID myImage into the Scroll Content parameter input field. You can leave the other default settings as they are. If you test the movie (CTRL+ENTER), the movie clip you created will be displayed in the panel instance:

5. If you wanted to load the content using ActionScript, you could add the following line of code onto frame 1 of an actions layer instead of entering the Identifier ID on the main timeline:

```
panel.setScrollContent("myImage");
```

Customizing components

Components can be customized in several ways. The Flash MX UI component set can *listen* to a global style format. This style format is an instance of the FStyleFormat object. However, you can also make your own custom style format, and select instances of components to listen to the new format. Alternatively, you can alter part or all of the global style format and have every component listen to these changes.

Both of these options involve using ActionScript to change the properties assigned to the components. To change the global style format, you change the properties of the globalStyleFormat object instance. To make your own style format, you use the FStyleFormat constructor and properties, like we saw earlier in the RadioButton example. Components will continue to listen to the globalStyleFormat of whichever properties are *not* changed in your custom style format. If you only need to change a few properties of a single component instance, it's much easier to simply use setStyleProperty() instead of constructing a new FStyleFormat custom style. Remember that the changes you make to any of these style properties are only seen once you run the FLA file.

Making changes to style formats only makes changes to text and color in components. It doesn't actually change the shape or graphics of the instances. In order to do this, you have the option of *skinning* your components by registering new skins to them using registerSkinElement(). Taking these steps allows you to give the Flash UI components an entirely new look and feel, while retaining the dependability of the components that ship with Flash MX.

For more information on customizing your component instances, refer to **Chapter 9**.

Creating new components

Creating an entirely new component is worthwhile if you find that you reuse the same function repeatedly in your designs. You may want to keep this task on hand, and drag-and-drop it onto a movie clip when you need it, to save yourself time and energy in the long run. Custom components are also ideal if you want to share something you've made, which can be used by others for a common task.

Let's create a very simple component. Once you've worked through this example, you'll be ready to start creating your own custom components containing whatever functionality you can dream up for your user interfaces!

Earlier in this chapter we looked at creating draggable elements for our UIs. Wouldn't it be useful if we could simply take that functionality and drop it onto whatever movie clip we wanted to add it to? By building a custom component, adding such properties to a movie clip is very easy to do.

In this exercise, we'll create a custom component that will make any movie clip instance draggable within the confines of the stage it is on. For reference, you'll find the finished product in customComponent.fla on the CD – to look inside the component, just select it in the Library, right-click on it, and choose Edit.

1. Open a new FLA file, and create a new movie clip called `dragIt`. Inside the `dragIt` movie clip, make a graphics layer and an actions layer. Select the graphics layer and make a small icon. Ultimately, this icon will snap to movie clips when you add the component to each instance:

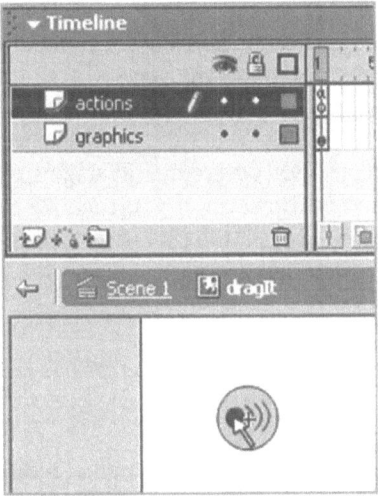

2. Open up the Library (F11), right-click on your `dragIt` movie clip, and select Component Definition... from the menu. The Component Definition window will open, and the first thing you want to do is press the + button, which will add a new line. Where it says `varName` on this line, select it and enter `dragger`. Under the Variable heading, enter `_targetInstanceName`. The other values in this line can be left at their default settings:

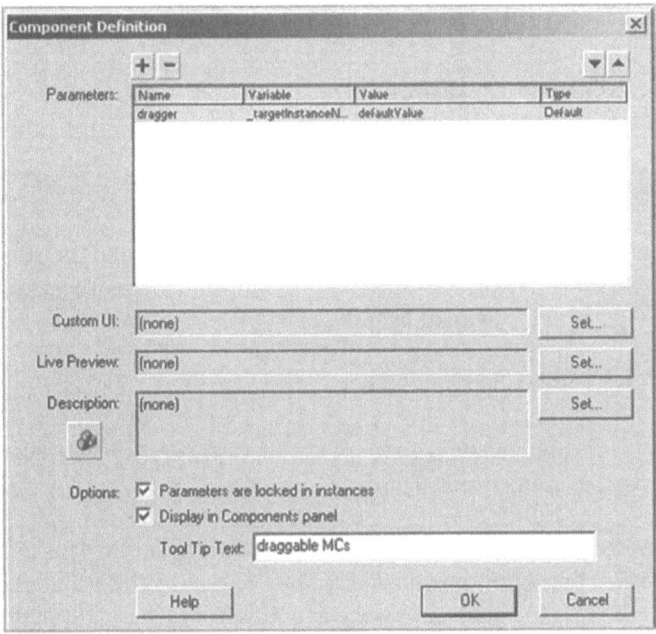

3. You can also select the Display in Components panel check box, which will also allow you to add an optional Tool Tip message – this is what users will read if they mouse over your component in their Component panel. Close the Component Definition window for now – we'll add some parameters soon.

4. Now let's add some code to the movie clip. We want this component to make any movie clip it snaps to start dragging, and not go off the stage. If you remember the code we used earlier in this chapter in the section on drag-and-drop control, this shouldn't be too difficult. What is different this time is that we have to consider that our code will have to work on different sized stages. There are two ways we can account for differences in stage size. The Stage object has Stage.height and Stage.width properties. However, if you trace what these properties actually return, you'll notice that it's slightly different from the real size of the stage. Therefore we'll allow our end users the option of entering in their own amounts – which will also allow us to demonstrate how to set up some parameters.

So, let's enter some code into the actions layer of our dragIt component. Start by entering the following two lines:

```
dragger = this._parent[this._targetInstanceName];
_visible = false;
```

These two lines create a path from our component to the movie clip we want to drag (the dragger). The _targetInstanceName is just that – the instance name of our target. You'll see where this is defined in the next section. The second line sets the visibility of our component icon to false at runtime.

5. Next, enter these lines of ActionScript after the first two:

```
halfWidth = dragger._width/2;
halfHeight = dragger._height/2;
maxLeft = maxLeft-halfWidth;
maxTop = maxTop-halfHeight;
```

This may seem a bit confusing. First of all, we're dividing in half the size of the movie clip instance that we're dragging. We'll use the number in our startDrag() method. Remember, the startDrag() method is defined like this:

```
MovieClip.startDrag(target, left, top, right, bottom);
```

where the first two boundary values, left and top, need to be defined by our users, which we have called maxLeft and maxTop above.

6. Let's now open up the Component Definition window again by right clicking on our component in the Library. Press the + button, and add stage width as the parameter name, maxLeft as the new Variable, 550 to the Value, and Number to Type. Our next parameter is almost the same. Press the + button again, and enter `stage height` under Name, `maxTop` under Variable, `400` under Value, and `Number` under Type. Here we've added the default stage size of Flash (550 x 400) as our `maxLeft` and `maxTop`:

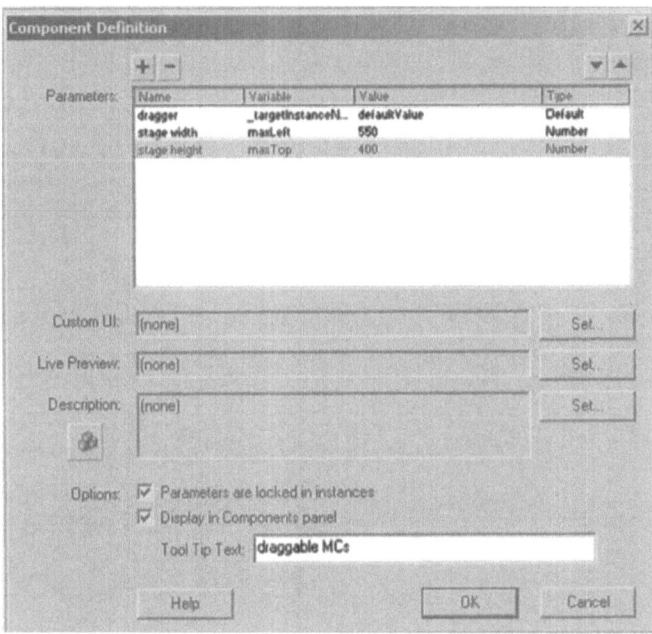

7. Close the Component Definition window, and let's go back and add some more ActionScript to our component. Type the following lines of code after the line `maxTop` definition:

```
dragger.onPress = function() {
      dragger.startDrag(this, maxLeft, maxTop, 0, 0);
};
dragger.onMouseUp = function() {
      dragger.stopDrag();
};
```

These function definitions should already be familiar to you from the earlier section on draggable elements. They use the variables taken from the user entered into the Parameters tab of the Property inspector.

8. Now, go back to the main stage, draw a shape and make it into a movie clip. Drag the component from your Library onto the movie clip, and it will snap to the instance (as long as you have View>Snap to Objects option turned on). Enter your stage dimensions in the Parameters tab of the Property inspector and test your movie!

    The completed example file for this exercise, `custom_component.fla`, is located on the CD along with all the code featured in this chapter.

3 The Drawing API

Objectives

- Introducing the drawing API and its associated methods

- Creating empty movie clips to contain images drawn at runtime

- Using the drawing API to create content:

  - Lines

  - Curves

  - Circles

  - Single color and gradient fills

- Advanced drawing techniques

Introduction

The drawing API (**A**pplication **P**rogramming **I**nterface) of Flash MX provides us with some very powerful scripting tools. With this API, we're able to draw graphics with code alone, and the images are rendered entirely at runtime. With the drawing API, we can draw lines and curves to form any shape, which we can then fill with a solid or gradient, all purely with ActionScript.

Creating graphics with the drawing API can be divided into two distinct steps:

1. Creating an empty movie clip, using the `createEmptyMovieClip()` method, in which we can create our drawing.

2. Using various methods from the drawing API to generate dynamic graphics at runtime.

For reference, and as a teaser of what we'll be covering in this section, the following table provides an overview of the draw methods available to us:

Drawing Method	Description
`lineStyle()`	Defines the color and thickness for the line to be drawn by `lineTo()` and `curveTo()`
`moveTo()`	Sets the position of the 'pen' used for drawing lines. This is how any drawing is started.
`lineTo()`	Draws a line, as defined by `lineStyle()`, from the last position to the position specified by `lineTo()`.
`curveTo()`	Draws a curved line, as defined by `lineStyle()`, from the last position to the anchor position specified in `curveTo()`, with a curve defined by the control points
`beginFill()`	Toggles filling on. Fills in the shape that is drawn with the `lineTo()` and `curveTo()` methods
`endFill()`	Toggles filling off, and fills in the shape that has been outlined with `lineTo()` and `curveTo()`
`beginGradientFill()`	Like `beginFill()`, except creates a gradient based on the values specified.
`clear()`	Clears all items that have been drawn in a specific movie clip by the drawing API.

We'll soon see that by using these simple yet deceptively powerful commands we can create some really startling images and effects.

Creating the empty movie clip

As you most likely know by now, the most vital building block of all images and graphics in Flash MX is the movie clip – this presents us with a single unit that may combine dynamic graphics, ActionScript, and interactivity. When we want to create an image with the drawing API, we must first create an empty *container* movie clip to hold our drawing instructions, in which the image will ultimately be rendered.

This is achieved as follows from the root timeline:

```
_root.createEmptyMovieClip(instanceName, depth);
```

Here, the `instanceName` is a unique name that we're going to use to refer to the newly created movie clip, and `depth` is an integer describing the drawing order for stacking and layering (this was discussed in detail in **Chapter 1**). Suffice to say that each empty movie clip you create must have its own unique depth; no two movie clips can exist on the same depth layer.

We can also create a new empty movie clip as the *child* of a currently existing movie clip (called `parentClip` for the purpose of this demonstration) like this:

```
parentClip.createEmptyMovieClip(instanceName, depth);
```

So, for example, if we had a movie clip on the stage with the instance name `canvas`, and we wanted to create within it a new movie clip called `drawing`, at the arbitrarily chosen depth level of 5, then we would write the following:

This new empty movie clip would be referred to as `canvas.drawing`, rather than `_root.drawing` if it were created on the root timeline.

It's also important to note what the depth of the `canvas` object is – in order for `drawing` to appear above the `canvas`, the depth of the empty `drawing` movie clip must be greater than that of the `canvas` movie clip. If you're not sure, you can always set the depth of the parent movie clip with the `swapDepths()` method:

```
canvas.swapDepths(4);
```

This would force the canvas to lie on depth level 4, and then when you define the empty movie clip you'd make sure to create it at a depth higher than this (5 and above).

Once an empty movie clip has been created, you can modify any of its properties, like `_x`, `_y`, `_rotation`, `_alpha`, and so on, in the standard way (see **Chapter 1**). Remember, however, that until we draw anything inside it with the drawing API functions, the clip remains an empty, and therefore *invisible*, movie clip.

Using the drawing API

After creating an empty movie clip, we now want to bring it to life with some dynamic graphics. From shifting fluid shapes and dynamic text systems to totally real-time rendered 3D-effect graphics – the applications of the drawing API are far-reaching. As usual with Flash, your imagination is the limit!

Line

Let's first look at drawing lines. We need to create our empty movie clip – we learned how to do this in the previous section, so let's stick with our drawing example, but put it on the root timeline:

```
_root.createEmptyMovieClip("drawing", 5);
```

The next thing we need to do is define a line style via the lineStyle() method. This method takes up to three parameters: thickness, color, and alpha, and looks like this:

```
drawing.lineStyle(thickness, color, alpha);
```

- The thickness parameter describes the line thickness in points. If, for example, we pass a value of 0, then the line will be a hairline; the maximum thickness is 255.

- The color value is a standard hexadecimal number in the format 0xRRGGBB, where the RR, GG, and BB values correspond to a red, green and blue level to form the color. If no color is specified, then the default color of 0x000000 (black) is used.

- The alpha parameter determines the opacity of the line. If you specify 0, then the line will be completely transparent. If no value is specified, then the line will be 100% solid.

Note that if you call lineStyle() without passing *any* values, then it is set as undefined, and no line will be drawn with subsequent lineTo() and curveTo() commands.

OK, enough talking – let's see this in action. Open up the file line.fla from your source code folder. Notice that there's nothing on the stage (and there's nothing up my sleeve!), and test this movie. The code attached to frame 1 of the actions layer produces the following image of a big chunky red line.

The ActionScript in the movie looks like this:

```
_root.createEmptyMovieClip("drawing", 5);
drawing.lineStyle(10, 0xFF0000, 90);
drawing.moveTo(0, 0);
drawing.lineTo(240, 110);
```

We create our empty movie clip called drawing in the first line, as we've already seen. Next, we use the lineStyle() method to define a 10 point, red line, with an alpha of 90%. Once the line style has been defined, we're almost ready to start drawing.

First, however, we must tell Flash where to begin drawing from. This is where the moveTo() command comes into play. With moveTo(), we are telling Flash where we would like it to move to and place its 'virtual pen' down on the canvas, ready to start drawing. As parameters, moveTo() simply takes the x and y coordinates; so, by stating moveTo(0, 0), we are telling Flash to move to the origin, or registration point, of our drawing movie clip, in preparation to start drawing.

Now we're ready to add the line – the first three lines in the code above essentially set everything up, ready for input that will actually produce some graphics. In the final line we utilize the lineTo() method, giving the coordinates (240, 110) as parameters. So, when we test the code, a red line is drawn from position (0, 0) to position (240, 110) in the drawing movie clip. Pretty easy, huh?

So, the moveTo() and lineTo() methods each take two parameters: the x and y co-ordinates. This might not seem like much of a big deal, but it's the starting point for every other drawing task we may want to perform. With every subsequent lineTo() command we add, the lines will be drawn in a join-the-dots fashion.

Now open up triangle.fla – here we've simply added a couple more lines of code to that in the previous example:

```
_root.createEmptyMovieClip("drawing", 5);
drawing.lineStyle(10, 0xFF0000, 90);
drawing.moveTo(0, 0);
drawing.lineTo(240, 110);
drawing.lineTo(0, 220);
drawing.lineTo(0, 0);
```

Test it and see what happens (the filename is a bit of a giveaway!):

These two new ActionScript commands just add a couple of lines to our image, following the specified co-ordinates. Notice that, because our final lineTo() method has the origin (0, 0) as its parameters, the last line meets up with the starting point to form a triangle.

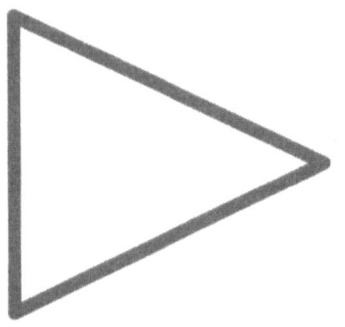

Curve

Now let's look at another method of the drawing API – the curveTo() command. Try replacing that last lineTo() command with a curveTo(), and see what we get:

```
_root.createEmptyMovieClip("drawing", 5);
drawing.lineStyle(10, 0xFF0000, 90);
drawing.moveTo(0, 0);
drawing.lineTo(240, 110);
drawing.lineTo(0, 220);
drawing.curveTo(150, 110, 0, 0);
```

Test this movie, `curve1.fla`, and the result will look like this:

Wow! How did we do that? Well, `curveTo()` acts just like `lineTo()`, except that we also apply a second point to the line, called a *control point*, which has the effect of pulling the line towards this point, almost like a rubber band. The `curveTo()` method takes this form:

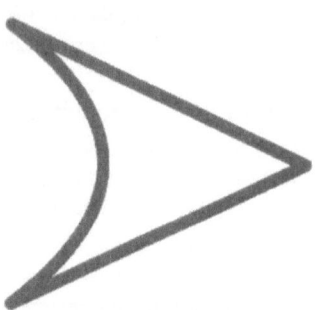

```
curveTo(controlX, controlY, destX, destY);
```

With these parameters we specify the x and y co-ordinate of the final destination of the line (`destX`, `destY`), and also the x and y co-ordinate of the control point (`controlX`, `controlY`). To understand how the control point works, it is necessary to understand the concept of a tangent. A tangent is a line that touches a curve at only one point, and the control point is the point which, when connected to the curve's starting point and (`destX`, `destY`) position, forms a tangent to the curve.

This concept is rather tricky to explain in words, so let's look at another example. You'll find the following code in `curve2.fla`:

```
_root.createEmptyMovieClip("drawing", 5);
drawing.lineStyle(10, 0xFF0000, 90);
drawing.moveTo(0, 0);
drawing.lineTo(240, 110);
drawing.lineTo(0, 220);
drawing.curveTo(150, 110, 0, 0);
drawing.lineStyle(1, 0x0000FF, 90);
drawing.lineTo(150, 110);
drawing.lineTo(0, 220);
```

You'll recognize the first half of this code from the previous example. We've then added a few new lines, starting with setting a new line style with `lineStyle(1, 0x0000FF, 90)`. What this is doing is setting the line style to a thin, blue line. Next, to demonstrate how a control point works, we draw a line to the control point of the previous curve (150, 110), and then another line back to the other end of the curve (0, 220). The end result is shown below:

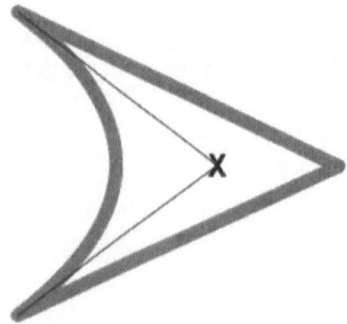

So, the thin blue lines coming from the control point represent the tangents to this curve – for clarity, we've marked the control point with an 'X' in this figure.

We can see how the curveTo() method works even better if we make a few more adjustments to the code. Have a glance at curve3.fla, and the relevant changes to our code are highlighted below:

```
_root.createEmptyMovieClip("drawing", 5);
_root.drawing.onEnterFrame = function() {
      this.clear();
      this.lineStyle(10, 0xFF0000, 90);
      this.moveTo(0, 0);
      this.lineTo(240, 110);
      this.lineTo(0, 220);
      this.curveTo(_root._xmouse, _root._ymouse, 0, 0);
      this.lineStyle(1, 0x0000FF, 90);
      this.lineTo(_root._xmouse, _root._ymouse);
};
```

Now we're creating an onEnterFrame function in the drawing movie clip that allows us to move the control point of the new curve and tangent lines according to the position of the mouse. Note that we've also used the clear() method to erase our drawing on each new frame – we'll learn more about this method shortly. For now, just try it out to see directly the effect that the control point and associated tangent line have on the look of the curve:

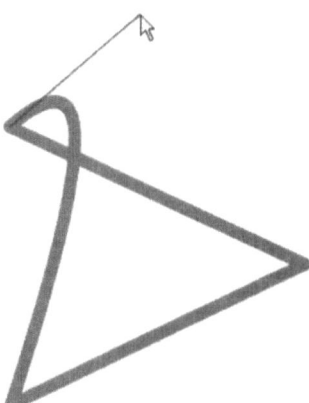

Using the curveTo() method takes a bit of getting used to, and it's recommended that you play around with it by moving the control point to different locations to get a feel for it. For example, you could simply reverse the x coordinate of the control point from our previous examples, like this (see curve4.fla):

```
_root.createEmptyMovieClip("drawing", 5);
drawing.lineStyle(10, 0xFF0000, 90);
```

```
drawing.moveTo(0, 0);
drawing.lineTo(240, 110);
drawing.lineTo(0, 220);
drawing.curveTo(-150, 110, 0, 0);
```

This has the effect of reversing the direction of the curve:

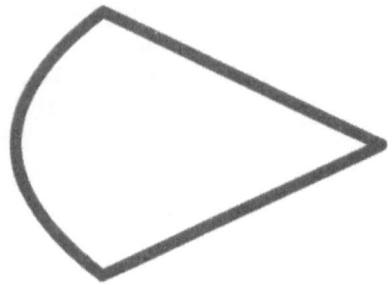

Circle

To draw a circle, you might think that we have to use hundreds of `lineTo()` commands. We can, however, draw an *approximation* of a circle by simply using four `curveTo()` commands, like this (see `circle1.fla`):

```
_root.createEmptyMovieClip("drawing", 5);
drawing.lineStyle(10, 0xFF0000, 90);
drawing.moveTo(0, 0);
a = 3.5;

drawing.curveTo(100-a, a, 100, 100);
drawing.curveTo(100-a, 200-a, 0, 200);
drawing.curveTo(-100+a, 200-a, -100, 100);
drawing.curveTo(-100+a, a, 0, 0);
```

Here we're adjusting the control points of our four curves by a constant defined by the variable a. The effect is to link up the four curves to roughly form a circle that is 100 pixels from left to right, and top to bottom. Try varying the `adjust` variable to tweak your circle:

OK, so an approximation of a circle is all well and good, but what if we want something a little more precise? Well, with a little bit of extra coding we can use eight curves, instead of the four in the rough version, and achieve a pretty much perfect circle. Take a look at `circle2.fla`, and here's what the relevant code looks like:

```
_root.createEmptyMovieClip("drawing", 5);
x = 275; // X-coordinate circle centre
y = 200; // Y-coordinate circle centre
R = 100; // Radius of circle
a = R*0.4086; // Radius multiplied by constant
b = R*0.7071; // Radius multiplied by constant
drawing.lineStyle(5, 0xFF0000, 90);
drawing.moveTo(x-R, y);
drawing.curveTo(x-R, y-a, x-b, y-b);
drawing.curveTo(x-a, y-R, x, y-R);
drawing.curveTo(x+a, y-R, x+b, y-b);
drawing.curveTo(x+R, y-a, x+R, y);
drawing.curveTo(x+R, y+a, x+b, y+b);
drawing.curveTo(x+a, y+R, x, y+R);
drawing.curveTo(x-a, y+R, x-b, y+b);
drawing.curveTo(x-R, y+a, x-R, y);
```

This time we define a few variables to start with – the co-ordinates of the center of the circle (x, y), its radius R, and a couple of constants, a and b, that are related to R. We then use these variables in the `curveTo()` commands to construct our eight curves. This time, the resultant circle is perfect!

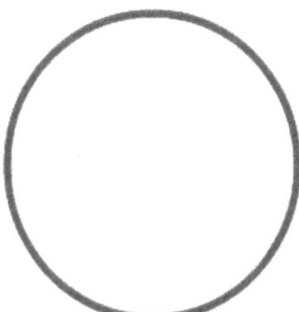

Fill

So far we've learned how to draw lines, curves, and some basic shapes. These shapes create a foundation for a filled solid object – so we can use the `beginFill()` or `beginGradientFill()` methods to achieve this.

Single color fills

The `beginFill()` method works by 'turning on' the filling of an outlined shape. If you place a `beginFill()` before a series of `lineTo()` commands, you're effectively telling the drawing API to "pay attention, because you're going to be filling all these in when I tell you to". But how do we indicate that we're ready to fill the shape? We just use the `endFill()` method.

Let's look at our triangle again – if we wanted a triangle to be filled in solid blue we'd simply wrap up the moveTo() and lineTo() methods with a beginFill() and endFill() command, inserting the appropriate values. The beginFill() method takes two parameters, color and alpha, like this:

```
drawing.beginFill(color, alpha);
```

The first, color, is the standard RGB color, and alpha is a percentage transparency value, where 100 is solid and 0 is invisible. If you don't specify an alpha value, then 100 is assumed. So, if we wanted to begin filling an object in blue at 100% alpha, we'd use this code:

```
drawing.beginFill(0x0000FF, 100);
```

Let's insert this code, along with an endFill() command, into our triangle drawing from earlier – look at triangle_fill.fla:

```
_root.createEmptyMovieClip("drawing", 5);
drawing.lineStyle(10, 0xFF0000, 90);
drawing.beginFill(0x0000FF, 100);
drawing.moveTo(0, 0);
drawing.lineTo(240, 110);
drawing.lineTo(0, 220);
drawing.lineTo(0, 0);
drawing.endFill();
```

Test the movie, and you'll see our new, improved solid triangle:

Now let's try a little experiment. Let's remove the last lineTo() command of this code, so that our code looks like this:

```
_root.createEmptyMovieClip("drawing", 5);
drawing.lineStyle(10, 0xFF0000, 90);
drawing.beginFill(0x0000FF, 100);
drawing.moveTo(0, 0);
drawing.lineTo(240, 110);
drawing.lineTo(0, 220);
```

```
        drawing.endFill();
```

Go ahead and re-test it and you'll see something rather interesting about the output – it's the same thing, even though we've removed the code that closes the shape. So how did it still work? Well, the drawing API is a little bit clever – when you throw in an `endFill()`, it will automatically draw a line back to the starting point, where `beginFill()` was called, if you haven't already done so in the code. Neat!

Gradient fills

We've looked at drawing solid color with `beginFill()`, now let's step up the pace a little and get to grips with the `beginGradientFill()` method. At its core, `beginGradientFill()` works just like `beginFill()` – you tell it to start filling and then leave an `endFill()` when it's time to stop filling. But that's about as similar as they get – it can be a little more complicated when it comes to specifying all the parameters (there are five of them!). Let's look at the function definition:

```
        drawing.beginGradientFill(filltype, colorArray, alphaArray,
        ➥ratioArray, matrix);
```

At first glance, this may look slightly overwhelming, but it's actually quite simple. Let's look at each parameter in turn before using this method to create a gradient fill.

Fill type

The first parameter, `filltype`, is just a string of text that is either `linear` or `radial`. It's used to determine what type of gradient we're going to be drawing, a linear or a radial gradient.

To get a feel for these options, open up the Color Mixer panel (SHIFT+F9), and take a look at the Linear and Radial options from the drop-down menu:

Linear gradients are rendered in succession from one end to the other, while radial gradients are rendered from a center point outwards.

Color

Another aspect of defining gradients is specifying the colors that make up the gradient. Again, have a look at the color options in your Color Mixer panel:

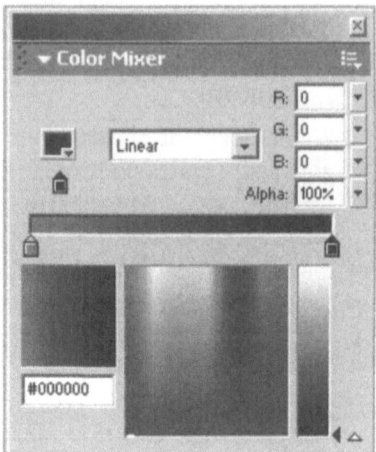

In the simplest case a gradient is made up of two basic colors – here we have a red (0xFF0000) to black (0x000000) transition. So, for this gradient we'd define its color array like this:

```
colorArray = [0xFF0000, 0x000000];
```

This array is made up of two elements. To look at the first element (or, color) in that array, we refer to it as colorArray[0], and the second element is referred to as colorArray[1]. However, we don't need to worry about this because beginGradientFill() takes the *entire* array as a parameter and does not require you to specify its individual elements.

Obviously, this array can get rather more complex, if you want it to:

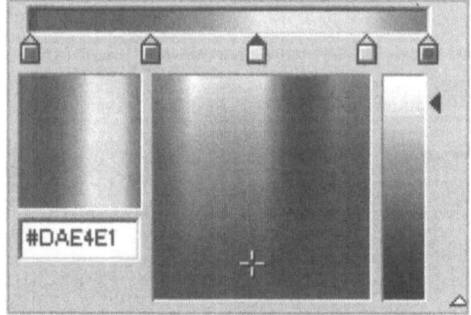

Here we have five colors making up the various gradients – we could do something like this with ActionScript by passing all the colors, as an array of numbers, to the beginGradientFill() command.

Alpha

Note that all the colors in the above gradients are 100% solid. However, because Flash MX uses alpha values with most of its colors, it's also possible to assign an alpha value to each color, as we have to the middle color in this gradient:

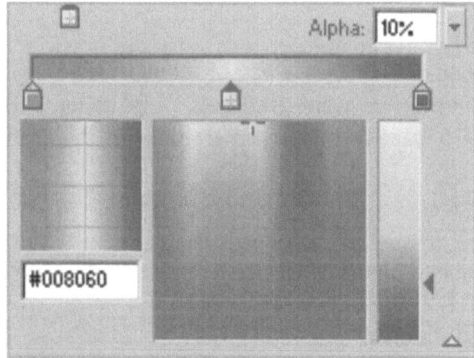

Notice that the middle color here has an alpha value of 10%, and its color is 0x008060. This is where the alphaArray parameter comes in – the third parameter of the beginGradientFill() method. It is defined in the same manner as the colorArray. In this case, we have the following:

```
colorArray = [0xFF0000, 0x008060, 0x000000];
alphaArray = [100, 10, 100];
```

Ratio

OK, so now that the colors are defined, we have to tell beginGradientFill() *where* in the gradient it will be placing these colors. Are they evenly spaced, left-biased, and so on? There are many possibilities, so that's where ratioArray comes in useful. This parameter is used to specify the position of colors from one end of the gradient to the other. Will a color be centered at the far left (0%) or at the far right (100%) of the gradient? What we're talking about here, is the position of the brightest spot of a particular color – that's its position value in ratioArray.

The catch is that the numbers within ratioArray are not actually defined as 0 to 100. They're actually defined from 0 to 255 (or 0x00 to 0xFF in hexadecimal form – we'll learn more about this when we discuss the color object in detail, in **Chapter 6**). It's not that difficult to do, just remember that if you want a color at 100% to the right, then that's actually 0xFF in the ratioArray. Halfway across (50%) is actually 0x80. The following table gives hexadecimal conversions of some of the more commonly used ratios:

Ratio (percent)	Hexadecimal value
0 %	0x00
10 %	0x1A
20 %	0x33
25 %	0x40
30 %	0x4D
40 %	0x66
50 %	0x80
60 %	0x99
70 %	0xB3
75 %	0xBF
80 %	0xCC
90 %	0xE6
100 %	0xFF

So, if we had a gradient, which had four colors: red, green, blue, and black, and each color had 100% alpha, and they were positioned at 0%, 30%, 60%, and 100% of the overall gradient, we would define the gradient like this.

```
colorArray = [0xFF0000, 0x00FF00, 0x0000FF,
➥0x000000];
alphaArray = [100, 100, 100, 100];
ratioArray = [0x00, 0x4D, 0x99, 0xFF];
```

Matrix

The final parameter is the `matrix` – this is a way of telling Flash MX just how to draw the gradient within its destination shape. Sometimes we want gradients to be taller, shorter, longer, or thinner depending upon the object. And we also want to position the center of the gradient.

Consider these two circles:

They both use identical radial gradients, with identical colors, alphas and ratios, but they look different! We've adjusted the center position of the matrix with respect to the shape, and thus moved the gradient and made it seem as if the light source has moved. So, let's look at how we define the matrix.

The `matrix` is not an array, it's an object, and so it is defined a little differently. Also, there are actually *two* forms of the matrix. One is a classical transformation matrix that you might have learned about in high-school math (but don't worry if you didn't – the second form is a lot easier to pick up!). Unfortunately, this form is not very intuitive to look at, for example:

```
matrix = {a:200, b:0, c:0, d:0, e:200, f:0, g:200, h:200, i:1};
```

This defines a 3x3 matrix, which encompasses the rotation, translation, skewing, and scaling of a standard mathematical matrix. This technique requires background knowledge of matrix math for the manipulation of a 2D co-ordinate system. In order to combine all the possible properties in one matrix, you would also have to know how to do matrix multiplication and definition – topics that are somewhat beyond the scope of this book.

Let's instead look at the second form of the matrix:

```
matrix = {matrixType:"box", x:100, y:100, w:200, h:200,
➡r:angleInRadians};
```

The key thing here is to specify `matrixType` as `box`. When this is set, the drawing API knows not to treat the `matrix` parameter as a transformation matrix, but rather as a simple box definition. With this form of the matrix, we specify the x and y position of the gradient center (relative to the registration point of the movie clip within which it's being drawn), the width and height of the gradient, and finally the rotation of the gradient (in radians, not degrees). To convert degrees into radians, we can use this simple formula:

```
angleInRadians = (angleInDegrees/180)*Math.PI
```

Using beginGradientFill

OK, now that we've described all of the parameters, let's see the `beginGradientFill()` method in action. Take a look at the following code, which you'll find in `gradientFill.fla`:

```
_root.createEmptyMovieClip("drawing", 5);
drawing.lineStyle(4, 0x000000, 90);
colorArray = [0xFF0000, 0x000000];
alphaArray = [100, 100];
ratioArray = [0x00, 0xFF];
matrix = {matrixType:"box", x:0, y:0, w:240, h:240, r:0};
drawing.beginGradientFill("linear", colorArray, alphaArray,
ÂratioArray, matrix);
drawing.moveTo(0, 0);
drawing.lineTo(240, 0);
drawing.lineTo(240, 240);
drawing.lineTo(0, 240);
drawing.lineTo(0, 0);
drawing.endFill();
```

Test the movie and you'll see that this code produces the following output:

It's really straightforward – the matrix parameter creates a 240 x 240 box, with a linear gradient from red to black as defined in the colorArray.

Let's try changing something in the matrix – change the rotation r to 90 degrees. Remember, we'll need to convert degrees to radians using the equation defined in the previous section, so the matrix definition line will look like this:

```
matrix = {matrixType:"box", x:0, y:0, w:240, h:240,
➡r:(90/180)*Math.PI};
```

The output is now:

As expected, the gradient has turned 90 degrees, and now runs from top to bottom.

Now check out `gradientFill_radial.fla` – here we've changed the fill type to `radial`:

Clearing drawings

When you've performed several drawing tasks within a blank movie clip, things can get a little bit busy, so the drawing API includes with one last method, `clear()`, and it is called like this:

```
drawing.clear();
```

This method doesn't take any parameters; it just removes everything that has been drawn with the drawing API in a specific movie clip. It does *not* remove things that have been drawn on the stage manually in the Flash authoring environment.

What happens if you only want to erase specific objects that have been drawn with the drawing API? You might, for instance, want something to remain persistent, while other elements are dynamic and changing – but they're both in the same blank movie clip. In such a case, you would need to constantly be clearing the dynamic part in every frame, but not the static part. The trick is to structure your drawings carefully with nested movie clips.

Open up `clear.fla`, in which you'll find the following ActionScript:

```
lines = 0;
_root.createEmptyMovieClip("drawing", 1);
drawing.createEmptyMovieClip("dancer", 2);
drawing.onEnterFrame = function() {
    lines++;
    if (lines<100) {
        this.lineStyle(4, 0);
        this.moveTo(Math.random()*200, Math.random()*200);
```

```
        this.lineTo(Math.random()*200, Math.random()*200);
        this.dancer.clear();
        this.dancer.lineStyle(4, 0xFF);
        this.dancer.moveTo(Math.random()*200, Math.random()*200);
        this.dancer.lineTo(Math.random()*200, Math.random()*200);
    } else {
        this.clear();
        lines = 0;
    }
};
```

First of all, we declare a variable called `lines` – we'll use this to keep track of how many lines we draw, and make sure that we don't draw so many that it slows down the Flash player. Next, we create a blank movie clip called `dancer` within a blank movie clip called `drawing`.

Within an `onEnterFrame` function we use the drawing API to create lines in the `drawing` movie clip that don't get cleared, and the same lines in the `dancer` movie clip that get cleared every frame, so the `dancer` will always be a fresh drawing every frame (and the random nature of the lines gives the impression that they're dancing around!). Note that these lines are simply one random point joined to another. Finally, so that the file doesn't get overrun with lines, we clear the drawing movie clip after every 100 lines are drawn. The output will look something like this:

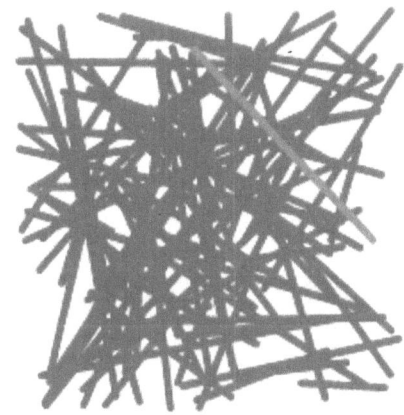

When you test the movie, you'll notice that the black lines are the drawing layer, while the blue line is in `dancer`. They both use the same code, but because of the `clear` command, only one dancer is ever seen.

Advanced Drawing

Now that we've seen how to draw simple items – lines, triangles, circles, squares, and so on – let's look at using ActionScript to draw something on a larger scale.

Creating faux-3D and detailed objects

In this example, we'll draw a shaded globe – using ActionScript alone! First, we'll draw a sphere as a series of boxes referred to as 'quads' (from quadrilateral, a four-cornered shape). There is some basic pseudo-3D math in here – just some perspective effects to make the sphere appear to have depth.

Open up `sphere1.fla` and test it – it's a wire-frame image of a sphere:

Each corner of a quad is called a vertex – with four vertices to one quad. The math here can be a bit daunting to look at the first time, but we'll use it to demonstrate the power of the drawing API – just take your time with it, and don't worry if you don't understand it at first glance.

Let's look at the first half of the code – this calculates the positions of every vertex:

```
_root.createEmptyMovieClip("sphere", 1);

sphere.onEnterFrame = function() {
    _x = 275;
    _y = 200;
};
with (sphere) {
    d = 400;
    pointx = new Array();
    pointy = new Array();
    pointz = new Array();
    numStrips = 10;
    degPerStrip = 180/numStrips;
    numAround = 20;
    degPerAround = 360/numAround;

    for (i=0; i<=numStrips; i++) {
        pointx[i] = new Array();
        pointy[i] = new Array();
        pointz[i] = new Array();
        for (j=0; j<=numAround; j++) {
            ang = j*degPerAround;
```

```
                    ang2 = i*degPerStrip;
                    rad = Math.sin(ang2*(Math.PI/180))*100;
                    x = rad*Math.sin(ang*(Math.PI/180));
                    z = (rad*Math.cos(ang*(Math.PI/180)))+500;
                    y = Math.cos(ang2*(Math.PI/180))*100;
                    pointx[i][j] = x;
                    pointy[i][j] = y;
                    pointz[i][j] = z;
            }
    }
```

Flash effectively sweeps around the sphere jotting down points in the arrays pointx, pointy, and pointz as it goes. The number of points it calculates is determined by numStrips (vertical) and numAround (horizontal around the sphere). degPerStrip and degPerAround are just variables that specify how many degrees (out of 360) are covered by each quad. If, for example, we were to double the values given to numStrips and numAround, the grid around our sphere would look even more detailed.

Wow, just like Star Wars!

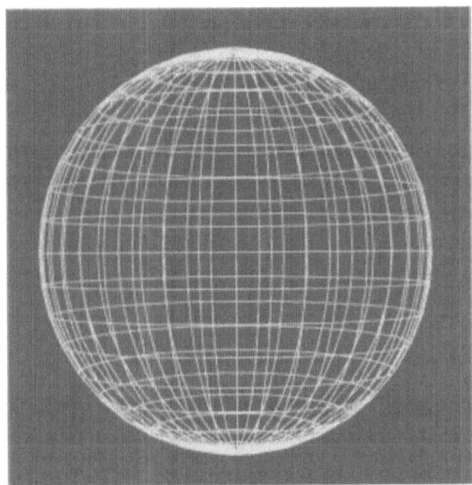

Let's continue with the code – once all the points have been calculated, we can proceed with drawing the sphere:

```
for (i=0; i<numStrips; i++) {
        for (j=0; j<numAround; j++) {

                // Grab the 4 points of the quad
                x1 = pointx[i][j];
                y1 = pointy[i][j];
                z1 = pointz[i][j];
```

```
x2 = pointx[i+1][j];
y2 = pointy[i+1][j];
z2 = pointz[i+1][j];
x3 = pointx[i+1][j+1];
y3 = pointy[i+1][j+1];
z3 = pointz[i+1][j+1];
x4 = pointx[i][j+1];
y4 = pointy[i][j+1];
z4 = pointz[i][j+1];
sx1 = (x1*(z1/d));

// Corner 1, on screen
sy1 = (y1*(z1/d));
sx2 = (x2*(z2/d));
// Corner 2, on screen
sy2 = (y2*(z2/d));
sx3 = (x3*(z3/d));
// Corner 3, on screen
sy3 = (y3*(z3/d));
sx4 = (x4*(z4/d));
// Corner 4, on screen
sy4 = (y4*(z4/d));
```

Here we're stepping through the points, and storing the four co-ordinates of each quad in temporary variables, (x1, y1, z1), (x2, y2, z2), (x3, y3, z3), and (x4, y4, z4). These are 3D space co-ordinates. To get them on screen, they're converted to screen co-ordinates, (sx1, sy1), (sx2, sy2), (sx3, sy3), and (sx4, sy4).

Finally, each quad is drawn in order from point 1, to point 2, to point 3, to point 4. The main drawing code is at the very end of the script:

```
this.lineStyle (1, 0xFFFFFF, 100);
this.moveTo(sx1, sy1);
this.lineTo(sx2, sy2);
this.lineTo(sx3, sy3);
this.lineTo(sx4, sy4);
        }
    }
}
```

Now, to give the sphere a solid look we could avoid drawing quads that are facing away from us. In sphere2.fla we've changed the final part of the script to:

```
// Test to see if this quad is visible or not
if (sx1<sx4) {
```

```
this.lineStyle(1, 0xFFFFFF, 100);
this.moveTo(sx1, sy1);
this.lineTo(sx2, sy2);
this.lineTo(sx3, sy3);
this.lineTo(sx4, sy4);
}
```

This modification results in only the front of the sphere being drawn:

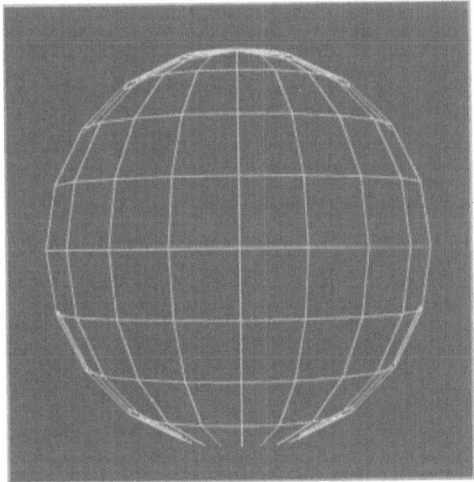

Finally, we could add a shaded fill to our globe, as we have done in sphere3.fla:

```
if (sx1<sx4) {
    dx = Math.abs(x4-x1);
    this.beginFill(dx*6, 100);
    this.moveTo(sx1, sy1);
    this.lineTo(sx2, sy2);
    this.lineTo(sx3, sy3);
    this.lineTo(sx4, sy4);
    this.endFill();
}
```

Notice that we've taken away the outlines by not defining a lineStyle(), and then added the fill. This code determined the shade of blue to use as our fill:

```
dx = Math.abs(x4-x1);
this.beginFill(dx*6, 100);
```

It's not 100% accurate shading, but it does the job. We just look at the width of the quad, and based upon that width, stored in dx, we determine the shade of blue to use. The shading works because the closest quads to us are the widest, so we get an additional perspective effect.

Here's the finished product – a solid, 3D, shaded sphere rendered entirely at runtime by the drawing API:

For reference, here's the complete script for sphere3.fla:

```
_root.createEmptyMovieClip("sphere", 1);
sphere.onEnterFrame = function() {
    _x = 275;
    _y = 200;
};
with (sphere) {
    d = 400;
    pointx = new Array();
    pointy = new Array();
    pointz = new Array();
    numStrips = 10;
    degPerStrip = 18;
    numAround = 20;
    degPerAround = 18;
    for (i=0; i<=numStrips; i++) {
        pointx[i] = new Array();
        pointy[i] = new Array();
        pointz[i] = new Array();
        for (j=0; j<=numAround; j++) {
            ang = j*degPerAround;
            ang2 = i*degPerStrip;
```

```
                    rad = Math.sin(ang2*(Math.PI/180))*100;
                    x = rad*Math.sin(ang*(Math.PI/180));
                    z = (rad*Math.cos(ang*(Math.PI/180)))+500;
                    y = Math.cos(ang2*(Math.PI/180))*100;
                    pointx[i][j] = x;
                    pointy[i][j] = y;
                    pointz[i][j] = z;
            }
    }
    for (i=0; i<numStrips; i++) {
            for (j=0; j<numAround; j++) {
                    // Grab the 4 points of the quad
                    x1 = pointx[i][j];
                    y1 = pointy[i][j];
                    z1 = pointz[i][j];
                    x2 = pointx[i+1][j];
                    y2 = pointy[i+1][j];
                    z2 = pointz[i+1][j];
                    x3 = pointx[i+1][j+1];
                    y3 = pointy[i+1][j+1];
                    z3 = pointz[i+1][j+1];
                    x4 = pointx[i][j+1];
                    y4 = pointy[i][j+1];
                    z4 = pointz[i][j+1];
                    sx1 = (x1*(z1/d));
                    // Corner 1, on screen
                    sy1 = (y1*(z1/d));
                    sx2 = (x2*(z2/d));
                    // Corner 2, on screen
                    sy2 = (y2*(z2/d));
                    sx3 = (x3*(z3/d));
                    // Corner 3, on screen
                    sy3 = (y3*(z3/d));
                    sx4 = (x4*(z4/d));
                    // Corner 4, on screen
                    sy4 = (y4*(z4/d));
                    // Test to see if this quad is visible or not
                    if (sx1<sx4) {
                            dx = Math.abs(x4-x1);
                            this.beginFill(dx*6, 100);
                            this.moveTo(sx1, sy1);
                            this.lineTo(sx2, sy2);
                            this.lineTo(sx3, sy3);
                            this.lineTo(sx4, sy4);
                            this.endFill();
```

```
                                    }
                            }
                    }
            }
```

Gradients in action

We have one more example to show, which this time relies on gradient filling. Open up `flightSim.fla` and you'll see an image on the stage that appears to be the cockpit of a plane:

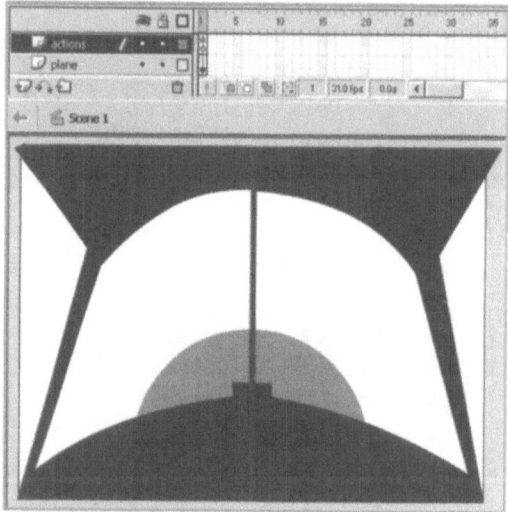

Now test this movie by hitting CTRL+ENTER:

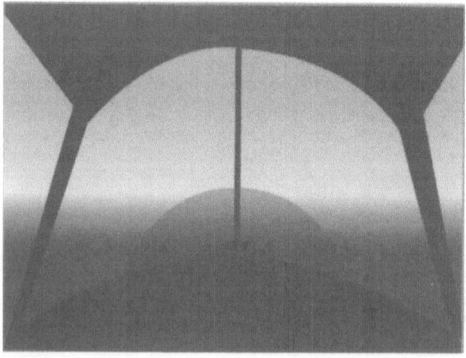 

It's a flight simulator! You can bank left and right with the left and right arrow keys, and climb or dive with the down and up arrow keys, like pulling back and pushing forward the joystick. OK, it's a rather basic simulator at present, but it's got all the makings of the early design stage of a pretty cool Flash game. Notice that we're relying on a gradient fill here to create the sky effects – the power of the dynamic gradient fill means that we can play with all sorts of things, like rotation, scaling, position, and the gradient ratios. For instance, notice in the movie that when we get close to the ground, the cloud haze vanishes from the horizon, giving a feeling of low altitude:

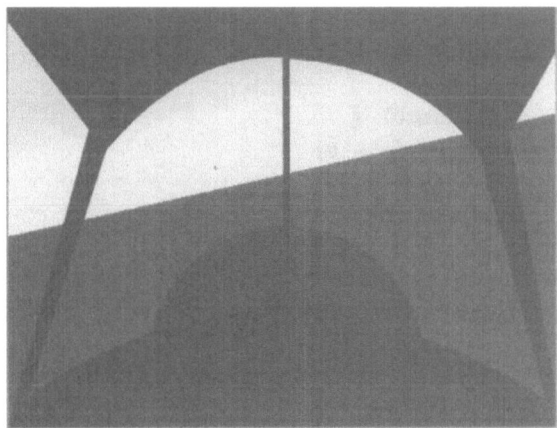

If we return to the Flash MX authoring environment, we can see that this movie consists of the cockpit movie clip on the stage, within which there is another movie clip to animate the plane's propeller. The interesting and powerful stuff takes the form of the ActionScript attached to frame 1 of the actions layer. Here's the code in full:

```
_root.createEmptyMovieClip("window", 1);
window.rot = Math.PI/2;
window.dr = 0;
window.xaim = 275;
window.yaim = 150;
window.altitude = 1500;
cockpit.swapDepths(2);
window.onEnterFrame = function() {
    this.clear();
    this.colors = [0xC4C4FF, 0xFFFFEE, 0x000099];
    this.alphas = [100, 100, 100];
    this.ratios = [0, 150, this.altitude];
    this.matrix = {matrixType:"box", x:this.xaim, y:this.yaim,
➥w:190,h:190, r:this.rot};
    this.beginGradientFill("linear", this.colors, this.alphas,
➥this.ratios, this.matrix);
    this.moveto(0, 0);
    this.lineto(0, 400);
    this.lineto(550, 400);
    this.lineto(550, 0);
    this.lineto(0, 0);
    this.endFill();
```

continues overleaf

```
        this.rot += this.dr;
        this.yaim += this.dy;
        this.altitude += this.uprate;
        this.uprate += (this.dy/100);
        if (this.altitude>255) {
                this.altitude = 255;
        }
        if (this.altitude<0) {
                this.altitude = 0;
        }
        if (Key.isDown(Key.LEFT)) {
                this.dr += 0.001;
        }
        if (Key.isDown(Key.RIGHT)) {
                this.dr -= 0.001;
        }
        if (Key.isDown(Key.UP)) {
                this.dy -= 0.1;
        }
        if (Key.isDown(Key.DOWN)) {
                this.dy += 0.1;
        }
    };
```

We're using a blank movie clip called `window`, and rendering our sky within it every frame. The altitude is controlled with a specific variable; likewise, movements like climbing and banking are managed with acceleration and deceleration variables that are controlled with the keyboard arrow keys. The result is a very smooth and realistic control, which enhances the look and authenticity of our Flash flight simulator.

The important lines are those where we define all the parameters to be used in the `beginGradientFill()` method, early on in the `onEnterFrame` function declaration:

```
        this.colors = [0xC4C4FF, 0xFFFFEE, 0x000099];
        this.alphas = [100, 100, 100];
        this.ratios = [0, 150, this.altitude];
        this.matrix = {matrixType:"box", x:this.xaim, y:this.yaim,
    ➡w:190,h:190, r:this.rot};
```

First we define the colors – a light blue sky, a yellowy-white horizon, and a dark blue ocean. The alpha values are all 100, and the ratios vary depending on the variable `altitude`. This is the key to making the clouds grow and shrink dynamically. Try playing with the simulator to get a feel for how the horizon gradient changes; fly up really high, and then dive back to the ground – you'll see the clouds fade in and out.

In the `matrix` definition we have the variables `xaim` and `yaim` that determine the heading of our plane, as determined by the keyboard presses detected by the `Key.isDown()` method. The last variable is `rot` – this controls the rotation, or banking, of your plane. The end effect, when everything works together, is a visually convincing flight simulator in Flash MX, thanks to the power of the drawing API.

4 Motion Control

Objectives

- Techniques for motion control in Flash MX:

  - Keyboard input

  - Mouse input

  - Local control

  - Control by a secondary movie clip

  - Timed events

- Using ActionScript-based motion control

- Multi-element animation

Introduction

In this section we'll study techniques enabling the dynamic control of our graphics through ActionScript. We'll be looking at motion that is entirely determined by code, to the point where it isn't predetermined by any frame-based animation and can therefore be considered *non-linear*. In the first half of this chapter we'll familiarize ourselves with the different control strategies available to us with ActionScript in Flash MX. Next, we'll use these techniques as we examine the solutions to and practicalities of some specific motion design problems and scenarios. Finally, we'll study the details of motion in a fairly complex example of a multi-element movie.

Motion control techniques

When dealing with script-based animation we should realize that there are many ways in which to control motion. The choices depend greatly upon the application for which the motion is intended. We'll examine the following techniques for motion control with ActionScript:

- **Keyboard Input** – Key presses cause objects to move.

- **Mouse Input** – Mouse movements and button clicks cause objects to move.

- **Local control** – Frame- and event-based functions are attached to events like onEnterFrame, so that all the motion code is attached to the object itself. The object therefore controls its own motion. This method is sometimes known as **anonymous** control.

- **Control by a secondary source** – Movie clips and timed events are used to orchestrate the motion of several different elements. An object is therefore controlled by another object.

- **Timed events** – Using the setInterval() function allows us to execute a function, thus giving the potential to move an object at a specified time interval.

Keyboard input

Keyboard input is one of the standard forms of input for Flash projects, such as (for example) a video game. There are two main techniques that we can use:

- **Key state testing** – Using this method we check to see if keys are being held down, on a frame-by-frame basis. As the keyboard is pressed its state will change, and we constantly check this. This is the best way to create real-time, non-repeating control of the keyboard. By non-repeating, we mean that when the key is pressed down, it will not continue to send a press event. Holding down an arrow key is a key state and will be taken as the key being held down, rather than pressed repeatedly.

- **Key event listening** – Using this method, we program Flash to respond to the key press events: *Press* and *Release*. As opposed to key state testing, these events will continue to be triggered as long as the key is held down, as in a computer game when a character is moved around the screen using the arrow keys.

Key state testing

Checking whether or not a particular key is pressed is easily done with the isDown() method of the Key object. It returns true or false, depending upon whether or not the key in question is held down. The syntax is as follows:

```
Key.isDown(KeyCode);
```

The parameter KeyCode corresponds to the object code of the key that we're looking at. Each key on the keyboard has a designated ASCII (American Standard Code for Information Interchange) scan code. In fact, the Key object contains several of these key codes stored as pre-defined variables. The following table shows these key object code variables, and their corresponding ASCII scan codes:

Key	Key object code	Scan Code Number
Up arrow	Key.UP	38
Down arrow	Key.DOWN	40
Left arrow	Key.LEFT	37
Right arrow	Key.RIGHT	39
Shift	Key.SHIFT	16
Control	Key.CTRL	17
Backspace	Key.BACKSPACE	8
Delete	Key.DELETEKEY	46
End	Key.END	35
Escape	Key.ESCAPE	27
Home	Key.HOME	36
Insert	Key.INSERT	45
Page Down	Key.PGDN	34
Page Up	Key.PGUP	33
Space	Key.SPACE	32
Tab	Key.TAB	9
Enter	Key.ENTER	13

For reference, the table on the next page lists the scan code values of the commonly used letter and number keys:

Key	Scan code number	Key	Scan Code Number
A	65	S	83
B	66	T	84
C	67	U	85
D	68	V	86
E	69	W	87
F	70	X	88
G	71	Y	89
H	72	Z	90
I	73	0	48
J	74	1	49
K	75	2	50
L	76	3	51
M	77	4	52
N	78	5	53
O	79	6	54
P	80	7	55
Q	81	8	56
R	82	9	57

An example of the usage of the Key.isDown function is like so:

```
if (Key.isDown(Key.SPACE)) {
        trace("Right arrow button is down!");
}
```

Note that we also need to attach this code to some kind of event or listener to trigger the action. We'll be looking at this in more detail soon.

Key event listening

The key listener differs from the key state test because it lets us react in a certain way when a key is either pressed or released. So a listener is simply an object that has functions defined within it. In the case of the Key object, we're going to define functions associated with two events, onKeyDown and onKeyUp, which correspond to the press and release actions of the keyboard.

Let's study how to write the code. First, we create a new listener object:

```
myListener = new Object();
```

Then, we define the onKeyDown function:

```
myListener.onKeyDown = function() {
     trace("Key pressed");
};
```

Next, we define the onKeyUp function:

```
myListener.onKeyUp = function() {
     trace("Key released");
};
```

Finally, we activate the listener by attaching it to the Key object:

```
Key.addListener(myListener);
```

When this code is tested, the Output window will display Key pressed when any key is pressed, and Key released when any key is released (note, however, that holding a key down may register multiple onKeyDown events until the key is released):

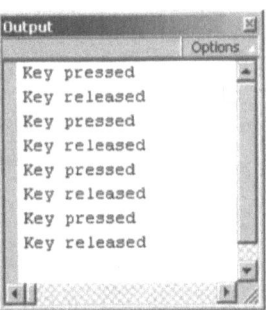

To determine which key has been pressed, we must use the Key.getCode() or Key.getAscii() methods. For example, we could add this new line (highlighted) to our previous code:

```
myListener = new Object();
myListener.onKeyDown = function() {
     trace(Key.getAscii());
     trace("Key pressed");

};
myListener.onKeyUp = function() {
     trace("Key released");
};
Key.addListener(myListener);
```

This will now trace out the code value of the ASCII key that has been pressed:

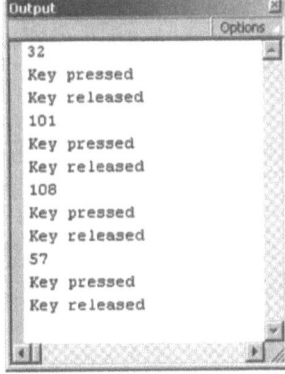

Note that in this case we'd get different values returned if we were to press an uppercase or a lowercase character, because they have their own individual ASCII codes.

If we want the key to stop trapping key presses, and disable the listener, then we must use the `removeListener()` method, like so:

```
Key.removeListener(myListener);
```

Mouse input

Detecting motion for mouse movement and button events is quite similar to the `Key` object, but with only one button, instead of numerous keys. Of course, there are two distinct properties associated with a mouse:

- The **position** – Corresponds to x and y co-ordinates of the mouse cursor's current position on the stage. There's an event called `onMouseMove`, which is triggered every time the mouse is moved.

- The **buttons** – Responds to the press and release of the mouse button on an event basis via `onMouseDown` and `onMouseUp`.

Mouse movement

Let's first consider using the mouse's position to control the motion. Fortunately, Flash provides us with a very simple mechanism for determining the mouse cursor position. There are two properties, `_xmouse` and `_ymouse`, which can be used to determine the position of the mouse cursor relative to the registration point of a particular target.

Perhaps the easiest thing to do is measure the position of the cursor relative to the root timeline, which is always relative to the upper left-hand corner of the stage. We do this like so:

```
xPos = _root._xmouse;
yPos = _root._ymouse;
```

Here, `xPos` and `yPos` will be two variables which will contain the on-screen x and y co-ordinates of the mouse cursor. To use these variables to gain feedback on the position of the mouse, we need to declare and add a new listener object, `myMousePosListener` for example, as shown below:

```
myMousePosListener = new Object();
myMousePosListener.onMouseMove = function() {
    xPos = _root._xmouse;
    yPos = _root._ymouse;
    trace(xPos+", "+yPos);
};
Mouse.addListener(myMousePosListener);
```

This will continually trace the position of the mouse cursor on the stage to the Output window, every time the mouse is moved:

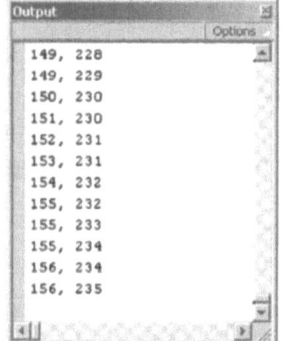

If, however, we use a movie clip as the source of the co-ordinates, then the co-ordinates returned to us will be relative to the movie clip's own registration point:

```
mcXpos = myMovieClip._xmouse;
mcYpos = myMovieClip._ymouse;
```

In this case, if myMovieClip is resting at (100, 100) on the stage, then the position of the mouse cursor will be told to us as if (100, 100) (relative to the root timeline) is the point (0, 0). So, when we move the cursor to (100, 100) on the stage, mcXpos, mcYpos will actually be set to (0, 0).

Mouse clicks

Let's now bring the mouse button into play using the onMouseDown and onMouseUp events. As usual, first we create the listener:

```
myMouseListener = new Object();
```

Then we define the functions:

```
myMouseListener.onMouseDown = function() {
     trace("Mouse button pressed");
};
myMouseListener.onMouseUp = function() {
     trace("Mouse button released");
};
myMouseListener.onMouseMove = function()
     trace("Mouse moved");
};
```

Finally, we add the listener to the Mouse object:

```
Mouse.addListener(myMouseListener);
```

Running this will cause the Output window to be filled with text as we perform different tasks with the mouse:

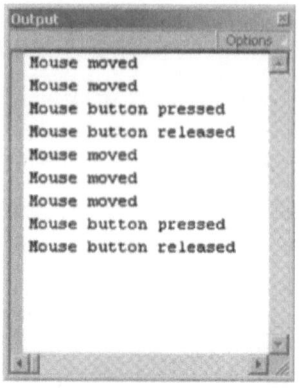

We can also create functions to react to the mouse events of individual movie clips rather than the root timeline. The syntax is simple:

```
myMovieClip.onMouseDown = function() {
    trace("Mouse button pressed in myMovieClip");
};
myMovieClip.onMouseUp = function() {
    trace("Mouse button released in myMovieClip");
};
myMovieClip.onMouseMove = function() {
    trace("Mouse moved in myMovieClip");
};
```

In such cases, we don't need to create a generic listener, because the movie clip acts as the listener, but the usage is the same.

In fact, to have an overall generic mouse handler, we need only apply these events to the _root, like this:

```
_root.onMouseDown = function() {
    trace("Mouse button pressed");
};
_root.onMouseUp = function() {
    trace("Mouse button released");
};
_root.onMouseMove = function() {
    trace("Mouse moved");
};
```

So, it's clear that there are several ways to respond to the press, release, and move events of the mouse.

Local control

The method of *local control* is possibly the most practiced technique for controlling the behavior of movie clips and using ActionScript to produce on-screen motion. With this technique we simply attach the onEnterFrame event to a movie clip, effectively allowing it to control itself. For example:

```
myMovieClip.onEnterFrame = function() {
    this._x++;
    this._y++;
    // Or any code that we want to run on every new frame...
};
```

This is the core of much work in this chapter. The concept is very straightforward: the code in the onEnterFrame function will run on every new frame. So, if our movie is set to run at 24 frames per second, then this code will attempt to execute 24 times per second (see **Chapter 1** for more information). Remember, any time we use the word this, we're referring to the movie clip to which the function is attached.

One of the nice things about using the onEnterFrame function is that we can remove it from action by simply nullifying it, like this:

```
myMovieClip.onEnterFrame = null;
```

Once this is done, then the onEnterFrame event for myMovieClip will stop being monitored, allowing us to gain back valuable processor resources. So, for instance, you could nullify the event when your movie clip reaches a certain position on the stage.

Another nice thing about local control is that the movie clip doesn't need to know anything about the environment in which it's residing. Hundreds of on-screen movie clips could be performing the same or similar tasks creating a complex web of motion, with only the simplest code. Rather than use an anonymous function (myMovieClip.onEnterFrame = function), we can use a named function, and thereby repeat its use over and over:

```
moveMe = function () {
    this._x++;
    this._y++;
};
myMovieClip1.onEnterFrame = moveMe;
myMovieClip2.onEnterFrame = moveMe;
myMovieClip3.onEnterFrame = moveMe;
myMovieClip4.onEnterFrame = moveMe;
myMovieClip5.onEnterFrame = moveMe;
```

We can have several movie clips all using the same function to perform motion actions. Of course, there's room for a for loop in the above code, but the modular nature of defining functions like this is a highly efficient programming practice.

Controller movie clip

We've just seen that movie clips can control themselves, but there's another type, commonly known as a *controller* movie clip, which is responsible for the motion of other movie clips. Here's an example of a controller movie clip's code in its simplest form:

```
myController.onEnterFrame = function() {
    myMovieClip1._x++;
    myMovieClip1._y++;
    myMovieClip2._x++;
```

```
        myMovieClip2._y++;
   };
```

Here we have a movie clip called myController with an associated onEnterFrame function. Within this function two different movie clips, myMovieClip1 and myMovieClip2, are being moved around the stage. However, they have no self-control – rather, myController is controlling them.

The advantages of this method are better understood when many complex objects are required to interact with each other. In a situation where objects must know about each other, a controller is the best bet. Rather than have hundreds of onEnterFrame functions executing every frame, if we keep all the actions in one function then the processor overhead will be minimized, and we can also keep a tight handle on which objects are where, and how they're interacting.

The complexity of such control schemes can become quite intricate. Accordingly, we'll take a look at a specific example of multi-element script-based animation at the end of this chapter.

Timed events

There is one more motion control technique to examine – the setInterval() method allows us to execute a function at a fixed time interval. In general, the setInterval() method looks like this:

```
setInterval(intervalFunction, milliseconds, optionalParameter1,
➡optionalParameter2, ...);
```

where *intervalFunction* corresponds to an arbitrary function that we define to create our timed event, and *milliseconds* is the time in milliseconds that Flash should wait before executing the function. They are just that, optional *containers* for passing any additional information into the function, should we so desire.

To use the setInterval() method in its simplest form, with two parameters, we first need to create the function:

```
myInterval = function () {
     myMovieClip._x++;
};
```

And then we can set the interval, and reference the function:

```
setInterval(myInterval, 10);
```

In this case, if we have a movie clip on the stage with the instance name myMovieClip, then we're going to see it move to the right by 1 pixel every 10 milliseconds (assuming that our processor can cope with this interval). It's that simple!

Note that you can see an example that features the `setInterval()` method used with its optional parameters in **Chapter 13**.

Motion control scenarios

Now that we have a thorough grounding in the different motion control techniques and strategies that are available in Flash MX, we can start to look at examples of the type of motion that models real life. This can be the type of motion that really adds an extra level of fluidity and realism to our Flash creations. Obviously, there are many different types of motion, so we'll start at a fairly basic level, and work upwards to some pretty impressive dynamics.

Standard motion

Open up `movingBall_wrap.fla` and test it by pressing CTRL+ENTER. This movie is pretty simple – it consists of a movie clip with the instance name `ball` that moves along at a fixed trajectory. When it reaches the edge of the screen, it wraps around to the opposite side:

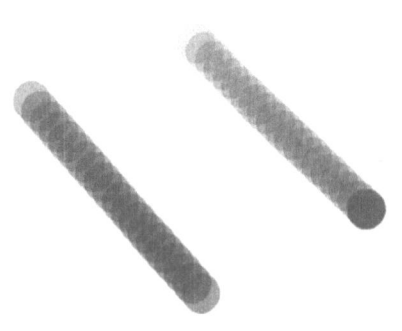

On frame 1 of the actions layer of the main timeline, we have the following code attached:

```
moveMe = function () {
     this._x += this.dx;
     this._y += this.dy;
     this._x = (this._x+550)%550;
     this._y = (this._y+400)%400;
};
ball.dx = 10;
ball.dy = 10;
ball.onEnterFrame = moveme;
```

Here we're moving a ball along a fixed trajectory by adding the values `this.dx` and `this.dy` to `this._x` and `this._y` respectively, in each frame (see also **Chapter 1**). This has the effect of moving the ball at a smooth, fixed speed. In this example, `ball.dx` and `ball.dy` (which correspond to `this.dx` and `this.dy` in the `moveMe` function) are both set to `10`. This means that in every frame the object attached to the `moveMe` function (in this case, `ball`) will move 10 pixels along `_x` and 10 pixels along `_y`.
We also have these two important lines of code:

```
this._x = (this._x+550)%550;
this._y = (this._y+400)%400;
```

These statements force `this._x` to remain within a range of 0 to 549, and `this._y` to remain within 0 to 399. We're using the modulus operator (`%`) here, which returns the remainder of dividing `this._x` by 550 and `this._y` by 400. For example, if `this._x` were 560, then `(this._x+550)%550` would return

10 – exactly where we would want the ball to be on screen to give the appearance that it had wrapped around on the same trajectory.

Limiting the area of travel

We've seen how to wrap around the screen when the ball zooms off the edge, so let's now look at the alternative – reflection, or bouncing off the sides of the screen. What we want to do is simple: when the ball reaches the right or left edge of the stage, reverse its horizontal speed (dx), and when the ball reaches the top or bottom of the screen, reverse its vertical speed (dy).

Open up `movingBall_bounce.fla` where you'll find the code necessary to achieve this:

```
moveMe = function () {
      this._x += this.dx;
      this._y += this.dy;
      if (this._x<0) {
            this.dx *= -1;
      }
      if (this._x>(550-this._width)) {
            this.dx *= -1;
      }
      if (this._y<0) {
            this.dy *= -1;
      }
      if (this._y>(400-this._height)) {
            this.dy *= -1;
      }
};
ball.dx = 10;
ball.dy = 10;
ball.onEnterFrame = moveme;
```

With this new code we're looking at the position of the ball every frame and checking to see if it has crossed the edge of the screen or not – if it has, we reverse the direction of the increments. For example, consider the first portion of the script:

```
if (this._x<0) {
      this.dx *= -1;
}
```

In simple terms, this says, "If the x position of the ball is less than 0 (meaning that it has crossed the left-hand side of the screen), then reverse its horizontal speed (dx)". That's literally it!

We also do this with _x on the right edge of the screen, but this time we must check to see if it has crossed the screen width minus the width of the ball, or `this._x>(550-this._width)`. This is because we need to know if the *right edge* of the ball has hit the screen's edge, not just _x, which is the left edge of the ball where its registration point is (top left).

The following image shows the edges of our ball, and how they're represented with ActionScript:

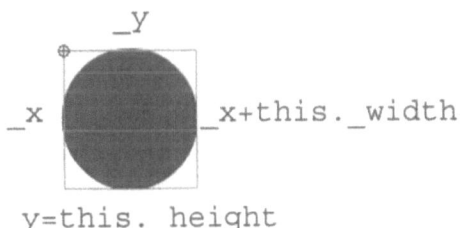

The formula to detect a collision with the wall is the same for _y as it is for _x, but instead of using the _width of the ball, we use its _height to detect the bottom of the screen. If we run this movie, the ball will bounce consistently around the screen. Because of the nature of the way we're calculating the direction change, the angle of reflection acts like a real-world ball would. We're only changing one direction at a time – if the ball hits the right or left edge, nothing is done to the vertical movement, but the horizontal movement is reversed.

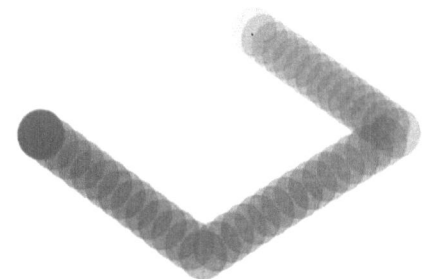

Rotational motion

All of the motion that we've looked at so far has been linear, based upon a system of _x, _y, dx, and dy coordinates, or *rectangular* co-ordinates. There is another form of motion called rotational motion, or *polar motion*, which consists of using two basic parameters, angle and speed, to derive dx and dy. In previous examples, dx and dy were maintained and adjusted every frame. With rotational motion, the movement is controlled via the angle and speed and, because of the screen being based upon a rectangular grid, dx and dy are simply calculated from these properties.

Angle and speed are simple concepts: angle is the direction in a circle that we're facing. The unit of measurement for angle will be either degrees or radians. There are 360 degrees in one full circle, as most people know. In Flash, the _rotation property is measured in degrees. However, when we're dealing with trigonometry functions in ActionScript, we measure angles in radians. There are approximately 6.28, or 2 times Pi, radians in one complete circle. Speed is basically the distance that we're moving, in pixels, in every frame.

When the angle (ang) and speed (speed) are combined we end up with enough information to determine the motion of an object (myObject), like so:

```
myObject.dx = Math.cos(myObject.ang)*myObject.speed;
myObject.dy = Math.sin(myObject.ang)*myObject.speed;
```

Here we're computing dx and dy, using the angle and speed of myObject. Note that the horizontal motion element, dx, is calculated using the cosine of the angle, while the vertical element, dy, is found with the sine of the angle. These are two mathematical functions that accept an angle, in radians, and return a number between -1 and 1. At this point, some readers may be having horrible flashbacks to high school math classes – but don't worry, that's really all the background we need!

Once we've computed dx and dy, we can use them as increments, as usual:

```
myObject._x += myObject.dx;
myObject._y += myObject.dy;
```

OK, let's see rotational motion in action – open up rotation.fla where you'll see that we've converted our ball from the previous examples into a cute little mouse (with the instance name mouse):

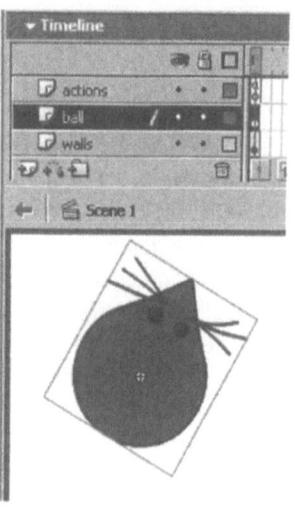

The code on frame 1 of the actions layer looks like this:

```
moveMe = function () {
        this.dx = Math.cos(this.ang)*this.speed;
        this.dy = Math.sin(this.ang)*this.speed;
        this._x += this.dx;
        this._y += this.dy;
        this.ang += 0.05;
        this._rotation = this.ang*(180/Math.PI);
        if (this._x<(this._width/2)) {
                this._x = (this._width/2);
        }
        if (this._x>(550-(this._width/2))) {
                this._x = 550-(this._width/2);
        }
        if (this._y<(this._height/2)) {
                this._y = (this._height/2);
        }
        if (this._y>(400-(this._height/2))) {
                this._y = 400-(this._height/2);
        }
};
mouse.ang = 0;
mouse.speed = 10;
mouse.onEnterFrame = moveMe;
```

Look familiar? Initially, we compute the dx and dy elements and use them to increment the object attached to the moveMe function (generically this until an object is specifically linked). Next, we set up an incrementing angle variable like this:

```
this.ang += 0.05;
```

What exactly are we doing here? We're changing the direction of the object slightly, each frame (when the onEnterFrame event is finally attached), by increasing the angle by 0.05 radians. The effect is that our object (that cute little mouse) will appear to be moving forward and turning as it goes. We also have this line:

```
this._rotation = this.ang*(180/Math.PI);
```

This is responsible for setting the _rotation property of the object, based upon this.ang. Remember, since these properties operate with two different angle formats (degrees versus radians) we must perform this calculation to convert the radians to degrees.

Next, we have some wall detection code, just to make sure that if we have hit the wall, we don't move past it. It creates the interesting effect of making the object continue to spin even though it is unable to move past the wall. This is somewhat like seeing a fly hit a window over and over until it is able to change direction.

Finally, we're creating the parameters for our mouse object. With ang = 0, the object starts off in the direction we place it on the stage, and a speed of 10 means that the object will move at 10 pixels per frame. Once the ang has been increased by 0.05, however, the next move will be nearly 10 pixels to the right, and a fraction of a pixel down (the increasing angle moves clockwise from due right). This is how the gradual curve is introduced.

```
mouse.ang = 0;
mouse.speed = 10;
```

Finally, we connect the onEnterFrame event of our mouse movie clip to the moveMe function defined previously:

```
mouse.onEnterFrame = moveMe;
```

Test the movie for yourself and watch the rotating mouse:

Random motion

One of the most interesting tricks to include in your dynamic designs is random motion. Here we move our objects by modifying their speed and direction of motion at a random rate. Take a look at randomMotion.fla to see this in action. Test the movie and notice that we've now got what looks like a small mole randomly moving around the screen as if he's exploring the stage and edges of the screen:

So what's the trick here? Well, the code is very simple, with only a subtle change from the previous example. This time on frame 1 of the actions layer you'll see the following code:

```
moveMe = function () {
        this.dx = Math.cos(this.ang)*this.speed;
        this.dy = Math.sin(this.ang)*this.speed;
        this._x += this.dx;
        this._y += this.dy;
        this.ang += (Math.random()-.5);
        this._rotation = this.ang*(180/Math.PI);
        if (this._x<(this._width/2)) {
                this._x = (this._width/2);
        }
        if (this._x>(550-(this._width/2))) {
                this._x = 550-(this._width/2);
        }
        if (this._y<(this._height/2)) {
                this._y = (this._height/2);
        }
        if (this._y>(400-(this._height/2))) {
                this._y = 400-(this._height/2);
        }
};
mole.ang = 0;
mole.speed = 10;
mole.onEnterFrame = moveme;
```

So the only difference between this example and the previous one (excluding the new mole movie clip), is this line:

```
this.ang += (Math.random()-.5);
```

In our previous example we were increasing ang by a constant amount (0.05) each frame. Now we're increasing it by a number that falls in the range of -0.5 to 0.5 (remember – without any parameters, the Math.random() method gives a random number between 0 and 1). At times, the mole will turn right and at times it will turn left. Overall, the little critter appears to scamper and scurry in a random, chaotic, and most important of all, realistic fashion.

Target-based motion

When we're talking about target-based motion, we mean the type of motion that involves moving an object towards a target with a specific amount of acceleration (and deceleration).

For example, a popular design trick in Flash is the 'ease into place' method, where an object zooms towards a target, and moves at a speed proportionate to the amount of distance remaining to the target. A real-world analogy will help to clarify what we mean here – if, for example, you are standing 6 feet from a wall, and you move 3 feet forward in one step, you have cut your distance in half. If you then step 1.5 feet, you have again cut your distance in half, but now you're moving slower. Step forward 50% of the remaining distance and you'll be closer, yet slower still. This is the basis behind the cool effect that we're talking about.

Now open `targetMotion.fla` to see a Flash version of this motion. In this example we're going back to using our `ball` movie clip, for simplicity. The code on frame 1 of the root timeline actions layer starts by defining a `moveMe` function:

```
moveMe = function () {
      this.dx = (this.targx-this._x)*.1;
      this.dy = (this.targy-this._y)*.1;
      this._x += this.dx;
      this._y += this.dy;
};
```

There are two variables, `targx` and `targy`, which represent the _x and _y co-ordinates of where we would like the object to end up. They can be set in any number of ways, but we'll do it in another function, appropriately named `setTarget`, to set the target to be the position of our mouse:

```
setTarget = function () {
      this.targx = _root._xmouse;
      this.targy = _root._ymouse;
};
```

The motion is simple: we compute a dx and dy value, based on the distance between the current _x, _y and the `targx`, `targy`. In this example, we set dx and dy to be 0.1, or 10% of the remaining distance (in the example where we discussed stepping towards a wall, above, this ratio was 50%). Changing this number (0.1) will change the speed at which the object arrives in place; the higher the number, the faster it will arrive. Setting the number to 1 will force the object to zoom into place instantly (in exactly one frame). Setting the ratio to be larger than 1 will have some pretty strange results – values between 1 and 2 are rather interesting... try it out yourself!

Finally, we set up our `ball` movie clip with an initial target position 10, 10, and connect it to the `moveMe` and `setTarget` functions via `onEnterFrame` and `onMouseDown` events:

```
ball.targx = 10;
ball.targy = 10;
ball.onEnterFrame = moveme;
ball.onMouseDown = setTarget;
```

Test the movie and you'll see that, after a mouse click, the ball will follow your cursor at a speed inversely proportional to its distance from the ball:

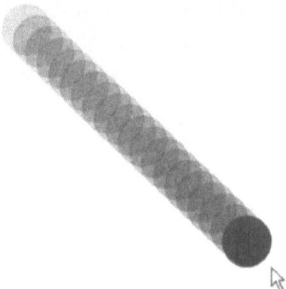

Real-time control of motion

So far, the motion we've seen has been fairly non-interactive and automated. OK, so we've seen the target-based clicking motion, but once we click, the motion is out of our hands. What about motion that is constantly changing in real-time? We want motion that the user can control on a frame-by-frame basis.

Time for another example – open `realtimeControl.fla` and test it. We see a ball on screen that appears to be stationary. However, once we press the arrow keys, the ball begins to move smoothly in the chosen direction, until it hits the edge of the screen, and bounces off. This clearly has the makings of some kind of Flash game.

How is this real-time motion control achieved? We simply adjust the movement variables, `dx` and `dy`, based on the state of the arrow keys. Here's what the code looks like:

```
moveMe = function () {
    this._x += this.dx;
    this._y += this.dy;
    if (this._x<0) {
        this._x = 0;
        this.dx *= -.9;
    }
    if (this._x>(550-this._width)) {
        this._x = 550-this._width;
```

```
            this.dx *= -.9;
      }
      if (this._y<0) {
            this._y = 0;
            this.dy *= -.9;
      }
      if (this._y>(400-this._height)) {
            this._y = 400-this._height;
            this.dy *= -.9;
      }
      if (Key.isDown(Key.RIGHT)) {
            this.dx += 0.5;
      }
      if (Key.isDown(Key.LEFT)) {
            this.dx -= 0.5;
      }
      if (Key.isDown(Key.UP)) {
            this.dy -= 0.5;
      }
      if (Key.isDown(Key.DOWN)) {
            this.dy += 0.5;
      }
};
ball.dx = 0;
ball.dy = 0;
ball.onEnterFrame = moveMe;
```

This is very much like the earlier ball bouncing example, except that we've also added a *friction factor* by multiplying each speed element by -0.9 each time the ball hits a boundary.

Additionally, we have a few more lines of code to allow the ball to be controlled by the cursor keys:

```
if (Key.isDown(Key.RIGHT)) {
      this.dx += 0.5;
}
if (Key.isDown(Key.LEFT)) {
      this.dx -= 0.5;
}
if (Key.isDown(Key.UP)) {
      this.dy -= 0.5;
}
if (Key.isDown(Key.DOWN)) {
      this.dy += 0.5;
}
```

We're using the `isDown` method of the `Key` object to adjust `dx` and `dy`. For instance, if the right arrow key is held down, then we add 0.5 to the `dx` every frame. On the other hand, if the left arrow key is held down, then we subtract 0.5 from the `dx` each frame. This will cause the ball to slowly increase in speed towards the right or left, depending upon which keys we press. The same applies for the up and down arrows and the `dy` variables, causing the ball to smoothly accelerate up or down.

When the horizontal and vertical motions are combined, the effect is a ball that can move smoothly around the screen with acceleration, velocity, and momentum. At the same time, it bounces off the walls when it strikes them. The combination of forces and motions are numerous, yet quite simple, all in the spirit of programming with ActionScript.

Real-time rotational motion control

Another scenario that we should consider is the real-time control of rotational motion. Let's look at what happens when we add real-time control to rotational motion – we'll use the friendly little mole that featured in the random motion example we studied earlier.

Open up and test `realtimeRotation1.fla` and, again, use the cursor keys to control the movement of the mole. Note that this time the up and down keys control the acceleration and deceleration of the mole, while left and right control its direction – this kind of motion control is reminiscent of those early video games, like Defender.

Let's look at the code:

```
moveMe = function () {
    this.dx = Math.cos(this.ang)*this.speed;
    this.dy = Math.sin(this.ang)*this.speed;
    this._x += this.dx;
    this._y += this.dy;
    this._rotation = this.ang*(180/Math.PI);
    if (this._x<(this._width/2)) {
        this._x = (this._width/2);
    }
    if (this._x>(550-(this._width/2))) {
        this._x = 550-(this._width/2);
    }
    if (this._y<(this._height/2)) {
        this._y = (this._height/2);
    }
    if (this._y>(400-(this._height/2))) {
        this._y = 400-(this._height/2);
    }
    if (Key.isDown(Key.RIGHT)) {
        this.ang += 0.05;
    }
```

```
            if (Key.isDown(Key.LEFT)) {
                    this.ang -= 0.05;
            }
            if (Key.isDown(Key.UP)) {
                    this.speed += 0.5;
            }
            if (Key.isDown(Key.DOWN)) {
                    this.speed -= 0.5;
            }
    };
    mole.ang = 0;
    mole.speed = 0;
    mole.onEnterFrame = moveMe;
```

The critical difference between this type of motion control and that of the previous example (in standard rectangular co-ordinates) is in the key control code. This time, the right and left keys control only the ang variable, and the up and down keys relate only to the speed variable.

The results are rather intuitive – when we press right, we turn right because our angle is increased by 0.05 radians each frame. As we press left, we turn left because the angle is decreased by 0.05 radians each frame. When we press up, the speed increases by 0.5 pixels per frame in each frame, and our mole begins to move faster. Finally, when we press down, the speed decreases and the mole slows down. In fact, if we continue to press down after the mole has stopped, then he'll start to move backwards, all in a smooth, fluid motion which mimics real life.

Now we'll look at a slight variation on this theme – in realtimeRotation2.fla, everything is similar, except for the key control code, and a few new lines beneath it:

```
            if (Key.isDown(Key.RIGHT)) {
                    this.da += 0.02;
            }
            if (Key.isDown(Key.LEFT)) {
                    this.da -= 0.02;
            }
            if (Key.isDown(Key.UP)) {
                    this.speed += 0.6;
            }
            if (Key.isDown(Key.DOWN)) {
                    this.speed -= 0.6;
            }
    this.speed *= 0.95;
    this.da *= 0.90;
    this.ang += this.da;
```

This time we're using different rates of accelerated and decelerated turning and moving. We're also applying decay to the speed, so that if the keys are released, the mole will come to a gentle stop. We have the new variable, da, which is somewhat like dx in as much as dx indicates 'a change in x'; da means 'a change in angle'. Rather than letting the left and right arrow keys control the angle itself, they instead control the rate of change of the angle. The result is that when we press the right arrow key, the mole begins turning slowly at first, and then gradually increases its turning speed, up to a maximum. The same applies to the left key.

This allows us to have a mole, which eventually stops turning once the keys are released. Since we have the decay code `this.da *= 0.90`, da will be reduced by 10% each frame. If we're holding down the arrow key, then da will be increasing each frame, so the decay will be negligible. However, if we are not holding down any arrow keys, then da will eventually decay, reach 0, and the mole will stop turning.

Multi-element scripted animation

So far in this chapter we've looked at the various motion control techniques for using ActionScript to create intricate and exciting dynamic designs, and we've studied various scenarios in which these techniques can be employed. Now, armed with a good grounding in the use of these scripting tools, we'll enhance our understanding by looking at a larger example that features some elaborate motion effects produced from a number of different elements.

Let's dive right into it – open up `molecules1.fla`, and test it:

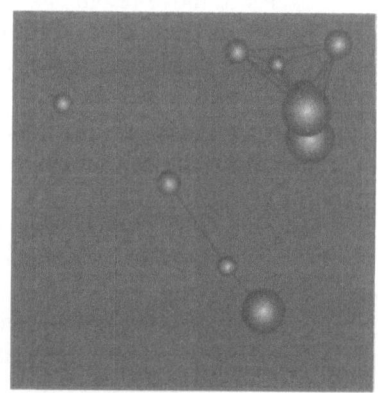

Spend a moment watching this movie to see exactly what is going on – there's actually some pretty complex motion taking place. This example is an artistic representation of the principles of nuclear and atomic physics, how atoms interact and the forces that bind them and affect their motion. We have ten atoms of various sizes (masses) floating around on screen, and if they pass within a given distance of each other then a line is drawn between them to indicate that forces are interacting between them. Larger atoms have greater pull and lower speeds, while smaller atoms are weaker but can travel faster. The overall system at work here is very simple yet the outcome is complex and unpredictable – so it's perfect as a case study to enforce some of the basic techniques that this chapter is concerned with.

From an ActionScript perspective, we're making use of movie clip (local) self-control, as well as using a controller movie clip to take care of the interactions between atoms. Let's break down the relevant code and discuss the methods being put into practice in each segment of script.

The molecule code

For reference, here's the code from `molecules1.fla` in full:

```
MovieClip.prototype.distanceTo = function(targ) {
    this.diffx = _root[targ]._x-this._x;
```

```
        this.diffy = _root[targ]._y-this._y;
        this.d = Math.sqrt((this.diffx*this.diffx)+(this.diffy*this.diffy));
        return (this.d);
};
moveMe = function () {
        this._x += this.dx;
        this._y += this.dy;
        if (this._x<0) {
                this._x = 0;
                this.dx *= -.9;
        }
        if (this._x>550) {
                this._x = 550;
                this.dx *= -.9;
        }
        if (this._y<0) {
                this._y = 0;
                this.dy *= -.9;
        }
        if (this._y>400) {
                this._y = 400;
                this.dy *= -.9;
        }
};
numatoms = 10;
for (i=0; i<numatoms; i++) {
        nm = "atom"+i;
        duplicateMovieClip(atom, nm, i);
        _root[nm]._x = Math.random()*550;
        _root[nm]._y = Math.random()*400;
        _root[nm].dx = Math.random()*4-2;
        _root[nm].dy = Math.random()*4-2;
        _root[nm].mass = Math.random()*180+20;
        _root[nm]._xscale = _root[nm]._yscale=_root[nm].mass;
        _root[nm].onEnterFrame = moveMe;
}
myController.onEnterFrame = function() {
        _root.clear();
        for (i=0; i<numatoms; i++) {
                nm = "atom"+i;
                for (j=0; j<numatoms; j++) {
                        if (i != j) {
                                dnm = "atom"+j;
                                if (_root[nm].distanceTo(dnm)<100) {
                                        _root.lineStyle(1, 0);
```

continues overleaf

```
                            _root.moveTo(_root[nm]._x,
                          ➡ _root[nm]._y);
                            _root.lineTo(_root[dnm]._x,
                          ➡ _root[dnm]._y);
                            _root[nm].dx +=
                          ➡ _root[nm].diffx*0.002*
                          ➡ (_root[dnm].mass/100);
                            _root[nm].dy +=
                          ➡ _root[nm].diffy*0.002*
                          ➡ (_root[dnm].mass/100);
                   }
              }
          }
      }
};
```

In order to fully understand this ActionScript, we'll break it down into these four sections:

- Defining the distanceTo prototype function

- Defining the moveMe function

- Setting up and initializing each atom movie clip

- Creating the controller code

Defining the disanceTo prototype function

One of the necessary pieces of functionality in this example is the ability to determine how far one particular atom is from another. Accordingly, we create a neat little function called distanceTo as a prototype method of the MovieClip object. We'll learn more about the prototype property, and object-oriented programming in general, in **Chapter 16** of this book.

This function declaration looks like this:

```
MovieClip.prototype.distanceTo = function(targ) {
     this.diffx = _root[targ]._x-this._x;
     this.diffy = _root[targ]._y-this._y;
     this.d = Math.sqrt((this.diffx*this.diffx)+(this.diffy*this.diffy));
     return (this.d);
};
```

By saying MovieClip.prototype.distanceTo, we're telling Flash to create this function as a method of the MovieClip object, which means that every single movie clip in our movie will have the distanceTo function automatically built into it.

The function takes one parameter, `targ`, which refers to the name of a movie clip instance. The function then uses the standard Pythagorean formula of $a^2 + b^2 = c^2$, the typical method for determining the distance between two points. Once the distance has been computed, it is returned.

Defining the moveMe function

The `moveMe` function is similar to other functions we've looked at in this chapter – it consists of a standard increment of _x and _y by dx and dy, and the code that makes the movie clip bounce off the walls when a collision occurs:

```
moveMe = function () {
        this._x += this.dx;
        this._y += this.dy;
        if (this._x<0) {
                this._x = 0;
                this.dx *= -.9;
        }
        if (this._x>550) {
                this._x = 550;
                this.dx *= -.9;
        }
        if (this._y<0) {
                this._y = 0;
                this.dy *= -.9;
        }
        if (this._y>400) {
                this._y = 400;
                this.dy *= -.9;
        }
};
```

This function will be applied to each atom so that it moves itself along in space. In this sense, the atoms have localized control.

Setting up and initializing each atom movie clip

In this segment of code we're creating all of our atom movie clips from one master movie clip called atom, which is sitting well off the main stage:

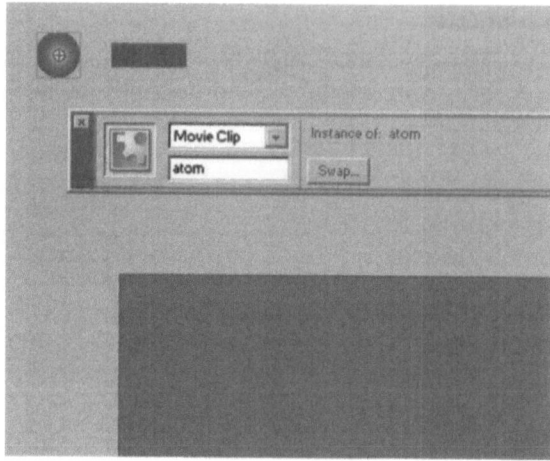

This is an old trick in Flash – just drop any movie clips that you want to use with ActionScript off-stage, and you can access them at runtime without the *parent* being seen in your movie. Note that in the image above we can also see our controller movie clip – more on this shortly.

As we create each atom using the duplicateMovieClip() method we set up a few things about its behavior, including its position, speed, and mass. We use the mass to determine its _xscale and _yscale so that atoms with a larger mass appear bigger. We also have a variable called numatoms that is used to determine how many atoms are created and active:

```
numatoms = 10;
for (i=0; i<numatoms; i++) {
       nm = "atom"+i;
       duplicateMovieClip(atom, nm, i);
       _root[nm]._x = Math.random()*550;
       _root[nm]._y = Math.random()*400;
       _root[nm].dx = Math.random()*4-2;
       _root[nm].dy = Math.random()*4-2;
       _root[nm].mass = Math.random()*180+20;
       _root[nm]._xscale = _root[nm]._yscale=_root[nm].mass;
       _root[nm].onEnterFrame = moveMe;
}
```

Note that we're choosing to place all the atoms on the root timeline to ensure the most efficient use of the controller movie clip (detailed next). With all atoms on the same timeline, their co-ordinate systems are all based on the same grid (in _root). This also accommodates an easy way of using the drawing API to create the interconnecting lines.

Creating the controller code

Finally, let's look at the code that checks for forces between atoms – this is contained within the onEnterFrame code for a movie clip called myController, which again is found off-stage. Here we're using the drawing API (discussed in detail in **Chapter 3**) on the root timeline to draw our black lines, so the first thing we do is _root.clear() to clear out any dynamically drawn lines:

```
myController.onEnterFrame = function() {
     _root.clear();
```

Next, we create a nested for loop that compares each atom with every other atom:

```
for (i=0; i<numatoms; i++) {
     nm = "atom"+i;
     for (j=0; j<numatoms; j++) {
```

making sure not to compare an atom with itself:

```
if (i != j) {
```

Then we check to see if the two atoms are within 100 pixels of each other, using the distanceTo function:

```
dnm = "atom"+j;
if (_root[nm].distanceTo(dnm)<100) {
```

and if they are, we draw a line between the two atoms:

```
_root.lineStyle(1, 0);
_root.moveTo(_root[nm]._x,
➥_root[nm]._y);
_root.lineTo(_root[dnm]._x,
➥_root[dnm]._y);
```

Then we perform some trickery with the velocity of each atom, based upon the forces acting upon it. Each atom has a specific amount of pull on each other atom based on its proximity and its mass. This effectively alters the velocities of the atoms enough to create bonds and orbits:

```
_root[nm].dx +=
➥_root[nm].diffx*0.002*
➥(_root[dnm].mass/100)
_root[nm].dy +=
➥_root[nm].diffy*0.002*
➥(_root[dnm].mass/100);
                }
            }
        }
    }
};
```

And that's it! The atoms are all interacting as well as moving of their own accord. To some, this example may seem a little too scientific in nature when we're concerned with designing with ActionScript, but the ultimate effect is very cool! Anyway, generally speaking we're demonstrating the possible interrelationships between different motion-generating techniques and various objects, and how it all works together as a whole.

Inter-atom communications

There is one more level of communication possible between movie clips in this scenario – we can define certain variables to tell all the atoms to behave a certain way. Load up molecules2.fla and test it. Nothing much different from the previous example at first glance, but now try clicking on any atom and dragging it to a different location – pretty neat! See if you can separate all the atoms, it's rather tricky. Now press the SPACE bar and keep your finger on it, and notice that everything comes to a gentle rest... let's see what additions we had to make to get these extra features.

The most obvious new chunks of code are the two new functions that come after the moveMe function:

```
dragme = function () {
    if (this.hitTest(_root._xmouse, _root._ymouse)) {
        this.canmove = false;
        this.startDrag();
    }
};
undragme = function () {
    this.stopDrag();
    this.canmove = true;
};
```

Here we see the dragme and undragme function definitions. These are also assigned to each atom in the initialization code:

```
numatoms = 10;
for (i=0; i<numatoms; i++) {
    nm = "atom"+i;
    duplicateMovieClip(atom, nm, i);
    _root[nm]._x = Math.random()*550;
    _root[nm]._y = Math.random()*400;
    _root[nm].dx = Math.random()*4-2;
    _root[nm].dy = Math.random()*4-2;
    _root[nm].mass = Math.random()*180+20;
    _root[nm]._xscale = _root[nm]._yscale=_root[nm].mass;
    _root[nm].canmove = true;
    _root[nm].onEnterFrame = moveMe;
    _root[nm].onMouseDown = dragme;
    _root[nm].onMouseUp = undragme;
}
```

They are responsible for setting the local variable of each atom canmove to true or false. If canmove is false, then this atom will not move in accordance with the new code in the moveMe function:

```
if (this.canmove) {
        this._x += this.dx;
        this._y += this.dy;
}
```

We also have some additional code attached to the onEnterFrame function of myController – when the SPACE bar is held down, then we set a variable on the _root level called slowdown to true, or otherwise it's false:

```
if (Key.isDown(Key.SPACE)) {
        _root.slowdown = true;
} else {
        _root.slowdown = false;
}
```

Along with this, we have a bit of code added to the bottom of the moveMe function that is attached to each atom:

```
if (_root.slowdown) {
        this.dx *= 0.9;
        this.dy *= 0.9;
}
```

Essentially, we're checking to see the state of the slowdown variable. If it is true, then each atom will react in its own way by decaying its own momentum, and coming to a stop.

What this ultimately means is that we can drag one atom around, while all the other atoms continue to fly around the screen. This allows us to set up particular groupings of atoms to build molecules. In theory we could hold the SPACE bar down so that all atoms come to rest, then position a few atoms in a nice

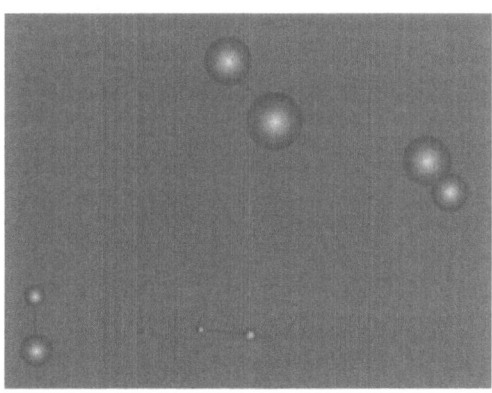

symmetrical arrangement, release the SPACE bar, and watch as the forces balance perfectly and we have what appears to be a molecule in equilibrium. This is what happens when we use good combinations of motion control techniques. These techniques give us a vast design potential – an intelligent web site, a cool game, or even just fun physics modeling experiments!

Objectives

- Importing sound

- Setting up and using the sound object:

  - Incidental sound

  - Background sound

- Sound properties and controls: methods and events associated with the sound object

Objectives

- Importing sound

- Setting up and using the sound object:

  - Incidental sound

  - Background sound

- Sound properties and controls: methods and events associated with the sound object

Introduction

The sound object in Flash MX ActionScript enables us to bring dynamic, script-driven sounds into our Flash movies. With the sound object we're able to play sound effects, songs, looped tracks, voiceovers, and just about anything else that requires dynamic sound. It gives us the ability to start and stop sounds, set their volume and pan, and detect the current position of playback for a current track, as well as use the completion of a sound as a trigger for our animations.

In this chapter, after a brief overview of how to import and configure a sound in Flash MX, we'll examine some specific methods to control the **volume** and **pan** of our sounds. For reference, let's take a quick look at some of the functionality that we're likely to come across – the table below describes the main methods associated with the sound object:

Method	Description
attachSound()	Attaches a specified sound to a specified sound object.
loadSound()	Dynamically (at runtime) loads an MP3 sound file into a specified sound object.
start()	Starts playing the attached sound object.
stop()	Stops the sound that is currently playing.
getBytesLoaded()	Gives the number of bytes loaded (streamed) for the attached sound object.
getBytesTotal()	Gives the size in bytes of the attached sound object.

Importing sound

In order to actually use the ActionScript sound object, we must either import a sound file into our Library and appropriately configure it for runtime export with the attachSound() method, or load the sound dynamically with the loadSound() method. We'll soon learn about these techniques when we look at scripting with the sound object, but first let's learn how to import sound into Flash.

Open up a new FLA file, select File>Import, or use the shortcut keys CTRL+R, to open up the Import dialog window. Next, browse to the directory containing the sound file that you wish to import. Don't forget that in order to *see* your sound files in the Import window you must have an option like All Formats selected in the Files of Type drop-down menu at the bottom of this window:

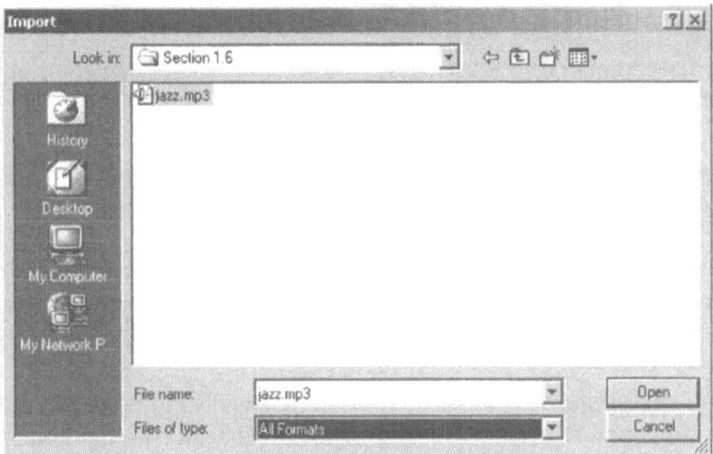

After locating the required file, select it and click Open. The sound file will then be imported.

Next, we must set up the linkage options of our sound file in order to access it with ActionScript. Press F11 (or CTRL+L) to open the Library, and select the sound file within it. Right click your file and choose Linkage... from the options available:

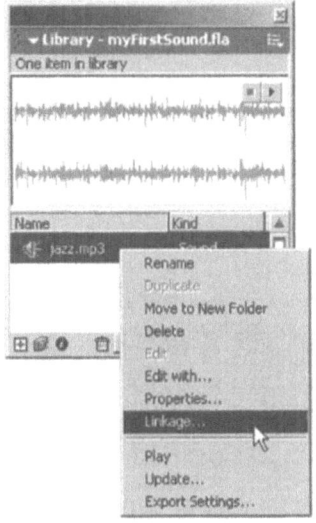

In the Linkage Properties window that appears, check the Export for ActionScript box (the Export in first frame box will also check itself by default – leave it like that), and then enter a unique name for your sound in the Identifier box. Finally, click OK. This declares the name that we'll use with ActionScript to reference and play the sound later using the sound object.

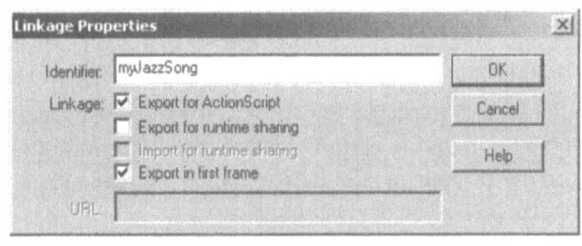

That's it! Our sound is now ready to be used with the ActionScript sound object.

Creating and using a sound object

Now we'll study the script required to set up and use the sound object. When it comes to implementing sound in our Flash movies, there are two types of sound to consider:

- **Incidental sound** – This is sound which plays based on distinct events. This might be in response to a click, or a game action, or any other one-off type of sound effect.

- **Background sound** – This is sound which may play in the background for a long period of time. This could include music, ambient sound effects (forest, waves, crowd). These are sounds, which may end up looping many times, and are therefore often specifically *seamless* in nature.

As mentioned earlier, we can use sounds that have been manually imported into the Flash MX Library. However, Flash also supports the dynamic loading of MP3 audio files via the `loadSound()` command, and these files can be configured to be either streaming or event sounds. If set up for streaming, however, the sound file will begin playing after only a few seconds – it won't load and then wait to play like an event-based sound.

Before we examine the difference between the use of incidental and background sounds, we'll look at a quick example that shows how to create a sound object. Defining a new sound object is very much like defining any other type of object in ActionScript – we use a constructor, like this:

```
mySound = new Sound();
```

It's as simple as that! Here we've created a new Sound object called mySound, and we can now link sounds from our Library to it. The constructor can also take a parameter, the name of a target movie clip, like this:

```
mySound = new Sound(mySound_mc);
```

By including the movie clip name mySound_mc we're telling Flash that we want to attach the sound mySound to that particular movie clip. If we don't provide a movie clip name, all sounds will be treated and acted upon by the Sound object in the same way, and any setting of volume or pan will be global to every sound in your movie. By specifying a target movie clip we're able to apply individual changes to certain characteristics of that sound alone.

Let's look at an example – open up myFirstSound.fla, and test it with CTRL+ENTER. Make sure you have your speakers or headphones turned on – we should hear some jazz music playing as the output.

Now return to the Flash authoring environment – notice that there's nothing on the stage, and indeed the root timeline has no sound waveforms in it as it would if we simply dragged and dropped an instance of a sound file onto the stage. Typically, in non-scripted sound, we would see the sound itself in the frame, configured to play as an event or a stream:

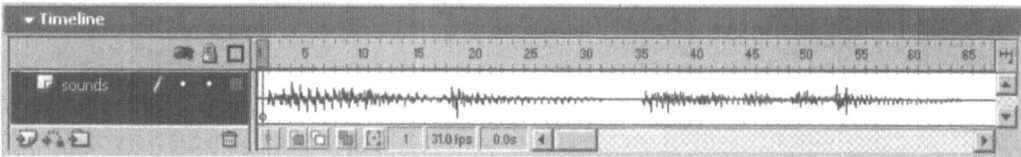

With a scripted sound object, however, our main timeline has nothing but an actions layer, and a frame full of ActionScript, as indicated by the small a symbol in frame 1 here:

Select frame 1 of the actions layer of myFirstSound.fla and open up the Actions panel with Window>Actions or F9 – you'll find the following code:

```
1  _root.createEmptyMovieClip("mySound_mc", 10);
2  mySound = new Sound(mySound_mc);
3  mySound.attachSound("myJazzSong");
4  mySound.start();
5
```

These 4 lines are essentially all that are required to start playing a sound dynamically with ActionScript.

Initially we need to use the createEmptyMovieClip() method to create a new, blank movie clip on the root timeline, called mySound_mc, at depth level of 10. We can use this movie clip as a distinct container within which our sound can be independently controlled. Next we set up our new Sound object called mySound and link it to the freshly created movie clip:

```
_root.createEmptyMovieClip("mySound_mc", 10);
mySound = new Sound(mySound_mc);
```

In the next line of code we're telling Flash that mySound will play the sound that has the linkage ID, myJazzSong, as was set up earlier in the library, using the attachSound() method:

```
mySound.attachSound("myJazzSong");
```

Finally, we're telling the sound to begin playing, using the start() method of the Sound object.

```
mySound.start();
```

Note that the start() method can take 2 optional parameters:

```
mySound.start(secondsOffset, loops);
```

The first parameter, secondsOffset, allows us to specify precisely where in the sound the playback will begin. If we don't specify anything, or pass in 0, then playback will start at the very beginning of the sound. The second parameter, loops, tells Flash how many times to loop through, or repeat this sound.

Incidental sound

In general, when dealing with incidental sound we create a sound object, attach to it a sound in the Library by referencing a linkage ID, and then tell it to start playing by association with some event. Let's look at an incidental sound in a common situation: a button press. Open incidentalSound.fla, and take a look on the stage:

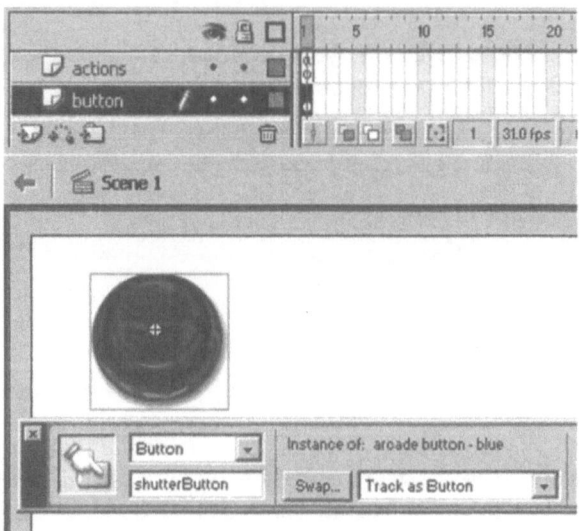

We've got a nice blue arcade-style button on the stage – this is taken from Window>Common Libraries>Buttons in Flash MX – and it has an instance name of shutterButton.

Attached to frame 1 of the actions layer we have the following code:

```
_root.createEmptyMovieClip("mySound_mc", 10);
mySound = new Sound(mySound_mc);
mySound.attachSound("shutter");
shutterButton.onPress = function() {
    mySound.start();
};
```

As before, we're creating a new sound object called mySound, and attaching it to the newly created mySound_mc movie clip. This time, we're attaching a sound with the ID shutter, which is in the Library:

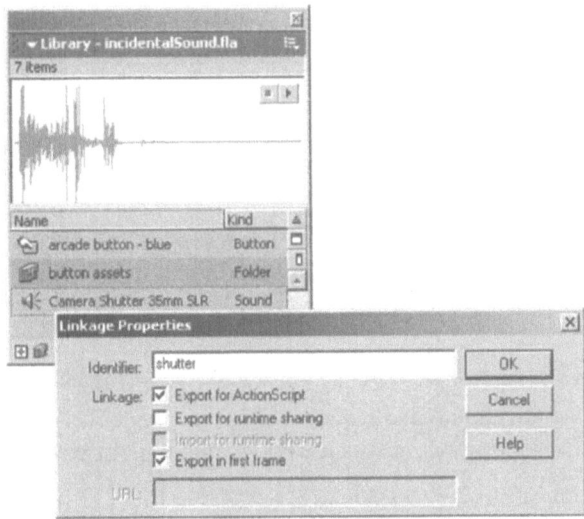

Note that this sound was taken from Window>Common Libraries>Sounds – here you'll find lots of intriguing sounds to play around with. Otherwise, we must import our sound as described at the beginning of this chapter.

Finally, we're creating some code in order to handle the pressing of the button. We use the onPress event of the button object, and within it tell mySound to start playing:

```
shutterButton.onPress = function() {
    mySound.start();
};
```

Test the movie and hit the button a few times to hear the camera shutter go off – pretty straightforward, right? The sound object is initialized as soon as frame 1 is played. Now we could fill our library with sound effects, giving them all unique linkage ID names and different triggering mechanisms. All we have to do is set up all the sound objects at the beginning of our code, and we're ready to bring our work alive with incidental sound.

Dynamic loading of an incidental sound

Another way that we can create incidental sound is to use the loadSound() method of the sound object. With this method we can load our sound effects from MP3 files straight off the hard drive, ready for us to begin playing when we need them. loadSound() is linked to an instance of a sound object and takes the following form:

```
mySound.loadSound("url", isStreaming);
```

Here, url is the name and location of your MP3 file – so, for example, if you have an MP3 file called mySoundFile in the same directory as the FLA file that references it, the url parameter would simply be mySoundFile.mp3. The other parameter, isStreaming, indicates whether the sound is a streaming or event sound – accordingly, it can be true or false, respectively.

Take a look at incidentalSound_dynamic.fla. The only code in this movie is found on frame 1 of the actions layer:

```
root.createEmptyMovieClip("mySound_mc", 10);
mySound = new Sound(mySound_mc);
mySound.loadSound("jazz.mp3", false);
mySound.start();
```

Everything looks similar to the earlier example, except we're now utilizing the loadSound() command to load the jazz.mp3 file at runtime and store it within mySound. The false parameter signals that we don't want to stream this sound since it's incidental – we'll look at streaming soon, when we come to study background music.

Once our sound has been loaded, we can tell it to begin playing with the start() command, just like a sound linked from the Library. Again, we can use this within buttons and actions to trigger our loaded sounds.

> *Note that it's probably a good idea to make sure that a loaded sound has completely finished loading on our website before we begin to play it. In fact, the sound object has the getBytesLoaded() and getBytesTotal() methods to tell us just how much of the sound has been loaded. We should be sure that it is 100% loaded before we begin playing an incidental sound.*

In fact, we can use the getBytesLoaded() and getBytesTotal() methods to issue a warning that the sound was loading like this:

```
if (mySound.getBytesLoaded() == mySound.getBytesTotal()) {
    mySound.start();
} else {
    trace("Sound not yet loaded... please wait!");
}
```

We can also make use of the onLoad event of the sound object, like so:

```
mySound.onLoad = function() {
    this.start();
};
```

When the sound has finished loading, this function will execute, and the sound will begin playing. This way there will be no unexpected behavior or confusing lack of sound for users accessing your site.

Background sound

Now let's look at adding background sound to our designs – perhaps a musical soundtrack or an ambient sound effect presence. Open backgroundSound.fla, to see how we use what we've learned so far in this module, and extend it for background sounds. If we test this movie, we can sit back and relax and listen to several hours of cool jazz music. Well, after several hours of a looping 30-second jazz sample, continually repeating itself, you might feel a little uneasy, but you get the general idea!

The following code, found in the actions layer of backgroundSound.fla, does the trick:

```
_root.createEmptyMovieClip("mySound_mc", 10);
mySound = new Sound(mySound_mc);
mySound.attachSound("myJazzSong");
mySound.start(0, 9999);
```

It's really quite simple – we're creating the sound object, attaching to it a linked sound from the Library, and then telling it to play 9999 times. This sound loop is 26.2 seconds long, so that equates to a good few days worth of music – the jazz fans will come flocking! Suffice it to say, this is how we tell Flash to repeat a loop *forever*.

And remember, we can tell Flash to stop a sound at any point by issuing the stop() command:

```
mySound.stop("myJazzSong");
```

Dynamic loading of a background sound

We can also use the loadSound() method to play a background sound. With this technique we would generally stream the sound in, because a background sound is typically longer, and therefore a larger file size, than an incidental sound.

Look at the code in the actions layer of backgroundSound_dynamic.fla:

```
_root.createEmptyMovieClip("mySound_mc", 10);
mySound = new Sound(mySound_mc);
mySound.loadSound("jazz.mp3", true);
```

This time, we're passing the value true as the second parameter of the loadSound() method to indicate that we want streaming sound. This means that our song will begin playing while it is still downloading –

this is ideal for sounds that are quite long but we don't want users to have to wait around in silence while the sound downloads.

> *Notice that if we run this movie the sound begins playing without us issuing a start() command. This is fundamental to nature of streamed sound - by starting the stream loading, we're also telling Flash to begin playing the sound when enough of it has loaded to smoothly begin playing.*

Unfortunately, when we perform streaming of a sound we really can't loop it like we can a non-streamed sound. This is because once a streamed sound has finished, it is no longer in memory. The best way to loop streamed sound is to put the loop in the sound file itself (creating a very long sound file!), or just use the `onSoundComplete` event to re-initiate the stream upon completion (don't worry, we'll learn how to do this at the end of this chapter).

Sound properties and controls

Now that we know how to use the sound object to create, set up, and play back sounds, let's look at some of the characteristics of the sound object that we can control.

There are two properties specifically associated with the sound object and they work on all types of sounds. They are `position` and `duration`, and they indicate how much of the sound has been played at any time, and how long the sound is in total.

Sound property	Description
position	The number of milliseconds that a sound has been playing for.
duration	The total length of a sound in milliseconds.

Additionally, there are several methods associated with the sound object that we can use to modify and adjust various aspects of its sound and playback. These methods are shown in the following table:

Sound control method	Description
setVolume()	Used to adjust the default volume of a sound object. A sound plays at 100% volume by default. The setVolume() method takes a percentage, where 0 is silent and 100 is full.
setPan()	Used to adjust the pan of a sound object. The pan determines how far left or right the sound will play in the speakers. The valid numbers range from -100, which is far left to 100; far right. 0 is properly centered.
setTransform()	Used to specify both pan and volume in specific ways via the use of a sound transform object.

Note that each of these *setter* methods has a corresponding *getter* method: getVolume(), getPan(), and getTransform(). These obviously return the current volume, pan, and transform object assigned to a sound object.

Let's look at some examples featuring these properties and methods.

Position and duration

We can use these position and duration properties to determine how far along in a sound we are, and to display the information in a status bar or similar type of indicator. Load the file soundStatusBar.fla and test it:

As the song plays, we have a status bar that indicates our current position in the song. The status bar is simply a movie clip image of a box with the instance name myIndicator, which has dimensions of 300 x 10 pixels. We can make use of the _xscale parameter nicely here because it is based on 100% being full size – if we then calculate a loading percentage, we can directly relate the two properties. To achieve this, the following code is attached to the main timeline:

```
_root.createEmptyMovieClip("mySound_mc", 10);
mySound = new Sound(mySound_mc);
mySound.loadSound("jazz.mp3", true);
myIndicator.onEnterFrame = function() {
    var pos = mySound.position;
    var dur = mySound.duration;
    var perc = (pos/dur)*100;
    this._xscale = perc;
};
```

We're setting up the sound object and telling it to stream in the sound file `jazz.mp3`. Then we have an `onEnterFrame` function attached to the `myIndicator` movie clip. In this function, we take the current position of the sound playback and divide it by the total duration of the sound, and then multiply that by 100 to get the percentage complete. This value is then directly applied to the `_xscale` of `myIndicator`. Note that this status bar relies on the registration point of the movie clip being in the top left corner – otherwise it would not just expand from left to right.

Beneath `myIndicator` on the stage, we also have a rectangular graphic of the same 100% size but a different color, to display the total length of the indicator so that we can compare and determine how much of the song is left to go.

> *It's important to note that with a streaming sound, the result of duration will take a few seconds to reach the actual length of the song. The sound must be buffered so that there is enough information for the MP3 decompressor to start playing. At this point, the full duration will be known to Flash.*

Volume

Now open `setVolume.fla`, and test it – what we hear is the music playing again, except this time it's very quiet. We're using the `setVolume()` method, with the following code attached to the actions layer:

```
_root.createEmptyMovieClip("mySound_mc", 10);
mySound = new Sound(mySound_mc);
mySound.attachSound("myJazzSong");
mySound.setVolume(10);
mySound.start();
```

In this case, we're setting the volume of `mySound` to 10%. It's also possible to turn up the volume to a value larger than 100%. But beware of setting it too loud – something like this, for instance:

```
mySound.setVolume(2000);
```

Produces an annoyingly loud, not to mention highly distorted sound. Choose the volume to suit the occasion and atmosphere set by your overall design.

Pan

Next, open `setPan.fla`, and test it. In this instance we can still hear the music but, assuming we have stereo set up, the sound is coming from the left speaker only, giving the impression that the sound is off to our left somewhere. Here's the code.

```
_root.createEmptyMovieClip("mySound_mc", 10);
mySound = new Sound(mySound_mc);
mySound.attachSound("myJazzSong");
mySound.setPan(-100);
mySound.start();
```

Again, notice the new code – just like turning the balance knob on our hi-fi, we're using the setPan() method to play the sound from the left output only by specifying -100. Similarly, if we were to say 100 here, we'd instead play the sound from right speaker only. If we specify a pan of 0, the default value, then the sound will be centered. Obviously, by changing the pan parameter between -100 and 100, we can get varying degrees of left and right sound.

Sound transform

The setTransform() method of the sound object gives us greater control on how to play the contents of each stereo channel. Rather than specifying a volume or a pan only, we can stipulate the volume of each channel, left and right, and therefore affecting both volume *and* pan at the same time.

Take a look at soundTransform.fla. When we test this movie, again the sound has a left bias because the way in which the sound transform has been set up:

```
_root.createEmptyMovieClip("mySound_mc", 10);
mySound = new Sound(mySound_mc);
mySound.attachSound("myJazzSong");
myTransform = new Object();
myTransform.ll = 90;
myTransform.lr = 0;
myTransform.rr = 10;
myTransform.rl = 0;
mySound.setTransform(myTransform);
mySound.start();
```

Here, the transform basically tells Flash to "play 90% of the left channel in the left speaker, but only play 10% of the right channel in the right speaker". The effect is a slightly more subtle favoritism for the left speaker and a higher degree of control compared to using setPan().

Let's look at how the sound transform is set up – the setTransform() method takes one parameter: a generic object, which contains 4 specific parameters. This is known as the sound transform object and its parameters are detailed in the table below:

setTransform parameter	Description
ll	The percentage of the left channel to play in the left speaker.
lr	The percentage of the right channel to play in the left speaker.
rr	The percentage of the right channel to play in the right speaker.
rl	The percentage of the left channel to play in the right speaker.

The onSoundComplete event

One of the most useful pieces of sound functionality in Flash MX is the onSoundComplete event. With onSoundComplete, we can make an event that triggers as soon as a sound finishes playing. We can do this with both event-based incidental sounds and streamed sounds.

Take a look at onSoundComplete.fla. Here's the code from frame 1 of the actions layer:

```
_root.createEmptyMovieClip("mySound_mc", 10);
mySound = new Sound(mySound_mc);
mySound.attachSound("myJazzSong");
loopnum = 1;
mySound.onSoundComplete = function() {
        trace("Completed loop number: "+loopnum);
        loopnum++;
        this.start();
};
mySound.start();
```

It's the same as usual – we're creating a sound object, attaching the jazz music to it, and then playing it. However, we've also defined an onSoundComplete function that prints the loop number in the output window, increments this number with each play of the track, and then starts the sound over again.

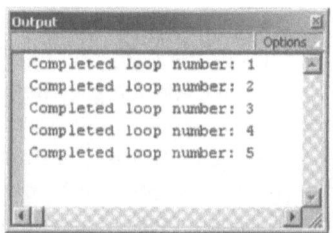

We can do any number of things in the onSoundComplete function. For instance, perhaps the sound is a little shorter than our jazz tune, in which case the onSoundComplete event could be used to update some on-screen animation – this would synch up sound events with on-screen events giving a really professional feel to your designs.

Open the file soundStatusBar_event.fla and take a look at the use of onSoundComplete with dynamically loaded streaming sound. This movie is very similar to an earlier example, except the we've now got a onSoundComplete function within it. The code looks like this:

```
_root.createEmptyMovieClip("mySound_mc", 10);
mySound = new Sound(mySound_mc);
mySound.loadSound("jazz.mp3", true);
mySound.onSoundComplete = function() {
    this.loadSound("jazz.mp3", true);
};
myIndicator.onEnterFrame = function() {
    var pos = mySound.position;
    var dur = mySound.duration;
    var perc = (pos/dur)*100;
    this._xscale = perc;
};
```

The new code is highlighted – again we're streaming the jazz.mp3 sound, and when it has completed playing we simply start it streaming again. With the dynamically loaded file in your machine's virtual memory, using the onSoundComplete event is an efficient way of making the sound play again without re-downloading the music.

That's the sound object – by utilizing its associated methods we can implement both incidental and background sounds, and bring our movies to life!

6 The Color Object

Objectives

- Creating a color object

- Using a color object with its two main methods:

  - `setRGB()`

  - `setTransform()`

- Advanced design ideas using the color object

  - Dynamic color changes and transitions

  - Color cycling

Introduction

When we create graphic content for Flash MX, we will often draw our images with an external graphic creation tool, like Adobe Illustrator, Adobe Photoshop, Macromedia FreeHand, or one of many more. Naturally, as we design our images, we design them in a certain color, with the intention of making them fit into our overall design.

However, what happens when we want to change the color of something in a slightly more subtle manner? For example, in a Flash space invaders game we might want to give players the option of customizing the color of their spaceship. Or in an interactive chat application we may want to allow users to change the skin and clothing color of their avatar to accurately reflect themselves.

This is where the color object comes into play in Flash MX. With it, we are able to dynamically change the colors of any movie clip or button with just a few simple lines of code. Color objects themselves are created and attached to movie clips, and can be used to achieve a number of different effects.

The color object can affect graphics in a couple of different ways:

- Using `setRGB()` we can fill in the entire contents of the graphics in one solid color. It doesn't matter how detailed our images are, when `setRGB()` is applied to them, they will be completely covered in one solid color.

- Using `setTransform()` we can subtly adjust the color of the current content. This is the technique we should use to color our graphics to conform to our web site's colour schemes, for instance, yet still maintain the finer details of each image.

Creating a color object

The creation of a color object is the same as the creation of any other object in Flash – we should use the `Color` constructor and create a new object, using the `new` operator, like this:

```
myColor = new Color(myMovieClip);
```

When creating the new color object, we pass it the instance name of a target movie clip to which the color effects will be applied (`myMovieClip`), and the color object that we've created is stored with the variable name that we initially define (`myColor`).

So, if we have a movie clip on the root level of the stage with the instance name `ball` and we want to create a new color object called `cObject`, we would initialize it like this:

```
cObject = new Color(_root.ball);
```

What's important to realize is that `cObject` will exist in the timeline that the object is created in. So, if that line of code was placed within frame 1 of the root timeline, as good Flash MX programming techniques suggest, then `cObject` would exist on _root, and would be referred to via `_root.cObject`.

In fact, to make sure we place our color object in a logical and intuitive place, it is good practice to initialize the cObject *within* the object that we're applying the color to. Take the following line, for instance:

```
_root.ball.cObject = new Color(_root.ball);
```

This creates a new color object as a parameter of the _root.ball movie clip, which will also apply its color to the _root.ball movie clip. This might seem like an obvious association, but we should explicitly define it this way.

Methods of the color object

So now that we know how to create a color object, let's see exactly how to use it with the two methods mentioned earlier: setRGB() and setTransform().

setRGB

First, we'll look at the setRGB() method, the syntax of which is as follows:

```
myColorObject.setRGB(0xRRGGBB);
```

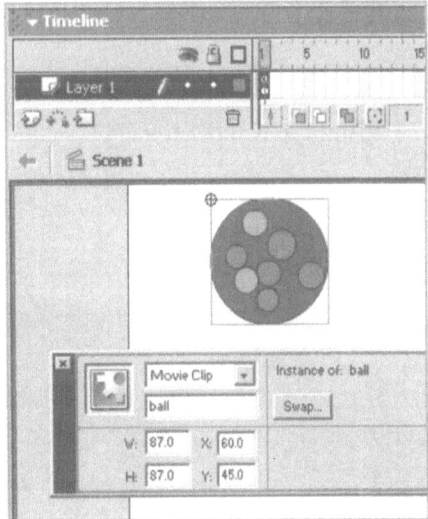

Here, 0xRRGGBB is the hexadecimal color value – more on this shortly. Let's assume we have a movie clip on the stage with the instance name ball and it looks like, well, a ball! Open up setRGB.fla to see our movie clip on the stage:

We'll attach the following code to frame 1 of the main timeline:

```
_root.ball.c = new Color(_root.ball);
_root.ball.c.setRGB(0);
```

Note that we've simplified the name of our new color object to c. Test this movie (CTRL+ENTER) and something truly not-so exciting will happen – can you predict what it is?

That's right, we've turned the ball completely black with the setRGB() method, using a parameter of 0 to indicate black.

You might think that this is pretty dull – indeed, why would we possibly want to black-out the details of our image? Well, how about if we want to produce some kind of shadow effect. Take a look at `setRGB_shadow.fla`:

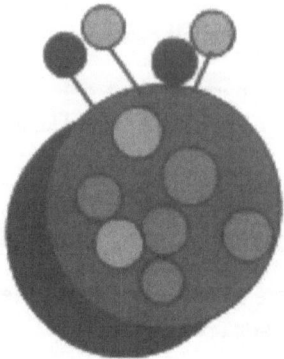

In this case we've created a copy of the ball, placed it above and to the right of the original instance, and renamed it. What happens? The instance named `ball` still turns black, but our new copy is not affected by the `setRGB()` command, and the end result is a completely accurate, dynamically generated drop shadow.

In fact, all we need to do is add a background, and an extra line of code:

```
_root.ball._alpha = 10;
```

And the end result will be a cool faded shadow effect (see `setRGB_fade.fla`):

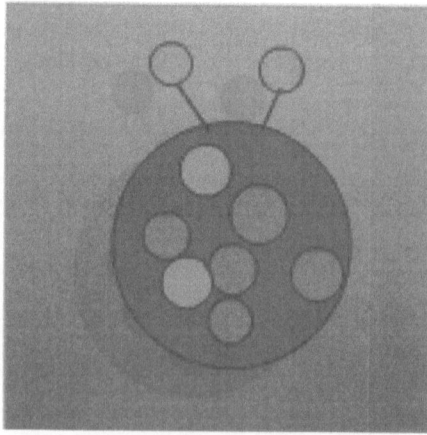

This same technique could be used for complete animations – imagine a movie clip that contained a frame-based animation. Its shadow could be dynamically generated, saving quite a bit of design time. Or perhaps change the frame of the shadow so that it follows a few frames behind the solid movie clip, creating a realistic animated shadow effect.

Hexadecimal vs. decimal color value systems

Now we'll make a brief but relevant detour relating to the hexadecimal number that is passed into the setRGB() method.

The hexadecimal numbering system starts at 0 through to 9, and then continues with A, B, C, D, E, and F, where A represents 10, B is 11, and so on until F which takes the place of 15. The series 0 to F forms a sequence of 16 digits that we can sum like binary numbers – for instance, decimal 15 equates to 0F in hex, and decimal 16 is hex 10. So the digit 1 in hex 10 represents the number 16. Whereas decimal numbering is a base-10 system, hexadecimal is what we call a base-16 system. Let's look at a few more examples to set this in stone – the following table gives the hex versions of a few decimal numbers:

Decimal numbers	Hexadecimal numbers
1	01
9	09
10	0A
25	19
26	1A
31	1F
32	20
100	64

In ActionScript, like many other programming languages, every color can be described by simply combining various proportions of red, green, and blue – this is the fundamental nature of color mixing in light. With computer languages it's the same, colors can be defined as a hexadecimal number from 00 to FF for red, green, and blue. This number is known as an RGB color – a color defined by a red, green, and blue component. Note that FF, as our maximum 2-digit hex number, equates to a decimal 255 (FF = 16*15 + 15) The following table shows examples of the hexadecimal values of some common colors:

Color	Hexadecimal value (0xRRGGBB)
100% Blue	0x0000FF
100% Red	0xFF0000
100% Green	0x00FF00
100% White	0xFFFFFF
100% Yellow	0xFFFF00
100% Magenta	0xFF00FF
100% Cyan	0x00FFFF
50% Grey	0x808080

So for example, if you had a red value of 80, a green value of 7F and a blue value of 2A, then your hexadecimal number would be 0x807F2A, which is actually a sandy dark yellow color of some sort:

> Hexadecimal numbers from 00 to FF correspond to decimal numbers from 0 to 255.

If you have red, green, and blue decimal values in mind, and you want to convert them into a 24-bit color code number to be used in setRGB() at runtime, you can use the following ActionScript formula:

```
RGBvalue = (r << 16) + (g << 8) + b
```

This takes the three values r, g, and b, which will be numbers from 0 to 255, and converts them into one big RGB value, which will actually be a number between 0 and 16777215 (24-bit color). We discuss the bitwise left shift operator << in the ActionScript dictionary in the latter half of this book. For the moment, it's probably sufficient to note that a << b is equivalent to multiplying the decimal version of a by 2^b. So in simpler terms we can get the RGB value from this equation:

```
RGBvalue = (65536*r)+(256*g)+b
```

OK, that's enough boring math for now - let's get back to learning how we can use RGB colors.

Along with setRGB() comes the getRGB() method, and its job is to retrieve the RGB value that has been applied to a color object. The syntax is as follows:

```
RGBcolor = myColor.getRGB();
```

If, however, you try and get the RGB value of a color object that has not yet been colored with setRGB(), it will simply return 0.

Let's look at an example of using the above-mentioned equation to combine red, green, and blue values to produce a unique color, and then using the getRGB() method to retrieve the number of the new color. Open up getRGB.fla and you'll see the following code attached to frame 1 of the root timeline:

```
_root.ball.cObject = new Color(_root.ball);
r = 255;   // 255 is the same number...
g = 0xFF; // ...as  0xFF in hexadecimal.
b = 100;   // 100 is 0x64 in hex
finalColor = (r << 16)+(g << 8)+b;
_root.ball.cObject.setRGB(finalColor);
```

```
gotColor = _root.ball.cObject.getRGB();
trace(gotColor);
```

Here we have defined a new color object in the usual way, specified our variables r, g, and b with explicit values, described the equation that we mentioned earlier and set our new color to be the outcome of this equation. Finally, we use the getRGB() method and the trace() expression to read and print the value of our new color. When you test this FLA, you'll see that it produces the following output:

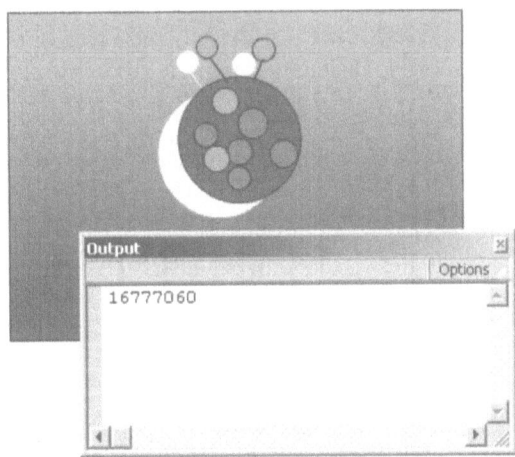

As you can see, the shadow is not colored black this time, but a creamy yellow. This corresponds to color 16777060, or 0xFFFF64.

Of course, gotColor must be equal to finalColor in this code. If you don't believe it, try the following code:

```
trace(gotColor == finalColor);
```

This will produce the word true in the trace window.

setTransform

As we have seen, with setRGB() we can color a movie clip in one solid color, as if we had brushed a thick layer of paint over it from top to bottom. However, we don't always want something so crude when creating color effects on the fly. What if we want to simply *adjust* the colors of a movie clip? We might want to make the clip a little bluer, a little bit darker, or give it a red glow, for example. This is what setTransform() can do for us.

The setTransform() method simply applies a color transform object to a movie clip, and adjusts the colors of the movie clip by a percentage or an offset. To use it, we first define a color object as usual:

```
cObject = new Color(myMovieClip);
```

Next, we must define an object known as a *transform object*. This is simply a generic object with specific properties applied to it, which the setTransform() method is expecting. We can create a new transform object with the following code:

```
cTransformObject = new Object();
cTransformObject.ra = 50;
```

Here, ra refers to the percentage adjustment of the any red color in our target movie clip – more on this and other color options shortly. Finally, we apply a color transform to a color object with the following code:

```
cObject.setTransform(cTransformObject);
```

Let's see this in action before moving on to more complex transforms. Open up setTransform.fla – on the stage you'll notice a simple movie clip with the instance name myColors:

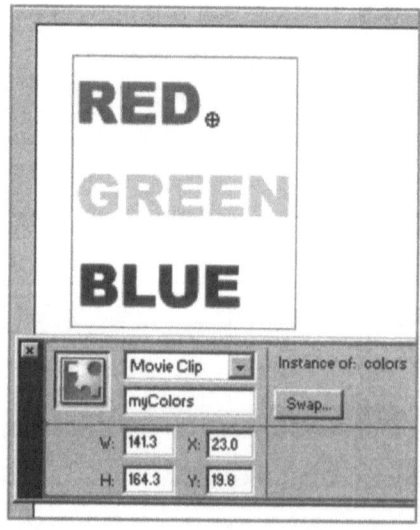

Now take a look in the Actions panel at the script attached to frame 1 of the root timeline:

```
1 _root.myColors.cObject = new Color(_root.myColors);
2 _root.myColors.cTransformObject = new Object();
3 _root.myColors.cTransformObject.ra = 50;
4 _root.myColors.cObject.setTransform(_root.myColors.cTransformObject);
5
```

Test this movie and you'll see that the red color in our movie clip is indeed reduced (darkened) by 50% (obviously you can't see so well in a black and white book, so go on and test it!):

RED

Now we'll look at the other options available to us when defining transform objects. Consider the following code:

GREEN

BLUE

```
cObject = new Color(myMovieClip);
cTransformObject = new Object();
cTransformObject.ra = 50;
cTransformObject.rb = 0;
cTransformObject.ga = 50;
cTransformObject.gb = 0;
cTransformObject.ba = 50;
cTransformObject.bb = 0;
cTransformObject.aa = 100;
cTransformObject.ab = 0;
cObject.setTransform(cTransformObject);
```

These are color transforms applied to the red, green, blue, and alpha values of the target movie clip. This code will produce a color transform which, when applied to the movie clip, will reduce each color by 50% of its original value.

> ra, ga, ba, aa *are the red, green, blue, and alpha percentage adjustments, respectively, while* rb, gb, bb, ab *are the red, green, blue, and alpha offset adjustments (between -255 to +255)*

These parameters correspond to the settings Advanced Effect window. For instance, if you select your movie clip, and then choose Advanced in the Color options drop-down menu of the Property inspector, and then hit the Settings… button, the following window will pop up:

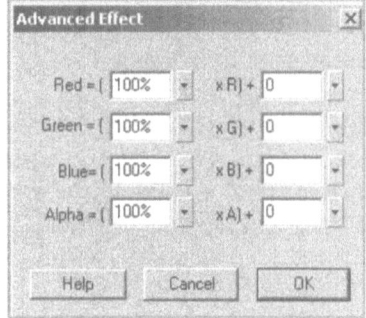

With this, you can play around with the specific proportions of red, blue, green, and alpha – it's useful to get a feel for what a certain color combination will look like before inserting it into your ActionScript.

So, with ra, ga, and ba you can scale the colors of the movie clip by the specified percentages, and set the transparency from 0% to 100% with aa. For example, if all the values are 0, then the movie clip will be black. However, if they are all set to 100, then the movie clip colors will not be changed from their initial design. In simple terms, every color in your movie clip can be individually scaled and adjusted by the percentage associated with each of the ra, ga, and ba values.

Alternatively, with the offset parameters: rb, gb, bb, and ab, we set the values to be between -255 and 255, and these numbers are *added* to the current red, green, blue, and alpha values of each parameter to produce a transformed color. If you were to set rb to 255, gb to 255, and bb to 255, your image would be solid white.

> *When using the transform object, it is important to be familiar with the differences between the percentage value and the offset. The percentage value will adjust the intensity of the specific channel, whereas the offset will add the value of the color across all color channels to effectively change the color.*

Let's look at another example using both percentage and offset adjustment parameters. A color transform that removes all the red from an image, reduces the green by 50%, adds 127 to the blue value, and reduces the alpha by 50% would look like this if applied to our myColors movie clip:

```
_root.myColors.cObject = new Color(_root.myColors);
_root.myColors.cTransformObject = new Object();
_root.myColors.cTransformObject.ra = 0;
_root.myColors.cTransformObject.rb = 0;
_root.myColors.cTransformObject.ga = 50;
_root.myColors.cTransformObject.gb = 0;
_root.myColors.cTransformObject.ba = 100;
_root.myColors.cTransformObject.bb = 127;
_root.myColors.cTransformObject.aa = 50;
_root.myColors.cTransformObject.ab = 0;
_root.myColors.cObject.setTransform(_root.myColors.cTransformObject);
```

Open up setTransform2.fla in which you'll find the code above attached to frame 1 of the root timeline. Test the movie, and check out the exciting results:

RED

GREEN

BLUE

Notice how all the red color has been completely removed from the screen, green has been reduced significantly, blue has been added to all colors, and the entire movie clip has been faded using the alpha property.

As a side note, an alternative and quicker way of writing the previous 11 lines of code is as follows:

```
_root.myColors.cObject = new Color(_root.myColors);
_root.myColors.cTransformObject = new Object();
_root.myColors.cTransformObject = {ra:'o', rb:'0', ga:'50', gb:'0',
➡ ba:'100', bb:'127', aa:'50', ab:'0'}
_root.myColors.cObject.setTransform(_root.myColors.cTransformObject);
```

Finally, like the getRGB() method, we can also issue a getTransform() command to find out the transform that has been applied by any previous setTransform(). For example, in setTransform3.fla we have added the following lines to the previous script:

```
gotTransform = _root.myColors.cObject.getTransform();
trace(gotTransform);
```

This will turn gotTransform into an object that will contain the transform object applied to cObject – the trace() command proves that it is indeed an object.

RED

GREEN

BLUE

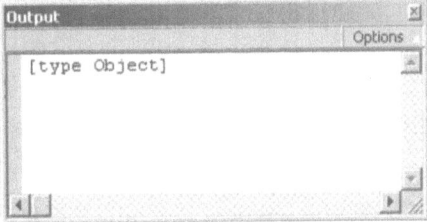

Advanced design with the color object

So far we've only looked at simple, rather abstract examples of using color objects – so now we'll demonstrate a couple of programs in which the color object is integral to the design. Although the scripting will still be fairly straightforward, we'll see that these examples have a greater potential to be used in real-world designs.

Dynamic color changes

When you're creating an interactive game or web site that will allow users to change the color of their spaceship, character, or whatever, then it's best to design the graphics so that they're ready to be colorized. The best way to do this is to create your objects in a grayscale color scheme, and then simply apply a color transform to them. Make sure to use as much shading and variations of gray as you can, so that your color application is as detailed and accurate as possible.

Open up `faceChange.fla` – this FLA will allow a user to change the face color of a character on screen. First you'll notice that there are four objects on the stage: three scrollbars with instance names `scrollRed`, `scrollGreen`, and `scrollBlue`, and a movie clip with the instance name `face`, which consists of a rather sinister-looking grayscale face. Our stage looks like this:

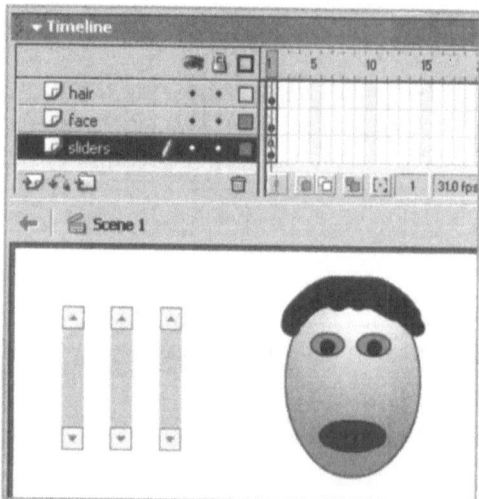

Before we look at the details, have a play with the effect first. Test the movie and use the scrollbars to adjust the color of our face:

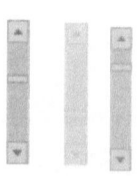

This program works using three Flash MX component scrollbars, each corresponding to a color offset to be used in a transform, which is then applied to the face. In this example, we're using the color offset portion of the transform, and leaving the percentage transform at 100% for the red, green, blue, and alpha channels.

Let's step through the scripting process of creating such a transform. Look at the code attached to frame 1 of the root timeline. First we create the scrollbars and set their limits and positions:

```
scrollRed.setScrollProperties(5, 0, 512);
scrollRed.setScrollPosition(255);
scrollGreen.setScrollProperties(5, 0, 512);
scrollGreen.setScrollPosition(255);
scrollBlue.setScrollProperties(5, 0, 512);
scrollBlue.setScrollPosition(255);
```

The three scrollbars are being created and initialized with scroll limits from 0 to 512. Then we're setting the start position of the scroll handle on all three to 255. Note that we actually want an offset value from -255 to 255, so when the scrollbar positions are read, we need to decrease them by 255 to produce the required offset values.

Next, we create a color object and a color transform object attached to the face movie clip, and set the initial colors to be the same as the face movie clip:

```
face.cObject = new Color(face);
face.cTransform = new Object();
face.cTransform.ra = 100;
face.cTransform.ga = 100;
face.cTransform.ba = 100;
face.cTransform.aa = 100;
```

Finally, we define an onEnterFrame function for the face movie clip, which constantly reads the positions of the scrollbars and applies their values to the color transform. The color transform is applied to the color object and the face changes color – simple!

```
face.onEnterFrame = function() {
    this.r = _root.scrollRed.getScrollPosition();
    this.g = _root.scrollGreen.getScrollPosition();
    this.b = _root.scrollBlue.getScrollPosition();
    this.cTransform.rb = this.r-255;
    this.cTransform.gb = this.g-255;
    this.cTransform.bb = this.b-255;
    this.cObject.setTransform(this.cTransform);
};
```

Remember that because the face is grayscale to begin with, as its colors are transformed it can take on a large array of colors and everything scales accordingly – dark gray becomes a dark color, and light gray becomes a light color.

Color cycling

Color cycling is a neat effect that can be applied to a number of different colors at a time. Basically, color cycling is when we change the color of a graphic dynamically, according to our own formula. For example, we could create a movie clip that cycles from black to bright red and back according to a sine wave. This would create the appearance of an emergency light. In fact, the theory behind our next example is that if we cycle the red, green, and blue values at different rates then we'll see some really cool color cycling effects.

Open up `colorCycle.fla` – here we have an innocent-looking gradient taking up the entire stage. It's actually a movie clip called `background` (named so that we can *talk* to it with ActionScript!). Note that `background` is 550 x 400 pixels in size, therefore the same as the stage:

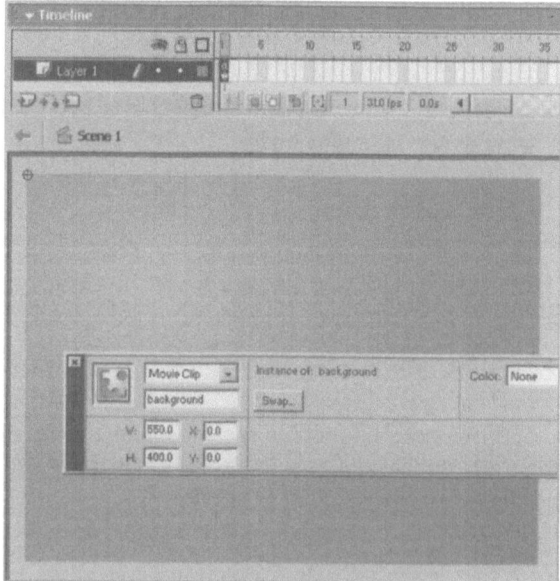

On frame 1 of our root timeline we have the script that controls this movie. Initially we create our color object and transform, and set the color offset parameters of the transform (`rb`, `gb`, and `bb`) to `0`:

```
background.cObject = new Color(background);
background.cTransform = new Object();
background.cTransform.rb = 0;
background.cTransform.gb = 0;
background.cTransform.bb = 0;
background.cTransform.ab = 0;
```

Next, with every frame, we're changing the r, g, and b values of the background color transform:

```
background.onEnterFrame = function() {
    this.r = Math.sin(angle1)*100;
    this.g = Math.cos(angle2)*100;
    this.b = Math.sin(angle3)*100;
    angle1 += 0.01;
    angle2 += 0.02;
    angle3 += 0.03;
    this.cTransform.rb = this.r;
    this.cTransform.gb = this.g;
    this.cTransform.bb = this.b;
    this.cObject.setTransform(this.cTransform);
};
```

More specifically, we're creating sine and cosine waves that vary from 0 to 100, at different rates. The blue color (this.b) cycles the fastest, according to largest angular increment (+= 0.03), while the red color cycles the slowest.

Test the movie to see the effect – we'll see almost every color of the rainbow fade in and out as we watch the show. In this case, the color object of ActionScript can be used to create some really cool dynamic background effects for our movies.

7 Performance and Optimization

Objectives

- Optimizing graphical elements:

    - Redrawing versus static regions

    - Gradients

    - Alpha transparency

    - Lines

    - Image complexity

    - Tweens

    - Frame rate

- Optimizing ActionScript:

    - Explicitly declaring variables

    - Variable and function name length

    - Code timing

    - Commenting out code

    - Optimizing your functions

Introduction

Working with ActionScript can sometimes make bizarre things happen to the performance of your movie. It's possible to spend days perfecting a game or a web site with tons of cool ActionScript effects, and then find that suddenly your creation is only able to achieve a frame rate of 10 frames per second.

> *The bottom line is this: if used inefficiently, ActionScript can slow down Flash performance just as much as graphics can. Accordingly, there are a number of performance and optimization issues that we must consider.*

Most designers are aware of what happens when they put hundreds of objects, bitmaps, alpha fades, tweens, gradients, lines, and shapes on screen at once: the performance slows down dramatically. However many designers, especially those new to ActionScript, aren't aware of the similar dangers of poorly written ActionScript.

We must pay equal attention to graphics and ActionScript if we're to make the best, most solid and stable performances possible.

Optimizing graphical elements

All Macromedia Flash movies with multiple frame actions are achieved through the use of animation contained within movie clips, often controlled with ActionScript. The first step we can take towards the optimization of such movies is to optimize our graphics. If we don't, these graphics can become a bottleneck that no ActionScript wizardry will be able to salvage.

Redrawing versus static regions

From frame to frame, Flash is required to redraw any areas of the screen that have changed (it's for this reason that animation is so expensive in terms of CPU and processor requirements). So, the first question to ask yourself when designing a graphic is, "How much will this be moving on screen, and thus how frequently will it need to be redrawn?". Even if we have a complex image that never moves, but has a very simple movie clip that moves over the top of it, both the simple and the complex images will need to be redrawn every frame.

For example, here we can see two consecutive frames. The only difference between them is the addition of a tent:

Frame 1

Frame 2

Since the region of *invalidation* (the area that Flash needs to redraw) must be a rectangular shape, Flash is required to draw the tent, but also redraw portions of the background, and even the tip of a frond of the palm tree. In the image below, we can see what must be redrawn because of this addition:

So, you can see how important it is to consider what Flash will be doing in the background while we're moving objects around the screen.

Different graphical elements require a different amount of work to redraw, but as long as you watch out for those ones that put a big strain on the system, you should be alright. In the first half of this chapter we'll look at which graphical elements you need to be wary of.

Gradients

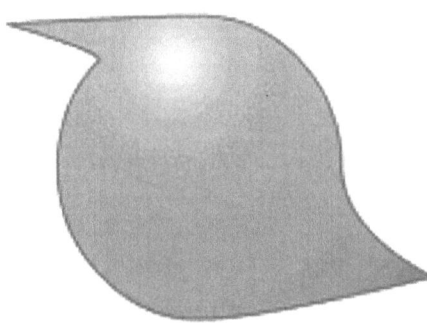

Flash takes a lot of processing power to draw gradients because all of the intricacies of shade and color at every pixel on the gradient must be computed. This is especially important to consider when the gradient is going to be part of a movie clip that may be animated. In such an event, Flash would be required to completely redraw and anti-alias the gradient at every frame.

> *As nice as gradients look, we're dramatically multiplying our demands on Flash when we place gradients in our objects.*

Linear gradients are easier for Flash to draw than radial gradients are, so if you must use a gradient, try to use a linear one. From the perspective of region redrawing, one of the most computationally expensive things that we can do with Flash and gradients is to create a background image that consists of a large gradient. Imagine we had a large full-screen sweeping sunset beneath an entire game. Flash would be required to redraw this entire gradient every time something moves or animates on a layer above it!

Alpha transparency

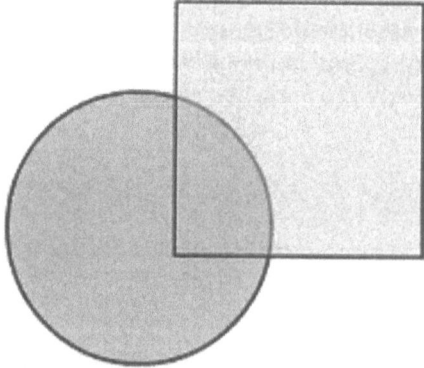

One of the coolest effects in Macromedia Flash is the alpha transparency effect. It can be used to create glass, water, gel, smoke, and all sorts of other effects. It will also single-handedly take your Flash movie from using 20% of the user's CPU, to 100% of the user's CPU! With an alpha transparency, we're practically telling Flash to redraw graphics several times as it writes, reads, and writes graphics again in order to create the layers.

If possible, try and place alpha transparency effects in areas which are static, or include smaller, limited animations. You'll thank yourself later as you're adding ActionScript and other elements to the movie, and the user's machine is still breathing.

Lines

As standard as they are, sometimes it's better to eliminate outlines from movie clips and graphics when you draw them, as long as your solid fill images are correctly and efficiently drawn, with enough contrast against the background. Lines demand an extra step in redrawing that we can often do without.

Don't be swayed from using lines if you need them; they're not as CPU-intensive as gradients and alpha transparency. But if you can get away with it, the benefits for usability might outweigh the shortfall in esthetics.

Image complexity

A lot can be said on the topic of image complexity, but the bottom line is this: the number of curves and points in graphics can make or break a movie's performance. All too often, designers create large complex images, which are then shrunk down to one or two inches on screen. They don't, however, endeavor to simplify and optimize the images, given the considerable change in detail when shrinking graphics.

Consider this fine piece of modern art:

Believe it or not, it contains 422 curves, which could be considered moderately complex. Let's say that we're going to be using this image as a logo, and it's going to be sitting in the lower right-hand corner of the screen. So we shrink it down like so:

Take a look at the two mini versions of our logo. One of them has just been shrunk, and still contains the original 422 curves, and the other one is an optimized version, now with only 249 curves. Can you tell which is which? No, neither can I! (In fact, the image on the right is the optimized version.)

The complexity in an image should never surpass the detail level that we're able to distinguish, so it's always a good idea to make use of the **Optimize Curves** window in Flash MX. You can pull up this tool by selecting an area of curves, and choosing from the Modify>Optimize menu(or press CTRL+ALT+SHIFT +C if you're a little more dexterous than me!):

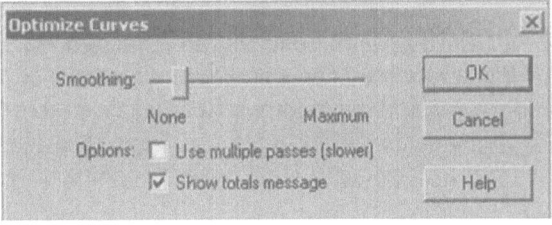

Notice the Smoothing values slider. You can use it to smooth out your curves, thus reducing the overall number of them by shifting the smoothing value from None to Maximum. To make Flash optimize, and then re-optimize your image, check the Use multiple passes option.

Hit OK, and Flash will go through the image and attempt to remove and smooth out curves which may be too small to see, or are redundant, as in a straight line which is made up of several line segments. When Flash has finished, we'll see a results box:

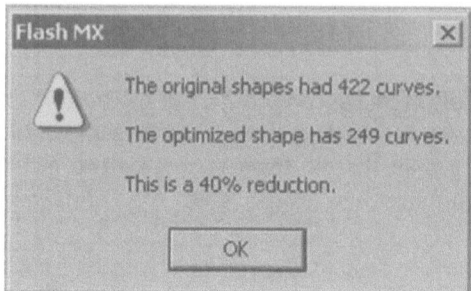

This will show us just how much of an optimization we were able to achieve. It may, however, be that smoothing your curves to the Maximum level reduces the detail of your image too much. Experiment with the slider until you reach a compromise that you're happy with.

Tweens

Complex tweens can dramatically slow down the performance of any Macromedia Flash movie. Not only are they mathematically complicated, they're also full of motion, so by using them, we're forcing Flash to do a lot of redrawing. The solution? Use ActionScript for animation as much as possible (see **Chapter 1**), and keep the tweens to a minimum. It's also best to keep the area that a tween covers small as well.

Frame rate

One of the most frustrating issues with Flash is the often idiosyncratic behavior of the frame rate system. For starters, Flash will only ever *attempt* to achieve a given frame rate. If we're choking Flash with complex alphas, gradients, and so on, it won't achieve the 30 frames per second we've requested in our movie layout. Perhaps it would work consistently if we manually reduced the size of the SWF window to a 10 x 10 pixel postage stamp, but this is obviously not a realistic solution.

It's worthwhile to compare the requested frame rate, as set in the Property inspector, with the actual frame rate of a couple of different methods of publication, as measured by an ActionScript-based frame rate timer. In the following table, we give these results for a SWF in a browser window and a standalone projector (File>Publish Settings... and then select a Projector as an output). This set of data was taken from a Macromedia Flash Player 6 running on a Pentium 4 1.8GHz PC:

Requested frame rate (fps)	Actual frame rate achieved in browser (fps)	Actual frame rate achieved standalone projector (fps)
1	1	1
2	1.93	1.93
5	4.8	4.8
10	9.7	9.7
15	14.1	14.86
20	18.7	19.7
30	25	30
40	33.3	38.7
50	44.4	49.7
60	50	62.5
70	50	71.2
80	50	83.3
90	51.1	90.9
100	98.1	100
110	100	111.1
120	100	124.9

As we can see, although the standalone Flash projector doesn't quite hit the mark spot on, it's pretty close. The SWF file in a browser, on the other hand, is even less accurate for high frame rates. Let's look at this data more graphically:

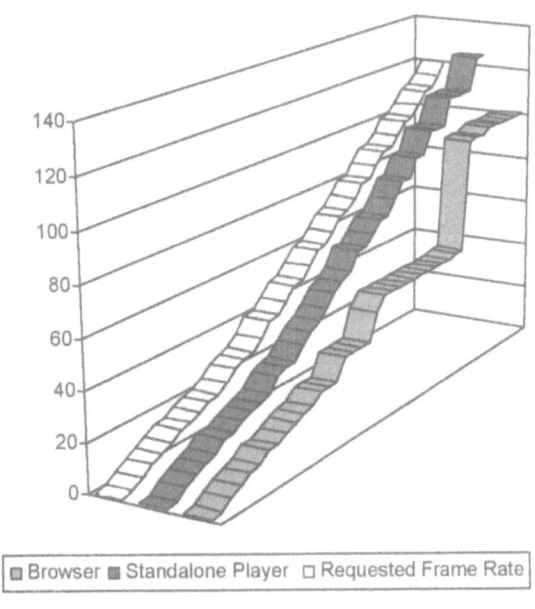

Browser ■ Standalone Player □ Requested Frame Rate

We can see that the frame rates tend to follow a trend of rises and plateaus. It's interesting to note that there is a range of frame rates from about 51 to 81 that the browser will not achieve, and will instead stick to 50 frames per second. Also, in our tests, the browser never seems to exceed 100 frames per second.

So what does all this mean? Basically, we have to be very careful what frame rate we choose because the results can be a lot different from what we expect. The bottom line is that we really can't get a movie to perform at a consistent frame rate if it's over about 24 frames per second, so we must choose a value that comes closest to our desired frame rate.

> *Keeping your frame rate low will also improve your file size, because increased frame rate in a movie means that more frames need to be redrawn.*

Optimizing your ActionScript

So far, we've looked at the visual and graphic elements that may slow down a Flash movie. Now we need to look at the other side to the equation: efficient use of ActionScript. As much as graphics can slow down our movie's performance, so too can carelessly written code. We'll take a look at some of the standard tips and tricks that we can adhere to in order to make our ActionScript super-fast.

Explicitly declaring variables

The fastest variables are local variables within functions which are explicitly defined with `var` before they're used. For example, consider the following function, in which we don't declare the variables `myLoop` and `mycount`:

```
myFunction = function () {
    for (myloop=0; myloop<10000; myloop++) {
        mycount++;
    }
};
```

This function will run substantially faster with the variables explicitly declared using the `var` keyword, like this:

```
myFunction = function () {
    var myloop;
    var mycount = 0;
    for (myloop=0; myloop<10000; myloop++) {
        mycount++;
    }
};
```

> *When a variable is defined with* var, *it is only local to the function. So once the function is finished, that variable ceases to exist. Note that a local* var *will override a* _global *or* _root *variable.*

Name length of variables and functions

This is quite an interesting point – Flash actually performs marginally faster if we reduce the amount of text in the ActionScript. So, this:

```
for (myLudicrousLoopVariable=0; myLudicrousLoopVariable<10000;
➥myLudicrousLoopVariable++) {
    myLudicrousInnerLoopVariable++;
}
```

will run slower than this:

```
for (i=0; i<10000; i++) {
    j++;
}
```

The reasons for this stem from the fact that ActionScript is actually a scripted language, rather than a compiled, token-based language (like Java or C++, for instance).
The same point applies to function names too.

> *Although using less ActionScript does allow Flash to work faster, it's just as important to use functional, easy to understand variable names. More specifically, using variable names such as* a *or* x *in place of names like* timeCounter *may not always be the best thing to do. It's a case of finding the right compromise between clear code and fast processing times.*

Code timing

A simple yet powerful trick in Flash MX scripting is code timing using the getTimer() method (see **Chapter 13** for more details). Essentially we measure, in milliseconds, how long a particular piece of code took to execute and, using this information, we can determine which areas in our code are the slowest.

First, we use the `getTimer` command to get a start time (st):

```
st = getTimer();
```

Then, we add the code we want to measure, for example:

```
st = getTimer();
for (j=0; j<100000; j++) {
    m = Math.random();
}
tt = getTimer()-st;
```

The final line here, `tt = getTimer()-st` takes the new current time, and subtracts from it our start time, in order to determine how much total time has elapsed.

So we're left with a value in `tt`, which corresponds to the number of milliseconds that our measured code took to execute. We could then trace `tt` to see how long it took.

We can use this concept to determine where, for example, our programs are slowing down the most, by isolating the pieces of code, one at a time.

Commenting out sections of code

A classic and often overlooked method of code optimization is the use of comments. With comments, we can turn different pieces of code on and off to determine which ones are causing problems and slowdowns. Take for example, this segment of pseudo-code:

```
st = getTimer();
myFunction1();
myFunction2();
myFunction3();
tt = getTimer()-st;
trace(tt);
```

We may find that `tt` is tracing out to be, say, 50. So then we might change the code to this:

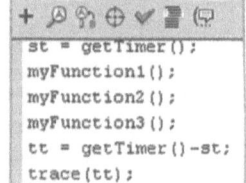

```
st = getTimer();
// myFunction1();
myFunction2();
myFunction3();
tt = getTimer()-st;
trace(tt);
```

Here, we've commented out the call to `myFunction1`, and now we may find that `tt` traces out to be 45. So, we know that `myFunction2`, or `myFunction3` are taking the bulk of the time. Next we do this:

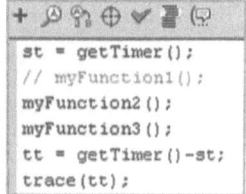

```
st = getTimer();
myFunction1();
myFunction2();
myFunction3();
tt = getTimer()-st;
trace(tt);
```

If `tt` then drops to 5, we know, that there's something in `myFunction2` that we need to optimize. We would then step into `myFunction2`, and go through it line by line to find the offending code. Don't forget to uncomment the function calls to `myFunction1` and `myFunction2` when you're done, otherwise the code will never be executed at all.

Function optimization

This is a cool code optimization technique that relates to the overhead required for function calls. The premise is that if you have a small function that's being called multiple times from within a loop, it may be better to include the contents of the function in the loop, rather than perform the function call multiple times.

Take a look at `function_vs_inline.fla` from the CD:

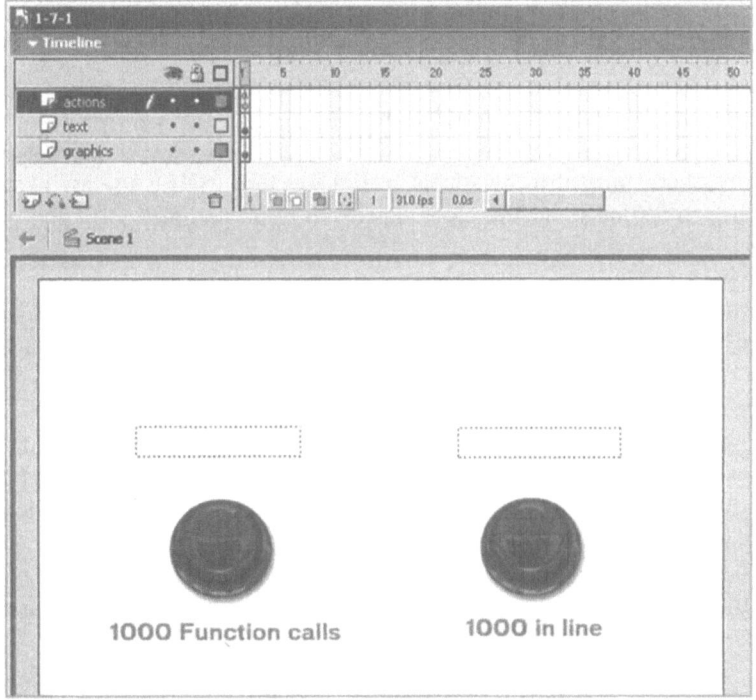

This movie consists of two buttons, with instance names of `testButton1` and `testButton2`, and above each button is a dynamic text field, `result1` and `result2`. The idea is that pressing each button triggers some code which is functionally identical, differing subtly only in structure. Attached to frame 1 of the actions layer, is the following code:

```
doSomething = function () {
    var h = Math.sin(Math.random());
};
testButton1.onRelease = function() {
```

continues overleaf

```
            var st = getTimer();
            for (var i = 0; i<1000; i++) {
                    doSomething();
            }
            var tt = getTimer()-st;
            result1.text = tt;
    };
    testButton2.onRelease = function() {
            var st = getTimer();
            var h;
            for (var i = 0; i<1000; i++) {
                    // Contents of doSomething are here...
                    h = Math.sin(Math.random());
            }
            var tt = getTimer()-st;
            result2.text = tt;
    };
```

Here we have a function called doSomething (which doesn't actually do much at all!) – it just computes a random number and stores it in a variable h. The function itself is useless because the variable h is defined as a var, so it's local and therefore destroyed upon completion of the function. The function doesn't actually return anything.

Next, we have the code for the two buttons. In testButton1, we call the doSomething function 1000 times in a loop. We're using a code timing technique to determine how much time elapses from the start of the loop to the end of the loop. Finally, we're setting the value of the text fields to be the result of the code timers.

In testButton2, we're doing exactly the same thing, except we're including the contents of the doSomething function in the loop rather than calling it from outside – this means that this function needs to actually perform 1000 calculations.

When we run this program, and press the buttons, we see something like the following:

130   67

1000 Function calls   1000 in line

Although the actual times will differ with different systems and processors, the ratio should generally be the same. In our case, 1000 function calls took 130 milliseconds, while 1000 in line instructions took 67 milliseconds. Notice that the 1000 function calls are over twice as slow as the 1000 in line instructions, yet each button is performing precisely the same calculations: h = Math.sin(Math.random()).

What does this tell us? It tells us that Flash has quite a bit of overhead surrounding each function call, and so, when optimization is the goal, we should keep the function calls to a minimum.

Now let's have a look at the file `walk_1000_lines.fla`, which takes this exercise one step further. In this file, we do something known as *unrolling the loop* – instead of having a loop, we explicitly right (well, copy and paste in my case!) the 1000 lines of code. It seems ridiculous, yes, but it's actually a useful demonstration. Take a look at the new code for the first function `testButton1`, which is the only thing that has changed from `function_vs_inline.fla`:

```
testButton1.onRelease = function() {
    var st = getTimer();
    var h;
    h = Math.sin(Math.random());
    h = Math.sin(Math.random());
    h = Math.sin(Math.random());
    h = Math.sin(Math.random());
    h = Math.sin(Math.random());
    h = Math.sin(Math.random());
    h = Math.sin(Math.random());
    h = Math.sin(Math.random());
    h = Math.sin(Math.random());

    .
    . up to 1000
    .

    h = Math.sin(Math.random());
    h = Math.sin(Math.random());
    var tt = getTimer()-st;
    result1.text = tt;
};
```

And the results?

46

67

1000 Unrolled Statements

1000 in line

So, by writing out each calculation we've achieved even more optimization. In fact, these speeds are now approaching that of professional compiled languages like C++ and VB. Of note here is that native functions, like `Math.random` seem to be faster than user defined functions.

Overall, we're now equipped with the tools to go forward and optimize our Flash movies to keep our code and graphics as fast as possible.

8 Advanced Components with ActionScript

Objectives

- Using ActionScript to enhance the Flash MX UI components:

  - Advanced ScrollBar control

  - Dynamic loading of content into the ScrollPane

- Integrating multiple components

Introduction

One of the coolest and perhaps most useful concepts in Flash is that of the Flash MX components that we can utilize in our movies, customize, or even create ourselves. In the past, if we wanted to make something as simple as a ScrollBar, we had to build it from scratch – there was no quick way of implementing a user interface element like that. Now, we can use the built-in UI components of Flash MX to perform a wide variety of tasks and easily construct striking UIs. The functionality offered by these basic components reflects the standard UI elements that users have come to expect from most visual-based applications and operating systems today.

In Chapter 2 we familiarized ourselves with the default components of Flash MX, learning that placing a component in a movie is as simple as dragging it from the UI Components panel (opened up by pressing CTRL+F7) and dropping it on the stage. Now, we're ready to look at the further potential of components when we combine them with ActionScript. As a teaser of what we'll see in this chapter, take a look at some of the methods associated with the Flash UI components by opening up the relevant sections of the ActionScript dictionary in the left-hand pane of the Actions panel (F9):

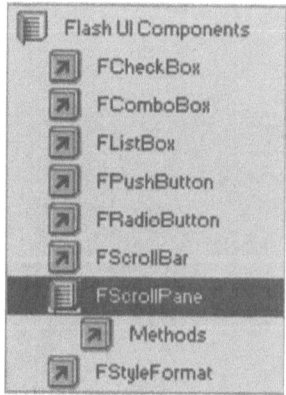

Note that in ActionScript the UI components are referred to with the letter F prefixing their name. So, for example, the CheckBox code is found under the FCheckBox section of the ActionScript dictionary.

In this chapter we'll use a couple of examples to demonstrate the use of some of these methods first hand. We'll start off with a look at how we can enhance our use of the ScrollBar component with ActionScript, and then we'll examine a larger example featuring the integration of several different components in one Flash movie.

Advanced ScrollBar control

Let's dive straight into an example – open up `advancedScrollBar.fla` from the CD and look at the stage:

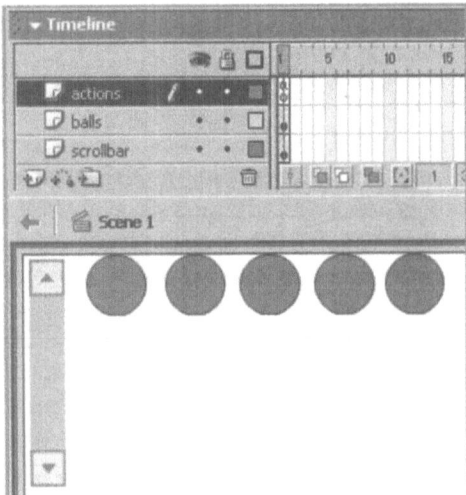

We have a ScrollBar and five red circles. The circles have instance names of ball1 to ball5, and the ScrollBar has an instance name of myScrollBar. When we run this movie and slide the ScrollBar up and down, the circles also move up and down, but at different rates:

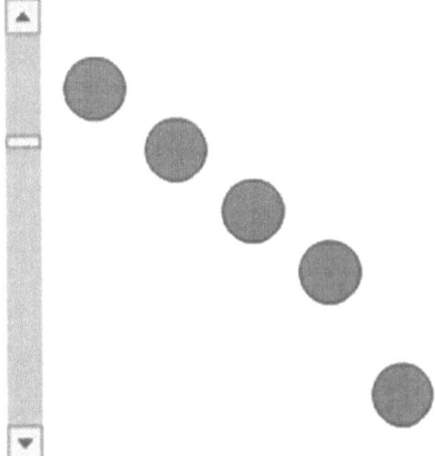

Attached to frame 1 of the actions layer we have the following code:

```
myScrollBar.setSize(200);
myScrollBar.setChangeHandler("myScrollHandler");
myScrollBar.setScrollProperties(1, 0, 200);
myScrollHandler = function () {
        var val = myScrollBar.getScrollPosition();
        ball1._y = val*.5;
        ball2._y = val*1;
```

continues overleaf

```
            ball3._y = val*1.5;
            ball4._y = val*2;
            ball5._y = val*3;
    };
```

First, we're setting the height of the ScrollBar to 200 pixels with the setSize() method. Next, we're telling the ScrollBar to call the function myScrollHandler every time it's scrolled. Then we're using the setScrollProperties() method to force the ScrollBar to be active, and give us something to scroll through. If we don't issue this command, the ScrollBar will be gray and inactive, by default.

The setScrollProperties() method takes three parameters: **page size**, **minimum value**, and **maximum value**. The minimum and maximum values are simply two numbers that represent a numerical range. An advanced ScrollBar works by essentially returning a number. The value of that number will vary depending upon the position of the *thumb* (the draggable square that you can control, which indicates how far you can scroll) within the range of values from minimum to maximum. If minimum was 0, and maximum was 1000, then scrolling the thumb at the bottom would set the scroll value to 1000, scrolling to the top would set the value at 0, midway would be 500, and so on.

The page size parameter is used to determine the size of the thumb. If the maximum value is 200, and the page size is set to 20, then that means that the thumb will be $1/10^{th}$ (20/200) the size of the ScrollBar itself. The smallest page size is 1, as used in our code. Try setting it to 50, for example, and notice how the thumb size changes.

Next, we have the myScrollHandler function – it's here that we move the circles to their new positions at different rates:

```
    myScrollHandler = function () {
            var val = myScrollBar.getScrollPosition();
            ball1._y = val*.5;
            ball2._y = val*1;
            ball3._y = val*1.5;
            ball4._y = val*2;
            ball5._y = val*3;
    };
```

We're using the getScrollPosition() method of the ScrollBar component to return the current scroll position. The result will be a number from 0 to 200, as per the minimum and maximum values that we set in the setScrollProperties() method. We store this value in the variable val, and then set the _y position of the circles to a multiple of val.

And that's it! We're essentially using the ScrollBar as a tool for numerical data entry. Next we'll look at a slightly larger scale example involving a few different components working together.

Dynamic loading into the ScrollPane

We introduced the ScrollPane component and its basic uses in **Chapter 2**, but let's now see an example of how we can combine the ScrollPane *and* ActionScript in our designs. We'll examine how to dynamically load content into the ScrollPane and create scrollable or draggable windows of graphics and animations. This component, like most of them, is very easy to use, and presents us with a very powerful tool.

An advanced application of the ScrollPane can be seen in `advancedScrollPane.fla`:

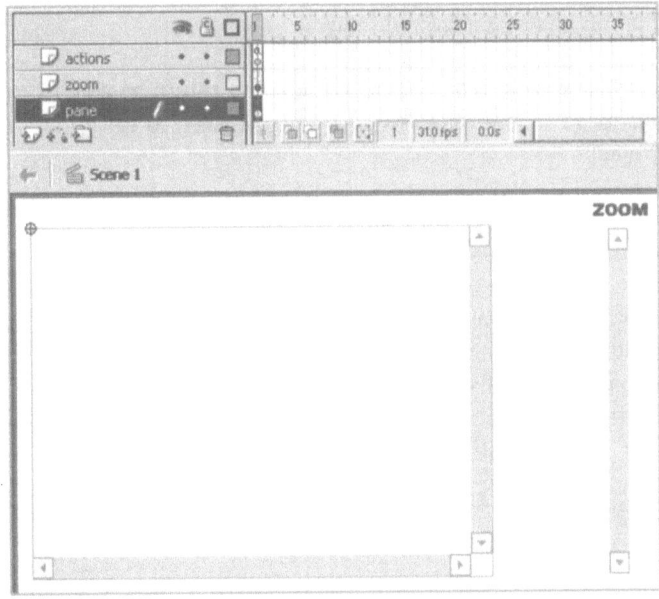

In this example we have a large ScrollPane on the stage with instance name `myScrollPane` and we also have a ScrollBar at the right-hand side of the screen called `zoomBar`. What we can do here is dynamically load a JPEG image into the ScrollPane (or a SWF file, for that matter), and then use another ScrollBar to zoom in and out, while the ScrollPane dynamically resizes its bars.

First let's look at the code that makes this possible. This is found on frame 1 of the actions layer:

```
myScrollPane.loadScrollContent("mypic.jpg", "loaded", _root);
zoomBar.setScrollProperties(100, 1, 1000);
zoomBar.setChangeHandler("zoommove");
loaded = function () {
    theContent = myScrollPane.getScrollContent();
};
zoommove = function () {
    var zoomlevel = zoomBar.getScrollPosition();
    theContent._xscale = zoomlevel;
    theContent._yscale = zoomlevel;
```

```
        myScrollPane.refreshPane();
};
```

We're using the `loadScrollContent()` method of the `FScrollPane` component. This loads a SWF or JPEG into the scroll area of the ScrollPane and allows us to scroll around it, or drag it with the mouse. In this case, we're loading the file `mypic.jpg`, which should be in the same directory as the master FLA file when we test the movie. The other two parameters that we've included in this method are `loaded`, which refers to a callback function that will be executed when the content is finished loading (defined below), and `_root`, which is the location of that function. So, in this case we're asking the ScrollPane to call `_root.loaded` when the JPEG has finished loading.

Next we set the ScrollBar with instance name `zoomBar` to return a value from 1 to 1000 when we scroll it – this corresponds to our zoom ratio. We also tell `zoomBar` to call the function `zoommove` whenever the `zoomBar` is scrolled:

```
zoomBar.setScrollProperties(100, 1, 1000);
zoomBar.setChangeHandler("zoommove");
```

The `loaded` function does one simple thing – it creates a variable named `theContent` and fills it with a reference to the contents of the ScrollPane. The `getScrollContent()` method of the `FScrollPane` returns a reference to the movie clip that is within its scroll area. We don't have to worry about this movie clip because it's maintained by the ScrollPane. However, in this case, we actually want a reference to it so that we can adjust its `_xscale` and `_yscale`, and hence change the zoom:

```
loaded = function () {
    theContent = myScrollPane.getScrollContent();
};
```

When the `zoomBar` is moved, it will trigger the `zoommove` function. This is defined as follows:

```
zoommove = function () {
    var zoomlevel = zoomBar.getScrollPosition();
    theContent._xscale = zoomlevel;
    theContent._yscale = zoomlevel;
    myScrollPane.refreshPane();
};
```

`zoommove` gets the `scrollPosition` of `zoomBar`, and then sets the `_xscale` and `_yscale` of the `myScrollPane`'s content (`theContent`) to that result. In our case, `zoomBar.getScrollPosition()` will always return a number from 1 to 1000, because that's what we set up the ScrollBar to do. Once the content of the ScrollPane has been resized, we must issue its `refreshPane()` method in order to get its associated ScrollBars to resize accordingly – notice that, as the image gets bigger, the thumb of the ScrollPane's bars must get smaller. Conversely, as the image shrinks to a size that is smaller than the ScrollPane, then its bars should become disabled.

When we test this movie and play around with the different zoom levels, we see the following results:

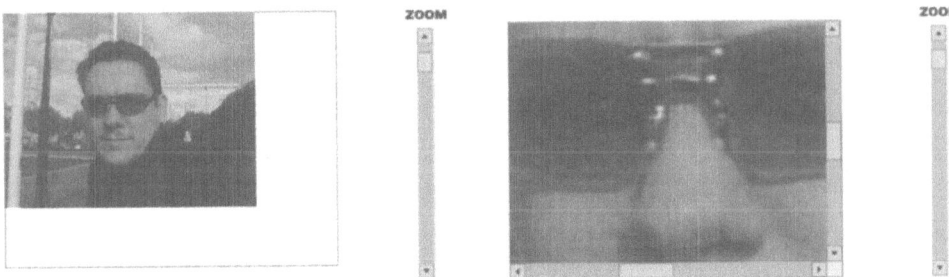

We can zoom in on the image up to 1000 percent, all with just two components and about a dozen lines of code. How cool is that?!

Integrating multiple components

As we've seen in the previous example, the properties within each UI component are accessible via ActionScript. We're now going to look at the some of the important ActionScript functions available for a few different components, and learn how they can interact to create a simple UI application. Open up `componentEntryForm.fla` – this movie contains an example UI user details form for gathering information about users of your Flash site. The stage of our FLA looks like this:

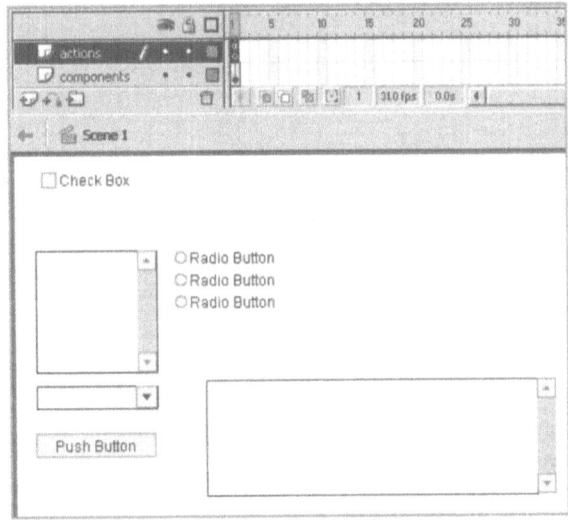

As usual, we have all of our components on one layer called components, and our ActionScript on an actions layer. Test the movie, fill out the form, and press the Submit button to see how the form processes your details:

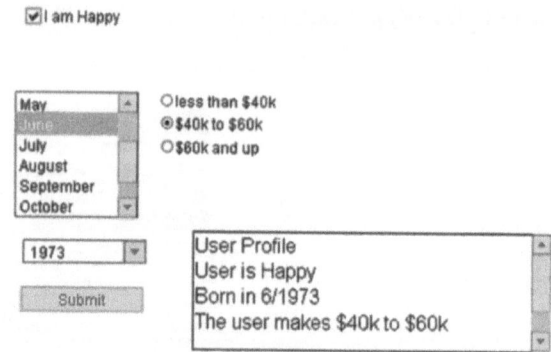

At the top, there's a CheckBox that is checked if the user is a happy person (OK, we said this was going to be a simple demonstration!). Below that is a ListBox of months referring to their month of birth, and then a ComboBox referring to their year of birth. We've also got a group of three RadioButtons indicating a salary range. At the bottom left of our form is the Submit PushButton that, when pressed, generates a report about the user, which is placed in the ScrollBar-controlled text field at the bottom right.

Remember, it's always possible to set the initial parameters of each component via the Property inspector (see **Chapter 2** for more details), but here we're going to use ActionScript to set up the components. Note, however, that we must still give each component on the stage an instance name in the Property inspector.

The complete code for this FLA shown below for reference, and we'll examine each part of it step-by-step in the subsections that follow:

```
// myCheckBox1 setup
myCheckBox1.setSize(333);
myCheckBox1.setLabel("I am Happy");
myCheckBox1.setValue(true);

// myComboBox setup
myComboBox.addItem("1970", 1970);
myComboBox.addItem("1971", 1971);
myComboBox.addItem("1972", 1972);
myComboBox.addItem("1973", 1973);
myComboBox.addItem("1974", 1974);
myComboBox.addItem("1975", 1975);
myComboBox.addItem("1976", 1976);
myComboBox.addItem("1977", 1977);
myComboBox.addItem("1978", 1978);
myComboBox.addItem("1979", 1979);
myComboBox.addItem("1980", 1980);
myComboBox.addItem("1981", 1981);
myComboBox.addItem("1982", 1982);
```

```
myComboBox.addItem("1983", 1983);
myComboBox.addItem("1984", 1984);
myComboBox.addItem("1985", 1985);

// myListBox setup
myListBox.addItem("January", 1);
myListBox.addItem("February", 2);
myListBox.addItem("March", 3);
myListBox.addItem("April", 4);
myListBox.addItem("May", 5);
myListBox.addItem("June", 6);
myListBox.addItem("July", 7);
myListBox.addItem("August", 8);
myListBox.addItem("September", 8);
myListBox.addItem("October", 10);
myListBox.addItem("November", 11);
myListBox.addItem("December", 12);

// myPushButton setup
myPushButton.setLabel("Submit");
myPushButton.setClickHandler("myClickHandler");

// myRadioButtons setup
myRadioButton1.setLabel("less than $40k");
myRadioButton2.setLabel("$40k to $60k");
myRadioButton3.setLabel("$60k and up");
myRadioButton1.setGroupName("salaryGroup");
myRadioButton2.setGroupName("salaryGroup");
myRadioButton3.setGroupName("salaryGroup");

// myClickHandler setup
myClickHandler = function () {
    feedback.text = "User Profile"+newline;
    if (myCheckBox1.getValue()) {
        feedback.text += "User is Happy"+newline;
    } else {
        feedback.text += "User is Not Happy"+newline;
    }
    feedback.text += "Born in
    ➥"+myListBox.getValue()+"/"+myComboBox.getValue()+newline;
    feedback.text += "The user makes "+salaryGroup.getValue()+newline;
};
```

FCheckBox

The first thing we do is set up the CheckBox instance myCheckBox1. We're setting it up with two parameters: size and label. The size parameter is used to determine how large the text field for the label should be. This is a value in pixels. If this value is too small, then the label of the CheckBox is likely to appear truncated. We use the method setSize() to define this size:

```
myCheckBox1.setSize(333);
myCheckBox1.setLabel("I am Happy");
myCheckBox1.setValue(true);
```

The next method called is setLabel(), and this simply defines the text associated with the CheckBox. We're setting it to I am Happy, so that user will leave it checked if they're happy, and uncheck it if they're not happy. We use the setValue() method to set it in the checked state to begin with (true is checked, and false is unchecked).

FComboBox

The next item we set up is the ComboBox instance myComboBox. All we're really doing here is populating it with a list of years from 1970 to 1985. The code to add each year is identical, except for the year itself:

```
myComboBox.addItem("1970", 1970);
myComboBox.addItem("1971", 1971);
myComboBox.addItem("1972", 1972);
      .
      .
      .
myComboBox.addItem("1985", 1985);
```

The first parameter, in the quotes, is the value that will appear in the label; the second value is the actual data to be returned when the ComboBox is accessed via the getValue() method (we'll come to that shortly). One good thing about ComboBoxes is that we can manually type in the value if we don't find it in the list, so we're not limited to what was created with ActionScript.

FListBox

The setup of myListBox is quite similar to that of myComboBox, except we're passing in months rather than years:

```
myListBox.addItem("January", 1);
myListBox.addItem("February", 2);
myListBox.addItem("March", 3);
myListBox.addItem("April", 4);
myListBox.addItem("May", 5);
myListBox.addItem("June", 6);
```

```
myListBox.addItem("July", 7);
myListBox.addItem("August", 8);
myListBox.addItem("September", 8);
myListBox.addItem("October", 10);
myListBox.addItem("November", 11);
myListBox.addItem("December", 12);
```

Again, we have the display label in quotes, and the actual data value as the second parameter. In this case, the data value corresponds to the month number, as used in standard numerical dates. Since all twelve months are being populated in the list, we have no need for a ComboBox, because no values will need to be typed in.

FPushButton

Setting up the PushButton is a simple task – first we set the label to Submit, and then we assign a click handler to the button. This is a function (detailed soon) that will be called whenever the user presses the button. In this case, we're going to be calling a function called myClickHandler:

```
myPushButton.setLabel("Submit");
myPushButton.setClickHandler("myClickHandler");
```

FRadioButton

The last components to be set up are the RadioButtons. We have three of them on the stage, named myRadioButton1, myRadioButton2, and myRadioButton3, and all we're doing is calling the setLabel() method of each one, and setting the label to be the value in quotes:

```
myRadioButton1.setLabel("less than $40k");
myRadioButton2.setLabel("$40k to $60k");
myRadioButton3.setLabel("$60k and up");
myRadioButton1.setGroupName("salaryGroup");
myRadioButton2.setGroupName("salaryGroup");
myRadioButton3.setGroupName("salaryGroup");
```

We're also setting up these three RadioButtons to be part of a group called salaryGroup. The functionality of a RadioButton is such that you should only be able to select one RadioButton in a given group of RadioButtons. In order to do this, we have to give each of our RadioButtons a common group name so that Flash knows that only one of these three can be selected at a time.

That's it for the component setup code – now we move on to the myClickHandler function.

Handling the button click

The `myClickHandler` function is responsible for taking the information from the form, compiling a report, and then displaying that report in the text field at the right. This function is called by the Submit PushButton when the user presses it:

```
myClickHandler = function () {
        feedback.text = "User Profile"+newline;
        if (myCheckBox1.getValue()) {
                feedback.text += "User is Happy"+newline;
        } else {
                feedback.text += "User is Not Happy"+newline;
        }
        feedback.text += "Born in
        ➡"+myListBox.getValue()+"/"+myComboBox.getValue()+newline;
        feedback.text += "The user makes "+salaryGroup.getValue()+newline;
};
```

Most of the code in the function is sending text to the text field (which has the instance name `feedback`) with `feedback.text`. The other action that we're performing is calling the `getValue()` method of the various UI components:

- `myCheckBox1.getValue()` returns the value of the CheckBox (`true` or `false`, depending upon whether or not it is checked).

- `myListBox.getValue()` gets the value of the month, the second parameter in the `addItem()` method (this is a number from 1 to 12).

- `myComboBox.getValue()` returns the value of whatever text is in the text field of the ComboBox, whether we select or type in a year.

Note that the ScrollBar in this example is not under our control; it has been attached to the feedback text field, and it updates itself automatically.

The extent to which we can use the UI Components is only limited by our own creativity.

9 Component Styles

Objectives

- Using the component style formatting object `FStyleFormat` andits associated methods and properties.

- Customizing your component skins.

Introduction

In **Chapter 2** we looked at script-based user interface elements and, more specifically, the Macromedia Flash MX UI components and how to use features like ScrollBars, PushButtons, CheckBoxes, ListBoxes, and so on. One thing that you may have noticed is that each component has an identical gray design scheme – which is pretty bland to designers like us! Wouldn't it be nice if we could change the look of different aspects of a UI component, like you can in HTML with **Cascading Style Sheets**? Well, fortunately, we can! In fact, the Flash MX components are highly customizable, allowing us to turn standard components like this:

Into this something a little more jazzy, like this:

In this chapter we'll look at the built-in style formatting object for components, known as FStyleFormat, and how we can apply it to each UI component via some simple ActionScript. After that we'll move on to what's known as *skinning* our components – where we'll actually replace individual graphical elements within a component with designs of our own creation. Let's get started...

FStyleFormat

All components use a standard set of properties that define the colors and attributes of every element within the component. For instance, take a look in the Flash UI Components section of the scripting dictionary pane on the left-hand side of your Actions panel (F9). Browse down to the FStyleFormat entry, and click open the Properties folder:

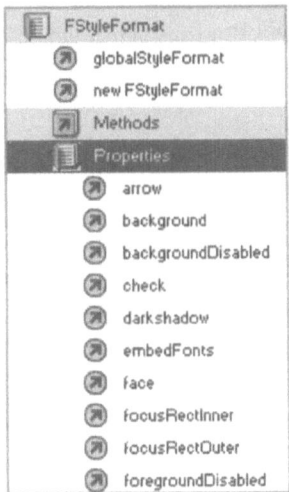

Here we see just a sample of the available properties in the `FStyleFormat` object. For example, the `face` property corresponds to the color of the surface of a component, the default being that dull old gray color. The result of changing these properties is that we can create UI components that look substantially different to the default components. So, how exactly do we go about changing these properties? Well, we can do it directly, like this:

`componentInstance.setStyleProperty("property", value);`

So, for example, we could write something like:

`myPushButton.setStyleProperty("face", 0xFFFFFF);`

This will change the property `face` to the color white (0xFFFFFF). Note that the color value must take the hexadecimal form of 0xRRGGBB (see **Chapter 6** for further details). This is the simplest way of changing component format properties, but also the most tedious. To make things much faster, we can make use of the `FStyleFormat` component.

Updating the properties of all UI components (and thus making our entire site take on a consistent look) is very simple. We just set the style properties of an `FStyleFormat` component, and then use the `applyChanges()` method of the `FStyleFormat` component to update the UI components.

There are actually two ways to use the `FStyleFormat` object to apply formatting changes to your components:

- **globalStyleFormat** – This is an instance of the `FStyleFormat` object that exists from the moment the movie begins running. Any changes we make to the `globalStyleFormat` are applied to the skin elements of *every* component in the movie, hence the term *global*.

- **new FStyleFormat** – We can create our own instance of the `FStyleFormat` object using the standard object constructor, modify its properties, and then apply those changes to specific UI components in our movie. This gives us more precise control over how each skin element will look in our final movie.

We'll take a look at each of these techniques in the following sections.

globalStyleFormat

Setting properties of the global `FStyleFormat` object and then applying them will cause all skin elements in a movie to inherit those changes. The only exception to this is if a specific UI component has had changes applied to it specifically with its own instance of an `FStyleFormat` object (discussed in the next section).

The best way to learn about global formatting is through an example – open up `globalStyleFormat.fla` from the CD. On the main stage we have four PushButtons, all of which are instances of the `FPushButton` component:

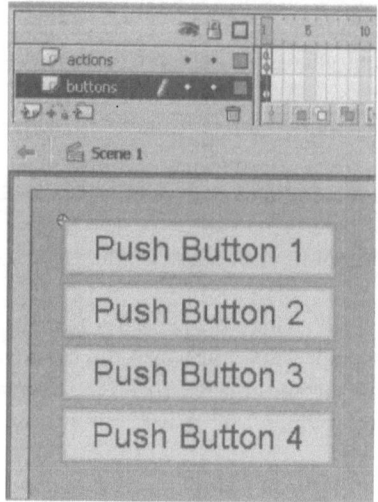

We also have another layer called actions, and in this layer we have a few lines of ActionScript. We'll get to this shortly, but for the moment test the movie (CTRL+ENTER) and see what happens. In the Flash MX authoring environment, the buttons are the plain, default gray style. When we run this movie, however, the look that we actually get is that of some sleek, colored buttons:

Look on your screen and you'll see that the differences are striking when viewed in full glorious color, rather than the grayscale of the image above. Here we've defined the face, shadows, highlights, and the text properties. Now let's take a look at that code on the actions layer:

```
globalStyleFormat.face = 0x3399CC;
globalStyleFormat.shadow = 0x000033;
```

```
globalStyleFormat.darkshadow = 0xF2FA5F;
globalStyleFormat.highlight = 0xFFECB5;
globalStyleFormat.textColor = 0xFFFFFF;
globalStyleFormat.textSize = 10;
globalStyleFormat.textBold = true;

globalStyleFormat.applyChanges();
```

So, we're applying our changes globally using the `globalStyleFormat` instance of the `FStyleFormat` object. The code is actually remarkably intuitive – we're putting color values in the `face`, `shadow`, `darkshadow`, `highlight`, and `textColor` properties. The `textSize` property expects a font point size, and the `textBold` property expects `true` or `false`, depending on whether or not we want the text in the button to be bold.

Finally, we apply these changes to all UI components with the `applyChanges()` method. Depending on the UI component, the applicable `FStyleFormat` properties will vary. Here's a list of the properties accompanied by a brief description of each:

Property Name	Description
arrow	The color of the small up and down arrow used in ScrollBars and ComboBoxes.
background	The color of the `background` of any component, like the background of a ListBox or the area of a CheckBox behind the check mark.
backgroundDisabled	Similar to background, except it's the color of a UI component that is currently disabled.
check	The color of the check mark in a CheckBox component.
darkshadow	The color of the lower and right outer border of a component:

`face`	The color of the main part of the component. For example:
`foregroundDisabled`	The foreground color of a disabled component.
`highlight`	The upper and left inner border of the component:

`highlight3D`	The upper and left outer border of the component:

`radioDot`	The color of the dot in the middle of a RadioButton.
`scrollTrack`	The color of the scroll track at the back of a ScrollBar component, as represented by the black region in this image:

selection	The color of the selection bar, which highlights an item in a ListBox or a ComboBox.
selectionDisabled	The color of the selection bar which highlights a disabled item in a ListBox or ComboBox.
selectionUnfocused	The color of the selection bar when the component does not have focus.
shadow	The color of the lower and right inner border of the component:
textAlign	The alignment of the text in any component with text in it, like button labels, ListBox text, CheckBox labels, and so on. The applicable values are: "left", "right", or "center".
textBold	A true or false value that specifies whether or not text within a component will be bold or not.
textColor	The color of the text in a component.
textDisabled	The color of the text in a disabled component.
textFont	The font to use in the text in the component.
textIndent	An indentation, measured in pixels, to apply to the text from the left margin.
textItalic	A true or false value specifying whether or not text is italicized.
textLeftMargin	The left paragraph margin for text in a component (measured in pixels).
textRightMargin	The right paragraph margin for text in a component (measured in pixels).
textSelected	The color of the text in a selected list item in a ListBox or ComboBox.
textSize	The size of the text in a component, in standard font point size.
textUnderline	A true or false value that specifies whether or not text in a component should be underlined.

Any of these properties can be applied to an FStyleFormat object with this generalization:

```
FStyleFormatName.property = value;
```

where `FStyleFormatName` is either the `globalStyleFormat` or an instance of the `FStyleFormat` object that you define yourself. `property` is the property name, and `value` is the appropriate value (as described in the table above).

new FStyleFormat

The other way of formatting our components is to create our own `FStyleFormat` instance, and use it to affect only a few of the skins in our movie, rather than every single component. We create a new `FStyleFormat` instance with the `new` constructor, like so:

```
myStyleFormat = new FStyleFormat();
```

And then we go on to set its properties like this (for example):

```
myStyleFormat.face = 0x7700FF;
myStyleFormat.shadow = 0x000000;
myStyleFormat.textColor = 0xFFFFFF;
```

This is very similar to how we worked with the `globalStyleFormat` object. The main difference comes in the fact that we then have to apply it to a specific UI component, so we cannot immediately jump to the `applyChanges()` method. We must first use the `addListener()` method of the `FStyleFormat` component. This is attached to the end of the existing code as follows:

```
myStyleFormat = new FStyleFormat();
myStyleFormat.face = 0x7700FF;
myStyleFormat.shadow = 0x000000;
myStyleFormat.textColor = 0xFFFFFF;
myStyleFormat.addListener(myButton);
```

This assigns `myButton` to make use of the format information in `myStyleFormat`. We can use this technique to apply formatting to any number of UI components, and they can all make use of the same `FStyleFormat` instance. Have a look at the file `myStyleFormat.fla` to see this code in action; when we test this movie, we're presented with a nicely colored PushButton (with the instance name `myButton`), formatted according to the `myStyleFormat` object. A second PushButton, without an instance name, has been placed in this FLA to demonstrate that the changes are only applied to the defined instance (`myButton`) and not to every component in the movie:

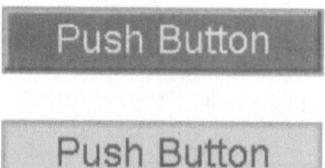

When we use the `addListener()` method, we can assign several UI components to draw their formatting information from one `FStyleFormat` component. This means that we can make changes to this `FStyleFormat` component, and then simply perform the `applyChanges()` method and all of the *listening* UI components will change accordingly. Take a look at `addListeners.fla` to see this in action – in this movie, we have some token components on the stage (a PushButton and a ScrollBar, with the instance names `myPushButton` and `myScrollBar`). The code on the actions layer looks like this:

```
myStyleFormat = new FStyleFormat();
myStyleFormat.addListener(myButton);
myStyleFormat.addListener(myScrollBar);
_root.onEnterFrame = function() {
    myStyleFormat.face = Math.random()*0xFFFFFF;
    myStyleFormat.applyChanges();
};
```

Test the movie and watch what happens. It's difficult to illustrate here, so look at your SWF – the faces of the buttons on both components are rapidly changing color because we're choosing a random color value between `0` and `0xFFFFFF` using the `Math.random()` function, and assigning it to the face property of the `myStyleFormat` component. When we apply the changes with `applyChanges()`, both UI components pick up on the changes, because of the fact that they're listening (they've both been told to with `addListener()`).

Next, open up and test `twoPushButtons.fla` (can you guess what it contains?), and we'll look at two different `FStyleFormat` components being used on two different UI items:

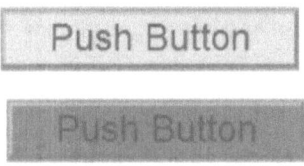

The following code accomplishes this effect:

```
myStyleFormat = new FStyleFormat({face:0xFFFF22, shadow:0x66666});
myStyleFormat.addListener(myButton);
myStyleFormat = new FStyleFormat({face:0x0066FF, shadow:0x66666});
myStyleFormat.addListener(myButton2);
```

Notice that we're specifying the `face` and `shadow` property values right in the constructor statement itself this time. Flash allows us to do this, because this is how it generically creates an object, and we then assign the properties based upon what's within the brackets. This is a more efficient coding technique than adding a new code line for each property, as we did earlier. Why use many lines of code when one will do?!

If we want to stop a particular UI component from listening to a `FStyleFormat` component for changes, then we must use the `removeListener` method as follows:

```
myStyleFormat.removeListener(myComponent);
```

Where `myStyleFormat` is an `FStyleFormat` component, and `myComponent` is the UI component that was previously assigned to it (in our previous examples this was `myButton`). If we want, we can also remove a component from the `globalStyleFormat` instance of the `FStyleFormat` component as follows:

```
globalStyleFormat.removeListener(myComponent);
```

This means that any changes we make to the `globalStyleFormat` will no longer be propagated to the specified component. This is useful for assigning a site-wide global style, but with scope for exceptions to the defined style.

Now that we're able to define the colors of the standard skin elements within UI components, let's look at changing the actual *look* of the skin elements themselves by changing the graphics and movie clips that make up a skin.

Changing skins

At the start of this chapter, we suggested the possibility of changing the default ScrollBar into something a little more flamboyant, like this:

Keeping in mind the previous section and our understanding of the `FStyleFormat` object, it's pretty clear that we've done more than just change `FStyleFormat` properties of this component. The graphics themselves have been modified – the arrows are a different shape, the background of the scroll track is a bitmapped texture, and the thumb is a metallic effect gradient. So how do we do this? Well, the easiest way is to go into the Library, and modify the skin elements themselves. It just so happens that every one of the `FStyleFormat` properties whose colors we were able to modify also happen to correspond to a single graphic or skin element in the UI component.

To start with, let's try a simple customization ourselves – open up `basicCheckBox.fla`:

This movie consists of two CheckBoxes, one labeled Fish, and the other Chicken. So when the movie is tested, we can select either option:

What we might like to do is change the check mark to something more appropriate – a chef's hat, for instance, if these options relate to what's on the menu. Back in the authoring environment, open up the Library (CTRL+L or F11) and you'll see that it contains the Flash UI Components folder. This folder is automatically imported into your Library when you drag and drop any component onto the stage. Double-click on the folder to open it, and then take a look at its contents:

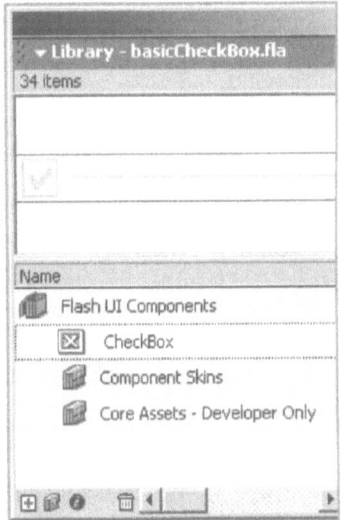

We can see here the main CheckBox component – this contains all the operational code for the functionality of the CheckBox, such as initialization, showing/hiding the check mark, and so on. Beneath that, we see a folder called Component Skins. Double click on this, and then the component skins folder will open up to reveal two more folders: FCheckBox Skins and Global Skins. It's within the FCheckBox skins folder that we're going to find the skin elements that we're looking for.

Double click to open this folder. We're now presented with the movie clips that make up our CheckBox:

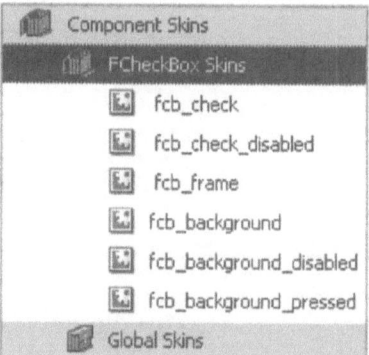

These six movie clips are the skin movie clips used to make up the FCheckBox component. Each of these movie clips are made up of one or more *skin elements*, which are themselves simply movie clips and graphics.

Let's take a closer look at the check mark skin – double click on the fcb_check movie clip, and we'll be brought into its timeline:

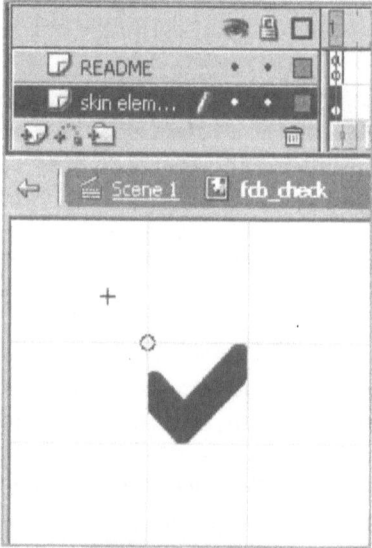

There are two layers within the timeline of this fcb_check skin: The README layer, and the skin element layer. Here we have all the skin elements and style format properties which make up the skin. Remember, when we want to change the color of the check in a CheckBox we use something like the following code:

```
check1.setStyleProperty("check", 0xFF0000);
```

The check property in this line comes directly from this fcb_check skin. Take a look at the code in the README layer, and find the following line near the bottom:

```
component.registerSkinElement(check_mc, "check");
```

Here we are issuing the registerSkinElement() command, and telling Flash to register the check_mc movie clip as the check style format property. Notice that registerSkinElement() is being applied to something called component; take a look at the top of the README code, and we'll see this:

```
var component = _parent._parent;
```

So our registerSkinElement() method actually translates to:

```
_parent._parent.registerSkinElement(check_mc, "check");
```

Every time we go into a skin and add a new skin element, then we must register it in this fashion if we want to be able to change the color of that skin element with the setStyleProperty method, or with an FStyleFormat component. All of the code in these default UI components comes pre-written, and for the most part we don't really have to worry about them unless we're writing our own UI components from scratch.

So, what about changing the actual graphic – that's what we're here for, right? For this, we need to focus our attention on the other layer, the skin element layer. Double click on the checkmark, and we'll be taken into its timeline. It too is called fcb_check:

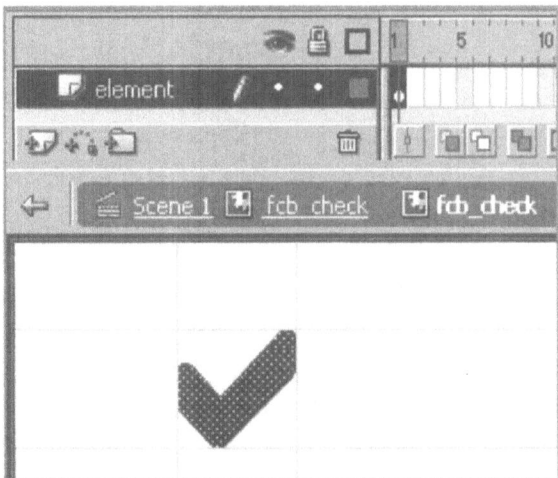

In here, we can edit the actual image, on a drawing tool level. Let's try drawing a chef's hat in place of the check:

Now if we test our movie and select an option for dinner, we see this:

Chicken it is! Open up see `chefCheckBox.fla` to see the finished version of this example. That's all we need to do to change the graphics of skin elements.

It's worth noting that, while the `fcb_check` is made up of one skin element, some skins are themselves made up of several skin elements. Let's go back to the Library in `basicCheckBox.fla` (or indeed in `chefCheckBox.fla`), and this time double click on the `fcb_frame` skin. This will take us into its timeline, and if we look at its README layer we'll see several skin elements being registered:

```
component.registerSkinElement(shadow_mc, "shadow");
component.registerSkinElement(darkshadow_mc, "darkshadow");
component.registerSkinElement(highlight_mc, "highlight");
component.registerSkinElement(highlight3D_mc, "highlight3D");
```

These style format properties should be familiar to us from the early part of this chapter (if not, just have another glance at the properties table we saw earlier). We'll need to zoom in on the frame image – now we can see the movie clips that they're associated with: shadow_mc, darkshadow_mc, highlight_mc, and highlight3D_mc. These four skin elements compose the fcb_frame. They break down like this:

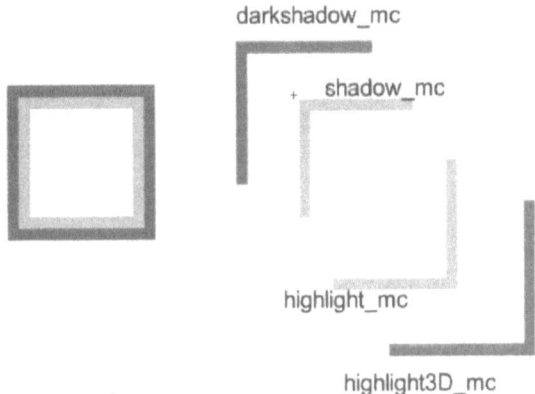

darkshadow_mc

shadow_mc

highlight_mc

highlight3D_mc

Double clicking on each skin element allows us to go in and change them to edit the frame to however we want it to look.

> *Components can be made up of several skins, and we can edit each skin element. It's worth spending some time playing with each skin, and seeing exactly what kind of effects can be created.*

Now that we've looked at a very simple component customization, we're ready to study something a little more advanced. So open up customScrollBar.fla – this is the modified ScrollBar that we saw at the beginning of this chapter. Look at the ScrollBar's individual elements in the Library to see how we've altered the basic ScrollBar characteristics to create our unique design. Now try one for yourself!

With the concepts we've learned in this chapter, we now know how to set the style format properties and change the skins of any UI component – we can use the Flash MX UI components, which offer a standard, well-known functionality to users, but we can make them look completely original and tailor them to fit in with the rest of our site's design.

10 Functions and Events

Objectives

- How events work with functions

- Flash 5 object scripts vs. Flash MX remote callbacks

- Setting up and using functions:

  - Callbacks

  - Listeners

  - Watchers

Introduction

In any robust programming language, like Visual Basic or C++, programmers have an important technique to ensure efficient coding: the use of **functions**. As Flash has evolved through its various versions, ActionScript has grown with it, from simple target-based instructions way back in Flash 3, to the introduction of functions in Flash 5. With the *robust* and *remote* functions and event definitions that are now possible in Flash MX, emphasis has been placed on the ability to write highly *modular* pieces of code.

Flash MX takes this modular approach one step further. In Flash 5, the general coding practice was to place functions on individual timelines, or attach them to specific movie clips and buttons, resulting in code being scattered throughout your movie. This old technique was known as *object scripting* – code could be located in any number of places within the Flash authoring environment, even deeply nested within several movie clips. As designers became used to the power of functions, and almost dependent on them, it soon became apparent that distributing code throughout a movie was not only inefficient, but also extremely difficult to housekeep when revisiting files at a later date.

Flash MX addresses this problem by giving designers a powerful new approach to scripting, more in line with traditional programming languages. As we've seen throughout this book, rather than attach code to buttons or movie clips, it can be placed centrally within your movie. The best design practice in Flash MX is generally to write all of your ActionScript on frame 1 of the root timeline – actions are executed from here and attached to the various objects and timelines throughout your movie using simple dot syntax referencing, paying particular attention to the scope of your functions and events. Keeping code in one place is extremely good programming practice – it makes life very easy when trying to debug, search through, update, or reuse chunks of code.

So, it is much more efficient to define all our code in a single location using **callbacks** instead of **object scripts** attached to individual buttons and movie clips – we just need to reference the instance name of the movie clip and the associated event from the main timeline, and pack them together in a single bite-sized function. But remember, callback functions have the same scope as the timeline that they are defined on. In addition, we now have **listeners** and **watchers** – we can use these to determine whether certain events have happened to particular objects. For instance, a listener can *listen* for the selection of objects that include key, mouse, movie clips, text fields, and so on.

Macromedia Flash is a constantly evolving application; each updated release has dramatically improved upon the previous one. Flash MX now brings us to a point where the coding practices and concepts of ActionScript are so similar to traditional programming languages that it is considered by many as one of the primary programming languages on the web. In this chapter we'll study the use of callback functions, listeners, and watchers to enhance our design functionality.

Using events and functions

In ActionScript, an event is recognized by Flash whenever certain incidents take place – for example, pressing or releasing a key, moving the mouse, tabbing into a text box, and so on. When attached to functions, all of these events, and more, can be used to trigger actions in our movies.

To put events into context, let's have a quick look at a listener function. A listener can receive and respond to an event. We can create a listener that monitors for certain events taking place, such as onEnterframe, onLoad, mouseDown, onMouseUp, and so on. In Flash MX we can define a listener object and associate it with virtually any event. Here's a simple example:

```
myListener = new Object();
Mouse.addListener(myListener);
myListener.onMouseDown = function() {
      trace("The mouse button is down.");
};
```

With this piece of ActionScript we create a new object called myListener with the standard constructor, add this listener to the Mouse object, and then define a function in the myListener object that acts on the onMouseDown event. So, when we test this code, the following message is traced into the Output window:

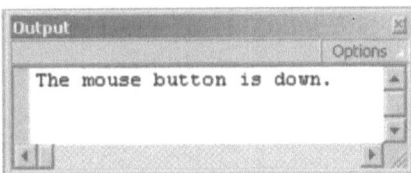

Another powerful feature of Flash MX is the ability to add and remove listeners, and change or delete the handling functions on the fly. The example above serves to introduce and demonstrate the basics of events and functions, but to show their full potential we need a more practical example. In fact, the best way to learn about callback, watcher, and listener functions is to build up a complete example, and go through its design, development, and implementation stages – so let's do just that!

Callbacks

Before looking at the more specific listener and watcher functions, we'll start by demonstrating a callback on the Mouse object. Let's put together a movie that customizes the mouse cursor in certain situations. More specifically, we'll make our mouse pointer change from the usual white arrow into an inverted black arrow when we click on a specific region within our Flash movie. This is a good example of a simple yet effective and eye-catching piece of design functionality.

Open up callbackCursor.fla from the CD – on the stage you'll see a simple box movie clip with the instance name myStageMC – for the sake of demonstration, this represents the stage or window that we want our mouse cursor to react to. So, this movie will display the normal system cursor outside of the stage movie clip, and then the system cursor will be replaced when the mouse pointer moves across this movie clip. Additionally, the appearance of our mouse cursor will change when the mouse button is pressed. Let's learn how to do it!

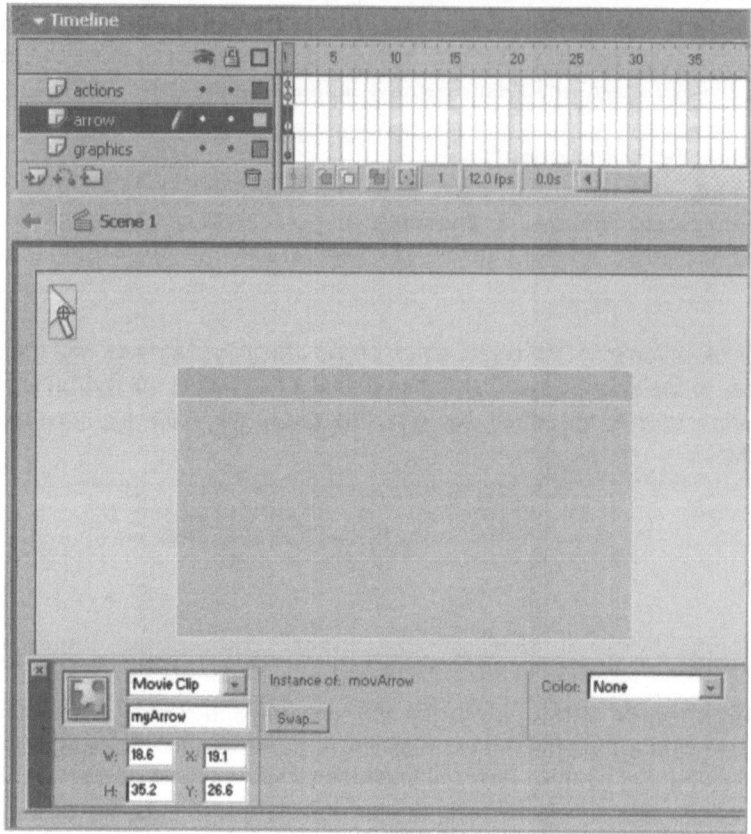

Also on the stage we've got a movie clip of a cursor arrow with the instance name of myArrow. Let's have a closer inspection of this movie clip – doubleclick on it to drill down to its own timeline:

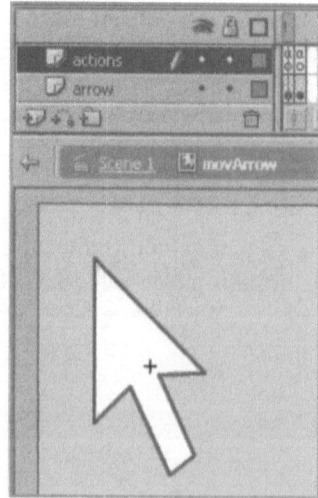

Now we see that it consists of two frames: in the first we've got the white arrow with a black outline, and in the second frame it's been filled in black with a white outline, and inverted:

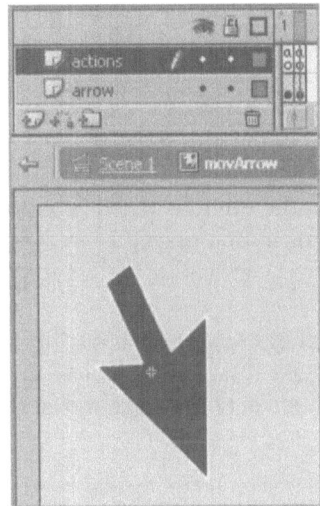

Note also that stop() commands are attached to both frames.

We now have the infrastructure in place to be able to start adding code. But first, let's remind ourselves of the initial brief – it's always a good idea to consider the bigger picture before getting down to the finer technical details of your design. We want to replace the operating system cursor with our enlarged white arrow while over the stage movie clip, but revert to standard mouse arrow when leaving this movie clip. On top of this, if the mouse is pressed when over the stage movie clip, we want the cursor to invert, hence the second frame in the movArrow movie clip.

OK, let's get down to defining some callback functions that will achieve our desired functionality. Return your attention to the main stage, and the root timeline. Select frame 1 of the actions layer and you'll see the following code:

```
myStageMC.onMouseMove = function() {
    if (this.hitTest(_root._xmouse, _root._ymouse, false)) {
        Mouse.hide();
        myArrow._visible = true;
        myArrow._x = _root._xmouse;
        myArrow._y = _root._ymouse;
    } else {
        Mouse.show();
        myArrow._visible = false;
    }
    updateAfterEvent();
};
```

continues overleaf 237

```
myStageMC.onMouseDown = function() {
      myArrow.gotoAndStop(2);
};
myStageMC.onMouseUp = function() {
      myArrow.gotoAndStop(1);
};
```

This ActionScript essentially monitors the mouse events onMouseMove, onMouseUp, and onMouseDown with three functions. Because we're assigning these events to a movie clip, myStageMC, the functions effectively listen out for changes in the events – this is very similar to how listeners work, but they don't need to be linked to a movie clip or button object, as we'll see later in this chapter. Once the specified event occurs, our functions respond by executing the associated code.

But don't worry about understanding everything about this code for the moment; we'll describe it at length very soon. Right now, test the movie (CTRL+ENTER) to see the finished effect. As expected, our dynamic cursor grows in size when it's over the stage movie clip, and then inverts and turns black when we click the mouse button:

  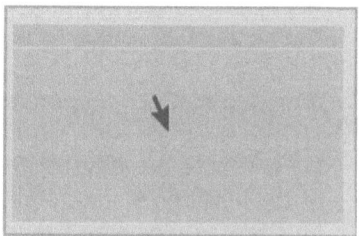

So, let's examine the finer details of our code. Initially we set up the first callback function that tracks the mouse movement. We attach it to the myStageMC movie clip, which acts like a listener:

```
myStageMC.onMouseMove = function() {
```

Remember, in Flash 5 we would have defined this code as an object script, placed directly on the movie clip, like this:

```
onClipEvent (mouseMove) {
```

The Flash MX callback technique is actually much clearer and easier to understand and maintain, and of course all your code is in one place.

Moving on, we come to the core code of the function – this is where we define the actions that we want to occur when the onMouseMove event occurs. This event will fire every time the mouse is moved, it is therefore important that code is lean, mean, and efficient. Our function code starts with this line:

```
if (this.hitTest(_root._xmouse, _root._ymouse, false)) {
```

Here we have the start of an if loop containing a hitTest() condition – this is a crucial piece of ActionScript. With this line we are checking to see whether the mouse is over our stage movie clip. The hitTest() method accepts three parameters: the x and y limits of the hit area that we are testing, and whether or not we want to test for an irregular shape object (true or false) – for more details on the use of hitTest(), see **Chapter 2**. In this case, we're giving the co-ordinates of the mouse as our hit area – so whenever the mouse cursor moves into the area defined by myStageMC, Flash will run the next batch of code in the if loop.

Another point worth noting about this line is the use of the term this attached to hitTest(). When writing callback type functions, we can use the this keyword to refer to the object targeted in our function definition. So in our case, this refers directly to the myStageMC movie clip.

So, if our cursor moves over myStageMC, the following code will run:

```
Mouse.hide();
myArrow._visible = true;
myArrow._x = _root._xmouse;
myArrow._y = _root._ymouse;
```

First, because we want our own customized pointer, we hide the system cursor using the hide() method of the Mouse object. Next, we must ensure that our replacement cursor, the myArrow movie clip, is visible. Then we want myArrow to move around as if it were the default cursor. We do this simply by tracking the mouse movement via the _root._xmouse and _root._ymouse properties, and setting our movie clip cursor's position to be the same co-ordinates.

At this stage, we have a basic if statement of our first callback function testing whether the mouse is over the hit area of our myStageMC. But what if it's not, and the hit test evaluates to false? Obviously, we need to include an else statement, which looks like this:

```
} else {
        Mouse.show();
        myArrow._visible = false;
}
```

This is fairly self-explanatory – when the mouse is not over the myStageMC movie clip, we just make the standard system mouse visible again, and hide our custom arrow.

Before closing this function definition, we can throw in a little method to optimize the movie's performance – the updateAfterEvent() method forces Flash to refresh the screen every time the onMouseMove event is fired:

```
        updateAfterEvent();
};
```

Try commenting this line out, and testing the code – you'll see that the movement of the cursor becomes extremely jerky, so `updateAfterEvent()` is really handy.

We are now ready to consider the code needed to change our cursor's appearance when the user presses the mouse down over the stage movie clip. Of course, we also need to cater for when the user releases the mouse button. This is done using two separate mouse events – `onMouseDown` and `onMouseUp`. Remember, we've already set up our cursor movie clip to contain frames for its up and down states, so this code is a simple case of setting which frame of the cursor movie clip to go to, depending on whether the mouse is down or up.

Let's deal initially with what happens when the mouse is pressed. Just as we did with the mouse move event, we'll attach this code to a callback function of the `myStageMC` movie clip:

```
myStageMC.onMouseDown = function() {
      myArrow.gotoAndStop(2);
};
```

Next, the code for the mouse button moving back up tells our cursor movie clip to go to its up state in frame 1:

```
myStageMC.onMouseUp = function() {
      myArrow.gotoAndStop(1);
};
```

And that's it for our three callback functions. As we mentioned earlier, strictly speaking movie clips are already a kind of listener – they listen for events such as `onLoad` and `onEnterFrame`. In fact, to see all of the events that are associated with movie clips, just have a look in your Actions panel (F9):

However, as we'll soon learn, the true power of events and functions in Flash MX is the ability to add listeners to *any* object.

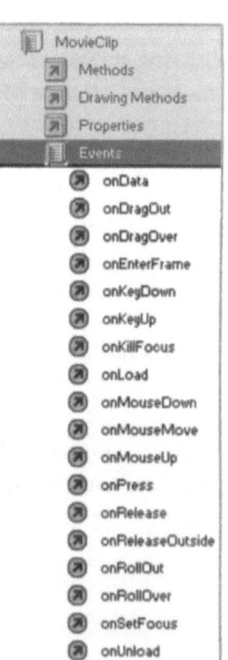

Listeners

A listener allows you to create an event handler function that responds to events raised by basic input and output techniques, other than the button and movie clip instances we use with standard callbacks. The list of available objects and their associated events is as follows:

- **Key** – onKeyDown, onKeyUp
- **Mouse** – onMouseMove, onMouseDown
- **Selection** – onSetFocus
- **Stage** – onResize
- **Text Field** - onChanged, onScroller

So what's the difference between a listener and a callback event? Well, a listener event is attached to objects other than the one generating the event. A side effect of this is that the initiating event can affect more than one other object. This is reasonable, given the nature of the objects listed above: more than one object may want to react to a key press, and *all* movie clips on stage may want to react to a stage resize. Another special feature of listeners is that the initiating object is predefined.

To demonstrate the use of listeners we'll create our own generic object that will monitor keyboard activity. Most games require some kind of keyboard interactions, so this example gives us the opportunity to investigate the type of code required when building a typical Flash game. Open up listenerKeys.fla and take a look at the stage:

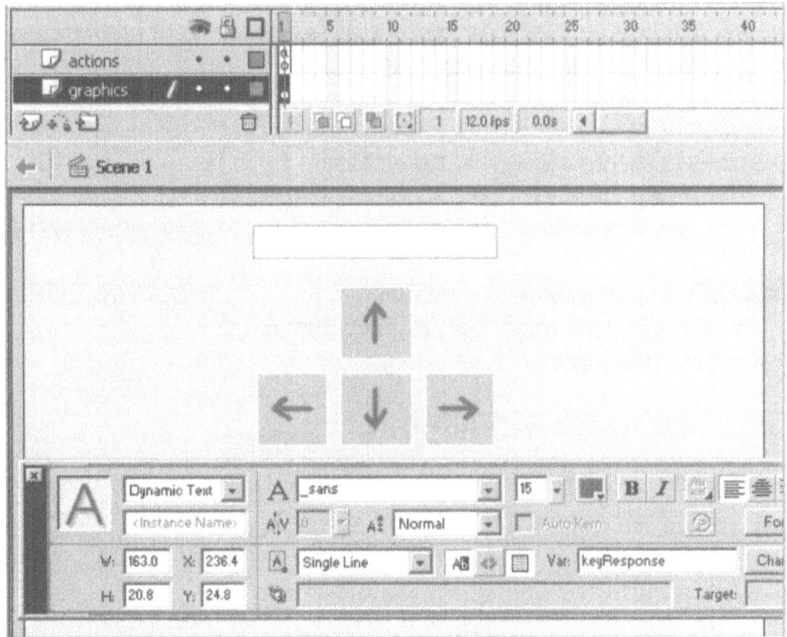

First of all we have a dynamic text field on the stage with an associated variable name keyResponse. Beneath the text box, we've got four instances of the key movie clip laid out like the arrow keys on your keyboard. These keys have instance names key37, key38, key39, and key40 for the left, up, right, and down arrows, respectively. These instance names reflect the key code values of the arrow keys – we'll soon see why this is necessary. Double-click one of the arrow movie clips and note that frame two has a slightly different graphic, representing the down state of the button (this is very similar to how we achieved the up and down states of our custom cursor in the previous example):

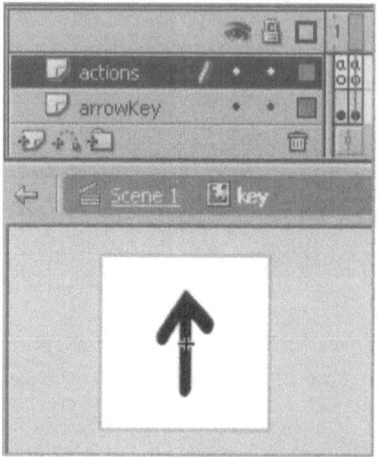

OK, time for some ActionScript – go back to the main stage, and open up the Actions panel on frame 1 of the actions layer. You'll see the following code:

```
checkKeyActivity = new Object();
checkKeyActivity.onKeyDown = function() {
    _root["key"+Key.getCode()].gotoAndStop(2);
    _root.keyResponse = "Key code pressed: "+Key.getCode();
};
checkKeyActivity.onKeyUp = function() {
    _root["key"+Key.getCode()].gotoAndStop(1);
    _root.keyResponse = "";
};
Key.addListener(checkKeyActivity);
```

As usual, we'll describe the code step by step. The first line creates a new object, checkKeyActivity, to handle our keyboard activity:

```
checkKeyActivity = new Object();
```

Next up, we want to add a callback function to this object that will listen for the onKeyDown event:

```
checkKeyActivity.onKeyDown = function() {
```

Now we need to add the action that actually does something when the specified event occurs. We will use the dynamic text field to deliver feedback to the screen, via the keyResponse variable. You'd use a similar process when coding the key feedback for a Flash game:

```
        _root["key"+Key.getCode()].gotoAndStop(2);
        _root.keyResponse = "Keycode pressed: "+Key.getCode();
};
```

The first line here finds the key code value corresponding to the arrow key that is pressed, using the getCode() method of the Key object, and joins this number to the word key. This string will therefore reflect the instance names of our key movie clips. The gotoAndStop(2) command subsequently moves the playhead to the key's down state in frame 2. The overall effect of these two lines is that we dynamically reference the arrow movie clips according to the key code values of the depressed arrow keys.

Similarly, we need another callback that takes our button movie clips back to frame 1 when onKeyUp event occurs, and resets the text box:

```
checkKeyActivity.onKeyUp = function() {
        _root["key"+Key.getCode()].gotoAndStop(1);
        _root.keyResponse = "";
};
```

Finally, after defining the onKeyDown and onKeyUp functions, we have to add a listener specifically for the checkKeyActivity object – this is a critical step when we're working with listeners on objects that we've defined ourselves. This is done like so:

```
Key.addListener(checkKeyActivity);
```

Here the addListener() method registers our checkKeyActivity object with the Key object so it can listen to the onKeyDown and onKeyUp events. When a key is pressed or released, regardless of the input focus, all listening objects registered with addListener() have either their onKeyDown or onKeyUp functions invoked. Note that multiple objects can listen for keyboard notifications – this is particularly relevant to games developers.

Now when we test your movie we should see that the arrow key movie clips appear to depress and release according to our keystrokes:

In this example, our listener monitors which keys are depressed, and then makes the arrow key movie clips mimic the arrow keys on our keyboard – a nice little trick, accomplished by utilizing the `addListener()` method.

Let's summarize our description of listener functions by noting the requirements for adding a listener:

1. Your listener object must have at least one listener event defined for it from one of these objects: **Key, Mouse, Selection, Stage, or Text Field.**

2. The listener object must then be *registered* as a listener with the `addListener()` method.

Watchers

So far in this chapter we've looked at callbacks and listeners. Let's now turn our attention to watchers. A watcher responds to a change in a variable or property that is updated through ActionScript. This can be useful in a number of different scenarios where we can respond to things like:

- User actions that change a continuous input value. For instance, if a slider value was at 59 and the user changed it to 84, you could use a watcher event to take the new value and change the volume of your backing soundtrack accordingly. Because the event reflects any change, the process is only required to run when something needs to be done – this is a far better solution than having to do it every frame, as with `onEnterFrame`.

- Filtering or processing values after a change. For example, if a variable changes to a value that is too high, the watcher can look out for this, and run a script to get it back to an in-range value.

The best way to understand how to set up and use watchers is to go through an example, and describe all the relevant code in detail. Open up `watcherProperties.fla` from the CD, in which you'll find a number of elements on the main stage:

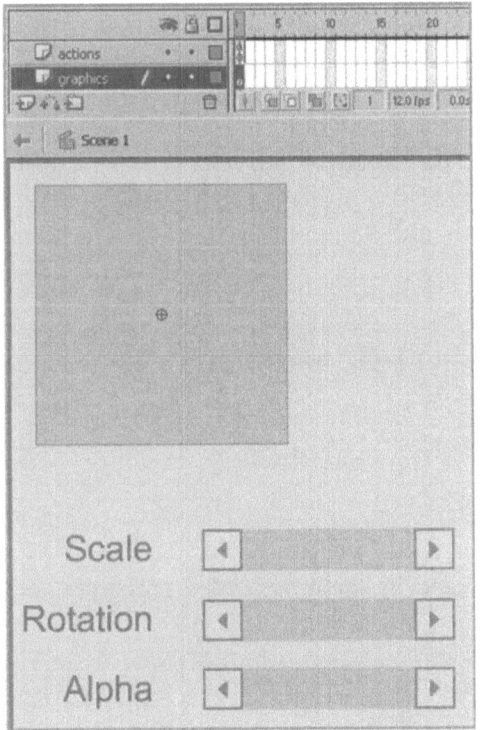

Firstly, we've got a simple square that's been converted into a movie clip and given the instance name mySq. There are also three ScrollBars, dragged onto the stage from the Components panel, with instance names scaleScroll, rotationScroll, and alphaScroll. Note that in the Property inspector each ScrollBar has been set up to scroll horizontally. Finally, we've got a label on the side of each scrollbar to indicate what it is for.

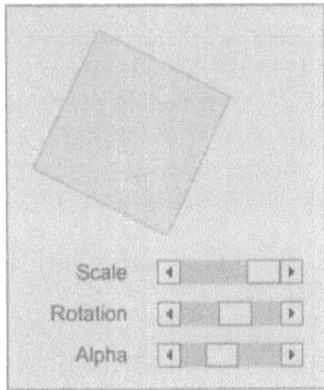

Before we go on to study the watcher code, let's take a sneak preview of the finished effect – test the movie by pressing CTRL+ENTER. You should see that all three scrollbars work correctly, and they adjust the scale, rotation, and alpha of your mySq movie clip as expected:

How does this work? ActionScript time! Open up the Actions panel (F9) on frame 1 of the actions layer and take look at the code, shown here in full for reference:

```
sqProperties = {scale:0, rotation:0, alpha:0};
scaleScroll.setScrollProperties(50, 0, 100);
scaleScroll.setScrollPosition(50);
rotationScroll.setScrollProperties(180, 0, 360);
rotationScroll.setScrollPosition(0);
alphaScroll.setScrollProperties(50, 0, 100);
alphaScroll.setScrollPosition(50);
_root.onEnterFrame = function() {
    sqProperties.scale = scaleScroll.getScrollPosition();
    sqProperties.rotation = rotationScroll.getScrollPosition();
    sqProperties.alpha = alphaScroll.getScrollPosition();
};
sqProperties.watch("scale", function (id, oldval, newval) {
    if (oldval != newval) {
        mySq._xscale = newval;
```

```
                mySq._yscale = newval;
        }
        return newval;
});
sqProperties.watch("rotation", function (id, oldval, newval) {
        if (oldval != newval) {
                mySq._rotation = newval;
        }
        return newval;
});
sqProperties.watch("alpha", function (id, oldval, newval) {
        if (oldval != newval) {
                mySq._alpha = newval;
        }
        return newval;
});
```

The first thing we do in this code is define an object and its three associated properties: scale, rotation, and alpha:

```
sqProperties = {scale:0, rotation:0, alpha:0};
```

With this line of code we're creating an object called sqProperties that has the properties of scale:0, rotation:0, and alpha:0. Next, we need to programmatically set up our ScrollBars:

```
scaleScroll.setScrollProperties(50, 0, 100);
scaleScroll.setScrollPosition(50);
rotationScroll.setScrollProperties(180, 0, 360);
rotationScroll.setScrollPosition(0);
alphaScroll.setScrollProperties(50, 0, 100);
alphaScroll.setScrollPosition(50);
```

Notice here that we're setting two object properties for each of the three scrollbars – for this we use the setScrollProperties() and the setScrollPosition() methods of the ScrollBar object. The first method has three arguments: pageSize, minPos, and maxPos, which represent the following information:

- pageSize – an integer representing the number of positions displayed in the page view, adjusting this directly affects the size of the *thumb* on the ScrollBar.
- minPos – an integer representing the minimum scrolled position.
- maxPos – an integer representing the maximum scrolled position.

The second method, setScrollPosition(), takes one argument representing the initial position of the thumb on the scrollbar.

Now, when the movie is running the user will interact with the ScrollBars by clicking or click-dragging the thumb bars. In order to determine the ScrollBar positions we need to use the `getScrollPosition()` method. This is a getter/setter property of the ScrollBar. These properties can *only* be accessed via this function and we need to access them regularly using the `onEnterFrame` event to efficiently *watch* for change.

> *This point is worth emphasizing – in order for a watcher to see a change in a specified property, the value must be explicit and require no additional evaluation. Some values might not exist in the form we want them, so they have to be converted via a function containing some getter/setter methods. Because the watcher doesn't actually use this function directly, the change may be masked from it until our ActionScript causes a re-evaluation of the calculated values by reading them explicitly.*

So, the code continues with our getter/setter methods attached to an `onEnterFrame` function:

```
_root.onEnterFrame = function() {
    sqProperties.scale = scaleScroll.getScrollPosition();
    sqProperties.rotation = rotationScroll.getScrollPosition();
    sqProperties.alpha = alphaScroll.getScrollPosition();
};
```

You will no doubt have deduced from these lines of code that we are setting our `onEnterFrame` event directly on the `_root` of the movie, and that we are also setting the `scale`, `rotation`, and `alpha` of the `sqProperties` object according to the scroll position returned by the `getScrollPosition()` method for each ScrollBar.

Now we're ready to begin to add our *watchers* to the script. We will be adding three watchers: the first to handle the scale of our square, the second to handle its rotation, and finally the third will handle the square's alpha setting. Our first watcher looks like this:

```
sqProperties.watch("scale", function (id, oldval, newval) {
    if (oldval != newval) {
        mySq._xscale = newval;
        mySq._yscale = newval;
    }
    return newval;
});
```

The watch() method is attached to the object in this form:

```
myObject.watch("myProperty", function (id, oldval, newval){
        // callback function code goes here...
});
```

where myProperty is a string indicating the name of the object property to watch, and function() is the callback to invoke when the watched property changes (note that the whole function is included as an argument!). The parameters of this callback function are as follows:

- id – the property identifier and will be sent as myProperty
- oldval – the last value that myProperty has the last time it changed
- newval – the new myProperty value that caused the watch event to trigger

Continuing with the code for watcherProperties.fla, we need two more watchers for the rotation and alpha properties. These are defined in a very similar manner to scale, as seen above:

```
sqProperties.watch("rotation", function (id, oldval, newval) {
        if (oldval != newval) {
                mySq._rotation = newval;
        }
        return newval;
});
sqProperties.watch("alpha", function (id, oldval, newval) {
        if (oldval != newval) {
                mySq._alpha = newval;
        }
        return newval;
});
```

Finally, an important point to notice is that the watch() method will trigger the callback function on *any* update of the property being watcher – this will occur even if the value has not changed. This means that if your watched property is being constantly updated (with an onEnterFrame script, for example), it will trigger the watch callback constantly even if it never changes.

Using callback functions, listeners, and watchers brings ActionScript one step closer to the established robust programming languages like Java and C++. These techniques are highly efficient and it's well worth the extra effort and mileage to learn them in the early days, as they will become second nature to you within no time at all.

Objectives

- How events work with functions

- Flash 5 object scripts vs. Flash MX remote callbacks

- Setting up and using functions:

  - Callbacks

  - Listeners

  - Watchers

Objectives

- Loading content to levels and targets

- Integrating content with the browser

- Integrating content via the user's computer:

  - System capabilities

  - Local shared objects

Introduction

Although this chapter's title suggests that we'll be learning specifically how to configure our designs for web browser presentation, in truth it's about much more than that. It's also about using Macromedia Flash MX to reach beyond the confines of the browser, and into the user's computer, allowing us a much greater degree of control over the details of their system, and the ability to do amazing things with that information. Before looking at the browser and user environments, we'll take a more general look at loading content into our movies, taking levels and targets into account.

Loading content

Let's look at loading content into a Flash movie. What we're interested in doing here is breaking down the loading process into its absolute necessities. For example, let's say that we have the main menu of a site that can take us to several different sections within that site. Rather than load everything at once, we can load different sections as the user requests them. Or, perhaps we don't require any user input, but we'd still like to load our movie in segments to evenly distribute loading times: our main movie can begin while we're loading peripheral sections.

There are a few ways of dynamically loading your content, some of which we've already seen in this book (in fact, we looked at loading sounds with the Sound object in **Chapter 5**, and dynamically loading graphics into components in **Chapters 2** and **8**). Accordingly, we'll concentrate on levels and targets in this section.

With Flash we can load external SWF files into a master SWF file *at runtime*. So, once our main movie is loaded, we can slot other movies into place like building blocks. These other movies can be anything, from entire web sites to single-framed graphics; the concepts and techniques are the same. We can use both **levels** and **targets** to load our external SWF files, but they work in slightly different ways. Let's take a closer look.

Levels

When our initial movie loads up, it loads into a location known as _level0. Any code in this movie that refers to _root, is referring to level 0 as well. Flash MX also allows us to load SWF files into other levels, layered on top of level 0. We refer to these as levels 1, 2, 3, and so on, depending upon which level we've used.

The levels are like layered sheets of glass – we see through them into the levels beneath, with _level0 as the base level:

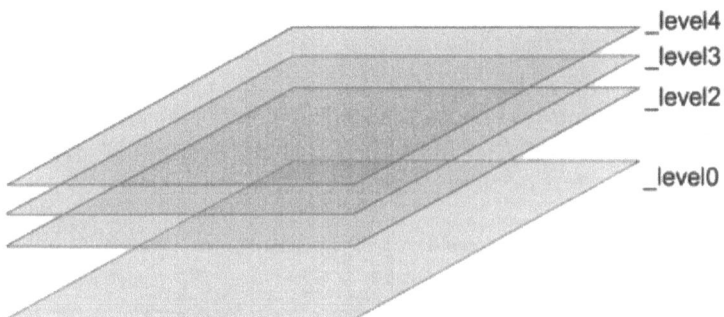

In this image, we see level 0 as the master level – it's our main movie. Then we've loaded three SWF files into level 2, level 3, and level 4 respectively. Notice that we've chosen not to load anything into level 1. This is fine; we can load SWF files into any level we want.

The order of level number determines the layering Flash will use to draw the levels, with level 0 always being on the bottom.

The movies loaded into level 2, level 3, and level 4 will all play independently of each other, as if they are each their own master movie – and this is exactly what we want. When we load a SWF file into a new level we don't want to have to worry about it interfering graphically or programmatically with our master movie. Even if each movie referred to variables in the _root, it still wouldn't affect our master movie. This is because the _root is specific to the level that a movie is on. So while code in the level 0 movie referring to _root would be referring to level 0, code in the _root of the level 2 movie would actually refer to just that: the root of level 2. The only time that there could be a code conflict would be if a loaded SWF specifically referred to a variable as _level0.*variable*, or a function as _level0. Aside from that, these movies might as well be running in different browser windows altogether.

One disadvantage to this approach is that we can't change any properties of our SWF files until they've started to load up. That is to say, we can't, for example, set the _x and _y position of an element within a level, until the content has begun to load into it.

Let's look at levels.fla from the CD. In it, we have a green background layer representing level 0, and there's an actions layer containing the following code:

```
loadMovieNum("movie1.swf", 2);
loadMovieNum("movie2.swf", 3);
loadMovieNum("movie3.swf", 10);
```

We're using the loadMovieNum() method to load three external SWF files into levels 2, 3, and 10 of our movie. loadMovieNum() expects at least two parameters to be passed with it, with another optional: the file name or URL of a SWF or JPEG file, a level number, and (optionally) a string that specifies the HTTP method for sending variables over a network (either GET or POST) – more on this optional parameter in **Chapter 17**. The three external movies that we are loading in here are movie1.swf, movie2.swf, and movie3.swf, which can also be found on the CD – remember to copy all these files into the same directory before you attempt to test this file.

When you test this FLA (CTRL+ENTER) you'll see the following output:

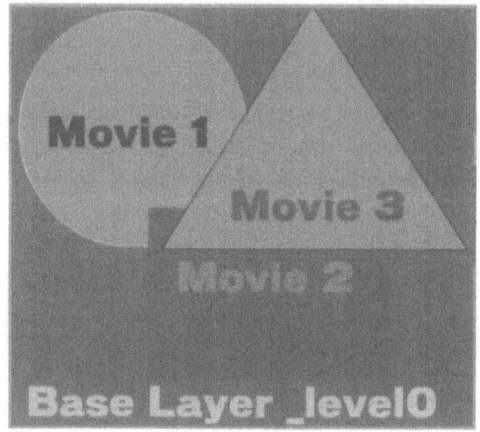

Notice that everything is loaded in, and they're layered in the correct order: movie3.swf is on top of everything because we've forced it to level 10, and all three loaded movies are above the base movie, on level 0. As you can see, the background of loaded movies is transparent; the root movie acts as their background.

> It's important to note that all loaded SWF files will take on the frame rate of the master movie. So, if our main movie is running at 30 frames per second, and we load in an animation that's designed to run at 8 frames per second, that animation will run substantially faster than we intended it to.

Now that we've loaded our external SWF files into this movie, we can use the unloadMovieNum() method any time we've finished with a particular loaded SWF file and want to gain back some performance speed – once a SWF is unloaded, it no longer runs and therefore does not use up any valuable processor resources. We could even attach this method to an event by defining a function. For example:

```
_root.onMouseDown = function() {
     unloadMovieNum(10);
};
```

With this code after our original three lines in `levels.fla`, when the mouse button is clicked in the movie, the `unloadMovieNum()` command is issued. This is responsible for unloading a movie that has been loaded into a level. It takes one parameter: the level number. In this case, we're unloading the movie in level 10, which happens to be the triangle of `movie3.swf`.

Targets

Targets, on the other hand, are movie clips sitting within our master movie. When using targets, we don't really think in terms of level 0, level 1, and so on. These are not levels, they are simply movie clips with different depth values:

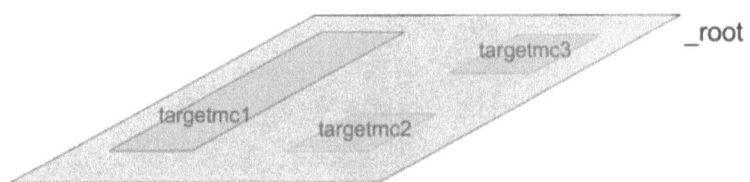

When we use a target-based method for loading external SWF files, we're loading them into actual movie clips in our master movie. Once loaded, we can treat them as we would any movie clip. In fact, we can move the target movie clip into position before we load anything into them, and then any loaded SWF files will align themselves relative to the registration point of the movie clip. Even if our target movie clip has nothing in it to begin with, we can still get it ready to receive the incoming SWF file.

Unfortunately, unlike the levels technique, with targets any ActionScript within the incoming SWF file that refers to code on the `_root` will be referring to the `_root` of our main movie. If we're not careful we can run into code collisions, where our incoming SWF files are overwriting variables unintentionally. However, if we just use targets for simple things like graphics or animations, or if we refer to any variables without using `_root` in our SWF files, then we should be fine.

Load up `targets.fla` – this time we have a movie that just displays the word `_root` on the stage. Of course, we've also got some ActionScript on frame 1 of the actions layer:

```
_root.createEmptyMovieClip("myMC1", 1);
_root.createEmptyMovieClip("myMC2", 2);
_root.createEmptyMovieClip("myMC3", 3);
myMC1._rotation = 30;
myMC2._xscale = 50;
myMC3._alpha = 50;
loadMovie("movie1.swf", myMC1);
loadMovie("movie2.swf", myMC2);
loadMovie("movie3.swf", myMC3);
```

What we're doing here is creating three empty movie clips as our targets in the _root timeline, and giving them instance names of myMC1, myMC2, and myMC3, on depth layers 1, 2, and 3 respectively. Next, we're changing some properties of these movie clips: namely, rotating myMC1 by 30 degrees, scaling the horizontal size of myMC2 by 50%, and setting the alpha transparency of myMC3 to 50%. Notice how we're able to perform these transformations *before* our movies are actually loaded in. For more details on using the createEmptyMovieClip() method, and changing the properties of movie clips via ActionScript, see **Chapter 1**.

Finally, we use the loadMovie() command this time to load in our three SWF files (the same ones that we used in the previous example for this simple demonstration). Like the loadMovieNum() command, loadMovie() takes three parameters: the SWF/JPEG file name or URL, the target movie clip, and the optional GET or POST variables. When we run this movie, we see this:

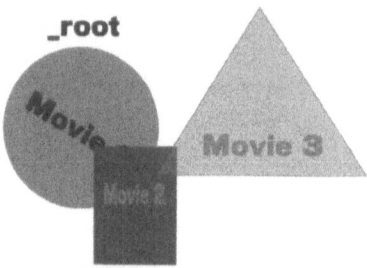

Notice that, as well as their properties being changed as specified, the SWFs are again stacked in order of their target movie clip's depth. However, rather than each imported SWF being isolated and relatively independent, like in the case of level loading, these clips are now an integrated part of our main movie.

With this technique we can still remove the contents we loaded with a click of a mouse button – this time by using the unloadMovie() method, like this:

```
_root.onMouseDown = function() {
    unloadMovie(myMC2);
};
```

If you add this code to targets.fla and test the movie, you can click the mouse button to unload the content that was loaded into myMC2 (the square of movie2.swf). Like unloadMovieNum(), unloadMovie() takes just one parameter: the name of the movie clip or target that contains the loaded movie you wish to unload.

> *Note that it's not possible to unload a movie that was actually contained within a movie clip in our master movie to start with –* unloadMovie() *only works on loaded movies.*

For further discussion and more examples of depth in Flash movies, see **Chapter 1**.

Integrating content with the browser environment

In Flash MX we have the Stage and Capabilities objects with which we're able to determine the size and state of the user's browser. Let's look at the Stage object in more detail; we'll return to the Capabilities object later in this chapter.

The stage

In the context of the Flash authoring environment, the stage is usually considered to represent the confines of our movie, and anything beyond the edge of the stage is considered off-screen. Although this is indeed true to a certain extent – we should consider the stage to be a fixed area within which we build our movies, when we use the onResize event of the Stage object with a non-scaling movie, we can genuinely support the creation of dynamically sizing movies where objects move around and reposition themselves relative to the screen edge.

This means we could take a movie with this general shape:

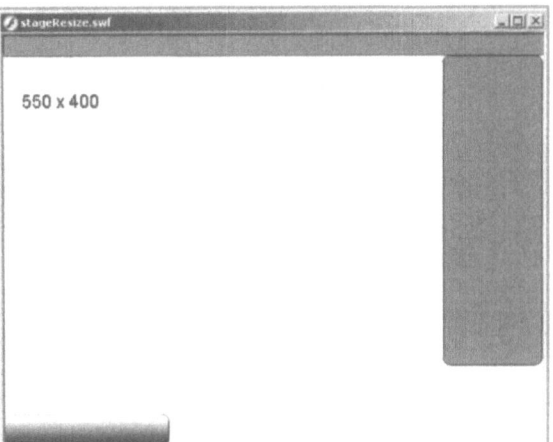

And resize it automatically so that it looks like this:

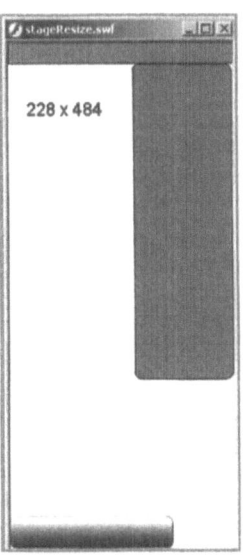

Notice that our SWF window has resized, but the items within it have not. Also, the tall box remains at the right edge, and the gradient bar remains at the bottom left of the screen. Only one item has been scaled, and that's the bar at the top – it scales to fit the width of the stage. The numbers displayed in the images above correspond to the stage dimensions. We can see that in the first image, the movie defaulted to 550 x 400, which is the stage size as specified in the Macromedia Flash MX design environment. One thing that must be noted here is that we cannot actually *change* the size of the stage with ActionScript – we can only *determine* the size of the stage after the user has resized it.

Take a look at `stageResize.fla` from the CD:

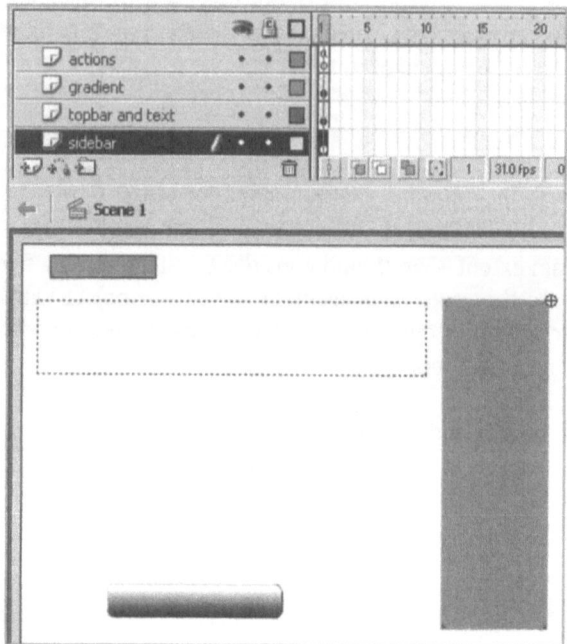

You can see we have an actions layer, and that various objects are sitting on the stage in no particular position. However, when we run this movie, we see something slightly different, as shown previously. The objects have stuck themselves to the walls – they've *docked* with the edges of the movie. We're using the `Stage` properties and `onResize` event to accomplish this. Let's take a look at the code itself. It's attached to frame 1 of the actions layer:

```
Stage.scaleMode = "noScale";
Stage.align = "TL";
myListener = new Object();
myListener.onResize = function() {
    _root.sizeDisp.text = Stage.width+" x "+Stage.height;
    topBar._x = 0;
    topBar._y = 0;
    topBar._xscale = Stage.width;
    toolbar._y = Stage.height;
    toolbar._x = 0;
    sideBar._x = Stage.width;
    sideBar._y = 21;
};
myListener.onResize();
Stage.addListener(myListener);
```

The first thing we do is set the scaleMode of the Stage to noScale. The scaleMode is used to tell Flash how to resize the stage when the user resizes the window. There are three other possible events we could use here: exactFit, showAll, and noBorder. However, for our sample, we're really only concerned with noScale. The other settings will stretch the contents of the window, thereby overriding our attempts to keep things uniform. In fact, the onResize event that we'll get to in a moment can **only** be triggered if scaleMode is set to noScale.

> *A movie that stretches everything might not even use the onResize event, because Flash would still see everything as being 550 x 400 (or whatever the original size was). It may be appear squashed on screen, but in Flash the dimensions would still be 550 x 400. So in this example we must use noScale.*

Next, with the line:

```
Stage.align = "TL";
```

We're setting the align property of the Stage object. This tells Macromedia Flash how to align the stage in its window. When the stage is the same size as the window, this property doesn't have any apparent effect. However, once we stretch or shrink the window, the align property determines what happens to the stage. When we set the property to TL, we're telling Flash to keep the stage in the top left hand corner of the window. This is the setting we need to position our objects properly, relative to the resized stage. The possible values of the Stage.align property are described in the following table:

align value	Position
T	Top (center)
B	Bottom (center)
L	Left (center)
R	Right (center)
TL	Top left
TR	Top right
BL	Bottom left
BR	Bottom right

Let's look at it this graphically:

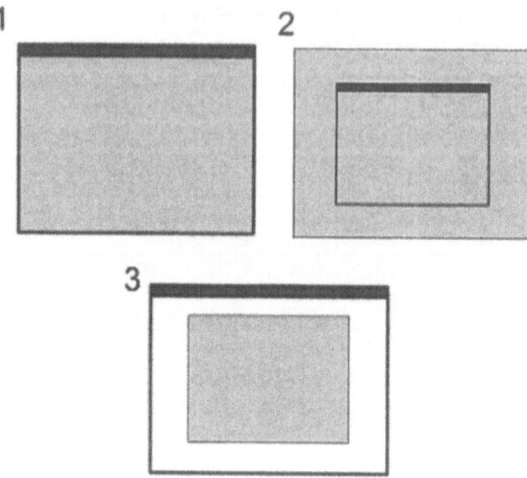

The gray area in each image is the stage, as defined in Flash MX. Here we're seeing the effects of the default align property, centered:

- In image 1, the window is not resized so the stage area fills the entire window.

- In image 2, the window has been shrunk and, since Stage.align is centered by default, the stage centers itself around the window. The problem with this is that the relative position of 0, 0 on the stage has moved off screen. So when we attempt to place an object at 0, 0 on the stage now, it will be out of shot.

- In image 3, the window is resized so it's larger than the default stage. Here, the stage centers itself within the window. Again, the problem is that the coordinate 0, 0 is now somewhere in the interior of the window, and not in the upper-left corner.

When we set Stage.align to TL, the effects are substantially different:

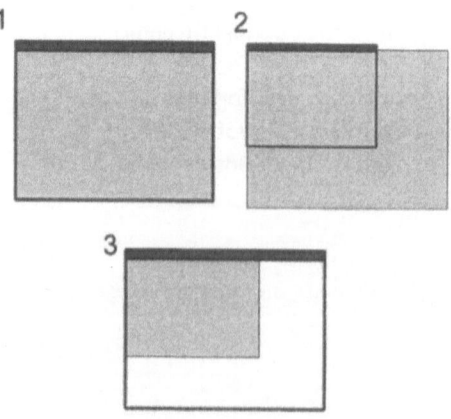

- In image 1, the window has not been resized, so the stage (the gray area) is still exactly the same size as the window.

- In image 2, the window has been shrunk, but the stage remains firmly in the top left corner of the window. Coordinate (0, 0) is still in the same place.

- In image 3, the window has been stretched so that it's larger than the stage, but it still remains aligned to the upper left-hand corner. With this align mode we can accurately move and position objects around the screen, relative to the edges.

Back to the code in stageResize.fla – next, we're creating a new Listener object, and creating within it a function called onResize. The function looks like this:

```
myListener = new Object();
myListener..onResize = function() {
    _root.sizeDisp.text = Stage.width+" x "+Stage.height;
    topBar._x = 0;
    topBar._y = 0;
    topBar._xscale = Stage.width;
    toolbar._y = Stage.height;
    toolbar._x = 0;
    sideBar._x = Stage.width;
    sideBar._y = 21;
};
```

First, in the sizeDisp text field, we're displaying the dimensions of the stage using Stage.width and Stage.height, with an x between them. Stage.width and Stage.height are both a pixel value, and they correspond to the actual on-screen dimensions of the window.

The topBar is a movie clip that is 100 x 20 in size, and its registration point is in its upper left corner. So, when we set its position to (0, 0) it will be placed in the upper left corner of the stage. Next, we set its _xscale to be the Stage.width. Since its original size was 100 pixels, setting the _xscale percentage will correspond exactly to an absolute width as well: – 200 percent is 200 pixels, 342 percent is 342 pixels, and so on. Then, by setting the position of the toolbar to 0 in _x and Stage.height in _y, it will always be docked to the lower left corner of the screen.

Finally, we come to the sideBar, which is a movie clip. Setting its _x to Stage.width forces it to be flush with the right edge of the screen. Setting its _y position to 21 will ensure that it's 21 pixels from the top, just below the topBar (which is 20 pixels in height).

The last two lines of code are as follows:

```
myListener.onResize();
Stage.addListener(myListener);
```

The first line is forcing the onResize function to execute just once, so that everything begins in the correct position. Then, we're using the addListener() method of the Stage object to make the stage know that it's supposed to call our onResize function whenever the user resizes the stage.

The browser

We can also get this to work perfectly in a browser by just changing a few HTML settings in the HTML tab of the Flash File >Publish Settings... options window:

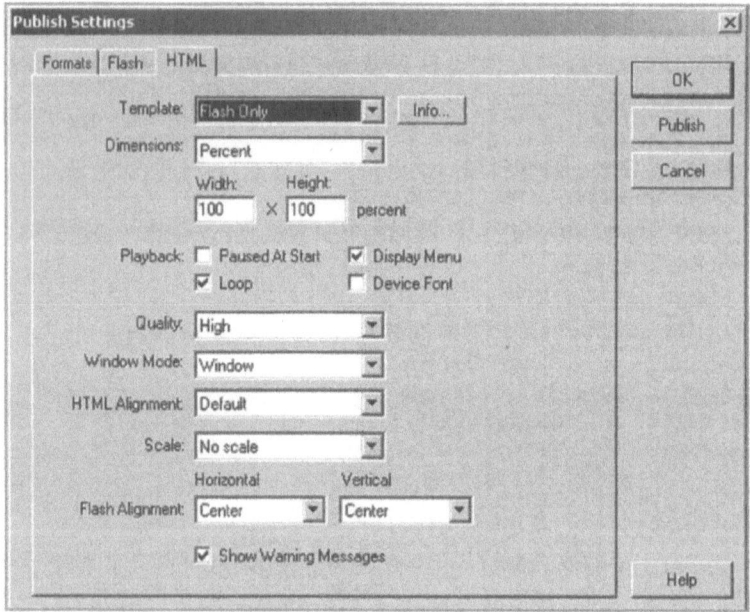

We need to make sure that the Dimensions option is set to Percent, and that the Width and the Height are both 100. This will ensure that our movie fills out the browser window. Finally, hit Publish to create the HTML file. Once created, open up stageResize.html in a browser window:

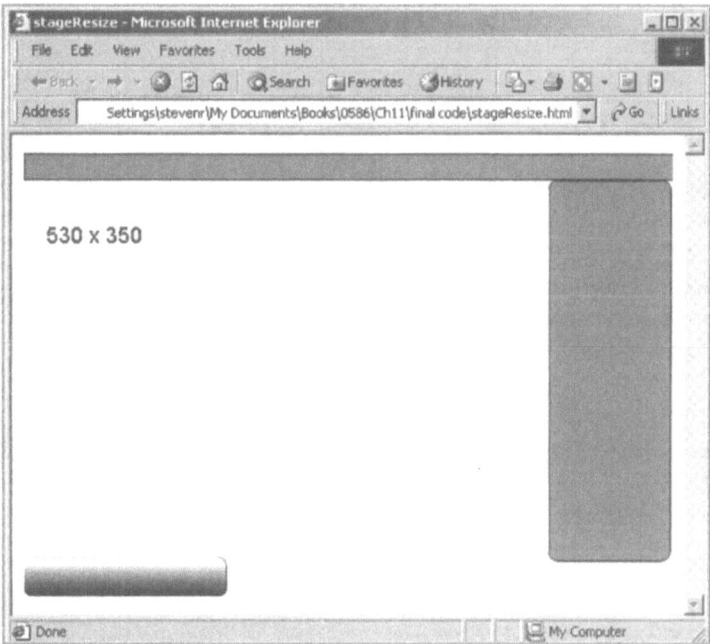

Notice that the Flash movie has resized to fill out the browser window. Indeed, if we resize the browser, the objects will move around the screen as we have told them to with the onResize function.

You may notice that there's a small border around the edge of our movie in the browser window. To make the movie completely fill to the edge of the browser, we need to add something to the HTML code. Open up the stageResize.html file in your favorite text editor, and find the following element:

```
<PARAM NAME=bgcolor VALUE=#FFFFFF>
```

Add the following attributes to specify the margin size as 0, before the closing >:

```
<BODY bgcolor="#FFFFFF" leftmargin="0" topmargin="0" marginwidth="0"
➥marginheight="0">
```

This will cause the Flash movie to stretch to the absolute frame of the browser window (in almost all new browsers, anyway).

Integrating content with the user's computer

Macromedia Flash MX has the ability to determine a large amount of information about the user's computer, browser, player, and so on. This ability resides in the Capabilities object. Flash MX also has the ability to respond to this information using what is known as a **local shared object**. Let's take a look at these objects in turn to find out what benefits they offer to our web interfaces.

System capabilities

As a starting point, take a look at the properties of the `Capabilities` object in the dictionary section of the Actions panel (F9):

Note that we must access all the properties of the `Capabilities` object through the `System.capabilities` object. Let's see this object in action – open up `systemCapabilities.fla` from the CD. Here we have a text field on the stage called `sysinfo` with vertical and horizontal ScrollBars around it. These are set to scroll automatically through the contents of the text field. What really matters here is the code attached to frame 1 of the actions layer:

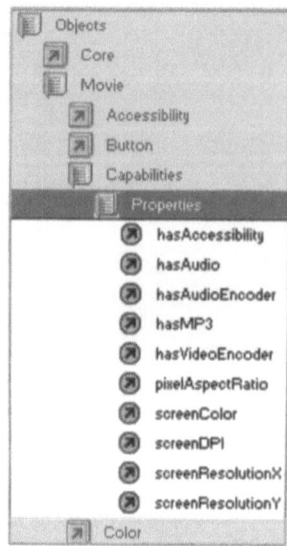

```
t = System.capabilities;
for (i in t) {
        _root.sysinfo.text += i+" == "+t[i]+newline;
}
```

We're simply stepping through each variable in the `System.capabilities` object, adding its name and value to the text field, separated by `==`. Test the FLA to see your system spec:

System Info

```
language == en
os == Windows 2000
input == point
manufacturer == Macromedia Windows
serverString == A=t&MP3=t&AE=t&VE=t&ACC=f&DEB=t&V=WIN%206%2C0%2C21%2
isDebugger == true
version == WIN 6,0,21,0
hasAudio == true
hasMP3 == true
hasAudioEncoder == true
hasVideoEncoder == true
screenResolutionX == 1024
```

In this list we're given, amongst other things, the user's language settings, their operating system, the version of Flash they're using, their screen resolution and dimensions, and so on. If we wanted to access a particular variable, we'd need to use the full path, like `System.capabilities.os` or `System.capabilities.screenResolutionX`, for example.

Putting all these together, we could load content based on a particular user's language, or if we're offering files for download, we could send them to the correct download file based on their operating system. How we choose to use these variables is really up to the project and the requirements.

The shared object

A really cool feature of Flash MX is the local shared object. With the shared object, we can save arbitrary variables and data to the user's hard drive (with permission, of course), and recall them at a later stage. In simple terms, shared objects are very much like cookies – you can store a user's profile so that they don't have to log into a restricted area every time, or you can present a custom page based on the client's previous buying habits for an e-commerce site. If we want to emulate what the browser and HTML/JavaScript can do, we can simply mimic the functionality of cookies, but because this is Flash we can go even further with them.

You could use shared objects for saving any of the following:

- Data to represent artwork created by the user within a Flash paint application created with the drawing API.

- The data required to re-create a sound mix created by an online Flash music mixing desk.

- User files for a desktop-based calendar/organizer.

- An online Flash form that remembers previous responses the user made in the same domain and auto-completes the user's name, address, e-mail address, and so on.

- Game data from an online Flash-based adventure game.

Take a look at `sharedObjects.fla`. Here we've got a very basic word processor. It's almost a text file editor really, and it allows us to save the content of our story, and then load it up later. Test it to see it in action – add some text to your text field:

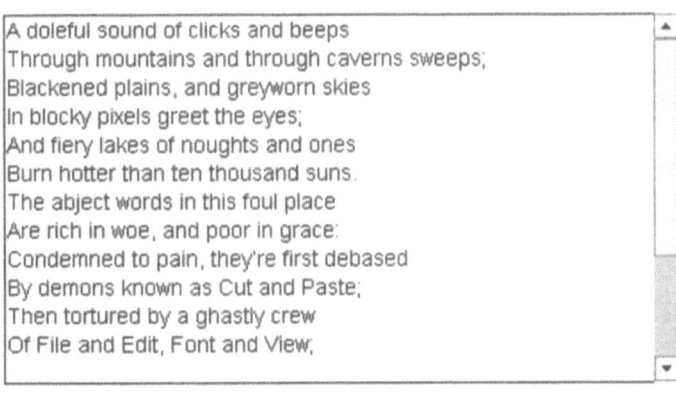

It's not particularly impressive to look at within a still screenshot, but if we hit Save we should then be presented with the Local Storage permission window:

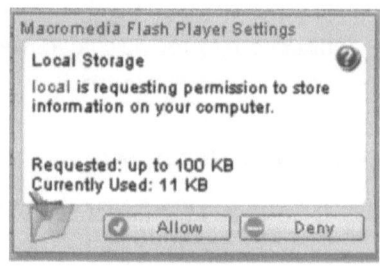

If we accept the local storage setting, we can then highlight and delete all the text from the text field, and simply hit Load to load it back in. We can even close down the SWF file completely, reload it, and hit Load again and our story will be brought back up exactly as we left it.

Now let's learn how we did this. In the FLA file, we have one text field and two push buttons. The Save button is set to trigger the saveStory function and the Load button is set to trigger the loadStory function. The code is attached to frame 1 of the actions layer:

```
saveStory = function () {
    var mySO = SharedObject.getLocal("myStoryFile");
    mySO.data.storyText = myStory.text;
    mySO.flush();
};
loadStory = function () {
    var mySO = SharedObject.getLocal("myStoryFile");
    myStory.text = mySO.data.storyText;
};
```

There's not a great deal to it is there? When the story is saved, saveStory is called:

```
saveStory = function () {
    var mySO = SharedObject.getLocal("myStoryFile");
    mySO.data.storyText = myStory.text;
    mySO.flush();
};
```

Here we create a new instance of the SharedObject called mySO, and use the getLocal constructor to open up, or create the file myStoryFile.sol. The file is created on the user's hard drive. We don't actually have to say .sol in the code, as that is assumed by Flash.

Next, we place the story in the data object of the shared object. In order to save the data to the disk, we must place anything we want saved in the data object, like so:

```
mySO.data.myVAR = thedata;
```

But *not* like this:

```
mySO.myVAR = thedata;
```

If we don't place the variables within the `data` object they will not be saved. We're storing the contents of the text field in a variable called `storyText` within `mySO.data`. Finally, we call the `flush()` method of the shared object, which saves the data to the disk at that point.

The next function is `loadStory`:

```
loadStory = function () {
      var mySO = SharedObject.getLocal("myStoryFile");
      myStory.text = mySO.data.storyText;
};
```

In this function we're opening the `myStoryFile` file again, but this time we're filling in the text field with the value of `mySO.data.storyText`, which will be the same text that was saved when we clicked Save.

The actual shared object file is located, by default, inside the user's documents and settings folder, in another folder that has the same name as the site URL that saved it. We can, however, specify a different location. If we change our code to this:

```
var mySO = SharedObject.getLocal("myStoryFile", "/");
```

Then we're specifying that Flash should store the file in the root shared object location, which on my Windows PC happens to be:

C:>Documents and Settings>Glen Rhodes>Application Data>Macromedia>Flash Player>localhost

This means that the file `myStoryFile.sol` will reside at this location. As data, we can save arrays, objects, strings, and numbers. We cannot, however, save movie clips and images locally.

12 Dynamic Text

Objectives

- Manipulating strings

- Creating and using text fields

- Properties and methods of the TextField and TextFormat objects

Introduction

The first step when working with dynamic text is to understand the base and native object of the text itself: the humble **String** object. Only then can we really get to grips with using text fields and text formatting. The String object can essentially be thought of as a type of variable, that holds text and numbers. Strings can be virtually any length and they're used to store textual information such as names, narrative, and just about anything else you care to think of.

When a string is filled with numbers, it isn't thought of by Flash as a 'number', but rather a character representation of those numbers. So, if we had the following two string variables:

```
varA = "6";
varB = "4";
```

...and then set a third variable called varC, like this:

```
varC = varA + varB;
```

In this case, varC will not equal 10. It will be 64, which is the strings "6" and "4" combined together. For varC to be 10, varA and varB need to be numbers instead of strings. In other words, you would define varA and varB like this:

```
varA = 6;
varB = 4;
```

Notice that the only difference between the two code examples here is that the strings are inside quotation marks "", while the numbers are not.

String objects versus string literals

It's also important to understand that a string literal is not the same as a String object. When a String object is created, it exists as an object for the rest of the movie or until it is destroyed. This String object has many built-in methods associated with it such as slice(), split(), and more, which can be used to perform manipulations and actions on the contents of the String object. For instance, take a look at its entries in the dictionary pane on the left hand side of the Actions panel:

When a string literal is created, it is simply a variable of type `string`. When we want to perform any of the String object's methods on it, we first need to convert it to a temporary String object, manipulate it, and then convert it back into a string literal.

String literal

There are two ways of creating a new string literal – the first of which we've just seen:

```
myString = "my string value";
```

or:

```
myString = String("my string value");
```

The second method is known as the string conversion function and can be used on any type of variable, for example:

```
theNum = 10;
theString = String(theNum) + "1";
```

Here we've created a number variable, `theNum`, with the value 10. We then use the string conversion function to turn it into a string of `"10"`, and then add 1 to it. Our final result? `theString` will be equal to `"101"`.

String object

The simplest way of creating a new `String` object is to use this standard constructor technique:

```
myString = new String();
```

Then, we can subsequently set the value of the string with:

```
myString = "Test String";
```

Or, we can set the value of the string at construction time like this:

```
myString = new String("My initial value");
```

By doing this we have created a `String` object that has several methods that can be used to perform complex string searching and manipulation operations. We'll look at these in detail in the next section.

Manipulating strings

We'll look at manipulating strings in detail in the next few subsections.

Concatenating strings

We can add strings together (also known as concatenating) simply by using the + character:

```
myString = "Hello my name is ";
myString2 = "Superman";
concatStrings = myString + myString2;
```

The result of these three lines is that concatStrings will be set to "Hello my name is Superman". We can also use the addition assignment operator += to join strings together:

```
myString = "Once upon a time there was a";
myString += " Fish";
```

Here, myString will be set to "Once upon a time there was a Fish". We can use this method to make a string continually increase in length, adding more and more information to create, for example, a log of system messages or errors.

Converting strings to numbers

The occasion may arise where we need to convert a string into a number so that we can perform mathematical calculations on it. For example, if we have a text field, that the user has typed a number into, we cannot perform any math with that number because it is actually a string. We must use the parseInt(), parseFloat(), or Number() conversion functions.

parseInt()

Take a look at these two lines of code:

```
myString = "999";
theNum = parseInt(myString);
```

Now, the variable theNum is set to 999, rather than "999". Any math operations such as addition, subtraction, multiplication etc., can be correctly performed on this number. The parseInt() function will ignore any trailing non-numeric characters. So this:

```
myString = "999joe";
theNum = parseInt(myString);
```

...will still be converted successfully to 999. If there is no number present in the string, Flash will return the value NaN, meaning "Not a Number".

The `parseInt()` function can also be used in this form:

```
parseInt(expression, radix)
```

This time the function accepts another additional parameter, called the `radix`. This is a number that tells Flash how many values of digits are used to make up that number. In standard **decimal** numbers the radix is `10`, because there are 10 numbers that a digit can be comprised of (0, 1, 2, 3, 4, 5, 6, 7, 8, and 9).

If we specify a radix of `2`, then the only two valid digit values are 0 and 1 (**binary numbers**). If we specify a radix of `8`, then only the numbers from 0 through 7 are valid. This is an **octal** representation of a number. If we specify `16`, then the only valid characters are 0-9 and then A-F, which is standard **hexadecimal** representation (see **Chapter 6** for more discussion of decimal versus hexadecimal numbering).

Let's look at using different values of `radix` in practice:

```
theNum = parseInt("101101", 2);
```

Here, `theNum` is 45, which is the decimal equivalent of binary `101101`. Next:

```
theNum = parseInt("7724", 8);
```

`theNum` is 4052, the decimal equivalent of octal `7724`. And now for hexadecimal:

```
theNum = parseInt("33FF", 16);
```

In this case, `theNum` is 13311, which is the decimal equivalent of hexadecimal `33FF`.

> *Here's a neat one:* `theNum = parseInt("GLEN", 36);`
> *In this case* `theNum` *is 774239, which is the decimal equivalent of the name "GLEN", where any digit is valid from 0 through to Z. Radix values above 36 are not valid because we would run out of characters to use, and we would need to start including symbols such as -, =, *, and so on. However, these are reserved operators used in mathematical calculations.*

parseFloat()

The `parseFloat()` function is a little bit easier to understand than `parseInt()`. Here, all we do is find any floating point (decimal) numbers within a string, and convert them to numbers. For example:

```
theNum = parseFloat("3.5");
```

...will set theNum to 3.5. Or, we can use scientific notation to say:

```
theNum = parseFloat("3.5e6");
```

This means that theNum will be 3500000. e6 simply means "multiplied by 1 followed by 6 zeros", or 1000000 (in other words, 3.5 multiplied by 1000000 is 3500000).

Number()

This is the simplest of all the string conversion functions, for example:

```
theNum = Number("3.5");
```

This simply parses the expression as a decimal number. Note that if the expression is a Boolean value, the return value is 1 if the expression is true and 0 if it is false.

escape() and unescape()

These two functions are used to convert the contents of a string both to and from a standard URL-encoded string that can be safely transmitted over a network connection. Let's say we had a string with the following contents:

```
myString = "I am equal to 10 people &not=to 20 people";
```

This is a string, which may have made perfect sense when entered by a user, but remember we need to pay attention to how data can be transmitted between Flash and the server. Typically, we use a method called ampersand-delimited name/value pairs. So, the data sent to and from the server is in a long string of text, like this:

```
Name=Joe&Age=32&City=New York
```

Notice that the variable names here are Name, Age, and City. The values are Joe, 32, and New York. These are name/value pairs, and each name/value pair is separated (delimited) by the ampersand character &. Now, what would happen if we were to additionally transmit our example string, myString, as defined above? Our transmission now looks like this:

```
Name=Joe&Age=32&City=New York&myString=I am equal to 10 people
➥ &not=to 20 people
```

Can you see the problem? myString contains the & character and it basically appears as if we're going to create a new variable called not, which will be equal to to 20 people – this is clearly an error. In fact, myString would be transmitted only as I am equal to 10 people, while not would be equal to to 20 people. We need a way to disguise special characters such as & and = when we use them within strings, so that they're not actually transmitted like this, which is where escape() comes into play:

```
myString = "I am equal to 10 people &not=to 20 people";
```

```
mySendString = escape(myString);
```

Now we can safely send `mySendString` because it is now equal to:

```
I%20am%20equal%20to%2010%20people%20%26not%3Dto%2020%20people
```

> Another important point to note here is that it's illegal for URLs to contain spaces. While some browsers, such as Internet Explorer, let you get away with this, others like Netscape (at least in version 4) would throw up an error.

All blank spaces, = signs, and & characters are replaced with a % followed by the ASCII character code that defines each character. Once the string arrives on the other side we can `unescape()` it, converting it back into its original form like this:

```
// Assume that myEncodedString =
// "I%20am%20equal%20to%2010%20people%20%26not%3Dto%2020%20people"
myString = unescape(myEncodedString);
```

So, `myString` is now equal to `"I am equal to 10 people &not=to 20 people"`, and we've successfully transmitted all characters. It's important to `escape()` and `unescape()` strings before they're sent. However, we should always make sure that we're not escaping previously escaped strings, and not unescaping strings that have not been escaped in the first place.

Text fields

As well as displaying normal text typed directly on to the stage, text fields can be used for containing strings of dynamic text on screen, and also as input fields for users to type their own text into. We create the basic text field by clicking on the Text tool in the Tools panel, and then drawing a text field on the stage:

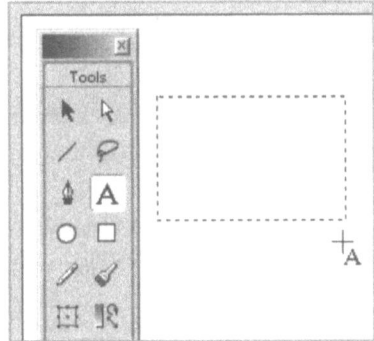

Once the text field is drawn on the stage, we need to change its settings in order to make it a useable TextField object on screen. With the text field selected, take look at the Property inspector:

In the Text type drop-down menu we can designate the text field as Static Text, Dynamic Text, or Input Text. Static text is non-selectable and is rendered by Flash as a graphic. We can change the contents of a dynamic text field at runtime in order to make the text change in response to events, server data, and so on. Finally, as selected in the image above, the input text field allows the user or the program to edit the text field's contents.

Below the Text type drop-down menu is the Instance Name box. An instance name is required to access the contents of the text field and in this example I've given the field the instance name myTextField.

At the right of the Property inspector are the standard text formatting controls including font, font size, text color, bold, italic, and various alignment options. Below this section are the various options used for controlling dynamic and input text fields. Take a look at the options available in the Line Type drop-down menu:

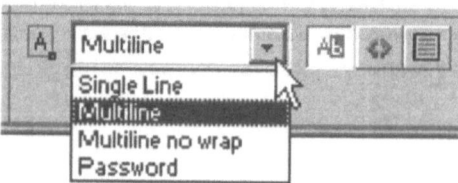

In Single Line mode, text will continue to scroll off to the left or right, even if it extends beyond the actual width of the text field. In Multiline mode, the text will fill within the edges of the text field and whole words are wrapped onto the following line, like this:

> This is an example of multiline text. In this example, whole words are wrapped around to the next line. No words are chopped in half.

In Multiline no wrap mode, the text will scroll to the right until it encounters a newline character, then it moves on to a new line. Take, for example, the following code:

```
myTextField.text = "Line 1 this is text from the first line";
myTextField.text += newline;
```

```
myTextField.text += "Line 2 this is text from the second line";
```

This formats the text like so:

Input text also has another option, namely Password. With this mode selected, all text typed into the text field is replaced with a password character, which by default is the asterisk symbol,*.

The next option, available to both dynamic and static text fields, is the Selectable option. With this selected, the user has the ability to highlight the text on screen, copy it to their clipboard, and then paste it into a third-party program:.

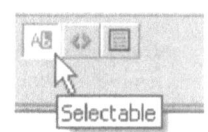

Next to this is the Render text as HTML button. With this switched on, any text in the field can include standard HTML tags (although the number of tags available is limited). This is necessary in order for text to be rendered correctly as HTML when using the `htmlText` property, and we'll be using this property to add text later in the chapter.

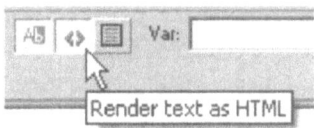

To the right of this, is the Show Border Around Text option, which , surprise surprise, tells Flash to render a box around the text field, to clearly define the dimensions of the text field. By default, the border is black and the background is white. This can be changed using the `borderColor` and `backgroundColor` properties of the TextField object, or can be completely turned on or off with the `border` property (more details below):

Finally, the box to the right is the Var entry field. We can enter the name of a variable with which this text field should be associated. However, this is actually a deprecated technique in Flash MX, as we now refer to text fields via their *instance* name rather than a variable name.

When we set our text field as an input text field, another option becomes visible in the lower right corner of the Property inspector: the Maximum Characters setting. Whatever number we specify here is the maximum number of characters that the user can type in our text field. This enables us to place useful limits such as a 5-digit zip code or an 8-letter password.

Working with numbers in text fields

Let's see how we can take the contents of two text fields, convert them to numbers, add them together, and then output the result in a new text field. Open up addNumbers.fla to see this in action. In this file there are three text fields. The top two fields are input text fields and have been given the instance names topNumber and bottomNumber. The lower text field has been named total, and is a dynamic text field.

Also present on the stage is a button named plusButton. This movie is simple; type a number into the top field, another number in the bottom field, and then click the plus button which adds them together numerically (not as strings). However, since text fields are strings, we must first convert the contents to numbers using either the Number(), parseInt, or parseFloat function. Let's look at the code in frame 1:

```
plusButton.onRelease = function() {
    var num1 = Number(topNumber.text);
    var num2 = Number(bottomNumber.text);
    total.text = num1+num2;
};
```

The only code in this movie is the code that's executed when the button is released. We create two variables, num1 and num2, which are taken from the text properties of the topNumber and bottomNumber text fields. Then, the two variables are added together and placed in total.text.

Test this movie (CTRL+ENTER), type 9 into the top field and 22 into the bottom field (for example), and then press the plus button:

We've successfully added the two numbers together, numerically.

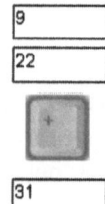

Properties and methods of the TextField object

Like movie clips, the TextField object has several methods and properties associated with it. Text fields have all the standard properties of the MovieClip object, properties such as _x, _y, _xscale, _yscale, _alpha etc. and so on, as well as their own text field-specific properties. There are a number of them, so, for quick reference, let's look at them in a detailed table:

TextField	PropertyType	Default Value	Description
autoSize	String	none	Determines how the text field will resize as its content changes. If the value is none, then the text field is a fixed square; if it's set to left or true, then the text field will expand to the right (the left size will be a fixed position). If the value is set to right, then the text field will expand to the left. If the value is set to center, then the text field will expand evenly to both the left and right..
background	Boolean	true	A true or false value, which determines whether or not the text field will display a background.
background Color	Color	0xFFFFFF (white)	The color of the background of the text field, if it is displayed.
border	Boolean	true	A true or false value, which determines whether or not the text field will display a border.
borderColor	Color	0x000000 (black)	The color of the border around the text field, if it is displayed.
bottomScroll	Number	1	The bottom-most line of text that is visible in the text field. Since the contents of a text field can be longer than the text field itself, this value tells us which line is at the *bottom* and *visible*. This property is read-only.
embedFonts	Boolean	false	A true or false value, this specifies whether or not the text in the field will be rendered as embedded font outlines, or as system fonts.
hscroll	Number	0	As the contents of a non-wrapping multiline text field can scroll horizontally, this specifies the current horizontal scrolling position of a text field.
html	Boolean	false	A true or false value, which indicatinges whether or not this text field uses HTML text or regular text. This is identical to the HTML button from in the text field
htmlText	String	false	A string of text used by the text field to display HTML text, rather than regular text. To update the HTML text of a text field, we do something like this: myTextField.htmlText = ➡Foobar"; This will display **Foo**bar in the text field, where the word Foo is in bold. This will only work if the html property is set to true

.length	Number	0	Indicates the current length of the contents of the text field. This property is read-only.
maxChars	Number	null	The maximum number of characters that can be contained within the text field. If the value is null, then there is no limit. This only affects characters entered by the user, whereas characters added with script can exceed maxChars.
maxhscroll	Number	0	This is read-only, and it indicates the maximum value of the hscroll property.
maxscroll	Number	1	This is a read-only property and it indicates the number of rows in the text field. This doesn't necessarily mean that's how many are visible, but if a 500 line essay was typed into a small text field, then maxscroll would be 500, meaning that this is the maximum amount we can scroll down to. We can use this to indicate when we've scrolled down to the bottom of a text field.
multiline	Boolean	false	A true or false value , which indicatinges whether or not a text field is a multiline or single line text field.
password	Boolean	false	Either true or false, this indicates whether or not an input field hides its input with asterisks or displays the characters as they are entered.
restrict	String	null	Used with an input text field, this specifies the characters that can be inputted. For example: myText.restrict = "HLOE"; This means that users can only enter the characters H, L, O, and E, so they could type HELLO. myText.restrict = "0-9 A-Z"; This restricts input to numbers, spaces, and upper case letters from A through Z. To restrict certain characters from input, pre clude them with a ^ symbol. For example: myText.restrict = "^a-z"; means that no lower case letters are allowed.
scroll	Number	1	Indicates the current vertical scroll position in the text field's contents.
selectable	Boolean	true	A true or false value that indicates whether or not a text field is selectable. When a text field is selectable, users can highlight sections of text, and copy it to their clipboard.

text	String		A string of text used by the text field to display regular text. Similar to htmlText, except that it does not accept any HTML codes. This is the default property used to fill the contents of a text field.
textColor	Color		Indicates the color of the font in the text field.
textHeight	Number	0	Indicates the height of the text.
textWidth	Number	0	Indicates the width of the text.
type	String	dynamic	The value of type is either dynamic or input, and determines how the text field behaves (as a dynamic text field or an input text field).
wordWrap	Boolean	false	Either true or false, this indicates whether or not the text will wrap or continue to flow horizontally past the edge of the text field.

The text field also has a few methods, most of which apply to the TextFormat object (which we'll get to shortly). Let's take a look at a couple of these methods right now.

getDepth()

There isn't too much to say about this relatively obvious method. It returns the current depth of the text field. Since text fields are treated like movie clips, they exist on a depth level (as do movie clips):

```
myDepth = myTextField.getDepth();
```

replaceSel()

With the replaceSel() method, we can tell Flash to replace all currently selected text with any text that we choose. Take a look at replaceSelection.fla from the CD. In this movie, there is a dynamic text field and two buttons. The text field is initially filled with a short passage of text and, when we roll over the buttons, any selected text is replaced with the word indicated next to the button. Here's a screenshot of the movie before any interaction has taken place:

This is an example of some text being replaced upon command. We went to the zoo and we saw a Monkey and a Lion.

Whale

Frog

Highlight the word Monkey, and then roll over the Whale button with your mouse. Also highlight Lion and roll over the Frog button (this has to be the strangest sentence I've ever written!):

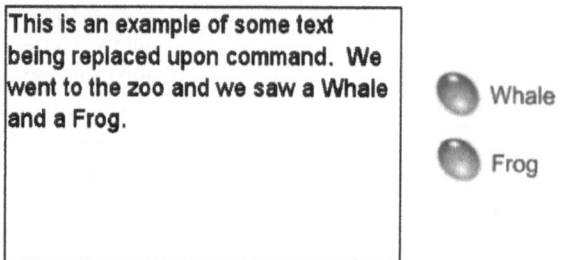

We've altered the text in the text field without actually typing anything (in fact, it's a dynamic text field so it's impossible to actually type anything in anyway). The code to accomplish this is simple:

```
myTextField.text = "This is an example of some text being replaced upon
➥command.  We went to the zoo and we saw a Monkey and a Lion.";
Whale.onRollOver = function() {
    myTextField.replaceSel("Whale");
};
Frog.onRollOver = function() {
    myTextField.replaceSel("Frog");
};
```

We need to use the onRollOver event for the buttons because when a button is pressed, the text field loses focus. This would mean that the selection would be lost and replaceSel would then have no text to act upon.

Dynamically creating text fields

It's possible for us to completely generate, position, and populate text fields in our movies without ever drawing any on the stage in the design environment. To do this, we use the createTextField() method of the MovieClip object like this:

```
myMovieClip.createTextField(InstanceName, depth, x, y, width, height);
```

This method takes the following parameters:

- instanceName – instance name of the newly created text field
- depth – depth of the newly created text field
- x – x-coordinate of the newly created text field
- y – y-coordinate of the newly created text field
- width – width of the newly created text field
- height – height of the newly created text field

To see this method in action, take a look at createTextField.fla. In this movie, we're creating 30 text fields on screen, and filling them with text that refers to their position in the series. Here's the code that makes it work, attached to frame 1 of the actions layer:

```
for (i=0; i<30; i++) {
    nm = "textfield"+i;
    _root.createTextField(nm, i, i*10, i*10, 120, 20);
    _root[nm].text = "This is TextField #"+i;
}
```

The text fields are named textfield0, textfield1, textfield2, etc, up to textfield29. The text field is created at i*10 on the x- and y-axes, which means that each new text field will be positioned to the lower right of the previously created field. Each text field is 120 x 20 pixels in size.

We're setting the text property of each text field to "This is TextField #", followed by the number of the TextField object (which also corresponds to its depth). The result, when tested, looks like this:

When a new text field is created, by default it is a dynamic text field with no border or background, single line, no word wrap, and with the html property set to false. The text is formatted as 12 point, black, Times New Roman text, and aligned left with no bold, italic, or underline.

HTML formatting

When a text field's html property is set to true we can then use the htmlText property to display HTML formatted text, in addition to simple, standard text. Most of the normal HTML tags are supported including font formatting, paragraph alignment, and hyperlinks. So, to make this work, we need to make sure that the text field is set to render HTML text either by selecting the Render text as HTML button in the Property inspector, or by using the following code:

```
myTextField.html = true;
```

Once we've done this, we can send text to the htmlText property of the text field, much like we do with the text property. Open up HTML_formatting_1.fla and look at the code on frame 1:

```
myTextField.htmlText = "This is Normal"+newline;
myTextField.htmlText += "<b>This is Bold</b>"+newline;
myTextField.htmlText += "<i>This is Italicized</i>"+newline;
```

```
myTextField.htmlText += "<u>This is Underlined</u>"+newline;
myTextField.htmlText += "<b><i><u>This is all three</u></i></b>"+newline;
```

This code produces the following output:

This is Normal
This is Bold
This is Italicized
<u>This is Underlined</u>
<u>This is all three</u>

We can perform further font formatting by using the `<font>` tag. Look at the code in frame 1 of the actions layer in HTML_formatting_2.fla:

```
myTextField.htmlText = "This is Normal"+newline;
myTextField.htmlText += "<font color='#FF0000'>This is RED</font>"+newline;
myTextField.htmlText += "<font size='33'>This is 33 point</font>"+newline;
myTextField.htmlText += "<font face='courier'>This is courier</font>"+new-
line;
```

This produces the following movie:

This is Normal
This is RED
This is 33 point
`This is courier`

We can also apply the standard paragraph alignment and formatting options, as in this example (this is HTML_formatting_3.fla):

```
myTextField.htmlText = "This is Normal"+newline;
myTextField.htmlText += "<p align='right'>This is right aligned</font>"+
➥newline;
myTextField.htmlText += "<p align='left'>This is left aligned</font>"+
➥newline;
myTextField.htmlText += "<p align='center'>This is centered</font>"+newline;
```

Test the movie to see how the text is formatted according to this code:

```
This is Normal
                                            This is right aligned
This is left aligned
                    This is centered
```

Finally, we can create standard hyperlinks, which that can be clicked on to open up links to other web pages (we can also trigger JavaScript functions within the current page). Look at the code in `HTML_formatting_4.fla`:

```
myTextField.htmlText = "This is Normal"+newline;
myTextField.htmlText += "visit <a href='http://www.friendsofed.com'>
➥friendsofed.com</a> today"+newline;
myTextField.htmlText += "and <u><a href='http://www.glenrhodes.com'>
➥glenrhodes.com</a></u> as well."+newline;
myTextField.htmlText += "This is Normal"+newline;
```

Here there are two hyperlinks, and the only difference between them is that we're also using the `<u>` underline tag for the second link. This may be required to make links more obvious to users.

```
This is Normal
visit friendsofed.com today
and glenrhodes.com as well.
This is Normal
```

The TextFormat object

Another technique used to apply text attributes such as bold, italics, and underline is via the `TextFormat` object. The `TextFormat` object provides us with a simple way of setting the text formatting of a specific text field without using HTML tags. The first thing we need to know is that when we want to create a `TextFormat` object we must define it with the standard constructor, like so:

```
myTextFormat = new TextFormat();
```

TextFormat objects are then applied to text fields using the `setTextFormat()` method:

```
myTextField.setTextFormat(myTextFormat);
```

When we do this, all the text in the text field is formatted according to the properties specified by `myTextFormat`. If we want, we can state a specific character in the text field to affect:

```
myTextField.setTextFormat(characterIndex, myTextFormat);
```

And finally, we can specify a range of characters to affect, like this:

```
myTextField.setTextFormat(beginIndex, endIndex, myTextFormat);
```

Alternatively, we can use the `setNewTextFormat()` method as follows:

```
myTextField.setNewTextFormat(myTextFormat);
```

This tells the `myTextField` to use the formatting specified in `myTextFormat` for any *future* text that is input by the user, or set with the `replaceSel()` method. With `setNewTextFormat()`, we will not see any immediate changes to the text field until the user begins to type, at which point the new formatting is applied to the new text. If we want to find out the `TextFormat` information for any text field, we can use the `getTextFormat()` method:

```
myTextFormat = myTextField.getTextFormat();
```

This tells us the `TextFormat` information for the entire text field. This returns an actual `TextFormat` object, and if there are several different `TextFormat`s throughout the text field, then any `TextFormat` property value that contains mixed formatting information will be set to `null`.

Alternatively, we can check the TextFormat of a specific character:

```
myTextFormat = myTextField.getTextFormat(characterIndex);
```

...or a specific range of characters:

```
myTextFormat = myTextField.getTextFormat(beginIndex, endIndex);
```

Finally, we can get the latest `TextFormat` object that is used to set new text, with this:

```
myTextFormat = myTextField.getNewTextFormat();
```

Properties of the TextFormat object

The TextFormat object consists of the following properties:

Property	Type	Description
align	String	Defines the alignment of the applied text field, or section of text in the text field. Valid values are left, right, or center.
blockIndent	Number	A number which specifies the number of points to indent the entire block of text by (applies to all lines in the text field).
bold	Boolean	Either true or false, this indicates whether or not the text is boldfaced.

bullet	Boolean	When this is set to `true`, the text will be indented, and new lines will begin with a bullet symbol at the left edge. For example:

```
myTextFormat = new TextFormat();
myTextFormat.bullet = true;

myTextField.setNewTextFormat(myTextFormat);
myTextField.text = "This is a
➥list"+newline;
myTextField.text += "Item #1"+newline;
myTextField.text += "Item #2"+newline;
myTextField.text += "Item #3"+newline;
```

- This is a list
- Item #1
- Item #2

color	Color	Indicates the color of the text. Uses a standard 24-bit color format, for example: `0xFF0000` for red (see **Chapter 6**).
font	String	The name of the font applied to the text as a string.
indent	Number	Indicates the amount of indent, in points, for the first line in a paragraph of text.
italic	Boolean	`true` or `false`, this indicates whether the text should be italicized or not.
leading	Number	The amount of vertical space between lines of text in points.
leftMargin	Number	The size of the left margin of a paragraph in points.
rightMargin	Number	The size of the right margin of a paragraph in points.
size	Number	The font size in points.
tabStops	Array	Takes an array of numbers, which define the custom tab stops, in points. Each time a tab character `\t` is placed in a text string, any subsequent text is placed at the next available tab stop.
target	String	Indicates the target for any URL, which is opened by clicking on any hyperlinks in the text. Normal values are `_self`, `_blank`, `_parent`, and `_top`.
underline	Boolean	A `true` or `false` variable defining whether or not underlining should be applied to text.
url	String	If a URL is specified in here, then clicking on any of this text will open up the specified URL. This will open up in a browser window specified by the `target` property.

getTextExtent()

Here's a neat method of the `TextFormat` object that's worth a mention – the `getTextExtent` method. Once we've defined our `TextFormat` object, we can find out the width and height of any text string that would be rendered on screen, by using the `getTextExtent()` method for example:

```
te = myTextFormat.getTextExtent("HOW BIG IS THIS TEXT?");
tWid = te.width;
tHt = te.height;
```

In this example, `tWid` and `tHt` are set to the width and height of the string `"HOW BIG IS THIS TEXT?"`, assuming that it has been formatted according to `myTextFormat`. This allows us to move and distribute text on the screen knowing exactly how much space it will occupy.

Dynamic fonts

One of the simplest applications of the `TextField` object is to dynamically change the font of a text field. Take a look at `dynamic_fonts.fla`. When we test it, the movie looks like this:

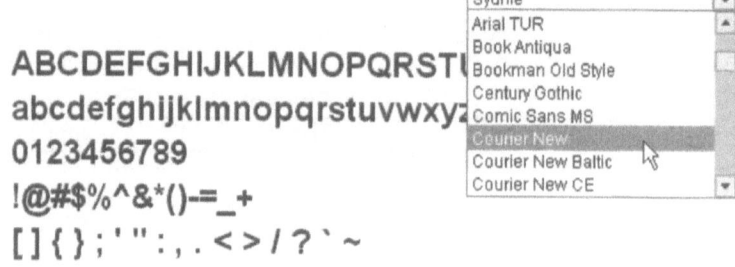

There is a ComboBox, that is populated with all the fonts on the user's system. When a font is chosen from this list, the font is applied to a text field containing a sample of characters from the ASCII character set. Here's the code:

```
myTextFormat = new TextFormat();
tl = TextField.getFontList();
for (i in tl) {
    fontDropDown.addItem(tl[i], i);
}
fontDropDown.sortItemsBy("label", "ASC");
function changeFont () {
    var f = fontDropDown.getSelectedItem().label;
    myTextFormat.font = f;
    myTextField.setTextFormat(myTextFormat);
};
fontDropDown.setChangeHandler("changeFont");
```

Here we create a new instance of the TextFormat object. Next, we use the getFontList() method of the TextField object to populate the ComboBox (with an instance name of fontDropDown). It turns out that the getFontList() method doesn't actually work with instances of text fields, but only the master TextField prototype object itself. After the list has been populated with all the fonts on the user's computer, the list is sorted according to the label field, in ascending order.

Next, there is a function called changeFont, which is triggered when a font is selected from the drop-down menu. First we get the label (the font name), and then set the font property of myTextFormat to that value. Finally, we use the setTextFormat() method to apply that font to the entire text field.

The last line simply tells Flash to trigger the changeFont function when items in the drop-down menu are selected.

User-defined attributes

Let's look at a simple application that allows the user to type text into a text field and, as they do so, they can toggle bold, italic, and underline formatting using the three CheckBox components at the right of the input screen. Open up is user_defined_fonts.fla and test it:

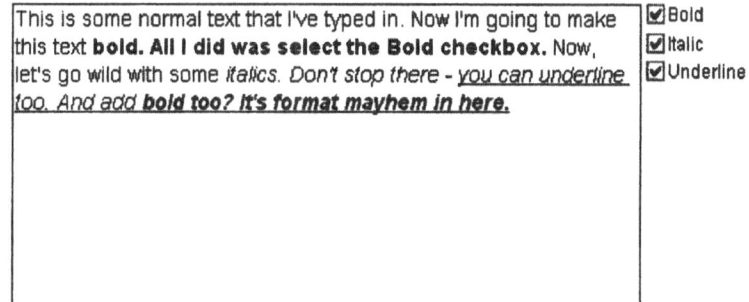

All these attributes were changed by toggling the check boxes. The check boxes have instance names boldCheck, italicCheck, and underlineCheck, and their change handlers are set to setBold, setItalic, and setUnderline. These are variables that hold references to functions that will handle the change events. Here is the code in full:

```
myFormatter = new TextFormat();
myTextField.setTextFormat(myFormatter);
function setBold() {
    myFormatter.bold = boldCheck.getValue();
    myTextField.setNewTextFormat(myFormatter);
}
function setItalic() {
    myFormatter.italic = italicCheck.getValue();
    myTextField.setNewTextFormat(myFormatter);
}
function setUnderline() {
```

```
                    myFormatter.underline = underlineCheck.getValue();
                    myTextField.setNewTextFormat(myFormatter);
          }
```

As each CheckBox is triggered, we take the value of the CheckBox (either `true` or `false`) and apply it to the appropriate `TextFormat` property (bold, italic, or underline). Once we've turned a parameter on or off, any new text entered into the text field is set to the new `TextFormat`. Notice that moving the cursor to the middle of a previously typed **bold** word, for example, means that we type in that format, (as you would in Microsoft Word, for example) because it isn't considered a new piece of text. We only really see the dynamic text formatting if we type new text at the *end* of the text field.

The Selection object

There is one more object that we're going to look at, the `Selection` object. We can only ever have one instance of it because we can only ever have one section of selected text at a time. Therefore, we don't need to create any instances of the `Selection` object as such; we just use the `Selection` object directly. The `Selection` object contains information about the currently selected text at any time. To determine the starting position of the current selection in the text field, we use the `Selection.getBeginIndex()` method like this:

```
          var selStart = Selection.getBeginIndex();
```

To determine the index of the last selected character we use the corresponding `getEndIndex()` method:

```
          var selEnd = Selection.getEndIndex();
```

Take a look at `one_betterselection.fla` for an interesting demonstration of the `Selection` object. Test the movie, and you'll see that there's a text field, which you can type into. It's a standard input text field but notice that, as you type, Flash substitutes the character you type with the subsequent character in the ASCII character set. For example, if you type in the word `Encyclopedia`, you'll see the following:

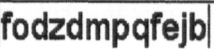

This jumble of characters actually represents all the letters in the word Encyclopedia, but each one has been increased to the next letter in the character set. The code used to achieve this is as follows:

```
      myTextField.onChanged = function() {
              var pos = Selection.getCaretIndex();
              Selection.setSelection(pos-1, pos);
              myTextField.replaceSel(chr(Key.getAscii()+1));
      };
```

This code is triggered whenever a character is added to the text field because it is attached to the onChanged event of myTextField. First, we're using the getCaretIndex() method of the Selection object, which returns the current position of the caret (the blinking cursor). We store this in a variable called pos. Next, we set the active selection to the previous character, and then replace that character with the next indexed character at the index of the recently pressed key plus one in the ASCII set.

The setSelection() method of the Selection object takes two parameters: start index and end index. Anything from start index up to and including end index is selected. What we do is select the range between the current cursor position minus one and the current cursor position. This effectively highlights the last character typed in. Then, we quickly replace the selected character with the character following the last typed character, using the replaceSel() method of the TextField object.

There's another method called Selection.getFocus(), which returns the name of the currently selected, or focused, text field. If we gave focus to a text field called myTextField, then Selection.getFocus would returns this result:

    _level0.myTextField

Alternatively, if we wanted to, we could force focus to go to a specific text field with the Selection.setFocus() method simply by saying:

    Selection.setFocus("_level0.myTextField");

This will cause myTextField to take focus, and then any Selection setting or manipulation we do will be performed on myTextField.

With the knowledge we've learnt in this chapter, we now know how to modify and use strings, text fields, and apply TextFormat objects to them to add some cool dynamic text features to our designs. We also know how to use the Selection object to manipulate text fields, and the contents of selected text.

13 Time and Timekeeping

Objectives

- The Date object and its associated methods

- Building an application timer and a clock

- Using the `setInterval()` function for various timed events

- Sound-based timing

Introduction

Date and time functions are a standard feature of most programming and scripting languages. ActionScript is no exception – it has all the expected functions that allow us to make our Flash programs convey the current date and time to the user. This date and time information is taken from the user's system clock, and is therefore local to the user's computer.

Of course, this also means that if the user has set their computer's clock incorrectly, Flash MX will also display the incorrect time, when the system date and time functions are used. We'll look at this in more detail shortly.

Flash also has another type of time, different from universal time: **execution time**. This is simply a timer that starts counting when the movie begins, and continues counting until the movie is closed. Because it is linked with your computer's system clock, this timer is very accurate: to within a thousandth of a second (that is, 1 millisecond). The timer has many uses, as we'll soon see.

Finally, Flash MX provides us with several different time-based features and functions. First, we can create a function that is triggered at a timed interval. There are many uses for this, such as timed animation, or perhaps updating an on-screen clock every second. This also allows you to call a function at a rate that is potentially much faster than the frame rate, thus outpacing onEnterFrame events. Additionally, we have the onSoundComplete event, which can trigger a function when a particular sound finishes playing, allowing us to synchronize graphics and animation with sounds for that truly professional touch to our movies.

The Date object

Flash refers to both the system time *and* date through the same type of object: the Date object. In its simplest form, this object consists of a single number: the number of milliseconds since the universal time reference point of midnight, January 1st, 1970 universal time (GMT).

The easiest way to create a new Date object is like this:

```
myDate = new Date();
```

This creates a Date object called myDate and, because we haven't specified any information about the date and time yet, it will use the current system date and time by default, as set in our computer.

On the other hand, if we entered a parameter of 0, like this:

```
myDate = new Date(0);
```

Then our Date object is set to zero milliseconds, referring to the universal reference date of midnight, January 1st, 1970; the output would be along the lines of Jan 1 1970 00:00:00.

You can find out what the current date and time is in milliseconds since New Year's Day in 1970 by making use of one of the Date object's built in methods – the getTime() method. Create a new Date object without specifying any parameters, and then use the trace() expression to get some feedback:

```
myDate = new Date();
trace(mydate)
trace(myDate.getTime());
```

Here, the first trace output will give you the current date and time in full, and the second trace uses the getTime() method, which will give you the date in milliseconds:

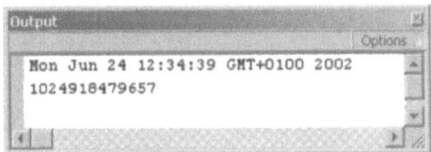

When you run it, you'll see the local date in full, followed by a nice long number – somewhere in the region of a trillion milliseconds (a billion seconds)! As you can see, as time goes by, the time in milliseconds will become rather large – so congratulations to anyone over 31 years of age; you've been alive for over 1 trillion milliseconds!

OK, so now we know how to create a date object using a very large number... but that's not very intuitive or practical, is it? How do we create a date out of time and date formats that we're already familiar with? Well, the Date object is flexible enough that when we use its constructor form, we can enter specific time and date values as parameters:

```
new Date(myYear, myMonth, myDate, myHour, myMinute, mySecond,
➡ myMillisecond);
```

The first two parameters are required, while the others are all optional (if, however, you declare only one parameter, Flash will assume that the value refers to the universal date in milliseconds). Let's examine these parameters in more detail – take a look at the table on the next page.

Date parameter	Description
myYear	This can be specified as a four-digit year, like 2002, or we can choose to specify only two digits, XX, in which case it will refer to a 19XX year. It's important not to get this confused: if you put 02, for instance, you're referring to the year 1902 (this might bring back flashbacks to the Y2K bug panic for some readers!).
myMonth	This is the month of the year from 0 to 11, where is January and 11 is December. Note that it starts at zero.
myDate	This is a number from 1 to 31 relating to the day of the month, where 1 is the first day of the month, so this parameter is not zero-based. Remember that this number isn't always valid right up to 31; depending on the month, the final day may well be 28, 29, or 30.
myHour	This is the hour portion of the time, from 0 to 23 (12 midnight to 11 pm).
myMinute	This is the minute portion of the time, from 0 to 59.
mySecond	This is the second portion of the time, also from 0 to 59.
myMillisecond	This is the millisecond portion of the time, with a valid range of 0 to 999.

With these parameters, we can create a date using the alternative form of construction – by specifying a logical date. Consider the following lines, for example, where I've entered my birthday for this year as the new Date object:

```
myDate = new Date(2002, 9, 29, 3, 50, 00, 00);
trace(myDate);
```

If we run this code, I can see that my birthday falls on a Tuesday this year:

Notice that this output says GMT+0000, suggesting that I've used a computer based in the UK to test this code on.

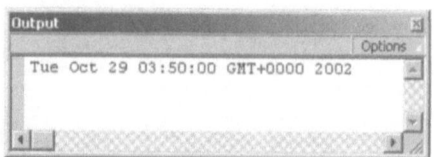

However, if I ran this same code from a machine in New York, I'd get a slightly different output:

Now we see GMT-0500 in the output. This means that the time being displayed is 5 hours less than GMT, which is EST. So, although the time is still displayed as 03:50:00, it is actually stored in the Date object as 08:50:00 in universal time (UTC). Flash interprets the time correctly because it looks at each parameter of the Date object, and also looks at our computer's time zone setting. It adjusts the output

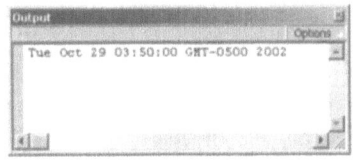

by the time zone offset and daylight savings (if applicable), and then gives out the adjusted time.

For example, if we now use the getHours() method and the getUTCHours() methods (more on these shortly), we can see the difference clearly. The former method simply returns the local hour of a Date object, while the latter returns the UTC hour of that Date object. First we create our Date object in the usual way, and then we trace out the result from the methods:

```
myDate = new Date(2002, 9, 29, 3, 50, 00, 00);
trace("Local hour = "+myDate.getHours());
trace("Universal hour = "+myDate.getUTCHours());
```

Test this code (you'll find it in the file createDate.fla) and, depending on where you are, you'll see something like this:

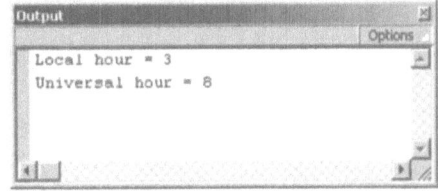

This shows that there's a 5 hour time difference between EST and GMT. Note that you may see different results, depending on your time zone. Readers in the UK, for example, will see no difference between the outputs of the two trace statements.

The important point to remember when you use the new Date() constructor is that whatever time and date you specify will be in your *local time zone*. If we wanted to specify our time in UTC, no matter what time zone we're in, we could use the Date.UTC() method. This creates a date object, but specifies the time in UTC, rather than local time. Open up createUniversalDate.fla to see this in detail:

```
myDate = new Date(Date.UTC(2002, 9, 29, 3, 50, 00, 00));
trace(myDate);
```

Running this code from our New York office again will produce this:

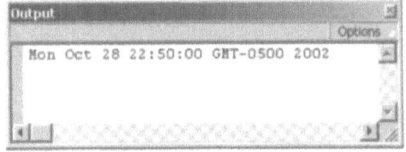

This creates the same date that we had earlier, except now we're explicitly saying that it's a UTC time, so it records the local equivalent. Notice that even though the Date object was specified as October 29th, at 3:50 in the morning, the output is October 28th at 10:50 at night. The UTC date that we created is automatically displayed in local time.

Methods for accessing the time and date

We've seen that creating a `Date` object and filling it in via its constructor function is easy. However, what if we already have a `Date` object and we want to modify some of the individual values, like just the minute, or year? Well, Flash MX has all sorts of date and time *setter* methods that can do just that. Additionally, we also have several *getter* methods that we can use to extrapolate certain information from a `Date` object, like hour or millisecond. Let's look at these in more detail.

Setter methods

The following table displays the setter methods of the `Date` object:

The setter methods	Description
`myDate.setDate(date)`	Sets the day of the month (1 to 31) of the `Date` object.
`myDate.setFullYear(year, month, date)`	Sets the year, month, and date of a `Date` object. The year must be a four-digit number otherwise, if a two-digit year is specified, it will be assumed to be a year within the range of 0 to 99 AD. Month and date entries are optional.
`myDate.setHours(hour)`	Sets the hour of a `Date` object, according to the local time zone. Valid numbers range from 0 to 23.
`myDate.setMilliseconds(millisecond)`	Sets the milliseconds of a `Date` object, in local time. Valid numbers are from 0 to 999.
`myDate.setMinutes(minutes)`	Sets the minutes value of a `Date` object, in local time. Valid numbers are from 0 to 59.
`myDate.setMonth(month)`	Sets the month of the year, from 0 to 11.
`myDate.setSeconds(seconds)`	Sets the seconds value of the time, from 0 to 59.
`myDate.setTime(dateTimeValue)`	Sets the complete date and time value by specifying a number of milliseconds from midnight, January 1st, 1970. A negative number will indicate a date earlier than this reference date.
`myDate.setYear(year)`	Sets the year of the `Date` object. If we specify only a two-digit year (XX), it will assume we mean 19XX, otherwise a full four digit year is required to explicitly declare a time prior to 1900 or after 1999.

Each of these methods, except for the last two `setTime()` and `setYear()`, also has a UTC equivalent, where all setting is done relative to UTC time rather than local time. So we have `setUTCDate()`, `setUTCFullYear()`, `setUTCHours()`, `setUTCMilliseconds()`, `setUTCMinutes()`, `setUTCMonth()`, and `setUTCSeconds()`.

Getter methods

The following table shows the getter methods associated with the `Date` object:

The getters methods	Description
myDate.getDate()	Returns the date of the month (1 to 31), according to the local time zone.
myDate.getDay()	Returns the day of the week (0 to 6), where 0 is Sunday and 6 is Saturday
myDate.getFullYear()	Returns a four digit year.
myDate.getHours()	Returns an hour from 0 to 23, local time.
myDate.getMilliseconds()	Returns the millisecond value of the Date object. This will be a number from 0 to 999.
myDate.getMinutes()	Returns the minute value of the Date object, from 0 to 59.
myDate.getMonth())	Returns the month of the Date object, from 0 to 11.
myDate.getSeconds()	Returns the number of seconds in the time of the Date object, a number from 0 to 59.
myDate.getTime()	Returns the number of milliseconds from midnight, January 1st, 1970, in UTC.
myDate.getTimezoneOffset()	Returns the number of *minutes* that the time in this Date object is offset from UTC. For example, an EST time would return 300 (5 hours).

Again, each of these methods except for the last two also has a UTC equivalent which returns their values relative to UTC: `getUTCDate()`, `getUTCDay()`, `getUTCFullYear()`, `getUTCHours()`, `getUTCMilliseconds()`, `getUTCMinutes()`, `getUTCMonth()`, and `getUTCSeconds()`.

Using these getter and setter methods, it is possible to create a `Date` object and then continually modify and update it as our Flash application runs.

Application timers

Earlier, we mentioned the timer that measures the execution time of a movie and records how long the movie has been running. To access the timer, we use its `getTimer()` method, like this:

```
appTime = getTimer();
```

Here, `appTime` will be set to a number corresponding to the number of milliseconds that the program has been running. Take a look at `appTimer.fla` – on the stage you'll find a dynamic text box, linked to the variable name `output`:

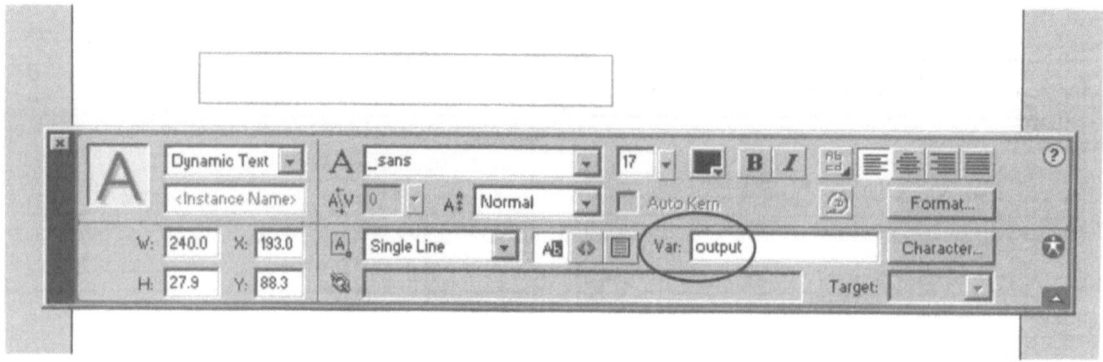

The ActionScript on frame 1 of the root timeline looks like this:

```
_root.onEnterFrame = function() {
      appTime = getTimer();
      output = appTime;
};
```

This code uses a function triggered by the `onEnterFrame` event to display the value of the timer in a dynamic text box on the stage, via the `output` variable. When we test this movie, we'll see a number in the middle of the stage counting up very quickly.

So, what are some good uses of the timer? Well, because the timer never stops counting, no matter how busy or tied down Flash is, we can use it to determine how long certain bits of ActionScript are taking to execute. This can help us eliminate processor hogs, and optimize our movies.

Take a look at `loopTimer.fla` for a sample of this. Here we're running a very simple loop of a `Math.sin` function, which repeats 1000 times:

```
_root.onEnterFrame = function() {
      startTime = getTimer();
      for (i=0; i<1000; i++) {
            h = Math.sin(i);
      }
      endTime = getTimer();
      output = endTime-startTime;
};
```

The startTime is being taken at the beginning of our code segment, then we're performing 1000 Math.sin functions, and then we're taking endTime to be the current timer value. Finally, we're outputting the difference (endTime–startTime) to the dynamic text box. On my system the value fluctuated around 56, meaning that it took 56 milliseconds to perform those 1000 Math.sin calculations.

Here's an optimization tip: if we declare the function s = Math.sin at the top of our code, and then replace h = Math.sin(i) with h = s(i), we should notice a marked improvement in performance speed.

You'll find this code in the FLA file loopTimer_tweak.fla on the CD:

```
s = Math.sin;
_root.onEnterFrame = function() {
    startTime = getTimer();
    for (i=0; i<1000; i++) {
        h = s(i);
    }
    endTime = getTimer();
    output = endTime-startTime;
};
```

Test it to see what value the timer gives now – it brought my time down from 56 to about 48 milliseconds! This is most likely because Flash uses script parsing at runtime, and when the string itself is longer, it takes more time to parse. It's a strange idiosyncrasy of Flash, but knowing about it means we can make our movies perform that much better.

Building a clock

So far we've talked lots about the Date object, and the getTimer() method. Let's now see these in use – we're going to learn how to create a simple visual clock and calendar application. The goal is to design an analog clock (with rotating hands), that includes the full date beneath it, as a small scripted application that we could potentially keep open on our website. As we'll see, all of the relevant code is in a function that is applied to a specific movie clip, so it could be easily copied and linked to any other movie clip.

Open up clock.fla to see it in action – our clock movie clip is on the stage, and looks like this:

Within this movie clip we have the clock face and three movie clips representing the hands of the clock (the secondHand, minuteHand, and hourHand) – these are simply lines of varying length, color, and thickness. Each of these hands has their center point at the bottom of the line, so that they point upwards. Notice also that the registration point of the clock movie clip doubles as the center of the clock – we'll soon see why this is useful.

We also have four dynamic text boxes in the calendar area with variable names: theWeekDay, theDate, theMonth, and theYear. When you test the movie it will look something like this:

We're making use of the timer and the date objects to make it all happen. Consider the first half of the code attached to the frame 1 of the root timeline – here we use an onLoad event to run this code when the clock movie clip is loaded:

```
_root.clock.onLoad = function() {
    this.myDate = new Date();
    this.ms = this.myDate.getTime();

    // Center the hands
    this.hourHand._x = 0;
    this.hourHand._y = 0;
    this.minuteHand._x = 0;
    this.minuteHand._y = 0;
    this.secondHand._x = 0;
    this.secondHand._y = 0;
    this.weekDayName = new Array("Sunday", "Monday", "Tuesday",
    ➡"Wednesday", "Thursday", "Friday", "Saturday");
    this.monthName = new Array("January", "February", "March", "April",
    ➡"May", "June", "July", "August", "September", "October", "November",
    ➡"December");
};
```

In this code we're creating our new Date object, myDate, and then grabbing its universal millisecond time value (from midnight, January 1, 1970). Next, we're placing the three hand movie clips at position (0, 0), which is the center of the clock. This causes all three hands to be aligned and pointing up at the 12, that is, indicating the time 00:00:00. Finally, we declare two string arrays: weekDayName and monthName, which will be used to fill out our calendar.

In this clock we make use of the _rotation property of the clock hand movie clips in order to display the time. The full sweep of the circle is 360 degrees, and because of the way our hands are drawn, 0 degrees is pointing straight up, 90 degrees is pointing at the 3 on the clock, 180 degrees is pointing straight down at 6, and 270 degrees is pointing left to the 9.

Next comes our `onEnterFrame` function, which controls and updates the hands of the clock in each new frame:

```
_root.clock.onEnterFrame = function() {
    this.newms = this.ms+getTimer();
    this.myDate.setTime(this.newms);

    // Get the second, minute, and hour
    this.second = this.myDate.getSeconds()+
    ➥(this.myDate.getMilliseconds()/1000);
    this.minute = this.myDate.getMinutes()+(this.second/60);
    this.hour = this.myDate.getHours()+(this.minute/60);

    // Set the rotation of the hands
    this.hourHand._rotation = this.hour*30;
    this.minuteHand._rotation = this.minute*6;
    this.secondHand._rotation = this.second*6;

    // Get the calendar information
    this.month = this.myDate.getMonth();
    this.weekDay = this.myDate.getDay();
    this.dayOfMonth = this.myDate.getDate();
    this.year = this.myDate.getFullYear();

    // Draw the calendar
    this.theMonth = this.monthName[this.month];
    this.theWeekDay = this.weekDayName[this.weekDay];
    this.theDate = this.dayOfMonth;
    this.theYear = this.year;
};
```

Now remember, when we created our `Date` object, we used a `new Date()` constructor, which grabs the current date and time and assigns it to `clock.myDate`. However, there's something that we must be aware of: `myDate` will not change on its own accord. Once it is created, it is initialized with the current date and time, but it doesn't change along with real time. It is only a snapshot. If we want it to reflect the actual time, we have to increment it ourselves – this is where the `getTimer()` method comes into play.

We already have `clock.ms`, which contains the millisecond value of our initial date. We also know that `getTimer()` returns the number of milliseconds that our program has been running. This gives us the correct time without having to grab the system time all over again. So, we always know what the current time is just by adding the two together, like we did with this code:

```
this.newms = this.ms+getTimer();
this.myDate.setTime(this.newms);
```

We're storing the new time as `clock.newms`, and then telling `myDate` to adjust itself, with the `setTime()` method.

After that, we're getting values for the second, minute, and hour hands. However, we want our hands to move smoothly around the clock. If we use `getMinutes()` on its own, for example, it returns a number from 0 to 59. But, in most analog clocks you'll notice that the minute hand slowly moves as the second hand moves. This means that we actually need `getMinutes()` to return a fraction to us. So, 10 minutes and 30 seconds should return a minute value of 10.5 – rather than just 10. Unfortunately, `getMinutes()` only returns a whole number for our current minute. So, we need to calculate the decimal portion on our own.

Luckily, we can get that information from the second hand! If we take the current second value and divide it by 60, then we'll have the fractional portion of the minute. We do this for each clock hand with this code:

```
this.second = this.myDate.getSeconds()+
➥(this.myDate.getMilliseconds()/1000);
this.minute = this.myDate.getMinutes()+(this.second/60);
this.hour = this.myDate.getHours()+(this.minute/60);
```

We want our clock to be as smooth as a Rolex, so the second hand is adjusted to include milliseconds, the minute is adjusted to include the seconds and finally, the hour is adjusted to include the minutes. This may seem complicated at first, but if you think about it for a moment, it should become clear.

Next, we're setting the `_rotation` of the hands so that they visually reflect the time. Remember that a full sweep of the circle goes 360 degrees, so with this code:

```
this.hourHand._rotation = this.hour*30;
this.minuteHand._rotation = this.minute*6;
this.secondHand._rotation = this.second*6;
```

We're taking the time values of each hand, and converting them into degree rotation values. There are 60 seconds in a minute, so if you multiply the seconds by 6, you get 360: the number of degrees in the circle. The same formula applies for minutes. The hour formula is a little bit different because there are only 12 hours in a complete circle. However, multiplying 12 hours by 30 gives us 360 degrees again – once around the circle in a 12-hour period.

Finally, we're using some date getter methods to retrieve calendar information, and we're then displaying that information in our 4 text fields: `theMonth`, `theWeekDay`, `theDate`, and `theYear`. With the month and the weekday, however, rather than display the number directly (from 0 to 6 for weekday, and from 0 to 11 for month), we're going to use our `monthName` and `weekDayName` string arrays to display the actual name of the day and month in our calendar.

Remember, this is the time on our local system – the computer that runs the SWF file. Don't expect people to visit a website and see the time that's on the server. For this, we require time information from the server before we build our Date object (more on that in the final chapters of this book).

Now for a little fun – if we change this line of code:

```
this.newms = this.ms+getTimer();
```

To this:

```
this.newms = this.ms+(getTimer()*2);
```

Then our clock will run twice as fast! Now try setting this factor to 100000 and watch the days fly by. Or, make this a negative number, and watch as the clock counts backwards. This works because we're computing our own time, rather than updating the system time every frame. Furthermore, since we're using the getTimer() function, our calculated time will remain very accurate.

Timed events

By its very nature, Flash is a timed system – frame rates keep graphics and code running at a fixed and consistent interval (although complex actions can sometimes slow down the frame rate a little).

We often attach code to the timeline with the onEnterFrame event of a movie clip. But what if we want some code to occur at a specific, fixed time interval that is independent of the frame rate? For example, say we want an on-screen counter to update every second, or we want an object to move around the screen much faster than the frame rate will allow.

Using setInterval()

This is where the setInterval() function comes into play – this is a way of interrupting the flow of your animation that enables Flash to execute a function at a rate of up to once every millisecond. Practically speaking, achieving true *once per millisecond* accuracy is actually quite difficult for Flash, especially if you have lots of code in the interrupt function, but setInterval() can clearly set shorter intervals than onEnterFrame using even the fastest frame rate – in the following example we achieve a 3 millisecond interval.

So, how does it work? Let's try attaching an 'interupt function' to a blank movie – open up interruptFunction1.fla, and you'll see the following code on frame 1 of the main timeline:

```
myInterrupt = function () {
      trace(getTimer());
};
id1 = setInterval(myInterrupt, 1);
```

Test it out (CTRL+B), but be careful when running this – it's going to fill up our trace window *very* quickly, so be prepared to stop it after a few seconds. When we run it, we'll see an output like this:

When we took this screenshot, the program had been running for only 3 seconds and, as you can see, the Output window was already quite full.

So what's happening here? Well, first we create a function called myInterrupt() that does one thing: displays the results of the getTimer() function in the trace output window. Remember, getTimer() never loses accuracy because it makes use of your computer's internal system clock (which is actually responsible for keeping your entire computer running).

Next, we set up our interval function by calling setInterval() with the name of the function we want executed, and how often we want it to be executed. The number we're using is 1, which represents 1 millisecond. We're asking Flash to run the myInterrupt() function every millisecond. When the interval is created, it is given a unique ID, id1 in this case, that is used by Flash.

Looking at the output window, we can see that it is in fact taking Flash about 3 milliseconds to set the interval. This is unavoidable because a program can only execute code so fast – there are physical limits to the processing speed, and it must share the computer with the operating system and many other programs.

> setInterval() *works differently from, say, a timeline action. The frame action will execute no matter what, even if it means slowing the actual frame rate, whereas the* setInterval() *will only be executed as many times as it can, without having to queue.*

OK, so that's how the setInterval() function works. Let's change our myInterrupt() function a little bit (see interruptFunction2.fla):

```
myInterrupt = function () {
        g = getTimer();
        trace(g);
        if (g>1000) {
                clearInterval(id1);
        }
};
id1 = setInterval(myInterrupt, 1);
```

Now, we're telling Flash to clear the interval when 1000 milliseconds have passed. Note that we're now using the clearInterval() function, which simply clears the id1 variable that we set when we created the interval in the first place. When we test this code, you'll see that the getTimer() output will cease on or around 1000 milliseconds:

So now that we know how to create intervals, let's try controlling some motion with the setInterval() function. Take a look at interruptFunction3.fla, where we have two instances of a movie clip on the stage with instance names ball1 and ball2. We'll use these two movie clips for a direct comparison between the onEnterFrame event and the setInterval() function:

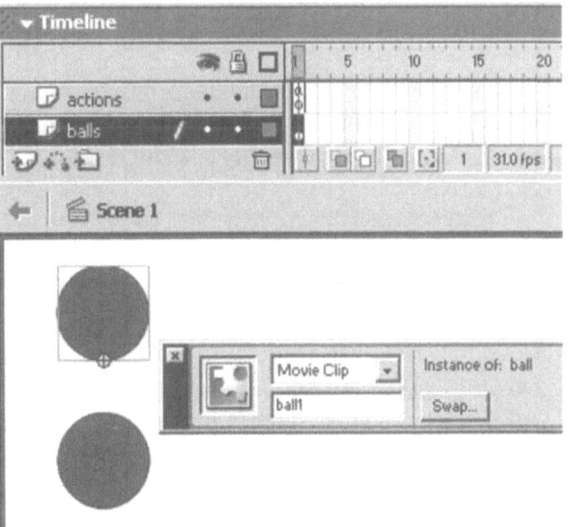

The following code is attached to the root timeline on frame 1 of the actions layer:

```
moveBall1 = function () {
     ball1._x++;
     ball1.count++;
};
id1 = setInterval(moveBall1, 0);

ball2.onEnterFrame = function() {
     this._x++;
};
```

Notice that we're moving both of the movie clips, but we're using two different methods. Firstly, `ball1` is being moved with a `setInterval()` – every 1 millisecond (in theory) the ball's _x position is being incremented by 1. Next, `ball2` is also having its _x position incremented by 1, however it is using the `onEnterFrame` event, which means that it's occurring a maximum of 31 times per second (according to this movie's frame rate – click anywhere on the stage and look in your Property inspector to see this value).

Well, when we test this movie, after a few seconds it's clear that `ball1` (the top one) has moved quite a bit further than `ball2` – the _x position of the `ball1` is being incremented at a much faster rate:

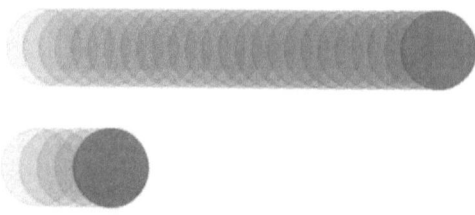

If we were now to reduce the frame rate of our movie clip, then `ball2` would move slower, but the speed of `ball1` would be unaffected. Try it out – enter 10 in the Frame Rate box of the Property inspector, hit ENTER, and the re-test the movie with CTRL+ENTER.

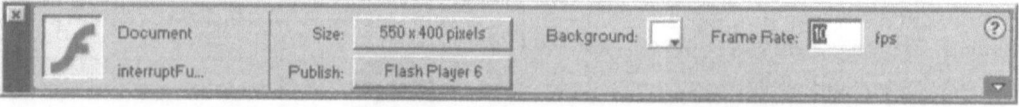

Note, however, that although `ball1` is still moving faster, it is now only being updated on screen at the new (lower) frame rate, like everything else in the movie. So `ball1` now moves across the screen in a jerky series of jumps. Later in this section we'll see how to use the `updateAfterEvent()` command to keep our `setInterval()`-animated movies running smoothly.

setInterval() for displaying dynamic content

How about another example of this important function? In countdown.fla, we have some simple ActionScript that produces a countdown at runtime. On the stage, we have a dynamic text box with the variable name counter, and we have labeled this box COUNTDOWN:

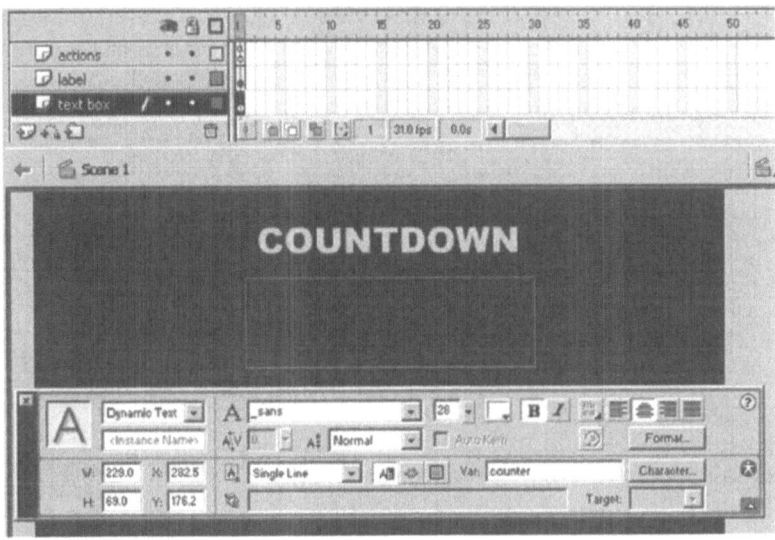

Attached to frame 1 of the actions layer on the root timeline, we have the following code:

```
counter = 10;
doCount = function () {
        counter—;
        if (counter<0) {
                counter = "Lift off!";
                clearInterval(id1);
        }
};
id1 = setInterval(doCount, 1000);
```

Here we have a variable called counter that is initially set to 10. Then, we've got a function called doCount, which simply decrements the counter, updating the dynamic text box on screen, and then checks to make sure that countdown hasn't yet reached 0. If it has, then it puts the words Lift off! in the text box, and clears the interval. Finally, the interval is actually set with setInterval() telling Flash to execute the doCount() function every 1000 milliseconds, or in other words, every second. When we run this movie, we'll see the counter start at 10, and begin counting down until if finally reaches 0, and displays:

setInterval() for changing playback speed

Another potential use of `setInterval()` is to dynamically change the speed at which a movie clip plays. Even if we set our overall movie's frame rate at 15, 20, or 30 fps, we can use `setInterval()`, along with the `updateAfterEvent()` command, to step through the frames of any movie clip at our own desired pace.

So, what does `updateAfterEvent()` actually do? Well, remember that if a `setInterval()` event is triggered at a rate that exceeds the frame rate, we may not see the visual changes represented on the screen, even though something may have moved position several times – `updateAfterEvent()` allows us to continuously update the screen to show changes *as they happen*.

Open up `changePlaySpeed.fla` and we'll see `updateAfterEvent()` in action. There are 3 instances of the same movie clip on the stage, called `box1`, `box2`, and `box3`. The movie clip itself is just a 500-frame shape tween, which changes from a rectangle to a circle – open up the Library (F11*) to see it play through:*

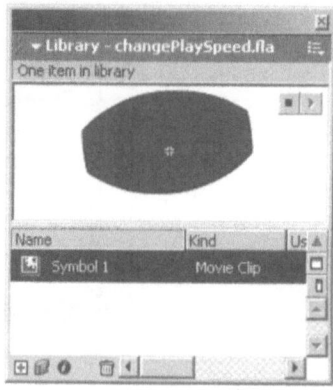

Note that a single `stop()` action is attached to frame 1 of the movie clip, because we don't want it to play on its own accord, we want to remotely control the progress ourselves using some more ActionScript.

Attached to frame 1 of the root timeline is the following code:

```
frameInc = function (who) {
    who.nextFrame();
    updateAfterEvent();
};
id1 = setInterval(frameInc, 2, _root.box1);
id2 = setInterval(frameInc, 15, _root.box2);
id3 = setInterval(frameInc, 30, _root.box3);
```

We create a function called `frameInc`, which simply takes a reference to a target movie clip as a parameter, and then tells that target to go to the next frame. Then, `updateAfterEvent()` is called so that the frame will be redrawn, no matter what our frame rate is set to.

Notice that the function takes a parameter this time: `who`. With `setInterval()` it's possible to pass parameters to the linked function by specifying them *after* the second `setInterval()` parameter (the time delay). Here, we declare our `setInterval()` functions like this:

```
id1 = setInterval(frameInc, 2, _root.box1);
id2 = setInterval(frameInc, 15, _root.box2);
id3 = setInterval(frameInc, 30, _root.box3);
```

All three `setInterval()` functions are linked to the `frameInc` function, with increasing delay values, and we additionally pass the target movie clip as the `who` parameter. If we test the movie, after a few seconds we'll see something like this:

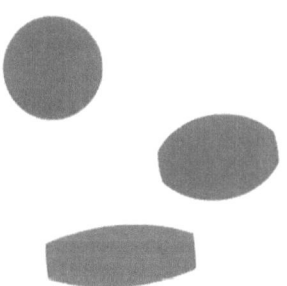

Notice that the movie clips are all playing at different speeds. Using this method, we can play back movie clips at almost any frame rate, regardless of what our master frame rate is set at.

There's one more potential use of `setInterval()` and that's for polling – we can use the `setInterval()` function to poll a server for information at regular intervals. We'll study this at length in the latter chapters of this book when we come to look at communicating with the world outside Flash...

Sound-based timing

The final major type of timing that we have in Flash MX is sound-based timing. With this technique we can cause a function to be executed whenever a given music track or sound finishes playing.

Take a look at `soundTiming.fla`. In this movie we've imported the sound file `song.mp3` into the Library – it's a small (8 second) piece of trance music:

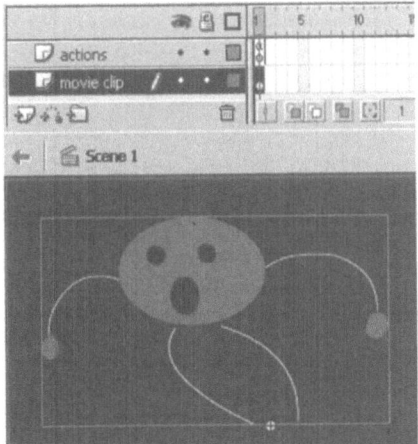

On the stage, we have a movie clip of a little dancing character (`dancer`) that sways from left to right and back when the movie clip plays:

When this movie is tested, we see the character dancing to the music and, whenever the music finishes, the music loop restarts and the character moves to a new position on the screen, giving the effect that he's dancing to the music – he is in fact moving around according to the timing of the music.

Now let's learn how we achieved this – attached to frame 1 of the actions layer on the root timeline, we have the following code:

```
moveChar = function () {
     dancer._x = Math.random()*500;
     dancer._y = Math.random()*300;
     s.start();
};
s = new Sound();
s.attachSound("theSong");
s.onSoundComplete = moveChar;
s.start();
```

The moveChar function simply relocates the dancer movie clip to a random _x and _y location on the stage, and then starts the sound s, defined later, playing again, with s.start(). Next, we initialize a sound object called s by creating a new Sound() object (see **Chapter 5**) and linking it to sound using the linkage identifier theSong. Note that our MP3 music file has been marked for ActionScript export using this identifier. To do this, simply open up the Library (F11), right click on the sound object, and choose Linkage.... You'll then see the Linkage Properties window appear:

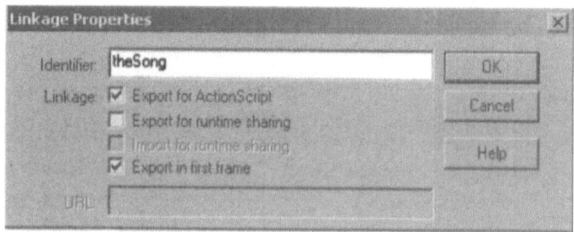

This is where we declare the identifier to be used in the code, and specify the export linkage properties.

After this, we set up the onSoundComplete event, by equating it to our moveChar function – this is the key to sound-based timing. Lastly, we need to start the sound playing with s.start(). And that's it! Test the movie, and the character will move around the screen as the song loops. This gives a simple taste of how we can utilize sound-based timed events to produce intelligent-looking designs.

14 Feedback and Debugging

Objectives

- Understanding techniques for gaining feedback from scripting and graphical content

- Using the Output window and its associated options:

  - List Objects

  - List Variables

  - The `trace()` command

- Using dynamic text fields for feedback

- The Flash MX Debugger for debugging ActionScript:

  - Linear scripts

  - Nonlinear scripts

  - Distributed scripts

Introduction

In this chapter we'll be considering the various techniques that we can use to get feedback on our movies during the design and development stages. Initially, we'll concentrate more on quick and dirty debugging techniques – we'll look at how to get instant feedback during testing, and how to review and check properties on the fly. Then, in the latter half of this chapter, we'll turn our attention to debugging scripts specifically through the use of the Flash MX Debugger tool. We'll highlight the programmatic debugging techniques for the various different types of scripted Flash movies.

The Output window

Not all feedback warrants using the Debugger tool in Flash MX, as it's often much more useful to get instant feedback from your code – this typically takes the form of the `trace()` expression to produce results in the Output window. In this section, we'll concentrate on the use of the Output window and the `trace()` command to get quick details of how our ActionScript is working. In addition, we'll look at the use of text field feedback, setting up what are known as *feedback panels* to give runtime details at the end of your movie, and general tips and tricks to enhance your design and creation process.

The most commonly used method of getting immediate feedback is to send information to the Output window. This is pretty much your quickest tool for finding bugs or simply getting feedback when building and testing your code. The Output window can display errors, variables, and objects within loaded movies; it'll even tell you the specific path to variables, whether they're within nested movie clips or loaded levels, and so on. To view your Output window, select Window>Output, or just hit F2.

Obviously, there's not much happening in it at the moment, but don't worry - we'll soon be using it:

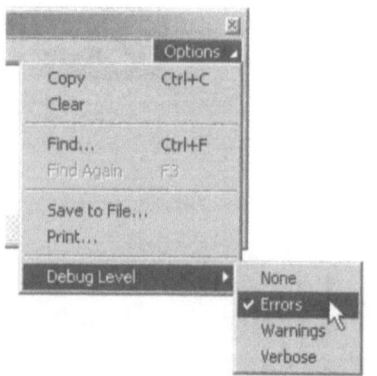

Take a quick look at the Options menu in the upper right corner of this window. It's worth mentioning something called the Debug Level of this window. In fact, many designers aren't aware of this option and leave it set at its default setting (Errors). There are actually four settings available, as seen opposite:

These options are self-explanatory – if you want to see both errors *and* warnings set the debug level to Verbose. You can imagine how unhelpful (and potentially dangerous) the setting None could be!

In this section, we're going to look at the various features of the Output window that are valuable for gathering information about your movie. Firstly, we'll look at the List Objects and List Variables options, both of which result in specific information being sent to the Output window – it's surprising how often designers post questions to Flash forums which could have been answered using one of these features. Then we'll look at more general uses of the Output window using the `trace()` command.

List objects

To invoke the List Objects command, test your movie (CTRL+ENTER), then choose Debug>List Objects from the Flash Player menu, or use the shortcut key combination CTRL+L. Even a seemingly empty movie has some information to offer:

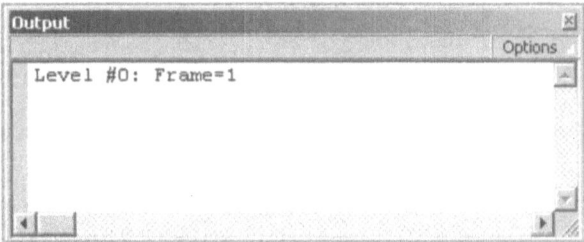

As its name suggests, List Objects displays details about all the objects in your movie. For example, the output for a movie with some content will typically look something like this:

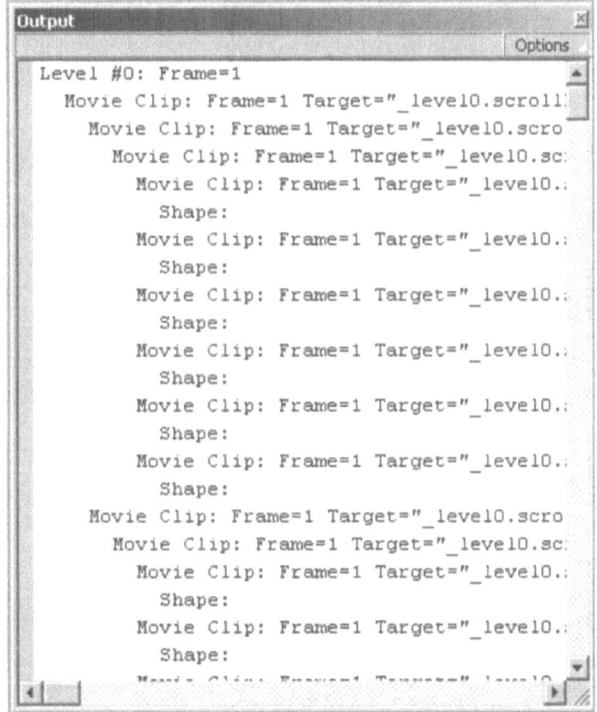

Try it out with your own movies to see what's going on under the hood – you should get a hierarchical list of all the objects, including levels, frames, object types (shape, movie clip, button, and so on), target paths, and instance names of movie clips, buttons, and text fields. One thing to note is that once the information has been sent to the Output window, it does not refresh or update until you force List Objects to run again.

List Variables

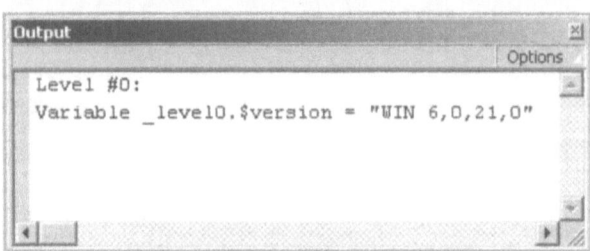

List Variables displays a list of all the variables currently in the movie. This is great for finding the correct path of specific variables buried deep within nested movie clips – and it takes no time at all! Again, note that just like List Objects, the information in the Output window does not refresh or update until you force List Variables again. To use this command, test your movie as before, and then select Debug>List Variables, or just press CTRL+ALT+V. You'll then get an Output window displaying every variable used in the movie – again, even an empty movie has something to say:

However, it's more interesting to see what List Variables produces from an action-packed movie, perhaps like this one:

```
Output                                              ×
                                         Options
Global Variables:                              ▲
  Variable _global.FStyleFormat = [function
    prototype:[object #2, class 'Object'] (
      addListener:[function 'addListener'],
      removeListener:[function 'removeListen
      applyChanges:[function 'applyChanges']
      isAStyle:[function 'isAStyle']
    )
  )
  Variable _global.globalStyleFormat = [obje
    nonStyles:[object #8, class 'Object'] (
      applyChanges:true,
      nonStyles:true,
      removeListener:true,
      addListener:true,
      isAStyle:true,
      isGlobal:true,
      listeners:true
    ),
    listeners:[object #9, class 'Object'] (
      _level0.scrollRed:[movieclip:_level0.s
      _level0.scrollRed.instance4:[movieclip
                                               ▼
```

Note that with this option the Output window even displays global variables declared with the _global identifier. All global variables will be displayed at the top of the List Variables output in a section titled Global Variables, and each variable is prefixed with _global, as shown above.

In addition, the List Variables command also displays getter/setter properties – those that are created with the `Object.addProperty` method and invoke `get` or `set` methods. A getter/setter property is displayed alongside any other properties in the object it belongs to. To make these properties easily distinguishable from ordinary variables, the value of a getter/setter property is prefixed with the string `[getter/setter]`.

trace()

The most common way to send information to the Output window is by using `trace()`. Most developers will be familiar with `trace()` and its usage, in fact we've often relied upon it in this book, but it's still worth spending a little time going through how to use it and how to enhance the actual output messages.

> Remember that `trace()` only functions when in test mode within the Flash authoring environment; published movies don't let `trace()` statements produce any output.

Although a published SWF will still contain `trace()` commands, you won't be able to see their output. If you want your finished movie to omit `trace()` altogether (and potentially save some processing time if you have a large number of them in your movie), simply click on the Omit Trace actions option in the Flash tab of the Publish Settings window (File>Publish Settings or CTRL+SHIFT+F12):

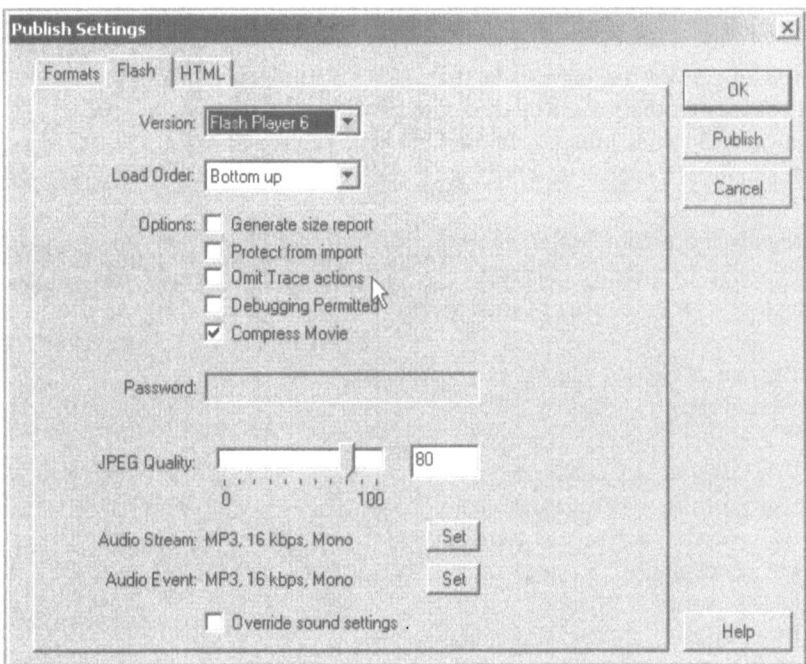

Let's look at the basic usage of `trace()`, and then how to enhance its output. Consider the following simple variable declaration as a starting point:

```
var x = 100;
trace(x);
```

If you type this into your Actions panel on, say, frame 1 of the root timeline and test the movie, you'll get the following rather predictable result:

First we set our variable x to be equal to 100, and then `trace()` returns the value of x in the Output window. This is very straightforward and easy to do, however it's not particularly meaningful – the Output window is an expanse of white, with the number 100 sitting in the top left corner. Imagine if you have scattered `trace()` statements throughout your code. All of a sudden, you'll have an Output window with a whole load of seemingly meaningless numbers in a list, with no indication of what they refer to.

So, let's include some simple concatenation to clarify our output. Concatenation simply joins strings and values together into one long line. To give our example above a little more meaning, we could change it to look like this:

```
var x = 100;
trace("var x = "+x);
```

This time, the output display is much more helpful:

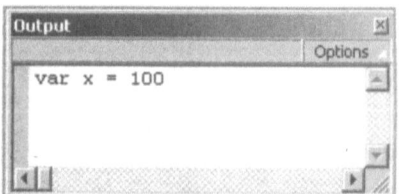

Seasoned developers will not leave it at that. Using a `trace()` statement to separate other `trace()` uses, and concatenation in front of and behind values brings a whole new light to using a command as simple as `trace()` to check your code.

Let's try a slightly more complicated example for the sake of showing how to extract information via `trace()`. Although it's a rather unrealistic use of scripting, for the sake of demonstration let's assume the following list of variables exist in your movie:

```
var UKfirstName = "Tony";
var UKlastName = "Blair";
var UKaddress1 = "10 Downing Street";
var UKaddress2 = "London";
var UKaddress3 = "England";
var UKjobTitle = "Prime Minister";
var USfirstName = "George W.";
var USlastName = "Bush";
var USaddress1 = "The Whitehouse";
var USaddress2 = "Washingon DC";
```

```
var USaddress3 = "USA";
var USjobTitle = "President";
```

Open up `trace_test.fla` to run this example as we go along. We'll being using `trace()` to separate, arrange, and concatenate these variables into readable output. First off we'll use `trace()` as a separator in order to visually group our output:

```
trace("---------------------------");
```

All this does is output a line of dashes to the Output window. Now we want to start building up our group of values from the available variables. As stated earlier, for the sake of demonstration we'll build something that is a little over the top, but gives us opportunity to really see what `trace()` can do. We will start by concatenating the details, then finish with a sentence, made up of the various parts.

```
trace(UKjobTitle+": "+UKfirstName+" "+UKlastName);
```

Note that we're using concatenation throughout to join several pieces of information stored in various variables. The other thing to note is the use of quotation marks, spaces, and punctuation to give the sentence a readable format. The Output window, at this stage is thus:

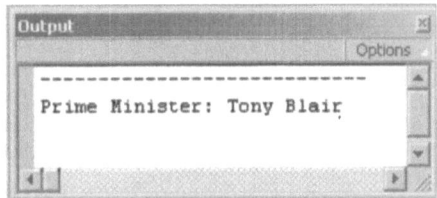

Continuing with this example, let's add the following line:

```
trace(UKaddress1+", "+UKaddress2+", "+UKaddress3+"\n");
```

Notice here that we are separating the lines of information by forcing a new line with the \n line marker notation. We can finish up this segment by adding a couple more `trace()` statements, concatenating some text into the statement so that we end up with a readable formatted sentence:

```
trace("Today, the "+USjobTitle+" of the "+USaddress3+", "+USfirstName+"
➥"+USlastName+", ");
trace("left "+UKaddress1+" to tour "+UKaddress3);
```

To conclude this part of our output, we should add another line break:

```
trace("---------------------------");
```

Finally, when we test our movie (CTRL+ENTER), the Output window will display the following message:

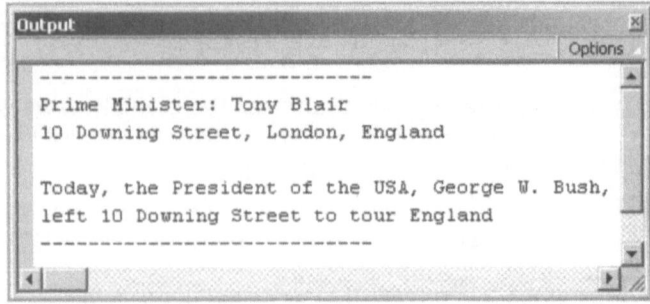

This example serves to demonstrate that something as simple and quick to use as `trace()` can actually deliver extremely informative output to the developer, after some basic string concatenation to add context to the variables.

Similar techniques can be used to view the contents of arrays, movie clip paths, and so on. Clever use of these techniques can deliver a formatted appearance to your output message. For instance, we can actually get `trace()` to output the contents of an array to look similar in context to the way it is written within our code. If we define an array as follows:

```
myArray = ["Tony", "Blair", "Prime Minister"];
```

We can use a structured `trace()` command like this:

```
trace("myArray ["+myArray[0]+" "+myArray[1]+"]");
```

which will output the following:

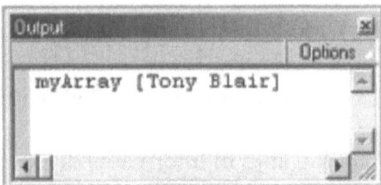

These rather abstract examples demonstrate the power and potential of the simple `trace()` command.

Dynamic text fields for feedback

Another quick and easy way to get feedback is to place a dynamic text field directly onto the stage, and use it to reference the variable you want to check.

Note that it's always good practice to place text boxes for this kind of feedback in a separate layer and put a label to the side of it:

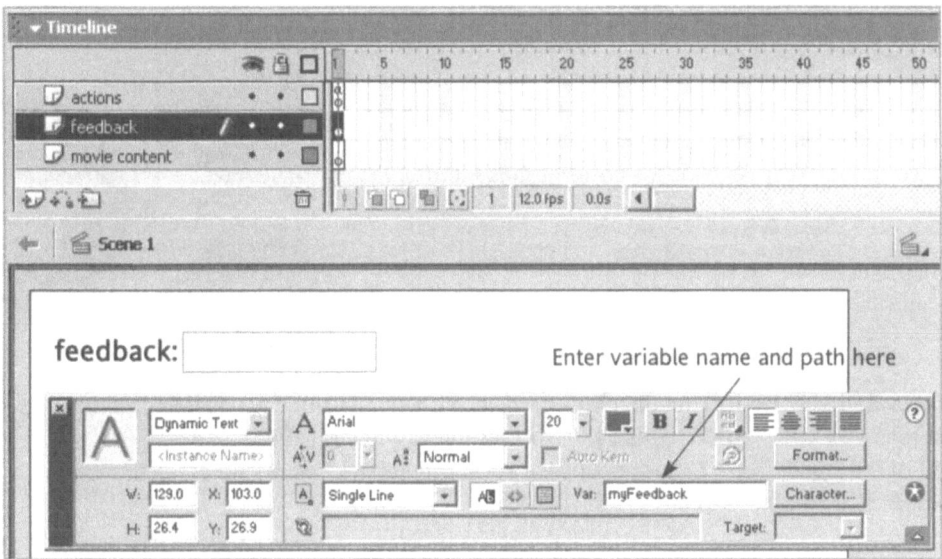

By entering the name of the variable in the Var field of the Property inspector, we can force the dynamic text field to display the contents of the variable. If necessary, you can even use a fully qualified path to the variable, for example: `_root.movieClip.VariableName`.

This technique is great when you simply want to see a specific variable, but it becomes a bit limited when you want to use one text field to display a series of variables or property information. Another trick is to use a combination of dynamic text fields and buttons. Give the dynamic text field an instance name and set its text via a button. Of course, the text set by the button can be anything you like, so you simply write code that investigates the content of a variable, or an object property, and then send that to the text field.

OK, time for an example; open up `dynamic_feedback.fla`. On the stage you'll find a simple circle, instance name `myCircle`, alongside a couple of buttons with instance names `myButton1` and `myButton2` (we've just dragged these arcade-style buttons from the Window>Common Libraries>Buttons Library for this demonstration). There's also a dynamic text field on the stage with a variable name of `myFeedback`, as described above. Now for the ActionScript – you'll find the following code on frame 1 of the root timeline:

```
myButton1.onRelease = function() {
    myFeedback = myCircle._width;
};
myButton2.onRelease = function() {
    myFeedback = myCircle._x;
};
```

Test the movie with CTRL+ENTER and notice how after clicking and releasing each button, the text field displays either the width or x-position of your circle. This simple example gives an idea how easy it is to get feedback on various properties in your movie at the click of a button:

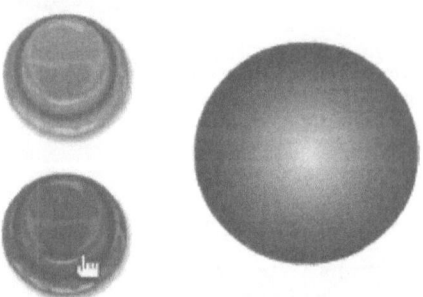

feedback: 226.5

So, what we've done here is build a quick and dirty feedback window. There are a few developer tricks and tips that we should keep in mind when using this kind of feedback:

- Always add this kind of feedback in its own layer, and name that layer something to reflect its content – Feedback or Trace Layer – so that it's easy to track down and delete or disguise at the end of the build. Don't be afraid to have several feedback layers and place them all in a feedback folder.

- While building and testing, you don't want to obscure your actual movie, so another trick is to place all your feedback buttons and text fields into a single movie clip. Of course, this way you will need to pay attention to the movie clip hierarchy and give the appropriate path names in your script. With this technique, you can turn the visibility of the movie clip on and off as you wish. You could even give it drag-and-drop functionality (see **Chapter 2**) so that you can position it wherever you want on the stage. In fact, the best way to think of your feedback content is as if it were an object within your movie – manipulate it just as you would any other object, make it draggable, visible or invisible, change its coordinates as you wish, and so on.

- Once you are ready to publish, simply change the state of your feedback layer to be a Guide layer (right-click on the layer).

    This layer then gets ignored by Flash when you compile your SWF, resulting in no worries about increased movie size, but lets you return to the source file and have access to a complete panel of information at any time.

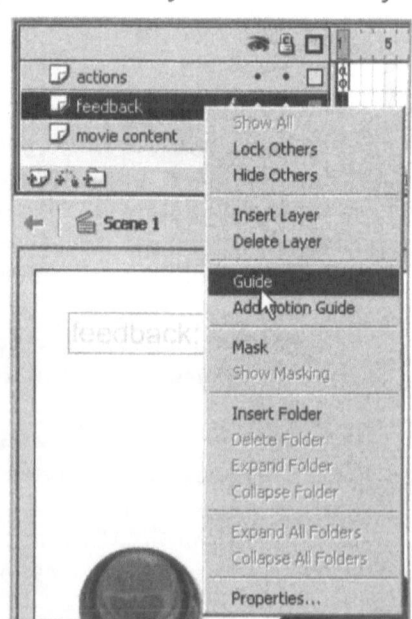

As mentioned at the outset of this chapter, we've covered the quick and easy ways of getting instant feedback on your scripting via the Output window and through dynamic text fields. This is not to imply that the Flash MX Debugger tool is anything but straight forward to use – it's also very simple to utilize! We'll look at programmatic debugging in depth in the next section.

The Debugger

In this second half of the chapter we'll look at the debugging environment, and show exactly what **breakpoints** are and how they can be effectively used to debug your code. Then, we'll look in detail at a few examples of specific debugging scenarios. We'll begin by examining the Flash MX debugging environment.

The Debugger window

The **Debugger** window will appear if you test a movie using Control>Debug Movie (or CTRL+SHIFT+ENTER). The debugger will only appear if your FLA contains scripts in it; this is reasonable, since if there is no code there will certainly be nothing to debug! So, to get the debugger up for now to see how it works, simply add a stop() action to frame 1 of a new movie, and go to Control>Debug Movie:

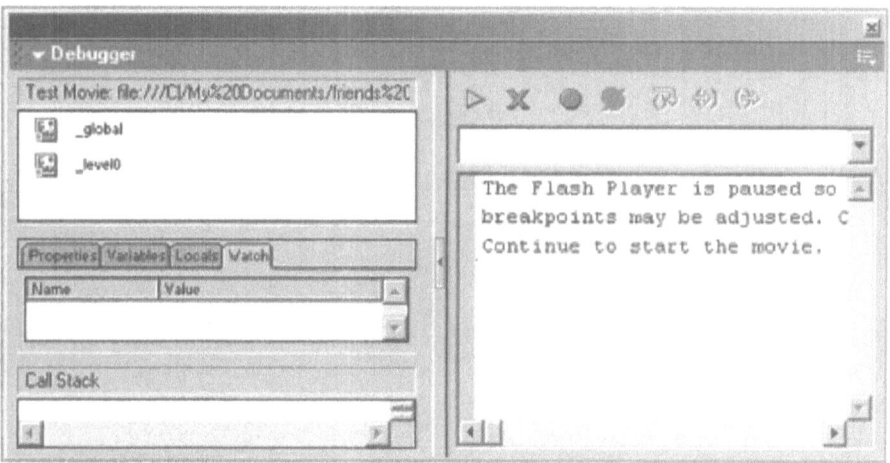

We should note the following important features of the Debugger window:

- The objects pane at the top left of the window allows you to view all of the objects in a tree format. Selection of objects in this pane only affects the left-hand side of the debugger window, allowing you to view its properties and variables and so on.

- The Properties tab lets you view and sometimes modify the properties of selected movie clips. These amendments are temporary, only effective in the debug session.

- One of the most powerful features of the debug window is within the Variables tab. During testing, you can edit variable values to see how they react, which may in turn affect an object. Values are editable in the same way as in the Properties tab – by double-clicking on them.

- The Locals tab allows you to see the values of **local** variables. Locals are variables that are created in function code blocks, and cease to exist when the block is completed; they are only *alive* at the time of execution.

- The Watch pane allows you to single out and monitor specific variables. You can mark variables to appear in the Watch list, which displays the absolute path to the variable and its value.

- The Call Stack pane displays information about nesting (hierarchy) of calls to functions, displaying the functions that are currently being run and the function that started them. For example, the stack would allow you to see that function A is called by function B from the main timeline.

- A script pane on the right of the window – this is the real meat of the debugger!

The script pane has a menu at the top as shown in close-up below:

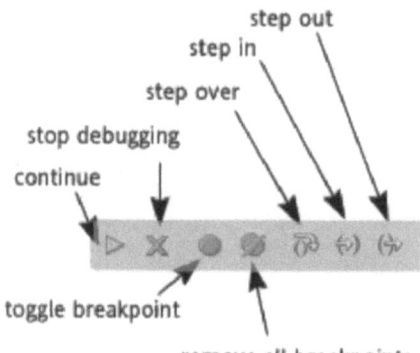

When you first debug a movie, the debugger will pause your movie. To actually begin the debug session (that is, play until the first breakpoint – or, if none are seen, play indefinitely) you need to hit the Continue icon. Hitting it a second time will make the SWF run until the next breakpoint is reached. If there is no subsequent breakpoint, you will end up with real-time debugging.

The Stop Debugging icon does exactly what it says – it halts the debugger. So why would you want to do this rather than just quit? Well, remember that you can change the values of any variables in the tabbed area on the fly, so one reason to create a breakpoint may not be to check your code, but to insert test values of variables at a certain point. You might want to stop debugging if you have found the error, confirm this by setting the erroneous variable to the correct value, and then confirm that correct program execution is seen from that point by exiting debug mode, allowing the SWF to continue.

Similarly obvious, the Toggle Breakpoint icon toggles the selected breakpoint. To use this of course, you have to activate a breakpoint before the program execution gets to it. Likewise, Remove All Breakpoints does exactly what it says.

The final three options allow you to step through the code one line at a time, and let you define what happens when the debugger comes across certain code structures:

- Step Over - executes the current line, and stops at the next line in the script. If the current line is a function, the debugger will execute it without making you step through every line of it as well (so the thing you are *stepping over* is the function).

- Step In – executes the current line and, if that line is a function call, the debugger will let you step through every line of it by jumping across to the script that contains the function. If the current line is *not* a function call, then both Step Over and Step In do the same thing: execute the current line and stop at the next one.

- Step Out – executes all lines up to the end of the current code block. For example, if you were in a long for loop that looped 100 times, you might just want to execute all the lines in the loop at once, and see what the variables were doing at the end of a loop.

Linear scripts

In the following example, we'll add a couple of breakpoints to a script, and also run it by single stepping. Open up linear.fla from the CD; on frame 1 of the main timeline you'll find the following code:

```
pie0 = "apple";
pie1 = "blueberry";
pie2 = "cherry";
pie3 = "lemon";
pieEaten = new Array();
for (i=0; i<4; i++) {
        pieEaten[i] = _root["pie"+i];
        _root["pie"+i] = "gone!";
}
```

At the beginning of this script, we define pie0 to pie3 as strings that represent various types of pies. We then use a loop to add each pie to an array of eaten pies. As each pie is added to the array, we reassign the pie variable as gone! (because we've eaten it!). If you debug the FLA (CTRL+SHIFT+ENTER), you'll see the Debugger window appear in its initially paused state. Hit the Continue icon to run the debugger. The script will run through to the end, and the Variables tab of the debugger shows the final result:

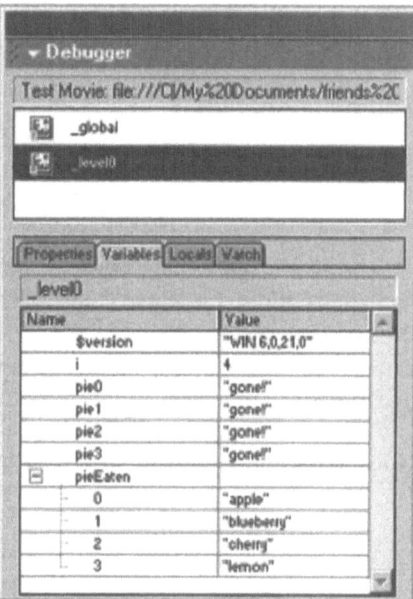

As you can see, all of the `pie` variables have now `gone!` and we've placed them in the `pieEaten` array. That's fine when it works, but there are all sorts of things that we could have done wrong, such as make the loop start with `i=1`, which would have given me this:

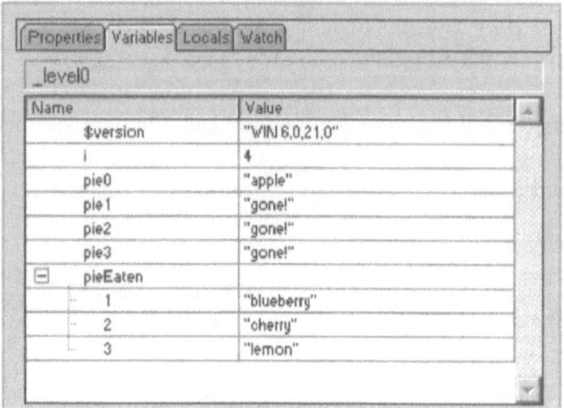

Although we know which line contains our error (`i=1` instead of `i=0` in line 6), the debugger isn't all that helpful in telling us this. This is because it doesn't let us see inside the loop; it only gives us a snapshot at the end of the script. To see what is going on in our script, let's add some breakpoints. It would be nice to see that all the `pies` are properly defined, and that the results at the end of each loop are correct. To do this, we need a snapshot at line 4 and one at the end of each loop, on line 8.

Note that the end of the loop is not the brace. If you try to add a breakpoint on a line containing a brace, Flash will raise an error during the debug session, stating that "One or more breakpoints have been removed because they are not on valid lines of code". You cannot add a breakpoint to any line of script that will not compile to a byte of code in the final SWF (which leaves Flash nothing to attach the breakpoint to). This includes:

- Braces

- Function definition heads (that is, the line with `something = myFunction()` { at the top of a function definition)

- Lines containing only comments

To add a breakpoint to a line, place the text cursor on the line and then right click anywhere in the script editing pane of the **Actions** panel and select Set Breakpoint from the pop-up menu.

Alternatively you can click the Debug Options icon (top right of the **Actions** panel) and also select Set Breakpoint.

Add breakpoints to lines 4 and 8 of our code in `linear.fla`:

```
 1 pie0 = "apple";
 2 pie1 = "blueberry";
 3 pie2 = "cherry";
 4 pie3 = "lemon";
 5 pieEaten = new Array();
 6 for (i=1; i<4; i++) {
 7     pieEaten[i] = _root["pie"+i];
 8     _root["pie"+i] = "gone!";
 9 }
```

Now start the debugger. You'll see the script appear as shown below. Select _level0 (noticing that the debugger also allows you to see global values via the *_global* level) and click the Variables tab to see the current state of the variables on the main timeline:

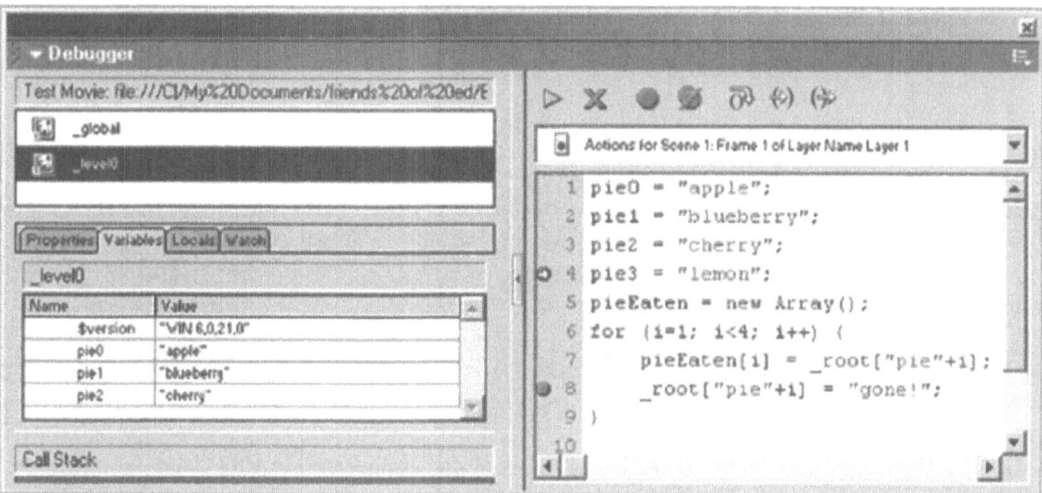

The first breakpoint has a little arrow over it, which will always point to the next line to be executed (we can tell when the script has finished if you can no longer see the little arrow pointer). The debugger has run through all lines up to the breakpoint, executing lines 1, 2, and 3. You can see this in the Variables tab: pie0, 1, and 2 have been defined, but there is no pie3. To run the script up to the next breakpoint, hit Continue:

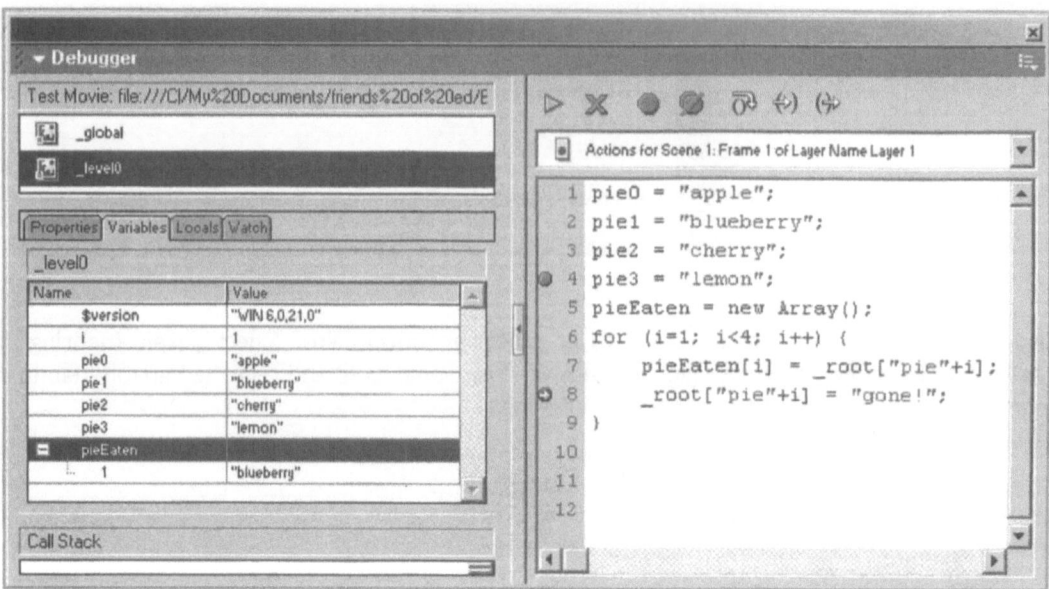

The script will now execute up to (but not including) line 8. This already shows us the error: the loop starts at 1, not 0, so the first pieEaten is the blueberry rather than the apple pie. Hit Continue. You'll see that nothing much changes – the arrow stays at line 8. This is because we are in a loop. Program execution has run the first loop, and the breakpoint stops execution on the next loop. You can continue looping round by hitting Continue, and see the Variables tab update to reflect changes made per loop.

OK, so we've found our error, but what if the error was a little more subtle? We might want to look at each line in turn, a process called *single stepping*, which is just like having a breakpoint on every line.

Quit the debugger and delete all the breakpoints by selecting Remove All Breakpoints from either of the two menus described earlier. Fix the for-loop so that it starts at i=0. Now, add a single breakpoint at line 1, and select Control>Debug Movie again. This time, the breakpoint will stop the script at line 1. No parts of the script have been executed yet.

Select _level0, hit the Variable tab, and click on the Continue icon once:

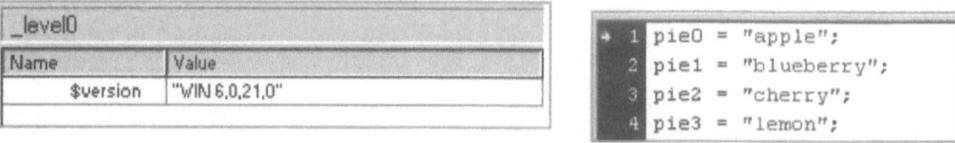

No variables have been defined, except for the system variable $version that tells you what version of the Flash Player you are debugging with.

Now single step by hitting the Step In icon [·] This will execute the current line, and stop at the next one:

_level0	
Name	Value
$version	"WIN 6,0,21,0"
pie0	"apple"

```
1  pie0 = "apple";
2  pie1 = "blueberry";
3  pie2 = "cherry";
4  pie3 = "lemon";
```

This causes line 1 to create pie0 and set it to the value apple. If you continue single stepping through to line 5 you'll eventually see this:

_level0	
Name	Value
$version	"WIN 6,0,21,0"
pie0	"apple"
pie1	"blueberry"
pie2	"cherry"
pie3	"lemon"

```
1  pie0 = "apple";
2  pie1 = "blueberry";
3  pie2 = "cherry";
4  pie3 = "lemon";
5  pieEaten = new Array();
```

All the pies have been defined, and we're just about to enter the loop. Hit Step In once more – you'll jump to line 6, and the pieEaten array will now be defined. It doesn't have a value yet, because it is still undefined. Hit Step In again:

_level0	
Name	Value
$version	"WIN 6,0,21,0"
i	0
pie0	"apple"
pie1	"blueberry"
pie2	"cherry"
pie3	"lemon"
pieEaten	

```
6  for (i=0; i<4; i++) {
7      pieEaten[i] = _root["pie"+i];
8      _root["pie"+i] = "gone!";
9  }
```

At line 7, our loop variable is set to 0. Hit Step In a few times to see the execution loop round the for, and you'll see the effects of eating the pie; the pie becomes gone!, and pieEaten is updated appropriately. Also notice the counter updating itself.

The process we are going through here is actually a very powerful debugging technique. We are seeing snapshots of the Flash Player at every single line, and can see everything that is changing. However, it is only useful if we already have a good idea of what we expect to happen, so it's helpful to jot down a few notes before you start debugging at this low level. Work out where you want the breakpoint and what you expect to happen to key variables involved with the error. In large scripts, you'll want to start single stepping a few lines before the place you think the error is occurring – and you must know roughly where the error is for single stepping, otherwise you are in for a long debugging session.

We are looping only four times (0, 1, 2, 3), but what if I were a particularly hungry designer and I were eating a hundred pieces of pie? Single stepping becomes a rather long process as soon as we hit a loop that big. We might have got all the usefulness of looking at individual loops by the third or fourth loop iteration. That's where the Step Out icon comes in. Hit it and the loop (or any block, such as a function or do loop) will run through until it is finished:

Name	Value
$version	"WIN 6,0,21,0"
i	4
pie0	"gone!"
pie1	"gone!"
pie2	"gone!"
pie3	"gone!"
⊟ pieEaten	
0	"apple"
1	"blueberry"
2	"cherry"
3	"lemon"

_level0

The script we have just looked at is fairly simple; all the action takes place in one script on a single frame. However, we may have functions that make multiple calls and jump all over the place in the timeline, so let's have a look at this scenario next.

Scripts that call other scripts

When you call a function that you have defined earlier in your ActionScript, the debugger must jump backwards out of the current script and resume execution at the function. Once the function has finished, execution will resume at the call point. Let's have a look at this in action.

> As we mentioned earlier, the debugger is not just for debugging. When you call many functions in a small script, you may not be aware of the total number of lines that end up being executed. When writing code loops in which performance is critical (such as those within games, communication loops, or XML parsing), the debugger will show you how many lines are executed; in this context, the debugger is an aid for **code optimization**.

For this example, open up `nonlinear.fla` and look at the script on frame 1 of the scripts layer:

```
function tax(value) {
    var taxPercent = 0.175;
    var taxAmount;
```

```
        taxAmount = value*taxPercent;
        return (taxAmount);
    }
```

This function works out the amount of tax due on the argument `value`, and returns the amount of tax payable, calculated at 17.5%. It uses `var` to define two local variables `taxPercent` and `taxAmount`.

Next, have a look at the code on frame 2 of the scripts layer:

```
    salaryAmount = 1000;
    taxAmount = tax(salaryAmount);
    myTakeHome = salaryAmount-taxAmount;
    stop();
```

This script uses the `tax` function to work out the tax I have to pay (`taxAmount`) on my salary `salaryAmount`, and works out my take-home pay as `myTakeHome`. Notice that there is already a variable `taxAmount` in the function we just created in frame 1; we have a variable local to the function and another variable of the same name in our main script. So, as well as looking at how functions affect program execution, this simple bit of accounting will also tell us how Flash handles variables that are local to a function block.

Debug the script with CTRL+SHIFT+ENTER. By clicking on Continue and going to the Variables tab of _level0 you'll see the final results:

_level0	
Name	Value
$version	"WIN 6,0,21,0"
myTakeHome	825
salaryAmount	1000
tax	
taxAmount	175

We have our function `tax` defined, as well as our variables `myTakeHome`, `taxAmount`, and `salaryAmount`. Although this tells us that the scripts have worked (because we can see that the answers are correct), it does not tell us anything about the interactions that occurred within the code because it all occurs within the space of a single frame. Let's have a look at that now.

Add a breakpoint to line 1 of the script on frame 2, and then debug the movie:

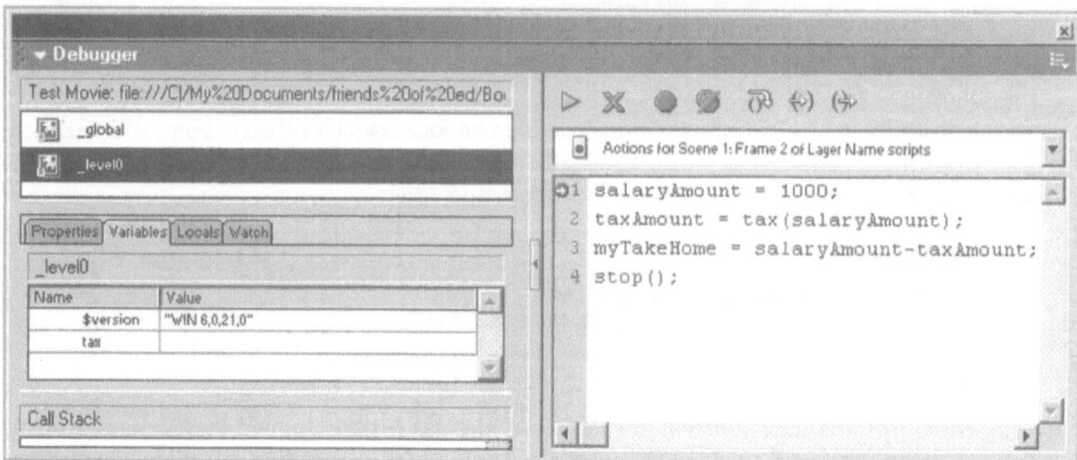

There are a couple of things to notice as soon as the script starts:

■   The debugger has already run through the script at frame 1 and the function `tax` has been defined. When using functions, it's always important to check that all functions are defined before you actually call them. Obvious perhaps, but still a common mistake!

■   We are now looking at the script at frame 2 of the **scripts** layer; the title bar at the top of the script pane indicates this. If we want to recap what the function `tax` actually looks like, we can click on this title and select it from the drop-down menu of available scripts:

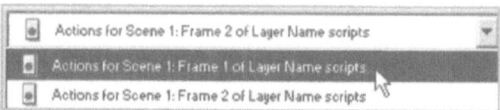

This is a very useful feature for FLAs that contain a large number of scripts; you may need to look at other scripts to help you deduce what has happened.

Hit Step In. Irrespective of which script you are currently looking at, the debugger will jump to the script line that is currently about to be executed – line 2 of the script on frame 2:

```
1  salaryAmount = 1000;
2  taxAmount = tax(salaryAmount);
3  myTakeHome = salaryAmount-taxAmount;
4  stop();
```

To execute this frame, Flash has to jump to the function `tax`. We can do one of two things here: either watch Flash as it does this, or we can stay within the current script. We'll do both to demonstrate, starting with the full deal.

Hit the Step In icon again. The function script appears because this is where program execution has jumped to, in order to evaluate `tax(salaryAmount)`:

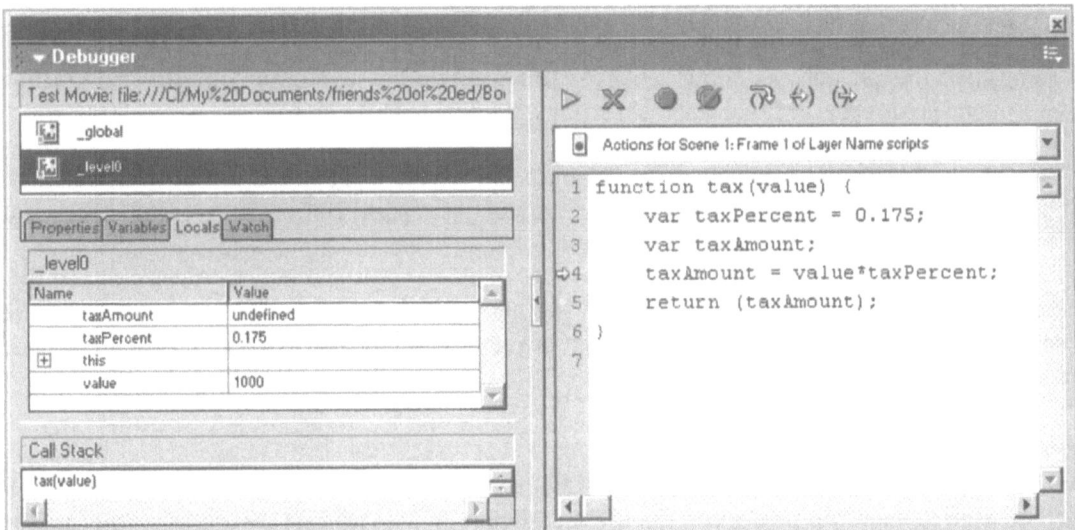

Use Step In to step down to line 4, as shown above. We want to look at a different `taxPercent` here: the version that is local to our function. To do this, look at the Locals tab. Hit Step In until you return to the main script, and Step In to the end. Notice that when you return to the main script, the Local variables disappear. This is to be expected – the variables defined with `var` have a lifetime only within the function block that they are defined in, and once program execution has moved out of the function, they cease to exist.

> *Local values can only be defined in a function block. Using* var *in any other block (such as a* while *or* for*) does not create local variables.*

We have not only proven that the script works by looking for the final result, we have also shown that the *route* to the result is correct:

- The function executes as expected.

- There are no collisions between the two versions of `taxAmount`.

- We now have a better understanding of the lines that are executed and their ordering, something that can only make us better scripters!

OK, so assuming we are meticulous scripters and we've fully tested our function, what if we know it works and don't want to jump to it, or don't want to run through all lines? If we debug the FLA again, from line 2 of the main script we can:

- Hit Step Over – this will evaluate the line `taxAmount = tax(salaryAmount)` without actually jumping to the function `tax` in the debugger. You might do this if you were sure that the function was running correctly, and that the main script was jumping to it correctly.

- Hit Step In to jump to the function `tax`, but once you are there, hit Step Out. This will evaluate all lines in the function in one go and jump back to the main script. This option is useful if you want to be sure that the function is actually being invoked by a line in the main script.

Although we have looked at a script that relies on another script to work, real FLAs contain much more complexity than this; they may use a large number of totally different scripts that all run on the same frame – we'll look at this in the next example.

Distributed timelines

In the following example, `distributed.fla`, we'll look at how multiple scripts are executed by the Flash player. You need to know this before you can use breakpoints in most typical FLAs, because you typically have more than one script in more than one place, and it will also give you some insight into how scripts actually run. So, open the `distributed.fla` file, which you'll find on the CD. Look at the ActionScript attached to frame 1 of the fruit layer:

```
x = "apple";
y = "pear";
```

Here we've simply defined a couple of variables with fruit-related values. Next, in frame 1 of the islands layer, we've got some script that gives our variables values corresponding to the names of islands:

```
x = "Sumatra";
y = "Ireland";
```

In the graphics layer you'll find a movie clip with the instance name `clip`; if you double-click on this movie clip, you'll see that there is some script on frame 1 of its timeline:

```
x = "dog";
y = "cat";
_root.x = "monkey";
_root.y = "budgie";
```

This script makes our main timeline variables the names of some animals, and also creates a pair of variables local to `myClip`, also animals. Now the question is, when we run this FLA, what will all the variables be equal to? We have three scripts; all three are on the same frame, but in different places. Which order will they be executed in?

Well, we know that all of the variables are executed by the end of the frame. It is, however, a whole different ball game when looking at the scripts line by line, because there has to be a definite order. Flash doesn't execute them all at the same time, so it's important to know the execution order before we can understand how the debugger is used in single step or breakpoint mode.

> *The order of execution may cause problems during initialization, where one script will try to reference variables before they are created and defined.*

The first thing we have to do is add a breakpoint. In the Actions panel, bring up the script for the fruit layer and add a breakpoint at line 1:

```
1 x = "apple";
2 y = "pear";
```

We've put the breakpoint on the first line of this script for a reason: it's the first script to be run, so line 1 of this script is the first line to be executed. Test the FLA in debug mode, and press Continue once to start the debugger, and again to run from the breakpoint to the end of the frame:

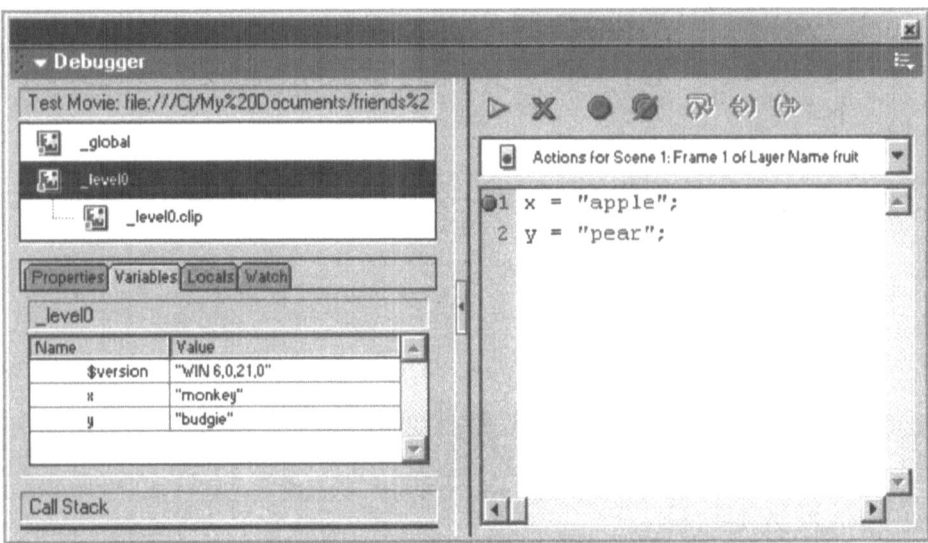

You'll end up with the rather confusing display shown above. The script tells us that x = "apple", but the actual value of x is "monkey". This is because we have ignored the order of execution; if we want to debug frames with multiple scripts, we must place a breakpoint at the start of each script, because the debugger will then give us some important information including:

- The order that each script executes in

- The variables that exist at the start of each script

■ The variables that exist at the end of each script

If you now add a breakpoint at the start of the other two scripts, you will see the order of execution. First:

```
x = "apple";
y = "pear";
```

Then:

```
x = "Sumatra";
y = "Ireland";
```

And finally (from the timeline of the movie clip):

```
x = "dog";
y = "cat";
_root.x = "monkey";
_root.y = "budgie";
```

The way Flash runs scripts is related to the layer order, but actually equal to the depth order. Layers only have meaning in FLA files; they don't even exist in the SWF file, which runs scripts in depth order, running the script with the lowest depth first.

If you do not use duplicateMovieClip or createEmptyMovieClip, the depth order is the same as the layer order, and goes from the top layer downwards. Any scripts that you place on the timelines at authoring time will be given a *negative* depth, which means they will always run before any scripts you define that are attached to clips you create at runtime (because they have positive depths). After all the scripts have been run in layer order, the first level of embedded timelines (such as our movie clip, which is embedded on _*level0*) are executed, and so on, moving deeper through the embedded timelines.

You can see how the layer order will change the depths, and therefore the execution order, by re-ordering the layers or by moving the clip to another layer, and then rerunning the debugger to see the new order of execution. Although this is a trivial FLA, it actually displays some fundamental principles about how Flash scripting works.

Remote debugging

If you debug an FLA, you'll see an additional **SWD** (Shockwave debug) file created alongside the SWF in the same location as the FLA. The SWD contains all the runtime debug data, including your scripts and breakpoint data. If you look inside a SWD file with a text editor (such as WordPad), you'll see that it contains all the scripts from the FLA. The SWF contains **byte code**, which is not readable, or rather, not easily readable, especially if the SWF is also compressed, so there's no need to worry about including all your scripting secrets into the SWF for all to see.

You should not upload the SWD file to a server unless you specifically want to debug online, and you should always remove it when you are done.

If you want to debug your movie remotely, choose File>Publish Settings and ensure that Debugging Permitted is checked in the Flash tab of the Publish Settings dialog box:

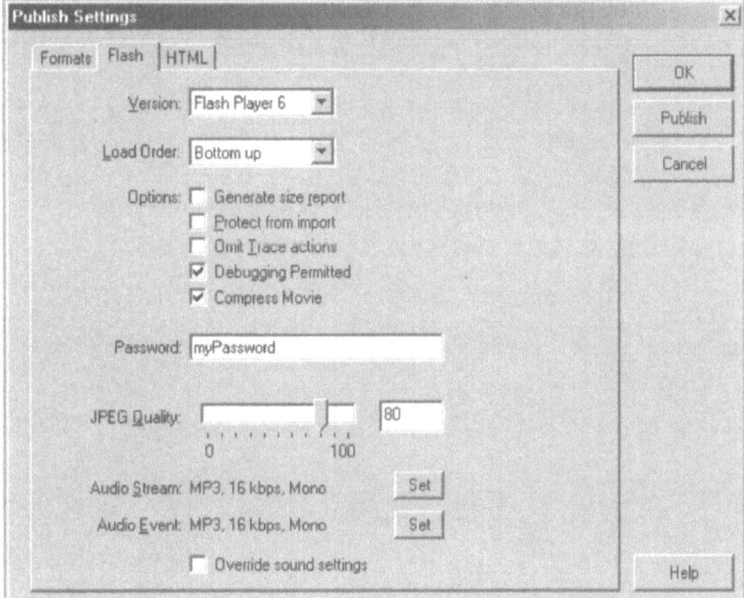

Notice when you check Debugging Permitted that the Password text field becomes available. It is highly advisable to enter a password here to keep your code secure. Once you set this password, no one can download information to the debugger without it.

The next step is to return to the debugger window, and select the Enable Remote Debugging from the options pop-up menu in the top right corner. Publish the movie and Flash will create the SWD file alongside the SWF file on your hard disk. The SWD file contains information that allows you to use breakpoints and step through code.

If you want to activate the debugger from a remote location, open up both the Flash authoring application and the published movie remotely. You should see the Remote Debug dialog box. If it doesn't appear, it probably means that Flash couldn't find the SWD. Try displaying the context menu by right clicking on the movie, and then selecting Debugger. Specify whether the file is stored locally or remotely,and enter the IP address of the computer running the Flash authoring application.

15 Modular Programming Techniques

Objectives

- Structured programming practices to enhance the scripting behind your creative motion graphics

- Understanding of the differences between Flash 5 and Flash MX modular code

- Understanding the concepts of modularizing your movies via timelines

- Defining and using functions and localized variables

- Developing common reusable code routines

- Components and their relevance to creating reusable, configurable, and modular scripts

Introduction

One of the most significant developments in Flash MX is the way that it not only allows you to write truly **modular** code – it almost *requires* it. Although this chapter, and **Chapter 16** on object oriented programming, will be firmly centered on Flash MX, we will at times refer to Flash 5 scripting practices to give some context to the updated techniques.

There will come a time when you decide that code efficiency is at the top of your priorities. You've moved away from the 'keep hacking away until it works' school of thought, and are beginning to think about your code *before* you start writing because it will save you time. Everyone tells you that you should not only be a visual designer, but also stand back and think about the code that drives it all; this is just as important as the graphic creation and interface design stages.

Most of all, you know that Flash MX is different from Flash 5 and all that came before it, in a big way. You know the real difference between Flash 5 and MX is in the code. You've heard that many Flash ActionScripters are getting really excited, and it's somehow all tied into the ideas of structured programming and modular code. Also, this is all part of the greater, overall concept of object oriented design.

Well, this is all true. Flash MX is radically different in the way it treats the scripting environment and, in most cases, this is not due to new features but it's down to the way you work. If you use a particular workflow, Flash MX is a different country altogether. Modular code is the starting point, the border crossing into this new country. It's when you stop thinking "Wow, that's a cool idea, let's hack together some script to make the graphics move," and consider broader questions such as:

- What is the basic effect and what are the separate elements that form this effect?

- How can I code all these elements so I can easily mutate it into something else at a later date?

- How do I take all these separate elements that I've just defined and combine them to form the final effect, and how do I plan it all out in advance of implementing it?

This is obvious, right? Time spent planning, rather than just hacking the code together as you go along, must be time well spent. The difficulty arises when you start listening to programmers: they may all live in this country that is MX, but they work very differently, talking in a different language to designers. Thinking with a programming mindset, the questions listed above now become:

- How can I split up my problem into *modular* code?

- How can I *generalize* my problem?

- How do I *structure* my solution?

In this chapter we'll be looking at structured and modular programming. We'll be sure to stay firmly rooted in the Flash world and the concepts and conventions of motion graphics, rather than think about them in general abstract programming terms (which, as we will see, can sometimes kill the creative input that Flash is all about).

The good, the bad, and why it can get ugly!

Like most things, writing code in a structured manner has both advantages and disadvantages. The trick is in knowing when to use it, and when the problem or process doesn't justify it.

Advantages of modular coding

If you make your code non-specific, you can reuse it. This isn't the only good thing; you can also easily modify it. Imagine your effect is a text message that starts life as 'Welcome to my site', then splits off into a snowstorm of flying dots, and finally coalesces into the new text 'Hope you like it!' Conceptually, there's one crucial point to realize here: each dot in your snowstorm represents the same basic problem, and the code that drives one dot is the same as the code that drives any other. This makes your overall problem much easier to define. Once you've worked out how to control one dot, the code can be modified slightly to work with any number of dots.

So, continuing with the snowstorm text scenario, start with one dot and sub-divide the problem further:

- We need to make the dot start at a location that corresponds to a pixel in the start text message.

- We need to make the dot fly off around the screen for a while.

- We then need to make it take up a new position that is part of the end text message.

This is what makes our solution modular. When we actually come to code the sub-divided bullet points *we tackle each point as a separate part of the problem*. We code the elements *separately*, even testing them in isolation, before joining them together to form the final effect. This is all modular coding really is.

Joining them together is where **structured programming** comes in. We require a degree of forethought before we start coding in order to make sure that we can actually join all the little bits (our modules) together at the end. We also need to know something about the ActionScript structures that will allow us to do this. Recognizing that all your dots are alike is known as **generalization**.

The reasons why programming in a modular fashion like this is advantageous are many.

Reusing code

This works on at least two levels. Firstly, the code required to drive each dot (going back to our earlier example) is essentially the same, so our final code is smaller. Secondly, the separate code modules are just that; they are separate from each other. This means that we can take one or more modules and use *them in another movie*.

Similar code, different effect

Because we have split the solution into smaller parts, these parts become more general. For example, we could replace the 'make the dots a snowstorm' module with a 'make the dots a star field' effect. We only change one of the modules, but the final effect is very different. The important point to note is that the majority of the code is the same but we have reused it to create a new effect.

Graphic-independent code

We have created code that can control a dot. It can also control many dots to produce a snowstorm effect. A side effect of this ability is that it can be separate from the dot graphic itself. In Flash MX, the code really can be separate from the graphics and stored in one easily accessible place; in its own layer in frame 1 of the root timeline. This is one of those subtle features of Flash MX that a workflow based on graphic design alone would miss. It is fundamental to Flash MX and the modular code creation process.

Eliminate debugging

This is an obvious benefit, but an important one nevertheless: if we make the code modular it can be reused and, as the code has already been tested and we know it works well, this eliminates the need for further debugging.

Modular structures limit errors

If we code our solution using modules, we have a number of 'ring-fenced' sections of code. It is very difficult for bugs to cross over these boundaries, so we limit the effects of individual bugs by restricting their scope for interacting with healthy code and confusing us with odd results that are not really the bug itself, but side effects of it.

Also, each module forms a particular part of our problem so, if there is a bug, we can find out which section of code contains it, just by examining the part of our problem that doesn't work. As we divide the problem into more and more modules, any potentially erroneous code blocks become smaller in size, making them easier to debug. As you move on to create larger code listings, you'll find that increasing amounts of time are spent debugging (the number of ways a program can go wrong increases almost exponentially with size), so although debugging is less of an issue when creating small one-trick FLAs, it becomes extremely relevant when you start thinking big.

Project management

Because modular code splits your solution into small well-defined steps, it is far easier to change the way your code works if you return to the project at later date. Also, this makes it much easier to collaborate with other people on a single project.

Precursor to object-oriented programming

The basic structures you need to establish for a modular approach (specifically, functions) are very similar to those you need to create object-based solutions. The latter is a natural progression from the modular approach. There are many people out there trying to get into OOP who don't realize this progression. You need to come here first before striding out into the world of OOP.

Disadvantages of modular coding

Now you may be thinking, "If modular programming is that good, then how have I got away without using it for so long?" Well, there are also disadvantages.

Short code doesn't require modular programming

If you're writing short FLAs, or large graphic web sites that only contain a small code core, then you can manage your script creation without jumping through hoops. In single-effect FLAs, the whole script is essentially one code module anyway, so you won't gain any of the benefits listed above by subdividing the movie any further. Also, some problems are so simple that they can be solved right away. Indeed, some Flash projects are not a problem as such, but more of an artistic exploration, so there is no solution, modular or otherwise. We will look at this issue in more detail shortly, because it is often missed.

Errors can creep in between modules

When writing modules separately, they may not fit together as expected at the join. This is actually the most common problem with structured code at any level; boats don't veer off course because their navigation software is *wrong*. They do so because two code modules (or, more likely, two software systems) stop talking to each other properly in a particular situation. This sort of problem is called an **interfacing error** and is not caused by incorrect code, but a misunderstanding in the definition of the problem. You'll get very used to it, and the general design method we'll introduce avoids this problem anyway.

Extra development time or commercial reality?

The client is on the phone and she's over the moon: "Love the graphics and interface design, but we're especially knocked out with those modular scripting techniques you used when building up the code; the site's visitors will really appreciate that! Here's another $10,000 for the extra time you put in to do this."

Obviously, this will never happen. The client wants a site that works, looks cool, and is certainly not concerned with your groundbreaking voodoo ActionScript. From your perspective, the code works but you couldn't swear you'll still know how it works six months down the line. If the development deadlines don't justify it, or the client isn't paying for it, you can only take modular coding as far as it takes you in meeting deadlines and getting paid.

Performance

While this isn't particularly important for other structured languages such as JavaScript and C, performance is a very important issue for Flash, as a slow ActionScript-controlled Flash animation looks pretty poor. If you write your code with modularity as the main concern, you can end up with less than optimized routines.

This puts many designers off, but is not actually the big problem that it appears to be. By identifying those modules that are critical to the overall performance, you can consider speed issues. When writing with performance uppermost in your mind – writing optimized code is actually a longer process than writing any other form of code – the ability to target critical modules and only optimize these (as opposed to optimizing everything) can actually work out as an advantage, especially when coding large applications such as games.

When code gets ugly

There are many people who get the wrong impression by reading too many books and newsgroup posts about code-cool. This takes hold, and you start thinking that if you can't create great visuals and interfaces while simultaneously churning out elegant code, then you're not a Flash master. This is a mistake because writing structured modular code or OOP simply because 'everyone else says it's king' is a subtle trap.

Unstructured raw ideas

If you completely subscribe to the concept of structured/modular programming techniques without knowing why, you're missing the point; we don't naturally think in a modular way, particularly when exploring creative avenues. Raw ideas that are modularized too early can lose the random edginess that actually generates the innovation and verve we strive for. When you look at a painting, you look at the overall scene and ambience before you move in closer to the canvas and notice the individual brush strokes. The big idea defines a work of art, not the individual modular strokes that form it.

For sure, there comes a point when you have to sit back and take stock, modularizing your code to give it the flexibility to be developed further, but art and science don't mix too well. It's a stop/start process, and sometimes you just have to turn the structured programming sensors off for a morning while you just *play*.

Graphic design is not a modular process

Applying modular principles to the visual and graphic design process that gives your site its look and feel, you may end up with a disjointed design, a trap that's easier to fall into than you may think. Designing many one-trick FLAs and then cramming them into a single site is not called modular design; it's called 'designing many one-trick FLAs and then cramming them into a single site'. It's the sort of thing that other designers will laugh at you openly in the street over.

Create or copy

Once you discover modular programming, a modular and structured thought process will quickly develop, but watch out for two dangerous pitfalls that come with it:

- You may not develop your raw ideas for long enough before hitting the modular object-oriented trail and making your idea general. This may *dilute* your idea.

- A modular approach allows you to reverse-engineer other people's interface and design ideas very quickly. By picking out the basic elements of a technique, you can replicate them rapidly; yet the result is simply *copying*.

We won't dwell on this too much other than to say that we all know when this happens, and if it's what you want, it's what you get. There are many very good ActionScripters out there who don't let a good knowledge of coding kill the creative spark. For example, the James Paterson/Amit Pitaru collaborations work so well specifically because they know where the jump point from creativity to coding is, and don't force it based on any fashion of code as king. Having said that, their techniques would not work without a high level of modular code and generalization so, as always, it's a fine balancing act... something that all motion graphics people should be aware of, and the reason why this book has 'designer' on the cover, not 'programmer'.

OK, now that the big overview is done, let's get our hands dirty. First up are some general thoughts on building timeline modularity using different levels. This is not strictly about the creation of modular code, but is modularity at a higher level, as it allows you to separate your site content from the site interface, therefore allowing you to modularize the two and treat them separately.

We will then look at the most important building block of modularity within code: **functions**. Finally, we'll look at the #include ActionScript compilation directive and **components**.

Modular timelines

Modular timelines are like a halfway house towards true code modularity based on functions. Your code isn't modular in the true programming sense, but because you are using movie clips and timelines as code or asset containers, you achieve some level of separation. This can actually give you something very similar, because you retain many of the advantages of modularity, and also gain some other nice benefits regarding bandwidth.

Level structure in Flash

As we saw in **Chapter 11**, Flash allows us to divide our applications into a number of separate SWFs that can be layered on top of each other. When loaded in this way, the individual SWFs are referred to as **levels**. This has two advantages:

- Separating a site into several SWFs reduces the initial download time

- The SWFs can all be written separately

We mention load levels as a modular device because this is a practical book, and modularity is not just about code in real life; it can be about site content as well. Loading movies into separate levels allows you to separate content from the site's user interface, a truly modular concept.

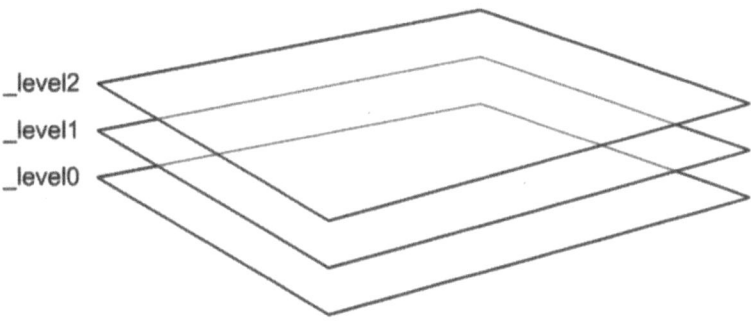

Think of levels as a stack of... well, levels. _level0 is at the bottom and possesses some unique properties, which it assigns to the overall SWF document: the movie's background color; the frame rate; and the stage's width and height. These are those properties you specify when setting up a new document in the **Document Properties** window (Modify>Document...):

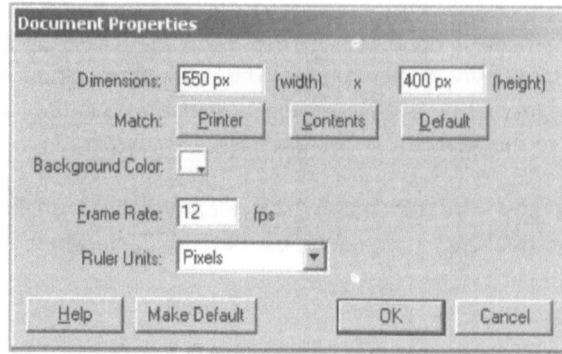

Subsequent levels are stacked on top of _level0, and their background color, frame rate, and size are ignored. This has a number of implications.

As the extra levels don't have a background color, their background is effectively transparent, and can be thought of as layers of stacked glass. For those of you familiar with film animation, a better analogy is the layers of transparent acetate used in hand-painted cel animation. The graphics on the cel sheets are visible, and can be seen in the background and foreground order they are stacked in, but the plastic of the sheets is invisible due to its inherent transparency.

For more discussion on levels in Flash movies see **Chapters 2** and **11**.

Functions

Functions are the main element of modular code, although timelines can also play a part in modular techniques, even if we are not using load levels, as we shall see later. There's also another reason to get into functions even if you are not that excited by modular techniques; functions in Flash MX are one of the core concepts you need to grasp before you can use ActionScript effectively. Using them in modular code is a precursor to using them (and more importantly, understanding *why* you use them) in the Flash MX event model and object-oriented programming (OOP) – OOP is discussed in greater detail in **Chapter 16**.

A function can be used in several ways. At the simplest level, functions are bits of code that are used in several places within your code. Rather than keep re-inventing the wheel, it is better to use the *same* code module. This is the *classical* way of using functions. Functions can also be used in slightly more complex structures. In particular, they can have inheritance and you can define a function as a reference.

Flash 5 allowed you to define a function as a reference (although it wasn't documented until late on in the revisions cycle). Flash MX documents this usage and it is slightly more involved than the classical use of a function. We can actually start treating functions as objects because inheritance and being able to pass references is usually associated with objects. Flash MX actually comes clean on this and allows us to use the **methods** of the Function object (note the use of a capital 'F' when we discuss functions as an object in MX, because it really is an object in this version). One of the most useful Function methods for modular programming is `Function.apply` and we will look at this later.

For advanced users (or those just trying to learn everything about functions in MX – which will probably include Flash 5 users trying to get their head around why MX relies so heavily on functions), here's a quick summary and set of cross references to the appropriate sections. The important thing to realize here is that both usages listed below are actually just extensions of using functions as modular code carriers.

Some people think Flash MX is more difficult to learn than the previous version, bit this isn't particularly true. There's an extra hidden step in the learning process required by MX, which is gaining an understanding of the function as modular code. This is what we're doing now. The next step is simply realizing that it's also an object (which we will also start looking at in this section).

Flash MX object model

We studied functions and how Flash MX allows you to use functions as event handlers in **Chapter 10**. This is possible because a function is also an object. We'll see later in this chapter how MX allows you to use functions as **callbacks in a modular context**.

Prototypes and OOP

Functions form the backbone of OOP, which we'll look at in more detail in **Chapter 16**. Functions can be used as **constructor** functions. This allows you to use functions to create a structure to your Object objects. Constructor functions allow you to add **properties** to your structure, but do not allow you to add **methods**.

Functions can be used to build a **prototype**. In MX, the fact that a function is an object means that they can be used to build other functions. We use both the facts that Function objects have inheritance and can be defined as references here. Beginners who want to get into this area of Flash will do well to stay with this chapter and learn modular code first, particularly the use of `Function.apply()`, because using prototypes in OOP is very much the same process in practice (if not in theory).

Syntax and basic structures

Functions are simple to start off with, but can become very complicated quite quickly if you blink, so stay with it! Imagine a basic function that doubles a number. We could write this:

```
function double() {
      x = x*2;
}
x = 4;
double();
```

continues overleaf

```
trace(x);
```

This code will run through the function definition code (lines 1 to 3) and **define** our function. It will not execute it until we call it with `double`. We then set `x` to 4 and call the function. This finally runs the function and performs the doubling operation via the line `x = x*2` to give a result of 8.

This is fine but we can do better. We really want to double *any* number before we can claim we've written good code, and we do this by passing an **argument**:

```
function double(myNumber) {
      myNumber = myNumber*2;
      return myNumber;
}
x = 4;
y = 5;
x = double(x);
y = double(y);
trace(x), trace(y);
```

You can also pass a literal value, so you could just as well make this function call:

```
z = double(1.5);
```

This time we are using an argument `myNumber`. When you pass an argument, the value is assigned to the variable in the parentheses of the function automatically, and you can assume that the argument is the variable in your code. This is cool, because it allows your code to be general. Our simple function calculates twice the value of `myNumber`, but is actually used to double `x` and `y`. We've also added the extra line `return myNumber` at the end of the function. This tells Flash to return the value of `myNumber` every time it sees the code `double(anything)`. So, for example, the line:

```
x = double(x);
```

...is evaluated as if it were:

```
x = myNumber;
```

Note that as well as causing the function to return a value, the `return` action also makes the function return program execution to the calling code:

```
myFunction = function () {
      if (something) {
            return firstThing;
      } else {
            return secondThing;
      }
};
```

This pseudo-code will return one of two values. The thing to remember is that a function will stop at the first return actions it sees. There are three other ways you can make your functions more flexible:

- You can make your functions more flexible by sending and receiving objects to and from them. This is covered in the following two sections and is a little involved, so if you start struggling, it may be a better idea to wait until you have got past **Chapter 16** before tackling them.

- You can use **local variables**. Although this is important from a pure programming perspective, motion graphics can also use the `this` path to do the same thing, so it's not as critical in Flash.

- You can treat functions as if they were objects. This is an important concept and we can't really wait until **Chapter 16** to discuss this because it's relevant to modular techniques.

Return an object

It would be reasonable to think that the function return is limited to a single value but this just isn't true because you can return any object type. The most useful object to return is an Object object. Suppose you not only want to double the argument, but also want to return treble the input. You could have a separate function but sometimes you want to have multiple values coming from a single function because the data is related (or can be calculated at the same time). Take a look at this:

```
function multiply(myNumber) {
        numbers = new Object();
        numbers.double = myNumber*2;
        numbers.treble = myNumber*3;
        return numbers;
}
x2 = multiply(2).double;
x3 = multiply(2).treble;
trace(x2);
trace(x3);
```

This will return x2 as 4 and x3 as 6. This code returns two values as properties of the function call returned value. Think of the properties in the returned values as you would the properties of a movie clip (or revisit this section once you've had a look at the next chapter). So, if we want to know what double and treble 3 are, we just look at `multiply(3).double` and `multiply(3).treble`. This is cool in terms of structured and modular programming, but isn't actually efficient enough for most motion graphics. When we access `multiply(3).double`, we also force Flash to calculate `multiply(3).treble`, and the same problem occurs when accessing `multiply(3).double`. We make Flash calculate all the properties every time we call `multiply` because the function has no way of knowing which property you actually want. This sounds like a bad thing, but actually isn't when you are working with true objects. If you add the line:

```
x = multiply(2);
```

...and then test the movie in debug mode (see **Chapter 14**) you will see that rather than x having a **single** value, it has inherited the properties *double* and *treble*. Rather than calling the function twice, you can now look at x.double and x.treble at your leisure:

⊟	╳	
┊··	double	4
┊··	treble	6
	╳2	4
	╳3	6

This type of function code is not just returning values for you; it is also structuring related data into a single object, something that is very useful.

Side note for advanced programmers

You can also return your values as an array:

```
function multiply(myNumber) {
        numbers = new Array();
        numbers[0] = myNumber*2;
        numbers[1] = myNumber*3;
        return numbers;
}
x = multiply(10);
trace(x[0]);
trace(x[1]);
```

This will return an array with x[0]=20 and x[1] = 30.

You could use something like this to return a table of values or look up a table. This is very useful for advanced motion graphics because you can pre-calculate difficult or processor-intensive values before you begin animating. You would use this when writing optimized 3D engines, because trigonometric values are slow to calculate and you should not normally try to calculate them at run-time if optimized (fast) code is your priority.

As you can see here, we have turned around something that initially sounded like it might be along the lines of a 'cool programming concept designed by someone who doesn't realize that programming techniques resulting in slower code are useless to the motion graphics designer' to a useful 'this can be used as a building block to create an optimized 3D engine'. As with all modular techniques, the theory isn't the important part; it's the creative application of this theory that is paramount.

The Arguments object

A function uses an array to hold your function arguments, but you can also access this array directly via the **Arguments** object (this is only possible in Flash MX and above). This is useful because sometimes you may not know how many arguments you want. For example, suppose that you have a function to calculate the average of four values:

```
function average(a, b, c, d) {
      return(a+b+c+d)/4;
}
x = average(1, 2, 3, 4);
trace(x);
```

This would give 2.5 as the result.

You can make your code more general by using the Arguments object. Here is an array that contains all your arguments:

```
function average() {
      av = 0;
      for (i=0; i<arguments.length; i++) {
            av += arguments[i];
      }
      return av/arguments.length;
}
x = average(1, 2, 3, 4);
trace(x);
y = average(1, 2, 3, 4, 5, 6, 7, 8, 9, 10);
trace(y);
```

The first call will create an arguments array with:

```
arguments[0] = 1;
arguments[1] = 2;
arguments[2] = 3;
arguments[3] = 4;
```

You also have an important property called arguments.length which gives you the length of the array, in this case 4. The loop can therefore simply loop through all the sent arguments to return the final average value. The great thing here is that we've created a very modular and general piece of code because it can handle a list of any length, so we can use the code to work out the average of the numbers 1 to 4 just as easily as 1 to 10. The only additional thing you need to know about the Arguments object is that there is effectively only one, and it is always set up to reflect the currently running function.

When you use functions that return objects (or arrays) *and* take an arguments array list as its input, you have a very flexible and modular section of code. Not only can it handle variable length input lists, it can also output a variable amount of data. This makes for a general reusable code.

The final piece in the modular function jigsaw is one of the more important ones for the programmer, but in practice, may be less important for the motion graphics designer: **localized variables**.

Local variables

When you write a function as part of a modular design, you don't know what the code external to it will be. More to the point, you may not even be the one writing the external code, so you can safely assume it will do the one thing that kills your function, which you assumed could never happen! More often than not, this involves collisions between variable names.

In the last example, we used a loop variable i. Using loop variables named i, j, and k is common practice and, in some older computer languages, is a common convention. This means that there is a good chance that your function will corrupt the external code if the function call occurs within a loop. The var action comes to our rescue here.

Using var tells Flash that this variable is local to the function. If we use var in the definition of a variable, that variable will only exist within the function block. This means that:

- It is not confused with any other variable of the same name outside the function.

- It is destroyed as soon as you leave the function block, so you cannot assume that a local value you set inside the last function call will be the same value the next time you are in the function.

So local variables may be constrained within the function code but they have no persistence. This isn't actually a bad thing for most programmers, but it can sometimes cause problems for motion graphics designers because we need persistence. When you begin an animation, you are usually controlling the animation using gradually changing variables, and you want these to remain at the last value you set. This brings us to an important side issue. Unlike most languages, Flash has two kinds of localization. The second type of localization is concerned with timelines and this type of variable *is* persistent.

Anyway, this is our function with local variables:

```
function average() {
    var av = 0;
    var i;
    for (i=0; i<arguments.length; i++) {
        av += arguments[i];
    }
    return av/arguments.length;
}
```

You can also use the following syntax for the new code:

```
var av, i;
av = 0;
```

This may seem like a small change but it's actually a crucial part of creating modular code. Code modules are separate and do not interact except at the defined interfaces. Programmers like to think of code modules as black boxes that you can throw values at without worrying about what is actually going on inside them. Local variables keep the internal workings of your function separate from other code modules.

As mentioned earlier, timelines also provide localization and do so implicitly, which means you don't have to set it all up, so it's faster. Performance is crucial for the motion graphics programmer, and this necessity can make timeline localization a better bet than function localization.

Treating functions as objects

As well as returning an object from a function, you can also treat a function itself as an object. There are two implications of this, one of which is that we can equate an event handler to a function reference, which is what we do when we use the Flash MX event model. The other implication is that we can define a function as if it were an object. We already know it is, but we have so far used the classic Flash 5 way of defining a function:

```
function myFunction() {
      // yadda yadda
}
```

This is fine but... well, it's a bit dull and simple. It defines our function but doesn't allow us any flexibility. If we treat the function as an object, we use the following syntax:

```
MyFunction = function() {
      // yadda yadda
};
```

So what does this let us do that isn't dull and simple? It lets us assign functions. We can equate something to a function, and we can now do things like:

```
_root.myClip.myFunction = function() {
      // yadda yadda
};

myFunction1 = myfunction2;
myFunction = undefined;

myClip.onEnterFrame = function() {
      // yadda yadda
};
```

The first function is placed on the root timeline irrespective of the timeline that the code that defines it is on. This is important because it allows you to create **position-independent code** that is portable to other timelines. This is a very useful feature, and we'll see how to use this along with `Function.apply` and `this` in the worked example later on in this chapter.

The fourth and fifth lines of code here illustrate that you can make a function a reference to another function. This may not seem like such a big deal but it does allow you to do some cool things with **nested functions**, which we'll also be looking at.

> *You know you are not calling the function* `myFunction2` *because there are no brackets after it.* `myFunction1 = myFunction2()` *is a* **function call***, something completely different!*

Finally, the last three lines are simply an extension of the previous ones. You may already know that this is the MX way of creating event handlers (if you've read **Chapter 10** already!), but it is really just nothing more than a consequence of treating functions as objects.

There is one more thing we need to discuss before we can start using functions in a truly motion graphics-centric way, whilst maintaining modularity, and this relates to **scope**.

Function scope

The scope of a function is important to the motion graphics programmer, because it is what a function will actually control. If you get it wrong, your code will not control the movie clips and other objects you are trying to control. It's also important when looking to write modular motion graphics code because modular code must be general, and therefore your functions need to be able to work with any movie clip. The way we do this in Flash is by making our functions reference a general scope called `this`.

To recap, the `this` path is synonymous with scope, which is important because as animation programmers we would like to write code like this:

```
// move a movie clip to the left
this._x += speed;
```

...as opposed to writing it like this:

```
// can only move myClip
myClip._x += speed;
```

The first example has the potential to be modular because the reference to the thing it controls is general, and this means that we can re-purpose it to control several movie clips. Rather than go through the theory of `this`, it's far easier to illustrate it by example because if we start talking programmer's language, this will look much more complicated than it actually is. Plus, there is only one exception to the general rule of thumb, so it won't take long!

```
function myFunction() {
      // yadda yadda
}
```

Again, this is the classic function syntax, and the scope is the timeline that the function code is located on. This is the default case.

The only special case here is when you *refer* to it rather than *call* it. In this case you are not actually calling myFunction but the thing you have equated it to, so that is where the scope is derived from. Although there is only one special case, it has several forms:

```
function myFunction() {
      this.myVariable1 = 1;
      myVariable2 = 1;
      var myVariable3 = 1;
}
myFunction();
```

this.myVariable1 refers to the variable myVariable1 on the current timeline. The variable myVariable2 will default to the place the function is located at (that is, the timeline the keyframe containing the function code is on). Lastly, myVariable3 is local to the function and therefore we don't have to worry about it.

You can see this if you test the movie in debug mode. The debugger will show myVariable1 and myVariable2 in the same place:

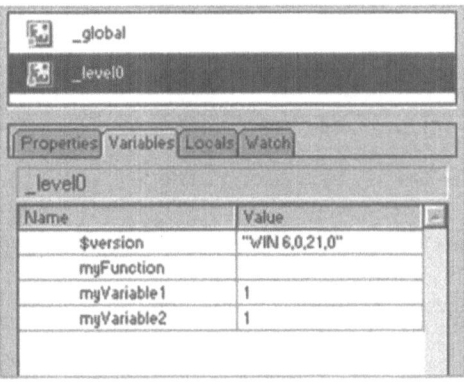

Take a look at the following code:

```
_root.myClip.onEnterFrame = function() {
    this.myVariable1 = 1;
    myVariable2 = 1;
    var myVariable3 = 1;
};
```

Here is a function that is equated directly to an onEnterFrame event and is called an **anonymous** function because, in keeping with our Western analogy, it is the Man With No Name. This is our special case, and we now look to the thing we equate the function to: _root.myClip.onEnterFrame.

The scope of this is _root.myClip. So, this.myVariable1 is actually _root.myClip.myVariable1. myVariable2 has no path, and so will use the default (the timeline this code is on). It is likely that this will *not* be the same as this. myVariable3 is again something we don't have to worry about because it ceases to exist outside the function body.

You can see this in action if you put an instance called myClip on the stage and attach the script to _root. You will get the following output, with myVariable1 and myVariable2 in different places. Obviously, this has now become very important; omit it at your peril!

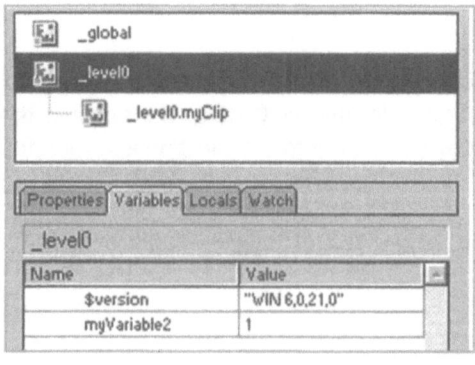 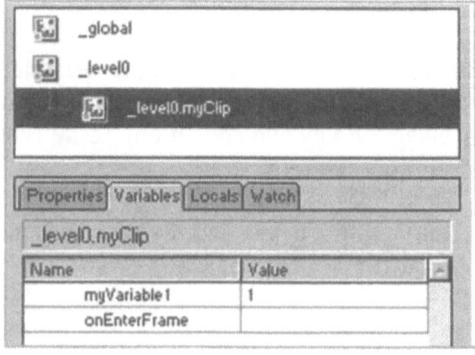

Now look at this code:

```
function myFunction() {
    this.myVariable1 = 1;
    myVariable2 = 1;
    var myVariable3 = 1;
}
_root.myClip2.onEnterFrame = myFunction;
```

This is another way of expressing our special case (and will give exactly the same sort of output as the last example). this.myVariable1 becomes _root.myClip2.myVariable1. myVariable2 will again default to the timeline the function code is actually attached to, and myVariable3 is still a 'don't care' because it is a short-lived local variable.

We have one final trick up our sleeves, the `Function.apply()` method. It works like this:

```
myFunction.apply(myClip);
```

...which runs `myFunction` with `this` equal to `myClip` (or whatever path you choose). So, for example:

```
myFunction.apply(myClip);
function myFunction() {
        this.x = 2;
}
myFunction.apply(_root.myClip);
```

...would put a variable x equal to 2 on the timeline _root.myClip. This is the same as temporarily changing the scope of a function and then running it.

You may well be thinking, "But what's that got to do with anything?" Well, as we've realized by now, scope is crucial to code-controlled motion graphics. By changing the scope, you change the thing you are affecting or controlling. `Function.apply()` allows us to change a scope dynamically, and this is very powerful when using advanced modular code.

A particularly subtle trick is to use `myFunction` as a **wrapper** function that contains other functions and events:

```
function myFunction() {
        this.onEnterFrame = function() {
                // do this
        };
        this.init = function() {
                // do this too
        };
        this.init();
}
myFunction.apply(myClip);
```

The function `myFunction` is run once, scoping `myClip`. When it runs it does something very sneaky. It creates a bunch of functions, event handlers, and code that are created in `myClip`. As long as you write modular functions, you can simply drop a few into a wrapper function and apply it to any number of clips, which is manna from heaven for the motion graphics designer who wants to write code quickly. The `Function.apply` method, when used in this way, creates the same end result as a `prototype`, and does it without requiring any nasty scratching the top of the head.

Having said that, if you have understood everything so far, you are about 70% of the way towards mastering object-oriented design; the programming concepts are already in place, it's just the world view that needs to change slightly. At the simplest level, all you have to do is change the word 'movie clip' in the last section to 'object', and you've almost cracked it!

Anyway, where were we? High Noon. Time to walk the walk...

Modular motion graphics in practice

As you can see, functions are a pretty flexible structure to have around because they are so open-ended. Here's a quick run through of a simple example that amplifies what we've discussed so far, and lets you sit back and look at the advantages of modular code. Our code is short, but the advantages we have touched on become greater as the code increases in size.

This example will illustrate two things to watch out for that we haven't really touched on yet.

For experienced Flash 5 users, it will show that modular code is not the same as anonymous targeting. That is a Flash 5 workaround of the fact that modular code in Flash 5 was not supported well enough to create large applications (it is now in MX).

Beginners will see how we can use modular code to set up general code, and why this is not just a beardy programming ideal. Once we have set up modular functions, we can easily mutate the effect, and this opens up all sorts of experimental avenues. This is due to the general nature of modular code. Because you know what each of your modules do, it's easy to just modify the effect of that code (James Paterson and Amit Pitaru actually use sliders, something we will also do in our example as it's a great motion graphics development trick).

When we write modular code in other languages, we end up with a long code listing, compartmented into lots of short, well-defined code modules. We wouldn't be thinking straight if we applied this high-end programming utopia to Flash. FLAs are relatively short. This is still true if you are writing cutting-edge applications in Flash – compare and contrast the number of lines it would take to write a similar application that was a single version compatible with a number of different operating systems, that runs from the desktop as a standalone application.

FLAs by contrast will be shorter with a more edgy design process behind them, rather than the monolithic programming prerogatives that operating system compatibility requires for modular coding. This means that flow charts etc. are out. We need a quick, motion graphics route that smells the flowers of reality and recognises that any technique taking longer than 'hacking' will never get off the pages of a text book...

A flower by any other name...

We will do a quick run through some motion graphics I coded up from scratch a while ago. It took me about a morning to build it from start to finish, and it gives a good idea of the way we can use modular code to underpin a graphic effect we are developing.

Open up `flower01.fla`. We're just using the drawing API to animate a filled shape with two curved edges:

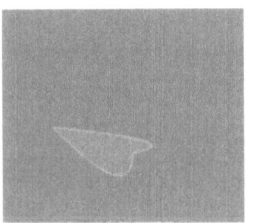 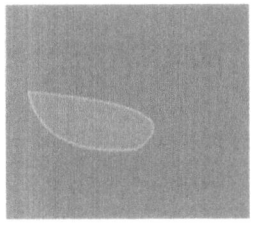 

To draw a petal we are using the `Movieclip.moveTo()` and `Movieclip.curveTo()` methods. Don't worry if you haven't used the drawing API yet, the important thing is the code structure that is driving this, rather than the code itself. For a detailed study of the drawing API, refer to **Chapter 3**.

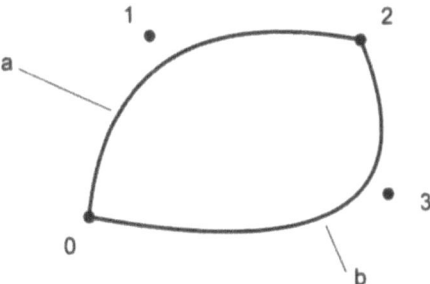

To draw the filled petal, we do the following:

```
beginFill(0xB0B0B0, 100);
moveTo(x[0], y[0]);
```

This defines the points seen between now and the `endFill()` action as part of a filled shape. The 'pencil' then moves to the point (x0, y0). Here's the next line:

```
curveTo(x[1], y[1], x[2], y[2]);
```

This makes the line curve to point 2, with the curve control point being point 1, creating line a.

```
curveTo(x[3], y[3], x[0], y[0]);
```

This makes the line curve back to point 0, with the curve control point being point 3, creating line b.

```
endFill(x[0], y[0]);
```

Lastly, this fills the outline shape we have just created. Here's the basic drawing API code to draw the petal:

```
this.clear();
this.lineStyle(0, 0xFFFFFF, 100);
this.beginFill(0xB0B0B0, 100);
this.moveTo(x[0], y[0]);
this.curveTo(x[1], y[1], x[2], y[2]);
this.curveTo(x[3], y[3], x[0], y[0]);
this.endFill(x[0], y[0]);
```

The only additional lines are the clear() and lineStyle() methods, which respectively clear the previous shape and format the line style (hairline, white, 100% alpha). Play around with the code if you wish, that's what it's there for after all; this is the creative 'driving down all the options' phase, and the code can be cleaned up later.

No real attempt was made to structure or modularize this code but having a look at this code is cool, because it shows us what modular code is *not*. There are no general routines, and all the data is just dumped straight on the root timeline. It works, but only just. The thing is, I wrote this code with the hunch that if I created several of these vaguely petal-shaped filled curves, I might end up with a flower. Well, the code tells me I *can* create a single petal, but I *can't extend it*.

There are two clear reasons why this is not modular. Firstly, all the code is specific. It would be very difficult to re-purpose it to do anything else without changing a lot of the code. For example, we can't make it draw a petal anywhere else but in the center of the screen, and to change the petal size, we would have to go in and change everything around. More importantly, we can't make our code control a general number of petals... it's hardwired for one. The data is not *general*. You can see this if you look at the movie in debugging mode:

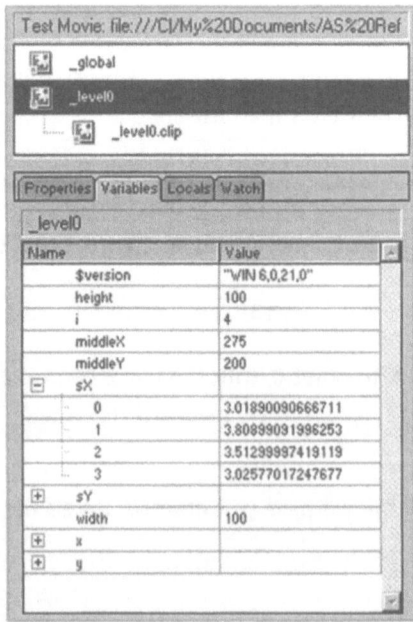

As mentioned above, all the data to drive this animation is simply dumped on _root. If we wanted two (or more) petals, we would have to do something about this.

The file `flower02_05.fla` is a Flash 5 style attempt at modular code. When writing this section we thought long and hard about what Flash designers will know about modular code already, and realized that anyone who knows Flash 5 will point at something that is actually *not* modular code (although it is modular in other ways). Let's have a look at this movie.

It all starts innocuously with the following code on frame 1 of the root timeline:

```
// create flower
_root.attachMovie("flower", "flower", 0);
```

This creates a movie clip called `flower` that is a copy of the movie clip with the same linkage name in the Library but this is where the code breadcrumb trail starts. You look in the movie clip ma.flower as you've worked out that this is what `flower` is actually an instance of and then, because in a normal FLA the Library would be full of other clips, it takes you ages to work back and realize that ma.flower uses the code in ma.petal to set up the 16 onEnterFrame events that actually run the effect. ma.flower is the initialization script, and the main workhorse of the effect is the ma.petal script.

Although we are finally using functions in this script, we're not using them as modular code. They are still simply fixed event handlers. The generality comes from the fact that we are using the _parent path to define our relationship between the petals and the flower. This is what we mean by anonymous targeting, and it occurs in the ma.petal clip:

```
this.onEnterFrame = function() {
    clear();
    lineStyle(0, 0xFFFFFF, 20);
    beginFill(0xB000B0, 20);
    moveTo(_parent.x[0], _parent.y[0]);
    curveTo(_parent.x[1], _parent.y[1], _parent.x[2], _parent.y[2]);
    curveTo(_parent.x[3], _parent.y[3], _parent.x[0], _parent.y[0]);
    endFill(_parent.x[0], _parent.y[0]);
};
```

We won't define this term exhaustively (it's not as important as it used to be, and the this path is much more relevant in Flash MX), but we're pointing it out for particular attention for the benefit of Flash 5 coders. Although we all thought this was cool in Flash 4 and 5, it is very rigid, as it depends on a very particular hierarchy. This rigidity makes it inflexible in the MX world, and we can't call the resulting code modular any more. It may be easy to code, but it's hard work to identify what is happening because of the distributed code that is splashed all over the timelines.

Now take a look at `flower02_MX.fla`. Although this is written in an MX style, the intent and feel of the code is actually the same as the Flash 5 version we've just looked at. Although the structures look as if they are MX (the code is now all on frame 1 of _root), the coding mindset is still firmly fixed in Flash 5.

This is another cool FLA to look at, because it illustrates how different the MX style is, and why it facilitates true modular code.

Old Flash 5 hands may recognize that this FLA is still using anonymous targeting. The only real difference is that this time we are creating it all dynamically (something else that is far easier to do in MX):

```
this["petal"+i].onEnterFrame = function() {
      this.clear();
      this.lineStyle(0, 0xFFFFFF, 20);
      this.beginFill(0xB000B0, 20);
      this.moveTo(this._parent.x[0], this._parent.y[0]);
      this.curveTo(this._parent.x[1], this._parent.y[1], this._parent.x[2],
      ➥this._parent.y[2]);
      this.curveTo(this._parent.x[3], this._parent.y[3], this._parent.x[0],
      ➥this._parent.y[0]);
      this.endFill(this._parent.x[0], this._parent.y[0]);
};
```

The file `flower03.fla` shows our first bit of modular code. We no longer have the Flash 5 anonymous targeting and little chunks of distributed code, but a large single script.

It started off life as `flower03skeleton.fla`, and was then animated. It's always good to do this in motion graphics because not only can you check your code modules are connected up properly, you also get to check the order of execution. This is something that pencil and paper design cannot offer because motion graphics depends on events, and they are never linear or ordered.

Here's the code that forms `flower03skeleton.fla`:

```
createFlower = function (flower, numberOfPetals, fWidth, fHeight, fX, fY) {
        // create the empty movie clip 'flower' that will become the flower,
        // and inside it create the movie clips that will become the
        // petals...
        trace("\ncreateFlower:");
        trace("creating the flower timeline...");
        _root.createEmptyMovieClip(flower, fDepth);
        trace("positioning flower and initializing its parameters...");
        initializeFlower.apply(_root[flower]);
};

initializeFlower = function () {
        trace("\ninitializeFlower:");
        trace("I am applying the code modules to drive the flower...");
        // initialize the flower variables and events...
        this.createPetals = function() {
                trace("\ncreatePetals:");
                trace("I am creating the petals...");
        };
        this.drawpetal = function() {
                trace("\ndrawPetal:");
                trace("I am drawing the petal graphics within the petal
                Âclip...");
        };
        this.petalControl = function() {
                trace("\npetalControl:");
                trace("I am working out the petal geometry...");
                this.drawPetal();
        };
        this.init = function() {
                trace("\ninit:");
                trace(" I am intializing this flower...");
        };
        this.init();
        this.createPetals();
        this.onEnterFrame = this.petalControl;
};

fDepth = 0;
// createFlower (flower, numberOfPetals, fWidth, fHeight, fX, fY)
```

```
createFlower("daffodil", 8, 100, 20, 200, 200);
```

So what is this? Well, it's a set of empty functions (sometimes called 'stubs') I wrote that I think solves the problem I am looking at. It draws and animates my flower or, rather, it tells me whether the structure I want to use will actually work. It's easier to see this working than trying to explain it. Here's its output:

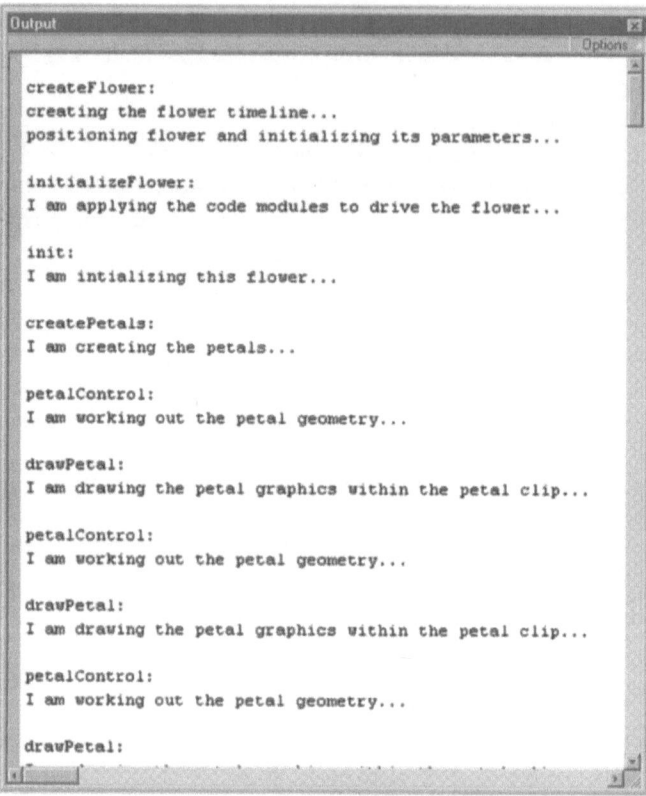

First, createFlower takes a call of the form createFlower (flower, numberOfPetals, fWidth, fHeight, fX, fY) where:

- flower is the name of the flower instance I want to create
- numberOfPetals is the number of petals the flower should have
- fWidth is the width of each flower petal
- fHeight is the height of each flower petal
- fX is the x position on the stage that I want to place the flower at
- fY is the y position on the stage that I want to place the flower at

The next thing to run is initializeFlower. This is one of those **wrapper functions** we talked about earlier. It's a large function that contains embedded 'sub-functions' that create my flower animation, and

I need to apply them all to each flower I make. It organizes my sub-functions, and this includes defining what each function is (an event handler, function, intializer/constructor etc.), and defines the order that my functions should run in. Let's go through the sub-functions.

init is the first function to run (although note that it is not the first one to be defined). This initializes the flower variables.

Next up is petalControl. This is actually configured as an onEnterFrame of the flower, and will run every frame. It calculates the point data changes that have to be made to make our petals appear to move.

petalControl calls drawPetal to actually draw the final petals once petalControl has performed its calculations.

So this output shows the order of my code execution and the relationship between my modules. It defines my code structure and shows me that the function order hangs together well enough to actually do what I want it to do. More importantly, you will remember me saying that the reasons why modular code often fails is when interfacing between modules. Our boat won't veer off course because we are looking at this important thing *first*, and we are actually doing it *before* getting down to write the modules.

Let's look in detail at how the ActionScript was built in flower03skeleton.fla.

Initially, I need to create my flower timeline and this is what the drawing API code will draw the graphics on. The code module that takes care of this is createFlower:

```
createFlower = function (flower, numberOfPetals, fWidth, fHeight, fX, fY) {
    trace("\ncreateFlower:");
    trace("creating the flower timeline...");
    _root.createEmptyMovieClip(flower, fDepth);
    trace("positioning flower and initializing its parameters...");
    initializeFlower.apply(_root[flower]);
};
```

This then applies the rest of the modules (functions) that will actually do the work. This set of functions are all inside initializeFlower, so createFlower simply applies that to the movie clip it has just created. Notice that I am not specifying what the flower will be called; I am allowing the user to specify the name of the flower by making it an argument. In fact, I am specifying everything about the flower as an argument, and this makes everything else customizable.

Next, I need to create the initializeFlower function. This function started off life like this:

```
initializeFlower = function () {
    trace("\ninitializeFlower:");
    trace("I will take care of the drawing and animating of the");
```

```
          trace("flower, based on the parameters passed on to me by");
          trace("createFlower...");
     };
```

...giving me the following output:

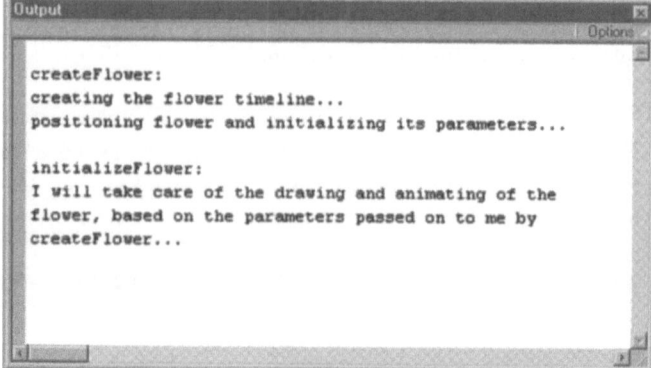

...and then I simply added further functions inside it to modularize the larger task of 'I will take care of almost everything' into smaller modules:

```
     initializeFlower = function () {
          trace("\ninitializeFlower:");
          trace("I am applying the code modules to drive the flower...");
          // initialize the flower variables and events...
          this.createPetals = function() {
               trace("\ncreatePetals:");
               trace("I am creating the petals...");
          };
          this.drawpetal = function() {
               trace("\ndrawPetal:");
               trace("I am drawing the petal graphics within the petal
               ➥ clip...");
          };
          this.petalControl = function() {
               trace("\npetalControl:");
               trace("I am working out the petal geometry...");
               this.drawPetal();
          };
          this.init = function() {
               trace("\ninit:");
               trace(" I am intializing this flower...");
          };
          this.init();
          this.createPetals();
          this.onEnterFrame = this.petalControl;
     };
```

> *A common question here is "how do you know when to stop sub-dividing the problem?" A general rule of thumb is that you can stop modularizing (sub-dividing) your function code blocks when the comments inside each one are recognizable as tasks that could be readily coded by yourself.*

We have created our structure in this skeleton, but haven't created the flow of data in it. Before we can write in a modular way, this also has to be well-defined. The way we do this is by defining our arguments and variables that exist *between* the functions (see `flower03skeleton2.fla`):

```
createFlower = function (flower, numberOfPetals, fWidth, fHeight, fX, fY) {
     // create the empty movie clip 'flower' that will become the flower,
     // and inside it create the movie clips that will become the petals
     trace("\ncreateFlower:");
     trace("creating the flower timeline...");
     _root.createEmptyMovieClip(flower, 0);
     trace("positioning flower and initializing its parameters...");
     _root[flower]._x = fX;
     _root[flower]._y = fY;
     _root[flower].numberOfPetals = numberOfPetals;
     _root[flower].fWidth = fWidth;
     _root[flower].fHeight = fHeight;
     initializeFlower.apply(_root[flower]);
};

initializeFlower = function () {
     trace("\ninitializeFlower:");
     message = "I am applying the code modules to drive the flower
  ➡ '"+this._name+"'";
     trace(message);
     // initialize the flower variables and events
     this.createPetals = function(numPetals) {
            trace("\ncreatePetals:");
            message = "I am creating "+numPetals+" petals...";
            trace(message);
            var numPetals, petals;
            for (petals=0; petals<numPetals; petals++) {
                   this.createEmptyMovieClip("petal"+petals, petals);
                   this["petal"+petals]._rotation = petals*(360/numPetals);
            }
     };
```

continues overleaf

```
        this.drawpetal = function(petal, color, alpha) {
            trace("\ndrawPetal:");
            message = "I am drawing the petal graphics within "+petal;
            trace(message);
        };

        this.petalControl = function() {
            trace("\npetalControl:");
            trace("I am working out the petal geometry...");
            for (i=0; i<this.numberOfPetals; i++) {
                this.drawpetal("petal"+i, null, null);
            }
        };

        this.init = function() {
            trace("\ninit:");
            trace(" I am intializing this flower...");
        };

        this.init();
        this.createPetals(this.numberOfPetals);
        this.onEnterFrame = this.petalControl;
    };

    // createFlower (flower, numberOfPetals, fWidth, fHeight, fX, fY)
    createFlower("orchid", 3, 40, 40, 100, 200);
```

So what's new and different? All our functions now have their arguments, and any variables that need to be passed between timelines are defined. We have also created all the empty movie clips that we will use.

The code is invoked with the final call:

```
    // createFlower (flower, numberOfPetals, fWidth, fHeight, fX, fY)
    createFlower("orchid", 3, 40, 40, 100, 200);
```

We want a flower called orchid with three petals. Does the code structure actually set this up?

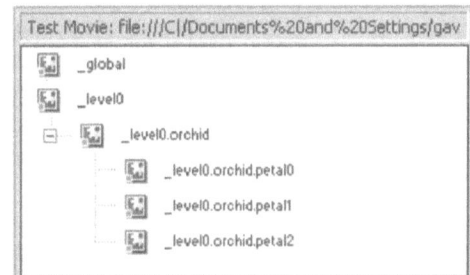

```
Output                                                    ×
                                                   Options ▲
createFlower:
creating the flower timeline...
positioning flower and initializing its parameters...

initializeFlower:
I am applying the code modules to drive the flower 'orchid'

init:
I am intializing this flower...

createPetals:
I am creating 3 petals...

petalControl:
I am working out the petal geometry...

drawPetal:
I am drawing the petal graphics within petal0

drawPetal:
I am drawing the petal graphics within petal1

drawPetal:
I am drawing the petal graphics within petal2

petalControl:
I am working out the petal geometry...

drawPetal:
I am drawing the petal graphics within petal0

drawPetal:
I am drawing the petal graphics within petal1
```

Test Movie: file:///C|/Documents%20and%20Settings/gav
- _global
- _level0
  - _level0.orchid
    - _level0.orchid.petal0
    - _level0.orchid.petal1
    - _level0.orchid.petal2

Looking at the movie clips created (in the Display list window of the debugger), the code does create the graphic structure we need. It generates a flower called _root.orchid with three petal clips inside it called petal0, petal1, and petal2.

Now we'll move on to the modules. initializeFlower correctly knows that it is creating the flower orchid, and createPetals correctly tells us it is creating three petals. The petalControl function has three calls to drawPetal after it, each of which name the petal instances in order. This tells us that the module structure does support the ability to animate our petals. If we change the call, the modules are automatically configured to handle a new flower structure. You can check this is true by changing the call to:

```
createFlower("daisy", 5, 40, 100, 300, 200);
```

Test Movie: file:///C|/Documents%20and%20Settings/gav
- _global
- _level0
  - _level0.daisy
    - _level0.daisy.petal0
    - _level0.daisy.petal1
    - _level0.daisy.petal2
    - _level0.daisy.petal3
    - _level0.daisy.petal4

When we look inside the instance `daisy`, we see the correct numbers of movie clips and the relationship between them also stays the same. You can really push it by asking the code to create both instances at the same time:

```
createFlower("orchid", 3, 40, 40, 100, 200);
createFlower("daisy", 5, 40, 100, 300, 200);
```

It doesn't actually work, but it doesn't take much to realize the mistake; we need to update the movie clip depth every time we create a new flower. We set up the flower in `createFlower`, so we immediately know that the problem is in there somewhere. Our error is contained in one function and we know which one immediately. This is a consequence of using code modules, and to make a seemingly large change (being able to handle any number of flowers) requires only three lines of new code (see `flower03skeleton3.fla`):

```
createFlower = function (flower, numberOfPetals, fWidth, fHeight, fX, fY) {
        // create the empty movie clip 'flower' that will become the flower,
        // and inside it create the movie clips that will become the petals
        trace("\ncreateFlower:");
        trace("creating the flower timeline...");
        _root.createEmptyMovieClip(flower, fDepth);
        fDepth++;
        trace("positioning flower and initializing its parameters...");
        _root[flower]._x = fX;
        _root[flower]._y = fY;
        _root[flower].numberOfPetals = numberOfPetals;
        _root[flower].fWidth = fWidth;
        _root[flower].fHeight = fHeight;
        initializeFlower.apply(_root[flower]);
};

initializeFlower = function () {
        trace("\ninitializeFlower:");
        message = "I am applying the code modules to drive the flower
    '"+this._name+"'";
        trace(message);
        // initialize the flower variables and events
        this.createPetals = function(numPetals) {
                trace("\ncreatePetals:");
                message = "I am creating "+numPetals+" petals...";
                trace(message);
                var numPetals, petals;
                for (petals=0; petals<numPetals; petals++) {
                        this.createEmptyMovieClip("petal"+petals, petals);
                        this["petal"+petals]._rotation = petals*(360/numPetals);
                }
```

```
        };

        this.drawpetal = function(petal, color, alpha) {
                trace("\ndrawPetal:");
                message = "I am drawing the petal graphics within "+petal;
                trace(message);
        };

        this.petalControl = function() {
                trace("\npetalControl:");
                trace("I am working out the petal geometry...");
                for (i=0; i<this.numberOfPetals; i++) {
                        this.drawpetal("petal"+i, null, null);
                }
        };

        this.init - function() {
                trace("\ninit:");
                trace(" I am intializing this flower...");
        };

        this.init();
        this.createPetals(this.numberOfPetals);
        this.onEnterFrame = this.petalControl;
};
fDepth = 0;

// createFlower (flower, numberOfPetals, fWidth, fHeight, fX, fY)
createFlower("orchid", 3, 40, 40, 100, 200);
createFlower("daisy", 5, 40, 100, 300, 200);
```

Our structure and interfaces are now complete. We have a general set of functions that can be configured via a single call to create a particular flower. We can also create multiple flowers by simply reusing the same code in a different movie clip configuration. I think we need a recap to see how far we've gone. We've defined all the functions we need to build our effect. We have done this firmly in the motion graphics environment, without needing to go away and draw time-consuming flow charts. In short, we have defined our problem simply by writing out the solution in a skeletal form. It's important to see that we haven't wasted any time by doing it this way because we haven't wandered away from the required solution by creating extra features that the client will not be paying for. We've also seen that our functions talk together properly. Again, we have done this in a way that advances directly towards the solution, rather than leaving the Flash environment. We know that the order of our events will work because we have tested it all out in real time.

What we haven't done is actually write the modules inside the functions themselves! However, we're now in a position to do this, and have placed ourselves in a very good position to pull it all off.

We know the order the functions will execute in at runtime and, if we write them in that order, we can test each new function within the final code environment. When we test the first function we have written, the skeleton code around it will simulate the other functions as if they were actually there, and this reduces our debugging effort. The skeleton code will disappear rather like scaffolding around a building under construction, and is a useful component in our design process, not just wasted effort. If we locate a problem, we can simply add a few extra trace actions to illustrate what our function is getting/sending through the module structure, something that you can't do if you write the modules in isolation without the skeleton.

We have the ability to play with our code structure at this point, and can optimize the relationships between them to create a fast and efficient solution. We will know the speed that our final effect will run at, rather than writing it all and realizing it's too slow at the end. As each function comes online, we can check that our motion graphics are running acceptably.

A point to make here is that when looking at the skeleton, you will see that we sometimes use local variables and arguments to pass data around, but pass them around timelines at other times. This is due to two issues.

Whenever we use var there is a performance hit. Flash has to create the variable at the start of the function and destroy it at the end. If you use var in an onEnterFrame script then you are asking for trouble, because Flash is forced to create/delete a sizable number of variables at the speed set by the frame rate! Consequently, we only use var to tidy up code that is not on the performance critical path. The rest of the code needs to run quickly.

Secondly, local variables are not permanent, whereas those that you send to a timeline are. When we need to send variables with permanence, we send them directly to the timeline:

```
_root[flower].numberOfPetals = numberOfPetals;
```

...and when we only need to communicate data that is used once, we send it directly to a function as an argument:

```
this.createPetals = function(numPetals) {
```
Programmers may balk at this by saying there are more elegant ways around this, but motion graphics (and games) programmers don't want to know; we need things to be fast, and cannot compromise on this by writing slow but elegant code. id Software's *Quake 3* sells because it is fast and furious, and Joshua Davis's inertia effect equations do the trick by simplifying the issue to create something that only looks like inertia, but is fast.

After all that legwork, it will come as no surprise that actually coding the piece up is easy. We've done all the important work already, and tackled the difficult areas early on. We won't even talk through the code, because you know it already. Here it is in flowerFinal.fla:

```
createFlower = function (flower, numberOfPetals, fWidth, fHeight, fX, fY) {
```

```
        // create the empty movie clip 'flower' that will become the flower,
        // and inside it create the movie clips that will become the
petals...
        var flower, numberOfPetals, petals, fWidth, fHeight, fX, fY;
        _root.createEmptyMovieClip(flower, fDepth);
        fDepth++;
        Stage.scaleMode = "exactFit";
        _root[flower]._x = fX;
        _root[flower]._y = fY;
        Stage.scaleMode = oldMode;
        _root[flower].numberOfPetals = numberOfPetals;
        _root[flower].fWidth = fWidth;
        _root[flower].fHeight = fHeight;
        initializeFlower.apply(_root[flower]);
};

initializeFlower = function () {
    // initialize the flower variables and events
    this.createPetals = function(numPetals) {
            var numPetals, petals;
            for (petals=0; petals<numPetals; petals++) {
                    this.createEmptyMovieClip("petal"+petals, petals);
                    this["petal"+petals]._rotation = petals*(360/numPetals);
            }
    };

    this.drawpetal = function(petal, color, alpha) {
            path = this[petal];
            path.clear();
            path.lineStyle(0, 0x505060, 30);
            path.beginFill(color, alpha);
            path.moveTo(this.x[0], this.y[0]);
            path.curveTo(this.x[1], this.y[1], this.x[2], this.y[2]);
            path.curveTo(this.x[3], this.y[3], this.x[0], this.y[0]);
            path.endFill(this.x[0], this.y[0]);
    };

    this.petalControl = function() {
            for (i=0; i<4; i++) {
                    this.x[i] += this.sX[i];
                    this.y[i] += this.sY[i];
                    if (Math.abs(this.x[i])>this.fWidth) {
                            this.sX[i] = -this.sX[i];
                    }
                    if (Math.abs(this.y[i])>this.fHeight) {
```

continues overleaf

```
                              this.sY[i] = -this.sY[i];
                      }
              }
              this.col = 0xFF0000;
              for (i=0; i<this.numberOfPetals; i++) {
                      this.drawpetal("petal"+i, this.col,
                   ➡ 200/this.numberOfPetals);
                      this.col += 0x001040;
              }
      };

      this.init = function() {
              this.x = new Array();
              this.y = new Array();
              this.sX = new Array();
              this.sY = new Array();
              this.x[0] = 0;
              this.y[0] = 0;
              this.x[1] = 0;
              this.y[1] = -this.fHeight;
              this.x[2] = -this.fWidth;
              this.y[2] = -this.fHeight;
              this.x[3] = -this.fWidth;
              this.y[3] = 0;
              for (i=0; i<4; i++) {
                      this.sX[i] = Math.random()*4+2;
                      this.sY[i] = Math.random()*4+2;
              }
              this.col = 0xFF0000;
      };

      this.init();
      this.createPetals(this.numberOfPetals);
      this.onEnterFrame = this.petalControl;
};

fDepth = 0;
// createFlower (flower, numberOfPetals, fWidth, fHeight, fX, fY)
createFlower("daffodil", 8, 100, 20, 200, 200);
createFlower("orchid", 3, 40, 40, 100, 200);
createFlower("daisy", 5, 40, 100, 300, 200);
```

Also included on the CD is flowerMutator.fla, which is there to demonstrate how modular code can be easily interfaced to/from other code. Because our set of code modules can be accessed via a simple function call to the top level function `createFlower`, it's child's play to wire this call up to a set of sliders to allow us to manually tweak the effect as desired and start playing around.

Play around and see if you can come up with a 3D version I'm playing with at the moment. Stop thinking spinning petals, and start thinking radial segments as in an orange. Spin them around in 3D to get something that hasn't been created before, but most importantly, play!

But we haven't finished yet! There's modular, and then there's *modular*.

Packaging modular code

Modular code really comes into its own when you make it portable. We can do this easily with our code by making no absolute references (that is, never using `_root` at the beginning of a path). Open up `flower04.fla`:

```
createFlower = function (flower, numberOfPetals, fWidth, fHeight, fX, fY) {
        var flower, numberOfPetals, petals, fWidth, fHeight, fX, fY;
        this.createEmptyMovieClip(flower, fDepth);
        this.fDepth++;
        this[flower]._x = fX;
        this[flower]._y = fY;
        this[flower].numberOfPetals = numberOfPetals;
        this[flower].fWidth = fWidth;
        this[flower].fHeight = fHeight;
        initializeFlower.apply(this[flower]);
};

initializeFlower = function () {
        // initialize the flower variables and events
        this.createPetals = function(numPetals) {
                var numPetals, petals;
                for (petals=0; petals<numPetals; petals++) {
```

continues overleaf

```
                                this.createEmptyMovieClip("petal"+petals, petals);
                                this["petal"+petals]._rotation = petals*(360/numPetals);
                        }
                };

                this.drawpetal = function(petal, color, alpha) {
                        path = this[petal];
                        path.clear();
                        path.lineStyle(0, 0x505060, 30);
                        path.beginFill(color, alpha);
                        path.moveTo(this.x[0], this.y[0]);
                        path.curveTo(this.x[1], this.y[1], this.x[2], this.y[2]);
                        path.curveTo(this.x[3], this.y[3], this.x[0], this.y[0]);
                        path.endFill(this.x[0], this.y[0]);
                };

                this.petalControl = function() {
                        for (i=1; i<4; i++) {
                                this.x[i] += this.sX[i];
                                this.y[i] += this.sY[i];
                                if (Math.abs(this.x[i])>this.fWidth) {
                                        this.sX[i] = -this.sX[i];
                                }
                                if (Math.abs(this.y[i])>this.fHeight) {
                                        this.sY[i] = -this.sY[i];
                                }
                        }
                        this.col = 0xFF0000;
                        for (i=0; i<this.numberOfPetals; i++) {
                                this.drawpetal("petal"+i, this.col,
                                ➥200/this.numberOfPetals);
                                this.col += 0x001040;
                        }
                };

                this.init = function() {
                        this.x = new Array();
                        this.y = new Array();
                        this.sX = new Array();
                        this.sY = new Array();
                        this.x[0] = 0;
                        this.y[0] = 0;
                        this.x[1] = 0;
                        this.y[1] = -this.fHeight;
                        this.x[2] = -this.fWidth;
```

```
                    this.y[2]  = -this.fHeight;
                    this.x[3]  = -this.fWidth;
                    this.y[3]  = 0;
                    for (i=0; i<4; i++) {
                            this.sX[i] = Math.random()*4+2;
                            this.sY[i] = Math.random()*4+2;
                    }
                    this.col = 0xFF0000;
            };
        this.init();
        this.createPetals(this.numberOfPetals);
        this.onEnterFrame = this.petalControl;
    };

    this.fDepth = 0;
    // createFlower (flower, numberOfPetals, fWidth, fHeight, fX, fY)
    createFlower("daffodil", 8, 100, 20, 200, 200);
    createFlower("orchid", 3, 40, 40, 100, 200);
    createFlower("daisy", 5, 40, 100, 300, 200);
```

So now we have code that is position-independent. We can place this code anywhere and it will create flowers there. I'll leave it up to you to find out how you can create flowers that are themselves made up of embedded rotating flowers (rather than embedded rotating petals), but we now have a very special piece of code; something that is **portable**.

There are two ways you can move your code physically to a new location, one of which is simply making the code a text file. The other method is to encapsulate the code in a component.

#include

#include is a compilation directive that tells Flash to use a block of external code and replace the #include with it. Although the end user can place an #include on any timeline, our code is covered for this.

Open flower04.fla and with the code visible in the Actions panel, click on the options menu (at the top right of the panel) and select Export As File.... This will simply export the file as a text file with the extension .as. Save it as flower.as in its own separate folder.

Now open a new movie and save it in the same folder as the AS file you just created. Add the following line to frame 1 of the default layer (this is flower05.fla on the CD):

```
#include "flower.as"
```

Note that this is not really an action, but more of an instruction to the Flash Player to include some external code. This is why it doesn't have a semi-colon at the end of the line (including one will raise an error).

Test the movie and you'll now see the flowers appearing in the new movie. You have simply transferred the code into a new movie and, because it is position-independent, it will still work. In a more general case, you would want to save your AS files in a project-specific folder, or one set aside for AS files to form a library of code modules to re-use. You can then specify an absolute path to your AS file like this:

```
#include "c:\Program Files\Macromedia\aslibs\flower.as"
```

This would allow you to add the flower animation into any FLA you are developing, assuming you have saved `flower.as` in the location shown.

Components

Components are one of the cool new features of Flash MX. These allow you to simply drag and drop a component building block onto the stage, and the code that makes it work takes care of itself automatically. This is like a visual form of `#include`, and also has the advantage of allowing you to add graphics into the component building block (whereas the AS file is strictly for code).

Because our code is both portable and configurable, it already possesses the necessary qualities needed to become a component, which is quite a bonus! So, although you might think that this section is going to be huge, it isn't; we've already done the hard work and are now simply using taking advantage of that fact.

Have a look at `flower06.fla`. It has an empty stage and a component called `flower` in the Library. With the Library open, you can do one of the following:

- Drag an instance of the component onto the stage.

- Open one of your own FLAs and drag the component onto a keyframe that you think is in need of some psychedelia (and this keyframe can be anywhere).

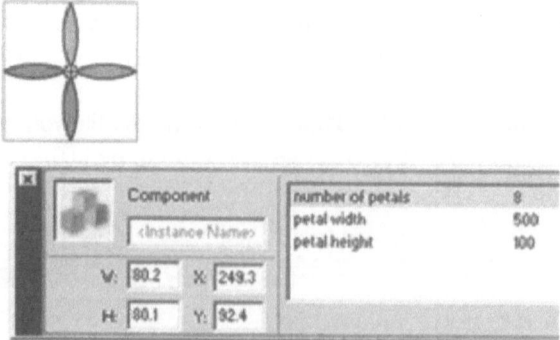

Next, using the Property inspector, set the number of petals and the petal height/width values:

Test the movie and you'll see the static flower shape replaced by our `flower` component. Cool! Nobody ever needs to write the flower code again!

So how does it work? Well, our code is actually more general than it needs to be. The flower is encapsulated inside the component so we no longer need to give it a name. We also specify its (x,y) location when we drop it onto the stage, so we don't need to state this either. All we really need to specify is the number of petals and their dimensions.

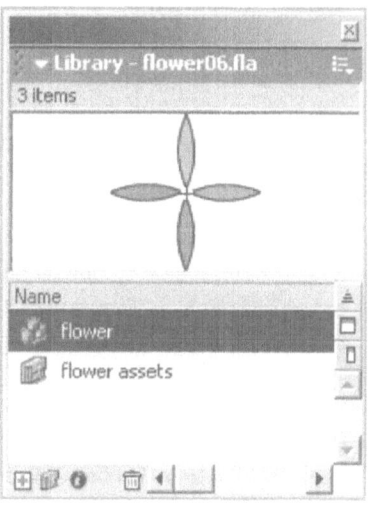

We do this in the Component Definition window, which you can access by selecting the flower component in the Library and selecting Component Definition... from the Library options menu window menu at the top right:

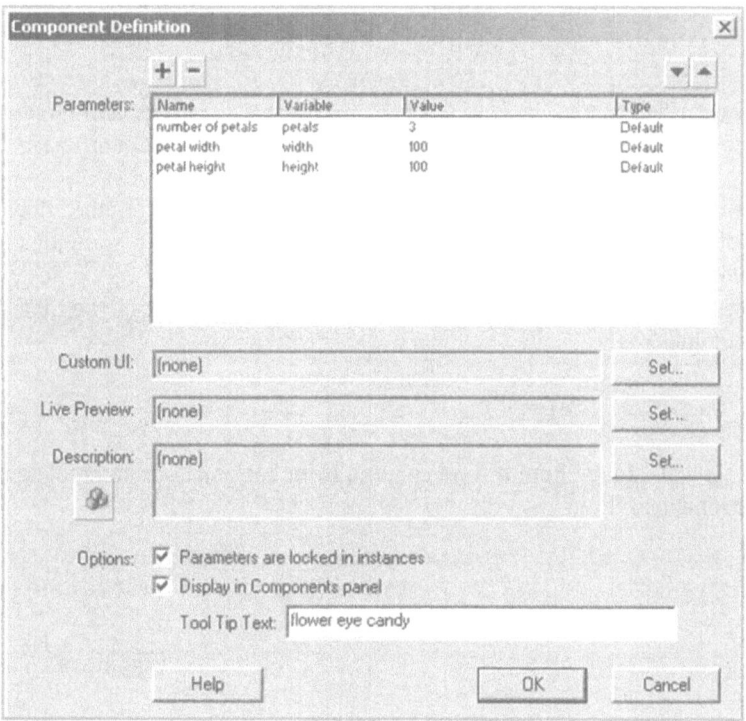

The Parameters pane is the important one for the programmer; it defines the variables that will be passed to the component (and which will appear in the Property inspector). The Name field contains the text that appears for each variable, and the Variable is the actual variable name that our encapsulated code will see. Value is the initial value the variables will take, and the Type is the variable type. If you leave it as Default, Flash will assume the type based on the value field (in our case they will all be numbers).

The code itself is inside the `flower` component and the only changes we have made are to the parameters in the top level `createFlower` module. Because this function interfaces with the other lower level modules, all we have to do to change our function call is change this function:

```
createFlower = function (flower, numberOfPetals, fWidth, fHeight) {
    var flower, numberOfPetals, petals, fWidth, fHeight, fX, fY;
    this.createEmptyMovieClip(flower, 0);
    this[flower].numberOfPetals = numberOfPetals;
    this[flower].fWidth = fWidth;
    this[flower].fHeight = fHeight;
    initializeFlower.apply(this[flower]);
};
```

I have deleted the `fX` and `fY` parameters to change `createFlower` accordingly. We also only create one flower per instance, so no longer need to mess about with `depth`, meaning this has been cut as well. I have left the `flower` parameter in because it appears in the code so often. A quicker way is to just give it a default value, as we shall see in a moment. At the end of this listing is the call to our code:

```
createFlower("myFlower", petals, width, height);
```

The flower is always called `myFlower`, and the `numberOfPetals`, `width`, and `height` parameters (set in the Property inspector) are picked up here and sent straight to our `createFlower` function. That's it!

One final element in this file that has nothing to do with the code is the little flower shape that forms the appearance of the component when you drag it onto the stage. It's a good idea to give it a graphical representation when authoring because an empty movie clip can be lost very quickly. The icon is a movie clip stored in the flower assets folder, and we make it invisible as soon as the SWF runs using the code in the penultimate line:

```
icon_mc._visible = false;
```

It may have taken a while to get here but we've gone from hacking code to creating totally encapsulated component functionality!

16   Object Oriented Programming Techniques

Objectives

- Understand why scripting in Flash is built around objects

- Understand the concepts of object and prototype inheritance

- Be able to code extensible and reusable ActionScript using OOP principles

Introduction

As a designer starting out in Flash, you may well have thought that when you created a few tweens and buttons on the stage to make a basic site, that you were well away from all this object/prototype deal. The truth is that the Flash authoring environment was shielding you from the truth; almost everything you do in Flash uses objects whether you realize it or not. You watch football, but may not fully understand the rules.

So, fine, you investigate all this object stuff and realize that the movie clip is an object, with properties such as `MovieClip._x` and `MovieClip._rotation`. You know it has methods like `MovieClip.gotoAndPlay()` and `MovieClip.stop()`, and that using actions such as `gotoAndPlay` and `stop` is just Flash shielding beginners from the truth. So now you watch football and know the rules, you can appreciate the subtleties of the game.

Get further down the line and you may start to see bits of code that you don't understand at all. You thought you had this ActionScript thing sussed, but the new stuff might as well be hieroglyphics! Well, that's the difference between being a programming spectator and a player. You can watch the game, absorbing what's on offer, or you can be a player and a part of it, defining the game itself. There is a world of difference from knowing about properties and methods and actually writing in the style that generated these terms.

This chapter is all about turning you into a player. It's about helping you understand the object oriented concepts, not so that you understand the terminology but to actually get you to write in this style yourself. We'll show you how to write in the super-structured style of OOP, but we will also show you how to hack it, so that your code isn't structured but still uses prototypes, constructors, and other OOP techniques. This is because we know that OOP is not for everyone, and some designers out there just want to play with this as a design avenue rather than a programming imperative. We won't be prescriptive one way or another on this (after all, maverick players are out there as well as the professional career sportsmen), but we will spend some time explaining how OOP is what makes Flash work, so even if you decide the programming style sucks, you'll still be left with an important and valuable insight.

In the previous episode...

This chapter is really part two of a running series. The first part dealt with modular code in **Chapter 15**, where we saw that functions are the crux of the advanced coder's repertoire. In that chapter, we also talked about the fact that modular coding in motion graphics is slightly a different beast. Motion graphics require a designer's eye, not a programmer's fixed view.

The same rules apply here. We won't be creating long code listings that look like horror stories, and neither will we pretend that we need to do that sort of thing in Flash. We're still designers that want to create code-controlled interfaces and animations. When we reach the point where Flash is fast enough to handle five thousand line code segments that exhibit true polymorphism as well as encapsulation and inheritance, then we'll tell you. Fortunately, we're not quite there yet.

We'll start by comparing and contrasting modular code to object oriented code, and illustrating how the difference in world view between these two stances are actually completely different (even though the code may look the same). Because OOP is a new country to many of you, we will also take some time out to get you talking in the language they speak there.

Hacking it

"Hacking it" is a well-known programming route. Just open up your scripting window and go for it with no advanced planning. Why go fixing bugs if a workaround will suffice?

We *should* say now that you should never do this, but who needs to structure a bit of ActionScript that's only ten lines long anyway? Even this programming style has its uses, particularly when you are following the scent of the initial creative idea, and don't want to pause in order to set up structures that constrain your creative path too early in the process.

Modular code and the top down structure

Modular code is based around a functional mindset. When we looked at the flower animation in the last chapter, we began with the top level function `createFlower` and then called a lower level function `initializeFlower`, whose job was to set up the code and graphics to drive the effect. `initializeFlower` does its thing but also creates `init`, `createPetals`, and `petalControl` (which isn't just a function, but an `onEnterFrame` event handler). `init` set up our variables and `createPetals` created our empty petal movie clips. Finally, `petalControl` updated the petal data and told `drawPetal` to actually draw the petals.

This diagram is one way of representing what we did:

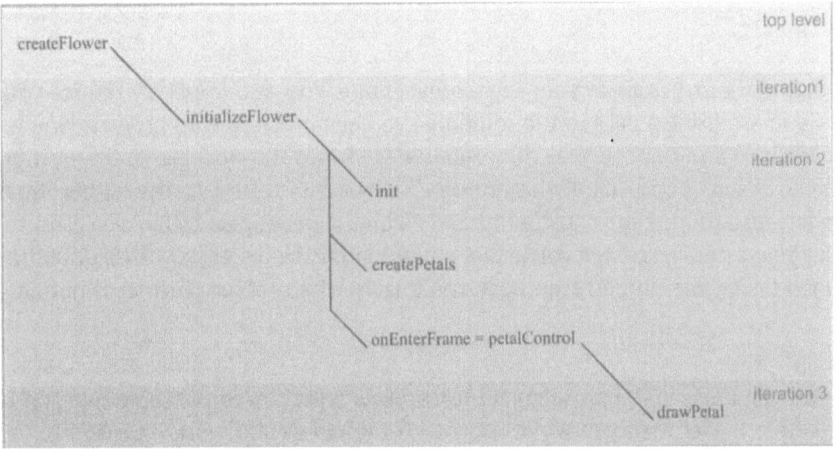

So, what does this show?

First of all, it shows that our design philosophy was the top down approach. When creating the skeleton, I sat back and thought "what do I want to do?" I wanted to create a flower so I made an empty module (function) called `createFlower`. This created the flower clip itself and copied the call information into it (almost like creating a flower seed and injecting the DNA that describes it). I now needed to form my flower based on this information.

Next, I said "how do I do that?" I wanted to set up my newly created flower for the effect, and to do this I created an empty function called `initializeFlower`. This is needed to initialize the flower parameters involved with the animation, create the petal clips, and then animate it.

So next I said "well how do I do that?" ... and so on.

The "what do I want to do?" question is what programmers call the **high level functional requirement**. The "how do I do that" questions are referred to as **iterations**. What you do is form the problem and keep on iterating, splitting up the problem until you have a solid skeleton solution. In our motion graphics world, we don't have the time for lengthy diagrams but, if we did, the one above accurately describes our code structure. It describes a **top down** solution. We started at the top of the problem and worked down, building functions that solved each level of the problem until we reached the bottom, iteration 3, where the petals are actually drawn.

Also, we created our code using a functional route. When we eventually came to code it, we worked through the diagram from left to right. This sounds like a sensible approach because we stick to the problem in hand, which is actually a very natural design process. The example we used was short because we don't want to hide the technique under the weight of the code, but this also hides some important disadvantages.

If you make a change to the problem, all iterations below the level where the change is made must also change, because their starting point has changed. The higher the level of your change, the more code you need to edit.

When you define the structure of your higher-level code, you also implicitly reduce your options for the lower levels; you are fixing a path to the solution. I've been involved with projects where we have reached the lower iterations and realized that the route we took was not necessarily the best one because there are unexpected results occurring at the bottom. Rather than return to the higher iterations, we started improvizing because of the time constraints, and when the going gets tough we resort to hacking it. What programming text books never tell you is that you don't hit the lower iterations until the end of a project, precisely when taking the time to step back and analyze the problem further is not an option.

OOP for designers

The OOP approach looks at the problem in the opposite direction to the top down approach. Rather than look at the whole flower first, you would start with the petals and work up like this:

First, create a petal module and encapsulate it. This means that, like the modular code, it is self-contained.

Create an interface to the petal. This will consist of petal **methods** and **properties**. If you want the petal to have points, for example (0,0) (200,200) (200,-200) and (0,100), you would use a method such as:

```
MyPetal.setPointList(0,0, 200, 200, 200, -200, 0, 100);
```

If you want it to rotate you would change a property:

```
MyPetal.rotation += 20;
```

The point of doing this is that you have built up a set of software interfaces to the module. Looking at it conceptually, you are no longer talking to a code module but are seeing the petal through its methods and properties. You no longer see the code modules behind the petal functionality. This is part of what we call **abstraction**. The collection of methods and properties that you use to access the petal module is what we call the petal **object**.

What you do next to create the flower is exactly the same as creating the petal; write a module called (say) flower. What is new here is that you assume the methods and properties of the petal to now be part of ActionScript, and you use them in creating the flower. Each time you build a new object you follow the same process using your collection of objects. You do not build up an application, but rather add more properties to ActionScript, changing it to become part of your solution.

It's important to note that this is no different from how you use the movie clip. You are assuming that there is a "thing" (an object) called a movie clip, but all it really is a set of properties and methods. You don't see the code modules that make it up and probably never thought about it that way! There is almost no difference between the way you use the Petal object to create a flower, and the way you use the MovieClip object to create the petal, except that you did not write the MovieClip object code. When you hear the phrase "Flash thinks with an object oriented approach", this is what we mean. Creating objects to build up your application is just the same as how Flash was built. All you are doing is carrying on the process.

Looking at it this way, what is actually happening is that the whole Flash environment is a set of open-ended objects that you can use to build more objects specific to your needs (or configure the existing ones so that they do what you want them to). You abstract away from this open-ended environment towards your problem. In building up an object oriented application, all you are doing is making the Flash coding environment more and more specific to your problem until it actually becomes the solution.

You may have thought that OOP was a code-centric beardy concept, but look at it now and it seems more like an organic thought process. Start off small and slowly build up to what you want. This is a **bottom up** approach and is physically different to the top down approach we looked at previously:

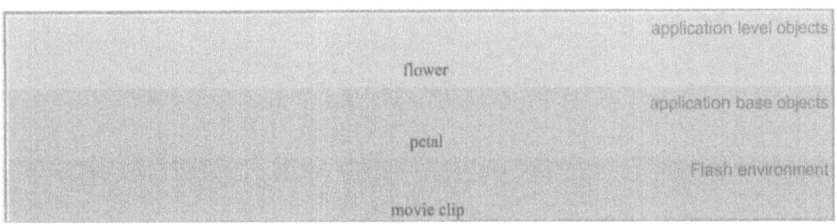

This time we have a Flash environment with many general objects, one of which is the MovieClip object. We use this to create our Petal object. So now we have another level where we have some base objects that will help us solve our problem. In the diagram above, I have called it application base objects (you may also hear the confusing term **base classes**, which is strictly irrelevant to Flash as we shall see when we get to the section headed 'Definitions').

We use these basic objects to build a foundation for our solution, and they rely on the Flash environment to give us the movie clip. That's a strict programming view but I sometimes prefer to just think of Petal as being the same as the MovieClip object, that it was always there at the 'Flash environment' level, but I'll leave that up to you – whatever works. Anyway, at the top level is the object that actually solves our problem; Flower. This assumes the application base classes below it, but when we use it all we see is the single method `flower.createFlower()`, or something similar.

Looking at it a different way, we can think of the MovieClip > Petal > Flower combination as if it were a Russian doll, where each doll contains a smaller doll inside:

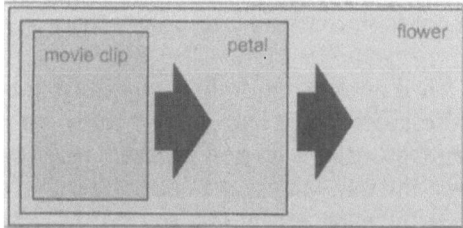

This is actually a nice way to think of it because it mirrors the workflow itself. You use the methods and properties of the MovieClip object as the building block for the Petal object, so the MovieClip is encapsulated inside it, and the petal is encapsulated inside the flower. During normal use you just use `flower.createFlower()` and you don't open up the Flower object to see the Petal and MovieClip 'dolls' rattling inside it.

This is the theory but there is one more way to think about objects, and I like this one most of all because it promotes creativity:

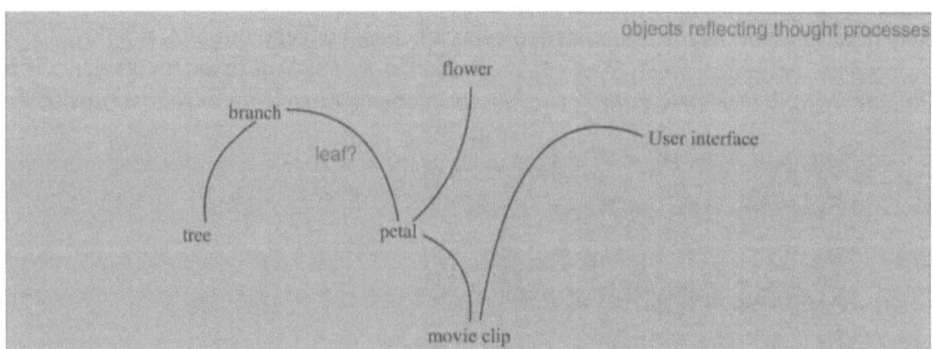

If you assume there is no hierarchy between objects except the ones you make, then you stop thinking in terms of an object based layered approach and more along the lines of how your exploration is developing.

Macromedia broadly intend that the movie clip is for use in user interface design; Flash is after all a web design tool and a means of creating animated content. They have, however, left it all up to you. You can use the movie clip to make a sprite object for a cool and nasty video game just as well as you can make it part of a scrollbar in an input form that has the faint and musty smell of JavaScript about it.

You can also create the Petal object and then, half way through building your flower from it, you think "hey, that petal is also like a leaf" and diverge to create a branch of leaves using your Petal object. This broadens further into many swaying branches to form a tree.

This open-ended approach is not used often in classic OOP, but they don't know kung fu like we do. This freeform 'create objects and then build other stuff on top of them in an open process' is what Flash is all about. Modular design is not open-ended enough to do this because it does not have the general method- or property-based interfaces between modules that OOP has, one big advantage of OOP.

The bad news is that OOP is different. It takes time to learn before you can use it in such a freeform manner. You need to know a bit of kung fu before you can get to this point.

Also, making truly general objects takes time and a lot of effort. There are people who will turn their nose up at objects that aren't built up in a structured way with base classes and elegant code routines, but most of us don't have much time to spare. Take OOP as far as it takes you, because the route you take is far less important than the working application you are attempting to create.

There is also much cross-talk of how difficult OOP can be. Well, maybe. If you stick to the hard programming conventions of OOP, then you will have difficulty. The sort of OOP that is used to build formal applications such as Windows XP is very well structured, with extremely layered and hierarchical software objects and associations between them. All we will say is that ActionScript is neither JavaScript nor is it Java. It doesn't have the high level structures of Java and, although it is syntactically very close to JavaScript, the fact that Flash is a visual environment and is time-based makes it a completely different beast in practice.

Definitions

In this book we will use the term object oriented programming, although ActionScript is not an object oriented language. It is object *based*. Languages that are object oriented use something called **class**, which you don't need to worry about in Flash so we won't even go there (but it is something that allows you to create totally new types of object). You may come unstuck when people start talking about class in Flash. Macromedia use this term. So do a lot of other people, and their definitions of class tend to vary with the tide. The differentiation between **instance** and **object** also causes some confusion, and people also use horror story terms like 'Object Class', which isn't meaningful whatsoever.

In Flash you must always base your objects upon one of the default objects (such as the MovieClip or Color object) using something called the **prototype**. This allows you to redefine bits of the default objects or add a bunch of new things to them.

For our purposes we will take a more pragmatic view and use the following definitions:

- **Class** does not exist in Flash. If you see it, mentally cross it out and change it to 'object', and any references to 'object' will probably now become 'instance'.

- A **prototype** is a simple structure based around functions that is the means of defining custom objects. It is not a class and neither is it misappropriated from Java or C++.

- An **object** is a group of entities that have the same method and property definitions. The MovieClip is one of the default objects, and if you created one of your own (via a prototype), then you have just created a new object.

- An **instance** is an individual member of your object. For example, a single movie clip that you drag on to the stage is an instance of the MovieClip object. You can define a particular instance by using a **constructor**.

- The difference between a **constructor** and a **prototype** is that the constructor works at the instance level, whereas the prototype works at the object level. Otherwise they are very similar in practice, and neither requiress any additional understanding over a knowledge normal functions.

Before we get onto the meaty bits, we have to revisit functions to show how to build prototypes and object constructors. We also have to reiterate how the whole Flash environment is really just a collection of objects and why it is a good idea to adopt this mindset. After that, we'll look at:

- How to modify the default Flash objects.

- How to create your own objects based on the default objects.

- Using the Object object.

Flash as an OOP playground

Except for graphic symbols, strokes, fills, and static text, everything you place on the stage is an object. As soon as you buy into this, you stop thinking of Flash as just a tween-based motion graphics system, but rather a tween-based motion graphics system with some nice general software objects to use as well.

For example, consider the Math object:

As a beginner we probably see its structure as odd. Why do you have to do this:

```
x = Math.floor(Math.random()*5);
```

...when you could just as well do this in Flash 4?

```
x = random(5);
```

Why is the long horror story at the top 'progress'? Well, both of them provide a random whole number between 0 and 4, but only the second line one actually looks like it does! The same thing applies to the movie clip. We were happy with this:

```
duplicateMovieClip(myClip_mc, "myNewClip_mc", 5);
```

...so why did Macromedia see fit to confuse us in Flash 5 by changing it to this?

```
myClip_mc.duplicateMovieClip("myNewClip_mc", 5);
```

To be fair, Macromedia still let you use the old version and, to maintain compatibility with the high volume of Flash 4 content still out there, a little bird tells me they always will. So, don't worry if you still use `x = random(5)` because it's easier, and `duplicateMovieClip(myClip_mc, "myNewClip_mc", 5)` because you see no reason to change, despite the hype about method-based scripting somehow being better.

Let's try to put this into some kind of perspective because, although people out there may well say "actions are bad, methods are good, even though the latter is usually longer", I've looked on the web and there's actually no real explanation why this is a good thing. Yet this object > method/property deal is supposedly much more 'elegant'. Why?

There are at least four very good reasons:

- When using object > method/property forms, you will find it much easier to navigate around the syntax.

- Most new additions to ActionScript (Flash 5 and later) only have the method-based forms.

- You can change the object methods and properties, making it extensible.

- You gain a deeper understanding of the way Flash works.

Let's look at each of these in detail.

Thinking in objects

The trouble with this form:

```
duplicateMovieClip(myClip_mc, "myNewClip_mc", 5);
```

...is that you have to know it before you can use it. If you want to duplicate a movie clip, you *have* to know that the action is duplicateMovieClip(). If you wanted to know more about it because you had forgotten the exact syntax, then you must already know it begins with the letter 'd' before you can locate the entry. The same applies to gotoAndPlay and stop.

So now you're thinking "Well, how else can I use it? Surely I *have* to know about it, or how else could I use it!" I don't blame you... but consider this. Suppose I want to duplicate a movie clip. I know there is an action that does it because I've used it before, but I've been playing with Director 8.5 and its 3D stuff for a while, so I've totally forgotten. That's okay. Happens to us all. So I think:

```
"MovieClip"
```

Then I look in the Reference panel under the MovieClip object and hit upon createEmptyMovieClip. It rings a bell but it isn't what I want. So I carry on and find duplicateMovieClip. **Bingo!**

```
"MovieClip.duplicateMovieClip"
```

> *By moving along the object > method/property tree, you can quickly find what you need in terms of what you want to do without knowing what the required scripting to perform this actually is.*

This is actually a very powerful concept to bear in mind. Flash ActionScript is a pretty simple structure, consisting of a number of definite objects. If you want to work with Flash but don't know all the syntax, you'd be better off starting with the object.method and object.property forms rather than the beginner stuff like gotoAndPlay and stop, because once you understand the general structure you can apply it to learning new objects such as System and TextFormat quickly.

Even if you don't understand OOP, think of the objects as chapters in a book. By knowing roughly what is in each chapter, you can get to the page you want pretty quickly, and it's much faster than thumbing through the whole book. Even better, Flash MX allows you to do this automatically in the Actions panel.

Type myClip_mc into the Actions panel and then add the '.' (period). You'll see this:

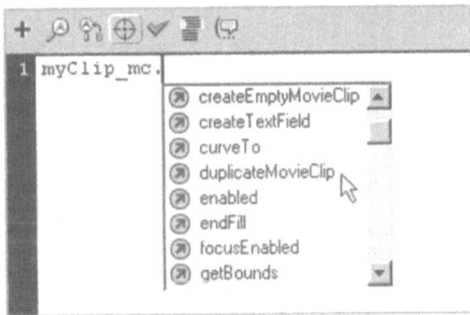

When you add the '.' you'll see that Flash knows that myClip_mc is an object and simply looks up all the relevant methods for you. So, from needing to know all 60 methods of the MovieClip object, you have can isolated the single method you want; you only need to know what a movie clip is and what it can do in general terms.

This is what objects are actually all about. They are *general*, and writing in the object.method form allows you to make use of this fact even at the beginner stage.

Also important is the fact that since Flash 5, all the new ActionScript additions are included in the object.method form only. There is no action-based form of the XML object or the new Shared object, and if you stick to random(5) or stop, you will never find them.

Extensibility and OOP

Extensibility is another important term to understand because, in the world of personal jewellery, this is the Crown Jewels of the Queen of England.

Remember this?:

```
X = random(5);
x = Math.floor(Math.random()*5);
```

We discussed earlier how the first form is short and sweet and, although the second line supposedly has the brains, it's a bit ugly. Well, try this below or use the file mathReplace.fla.

```
function myRandom(arg) {
        return Math.floor(Math.random()*arg);
}
Math.myRandom = myRandom;
x = Math.myRandom(6);
trace(x);
x = Math.sin(34);
trace(x);
```

Test the movie to see something like this:

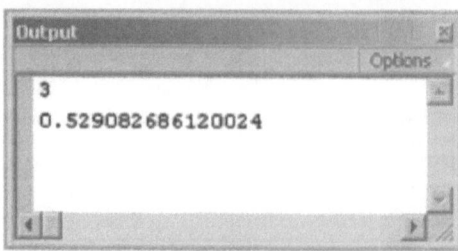

Hang on though. Look at what we've done here, because it's cool. You don't like:

```
x = Math.floor(Math.random()*5);
```

... so I have changed the Math Object so that you don't have to use it! All I've done is add a new method called `myRandom()` that gives you the same result as the `MathFloor(MathRandom()*5)` line above. So instead you could now just use:

```
x = Math.myRandom(5);
```

This gives us our 3, but it could just as well be 0, 1, 2, or 4. The second number in the Output window is the result from of `Math.sin(34)` just to show that the rest of the Math object still works. This is nice because you can go around changing objects in this way until the environment looks the way you want it, and that includes most of the default objects.

The way we have done it here is called **inheritance**, and all I have done is cause the Math object to inherit a new method. **You can't do this sort of thing with Actions such as `random` or `gotoAndPlay`.** This is what we mean about extensibility and OOP! Inheritance only takes you so far though as it only works on a single instance. There is actually only one instance of the Math object, so inheritance is okay for that. The next step up comes when you want to change all instances of a particular object, such as all movie clips, and you do that by altering the **prototype**.

The `MovieClip.gotoAndPlay()` method doesn't display an error if you try to go to a frame that doesn't exist. It simply goes to the last available frame. This is okay but it might be hiding an error, so it might be useful if `MovieClip.gotoAndPlay()` actually told us if we sent it on a fool's errand because we're the bigger fool. In fact, there are lots of bits of ActionScript that don't tell us when an error has occurred (called silent failure). Let's fix the movie clip case here as an example of extensibility (you can also just pull up `gotoAndPlayDebug.fla`):

```
MovieClip.prototype.newGotoAndPlay = function(arg) {
    var message;
    if (this._totalframes<arg) {
        message = "WARNING: "+this+" frame "+this._currentframe;
        trace(message);
        trace("debug error - can't jump past end of timeline!");
```

```
        } else {
              this.gotoAndPlay(Arg);
        }
    };
    _root.newGotoAndPlay(40);
```

Notice that the first line doesn't reference any particular movie clip instances; it is applied to the MovieClip object itself, which affects *all* movie clips. If you place this on _root and run it, all will be fine if the timeline is 40 or more frames long. If it happens to be 39 frames long (which this movie is) you get the following message:

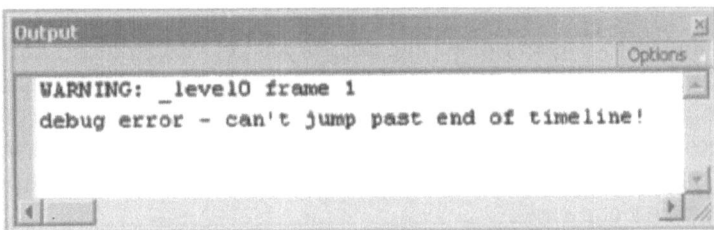

It looks like it might be an error message coming from Flash but isn't really. It's just us creating a new method MovieClip.newGotoAndPlay().

There are some very useful applications of this kind of thing. For example, you may want a special form of the MovieClip.gotoAndPlay() method called (say) MovieClip.gotoAndPlayStream(). This new method could be used in a streaming timeline where the frame you want to jump to may not exist yet. By halting the timeline and waiting 0.5 seconds before trying again, you could build in the functionality to handle streaming conditions in a transparent OOP way without any of those clunky preloaders.

Now we're really starting to talk extensibility and adding all the things that we wish Flash could do. Who needs a wish list when you can just add it yourself?!

Thinking in OOP

The thing about thinking in OOP terms is that you gain an insight into why things are the way they are in Flash. You get a feel for what is actually important and what isn't. We'll look at two examples of this. One is fundamental and the other is more like one of those little niggles that makes you think "what's the purpose in that?"

Under the hood of Flash

It's important to think about objects and how they can be treated the same. This isn't immediately apparent to a designer (or, for that matter, many programmers). We all intuitively see the MovieClip, Button, and TextField as being different to other objects, such as the Math and Sound objects, but the more we think about it, it starts to fall apart:

- MovieClips, TextFields, and Buttons are graphics and are attached to keyframes.

- Other objects like the Sound and XML objects are more concerned with the scripting side and are separate to this graphic environment.

- There are a few special objects, such as the Math object, that always exist and are not timeline dependent because they seem to exist everywhere at the same time. Are these a special case then?

- There's _root but hang on, what's that attached to?

- What is _global? ...a timeline? An all-encompassing god-like entity?

Well, it's pretty intuitive to begin with, but the deeper you get into an object-based view, the more you realize that you have to understand the overall hierarchy because that is the only way you can set up a hierarchy like the one we saw earlier with base objects growing up towards the application level. Don't worry though, because this structure is very simple; there are only two concepts involved, plus one special case. We have to make sure you get to this realization though because it's fundamental (and often missing in a true programming world view).

The only difference between the MovieClip and the XML object (once you forget what the **functional differences are**) is that you can *see* the MovieClip (it has a visual appearance), but the XML object is a data-only object. Stepping back a little, it soon becomes obvious that this is only really due to **properties**. Both objects have them, it's just that some of the MovieClip properties are related to things you can see. It also has properties such as _currentframe and _totalframes. Flash shows us these two properties *visually* as a timeline, and this construct has a lower base object called the **frame** which is expressed in a completely visual way. The frame might be visual when you see it in Flash but, to the Macromedia programmers that created it, it has properties that define what scripts and graphics are attached to it, so even the frame is essentially a data object.

> So, there is really no special case associated with the fact that you can see the MovieClip but not the XML object, as it's just down to the way they are represented in Flash.

The fact that you attach the visual objects to a keyframe is no different from any other object. When you attach a Button to a keyframe, you are defining a new instance of that Button. When you create a Sound object with new Sound in a script attached to the same frame, you are doing exactly the same thing but in a non-visual way. There is no difference between placing a graphic symbol on a keyframe and defining a non-graphic symbol programmatically via ActionScript:

- Both will have the same **scope** and are dependent on the timeline they are scoped to in exactly the same way.

■   Both can only be created on a keyframe.

Although _root looks as if it is a special case, it quickly becomes obvious that it is simply the top level MovieClip.

There's a new object that may not be immediately obvious to designers, and it is this object that causes many of the contortions in trying to work out how it all fits together. This object is called _global, and it is a special case as it is missing a very important implicit property: it has no scope. Therefore, all the objects within it are not attached to any timeline, and are available from *any* timeline. The Math object does this because it is scoped to _global, so you never have to attach it to anything. This is not a consequence of Math itself, but its **position**.

> Global objects are not a special case. They are just in a special position, and you can otherwise treat them exactly the same as you would any other object.

All of the ActionScript that doesn't appear to have a scope is actually in _global. This means that ActionScript itself is not a special case as the objects it uses are really no different from the ones we create. This is an important point because, as soon as we see that, we won't find it odd that we can go ahead and just change things in _global and, in doing so, change ActionScript itself.

Finally, as soon as the missing link that is _global fits into place, the whole idea starts to make sense… except for one thing. Now that we see that the MovieClip is just an object with properties that give it an appearance, making it no different from TextFormat for instance, we start to think "Well, if all objects follow the same structure (Object > method/property), then there should be a common base object, but I can't see it". It is there and, more importantly, you can use it. It's called the **Object object** and is the most important object, because it is the base that all other objects are built upon. Understand this object and you've cracked it!

We will look at this bit of angel dust later in the chapter, but you now have an important piece of information, as you know its context in the whole scheme of things.

> *As an aside, notice how we have defined* _global. *This gives an insight to how programmers think.* _global *exists everywhere, not because it is omnipotent and all pervading, but because it is missing something that would otherwise force it to conform to scope! For a programmer, special cases are not really all that special. They are usually different, not because they are more complex, but because they are simpler! A simple thing with less properties than its neighbours, stuck in a complex structure is always difficult to handle. Just think about all the IRS forms they make you fill in if you don't present all the personal details and numbers (i.e. properties) they expect!*

The discussion can be made much more concise now that we have developed it. There are only two important things: the object > .property/method structure and scope:

- All objects are fundamentally data structures, consisting of properties and methods. This structure is inherited from a base object called Object.

- Some properties are expressed as data and some are expressed as visual attributes, but neither are special cases, because the code that controls a property is fundamentally the same, irrespective of what the effect of changing the property will be.

- All objects conform to scope. There are two ways of assigning scope, one of which is visual (e.g. attaching MovieClips, Buttons, and TextFields to a keyframe), and the other is programmatical (defining an object within a script that is also attached to a keyframe). Neither is a special case, and both are actually different ways of doing the same thing.

- One object is unique because it has no scope and this is called _global. Rather than see this as a new object, it is better to see it as a special case of *position* (or scope==null or scope== everywhere, depending on how you prefer to see it). It is timeline-independent and therefore not a timeline itself, but a position. Objects that are global are not special cases, but simply normal objects in a special scope-less place.

Look up. Take a deep breath. Now say this: "I understand how Flash works." Breathe out. You now know kung fu.

ActionScript exceptions

There are some bits of Flash out on the edges that seem, well, odd. For example, take the _quality property. You can use:

```
_quality
MovieClip._quality
Button._highquality
TextField._highquality
```

The thing is, all of these apply the quality setting (the level of anti-aliasing) to the whole Flash Player. So, what's the point in having a Button._highquality property when it doesn't apply to every button instance? Well, think back a few pages to the discussion of base objects. This is what's happening here:

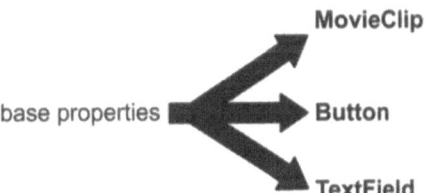

Because the MovieClip, Button, and TextField objects share the same low-level graphic properties (all of those that start with an underscore such as _x and _visible), all three objects must share the same base properties inherited from a common low-level object that isn't available directly to us (we don't need it; we can just use the MovieClip). Some of the properties are more useful to one of the three objects than the others, although they are still present in all three. It's a bit like the Russian dolls again. The MovieClip, Button, and TextField all share the same doll somewhere down the line.

So _highquality is only really relevant to _root (which is a MovieClip), but because the properties must come as a job lot, the Button and TextField need to have it too. This tells you that you don't really have to use Button._highQuality or TextField._highquality, as it makes more sense to just use _highquality (which will be using the MovieClip version because adding nothing in front of the property makes it default to the current timeline).

Thinking in an OOP-centric way almost always yields sensible and plausible answers, and is a good way of thinking through an anomaly in the way ActionScript works. Of course, it goes without saying that this works because OOP *is* the way ActionScript works, and you're beyond voodoo scripting and into classic kung fu moves now.

We will start on the slope to OOP now that we have a good idea of the terrain we will be covering and, more importantly, we have a good idea of what will be waiting for us when we reach the summit. To start off, we will look at the Object object, and then revisit our old friend the Function, whom we got so well acquainted with in the last chapter.

Deeper into Flash objects

So, all the Flash objects have methods and properties and if we think of ActionScript in that way, we will get further with it. But what are methods and properties anyway? Well, objects are only there to describe a problem. Language is there to describe the world we live in, so there's a pretty big correspondence between the two.

Objects as nouns

They represent something. Exactly what they represent depends on the way you are using the object. The Math object is a general math library of useful mathematical stuff. The MovieClip is a general timeline-based construction with a graphic appearance, and so on. Basically, all objects are simply collections of information. They are symbolic representations; the stage in Flash isn't really a white rectangle just as the rocket launcher in *Quake 3* doesn't really exist except as a set of points in a simulated 3D world.

Methods as verbs

These are the *doing* parts and cause change. If you use `MovieClip.gotoAndPlay()`, then the MovieClip timeline will do something, in this case moving to a new frame. Without methods to control our objects we would have no way of making our objects do things such as process data or animate. You could of course move a movie clip around yourself without using a method, using an event handler or other script. This is not the intention of OOP though. Instead, you should incorporate all the code associated with the 'doing' part of an object using either methods or lower level (base) objects that are encapsulated within your current object.

Properties as adjectives

Adjectives describe the noun in the same way that properties describe the object. A movie clip's `_x` and `_y` property describes its position, and its `_rotation` property describes its angle of rotation. Properties can also describe more than just appearance, which isn't a bad thing because some objects don't have an appearance at all (such as the Sound and XML objects). They can describe the **state** of an object. For example, the `_currentframe` property of a movie clip tells us how far along its timeline the playhead is.

Finally, they can describe **values** of some part of the object. The volume of a Sound object tells us how loud the sound it is controlling is. Because objects are software constructions rather than physical objects in the real world, their description can get, well, virtual. The value of a Number object has no meaning in terms of describing something real sometimes, but they are still descriptive of something about the object, so the analogy holds.

Using OOP in practice

Okay, we're finally there. We've got the basics under our belt. Time to start showing it.

Object inheritance

Because ActionScript isn't class-based, you cannot create totally new objects. They must all be based on one or more of the existing Flash objects. But what if you need a totally non-specific object to start you on your way?

As well as the more specific objects (such as Math, Sound, and XML, all of which have a very well defined area of functional expertise, as implied by their names), there is also a non-specific object. Programmers don't know what to call it, other than it is an object, so they call this beast (wait for it) the Object object. We've met it before briefly, but let's look at it in more detail:

- It has the ability to have methods and properties, but when you create one it won't have any, so you'll have a blank Object template to work with.

- It has no graphic portion so it is not an object in the sense that the MovieClip, Button, and TextField are.

You might be thinking "Stop there! I want to do motion graphics!" There are three reasons why it is important to learn the Object object, even though it's a data structure with no obvious use for motion graphics:

- The Object object allows you to drive your animations using more complex data structures than plain old variables.

- Learning the Object object enables you to understand the underlying Object > method/property structure.

- Explaining the basics with the Object object is fundamental to learning OOP with the other objects, because it is the base Object contained inside all the others. It's the center of the Russian doll.

The Object object is useful in its own right, particularly when it comes to **inheritance**, which we'll look at now.

You can create a new object like this:

```
MyObject = new Object();
```

This simply creates the object but, like a new movie clip with no graphics or script attached to its timeline, it's an empty structure with nothing going on. So we need to start filling it. To give it a single property say, prop1 equal to 10, we do the following:

```
myObject.prop1 = 10;
```

We can carry on doing this to add other properties:

```
myObject.prop2 = 20;
myObject.prop3 = "hello";
```

Your object will look like this if you test this code in debugging mode:

⊟	MyObject	
⋯	prop1	10
⋯	prop2	20
⋯	prop3	"hello"

You can also use the following shorthand form, which will create the object as well as populate it with properties:

```
MyObject = {prop1:10, prop2:20, prop3:"hello"};
```

You can add further levels of properties by nesting:

```
MyObject = new Object();
myObject.prop1 = 10;
myObject.prop2 = 20;
myObject.prop3 = "hello";
myObject.prop4 = new Object();
myObject.prop4.subprop1 = true;
myObject.prop4.subprop2 = false;
```

⊟	MyObject	
⋯	prop1	10
⋯	prop2	20
⋯	prop3	"hello"
⊟	prop4	
⋯	subprop1	true
⋯	subprop2	false

This time, we have added a new property of myObject that is itself an object, prop4. We have then given this the properties subprop1 and subprop2. So what does this give us? Well, it lets us structure our data in a form that is good for OOP coding. Lets look at this in detail.

Consider the standard classic; the bouncing ball movie clip, which is oopBall01.fla. This file consists of a ball movie clip called ball_mc, and the following code to drive it:

```
ballMover = function () {
     // calculate new x position
     this.xPos += this.xSpeed;
     if ((this.xPos<this.xLow) || (this.xPos>this.xHigh)) {
          this.xSpeed = -this.xSpeed;
     }
     // calculate new y position
     this.yPos += this.ySpeed;
     if ((this.yPos<this.yLow) || (this.yPos>this.yHigh)) {
          this.ySpeed = -this.ySpeed;
     }
     // animate to new position
     this._x = this.xPos;
     this._y = this.yPos;
};

// ball x stuff
ball_mc.xPos = 275;
```

```
ball_mc.xLow = 10;
ball_mc.xHigh = 540;
ball_mc.xSpeed = 5;

// ball y stuff
ball_mc.yPos = 200;
ball_mc.yLow = 10;
ball_mc.yHigh = 390;
ball_mc.ySpeed = 5;

// set event handler
ball_mc.onEnterFrame = ballMover;
```

This is all pretty standard stuff. The code sets up some data to control a clip called `ball_mc`, defining the position, speed, and boundaries for each of the x and y coordinates of the ball. The callback `ballMover` calculates a new ball position every frame, and then moves the ball to this new position.

The data for this FLA looks like this:

onEnterFrame	
xHigh	550
xLow	0
xPos	180
xSpeed	-5
yHigh	400
yLow	0
yPos	95
ySpeed	-5

Although the script is on the timeline of the movie clip it is controlling, it lacks any real structure.

Let's look at getting this to work using the Object object. The first major point to know about OOP is that data has to be structured, and this example will show why. The following code will give us the same data, but in a more structured form:

```
spriteData = new Object();

spriteData.xData = new Object();
spriteData.xData.pos = 275;
spriteData.xData.speed = 5;
spriteData.xData.low = 10;
spriteData.xData.high = 540;

spriteData.yData = new Object();
spriteData.yData.pos = 200;
spriteData.yData.speed = 5;
spriteData.yData.low = 10;
spriteData.yData.high = 390;
```

⊟	spriteData	
	⊟ xData	
	high	540
	low	10
	pos	275
	speed	5
	⊟ yData	
	high	390
	low	10
	pos	200
	speed	5

You can actually shorten this definition using a **constructor function**. This is simply a function that defines an object's properties (and, as we shall see later, methods) after you have instantiated it (created an empty object instance using `new Object`, for instance). To define our data, we can do this:

```
function constructPointElement(point, pos, speed, low, high) {
        this.pos = pos;
        this.speed = speed;
        this.low = low;
        this.high = high;
}

spriteData = new Object();
spriteData.xData = new ConstructPointElement(xData, 275, 5, 10, 540);
spriteData.yData = new ConstructPointElement(xData, 200, 5, 10, 390);
```

The function `constructPointElement` is a constructor. We simply pass an object to it, and it will fill in the structure. Why have we been able to shorten the code? Well, `xData` holds the same as `yData` in terms of the structure it contains and what these values actually represent. We have seen this and split a two-dimensional point into two general element values. By doing this, we have **abstracted**. We see that an x co-ordinate is really just like a y co-ordinate:

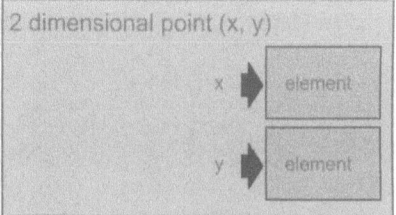

What are the advantages of this abstraction? Well, at the element level, we no longer know how many dimensions the point actually has anymore, when thinking purely along the lines of the code structure. It could be in a 3D point routine and all we would have to do is update the element code to create an extra element:

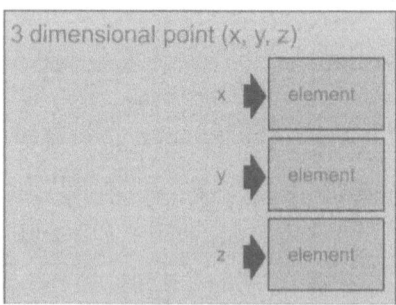

As long as we keep the code general and abstracted in this way throughout, as we build up from this point, it won't be long after creating a 2D ball that we'll be able to create a 3D ball bouncing about, and this is because our code structure allows it. We will only have to change the parts that actually need it when we do this, rather than rewrite the whole code because our structure doesn't allow it anymore. Our structure is extensible. The previous movie `oopBall01.fla` may be simpler, but it doesn't allow this to occur as easily because it expects a certain amount of data in a certain fixed format. No part of it is really general.

To create our spriteData object still requires two calls to the constructor, so we should really fix this. The following code uses another constructor to do this (see oopBall02.fla). So, now we have a general Object called ConstructTwoDeePoint that allows us to create our structured data.

```
function ConstructTwoDeePoint(xElement, xPos, xSpeed, xLow, xHigh,
yElement, yPos, ySpeed, yLow, yHigh) {
    this.xElement = new ConstructPointElement(xPos, xSpeed, xLow, xHigh);
    this.yElement = new ConstructPointElement(yPos, ySpeed, yLow, yHigh);
}
function constructPointElement(pos, speed, low, high) {
    this.pos = pos;
    this.speed = speed;
    this.low = low;
    this.high = high;
}
spriteData = new ConstructTwoDeePoint(xData, 275, 5, 10, 540, xData, 200,
➥5,10, 390);
```

Some of you may be wondering what use ConstuctTwoDeePoint is, and why it has more than the two values to represent a two-dimensional point. Surely you only need two values? No. We are not going for simple static points or casting for minnows. We're out there with Captain Ahab looking for much bigger fish; our data is describing a general *moving* point, and this is where we are still tied by the umbilical to Mother Motion Graphics.

So now we have our data. How do we actually animate it? Well, we don't want to keep talking about data anymore, but start incorporating movie clips into the mix. You may think this is a big change, but it isn't. Our data is an Object and so is the MovieClip, so we can swap them. Programmers call this feature **polymorphism** – the objects don't really care what their input objects are as long as they are properly defined, and that means that they must be general. We're almost doing this, but not quite. Polymorphism is actually a very complex area, and not really relevant to Flash OOP (although along with inheritance and encapsulation, it is one of the three requirements for true OOP), so we won't go further with this, but be aware that we are in the same ballpark as true OOP here.

Have a look at oopBall02b.fla:

```
function constructSprite(clip, xElement, xPos, xSpeed, xLow, xHigh,
yElement,yPos, ySpeed, yLow, yHigh) {
    this[clip].xElement = new ConstructPointElement(xPos, xSpeed, xLow,
    ➥ xHigh);
    this[clip].yElement = new ConstructPointElement(yPos, ySpeed, yLow,
    ➥ yHigh);
}
```

```
function constructPointElement(pos, speed, low, high) {
     this.pos = pos;
     this.speed = speed;
     this.low = low;
     this.high = high;
}
constructSprite("ball_mc", xData, 275, 5, 10, 540, yData, 200, 5, 10, 390);
```

Here, we have simply replaced the top level Object object spriteData with a movie clip. Although the data structure may look different in the debugger, it is the same. The only difference is that the top level of our object is now a timeline:

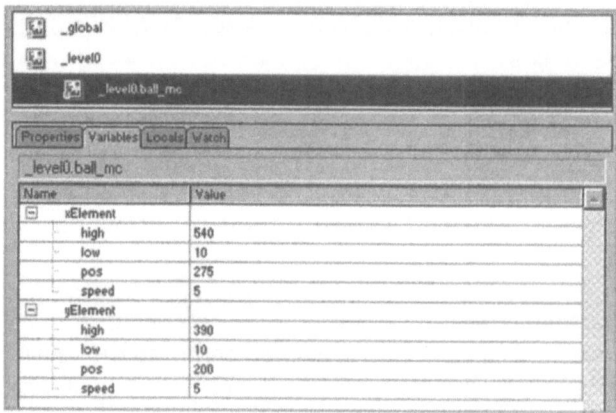

The ball doesn't move though, because we haven't added the code to do this yet. That doesn't actually matter too much because we have the structure of the data tied down, and this defines our code. This may seem odd to the modular programmer or hacker, but it's true; OOP is very hierarchical when you use it in the way we are doing now, and the code is defined by the data (i.e. objects and their structure) not the other way round, as happened in our previous non-OOP version. Then, I just created some functions and added the variables as I went along. This time round, I have spent almost all of the time thinking about **data**.

The final code to animate our ball is shown in the final example, oopBall03.fla:

```
function ballMover() {
     this.elementUpdate = function(pointElement) {
          pointElement.pos += pointElement.speed;
          if ((pointElement.pos<pointElement.low) || (pointElement.pos>
          ➡pointElement.high)) {
               pointElement.speed = -pointElement.speed;
          }
     };
     this.elementUpdate(this.xElement);
     this.elementUpdate(this.yElement);
```

```
    this._x = this.xElement.pos;
    this._y = this.yElement.pos;
}

function constructSprite(clip, xElement, xPos, xSpeed, xLow, xHigh,
yElement, yPos, ySpeed, yLow, yHigh) {
    this[clip].xElement = new ConstructPointElement(xPos, xSpeed, xLow,
    ➡ xHigh);
    this[clip].yElement = new ConstructPointElement(yPos, ySpeed, yLow,
    ➡ yHigh);
    this[clip].onEnterFrame = ballMover;
}

function constructPointElement(pos, speed, low, high) {
    this.pos = pos;
    this.speed = speed;
    this.low = low;
    this.high = high;
}

constructSprite("ball_mc", xData, 275, 5, 10, 540, yData, 200, 5, 10, 390);
```

All we have done is add an event handler definition in constructSprite that is referenced to ballMover, which becomes the callback that actually performs the animation.

An important thing to appreciate is how the ballMover code actually handles the object structure presented to it and why it is doing this, by simply reflecting the object structures presented to it:

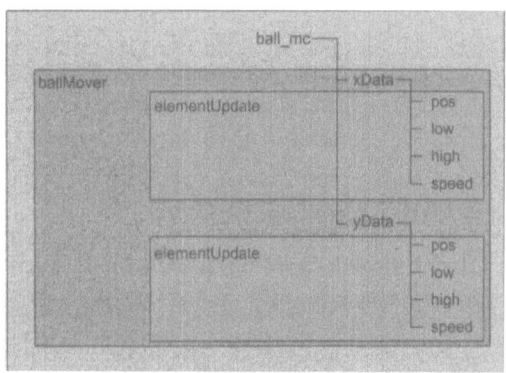

The ballMover event handler consists of an embedded function, and this reflects the structure of the objects presented to it.

The code in bold below handles xData and yData, but doesn't look inside them. It thinks in two-dimensional space, but thinks there are only the points (x,y) that represent position; it doesn't know about the high/low limits nor the speed value.

```
function ballMover() {
    this.elementUpdate = function(pointElement) {
        pointElement.pos += pointElement.speed;
```

continues overleaf (409)

```
            if ((pointElement.pos<pointElement.low) || (pointElement.pos>
            ➡pointElement.high)) {
                   pointElement.speed = -pointElement.speed;
            }
     };
     this.elementUpdate(this.xElement);
     this.elementUpdate(this.yElement);
     this._x = this.xElement.pos;
     this._y = this.yElement.pos;
}
```

The nested function elementUpdate handles the properties inside xData and yData, and it can handle both x and y data without differentiating between them because it only thinks in one-dimensional space and sees them as the same thing. This function does however know about speed and not leaving the screen (via the high/low properties):

```
function ballMover() {
     this.elementUpdate = function(pointElement) {
            pointElement.pos += pointElement.speed;
            if ((pointElement.pos<pointElement.low) || (pointElement.pos>
            ➡ pointElement.high)) {
                   pointElement.speed = -pointElement.speed;
            }
     };
     this.elementUpdate(this.xElement);
     this.elementUpdate(this.yElement);
     this._x = this.xElement.pos;
     this._y = this.yElement.pos;
}
```

This is the Russian dolls at work again, each checking only a particular layer of the problem. Everything reflects this layering:

- Our definition of the problem.

- The property structure of the objects.

- The code that handles the structure.

Once we defined the problem as the object structure, we forgot about the problem, and started thinking about this object structure as an entity in its own right. This is another facet of abstraction. Once we have defined our objects to reflect the problem, the object structure becomes our interpretation of the problem itself, and the code that solves it mirrors our problem.

We could stop here but since we're motion graphics people, and we know that our code may well be extensible and conform to OOP form, but if it isn't fast enough then it's useless. The files `oopTiming1.fla` and `oopTiming2.fla` test the main animation code in our OOP version and the original. I tested them on the slowest and fastest machines available to me (a Pentium 3 600 and an Athlon 2000+), and they both ran at about the same speed, which is cool, because we now have some extensible and easily modifiable OOP code that runs as fast as the corresponding hacked voodoo code. Time to play. See `oopBall04.fla`.

A point worth noting is that we have left our code more general than it actually needs to be. The parameters in bold are pretty much redundant in the function call:

```
constructSprite("ball_mc", xData, 275, 5, 10, 540, yData, 200, 5, 10, 390);
```

This is because the code as it stands is your cue to play about with it and tear it apart. You may want to look at reworking the code to add a **zData** set of parameters.

The trouble with inheritance at the instance level is that you have to apply it to every instance you want it to act on. This is not ideal because it would be better if we could just create a whole new object that was like the movie clip, but moved of its own accord like our ball instances. This is where we turn to the prototype...

Prototype inheritance

A prototype is Flash's way of defining objects. It works via inheritance again, but this time it is at the level of objects rather than instances. If you create a prototype object, all instances of that object have the full set of properties and methods you have assigned to the prototype as soon as they are created.

We have actually already covered all the theory to create a prototype. It is simply a set of embedded functions just like those we saw in **Chapter 15**. The only difference this time is what the embedded functions do:

```
function myObject() {
    this.prop1 = 1;
    this.prop2 = 2;
    this.method1 = function(arg1) {
            return ("you just called method1 with argument "+arg1);
    };
    this.method2 = function(arg1, arg2) {
            return ("you just called method2 with arguments "+arg1+" and
            ➡ "+arg2);
    };
}
```

This defines a prototype of an object myObject with the properties prop1 and prop2, and methods method1() and method2().

> Notice that we are using the this.myFuction = function () {
> form of function definition. We have to do this because the final code
> will be attached to each of our instances, so the functions must be
> position-independent (as does all the code in the prototype). To do this
> we have to use the this path, and this is the only form of the function
> that allows us to do so.

Now here's the catch. To make the prototype work, you have to add it to an existing Flash object. That's the 'no classes in Flash' deal at work again. The way it works out in practice is not as restrictive as it might seem, because there are really only two types of object you need:

- Those that act like the MovieClip object.

- Those that act like the Object object.

The latter are easier to work with so we will use that for now. The following line will use our prototype to create a new sort of object called **myObject**:

```
myObject.prototype = new Object();
```

What does this do? Well, it adds the methods and properties of our prototype to the Object object. Although the object doesn't have any methods and properties of its own (it's a non-specific object), it does have other features, and these make myObject begin to act like an object (the most important one being the ability to instantiate new instances of the object with new).

We can now create instances of our object, just like creating any of the normal Flash objects:

```
myFirstEverObject = new myObject();
mySecondOne = new myObject();
myThird = new myObject();
```

Unlike the last example with the ball, we don't have to apply any constructor to each instance as they are now true objects and come ready built:

Each of the myObject instances comes complete with the methods myMethod1(), myMethod2(), and the properties prop1 and prop2, all initialized and ready to go. You can try them:

⊟	myFirstEverObject	
	method1	
	method2	
	prop1	1
	prop2	2
⊞	mySecondOne	
⊞	myThird	

```
test = mySecondOne.method1("hello");
```

```
trace(test);
test = mySecondOne.prop1;
trace(test);
```

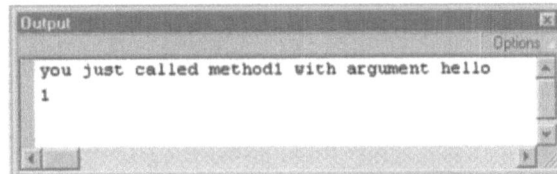

There's only one thing that myObject doesn't inherit, and that is scope. myObject doesn't inherit the 'globalness' of Object (recall that you can create an Object object on any timeline). If you try to do this with myObject, it won't work. This sounds like a bug in the process but the workaroud is easy – ;you give your prototype a global scope directly:

```
_global.myObject = function() {
      this.prop1 = 1;
      this.prop2 = 2;
      this.method1 = function(arg1) {
            return ("you just called method1 with argument "+arg1);
      };
      this.method2 = function(arg1, arg2) {
            return ("you just called method2 with arguments "+arg1+" and
            ➡"+arg2);
      };
};
```

If you now create a movie clip on _root and add this code to frame 1 of its timeline:

```
test = myRemoteObject.method1("hello");
trace(test);
test = mmyRemoteObject.prop1;
trace(test);
```

...you will see that the object is now working because you can see the outputs.

Although programming purists may not like this (programming etiquette specifies that it is bad form to clutter up the global scope), in the current revision of Flash we have no choice if we want to create objects that act just like Flash's default objects.

That's Object objects done, so what about movie clips? Well, the process is the same, except that you have to specify which movie clip in the Library you wish to become your new object.

Have a look at `prototype01.fla`. In the Library you'll find the ubiquitous `ball` movie clip. It has the linkage identifier `ball`.

Remember I said earlier that I prefer the OOP process to be open-ended? This time we're going to prove why this is beneficial. Rather than take the extreme structured view of the last example, we're going to just stick the 'non-OOP' example code from the same example into the prototype! Here's the code:

```
_global.myClipObject = function() {
    this.ballMover = function() {
        // calculate new x position
        this.xPos += this.xSpeed;
        if ((this.xPos<this.xLow) || (this.xPos>this.xHigh)) {
            this.xSpeed = -this.xSpeed;
        }
        // calculate new y position
        this.yPos += this.ySpeed;
        if ((this.yPos<this.yLow) || (this.yPos>this.yHigh)) {
            this.ySpeed = -this.ySpeed;
        }
        // animate to new position
        this._x = this.xPos;
        this._y = this.yPos;
    };

    this.initProperties = function() {
        // ball x properties
        this.xPos = 275;
        this.xLow = 0;
        this.xHigh = 550;
        this.xSpeed = undefined;

        // ball y properties
        this.yPos = 200;
        this.yLow = 0;
        this.yHigh = 400;
        this.ySpeed = undefined;
    };

    this.moveMe = function(arg1, arg2) {
        this.xSpeed = arg1;
        this.ySpeed = arg2;
```

```
                this.onEnterFrame = this.ballMover;
        };
        this.initProperties();
    };

    myClipObject.prototype = new MovieClip();
    Object.registerClass("ball", myClipObject);

    _root.attachMovie("ball", "ball1", 0);
    ball1.moveMe(5, 10);
```

This is a cool concept, because it shows how you can take on board OOP programming concepts but code them up in any style you see fit! That's a good thing because you can cater the style you write per prototype, and this decision can be based on anything from how much the client is paying for the work, to which programming head you happen to have on today.

This will turn the movie clip into our bouncing ball. This time, as well as the prototype inheritance line:

```
    myClipObject.prototype = new MovieClip();
```

...we also have this line:

```
    Object.registerClass("ball", myClipObject);
```

This does of course use the 'class' word but, apart from that, it's pretty cool. It applies the prototype myClipObject to the movie clip in the Library with linkage identifier `ball`. This will change the `ball` clip from being a standard movie clip to a myClipObject. "Um, it still looks like a movie clip to me" you are probably saying after taking a peek. Well, that's true; the prototype definition hasn't run yet... the transformation from MovieClip to myClipObject only occurs during runtime, and only on those movie clips you dynamically place onto the stage after the prototype has been set up.

I have added the method `moveMe()` which starts the animation, and it takes arguments equal to the x and y components of the speed of the ball. The ball will not move until you issue this at least once.

One final thing you can do is to change the prototype of the movie clip (or any other default object) directly. In this case, you are not creating a new object, but redefining the object globally. This isn't recommended though, because you can change more than you bargain for, especially if you change the Object object in this way (because all Flash objects use this object themselves, *all* objects will inherit your changes). It is, however, a very quick way of attaching a lot of event handlers to a lot of movie clips. The following code snippet shows a quick example (it creates a method `newStuff()` that will animate a movie clip from left to right across the screen):

```
    MovieClip.prototype.newStuff = function() {
        this.ballMover = function() {
                this._x++;
```

```
            };
        this.onEnterFrame = this.ballMover;
    };
    myClip.newStuff();
```

So we've come full circle here. From voodoo scripting to extreme structure via true object oriented programming (or as near as we can get to it in a quick example). We've then gone back to voodoo scripting, incorporating some OOP structures, but ignoring the unnecessary involved stuff, opting for a more freeform approach.

As always with Flash, the best advice is go your own way. You know the facts now, but your creativity and programming direction is entirely your own, and Flash will let you run with it whatever direction you choose. It's not about kung fu at the end of the day; it's knocking them out with the moves you pull that counts!

17 Talking to the Outside World

Objectives

- Basic communication in Flash MX:

  - `getURL()`

  - `loadVariables()`

- Introducing the communication objects:

  - The `LoadVars` object

  - The `XML` object

  - The `XMLSocket` object

- The `LoadVars` object and its associated methods

- Using `LoadVars` to communicate with server scripts

Introduction

To complete our study of ActionScript in Flash MX, a major piece of the puzzle is making Flash talk to the outside world through server communications. It's one thing to create a static Flash web site that never changes, but it's another thing to create a site that connects the user to the outside world, and to other users.

Imagine building a daily web log (or *blog*) on your site containing the latest sports scores, weather reports, news headlines, and perhaps messages from other users. To create this kind of functionality, we must take a look at the communication capabilities of Macromedia Flash MX, and the options that are available to us to make Flash really come to life.

Reaching outside of Flash

There are a few different techniques open to us for talking to the outside world. The first, getURL(), is mainly for opening up external web pages, and general browser level communication. The other methods deal with an open line of data communication without necessarily requiring the medium of a browser window:

- **getURL()** – This is one of the simplest and most commonly used methods of reaching outside of Flash. Essentially, what getURL() does is send an HTTP request to the browser. This means that we can make Flash open up other web sites, send emails, and activate JavaScript functions all by utilizing getURL(). The getURL() command doesn't actually return any data as such – it simply sends out HTTP requests.

- **loadVariables()** – Although loadVariables() is an old Flash 5 function, it's still highly useful today. With the loadVariables() command, we can call a web page, script, or text file, and retrieve data from it. The data comes back in a format that Flash can read, and we can use that data as variables. The data is sent in a format known as **name/value pairs**. A string of data in the name/value pair format might look something like this:

  variable1=data&variable2=moreData&variable3=lotsOfData&...

  Each name/value pair is separated by an ampersand (&). This data could be stored in a text file, or generated dynamically by a server script. Once a loadVariables() function is issued, the server responds and then the connection is closed.

- The **LoadVars** object – This is similar to loadVariables(), except that everything is neatly contained within an object, which allows for easy transmission and receipt of data. The LoadVars object has a number of associated send and receive methods, and data is also transmitted in name/value pairs. Once the send and response is complete, the connection is closed.

- The **XML** object – This object is similar to the LoadVars object, except it sends and receives its data formatted as an XML document rather than in name/value pairs. When an XML document is loaded, the connection is closed.

- The **XMLSocket** object – This object differs from the other data retrieval formats because once an XMLSocket connection has been established, the connection remains open, and any data can flow freely back and forth between server and Flash movie. Generally XML formatted data is sent across, but the XMLSocket object can actually transmit any format of data, as long as our Flash movie knows how to interpret and respond to it.

In this chapter we'll examine the getURL() and loadVariables() methods, along with the LoadVars object. We'll look at the specifics of XML, and the XML objects from Flash MX in the next couple of chapters.

getURL()

As mentioned above, the getURL() command allows us to perform various tasks at the HTTP browser level. Before we look at these in action, let's see how the getURL() function is actually structured:

```
getURL(URL, windowStyle, variableActions);
```

The first parameter here contains the URL you want to link to – this is the only required parameter (the other two are optional). The second parameter, windowStyle, describes how you want the window to open, and can take a few different values:

- _blank – Opens a new window. Flash will open up the web browser in a blank window, and display the URL there.

- _top – The top level frame in the current window (in this case the windows that are within a frameset).

- _parent – The parent of the current frame.

- _self – Specifies the current frame in the current window. That is, Flash will replace the SWF within the browser window with the URL we specify.

So, for example, to open up a web browser in a blank window, we could do this:

```
getURL("http://www.friendsofed.com", "_blank");
```

The third parameter, variableActions, is only necessary if we want Flash to pass variables to the URL that it's calling. These variables can be passed as either a POST or a GET standard of HTTP data transmission. Flash will automatically send *all* the variables of the timeline associated with the getURL() action. Sometimes, though, this is not what we want.

The getURL() command can also be sent as a method of a movie clip. For example, to send all the variables contained within the movie clip, myMovieClip via the POST method, we would write this:

```
myMovieClip.getURL("http://www.mysite.com/go.php", "_blank", "POST");
```

And to do the same via the GET method, we would do this:

```
myMovieClip.getURL("http://www.mysite.com/go.php", "_blank", "GET");
```

In both these instances, we're calling a PHP script called go.php. This script could be anything we want. As long as it knows how to handle our outgoing data, it will open up in a new browser window, with the results of our POST or GET.

The difference between POST and GET is the way the data is sent on the URL. With GET, the variables are all simply tacked on to the end of the URL string, as name/value pairs separated by ampersands. For example, if we had 3 variables in myMovieClip like this:

```
a = 5;
name = "Joe";
color = "Blue";
```

And we send the variables with getURL(), using the GET method shown above, then we'd see this URL string in our browser window:

The problem with this method is that we're limited to a maximum URL string of 256 characters. When we use the POST method, then our variables are sent embedded in something called the **HTTP Header**. This is a piece of data that we never see, which is sent to the server, and we're never made aware of. So the POST method allows us to send very long strings of data, much greater than 256 characters.

We can also use the variableActions parameter to make calls to built-in web browser functionality like mailto: and javascript:. These do not require windows to be opened, so we simply call them like so:

```
getURL("mailto:me@mysite.com");
```

This will open up an email window, with the To field filled in with the specified address:

Let's look at the form of the JavaScript action now:

```
getURL("javascript:myFunction();");
```

This will call the JavaScript function `myFunction`, which would most likely be defined on the page that contains the Flash movie – this demonstrates how easy it is to link your ActionScript with JavaScript, perhaps to create a universally accessible site.

Let's see all this in action – open up `getURL.fla`, and look on the stage:

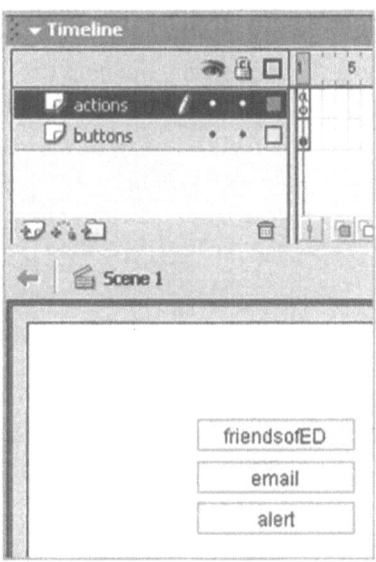

We see that there are three buttons, and an actions layer on the timeline. The buttons are labeled friendsofED, email, and alert, with corresponding instance names of `foedlink`, `mailbutton`, and `alertbutton`. The first button opens up the friends of ED web site, the second opens up an email with some specified details, and the third opens a JavaScript alert box. The code on the actions layer is as follows:

```
foedopen = function () {
    getURL("http://www.friendsofed.com", "_blank");
};
mailopen = function () {
    getURL("mailto:someone@somewhere.com?subject=test&body=This is the
    ⮡body");
};
javaalert = function () {
    getURL("javascript:alert('hello');");
};
foedlink.setClickHandler("foedopen");
```

continues overleaf

```
mailbutton.setClickHandler("mailopen");
alertbutton.setClickHandler("javaalert");
```

Each function contains a simple getURL() call. The first one, referenced by foedopen, opens up www.friendsofed.com in a new browser window. The second function, mailopen, opens up an email addressed to someone@somewhere.com, with some text in the subject line and body. Finally, the third function opens up a JavaScript alert box. In the last three lines, we're tying each button to the appropriate function.

When we run this code, and click on the friends of ED button, we're taken to the friends of ED web site. Remember, you can publish your FLA file by selecting File>Publish (SHIFT+F12), and this will automatically create an HTML file for your SWF that you can open up in your web browser (alternatively, just hit CTRL+F12 when you're testing a movie to publish *and* open up the HTML file in one go!). If you now click on the email button, a new email should pop up from your email client ready to send:

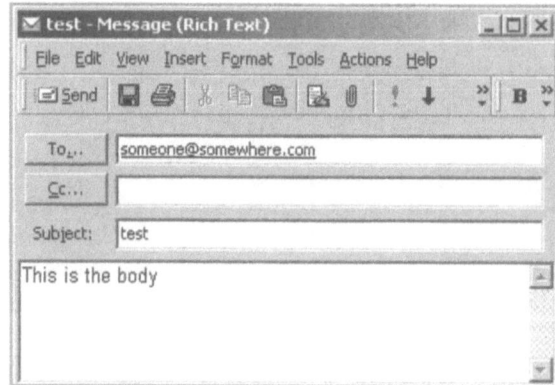

We filled in the various fields by specifying the mailto:, subject, and body variables in the getURL() string, like a standard GET string:

```
getURL("mailto:someone@somewhere.com?subject=test&body=This is the
➥body");
```

The third button opens up a JavaScript alert window:

To achieve this, we have a line of simple JavaScript code directly inside the `getURL()` string:

```
getURL("javascript:alert('hello');");
```

We're calling the `alert` function, which opens up a window on the screen containing the word, hello, as instructed.

loadVariables()

The `loadVariables()` command simply sends and receives data in the form of ampersand delimited name/value pairs. Its syntax is as follows:

```
loadVariables(URL, target, variableActions);
```

The `URL` is the filename or script containing our variables; `target` is the name of a movie clip or level number that we want the loaded variables sent to; `variableActions` works in the same way that it does with the `getURL()` command – using `GET` or `POST` to send data.

So, say we have a file called `scores.txt` that, when opened in a text editor, you can see contains the following information:

```
score0=Houston 3 Denver 2&score1=Detroit 4 Boston 5&score2=New York 6 New
Jersey 3&score3=Toronto 7 Los Angeles 5&
```

This is essentially one long string containing four variables made up of name/value pairs: `score0` to `score3`. Each variable is a string of text detailing the results of a sports game. All we need to get the data is a `loadVariables()` call, like this:

```
loadVariables("scores.txt");
```

We needn't specify a `variableAction` because we're not sending any variables *to* the text file, and, since we're not specifying a target, the variables will be sent to the location from which this call was made. For the purpose of this simple example, the `scores.txt` file is local, so we don't need to specify an HTTP URL, we only need the filename. When the data comes back, Flash will automatically parse it and convert it into variables.

Take a look at `loadVariables.fla` to see this in action. In this movie, we have a dynamic text field on the stage called `scoredisp`, and in it we're going to display a scrolling tickertape of scores. The code to do this is attached to the actions layer on the main timeline, as follows:

```
_root.loadVariables("scores.txt");
_root.onData = function() {
    i = 0;
    if (score0 != undefined) {
        scoredisp.text = "............................";
```

continues overleaf

```
            scoredisp.text += "...............................";
            scoredisp.text += "...............LATEST SCORES:    ";
            while (eval("score"+i) != undefined) {
                    scoredisp.text += "      "+eval("score"+i)+"      ";
                    i++;
            }
            scoredisp.text += "...............................";
            scoredisp.text += "...............................";
            scoredisp.text += "...............................";
        }
    };
    scoredisp.backgroundColor = 0;
    _root.onEnterFrame = function() {
        scoredisp.hscroll += 50;
        scoredisp.hscroll %= scoredisp.maxhscroll;
    };
```

In this code, first we issue the `loadVariables()` command as a method of the root timeline– because we're not specifying a target, the variables will be returned to the _root. We then have a function called _root.onData, which will be triggered when the data returns from the `loadVariables()` call. The relevant line to make sure of this is:

```
        if (score0 != undefined) {
```

So obviously the code in this function cannot run if the `score0` variable is undefined. The actions inside this `if` clause then go ahead and fill the `scoredisp` text field up with a list of scores derived from the `scores.txt` file.

Next, the `while` loop keeps adding on scores until we have no more score variables:

```
        while (eval("score"+i) != undefined) {
                scoredisp.text += "      "+eval("score"+i)+"      ";
                i++;
        }
```

Note the use of the `eval()` function here – this allows for the dynamic construction of an identifier based on a string (`score`) and an integer variable (`i`). With `eval()`, if the associated expression evaluates to a variable or property, the value of that variable will be returned. However, if the element named in the expression does not evaluate to a known object or variable, `undefined` is returned. After all the scores are printed, we send some *filler* dots to the text box.

Finally, we set the background color of the `scoredisp` text field to black, and then we've got an `onEnterFrame` function that is responsible for scrolling the text field horizontally, using the `hscroll` property of the TextField object, and then wrapping back around to the beginning when all is finished. When we test `loadVariables.fla`, we see the scores roll by in our text field, like so:

What we've done here is create a scrolling score ticker, where the data is retrieved from an external data source. The data in this example is hard coded in a text file, but it's also possible to call a script, in something like PHP or ASP, which would generate the results dynamically. All Flash really cares about is whether the data is sent back in the format it expects.

The LoadVars object

In its ability to load and send data, the `LoadVars` object is rather similar to the `loadVariables()` method. But now that we're dealing with an object, the load and send capabilities exist not as properties, but as part of a collection of methods that the `LoadVars` object offers us to make HTTP communications easy.

Creating a new instance of the `LoadVars` object is achieved in much the same way that we create other object instances:

```
myLoadVars = new LoadVars();
```

Once we've created our `LoadVars` object, we have two properties that we can access:

- `LoadVars.contentType` – This property contains the content type of the data, so we can ensure that the server knows what type of data we're sending. It's automatically set by Flash, and the default value is `application/x-www-form-urlencoded`.

- `LoadVars.loaded` – This property is simply a `true` or `false` Boolean variable. When we first send or load variables this property is set to `false`. Once the load has successfully completed, then `LoadVars.loaded` will be set to `true`. If the load failed for some reason (for example, if the data was missing or not returned), then this property will remain `false`.

LoadVars methods

Let's now examine all of the methods associated with the `LoadVars` object. First, we should note how we can add variables to our `LoadVars` object. For example, after creating a new `LoadVars` object called `myLoadVars`, we could write this:

```
myLoadVars.height = 44;
myLoadVars.aMessage = "Any Value";
myLoadVars.name = "Glen";
```

Then, if we were to issue a `send()` method, it would be these variables that would be sent. OK, on with our discussion of the methods we have available to us with this object.

send()

After defining our variables we can send them with the `send()` method, like so:

```
myLoadVars.send("http://www.mysite.com/go.php", "POST");
```

This will post all the variables associated with `myLoadVars` to a script called `go.php` at www.mysite.com. We can also use GET as the send type, but the default is POST.

Using this method, we don't expect anything back, as it's strictly for *sending* information to the server, and, assuming it's complete, Flash will ignore any responses from the server. However, if we want, we can tell Flash to redirect any responses from the server to a window, by adding a parameter to our code:

```
myLoadVars.send("http://www.mysite.com/go.php", "_blank", "POST");
```

If the server does send anything back, it will be sent to a new browser window. This can be helpful for debugging, and seeing whether or not our posts are working.

load()

This method just waits for a URL and then downloads all the variables at that URL. The code is as follows for a full URL:

```
myLoadVars.load("http://www.mysite.com/vars.php");
```

It's even simpler for a local file:

```
myLoadVars.load("vars.txt");
```

Once the load is complete, the `onLoad` event, if it has been defined, will be triggered, and the `loaded` property will be set to `true`. We'll look at the `onLoad` event in a moment.

First, let's look at a `LoadVars` version of our previous `loadVariables()` example. In the file `loadVars_load.fla` from the CD you'll find another score ticker. This time we'll load it up via the `LoadVars.load()` method. The code on frame 1 of the actions layer looks like this:

```
myLoadVars = new LoadVars();
myLoadVars.onLoad = function(success) {
    i = 0;
    if (this.loaded && success) {
        scoredisp.text = "............................";
        scoredisp.text += "............................";
        scoredisp.text += "...............LATEST SCORES:   ";
```

```
        while (this["score"+i] != undefined) {
                scoredisp.text += this["score"+i]+"      ";
                i++;
        }
        scoredisp.text += "..............................";
        scoredisp.text += "..............................";
        scoredisp.text += "..............................";
    }
};
myLoadVars.load("scores.txt");
scoredisp.backgroundColor = 0;
_root.onEnterFrame = function() {
    scoredisp.hscroll += 50;
    scoredisp.hscroll %= scoredisp.maxhscroll;
};
```

Everything is very similar to our previous example, except that here we're using the LoadVars object. We've created a new instance called myLoadVars, and then defined its onLoad function. In this function, we make sure that the data has completely loaded – this time by utilizing the LoadVars.loaded property, and that the load was successful. If everything is OK, we fill in the text field, as before.

We then issue the load() method of the myLoadVars object, and load the contents of "scores.txt". Finally, we scroll the text field in the onEnterFrame event of the root timeline.

getBytesTotal() and getBytesLoaded()

The two getBytes methods return values once a load has been initiated. At that point, getBytesTotal() will return the total number of bytes in the entire data stream and getBytesLoaded() tells us how much of it has already been loaded.

We can determine a percentage like so:

```
perc = (myLoadVars.getBytesLoaded()/myLoadVars.getBytesTotal())*100;
```

This will set perc to be a number from 0 to 100, depending on how much has been loaded. If there is currently no load in progress, then myLoadVars.getBytesTotal() will return undefined. It's also worth noting that the number of bytes may sometimes be undetermined if, for example, the size was not sent in the HTTP header from the server. In such a case, getBytesTotal() will again return undefined.

sendAndLoad()

Here we have a method that performs the functionality of both LoadVars.send() and LoadVars.load() at once. It's works like this:

```
myLoadVars.sendAndLoad("http://www.mysite.com/go.php", retVar, "POST");
```

What we're doing here is specifying a URL to upload variables to, and then we're stating a LoadVars, retVar, object to receive the results. We do this because we don't always want the results to be returned to the same LoadVars object that initiated the call. For example, we could have a case where LoadVars sends some variables, gets some back, and then the next time it sends variables it also sends those variables it just received from the server. To avoid sending lots of redundant data, we specify another return LoadVars object, so all sent and received data is kept separately. Optionally, in this method we can set the send type, be it POST or GET – when neither is specified, POST is used by default.

If we want, we can specify the same LoadVars object for both sending and receiving, like so:

```
myLoadVars.sendAndLoad("http://www.mysite.com/go.php", myLoadVars);
```

toString()

We can output all the variables contained within a particular LoadVars object, by simply calling the LoadVars.toString() method, like so:

```
trace(myLoadVars.toString());
```

If we run this method within the onLoad function in loadVars_load.fla that we looked at earlier, it will trace out the following data string:

```
score3=Toronto%207%20Los%20Angeles%205&score2=New%20York%206%20New%20Jersey%
203&score1=Detroit%204%20Boston%205&score0=Houston%203%20Denver%202&onLoad=%
5Btype%20Function%5D
```

Note that the function onLoad is also part of the variable list, the final entry, because it is a property of the object (see below).

onLoad

Although it's not actually a method, the onLoad event handler of the LoadVars object is worth a mention of its own. This event is triggered when any load has completed and with it we can activate whatever function we like. The structure of this function should generally be like so:

```
myLoadVars.onLoad = function(success) {
        if (success) {
                trace("Done Loading");
        } else {
                trace("Failed Loading");
        }
};
```

Here, the success parameter is passed into the function, and it returns simply true if the variables were successfully loaded, or false if there was an error.

So that's how we use the `LoadVars` object to talk to our servers and local files. Before we finish this chapter, let's take a look at a simple, yet very powerful, script and how we interact with it using the `LoadVars` object.

Using LoadVars to communicate with server scripts

In this section, we'll see how to load variables, and submit them to a server script file. The script we'll be referring to is a PHP script, chosen because it's simple, powerful, and free! It's also very similar to Actionscript, so it should be easy to read and understand.

> *If you're unfamiliar with PHP, and would like to get to know it better, check out Foundation PHP for Flash from friends of ED, ISBN: 1-903450-16-0. However, you should be able to follow this example whatever your level of PHP knowledge.*

Check out the file `serverscripts.fla`. The idea behind this Flash movie is simple – when the movie starts up, it connects to a server and calls a script named `servertime.php`. This script gets the current time from the server, and then returns it as a single variable called `servertime`. In this example, we're calling the PHP script from our imaginary site, www.mysite.com/servertime.php (If you want to test this code from your own machine, you can just change the relevant code to a local URL, like `servertime.php`).

So, if you were to use this code as it is you'd need to set up this script on a PHP-enabled site. A useful application of such a script could be a clock on your website, displaying the correct local time to each visiting user, no matter how the clock was set on their computer.

> *To run this example, you'll need PHP and an appropriate web server installed on your machine – we recommend using Apache. You might be surprised to learn that both PHP and Apache are free for personal and commercial use. You can download the current version of PHP from www.php.net/downloads.php, and the latest version of Apache from http://httpd.apache.org/dist/httpd/.*

If we set up the PHP script on our site and test this movie, we see something similar to the following in the `timedisplay` dynamic text field:

Server Time:Fri Jul 5 02:31:44 GMT-0400 2002

A string is displayed in a text field, and it's retrieved from the server script using the following Actionscript, attached to frame 1 of the actions layer:

```
myLoadVars = new LoadVars();
myServerTime = new Date();
myLoadVars.onLoad = function(success) {
      myServerTime.setTime(this.servertime*1000);
      timeDisplay.text = "Server Time:"+myServerTime.toString()+newline;
};
myLoadVars.load("http://www.mysite.com/servertime.php");
```

In this script, we're firstly creating a new `LoadVars` object, and then a new `Date` object. The `Date` object is necessary in order to take the server time, and then convert it into readable time.

When the server returns the time, it returns it as a system time, which is a measure of the time in seconds from a fixed date in history (midnight, January 1, 1970). By using this as a universal reference date, all computers can communicate the time to each other. So, if the system time for midnight, January 1, 1970 is 0, the system time at the time of writing is approximately `1025849135` seconds, and counting!

Flash uses this system of time calculation as well, but it actually counts the *milliseconds* since January 1, 1970, meaning the Flash system time will have three extra digits. That's why, in our `onLoad` event function, we're multiplying the variable `this.servertime` by 1000 – to transform the server time, set by our script in a variable called `servertime`, into a format that Flash understands. We set the value of our `Date` object, `myServerTime`, to the milliseconds time value with this line:

```
myServerTime.setTime(this.servertime*1000);
```

Then we display that value outputted as a nicely formatted time string:

```
timeDisplay.text = "Server Time:"+myServerTime.toString()+newline;
```

The result of this is that we see the full current time and date displayed in the text field `timeDisplay`.

Finally, we have the line of code that's responsible for actually calling the PHP script from which we'll obtain our original `servertime` value. We use the `load()` method of the `myLoadVars` object. Once this call is made to the server, the server returns a formatted name/value result representing the `servertime` variable. In fact, as far as Flash is concerned, we might as well be loading this from a text file because the results are exactly the same.

It's worth noting just how straightforward the PHP script that we've used is – open up `servertime.php` in a text editor:

```php
<?php
    $t = time();
    echo "servertime=$t";
?>
```

That's all there is to it! We're basically getting the current time, storing it in a variable called $t, and using the echo command to output to the data stream servertime=$t, which will be filled out by PHP with the actual server time. Since this script is run on the *server side*, the time value will be that of the server's internal clock. The PHP script must be opened with <?php, and closed with ?>.

In this section we've had only a brief look at the power of using scripting to create communication between Flash and the server. If we wanted to, we could send variables to the script using the sendAndLoad() method, and then PHP would make those variables available to itself immediately. So, for example, if we said in Flash:

```
myLoadVars.country = "Canada";
```

then in our PHP script the variable $country would now exist, which we could then make use of. The variable would be set to Canada, because that was part of the information Flash passed using the send() or sendAndLoad() method. We'll expand upon our knowledge of server-side scripting in the next bonus chapter-which is on the CD- by taking a look at the ColdFusion MX technology as part of an example.

ActionScript Dictionary

This ActionScript dictionary:

- Provides an authoritative description of each ActionScript operator, action, or method.

- Provides a practical resource for the working designer. Many actions and methods have at least one short FLA that shows their use and that are designed to make their operation transparent. These can be used as the starting point of code that uses the operator, action, or method.

- Is an aid to debugging, as well as providing information on how to use ActionScript, the dictionary shows how *not* to use it. This is to highlight pitfalls and common mistakes you may find in your code.

Each operator, action, or method will be laid out in a set way, as shown in the following example:

Title

```
Examples of typical syntax
```

or

general syntax

Description of syntax

Summary of the operator, method, or action. This will include *compatibility, summary of known issues, typical use, and reasons why you would/would not use it* and *a list of related entries elsewhere in the dictionary*. Major points are shown in **bold**.

Description

This section briefly describes the operator, method, or action, and then shows a table of typical uses, as shown below.

Code	Additional explanation	Notes
		White rows show typical uses
		Gray rows show common incorrect use (if any), and are presented as an aid to debugging code

Symbols

The entries in the following section appear in this order:

-=	Subtraction assignment p484
==	Equality p484
===	Strict equality p485
>	Greater than p487
>=	Greater than or equal to p489
>>	Bitwise right shift p491
>>=	Bitwise right shift and assignment p492
>>>	Bitwise unsigned right shift p493
>>>=	Bitwise unsigned right shift and assignment p494

- Subtraction and negation

```
a = -b;
c = d-e;
```

Where b, d, and e can be any expression that evaluate to a number. a will be returned as the negative value of the expression b (negation). c will be returned as the number value of d-e. If b, d, or e do not evaluate to a number, the returned value held in a or c will be NaN ("Not a Number", see **NaN** entry).

Compatible with **Flash 4 and above**. You should be aware that because ActionScript is not typed, **if you use Booleans in error, the returned value will assume true = 1 and false = 0**.

Description
This **operator** conforms to the usual rules of mathematical evaluation. If in doubt as to the order of such evaluation, you should use brackets.

Code	Returned value(s)	Notes
a = 5 - 1;	a = 4	

b = -10.5;
a = b;
c = -b;
	a = -10.5
	c = 10.5	

a = 5-(4-(3-2));	a = 2	a= 5-(4-(3-2)) = 5-(4-1) = 5-(3)
a = true-false; b = "10"-"3";	a = 1 b = 7	true is converted to 1 and false is converted to 0 before the subtraction is applied. This result is not usually meaningful, and an error has probably occurred if your code subtracts Booleans from each other or numbers. Strings that are numerals only will work with -, but this is not the case for other arithmetic operators (such as multiplication), so use this feature with caution.

a = "my cat" - "my";	a = NaN	Unlike addition, subtraction cannot be used with strings.

See the examples (subtractionandnegation).fla and (subtractionandnegation).swf on the CD.

-- Decrement (post/pre-decrement)

```
a--;
b = --a;
b = a--;
```

Where a is a variable, array element, or property that holds a number variable, b will be returned as a number value. If a is not a number, the result is NaN.

Compatible with **Flash 4 and above**. It is can be used as **a shorthand way of decrementing counter variables**, and **it is faster (in terms of code performance)** than if you used the longer versions of the same code.

Related actions include **for...** loops (where **--** is often used to decrement the loop counter) and **++** (which is similar to --, except that it increments).

Description

This **operator** can be used as a shorthand version of some often used expressions, as shown below.

Code	Shorthand version	Notes
a = a - 1;	a--;	
b = a; a = a - 1;	b = a--;	This form is called *pre decrement*
a = a - 1; b = a;	b = --a;	This form is called *post decrement*

See the examples (decrement).fla and (decrement).swf on the CD.

! Logical NOT

```
b = !a;
```

Where a is an expression that can be evaluated to a Boolean value (true or false). b will be returned as false if a is true and true if a is false.

Compatible with **Flash 4 or later**. You should be aware that because ActionScript is not typed, **if you use strings or numbers in error, ! will still return either** true **or** false, **(and never** NaN **or undefined) even though the result may be meaningless.**

Related actions include the **if...** branching structure, which uses this and other logic operators extensively to define its logical decision-making.

Description

This **operator** calculates the logical inverse of an expression or variable as a Boolean `true` or `false`. It first evaluates the expression as a Boolean `true`/`false`, and then calculates the inverse (`false`/`true`).

Code	Returned value(s)	Notes
`a = true;`	`c = false`	`!true = false`
`b = false;`	`d = true`	`!false = true`
`c = !a;`		
`d = !b;`		
`a = "dog";`	`e = true`	`true = 1, false = 0` (but 1 does not
`b = 5;`	`f = false`	always equal true when used as a
`c = 0;`	`g = true`	parameter, and the same goes for
`// d is undefined`	`h = true`	false, so be careful; always use true
`e = !a;`		and not 1 if you really mean true!)
`f = !b;`		The other results are not normally
`g = !c;`		meaningful, but worth knowing when
`h = !d;`		debugging.

See the examples (logicalnot).fla and (logicalnot).swf on the CD.

!= Inequality

```
b != a;
```

Where a and b are expressions that can be evaluated into a number, Boolean, or string. If b is unequal to a, `true` is returned. If b is equal to a, `false` is returned.

Compatible with **Flash 5 or later**. There are **no known issues** with any version of Flash that supports this operator. You should however be aware that type is ignored in the comparison; the number 1 and the string "1" are equal for example. You should use **strict inequality (!==)**, or more usually **strict equality (===)** if you want to consider type as well as value.

Description

This **operator** tests for inequality in two values, a and b, and gives `true` if they are unequal, and `false` if they are equal.

Also, note that, `(b != a) = (a != b) = !(b == a)`.
`(b <> a)` is the deprecated form, and should be avoided.

Code	Returned values	Notes

a = true;
b = false;
c = "1"
d = (a != b);
e = (a != c);
	d = true
	e = false
		a is unequal to b, so d = true.
		a and c are equal because
		true as a number is 1 and
		"1" as a number is 1,
		a and c are therefore not unequal, so
		e = false.

a = 123;
b = 123;
c = 123.00001;
d = (a != b);
e = (a != c);
	d = false
	e = true
		a is equal to b, so d = false.
		a is unequal to c so e = true.
		See the *Tips and precautions* section
		(on the CD) for further information on
		avoiding rounding errors

a = "dog";
b = "Dog";
c = " dog";
d = (a != b);
e = (a != c);
	d = true;
	e = true;
		The strings a, b, and c are all unequal
		to each other, because != is case
		sensitive and includes spaces in the
		comparison.

// a is undefined
// b is undefined
c = 10;
d = (a != b);
e = (b != c);
	d = false
	e = true
		Two valueless (undefined)
		expressions are assumed to be
		equal, hence d = false.
		If any of the two expressions
		compared is undefined, they are
		assumed to be unequal, hence e =
		true.

See the examples (inequality).fla and (logicalnot).swf on the CD.

!= Strict inequality

```
b !== a;
```

Where a and b are expressions that can be evaluated into a number, Boolean or string. If b is unequal to a and of different type, true is returned. All other combinations of value and type for a and b return false. This operator is rarely used, and using it can be confusing because there is only one (rather pointless) condition that yields true. You are recommended to use strict equality (===) in preference.

Refer to the entry for ===.

#endinitClip

#endinitclip forms part of the **#initclip... #endinitclip** structure. See the entry for **#initclip** for a description of both.

#include

```
#include "myFile.as";
```

Where `myFile.as` is the name and path to an .as script file.

Compatible with **all versions of the Flash player, although only the Flash 5 authoring environment and above** support it (this action is used by the Flash authoring environment as a code management feature, and compiled SWF code does not incorporate it).

Description

This **action** (although the #include action is really a "SWF compiler directive" rather than a true action) is used during runtime to include an external script within the current script. The script will be inserted in place of the #include during compilation. If the script file is not found during the compilation process, a syntax error will be raised.

#include is used during compilation time only. The action is replaced by the script it points to during compilation, meaning that #include does not exist in the final SWF. This means that compatibility with previous versions of the Flash player is not an issue; only the authoring environment ever sees this action.

Code	Contents of .as file	Notes

x = 2;
#include "myFile.as"
message = "x: "+x+" y: "+y+" z: "+z;
trace(message);
	y = 10;
	z = 20;
		Actual compiled code would be:
		
		x = 2;
		y = 10;
		z = 20;
		trace(x);

#include "c:\libs\init.as"		The specified path will be used when looking for init.as
#include "c:\bootlog.txt"	bootlog.txt is not an .as file	Flash does not discriminate between a true .as file and any other file that you may specify, and the specified file is always loaded in. This is a feature that may sometimes cause Flash to crash. You should always use the .as extension to avoid loading an incorrect file type.

See the examples (include).fla and (include).swf on the CD.

#initclip... #endinitclip

```
#initclip
// code
#endinitclip
```

```
#initclip order
//code
#endinitclip
```

Where `//code` represents the enclosed script that you want to run within the `#initclip` block. The enclosed script will be executed before the frame of the timeline it is seen on is started. If there are more than one `#initclip` blocks, the optional `order` parameter will be used to define which blocks are executed first (lowest `order` first). If no order is specified, 0 is assumed. If two order values of the same value are seen, execution will occur based on depth (and because this may be assigned at runtime, the exact order may not be known at author time).

Compatible with **Flash 6 and above**. This action **must exist in frame 1 of a movie clip timeline**, and executes before the frame it is seen on is started. **The scope of the enclosed script is always _root**, and not the timeline it is on. You would use the `#initclip... #endinitclip` if you wanted to define object prototypes and use the **Object.registerClass()** method to define custom object structures based on the movie clip object. You may also use it to define functions on **_root** or **_global** that will be referred to by scripts external to the movie clip the `#initclip` is on (when defining global or public functions). If your code is not object-oriented, then the chances are that you would be better off using the much easier **movieclip.onEnterFrame** method or the **onClipEvent(load)** action.

Description

This **action** is used to define code blocks you want to be processed before a timeline begins to run. It is useful in defining any object structures and ActionScript libraries (consisting of functions and other definitions) that must be in place before the movie clip timeline it is seen on is started. The diagram below shows the order of execution:

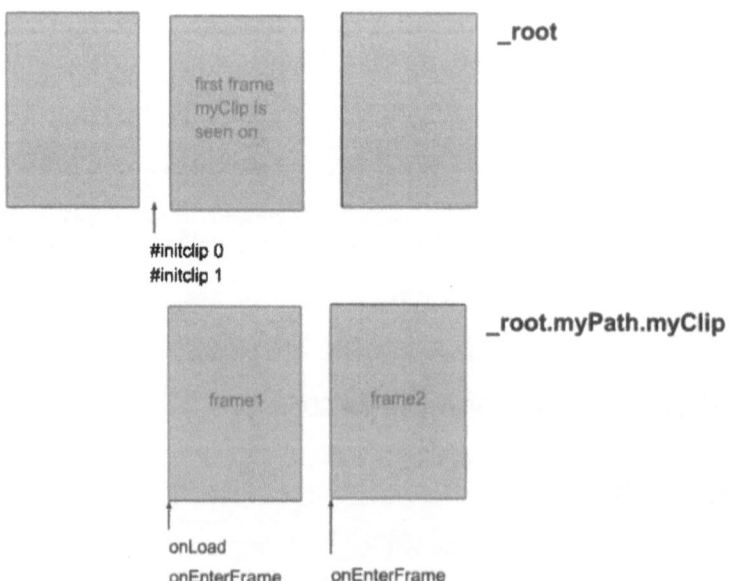

#initclip is associated with the definition of base prototypes associated with advanced object-oriented programming methods, as applied to component definition and/or extending the ActionScript language itself via new prototype chains that either modify or add to its default objects and methods. The discussion below therefore assumes an understanding of OOP and Flash's event model.

_root.myPath.myClip is a movie clip that has its linkage properties set to **Export for ActionScript** and **Export in first frame** (select the clip in the library window and then select **Linkage...** via either the right-click menu or the library windows **Options** menu). The clip will therefore be attached to frame 1 of the _root timeline (and this is crucial to the way #initclip is used – you *must* make sure that any clip using #initclip is attached to frame 1 of the _root timeline). When the SWF starts, frame 1 of the clip and frame 1 of myClip will both run immediately. The previous diagram shows the following:

- Any onLoad event associated with myClip will execute at the beginning of myClip's frame 1, and it will scope the _root.myPath.myClip timeline.

- Any onEnterFrame associated with myClip will run at the beginning of each new frame, and will scope the myClip timeline.

- The #initClip 0 action will force all code within the #initclip 0 ... #endinitclip block to run *before* frame 1 of the main timeline. It will run *before* any other code, and will also run *before* the myClip instance even comes into existence. It is effectively running whilst the myClip symbol is still in the Library. This means that it cannot scope the myClip timeline. Instead, it will scope _root. You can define any objects or prototypes at this point, and doing so will allow you to:

  - Define prototype classes and redefine one or more movie clips to be members of these classes.

  - Modify the default ActionScript classes and methods.

  - Create base prototypes (classes) that your components rely on.

The initClip structure allows you to do this *before* the main event model (and for that matter, the timelines) start up. This allows you to assume all your OOP structures are fully defined when the main SWF starts up. Essentially, this action allows you to predefine custom object structures or even redefine the ActionScript environment during SWF start-up. It is a very powerful concept, but requires a good knowledge of the Flash environment to use effectively.

  - The initClip 1 will do the same thing, but will run after initClip 0. It will still run *before* the standard movie clip events (onEnterFrame, onLoad).

The code within the #initclip ... #endinitclip actions is executed before frame 1 of the timeline it is seen on, _root.myPath.myClip. It is run before the first _root.myPath.myClip.**onLoad** or _root.myPath.myClip.**onEnterFrame** events are seen. The included code is executed as if it was attached to _root.

You should use the `#initclip`... `#endinitclip` structure to:

- Define any **object prototypes** and declare any **Object.registerClass()** definitions required by `myClip` or other movie clips. You would also need to export `myClip` for ActionScript to ensure that the definitions are in place before the main timeline, `_root`, starts. This ensures that the definitions are available throughout the SWF.

- To define any functions on `_root` that will be used by a component.

- To define any global methods that you may want to use to customize or extend the scripting environment.

If you simply want to initialize variables, properties, and other data to be used by `myClip` only, you would be much better off using the **MovieClip.onLoad** method (or the **OnClipEvent()** action with *load* as the argument).

Code	Notes

<pre>#initclip
  _global.message = function(msg) {
    var msg;
    trace(msg);
  };
#endinitclip</pre>
	This code would be on frame 1 of a movie clip (or more probably, frame 1 of a component) that is exported for ActionScript on frame 1 via the Linkage Properties window found in the library window dropdown menu.
	
	The code defines a global function called `message()` before frame 1 of the SWF is executed. Scripts within the FLA can call this from anywhere (and from frame 1 onwards) via, for example, the line:
	
	`message("hello");`
	
	This would output "hello" in the output window. `message()` can be thought of as a new action, and is an easy way to extend ActionScript without resorting to object-oriented programming.

<pre>#initclip
  MovieClip.prototype.giveMeFoos =
  function() {
    this.Foo01 = "I have Foo 1";
    this.Foo02 = "I have Foo 2";
  };
#endinitclip</pre>
	This code would be on frame 1 of a component that is exported for ActionScript on frame 1 via the Linkage Properties window found in the library window dropdown menu. It gives every movie clip in the SWF a new method via the Movie clip Object prototype called `giveMeFoos()`. Any movie clip can invoke it in the SWF via the line:

```
_root.myClipPath.myClip.giveMeFoos();
```

or if invoked from the timeline `myClip`:

```
giveMeFoos();
```

`giveMeFoos()` creates two new variables on the timeline of `myClip` called `Foo01` and `Foo02`.

This is a powerful way of extending the existing ActionScript methods by attaching additional custom methods directly to the default objects. See also **Object.registerClass()**, which is a method that allows you to do the same thing without polluting the default Movie Clip class.

See the examples (initclip).fla and (initclip).swf on the CD.

% Modulo

```
a = b % c;
```

Where `b` and `c` are variables, properties, or expressions that resolve to numbers, `a` is the remainder of the division `b/c`.

Compatible with **Flash 4 or later**, although Flash 4 uses an approximate method. This action allows you to tell if one number is divisible exactly by another.

Description

The modulo division arithmetic **operator** calculates a number corresponding to the "remainder" of a hand calculated long division sum. For example, recall the junior math sum below:

$$5\overline{)292.0}\ =\ 58.4$$

5 into 292 is calculated as follows:
5 into 2 doesn't go, so try 5 into 29.
5 into 29 is 5 carry 4. Write the 5 and carry the 4.
5 into 42 is 8 carry 2. Write the 8 and carry the 2.
5 into 20 is 4. Write the 4. Because there is no carry, the division is complete, and the answer is 58.4.

That division assumes knowledge of decimals, but most kids are taught division before decimal notation, and the division then becomes:

$$\begin{array}{r} 58\ r2 \\ 5\overline{)\ 292} \\ {}_4 \end{array}$$

5 into 2 doesn't go, so try 5 into 29.
5 into 29 is 5 with carry 4. Write the 5 and carry the 4.
5 into 42 is 8 with carry 2. Because we don't know about decimals, we can't carry the 2 anywhere, so we express it as a *remainder*, and at my school, we expressed this as 58 r2.

The "r2" or *remainder 2* is the value modulo returns, 292 % 5 is 2.

Code	Results	Notes
`x = 292%5;`	`x = 2`	Modulo will turn all arguments to
`y = "292"%5;`	`y = 2`	numbers before performing the
`z = 292.11%5.2;`	`z = 0.910000000000004`	modulo division.
`a = 292;`	`c = 2`	
`b = 5;`		Although modulo division is normally
`c = a%b;`		carried out between integers, using floating-point arguments is acceptable. The value returned, however, is less useful.
`// a is undefined`	`x = 0`	An undefined argument is treated as
`x = a%5;`	`y = NaN`	zero.
`y = 292%a;`	`z = NaN`	
`z = 292%0`		

See the examples (modulo).fla and (modulo).swf on the CD.

%= Modulo assignment

```
a %= b;
```

This is exactly the same as a = a % b. See the entry for **% Modulo**.

& Bitwise (binary) AND

```
a = b & c;
```

Where b and c are numbers that will be converted to unsigned 32 bit numbers and ANDed together to form a new unsigned 32 bit number, which will be returned as a. If b or c evaluate as anything else, the result will be 0 because b or c will be undefined (and taken to be 0).

Compatible with **Flash 5 and above**. Flash 4 used "&" to mean string concatenation, a feature that can now be done in Flash 5 and above via "+". Flash 4 files loaded into later releases will be automatically updated to reflect this change. & can be used as a *mask* or *filter* to ignore certain parts of a value. This usage is derived from digital circuit design, something not well known to web designers! Bitwise AND is therefore under-used, although very useful because it is **very processor-efficient**.

Description

This **operator** performs per bit (or bitwise) ANDing of two numbers. The arguments are assumed to be unsigned 32 bit numbers, and the returned value will be the same.

The following table shows how the & operator works:

```
c = a & b
```

a	b	c
0	0	0
0	1	0
1	0	0
1	1	1

c is 1 if both a and b are also 1. This binary table (sometimes called a *truth table* in Boolean math) can be applied to every bit position of two 32 bit values expressed as binary. For example:

```
c = 345 & 456
```

```
345 =      0000 0000 0000 0000 0000 0001 0101 1001
456 =      0000 0000 0000 0000 0000 0001 1100 1000
           0000 0000 0000 0000 0000 0001 0100 1000 = 328
```

Writing binary can be a long and error-prone exercise, and is more usually expressed in hexadecimal. A 32 bit unsigned number can express all integers between 0 and 4294967295 (0xFFFFFFFF).

Code	Results	Notes

`a = 23.985878;`
`a & 0xFFFFFFFF;`
`c = a & 0xFFFFFFFE;`
	`b = 23`
	`c = 22`
		ANDing any positive number with 0xFFFFFFFF results in a 32 bit *integer*. This is one way of discarding the decimal part of a number.

		c has been ANDed with a number that causes its least significant bit to be masked out and ignored. This has the effect of filtering out a jittering value.

`a = -10;`
`b = 45;`
`c = a & b;`
		AND assumes unsigned numbers. Using signed numbers will return a meaningless number in c.

```
d = b & "cat";
e = b & undefined;                          d and e will be zero because a non-
                                            numeric result is always assumed as
                                            zero.
```

See the examples (bitwisebinaryand).fla and (bitwisebinaryand).swf on the CD.

&& Boolean AND

```
a = b && c;
d = e && f && g;
```

Where b and c are expressions that evaluate to a Boolean true or false, and this Boolean value is returned as a. a will be true if b and c both evaluate to true, or false with any other combinations. Chains of expressions can be formed. d is true only if e, f, and g all evaluate to true. d will be false if any of the expressions in the chain are false.

Compatible with **Flash 4 and later**. If any of your expressions do not directly reduce to a Boolean, you will see odd results.

Boolean logic is different to bitwise logic (ANDing two numbers to form a third based on the truth table for bitwise AND). Refer to the entry for **&** if in doubt.

Description

This **operator** evaluates each expression as a Boolean true or false, and then performs a Boolean AND on the result. This will give true only if all the expressions are true, and false for all other combinations.

Note that:

```
a && b && c = (a && b) && c = a && (b && c).
```

Code	Returned values	Notes

a = true;
b = true;
c = false;
d = a && b;
e = a && b && c;
	d = true
	e = false	

a = 1;
b = 2;
c = "cat"
d = (c == "cat") && ((2*a)==b);
	d = true	

a = "cat"; b = "dog";	e = "cat"; f = 2	The results of (a && b) and (c && d) do not easily reduce to Boolean true

```
c = 1;
d = 2;
e = a && b;
f = c && d;
```

or false. The returned values are not
therefore meaningful.

&= Bitwise (binary) AND assignment

a &= b;

This is exactly the same as a = a & b. See the entry for **& Bitwise (binary) AND**.

() Parentheses

(expression)
action(parameters)

Where expression is any expression that can be evaluated by ActionScript, action is any ActionScript action or method that requires parameters, and parameters is the required parameter list.

Compatible with **Flash 4 and later**. Parentheses are used to define the evaluation order of an algorithm, or to define the set of parameters associated with a function, action, or method.

See also section 2.5.

Description

Parentheses are the first thing to be addressed in a mathematical equation; a programming algorithm is the same.

Parentheses are also required in the syntax of many actions or methods. Refer to the specific entries for more information.

Code	Returned values	Notes
a = 10 +4/2; b = (10+4)/2;	a = 12 b= 7	The order of mathematical execution is: Brackets Open Evaluate Divisions Evaluate Multiplications Evaluate Additions Evaluate Subtractions For a, the 4/2 is evaluated first, followed by 10 + 2. For b, the brackets are opened first, giving 10+4 = 14. This is followed by 14/2, giving 7.
a = !false || true; b = !(false ||true);	a = true b = false	The order of logic execution is: Brackets Open Evaluate Logic

> The evaluation for b makes the ! act on the result false || true, which is evaluated first. In a, the ! acts on false only.

‛ Multiplication

```
a = b * c;
```

Where b and c are expressions that can be resolved to numbers. a will be equated to a number that is the product of b and c. Anything that cannot be resolved to a number (such as a string) will be undefined, and the result will be 0.

Compatible with **Flash 4 and above**. There are no known issues with this operator.

Description
This **operator** will multiply two numbers.

Code	Returned values	Notes
a = 2;	e =6	The product of two integers is an integer.
b = 3;	f = 15.920205	The product of two floating-point numbers is a floating-point number.
c = 2.345;	g =7.035	The product of a floating point number and a floating-point number is a floating-point number.

d = 6.789;
e = a*b;
f = c*d;
g = b*c;		

a = true;
b = false;
c = a*23.2;
d = a*b;
	c = 23.2
	d = 0
		Booleans are converted to numbers before multiplication takes place. true is converted to 1 and false is converted to 0.

a = "2";
b = 3;
c = a*b;
	c = 0	A string is undefined when used in multiplication because it is not a number.

See the examples (multiplication).fla and (multiplication).swf on the CD.

*= Multiplication assignment

```
a *= b;
```

This is exactly the same as a = a * b. See the entry for *** Multiplication**.

, Comma

```
ActionScript line, ActionScript line, ... ActionScript line;
```

Where `ActionScript line` is any normal line of ActionScript.

Compatible with **all versions of the Flash player**. This operator is really just a quick way of writing code, or grouping related lines of code on a single line.

Description
This **operator** allows you to add a number of actions on a single line.

Code	Notes
`a = 2, b = 3, c = 4;`	Is the same as writing: `a = 2;` `b = 3;` `c = 4;`
`myClip._x = 100, myClip._alpha = 50;`	Is the same as writing: `myClip._x = 100;` `myClip._alpha = 50;`

. Dot operator

```
myInstanceName.property;
myInstanceName.method;
myInstanceName.variable;
myPath.myInstanceName.property;
myPath.myInstanceName.method;
myPath.myInstanceName.variable;
mypathStart[expression].property;
myPathStart[expression].method;
myPathStart[expression].variable;
```

Where:
- `myInstanceName` is the instance name of an object.

- `property`, `method`, and `variable` are a property, method, or variable of the object respectively.

Flash MX Designer's ActionScript Reference

NB: the object can only have variables associated with it if it also has a timeline, so this only applies to movie clip objects.

myPath is an optional path to the object if myInstanceName is not on the same timeline as the script. myPathStart.[expression] defines a dynamic path using dot notation.

myPathStart can be either _root or _parent, followed by [expression] where expression evaluates to a string of the form "myPathFromMyPathStart.myInstanceName".

Compatible with **Flash 5 and later**. There are no known issues with this operator.

Description

This **operator** allows ActionScript to reference the different layers of an object hierarchy, or to navigate through the Flash timeline structure to reference a unique instance. The path created can be absolute or relative, and can also be fixed or dynamic. Examples of all types of path are shown below.

Code	Notes
`myClip._x = 20;` `myObject.prop01 = 340;`	**Using dot notation to access properties**. The property _x of the movie clip myClip is set to 20. The property of the Object object myObject is set to 340. The path to both myClip and myObject is the timeline the code is attached to. If myClip and myObject do not exist on the current timeline, then the script will fail silently and no error will be issued by either the authoring environment or the Flash player during testing or runtime.
`myClip.gotoAndPlay(10);` `mySound.stop();`	**Using dot notation to access method**. The movie clip myClip is made to go to frame 10 and play using the movie clip object gotoAndPlay() method. The sound object mySound is made to stop playing via the sound object stop() method. Again, the path to both myClip and mySound is the timeline the code is attached to.
`_global.gVariable = 2;` `gVariable +=3;`	**Using dot notation to define global variables**. The variable gVariable is defined as existing on the _global

level. Subsequent references to gVariable do not need to refer to any path because gVariable exists on all timelines simultaneously.

The code can exist on any timeline and within code with any scope *except* if the current scope also has a local variable also called gVariable. You should avoid collisions between global and non-global variables via an appropriate naming convention. See also **_global**.

Using dot notation to form absolute paths. The script lines shown use _root as the starting point of the path. The paths are therefore relative to the "base level" or "absolute". You should note that:

```
_root.myClip._alpha = 50;
_root.myClip01.myClip02._y = 35;
_root._x = 45;
_level3.myClip03.gotoAndPlay(4);
```

- _root can be treated as a movie clip in its own right. The third line moves _root by accessing and changing its _x property.
- Where there are multiple loaded levels, _root is the same as _level0. To refer to the main timeline of a loaded level, you should refer to the level explicitly, as we do with the last example to reference myClip03, which exists on the main timeline of _level3.

The code can exist on any timeline because the paths are absolute and not relative to the code position. This is useful when you do not know the location of the target relative to your script, but it is better to use *relative* paths wherever possible because they are more general.

Using dot notation to form relative paths. The _parent path refers to

```
_parent.stop();
_parent.parent.gotoAndPlay(5);
```

```
this._x = 20;
_x = 20;
```

"the timeline below the one the script is referring to". If the code is in a movie clip, then _parent refers to the timeline the movie clip is on. this refers to the current scope of the script. this is *not* the same as the timeline the script is attached to in all cases. See the entry for **this** for more information.

In both cases, the path uses the scope of the current script as its starting point, making the path relative to where we are now.

```
myVariable = 12;
myString = "myClip"+myVariable;
_root[myString]._x = 10;
myString2 = "myClip1";
this[myString2]._alpha = 20;
```

Using dot notation to form dynamic paths. The [] brackets can be used to add variables to the path. The third line will form the path:

```
_root.myClip12._x = 10;
```

and the fifth line will form the path:

```
this.myClip1._alpha = 20;
```

```
x = Math.abs(-10);
myObject = new Object();
myObject.prop1= 2;
myObject.prop2 = 4;
y = myObject.prop1+myObject.prop2;
```

Using dot notation to access the object hierarchy. The paths above refer to timelines. More specifically, they refer to the movie clip object. This is really just a special case of the Object.property.subproperty and Object.method hierarchy.

The first line uses the **Math Objects** abs() method. The next three lines create an object with two properties prop1 and prop2 and you can see the myObject hierarchy below:

⊟	myObject	
	prop1	2
	prop2	4
	x	10
	y	6

The final line uses the dot path notation to access the property values and assign them to variable y.

See the examples (dotoperator).fla and (dotoperator).swf on the CD.

/ Division

```
a = b/c;
```

Where b and c are expressions that can be resolved to numbers, a will be equated to a number that is the result of the division of b into c. Anything that cannot be resolved to a number (such as a string) will be undefined, and the expression will be assumed to be zero.

Compatible with **Flash 4 and above**. There are no known issues with this operator.

Description
This **operator** will divide two numbers.

Code	Returned values	Notes

a = 2;
b = 3;
c = 2.345;
d = 6.789;
e = a/b;
f = c/d;
g = 6/3;
	e = 0.666666666666667
	f = 0.345411695389601
	g =2
		The result is specified to the accuracy of the Flash player. The last digit is rounded to the nearest significant figure.

a = "6";
b = "3";
c = a/b;
d = 2/true;
e = 2/false
	c = 3
	d = 2
	e = 0
		Strings and Booleans will be converted to a number if possible. Boolean true/false will be converted to 1/0 and strings will be converted to numbers as per the **Number()** function. Note that an "e" in a string will be taken to be the decimal point in the exponential representation of a number, so "6e1" = 6×10^1 = 60.
		
		Any number divided by zero will return zero.

See the examples (division).fla and (division).swf on the CD.

/* ... */ Comment delimiter

```
/* comment */

/* comment
comment */

/*
comment
comment
*/
```

Where comment is any text in the Actions window that you want Flash to ignore.

Compatible with **all versions of the Flash Player** (because comments are ignored by the Flash compiler and the Flash player never sees them). You cannot include comments on the same line as the "," (comma) operator.

Description

The **comment delimiter** is typically used when you want to comment out code or create a multiline comment block. The single line form of the comment (see **//**) can be used where the comment is one line long.

Code	Notes

`a = 2;`
`/*b = 3;*/`
`c = 4;`
	The line `/*b = 3;*/` has been commented out and will be ignored by the compilation process.

`/*`
`mySite.com Flash site v2.1`
`April 2002`
`Copyright 2002`
`Sham Bhangal`
`*/`
	Using the `/* ... */` to define a multi-line comment field allows you to add script headers that assign copyright or version control, as well as allowing you to embed long descriptions of how the code works.

`/*`
`event handlers are defined`
`below`
	If you fail to include a `/*` and `*/` pair, Flash will raise a syntax error.

// Comment delimiter

```
// comment
```

Where comment is any text in the Actions window that you want Flash to ignore.

Compatible with **all versions of the Flash Player** (because comments are ignored by the Flash compiler and the Flash Player never sees them). You cannot include comments on the same line as the "," (comma) operator.

Description

The **comment delimiter** is typically used when you want to comment out a single line of code or add a comment that you want the compiler to ignore. The multi-line form of the comment (see **/* ... */**) can be used where the comment is many lines long.

Code	Notes

`a = 2;`
`// b = 3;`
`c = 4;`
	The line `// b = 3;` has been commented out and will be ignored by the compilation process.

`// mySite.com Flash site`
`// v2.1`
`// April 2002`
`// Copyright 2002`
`// Sham Bhangal`
	This section of code will be ignored by the compilation process, although it is useful in documenting the attributes of the code, or how it works.

See also **/* ... */**

/= Division assignment

```
a /= b;
```

Is exactly the same as `a = a/b`. See the entry for **/ Division**.

?: Conditional

```
Form 1 (assignment);
a = b ? c : d;
```

Where b is an expression that can be reduced to `true` or `false` c and d are expressions of any type (string, and Boolean, number, or property). If b is `true`, a will be assigned the value of c. If b is `false`, a will be assigned the value of d.

```
Form 2 (logic);
a ? action1 : action2;
```

Where a is an expression that can be reduced to `true` or `false`. If a is `true`, then `action1` is executed. If a is `false`, then `action 2` is executed.

Compatible with the **Flash 4 Player or later**. The conditional is a shorthand version of a simple **if... else** structure, although no performance gains will be seen in the final code if `?:` is used over the longer **if... else** syntax.

See also section 2.4.

Description

The conditional ?: is a shorthand form of the same logic using **if... else**:

```
if (b) {
    a = c;
} else {
    a = d;
}
```

is identical to

```
a (b) ? c : d;
```

The expression b is evaluated as a Boolean. If it returns `true`, then a = c. If it returns `false`, a = d.

Code	Notes
message = (order<=stock) ? "accepted" : "error, not enough items in stock";	If order is less than or equal to stock, then message is "accepted", otherwise it is "error, not enough items in stock".
input = in ? Number(in) : 0;	input will equal a value in if in is a positive value (because any positive value will evaluate to `true`) or 0 if it is anything else (including zero or undefined). This is a quick way of making sure a value representing a positive quantity is never left undefined.
(a<=b) ? gotoAndPlay("lower") : gotoAndPlay("higher");	If a is less than or equal to b, then the timeline will go to frame "lower", otherwise it will go to "higher".

The examples `(conditional).fla` and `(conditional).swf` on the CD.

[ ] Array access index

```
a = [];
b = [c, d, e];
b[f] = g;
h = [ [ i0, i1, i2 ], [ j0, j1, j2 ] ];
```

Where a is a new empty array. c, d, e, and g are expressions that can be evaluated to a string, Boolean or number, and f is an integer.

b is a new single-dimensional array with elements:
```
b[0] = c,
b[1] = d,
b[2] = e,
b[f] = g.
```

h is a multi-dimensional array with two or three dimensional elements as follows:
```
h[0] = [ i0, i1, i2 ]
h[i] = [ j0, j1, j2 ]
```

Compatible with **Flash 5 or later**. Arrays are not typed by array but by element, so that you can mix different types within the same array.

See also section 2.7.

Description

Arrays allow you to store related multi-element data in an object that is structured for easy storage and retrieval via an *index-based* system. The array access index **operator** allows you to access, set, or define particular elements of the array. This entry only discusses the array access index. To find out more information on the array object itself, see the entry for **Array**.

Code	Notes

`myArray = [];`
`myArray = new Array();`
`myArray = [true, "ball", 3.14];`
	Initializing an array object. The first two lines shown create an empty Array object called myArray. You can use either of these two syntaxes to create an empty array. The third line creates and populates the array. myArray is created with the following elements:
	myArray[0] = true
	myArray[1] = "ball"
	myArray[2] = 3.14

`myArray = [2, 4, 6, 7];` `myArray[4] = myArray[0]+myArray[2];`	**Using the Array access index**. myArray is defined in line one, and consists of four elements myArray[0] to myArray[3]. Line two creates a new element, myArray[4] with value 2+6 = 8.
`myArray = [[23, 45], [0, 54]];` `myArray[0][1] = 30;`	**Creating and using complex array indexes**. myArray is defined as two embedded arrays, each with two elements. This index system can be used to represent two dimensional data.

The second line accesses the element [0] [1], which means look in entry zero ([23, 45]) element 1 (45) and equate it to 30. The array structure following this code is as follows:

⊟	myArray	
⊟	0	
	0	23
	1	30
⊟	1	
	0	0
	1	54

```
myArray = [23, 45, 56];
myArray[1.1] = 78;
x = myArray[1.1];
y = myArray[1.2];
```

This code will create an array element myArray[1.1] = 78. y will be undefined because there is no element myArray[1.2]. Although using non-integer arrays is allowed, it is not normally recommended.

See the examples (arrayaccessindex).fla and (arrayaccessindex).swf on the CD.

∧ Bitwise (binary) XOR (exclusive OR)

```
a = b ^ c;
```

Where b and c are numbers that will be converted to unsigned 32 bit numbers and XORed together to form a new unsigned 32 bit number, which will be returned as a. If b or c evaluate as anything else, the result will be 0 because b or c will be undefined (and taken to be 0).

Compatible with **Flash 5 and above**.

See also section 2.5.

Description

This **operator** performs per bit (or "bitwise") XORing of two numbers. The arguments are assumed to be unsigned 32 bit numbers, and the returned value will be the same.

The following table shows how the ^ operator works;

```
c = a ^ b;
```

a	b	c
0	0	0
0	1	1

```
1   0     1
1   1     0
```

c is 1 if a or b is also 1, but not both. This binary table (sometimes called a *truth table* in Boolean math) can be applied to every bit position of two 32 bit values expressed as binary. For example:

```
c = 345 + 678
```

```
345 =     0000 0000 0000 0000 0000 0001 0101 1001
456 =     0000 0000 0000 0000 0000 0001 1100 1000
          0000 0000 0000 0000 0000 0000 1001 0001 = 145
```

Writing binary can be a long and error-prone exercise, and is more usually expressed in hexadecimal. A 32 bit unsigned number can express all integers between 0 and 4294967295 (0xFFFFFFFF).

XOR was useful in early computer graphics draw routines because:

```
x ^ anything ^ x = x
```

Put another way, if you have a blank pixel on a screen, you can set it to white by XORing it with 1. You can then *undraw* it by doing the same thing; XORing it with 1. Early computers were memory-limited, and a XOR-based draw engine was both fast (because it operated on a per bit level) and memory-efficient (because the draw routine was the same as the undraw routine).

XOR is much less useful with the Flash Player, because Flash does not operate in the same way as early computers did (Flash uses a high level vector based draw engine that doesn't allow per bit operations direct to screen). XOR therefore has very few (if any) practical motion graphics applications in Flash.

^= Bitwise (binary) XOR (exclusive OR) assignment

```
a ^= b;
```

Is exactly the same as a = a ^ b. See the entry for ^ **Bitwise (binary) XOR (exclusive OR)**.

_focusrect

```
_focusrect = true;
_focusrect = false;
```

_focusrect is a **property** of the root timeline and affects the whole SWF globally. It defines whether or not a yellow bounding rectangle is shown around the currently focused button, movie clip, or textfield. _focusrect is the global version of **Button._focusrect** and **TextField._focusrect** and _focusrect can be overridden for instance by setting the instances _focusrect property explicitly.

See **Button._focusrect** and **TextField._focusrect** for more information.

_global

```
_global.a = b;
```

Where a is a non-timeline-based object or a variable, function, or class name and b is the corresponding expression, function definition, or class definition.

Compatible with **Flash 6 and above**. The global object allows you to create objects, functions, and definitions that can be accessed from any timeline without having to specify a path to _global, because the global level is, as its name suggests, global, and available directly from any timeline.

Description

The global object (sometimes also referred to as the *global level*) is the object within whose scope the default Flash data objects, functions, and definitions are contained. In non-programming terms, it is "where ActionScript lives". The **global object is not a timeline structure**, and therefore cannot hold movie clips, buttons, textfields, or other timeline-based objects. You can only attach objects that have no graphic appearance, and consist of data structures or definitions only.

To avoid misconceptions about what _global is, it is better to use the term *global object* rather than *global level* when describing _global.

The usefulness in the _global object is that:

- It allows you to create global functions and variables.
- It simplifies the control of typical mult-level SWF structures.

Code	Notes
`_global.gVariable = 20;`	Creates a global variable gVariable. You can access this variable on any timeline as gVariable (without having to specify a path).

`_global.gFunction = function(text) {`
`var text;`
`trace(text);`
`};`
	Creates a global function gFunction. You can access this function on any timeline as gFunction() (without having to specify a path) in exactly the same way as you do not have to specify a path for ActionScript actions and methods such as Math.abs() or evaluate(). This can make global functions look like native ActionScript actions.

`_global.x = 10;` `_root.myClip.x = 5;`	If you have a global and local variable (or object or function) of the same name, you will create "collisions"

between the two. See the *Tips and precautions* section (on the CD).

See the example (global).fla and (global).swf on the CD.

{} ActionScript braces

```
{
//code block
}
```

Where //code block is a number of lines of code.

Compatible with **Flash 5 and above**. ActionScript braces or 'curly brackets' are **used to define a code block**. You need to add such braces whenever you use conditional or looping structures. You also use them to define event handler routines and functions.

A number of actions require you to use code blocks, refer also to: (the following looping structures) **for, while, do... while**; (the following conditional structures) **if, then, elseif, case**; (the function definition) **function**; (the following miscellaneous actions) **with, for... in, ifFrameLoaded**; (the following event definitions) **on(mouseEvent)** and **onClipEvent**.

Braces can also be used as a shorthand way of defining properties of **Object** objects. See the entry for **{} object initializer** (below), which covers this separate usage.

Description

The ActionScript braces are used to group a set of actions together for associating them with a single loop, conditional, event handler, or function definition. The examples below include one of each type of usage.

Code	Notes
```for (i=0; i<=9; i++) { diagnostic = "I am loop number "+i; trace(diagnostic); }```	**Looping block**. The second and third lines are enclosed by a {..} pair, and this defines them as the actions that should be executed as part of the loop. The for action will execute the block ten times (0 to 9). Note that {} braces do not normally have a ; after them. The exception to this rule is the } that finishes a **function block** (see below).
```x = 6; if (x>5) { y = x+10;```	**Conditional block**. Lines 3, 4 and 6, 7 are two separate blocks. Either one or the other will be executed depending

```
  z = 5;
} else {
  y = 0;
  z = 0;
}
message = x+" "+y+" "+z
trace(message);
```
on the value of variable x.

```
double = function (x) {
  var x;
  return 2*x;
};
trace(double(4));
```

Function block. The second and third lines are part of the function double. The code block is executed every time the function is called.

You should note that it is good practice to add a ';' after the } brace that finishes defining a function block. This is purely a JavaScript convention that has been inherited by ActionScript. Flash adds them for you if you auto-format, although their omission is not a syntax error.

```
on (press) {
  x = x+1;
  diagnostic = "you have pressed me
"+x+" times!";
  trace(diagnostic);
}
```

Event handler. The code in lines 2-4 will be run every time the symbol that this script is attached to is pressed.

```
myDetails = {name:"Sham B", age:35};

myDetails = new Object();
myDetails.name = "Sham B";
myDetails.age = 35;
```

Object Initializer. The first listing (single line) is a shorthand version of the second listing below it. Both will produce the same result. For fuller coverage of the object initializer, see the **{} object initializer** entry below.

{} Object initializer

```
myObject = {prop1:value1, prop2:value2... ,propn:valuen};
```

Where myObject is an object that you want to define with properties myObject.prop1, myObject.prop2, ... myObject.propn with values value1, value2... valuen respectively.

This operator is compatible with **Flash 5 and later**. The object initializer is a shorthand version of doing the following:

```
myObject = new Object();
myObject.prop1 = value1;
myObject.prop2 = value2;
```

```
myObject.propn = valuen;
```

Both versions of this code will produce the following object (as seen graphically in the Debugger window):

Description

The object initializer braces are used to define properties of an object, and to populate the properties with values. If the object doesn't exist, then it is created. The object initializer is a quick way of defining both the object and its properties in one line, rather than the long hand version previously shown.

Code	Notes

`threeDeePoint = {x:20, y:34.3, z:0};`
 	
`threeDeePoint = new Object();`
`threeDeePoint.x = 20;`
`threeDeePoint.y = 34.3;`
`threeDeePoint.z = 0;`
	This will create an Object object threeDeePoint, with properties x, y, and z. These will be equal to 20, 34.3, and 0 respectively.
	
	The single line is equivalent to the second listing seen here. Both will produce the same object seen below:

`myText = {errorMsg:"error", okMsg:"accepted"};`	This will create an Object object myText with properties as shown below:

`_root.myClip = {_x:0, _y:5};`
 	
`_root.myClip._x = 0;`
`_root.myclip._y = 5;`
	You can only apply the object initializer to Object objects. You can't apply it to other objects such as the movie clip. Here, we have tried to use the object initializer to set the position of a movie clip, myClip, by setting the movie clip _x and _y properties. This will not work. You will instead end up with a new Object object called myClip, and this will

<table>
<tr>
<td></td>
<td>have only two properties, _x and _y. You should instead use the longhand version (second listing) if you want to change the properties of objects that are not Object objects.</td>
</tr>
<tr>
<td>myArray = {0:30, 1:45, 2:89.6};

myArray = new Array(30, 45, 89.6);</td>
<td>Again, the error in the first line here is that we are trying to initialize something that is not a true Object object. We are trying to initialize an array.

The correct shorthand way of initializing an array is shown as the second line.</td>
</tr>
</table>

Bitwise OR

```
c = a | b;
```

Where a and b are numbers. c will be returned as the bitwise result.

This operator is compatible with **Flash 5 or later**. | will convert the values a and b to 32 bit values, which in plain English means that c will always be an integer. Bitwise ORing is more usually used in Flash when forming RGB colors, and | is therefore associated with the **Color** object.

Note

Using bitwise operators requires a good understanding of binary and hexadecimal, and this dictionary entry assumes this is the case. It is, however, possible to use the color object without using bitwise OR. If you do not understand either binary or hexadecimal, then you should instead use the methods of the color object, and in particular **Color.setTransform**.

Description

A bitwise operation is performed at the bit (binary) level. Such operations are very processor-efficient because they are close to the low-level processes that digital computers use internally. The following example shows a bitwise OR operation.

```
val = 6 | 11
```

The first thing we need to do is convert our two values, 6 and 45, to 32 bit unsigned binary:

```
6  =     (0 * 231) + (0 * 230)...+ (0 * 23) + (1 * 22) + (1 * 21) + (0 * 20)
11 =     (0 * 231) + (0 * 230)...+ (1 * 23) + (0 * 22) + (1 * 21) + (1 * 20)
```

```
6:  0000000000000000000000000000110
11: 0000000000000000000000000001011
```

Note that any decimal part of either value would be omitted in this conversion, so 11.456 would still convert to the same bit pattern as 11.

A negative number -a as an unsigned bit pattern is simply ~a (see entry for ~ **bitwise NOT**). As we shall see below, the only real application of bitwise OR is with color, so ORing negative numbers in motion graphics is probably not something you will ever need to do.

Bitwise ORing looks at each bit position, and returns a 1 if either operand has a 1 in that position. If both bit positions are 0, then the result will be 0:

```
6:   0000000000000000000000000000110
11:  0000000000000000000000000001011
val: 0000000000000000000000000001111
```

The result is binary 1111 or 15 decimal.

Generally, bitwise OR is used with the `color` object, and values are expressed in hexadecimal (because it is more compact than binary). Expressed in this form, the example becomes:

```
6:       0x000006
11:      0x00000B
result:  0x00000F
```

The usefulness of OR and color is that ORing the three color components (0xRR0000, 0x00GG00, 0x0000BB) results in the correct RGB value. For example, if we wanted to create a color with values:

```
R = 240
G = 90
B = 200
```

We would:

1. Convert all our values to hex:

```
R = 0xF0
G = 0x5A
B = 0xC8
```

2. Shift the values to place each in the correct position:

```
R = R* 0x10000
G = G* 0x100
```

B (no change needed)

3.   OR each component to reach the final RGB value:

```
colValue = (R*0x10000) | (G*0x100) | (B)
```

The following code will give you the final RGB color value:

```
R = 240;
G = 90;
B = 200;
colValue = (R*0x10000) | (G*0x100) | (B);
trace(colValue);
```

The value returned, 15751880, is 0xF05AC8 in hex, and you can double-check this by putting the initial decimal values into the Color Mixer:

The final hex value is shown at the bottom left of the maximized window.

Note the two different ways of denoting a hexadecimal value:

- The Flash interface precedes hex values with '#'. This is the format used by HTML web design.
- Flash ActionScript precedes hex values with '0x' (zero-x). This is in line with JavaScript (amongst other programming languages, all of which tend to use this form).

See also **Color.getRGB()**, **Color.setRGB()**, **Color.getTransform()**, **color.setTransform()**.

Code	Notes

`a = 2;`
`b = 3;`
`c = a
	b;`	`c = 3`

`c = 0xCC0000	0x00AA00	0x000055;`	c will be returned as 13412949 (decimal) or 0xCCAA55 (hex).

`if (x | y){`
`  //do this`
`}`
	Although bitwise OR works much the same as logic OR, you are recommended to use **Logical OR** (||) in situations such as this example (decision-making).

`value = "dog"	"cat";`	Bitwise logic assumes that the input values can be converted to numbers. The result is meaningless if this is not the case.

See the examples (bitwiseor).fla and (biswiseor).swf on the CD.

|| Logical OR

`c = a || b`

Where a and b are expressions or variables that reduce to Booleans. c will take the value of the logical (Boolean) result a OR b.

This operator is compatible with **Flash 5 or later**. || will evaluate a and b to Boolean `true` or `false` (if they are not in this form already) and evaluate the result, c, as per the truth table shown in the Description section below. The OR logical operator is closely associated with the **if** conditional action.

Description

For the expression c = a || b, the following results will be seen for c:

a	b	c
false	false	false
false	true	true
true	true	true

It can be seen that the result, c, is `true` if *either or both* of the inputs a and b are also true. The || operator acts very much like the English usage of the word 'or'. For example:

I will get that coat if someone buys it for me *or* I have enough money to buy it myself.

This means that I will get the coat if *either or both* of the following statements are true:

- Someone buys it for me.
- I have enough money to buy it myself.

Code	Notes
```a = true || false;``` ```b = (x>4) || (y>6);```	a = true from the truth table shown above. b will be true if either x>4 or y>6, or both.

```if ((credits>0) || (freePlay==true)) {```
```   anotherGo = true;```
```}```
	If credits are greater than 0 (you still have some credits) or freePlay is equal to true (the game is on a 'free-play' mode where you can have as many goes as you want – heaven!), then the player can have another go.

```if (x || y || z){```
```   //do this code```
```}```
	The code in the if will only run if at least one of x, y, or z is true.

```a = 6 || 1;```
```b = "cat" || 3;```
```c = "cat" || "dog";```
	a = 6
	b = 3
	c = "dog"
	
	a will actually be 6 because of the way OR works internally. Flash looks at the left-hand side of the OR, and if it evaluates to true, it will return not true, but the value (in this case 6). If this returns false, it will instead return the value of the right-hand side of the OR.
	
	The upshot of this is that although OR can be used with non-Booleans, the results can look a little quirky, so avoid!
	
	Note that Flash takes any number above 0 to be true, and 0 and below to be false.

|= Bitwise OR assignment

```
b |= a
```

Where a is a number (or expression that will resolve to one), b will return the result of:

1. Converting the initial value of both a and b to unsigned 32 bit integers.
2. Performing the expression b = b|a.

In short, b |= a is a shorthand way of writing the following:

```
b = b | a;
```

This syntax is the normal bitwise OR operator. Refer to the entry for **| Bitwise OR** for further information.

~ Bitwise NOT

```
b = ~a;
```

Where a is a number. b will be returned as the twos complement (signed binary representation) of a, which is numerically equal to -a.

The bitwise NOT operator is compatible with **Flash 5 or later**. It returns the binary equivalent of -a. b **will be returned as the twos complement of** a, and is calculated as follows:

1. Convert a to an unsigned 32 binary number.
2. Replace all the 1s with 0s and all the 0s with 1s.

In terms of decimal numbers, this is the same as taking the negative value of a and then subtracting 1. Bitwise NOT has little or no application in motion graphics (or modern programming generally) when you consider its normal application (twos complement addition) because we now have the ability to work directly with decimal numbers.

Don't confuse Bitwise NOT with ! Logical NOT. The latter is the version you will almost always use, because it works with Booleans, whereas Bitwise NOT doesn't.

Description

Bitwise NOT (or more correctly, the twos complement of a number) is the way binary deals with signed numbers. Since digital systems are so stupid they can only add numbers, the cleverer humans have worked out a way of fooling computers into doing subtraction. This works by adding a binary pattern that gives results as if it were a negative number. This binary pattern is the twos complement, and is what you get from Bitwise NOT.

Signed 32 bit binary numbers are represented as a 32 bit unsigned number *except* that the most significant bit represents -2^{31} rather than 2^{31} as in normal unsigned binary. For the sake of a quick example, assume a 4 bit number instead of the full 32 bit number Flash actually uses. Then 6 is represented in binary as:

    0110

because $(0 * 23) + (1 * 22) + (1 * 21) + (0 * 20) = 4 + 2 = 6$

Now, in a **signed** binary representation, we have the most significant bit being **negative**, so to represent -6 we have to use -8, 4, 2 and 1. Now -6 = -8 + 2 or in our signed binary format:

1010

Now here's the clever bit. 6 = 0110 and -6 = 1010. To get from 0110 to 1010 is simple; just do the following:

1.   Change all the 1s to 0 and vice versa, so 0110 becomes 1001.
2.   Next, add 1. This gives us 1010. Bingo!

(Note that you cannot tell the difference between a signed and unsigned binary bit pattern just by looking at them – you have to know which one you are using.)

This is what Bitwise NOT gives us, but in decimal form.

Okay, so we have 6 and -6. Adding these together should give us 0...

$$
\begin{array}{r}
01 \\
10 \\
10 \\
10 \\
\hline
{}^{1}0 \\
00 \\
0
\end{array}
$$

It actually gives us 10000, but if we ignore the carry 1 at the end that takes us from a 4 bit number to a 5 bit one, we end up with 0000.

This is how signed binary works. For a 32 bit number, any carry to the 33rd bit is ignored (well, actually, the processor uses this carry to tell it something about the sum that has just occurred, but since Flash doesn't make it available to us, we will ignore it).

Code	Notes
a = ~6;	a = (-1 * (6+1)) = -7
b = ~(-3);	b = (-1 * (-3+1)) = 2
c = ~0	c = (-1 * (0+1)) = -1
a = ~true	a = -2
b = ~false	b = -1
	true is converted to 1 and false to 0 as 32 bit unsigned numbers, and the twos complement of these is -2 and -1 respectively. Note that ~true is **not** false and ~false is **not** true. Do not confuse ~ with **! Logical NOT**.

See the examples (bitwisenot).fla and (bitwisenot).swf on the CD.

+ addition

```
c = a + b
```

Where c is the result of adding a and b. a and b can each be any literal or data type holding numbers or strings.

This operator is compatible with **Flash 5 or later**. You should note that **the + operator in Flash 4 will add numbers only**. To add two strings or a number and string in Flash 4, you need to use the **add** operator.

When adding two values, the + operator will yield the following:

1. Flash 4 and above: If a and b are numbers or can be converted to numbers (or strings that can be converted directly into numbers), then c will be the numerical value a + b.
2. Flash 5 or above: If a or b (or both) are strings that cannot be converted into numbers then the result will be a new string that is formed by concatenating a and b together.
3. Flash 4 only: If a or b (or both) are strings, then the result will be **NaN** (Not a Number).

Description

The + **operator** provides both numerical addition and string concatenation. The table below assumes Flash 5 or above. See the Tips and Precautions section on the CD for working with versions of Flash before Flash 5.

Code	Notes
```a = 5, b = 6, c = -3.5;``` ```d = a + b + c;```	d = 7.5

```a = "cat", b = "cat ", c = "dog",```
 ```d = 2;```
 ```e = a + c;```
 ```f = b + c;```
 ```g = b + d;```
	e = "catdog"
	 f = "cat dog"
	 g = "cat 2"
	
	 Note that the two words "cat" and "dog" will only have a space between them following concatenation if you specifically make Flash do this. This has been done here by adding the space at the end of b.

```a = 1, b = 2, c = " 2 ";```
 	
 ```d = a + b;```
 ```e = a + c;```
	d = 3
	 e = "12"

```a = true + false;```
 	
 ```a = true;```
 ```b = false;```
 ```c = true;```
 ```if ((a+b+c)>=2) {```
 ``` trace("hi");```
 ```}```
	a = 1
	
	 When adding Boolean logic, Flash will first convert true to 1 and false to 0.
	
	 The if statement will work out as:
	
	 ```if ((1+0+1)>=2) {```
	
	 Which gives a true, so you will see the "hi".
	
	 This can sometimes be useful when counting 'how many things are true'. If you wanted to do something when two out of three things were true (also called a majority gate), you could simply add them as per the second listing.

```a = 1 + undefined;```
 ```b = 1 + NaN;```
 ```c = "cat" + true```
	a = 1
	 b = NaN
	 c = "cattrue"
	
	 When adding, Flash will ignore any values that are undefined, as long as at

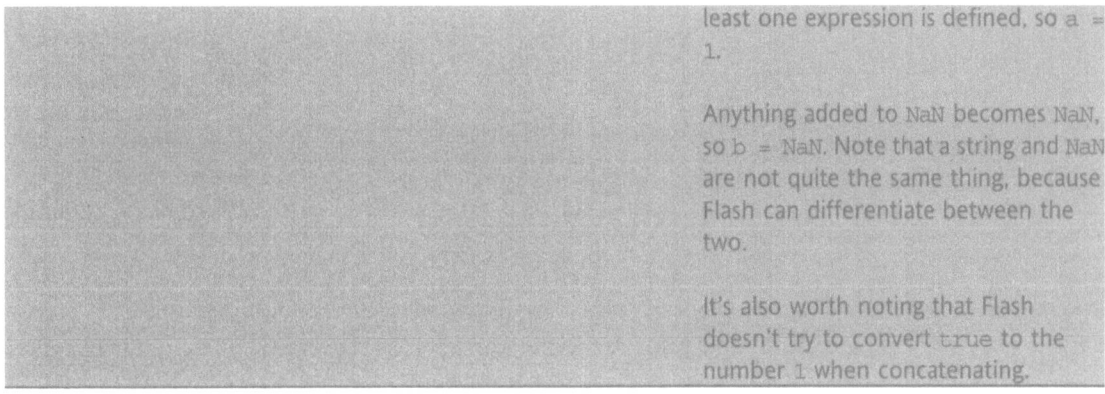

least one expression is defined, so a = 1.

Anything added to NaN becomes NaN, so b = NaN. Note that a string and NaN are not quite the same thing, because Flash can differentiate between the two.

It's also worth noting that Flash doesn't try to convert true to the number 1 when concatenating.

See the examples (bitwiseor).fla / (bitwiseor).swf and (global).fla / (global).swf on the CD.

++ increment

```
a = b++;    (post increment)
c = ++d;    (pre increment)
```

Where b and d are expressions that can be converted to numbers, a literal number or any data element holding a numeric value.

- In post increment, a is equated to b, and then b is incremented by 1.
- In pre increment, d is incremented by 1, and then c is equated to the new value of d, thus c and d end up with the same value.

This operator is compatible with **Flash 4 or above**. Because incrementing a value by 1 is a common programming requirement, **++ is a shorthand way of writing code that increments number values. The performance gains in doing this are not normally large, so if you are in any doubt, use the longhand versions (shown below) instead.** See the entry for **for**.

Description

The ++ **operator** adds no new logic to ActionScript; it is simply a typing shortcut. See table below.

Shorthand code	Equivalent longhand version	Notes
`a = b++;`	`a = b;` `b = b + 1;`	Post increment
`a = ++b;`	`b = b + 1;` `a = b;`	Pre increment
`++a;`	`a = a + 1;`	This is the most used form of the ++ operator.

Or

a++		Note that it doesn't matter here whether you use post or pre increment.

`for (i =0; i<100; i++)`
`{ trace(i)`
`}`
	`for (i =0; i<100; ++i)`
	`{  trace(i)`
	`}`
		Looping. This is the most common application of ++.

Or

`for (i=0; i<100; i=i+1) {`
`trace(i);`
`}`
	Again, it doesn't matter here if you use post or pre increment.

	Also see **for**.
`a = a++;`	a will never change. To increment a by 1, you need to use the ++a or a++ form noted above.

+= Addition assignment

```
ɔ += a;
```

This operator is equivalent to:

```
b = b + a;
```

It should be seen as a shorthand way of writing the latter, and adds no additional logic or real programming features to ActionScript. Refer to the entry for **+**, noting that the rules for providing string concatenation are the same as those for the + operator.

< Less than

```
c = a < b;
```

Where a and b are number or string literal values, or any data element holding number or string values. c will be true if a is less than b.

This operator is compatible with **Flash 5 or later. Flash 4 supports numeric comparisons, but not string comparisons**, so be aware that this operator may give you different results with the Flash 4 Player if you are performing string comparisons. This operator will also happily work with Booleans, but the results of such comparisons are not usually meaningful.

The < operator is most usually used with **if** and **for**.

Description
The process of evaluating c is as follows:

1. If a and b are number values, then c is true if a is less than b, otherwise it is `false`.
2. If a or b are strings (such as "3" or " 6") that can be directly converted to numbers, then they are converted into numbers and comparison occurs as per above.
3. If a and b are string values that cannot be directly converted to numbers, then the strings are converted to their ASCII character code numbers and the comparison proceeds based on that. To find the character code, `myCode` of a string, `myString` for yourself use:

```
myCode = myString.charCodeAt(0);
```

... or look up the value of each character using an ASCII table (search the web for 'ASCII character table' or for the purists, 'ISO 8859').

Note
ASCII is an acronym for **American Standard Code for Information InterChange**. All files, whatever they are, are merely a formatted collection of numbers. This means that:

- A text file that includes characters is really just a pattern of numbers that the computer has parsed into a pattern of text characters and control codes.
- When you hit a key on a keyboard, the computer sees a number corresponding to the letter you just pressed, and not the letter itself. It only converts the number back to a character when you want to see your input again (such as on the screen).

The fundamental reason for all this is that computers only see binary, and ways of representing anything on a computer (text, pictures, sound) must be based on a way of representing the format via raw binary numbers.

One of the oldest systems of converting raw numbers to/from text characters is ASCII. It was widely used for communications between a keyboard and a computer, and a way of representing raw text files (.TXT files are simply a series of ASCII-encoded numbers that are parsed into the corresponding ASCII defined characters when you view them on the screen). Later standards (such as ISO 8859) are either simply re-iterations of ASCII that are defined as part of a bigger international standard, or an extension of ASCII to cater for additional characters or slight modern differences.

It is important to have an appreciation of ASCII because almost all string manipulations that a computer does to a string are based on it, or a derivative of it.

The table below assumes **Flash 5 and above.** See the *Tips and Precautions* section on the CD for **Flash 4.**

Code	Notes

`a=10, b=8;`
`c = a < b;`
`d = b < a;`
	c = false
	d = true

`a = 5 < 5;`	a = false; If you want to detect 'less than or equal' (a = true for this sort of condition), use **<=** instead. See the entry for the **<=** operator.

`a = "10", b = 8;`
`c = a < b;`
`d = b < a;`
	c = false
	d = true
	
	"10" is converted to 10 before the comparison is made.

`a="cat", b="dog";` `c = a < b;`	c = true c is before d in the alphabet.

`a="anteater", b="aardvark";`
`c = a < b;`
`d = b < a;`
	c = false
	d = true
	
	Flash is clever enough to look further along the string if the first two letters are the same.

`a="Cat", b="cat";`
`c = a < b;`
`d = b < a;`
	c = true
	d = false
	
	ASCII has A-Z before a-z. If you want to make your alphabetic string comparisons case-insensitive, consider converting all text to the same case via the **toLowerCase** or the **toUpperCase** methods of the **String** object before making your comparison.

`a="cat", b=" dog";` `c = a < b;`	c = false Although c is before d, the string " "dog" has a space before the 'd', so the comparison is 'c' and ' ' (SPACE). Note that ASCII contains spaces, punctuation, brackets, control codes, and other stuff, not just letters, and

	you need to strip your strings of these if you want to make a proper alphabetical string comparison.

`a = true;`
`b = false;`
`c = b < a;`
	`c = true`
	
	`true` will be converted to 1 and `false` will be converted to 0 before the comparison takes place. Numeric comparisons applied to Booleans are not normally useful.

`a = undefined < 3;`
`b = 3 < undefined;`
	`a = true`
	`b = false`
	
	`<` returns odd values if either or both of the operators cannot be evaluated to a string or number. Be wary of making comparisons based on raw user input text without first checking the validity of those inputs.

<< Bitwise left shift

```
c = a << b;
```

Where a and b are literal numbers or data elements holding number values, or string values that can be directly converted to a number value (such as 5). b must be a positive number. c will be returned as a * 2^b. The sign of a will be preserved.

This operator is compatible with **Flash 5 or later**. It works by:

1. Converting a and b to 32 bit binary. If a or b are floating point numbers, then they will be converted to integers, so any decimal places will be ignored. If a or b are strings that can be directly converted to integer numbers (such as 2.3) then the process will occur (to give 2).
2. Shifting the bit pattern of a to the left b times.

Description
Shifting a bit pattern to the left each time is the same as multiplying the number it represents by 2.

For example, bit shifting the value 7:

7 in 32 bit binary is: 00000000000000000000000000000111
Bit shifting 1 gives: 00000000000000000000000000001110

1110 is 14, or 7 * 2, or 7 * 2^1

Bit shifting again gives: 00000000000000000000000000011100

11100 is 28 or 7 * 2 * 2, or $7 * 2^2$

Because binary shifting is less processor-intensive than multiplication and *much* less processor-intensive than working out 2^n by any other means, it can be useful in optimizing certain algorithms.

See also **<<= (Bitwise left shift and assignment)**, which is a quick way of doubling a number.

Bit shifted calculation	Equivalent arithmetic calculation	Notes
a = 4 << 2;	a = 4 * 2^2	
b = (b << 1) + b;	b = 3 * b	
c = "2.4" << 3;	c = 2 * 2^3	
d = -4 << 2	d = -4 * 2^2	
a = "cat" << 2	a = 0 << 2	a = 0
a = 4 <<-2		a = 0
		The number of shifts must be positive. To shift in the other direction, use the >> operator.

See the example (bitwiseor).fla and (bitwiseor).swf on the CD.

<<= Bitwise left shift and assignment

    b <<= a;

This is a shorthand way of writing:

    b = b << a;

See the entry for **<< (bitwise left shift)** for further details.

<=Less than or equal to

    c = a <= b;

Where a and b are literal number or string values, or data elements holding number or string values, c will be true if a is less than or equal to b.

This operator is compatible with **Flash 5 or later**. **Flash 4 supports numeric comparisons, but not string comparisons**, so be aware that this operator may give you different results with the Flash 4 Player if you are performing string comparisons. This operator will also happily work with Boolean values, but the results of such comparisons are not usually meaningful.

The <= operator is most usually used with **if** and **for**.

Description

The process of evaluating c is as follows:

1. If a and b are number values, then c is true if a is less than or equal to b, otherwise it is false.
2. If a or b are strings (such as "3" or " 6") that can be directly converted to numbers, then they are converted into numbers and comparison occurs as per above.
3. If a and b are string values that cannot be directly converted to numbers, then the strings are converted to their ASCII character code numbers and the comparison proceeds based on that. To find the character code, myCode of a string, myString for yourself use:

```
myCode = myString.charCodeAt(0);
```

... or look up the value of each character using an ASCII table (search the web for 'ASCII character table' or 'ISO 8859').

The table below assumes **Flash 5 and above**. See the *Tips and Precautions* section on the CD for **Flash 4.**

Code	Notes

```a=10, b=8;```
```c = a <= b;```
```d = b <= a;```
```e = a <= a```
	```c = false```
	```d = true```
	```e = true```

```if (a<=2) {```
   ```// do this```
```}```
	The do this code will be executed only if a is less than or equal to 2. This is one of two very common uses of this operator.

```for (i=1; i<=10; i++) {```
   ```trace(i);```
```}```
	The loop will execute ten times and i will take values 1, 2, 3, 4, 5, 6, 7, 8, 9, 10. This is the second of two very common uses of this operator. Note that you may also want to start looping from 0 to 9, and to do this, you would use the following first line:
	
	```for (i=0; i<=9; i++) {```

```a="10", b=8;```	```c = false```

`c = a <= b;` `d = b <= a;`	`d = true` `"10"` is converted to `10` before the comparison is made.
`a="cat", b="dog";` `c = a <= b;`	`c = true` c is before d in the alphabet.

`a="anteater", b="aardvark";`
`c = a <= b;`
`d = b <= a;`
	`c = false`
	`d = true`
	
	Note that the `<=` operator gives the same results as the `<` operator when considering strings. See also the entry for the `<` operator.

`a="Cat", b="cat";`
`c = a <= b;`
`d = b <= a;`
	`c = true`
	`d = false`
	
	ASCII has A-Z before a-z. If you want to make your alphabetic string comparisons case-insensitive, consider converting all text to the same case via the **toLowerCase** or the **toUpperCase** methods of the **String** object before making your comparison.

`a="cat", b=" dog";` `c = a <= b;`	`c = false` Although c is before d, the string "dog" has a space before the 'd', so the comparison is c and ' ' (SPACE). Note that ASCII contains spaces, punctuation, brackets, control codes, and other stuff, not just letters, and you need to strip your strings of these if you want to make a proper alphabetical string comparison.

`a = true;`
`b = false;`
`c = b <= a;`
	`c = true`
	
	true will be converted to 1 and false will be converted to 0 before the comparison takes place. Numeric comparisons applied to Booleans are not normally useful.

`a = undefined <= 3;`
`b = 3 <= undefined;`
`c = undefined <= undefined;`
	`a = true`
	`b = false`
	`c = true`

\<= returns potentially odd values if
either or both of the operators cannot
be evaluated to a string or number. Be
wary of making comparisons based on
raw user input text without first
checking the validity of those inputs,
otherwise you may inadvertently make
one of the comparisons shown here,
and all of which convert the undefined
value to a 'live' defined value.

= assignment

```
b = a;
c = d = e = f;
```

Where a and f are any literal, array element, or object property, or an expression that can be resolved to one of these data types, and b and c are any variable, array element, or writable object property. b will be returned with value a, and c, d, and e will be returned with value f.

This operator is compatible with **Flash 5 or later**. The = operator evaluates the right-hand side and assigns it to the left-hand. **Note that the Flash 4 = operator works with numbers only**.

Description
This section briefly describes the **operator**, and then shows a table of typical uses, as shown below.

Code	Notes

```a = 2;```
```b = c = a;```
```d = "cat";```
	a = 2, b = 2, c = 2, d = "cat"

```if (x = 2) {```
```   //do this```
```}```
```if (x == 2) {```
```   //do this```
```}```
	Make sure you know the difference between the = operator (assignment) and == operator (equality). The first listing will incorrectly make x equal to 2, and the do this code will always run irrespective of the original value of x, whereas the second one will check whether x is equal to 2, and execute the do this code only if it is.

-= Subtraction assignment

```
a -= b;
```

This is a shorthand way of writing:

```
a = a - b;
```

See the entry for the – **(subtraction)** operator for more details.

== Equality

```
c = a == b;
```

Where a and b are number, Boolean, or string literal values, or any data element holding number, Boolean, or string values. c will be true if the value held in a is equal to the value held in b. The type of a and b may be different.

This operator is compatible with **Flash 5 or later**. **Flash 4 supports numeric comparisons, but not string comparisons**, so be aware that this operator may give you different results with the Flash 4 Player if you are performing string comparisons. This operator will also happily work with Booleans (true and false will be converted to the numbers 1 and 0 before the comparison takes place).

The == operator is mostly used with **if**.

Description
The process of evaluating c is as follows for Flash 5 or above:

1. If a and b are number values, then c is true if a is equal to b, otherwise it is false.
2. If one of a or b is a string that can be directly converted to numbers (such as "3" or " 6") and the other is a number, then the string will be converted to a number and the comparison made as per 1.
3. If a and b are both strings, then they will be compared as strings.
4. If a or b are Booleans, then true will be converted to 1 and false to 0, and the comparison will then occur as per 1 or 2 above.

Flash 4 does not support steps 2 or 3.

The table below assumes **Flash 5 and above.** See the *Tips and Precautions* section on the CD for **Flash 4.**

Code	Notes

```a=10, b=8, c="10";```
 ```d = a == b;```
 ```e = a == a;```
 ```f = a == c;```
	d = false
	 e = true
	 f = true

```if (a==b) {```
   ```//do this```
 ```}```
	The do this code will be executed if a is equal to b. This is the most common usage of this operator.

```a = true, b = 1, c = 0;```
 ```d = a == b;```
 ```e = c == false;```
	d = true
	 e = true

```a="cat", b=" cat";``` ```c = a == b;```	c = false "cat" does not equal " cat" because there is a leading space in the latter.
```a = undefined == undefined;```	a = true A comparison between two undefined values gives equality, even though both are by definition valueless and therefore not strictly equal to anything.

```if (a=b) {```
   ```//do this```
 ```}```
	The first listing uses the = operator in error. This will cause a to become equal to b rather than just checking if a is equal to be, and the do this code will always be executed

```if (a==b) {```
   ```//do this```
 ```}```
	The code should be as per the second listing. This will run the do this code only if a is equal to b.

=== Strict equality

```
c = a === b;
```

Where a and b are number, Boolean, or string literal values, or any data element holding number, Boolean, or string values. c will be true if the value held in a is equal to the value held in b. The type of a and b must also be identical.

This operator is compatible with **Flash 6 or later**. Strict equality is used to compare value **and** type. This comparison is sometimes called **identity** because the two values compared have to be identical in every respect.

The === operator is most usually used with **if**.

Description

The process of evaluating c is as follows for Flash MX:

1. If a and b are number values, then c is true if a is equal to b, otherwise it is false.
2. If a and b are both strings, then they will be compared as strings. No conversions take place with this operator and both value and type must be the same for a true value to be returned.
3. If a or b are both Booleans, then comparison will occur, and a true result will only occur if the values are identical.

Code	Notes

`a=10, b=8, c="10";`
`d = a === b;`
`e = a === a;`
`f = a === c;`
Compare these results with those listed operator.
	d = false
	e = true
	f = false
	
	in the entry for the ==

`if (a===b) {`
`  //do this`
`}`
	The 'do this' code will be executed if a is equal to b in value and type. . This is the most common usage of this operator

`a=true, b=1, c=0;`
`d = a === b;`
`e = c === false;`
`f = a === true;`
 	
Compare these results with those listed in the entry for the == operator.
	d = false
	e = false
	f = true

`a="cat";`
`b = a === "cat";`
`c = a === " cat";`
 	
"cat" does not equal " cat" because there is a leading space in the latter.
	b = true
	c = false

`a = undefined === undefined;` A comparison between two undefined values gives strict equality, even though both are by definition valueless and therefore not really equal to anything.	a = true

> Greater than

```
c = a > b;
```

Where a and b are number or string literal values, or any data element holding number or string values. c will be `true` if a is greater than b.

This operator is compatible with **Flash 5 or later. Flash 4 supports numeric comparisons, but not string comparisons**, so be aware that this operator may give you different results with the Flash 4 Player if you are performing string comparisons. This operator will also happily work with Booleans, but the results of such comparisons are not usually meaningful.

The > operator is mostly used with **if** and **for**.

Description

The process of evaluating c is as follows:

1. If a and b are number values, then c is `true` if a is more than b, otherwise it is `false`.
2. If a or b are strings (such as "3" or " 6") that can be directly converted to numbers, then they are converted into numbers and comparison occurs as per above.
3. If a and b are string values that cannot be directly converted to numbers, then the strings are converted to their ASCII character code numbers and the comparison proceeds based on that. To find the character code, myCode of a string, myString for yourself use:

```
myCode = myString.charCodeAt(0);
```

...or look up the value of each character using an ASCII table (search the web for 'ASCII character table' or for the purists, 'ISO 8859').

The table below assumes **Flash 5 and above.** See the *Tips and Precautions* section on the CD for **Flash 4.**

Code	Notes

a=10, b=8;
c = a > b;
d = b > a;
	c = true
	d = false

a = 5 > 5;	a = false
	If you want to detect 'less than or equal' (a = true for this sort of condition), use >= instead. See the entry for the >= operator.
a = "10", b = 8; c = a > b;	c = true d = false

`d = b > a;`	"10" is converted to 10 before the comparison is made.
`a="dog", b="cat";` `c = a > b;`	`c = true` d is after c in the alphabet.

`a="anteater", b="aardvark";`
`c = a > b;`
`d = b > a;`
	`c = true`
	`d = false`
	
	Flash is clever enough to look further along the string if the first two letters are the same.

`a="Cat", b="cat";`
`c = a > b;`
`d = b > a;`
	`c = false`
	`d = true`
	
	ASCII has A-Z before a-z. If you want to make your alphabetic string comparisons case-insensitive, consider converting all text to the same case via the **toLowerCase** or the **toUpperCase** methods of the **String** object before making your comparison.

`a=" dog", b="cat";` `c = a > b;`	`c = false` Although d is after c, the string "dog" has a space before the d, so the comparison is SPACE and c. Note that ASCII contains spaces, punctuation, brackets, control codes, and other stuff, not just letters, and you need to strip your strings of these if you want to make a proper alphabetical string comparison.

`a = true;`
`b = false;`
`c = b > a;`
	`c = false`
	
	true will be converted to 1 and false will be converted to 0 before the comparison takes place. Numeric comparisons applied to Booleans are not normally useful.

`a = undefined > 3;`
`b = 3 > undefined;`
	`a = false`
	`b = true`
	
	> returns odd values if either or both of the operators cannot be evaluated to a string or number. Be wary of making comparisons based on raw

user input text without first checking the validity of those inputs.

>= Greater than or equal to

```
c = a>=b;
```

Where a and b are literal number or string values, or data elements holding number or string values. c will be true if a is greater than or equal to b.

This operator is compatible with **Flash 5 or later**. **Flash 4 supports numeric comparisons, but not string comparisons**, so be aware that this operator may give you different results with the Flash 4 Player if you are performing string comparisons. This operator will also happily work with Boolean values, but the results of such comparisons are not usually meaningful.

The **>=** operator is mostly used with **if** and **for**.

Description

The process of evaluating c is as follows:

1. If a and b are number values, then c is true if a is more than or equal to b, otherwise it is false.
2. If a or b are strings (such as "3" or " 6") that can be directly converted to numbers, then they are converted into numbers and comparison occurs as per above.
3. If a and b are string values that cannot be directly converted to numbers, then the strings are converted to their ASCII character code numbers and the comparison proceeds based on that. To find the character code, myCode of a string, or myString for yourself use:

```
myCode = myString.charCodeAt(0);
```

... or look up the value of each character using an ASCII table (search the web for 'ASCII character table' or 'ISO 8859').

The table below assumes **Flash 5 and above**. See the *Tips and Precautions* section on the CD for **Flash 4.**

Code	Notes

`a=10, b=8;`
`c = a >= b;`
`d = b >= a;`
`e = a >= a`
	c = true
	d = false
	e = true

`if (a>=2) {`
`    // do this`
`}`
	The do this code will be executed only if a is greater than or equal to 2. This is one of two very common uses of this operator.

```for (i=10; i>=1; i-) { trace(i); }```	The loop will execute 10 times and i will take values 10, 9, 8, 7, 6, 5, 4, 3, 2, 1. This is the second of two very common uses of this operator. Note that you may also want to start looping from 9 to 0, and to do this, you would use the following first line: ```for (i=9; i>=0; i-) {```
```a = "10", b = 8; c = a >= b; d = b >= a;```	c = true d = false "10" is converted to 10 before the comparison is made.
```a="dog", b="cat"; c = a >= b;```	c = true d is after c in the alphabet.
```a="anteater", b="aardvark"; c = a >= b; d = b >= a;```	c = true d = false Note that the >= operator gives the same results as the > operator when considering strings, and doesn't just return true for both c and d because a=a. See also the entry for the > operator.
```a="Cat", b="cat"; c = a >= b; d = b >= a;```	c = false d = true ASCII has A-Z before a-z. If you want to make your alphabetic string comparisons case-insensitive, consider converting all text to the same case via the **toLowerCase** or the **toUpperCase** methods of the **String** object before making your comparison.
```a=" dog", b="cat"; c = a >= b;```	c = false Although d is after c, the string "dog" has a space before the d, so the comparison is SPACE and c. Note that ASCII contains spaces, punctuation, brackets, control codes, and other stuff, not just letters, and you need to strip your strings of these

	if you want to make a proper alphabetical string comparison.
| ```
a = true;
b = false;
c = b >= a;
``` | `c = false`

true will be converted to 1 and false will be converted to 0 before the comparison takes place. Numeric comparisons applied to Booleans are not normally useful. |
| ```
a = undefined >= 3;
b = 3 >= undefined;
c = undefined >= undefined;
``` | `a = false`
`b = true`
`c = true`

>= returns potentially odd values if either or both of the operators cannot be evaluated to a string or number. Be wary of making comparisons based on raw user text input without first checking the validity of those inputs, otherwise you may inadvertently make one of the comparisons shown here, and all of which convert the undefined value to a 'live' defined value. |

>> Bitwise right shift

```
c = a >> b;
```

Where a and b are literal numbers or data elements holding number values, or string values that can be directly converted to a number value (such as "5"). b must be positive. c will be returned as the integer part of a / 2^b. The sign of a will be preserved.

This operator is compatible with **Flash 5 or later**. It works by:

1. Converting a and b to 32 bit binary. If a or b are numbers, then they will be converted to integers, so any decimal places will be ignored. If a or b are strings that can be directly converted to integer numbers (such as "2.3") then the process will occur (to give 2).
2. Shifting the bit pattern of a to the right b times.

Description
Shifting a bit pattern to the right each time is the same as dividing the number it represents by two and then truncating the result to discard the decimal part.

For example, bit shifting the value 7:

7 in 32 bit binary is: 00000000000000000000000000000111
Bit shifting 1 gives: 00000000000000000000000000000011

11 binary is 3, or the integer part of 7/2, or the integer part of $7 / 2^1$.

Bit shifting again gives: 00000000000000000000000000000001

1 is the integer part of $7 / (2 * 2)$, or the integer part of $7 / 2^2$.

Because binary shifting is less processor-intensive than division and *much* less processor-intensive than working out 2^n by any other means, it can be useful in optimizing certain algorithms.

See also **<<= (Bitwise left shift and assignment)**, which is a quick way of halving a number.

Bit shifted calculation	Equivalent arithmetic calculation	Notes
`a = 8 >> 2;`	`a = 8/22 = 2`	
`b = 20;`		
`b = b >> 1;`	`b = 20/2 = 10`	
`c = "50" >> 3;`	`c = 50/23 = 50/8 = 6`	
`d = -8 >> 2`	`d = -8/22 = -2`	
`a = "cat" >> 2`	`a = 0 >> 2`	`a = 0`
`a = 4 >> -2`		`a = 0`
		The number of shifts must be positive. To shift in the other direction, use the << operator.

See the examples `(bitwiserightshift).fla` and `(bitwiserightshift).swf` on the CD.

>>= Bitwise right shift and assignment

`b >>= a;`

This is a shorthand way of writing:

`b = b >> a;`

See the entries for **>> (Bitwise right shift)** and **<<= (Bitwise left shift and assignment)** for further details.

>>> Bitwise unsigned right shift

```
c = a >>> b;
```

Where a and b are literal numbers or data elements holding number values, or string values that can be directly converted to a number value (such as "5"). b must be a positive integer. c will be returned as the integer part of a / 2^b. The sign of the result will always be positive, although it will give incorrect answers if you use a negative value for a, because the conversion process uses unsigned binary and this is unable to handle negative numbers.

This operator is compatible with **Flash 5 or later**. It works by:

1. Converting a and b to unsigned 32 bit binary. If a or b are floating point numbers, they will be converted integers, so any decimal paces will be ignored. If a or b are strings that can be directly converted to integer numbers (such as "2.3") then the process will occur (to give 2).
2. Shifting the bit pattern of a to the right b times.

Description

Shifting a bit pattern to the right each time is the same as dividing the number it represents by two and then truncating the result to discard the decimal part.

For example, bit shifting the value 7:

7 in 32 bit binary is: 00000000000000000000000000000111
Bit shifting 1 gives: 00000000000000000000000000000011

11 binary is 3, or the integer part of 7/2, or the integer part of 7 / 2^1

Bit shifting again gives: 00000000000000000000000000000001

1 is the integer part of 7 / (2 * 2), or the integer part of 7 / 2^2

If you used -7, then the conversion process will do the following:

-7 in 32 signed binary is: 11111111111111111111111111111000
Assume this is **unsigned** or $2^{32}-2^2-2^1-2^0$ = 4294967295

Because binary shifting is less processor intensive than division and *much* less processor intensive than working out 2^n by any other means, it can be useful in optimizing certain algorithms.

See also >>>=.

Bit shifted calculation	Equivalent arithmetic calculation	Notes

a = 8 >>> 2;
b = 20;
b = b >>> 1;
c = "50" >>> 3;
d = -8 >>> 2;
	$a = 8/2^2 = 2$
	
	$b = 20/2 = 10$
	$c = 50/2^3 = 50/8 = 6$
	$d = (2^{32}-8)/2^2$
	$= 1073741822$
		The use of a negative a is not !usually useful in Flash programming, unless you want to try your hand at creating encryption routines.

a = "cat" >>> 2	a = 0 >> 2	a = 0
a = 4 >>> -2		a = 0
		The number of shifts must be positive. To shift in the other direction, use the <<< operator.

>>>= Bitwise unsigned right shift and assignment

```
b >>>= a;
```

This is a shorthand way of writing:

```
b = b >>> a;
```

See the entry for **>>> (Bitwise unsigned right shift)** for further details.

A

gotoAndStop()
hitTest()
loadMovie()
loadVariables()
loadVariables() play()
nextFrame()
prevFrame() setMask() startDrag()
removeMovieClip()
swapDepths() startDrag()
unloadMovie() attachMovie()
createEmptyMovie()
createTextField()
duplica...

add

```
c = a add b;
```

Where a and b are strings, c is the result of concatenating a and b together. If a or b are numbers, they will be converted to strings before concatenation.

This operator is compatible with **Flash 4 or later**. This operator is deprecated in Flash 5 and above, where the **+** operator can concatenate strings (as well as add numbers).

Description

The add **operator** provides string concatenation for Flash 4. The use of this operator is deprecated, and you should use the **+** operator instead in Flash 5 and above.

Code	Notes
`a-"crab", b-"apple";` `c = a add b;`	`c - "crabapple"`
`a = 2 add 1;`	`a = "21"`

and

```
c = a and b;
```

The and **operator** is the deprecated **Flash 4 version** of the **&&** operator, and you are recommended to use that in preference. and is functionally identical to **&&** (the latter was introduced to conform to the ECMA262 specification).

appendChild

See **XML.appendChild**.

apply

See **Function.apply**.

applyChanges

See **FStyleFormat.applyChanges**.

arguments

This object is addressed in Chapter 10.

General

Whenever a function is called, an object called the **call object** is created, one per nested function call depth. This object is used to create the scope chain amongst other things. It also has an additional associated object called **arguments**, and this object is available for the programmer to interrogate. The arguments object is actually an **array** holding the function argument values.

> *The following discussion is fairly advanced and assumes a good knowledge of the properties of the* arguments *object, so you may do well to have a look at the entries for* **arguments.callee**, **arguments.caller**, *and* **arguments.length** *first, plus have a good understanding of arrays.*

For example, consider the function below:

```
function 3D(x, y, z) {
  // code goes here
}
```

This function would have an array arguments as follows:

- arguments[0] holds the value of argument x.
- arguments[1] holds the value of argument y.
- arguments[2] holds the value of argument z.

More subtly, because the arguments object is really just an array, you can pass it from one function to another, as shown by the following code:

```
function sendArguments() {
    receiveArguments(arguments);
}
function receiveArguments(received) {
    trace(received[0]);
    trace(received.length);
}
sendArguments("cat", "dog", "hamster", 3, 5, 9);
```

The arguments "cat", "dog", "hamster", 3, 5, 9 are placed in an array `arguments[0]` = "cat" to `arguments[5]` = 9 by the function `sendArguments()`. This function sends the arguments to another function `receiveArguments()`.

`receiveArguments()` sees these arguments as the object `received`, and `arguments[0]` to `[5]` of `sendarguments()` can be read in the new function as `recieved[0]` to `[5]`.

The output for this FLA is shown below:

Note that `receiveArguments` has its **own** arguments, and you can see them by modifying `recieveArguments` to show them rather than those of `sendArguments`:

```
function recieveArguments(recieved) {
     trace(arguments[0]);
     trace(arguments.length);
}
```

This modification will give the new outputs shown. Note that the arguments for `receiveArguments` are a single argument with one element: the whole arguments object of the `sendArguments` function.

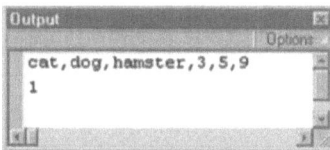

Practical uses

Using the arguments object instead of the traditional function calls of the form `myFunction(arg0, arg1, arg2…. argn)` allows several benefits:

- If you can get your functions working for one argument (or dimension), you can make it handle any number of dimensions simply by adding more arguments to the first call, and changing your main function code to read an array rather than a single value. In short, it makes it easy to extend your code to handle more parameters.
- Your functions don't have to know the number of arguments they should expect. This is *very* useful for statistical functions and other applications where the function may be asked to handle a variable number of similarly structured data sets depending on the sample size.

arguments.callee

```
arguments.callee();
```

Where the `callee` property is a reference to the currently running function.

This property of the `arguments` object is compatible with **Flash 5 or later**. It will only exist within the scope of the currently running function, and will cease to exist as soon as program execution returns to the code that called the function.

Description

The `arguments.callee()` **property** provides a reference to the current running function. You would refer to this property if you did not know the name of the currently running function and you wanted it to call itself recursively. The only time you would not know the name of the currently running function would be if it were defined anonymously, for example, in the form:

```
myFunction = function() {
  //function code goes here
};
```

or if you define an event handler as an anonymous function (which is a very common programming structure in Flash MX):

```
myClip.onSomeEvent = function() {
  //event code goes here
};
```

To make the function call itself, you would use code as shown in the examples below.

Code	Notes

`_root.onMouseDown = function() {`
`    var diagnostic = _root.count;`
`    _root.count++;`
`    if (_root.count<20) {`
`        arguments.callee();`
`    }`
`    message = "I am function call`
`number " + diagnostic;`
`    trace(message)`
`};`
`count = 0;`
`factorial = function (x) {`
`if (x <= 1) {`
	When using anonymous functions to define event handlers, the `arguments.callee` property is a way of running the event handler more than once in response to the event. In this example, the **onMouseDown** event handler will run 20 times for each press of the mouse

	Although the standard 'factorial of a number' algorithm is usually wheeled

```
return 1;
  } else {
    return x * arguments.callee(x-1);
  }
};
trace(factorial(300))
```

out as a good example of both
recursion and arguments.callee, it
is actually questionable as a real-life
programming solution, and this
example shows why. Running this
code will raise an error because only
256 levels of function call are allowed,
so recursive routines are a poor
general solution unless you know that
the number of iterations will be small.

```
function myFunction() {
    trace(arguments.callee);
}
myfunction();
```

This code will not trace the name of
the current function (myfunction) to
the output window, because the
arguments.callee property is a
reference and not a printable string. If
you want to know the order of
execution of functions, you should use
the debugger with breakpoints set up
in your code.

arguments.caller

```
arguments.caller();
```

Where the caller property is a reference to the function that called the currently running function.

This property of the arguments object is compatible with **Flash 5 or later**. It will only exist within the
scope of the currently running function, and will cease to exist as soon as program execution returns to
the code that called the function.

Description
The caller **property** becomes defined when one function calls another. The caller function allows
the second and subsequent functions to know the name of the function that called them:

If function1 calls function2, and function2 calls function3, then:

- function2 is the caller of function3
- function1 is the caller of function2

You may recognize this as the call scope chain, and the `caller` property refers to the previous nested function level in this chain.

Because in Flash MX, functions can be **event handlers**, the ability to know the calling event can be very useful in building complex event handling systems for advanced ActionScript applications.

Code	Notes
| ```
function myCaller01() {
    mainfunction();
}
function mycaller02() {
    mainfunction();
}
function mainfunction() {
    if (arguments.caller == myCaller01) {
        trace("I was called by
myCaller01()");
    } else {
        trace("I was called by
myCaller02()");
    }
}
myCaller01();
``` | The function `myCaller01` calls `mainfunction()`, and the trace text `"I was called by myCaller01()"` will appear in the Output window if you run this. |
	You can change the last line in this listing to:
	`myCaller02();`
	... to see that `mainfunction()` will recognize the change in calling function.
	Note that the code refers to the calling functions as `myCaller01` and `myCaller02` rather than `myCaller01()` and `myCaller02()`. This is to denote that we are referring to the functions as objects rather than calling them.
| ```
function myCaller01() {
    mainfunction();
}
function mycaller02() {
    mainfunction();
}
function mainfunction() {
    diagnostic = "I was called by
➡"+arguments.caller;
    trace(diagnostic);
}
myCaller01();
``` | You cannot treat `arguments.caller` as a string because it is a *reference* and not a literal. You cannot print it to screen as this code tries to do. Rather than see the function name `myCaller01` or `myCaller02`, you will see the message |
| | `"I was called by [type ➡Function]"` |

See the example `argumentscaller.fla` and `argumentscaller.swf` on the CD.

arguments.length

```
x = arguments.length;
```

x will be returned as the number of expected arguments of the currently scoped function.

This property of the arguments object is compatible with **Flash 5 or later**. It will only exist within the scope of the currently running function, and will cease to exist as soon as program execution returns to the code that called the function.

Description

The length **property** of the arguments object becomes defined when a function is called, and defines the number of arguments that have been included with the call.

Code	Notes

`function myFunction() {`
`   trace(arguments.length);`
`}`
`myfunction(10, 20, 30);`
	The function myfunction shows how you can capture the number of arguments received by a function. Note that the number of arguments sent is greater than the number of arguments myFunction is set up to receive (it isn't actually set up to receive any!).

	The Output window will display "3" if you run this script.
	Note that the value of the arguments sent to a function can be more or less than the function is set up to receive, and neither case will raise an error, because ActionScript does not check this.

`function myFunction() {`
`   for (i=0; i<arguments.length; i++) {`
`      trace(arguments[i]);`
`   }`
`}`
`trace("first call...");`
`myfunction(10, 20, 30);`
`trace("second call...");`
`myfunction(2, 4, 6, 8, 10);`
	The function myFunction shows how you can send a variable number of arguments to a function. The first call sends three numbers, whereas the second call sends five.
	
	This code also illustrates the true nature of the arguments object: **it is an array**.

The output of this code is shown below:

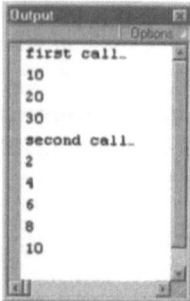

Note that the arguments object should really be described as 'array-like'. The arguments object has a very small subset of the features of the Array object (it only has the length property of the true Array object).

See the example argumentslength.fla and argumentslength.swf on the CD.

Array

General

The Array object is a data type derived from the **Object** object that is specifically designed to handle **lists** or sequential data. Although you can use the **Object** object to solve the same problems, using arrays is generally easier because the Array object has a rich set of pre-built methods and properties that allow it to be used much move easily where list-based data is to be handled.

A simple array list is created and initialized by the code shown below:

```
myArray = new Array("cat", "dog", "pig", 20.2, true);
myArray[6] = 10;
trace(myArray[0]);
trace(myArray[4]);
```

The output from this script is shown below:

... and the structure of the array itself, as seen in the debugger is shown below:

⊟	myArray	
	0	"cat"
	1	"dog"
	2	"pig"
	3	20.2
	4	true
	6	10

Notice that:

- An array can hold different types of data in the same list.
- Each element is denoted by a number n and the corresponding data is held in myArray[n].
- The first element is 0 and not 1.
- You can leave some elements in the array undefined. In our case, we have left myArray[5] undefined. This is perfectly legal and will not raise an error.

Some lists require multi-dimensional lists. There are several ways to do this, depending on how you want your data organized. Supposing for example, that we wanted to store the (x, y) data for five points, and wanted to initialize them all as (0,0). There are several ways of doing this, three of which are shown below.

```
myArray = new Array();
for (i=0; i<5; i++) {
    myArray[i] = new Array(0, 0);
}
```

⊟	myArray	
⊟	0	
	0	0
	1	0
⊞	1	
⊞	2	
⊞	3	
⊞	4	

```
myArray2 = new Array();
for (i=0; i<5; i++) {
    myArray2[i] = {x:0, y:0};
}
```

⊟	myArray2	
⊟	0	
	x	0
	y	0
⊞	1	
⊞	2	
⊞	3	
⊞	4	

```
myArray3 = new Array();
for (i=0; i<5; i++) {
    myArray3[i] = new Object();
    myArray3[i].point = new Array();
    myArray3[i].point[0] = 0;
    myArray3[i].point[1] = 0;
}
```

⊟	myArray3		
⊟	0		
	⊟	point	
		0	0
		1	0
⊞	1		
⊞	2		
⊞	3		
⊞	4		

- `myArray` is an array of arrays.
- `myArray2` is an array, each element of which is an object with properties.
- `myArray3` is an array, each element of which is itself an array containing two further elements ('an array of arrays').

See also **Array.push** for at least one other way of combining single-dimensional arrays to form matrices of values.

You can continue mixing arrays and/or `Object` objects to achieve the desired structure. As can be seen, the creation of complex data structures is very flexible, and it is relatively easy to structure them exactly how you want them. This level of flexibility is not well known, and many designers tend to stick to a single form of multi-dimensional array that they know works. Obviously, it is not necessary to restrict yourself in this way!

Note also that the **arguments** object can also be used to structure your functions so that they accept variable length `Array` objects as their argument. This allows for *very* flexible data structures when considering complex data, as would be required for more onerous applications such as 3D engines and other advanced motion-graphics-related tasks.

Practical uses

As mentioned earlier, the `Array` object is useful in handling lists of information. Arrays are, however, very flexible, and you can embed arrays to create multi-dimensional lists (matrices) or arrays of objects to create more complex data structures. These are all useful in any application that requires anything other than simple variables, from parsing XML trees to creating the data structures for holding point data for a Drawing API based vector engine.

The greatest advantage of the `Array` object is that it provides a very rich set of properties and methods, more so than the alternative, the `Object` object. This makes the `Array` easier to understand than the `Object` object (and the associated object-orientated programming (OOP) approach, where you have to build everything up from scratch yourself) for the non-programmer.

Additionally, arrays do not have to refer to data. A little known trick is that arrays can be made to refer to graphical objects, such as movie clips.

For example, supposing you had three movie clips called `myClip1`, `myClip2`, `myClip3` on `_root`, and `anotherClip` on `_root.someplace`. The following code will place them all at a position `_x = 0` relative to their co-ordinate system:

```
myArray = ["myClip1", "myClip2", "myClip3", "someplace.anotherClip"];
for (i=0; i<myArray.length; i++) {
    _root[myArray[i]]._x = 0;
}
```

The following code will attach **onEnterFrame** scripts to each of six named movie clips:

```
myArray = ["menu", "subBar", "mainbar", "clip4", "b5", "b6"];
for (i=0; i<myArray.length; i++) {
        _root[myArray[i]].onEnterFrame = function() {
                this._x++;
        };
}
```

This is a really cool feature of arrays; you can treat movie clips and buttons (or rather, the path to each movie clip/button) as array elements, and in doing so you can:

- Use the array sort features to divide out your movie clips based on particular property values they have, and treat each group separately (by for example, coloring them differently or giving them different event scripts).
- Dynamically reassign the groups based on the normal array editing features (**Array.push**, **Array.pop**, **Array.slice**, etc).

Array constructor

```
myArray = new Array();
```

This defines an empty array called myArray.

This constructor is compatible with **Flash 5 or later**. You must construct an array before you can use it. There are a number of alternative ways of constructing an array, which allow you to define the length and/or populate the array with values at the same time, and these are shown below.

Description

An array must be constructed before it can be used. Once constructed, the array elements can be populated individually. You can also populate or define the length of the array at the same time as defining it. See the examples below.

Once constructed, an array will grow automatically to include all elements you have defined. Arrays can quickly use up system memory (especially multi-dimensional arrays), so some care in optimizing your array structures should be considered.

Code	Notes
someArray = new Array()	This line will create an empty array with no elements in it. You can confirm that the array is empty by adding the following line after it (which will print a length of 0 in the Output window if you run the script).
	trace(someArray.length)

	See also **Array.length**.

`myArray = new Array();`
`myArray[0] = 23;`
`myArray[1] = "spider";`
`myArray[2] = false;`
 	
`myArray = [23, "spider", false];`
	Both these listings will produce the same array:
	
	`myArray[0] = 23`
	`myArray[1] = "spider"`
	`myArray[2] = false`

`months = new Array(12);`	This defines an array with 12 elements, `myArray[0]` to `myArray[11]`. You can confirm the arrays length by adding the following line: `trace(myArray.length)` See also **Array.length**.

See the examples `arrayconcat.fla` / `arrayconcat.swf` and `arraylength.fla` / `arraylength.swf` on the CD.

Array.concat

```
myArray = myArray.concat(value0, value1…. valuen);
```

value0…valuen are values or arrays that you want to add to the end of `myArray`. If `myArray` doesn't already exist, it will be created. You can also create a new array with:

```
myNewArray = myArray.concat(value0, value1…. valuen);
```

In this case, a new array `myNewArray` is created by concatenating value0 to value1 to the end of `myArray`, and storing the result in `myNewArray`. The initial state of `myArray` is preserved.

Description

`Array.concat` allows you to:

- Join one array onto another
- Join two or more arrays together to form a new array
- Add new elements onto the end of an existing array
- Add new elements onto the end of an existing array to form a new array

Code	Notes

`myMonths1 = ["jan", "feb", "march",`
➥`"april"];`
`myMonths2 = ["may", "jun", "jul",`
	Lines 1 and 2 create two arrays, `myMonths1` and `myMonths2`. Line 3 adds `myMonths2` onto the end of

```
➡ "aug"];
myMonths1 = myMonths1.concat(myMonths2);
myMonths1 = myMonths1.concat("sept",
➡ "oct", "nov", "dec");
```

contains 12 elements, "jan" to "dec":

myMonths1. Line 4 adds new elements "sept" to "dec".

At the end of this code, myMonths1

⊟	myMonths1	
	0	"jan"
	1	"feb"
	2	"march"
	3	"april"
	4	"may"
	5	"jun"
	6	"jul"
	7	"aug"
	8	"sept"
	9	"oct"
	10	"nov"
	11	"dec"
⊞	myMonths2	

```
mammals =["cat", "dog", "donkey"]
insects = ["bee", "centipede",
➡ "grasshopper"]
creatures = mammals.concat(insects,
➡ "wasp", "horse")
```

The new array creatures is created by concatenating insects to mammals, and then adding "wasp" and "horse". The final contents of creatures is shown below

⊟	creatures	
	0	"cat"
	1	"dog"
	2	"donkey"
	3	"bee"
	4	"centipede"
	5	"grasshopper"
	6	"wasp"
	7	"horse"
⊞	insects	
⊞	mammals	

See the example arrayconcat.fla and arrayconcat.swf on the CD.

Array.join

```
myString = myArray.join();
myString = myArray.join("separator");
myString = myArray.join(mySeparatorString);
```

Where `"separator"` is a string literal, and `mySeparatorString` is a string variable.

This method is compatible with **Flash 5 or later**. `myString` will be returned as a single string consisting of all the elements of `myArray`, separated by commas (if you do not give the method any arguments). You can also define your own separator as a literal string (`"separator"`) or a string variable (`mySeparatorString`).

Description

The `join` **method** converts an array to a single string.

Code	Notes
`numbers = [2, 4.5, 6];` `numString = numbers.join();`	`numString = "2,4.5,6"` Note that if you wanted to display numbers in a text field in the format shown for `numString`, you could do so much more easily simply by displaying `numbers` in the text field.

`menu = ["home", "about", "links",`
➡`"contact"];`
`menuText = menu.join(" | ");`
	`menuText = "home | about |`
	➡`links | contact"`
	
	The separator is defined as " | ".

See the examples `arrayconcat.fla` / `arrayconcat.swf` and `arraypush.fla` / `arraypush.swf` on the CD.

Array.length

```
myArrayLength = myArray.length;
```

Where `myArray.length` returns the current length of the array `myArray`.

This property is compatible with **Flash 5 or later**.

Description

`myArray.length` is equal to the length of the array `myArray`. This value is a positive integer. This property is perhaps one of the most useful things to know about an array. In many cases, you *have* to know it before you can do anything useful with the array.

Knowing the length of an array is useful because you then know that the array has elements 0 to length, and can use this fact to sequentially access all the elements in the array. This property is not available in the other complex data structure, the `Object` object, and this fact makes the array more useful in a number of applications where you need to handle basic lists of data.

Code	Notes
| ```
list = [23,"pies", "cakes", false, 40,
➡ "beer"];
trace (list.length);
``` | |

⊟	list	
	0	23
	1	"pies"
	2	"cakes"
	3	false
	4	40
	5	"beer"
	listLen	6

Notice that the last element in `list` is `list.length-1`, because arrays start at element 0.

Code	Notes
| ```
spectrum = ["red", "orange", "yellow",
➡ "green", "blue"];
spectrum[spectrum.length] = "indigo";
spectrum[spectrum.length] = "violet";
``` | Adding an element at position [array.length] of an array has the effect of appending the element at the end of the array. Because you have now added one to the length, the length is also updated by one, so this value always points to the first free element at the end of the array. |

⊟	spectrum	
	0	"red"
	1	"orange"
	2	"yellow"
	3	"green"
	4	"blue"
	5	"indigo"
	6	"violet"

If you want to add a number of elements to the end of an array (as we have done here) you will find the **Array.push** method more useful than the technique shown here.

Code	Notes
| ```
myArray = ["John", "Paul", "Ringo", "George"];
for (i=0; i<myArray.length; i++) {
     trace(myArray[i]);
}
``` | Using a **for** loop that cycles between 0 and myArray.length-1 is the quickest way to sequentially read through an array. The code shown would produce the following output: |
```

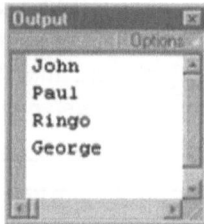

```
myArray = new Array();
myArray[12] = "23";
myArray[myArray.length] = "damn";
```

The array myArray has only one defined element myArray[12]. If you use myArray.length to add a new element to the end of myArray, the new element will go into a *new* element, although there are plenty of free elements already.

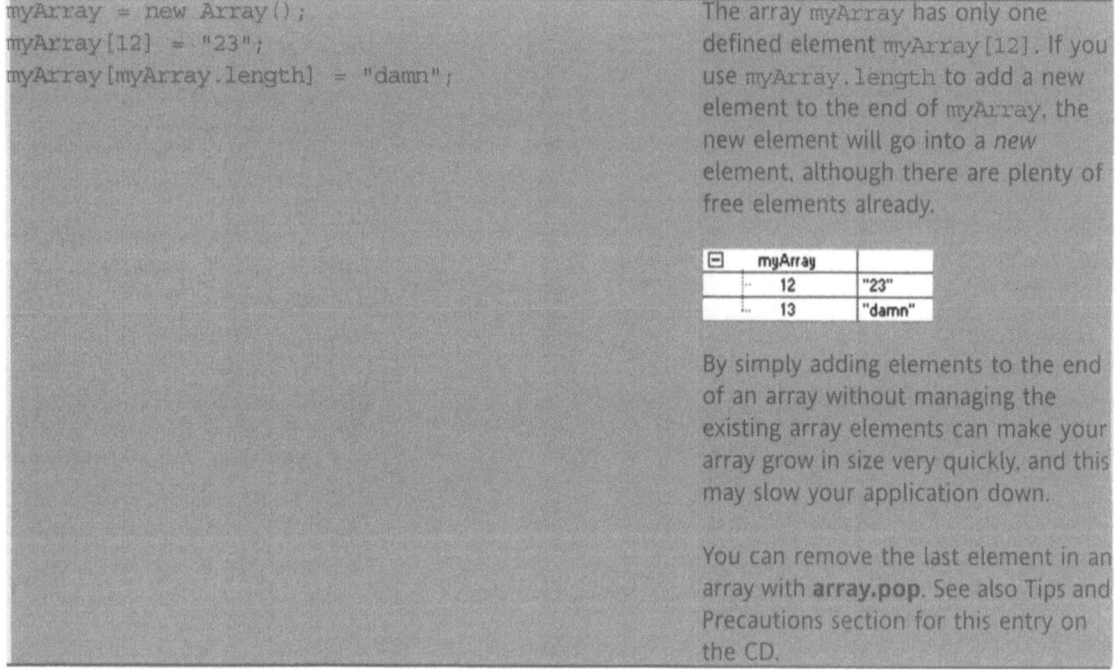

⊟	myArray	
⋯	12	"23"
⋯	13	"damn"

By simply adding elements to the end of an array without managing the existing array elements can make your array grow in size very quickly, and this may slow your application down.

You can remove the last element in an array with **array.pop**. See also Tips and Precautions section for this entry on the CD.

See example `arraylength.fla` and `arraylength.swf` on the CD.

Array.pop

```
myLastElement = myArray.pop();
```

where MyArray is an array, and myLastElement is a variable that will be returned with the last element in myArray.

This method is compatible with **Flash 5 or later**. It returns the value of the last element in an array, and deletes that element. The length of the array is reduced by one because of this.

Description

The pop **method** 'pops' the last value in an array. It returns this value before deleting the element containing it. If you have an array myArray, then val = myArray.pop() will delete the last element in the array (which you can also access before the pop by reading `myArray[myArray.length-1]`). See also **Array.length**.

Code

```
days = ["mon", "tue", "wed"];
lastDay = days.pop();
trace(lastDay);
trace(days);
```

Notes

The second line will make `lastDay` equal to `"wed"`, and then remove `"wed"` from the array days. The output from this code is shown below:

```
days = ["mon", "tue", "wed"];
days.pop();
```

If you want to discard the last element without reading it, you can simply use `myArray.pop()` without assigning the result to a variable.

After line 2:

```
days = ["mon", "tue"]
```
This shows how you can use the **Array.length** property within a loop

```
days = ["mon", "tue", "wed"];
while (days.length>0) {
to
        lastDay = days.pop();
        trace(lastDay);
}
```

Make sure that you pop each element in turn from array days.

Note that there is no guarantee that all elements popped from an array in this way will be defined.

Also, note that the array elements are popped from the end rather than the start, so your `lastDay` values will be backwards, as shown by the output from this code:

See the example `arraypoppush.fla` and `arraypoppush.swf` on the CD.

Array.push

`myArray.push(value0, value1,… valuen);`

Where `MyArray` is an array, and `value0` to `valuen` are values that will be added to the end of `myArray`.

This method is compatible with **Flash 5 or later**. It is used to add new elements to the end of an array.

Description
The `push()` **method** adds new elements to the end of an array. You can perform more complex array concatenation using the **Array.concat()** method.

Code	Notes
`days = ["mon", "tue", "wed"];` `days.push["thur", "fri"];`	Array days = ["mon", "tue", ➥"wed", "thur", "fri"]

`points = new Array();`
`point0 = [20.0, 30.1, 70.5];`
`point1 = [10.0, 50.0, 10.5];`
`point2 = [30.0, 20.0, 50.2];`
`points.push(point0, point1,`
`➥point2);`
	You can push objects onto an array as well as values. The code shown pushes arrays representing 3D points onto an array points.
	
	The structure of the resulting array is shown below:

⊟	0		
		0	20
		1	30.1
		2	70.5
⊞	1		
⊞	2		

Array.reverse

```
myArray.reverse();
```

Reverses the element order of the array myArray.

This method is compatible with **Flash 5 or later**. It reverses the indexes of all elements in an array, so that the first element becomes the last one, and so on throughout the array.

Description

The reverse **method** allows you to reverse the order of an array, as shown by the example below.

Code	Notes
```fruit = ["apples", "pears", "oranges", ➡ "limes"]; fruit.reverse(); trace(fruit);```	When reversed, the fruit array becomes [limes,oranges,pears,apples].

Array.shift

```
myFirstElement = myArray.shift();
```

where myArray is the array that you want to shift the elements of, and myFirstElement is the value of myArray[0] prior to the shift.

Description

The Array.shift() **method** shifts all the elements one place to the left. Consider the array below:

```
MrJones = ["John", "Fred", "Mr Strong", "Mr Happy"];
```

Before shifting, it looks like this:

MrJones[0]	MrJones[1]	MrJones[2]	MrJones[3]
"John"	"Fred"	"Colin"	"Roger"

Following the line:

```
shiftedMr = MrJones.shift();
```

... the array becomes:

MrJones[0]	MrJones[1]	MrJones[2]
"Fred"	"Colin"	"Roger"

... and `shiftedMr` is returned as `"John"`, the Mr Jones who has been shifted out of the array.

During this shift, element `MrJones[0]`, the first element in the array, becomes deleted, and this reduces the original length of the array, `MrJones.length` by 1. See also **Array.length**.

Code	Notes

```books = ["foundation", "studio",```
➥ ```"upgrade essentials"];```
```firstBook = books.shift();```
	After the shift, `books[0]` = `"studio"` and `books[1]` = `"upgrade essentials"`. Also, `books.length` will be reduced by one after the shift to now equal 2.
	
	`firstBook` will be equal to `"foundation"`.

```books = ["foundation", "studio",```
➥ ```"upgrade essentials"];```
```books.shift();```
	This listing is exactly like the previous one, except we discard the `"foundation"` entry without reading it.

See the example `arrayshift.fla` and `arrayshift.swf` on the CD.

Array.slice

```
mySlice = myArray.slice(start, end);
```

Where `myArray` is an array, and `start` and `end` are the start and end index of the slice you want to extract from `myArray`. This slice is returned as a new array, `mySlice`. The original array, `myArray` is not affected by the slice process.

If you want to extract a slice from the end of the array, you should specify a negative value for `start` and `end`, with the last index being `-1`.

If the `end` parameter is omitted, the slice will take a slice from the `start` index to the end of the array (or from the `start` index to the start of the array if you specify a negative `start` value).

This method is compatible with **Flash 5 or later**. It allows you to extract a portion of an array from an existing array to create a new array.

Description

The `Array.slice` **method** allows you to extract and copy a section of one array and use it to create a new array. The original array is unaffected by the process.

Note that taking slices from an array can be confusing. When taking slices from an array, it is recommended that you draw quick sketches of the portion you want to extract in relation to the rest of the array, as we have shown below.

To describe the slice, you have two arguments, `start` and `end`. (The `end` argument can be omitted, leaving you with the end of the array as `end`.)

For the purpose of example, assume we have an array `myArray`:

```
myArray = [0, 10, 20, 30, 40, 50, 60, 70, 80, 90];
```

0	1	2	3	4	5	6	7	8	9
0	10	20	30	40	50	60	70	80	90

If we specify a slice of the form `myArray.slice(start)` then we will extract a slice starting from index `start` and ending at the last index, `myArray[9]`.

If we extracted a slice with the line:

```
mySlice = myArray.slice(3);
```

... we would extract the shaded part of `myArray` below to create `mySlice`, which would be an array of 7 elements, with values `mySlice[0]` = 30 to `mySlice[6]` = 90.

0	1	2	3	4	5	6	7	8	9
0	10	20	30	40	50	60	70	80	90

If we instead want to extract a section of `myArray` from a start index up to an end index before the end of the array we specify a slice of the form `myArray.slice(start, end)`.

If we extracted a slice with the line:

```
mySlice = myArray.slice(3, 7);
```

... we would extract the new shaded part of `myArray` to create `mySlice`, which would be an array of four elements, with values `mySlice[0]` = 30 to `mySlice[3]` = 60.

0	1	2	3	4	5	6	7	8	9
0	10	20	30	40	50	60	70	80	90

The last slice index points were specified from the first index (leftmost end) of our original array `myArray`. Sometimes, it makes more sense to extract a slice that is defined by start and end points measured from the rightmost end. This occurs more often than you might expect, because this is the end that the array most often grows from.

To specify the same slice as the last example, measured from the rightmost end of `myArray` you would use the following line of code:

```
mySlice = myArray.slice(-7, -3);
```

With negative indexes, the slice method takes the index of the last (rightmost) element to be -1:

-10	-9	-8	-7	-6	-5	-4	-3	-2	-1
0	10	20	30	40	50	60	70	80	90

Finally, you can take a slice measured from the end (rightmost) element of the array from a start point measured from the right by using a line of the form `myArray.slice(-start)`. To create a slice `mySlice` of the array `myArray` that includes the last three elements, you would use the line:

```
mySlice = myArray(-3);
```

-10	-9	-8	-7	-6	-5	-4	-3	-2	-1
0	10	20	30	40	50	60	70	80	90

This would create an array `mySlice` with three elements `mySlice[0] = 70` to `mySlice[2] = 90`.

Note that for negative arguments, the new array is still read from left to right. To create a slice that is flipped as well so that it reads backwards, see the **Array.reverse()** method.

Code	Notes
`mySlice = myArray(7, 3);`	The start value must be less than the end value for positive arguments, otherwise the slice returned `mySlice` will be empty.
`mySlice = myArray(-3, -7);`	The start value must be greater (less negative) than the end value for negative arguments, otherwise the slice returned `mySlice` will be empty.

Array.sort

```
myArray.sort();
```

where `myArray` is the function you want to sort. The `sort` will sort:

- Numbers in ascending order, with `myArray[0]` been assigned the lowest value.
- Strings in ascending ASCII order (or more correctly, the character order defined by ISO 8859).

If you want to use a sort on another order, you can define it using the following:

```
myArray.sort(myOrderFunction);
```

where `myOrderFunction` is a function that defines a custom ordering scheme.

This method is compatible with **Flash 5 or later**. It allows you to reorder the position of the values that make up the array. This ordering can be user-defined.

```
function myOrderFunction(a, b){
  // code
  return val
}
```

- If value a should come before b in the list, then `val` should be positive.
- If value a should come at the same position as b, then `val` should be 0.
- If value a should come after b, then `val` should be negative.

Description

The `Array.sort` **method** allows you to sort the array. By default, it will sort numbers in numerical order, lowest first, or character order, lowest character first (this approximates alphabetical order, but is not true alphabetical order. See the < operator for more information on ASCII/ISO 8859, which is the character set used).

For example, the following code will sort an array `myNumbers` in ascending order:

```
myNumbers = [20, 40, 1, 0.2, 100, -5];
myNumbers.sort();
trace(myNumbers);
```

This code will give the following output:

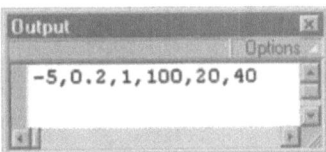

You can also use the default sort scheme to sort alphabetically, but be aware that for the sort to work, you should either make sure that all the characters are the same case, or force this to be the case by using the **String.toUpperCase** or **String.toLowerCase** methods on each element in the array before sorting. The following listing will perform an alphabetical sort, and the output is shown below:

```
myStrings = ["sham b", "glen rhodes", "john davey"];
```

```
myStrings.sort();
trace(myStrings);
```

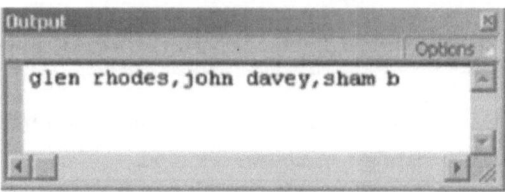

If you want to define your own order, you have to use the form:

```
myArray.sort(myOrderFunction);
```

`myOrderFunction` is the name of a function, which should look something like this:

```
function myOrderFunction(a, b){
  // code
  return val
}
```

- If value a should come before b in the list, then `val` should be positive.
- If value a should come at the same position as b, then `val` should be 0.
- If value a should come after b, then `val` should be returned as negative.

The following code will sort numbers in descending order:

```
function descending(a, b) {
  return (b-a);
}
myNumbers = [1, 2, 4, 7, 1234, 5632,7, 3211, 6];
myNumbers.sort(descending);
trace(myNumbers);
```

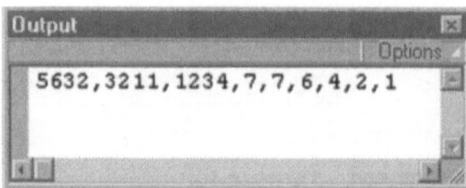

This works because if b is the greater of the two numbers, a positive number is returned, and a negative number returned if b is the lesser number. If b = a, then zero is returned.

You can also create sorts that are not based on size. The following sort will list even numbers, followed by all the odd numbers:

```
function evenOdd(a, b) {
 if (b/2 == Math.round(b/2)) {
return 1;
 } else {
    return -1;
 }
}
myNumbers = [1, 2, 4, 7, 1234, 5632, 7, 3211, 6];
myNumbers.sort(evenOdd);
trace(myNumbers);
```

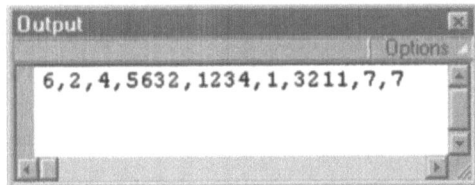

Array.splice

```
myArray.splice(start, numberOfDeletions);
```

where myArray is an array. Starting from index start, a number of elements equal to numberOfDeletions are deleted.

You can also insert new elements starting from the start point with the following form:

```
myArray.splice(start, numberOfDeletions, newValue0, newValue1, … newValueN);
```

Where newValue1… newValueN are the new elements that will be added.

This method is compatible with **Flash 5 or later**. Array.splice() allows you to add/delete/replace portions of an array.

Description

See the examples below.

Code	Notes
| ```
smiths = ["Mike", "Mark", "Bob", "Bill",
➡"Betty", "Sarah", "Sidney", "Jane"];
smiths.splice(3,2);
``` | **Deleting Elements**<br><br>Before the splice: |

After the splice, two elements, starting from smiths[3] and ending with smiths[3+1] (two elements) are deleted, so we lose Bill and Betty. The space left by this deletion is closed up by moving down smiths[5] to [7] to become smiths[3] to [5].

Code	Notes
| ```
smiths = ["Mike", "Mark", "Bob", "Bill",
➡ "Betty", "Sarah", "Sidney", "Jane"];
smiths.splice(3,0, "Fred", "Brenda");
``` | **Adding elements**<br><br>This time we delete zero elements starting from smiths[3], and add two new elements. This is the same as adding two elements starting from index 3, to give you the array shown below, with Fred and Brenda added between Bob and Bill: |

⊟	smiths	
	0	"Mike"
	1	"Mark"
	2	"Bob"
	3	"Fred"
	4	"Brenda"
	5	"Bill"
	6	"Betty"
	7	"Sarah"
	8	"Sidney"
	9	"Jane"

```
integers = [0, 1, 2, 3, 4, 5, 6];
integers.splice(2,2, 90, 91);
```

Replacing Elements

Replacing elements is a delete and an equal replace.

Prior to the splice, integers is equal to:

⊟	integers	
	0	0
	1	1
	2	2
	3	3
	4	4
	5	5
	6	6

Following the splice, it becomes:

⊟	integers	
	0	0
	1	1
	2	90
	3	91
	4	4
	5	5
	6	6

Two elements starting from integers[2] are deleted, and two new elements with values 90 and 91 take their place. The effect as if the values of integers[2] and integers[3] were simply overwritten.

You can also add more or fewer elements than you delete, allowing you to remove/add new elements at the same time as the deletion.

```
integers = [0, 1, 2, 3, 4, 5, 6];
integers2 = [90, 91];
integers.splice(2, 2, integers2);
```

Looking at the last example, you may be fooled into expecting that this code will insert an array integers2 into integers so that you finish with the same end result. In fact, the splice will create a **nested array** by inserting integers2 into integer[2]. Because integers2 counts as a single element, integer[3] ends up being deleted, and the other elements move down to fill the space.

⊟	integers	
	0	0
	1	1
⊟	2	
	0	90
	1	91
	3	4
	4	5
	5	6

Array.toString

```
myString = myArray.toString();
```

where myArray is an array. myString will be returned as all the elements of myArray turned to strings and concatenated, separated by commas.

For example:

```
numbers = [2, 4.5, 6];
numString = numbers.toString();
```

... would give numString = "2,4.5,6"

myString = myArray.toString() is exactly the same as myString = myArray.join() (toString is the same as join using the default argument). See **Array.join()** for more details.

In general, you should use the **join** method in preference to toString because:

- **Array.join()** largely deprecates **Array.toString().**
- **Array.join()** gives you more options as to how the final string will appear.

Array.unshift

```
myNewLength = myArray.unshift(value1, value2, value3,… valueN);
```

Where myArray is an array. One or more new elements with values value1,… valueN are added to the start of myArray, and the new length of myArray is returned as myNewLength.

This method is compatible with **Flash 5 or later**. Note that the **Array.splice** method may provide more array editing options (although it doesn't return the new length of the array, as unshift does).

Description
See the examples below.

Code	Notes

`favoriteGames = ["I-War2", "Unreal`
➥ `Tournament", "Operation`
➥ `Flashpoint"];`
`newLength = FavoriteGames.unshift`
➥ `("Defender", "Galaga");`
	Before the unshift, the length of favoriteGames is 3 and the array contains the following elements:
	
		⊟	favoriteGames	

---	---	---
	0	"I-War2"
	1	"Unreal Tournament"
	2	"Operation Flashpoint" | After the unshift, the array looks like this: | ⊟	favoriteGames	
---	---	---
	0	"Defender"
	1	"Galaga"
	2	"I-War2"
	3	"Unreal Tournament"
	4	"Operation Flashpoint"	 The new array elements have been inserted from favoriteGames[0], and the existing elements have been moved right to accommodate the new data. The new length of the array, 5, is available via variable newLength.

`favoriteGames = ["I-War2", "Unreal`
➥ `Tournament", "Operation Flashpoint"];`
`"Galaga");`
	If you don't need to know the length of the unshifted array, you can modify
	`favoriteGames.unshift`

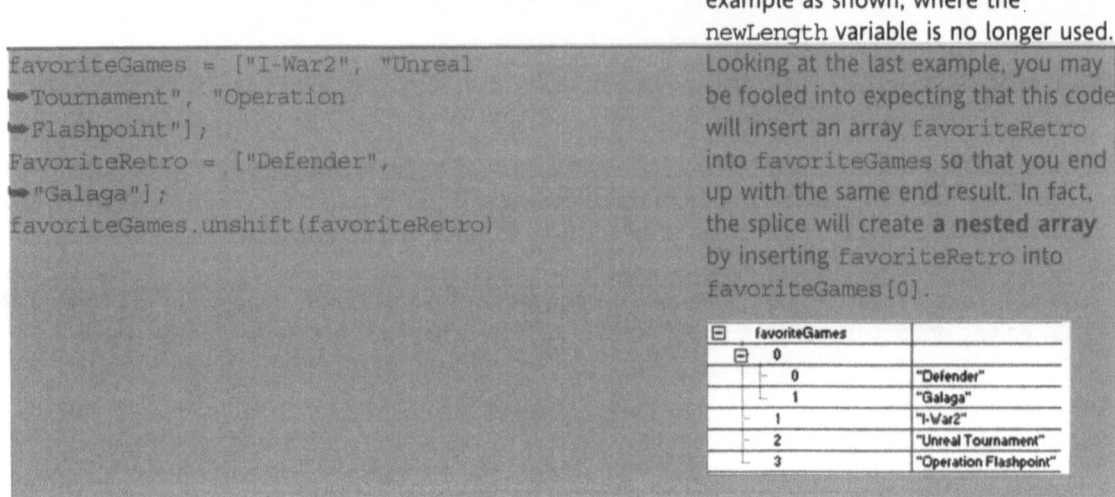

```
favoriteGames = ["I-War2", "Unreal
➥Tournament", "Operation
➥Flashpoint"];
FavoriteRetro = ["Defender",
➥"Galaga"];
favoriteGames.unshift(favoriteRetro)
```

("Defender", the code in the last example as shown, where the newLength variable is no longer used. Looking at the last example, you may be fooled into expecting that this code will insert an array favoriteRetro into favoriteGames so that you end up with the same end result. In fact, the splice will create a **nested array** by inserting favoriteRetro into favoriteGames[0].

favoriteGames		
0		
	0	"Defender"
	1	"Galaga"
	1	"I-War2"
	2	"Unreal Tournament"
	3	"Operation Flashpoint"

ASNative

```
x = ASNative(a, b);
```

or

```
x = ASNative(a, b)(c);
```

Where a, b,and c are *probably* direct references and arguments into hard-coded (native) functions that define how the Flash Player works. It is thought that a is most likely a reference to an internal Flash object or a reference to the internal function(s) that define it, and b and c are references and arguments to the code that handles the functionality for that object.

This action is undocumented and unsupported by Macromedia, and its functionality is open to change. The ASNative action is not normally required in any code, since legal ActionScript calls to the Flash Player usually do the same thing as most known ASNative calls. ASNative does, however, allow access to undocumented or beta functionality.

Description

The ASNative **action** allows direct access to the low-level Flash Player functions normally accessed indirectly by ActionScript. Code using ASNative is not supported, and its operation may change for subsequent point and version releases of the Flash Player. Although this prevents its use in commercial sites, some designers have used this action in the past for home sites and experimental/personal-fun work, (which is why it is included in this reference).

The following `ASNative` calls are the only ones that give the user additional features over standard ActionScript, and have appeared in both the current revision and last revision of the Flash Player (MX and 5):

Code	Notes
`x = ASNative(800, 2)(2);` `y = ASNative(800, 3)(2);`	x is `true` if the right mouse button is down, and `false` if it is up. y is toggled every time the right mouse button is click-released.
`x = ASNative (800, 2)(4);` `y = ASNative (800, 3)(4);`	x is `true` if the mouse middle button (or mouse wheel) is down, and `false` if it is up. y is toggled every time the middle button (or mouse wheel) is click-released.

See the examples `asnative.fla` and `asnative.swf` on the CD.

ASSetPropFlags

```
ASSetPropFlags(Object, properties, protection, permit);
```

Where `Object` is a Flash 6 object (such as `MovieClip`, `Math`, `TextField`, etc), `properties` is the list of properties of the object you want to hide/unhide, `protection` is the new values for property hiding and overwrite access you want to set for the `Object`, and `permit` is a flag that specifies whether or not you can set values to "unprotect".

This is an undocumented action that allows you to make the underlying object structures of ActionScript both visible and accessible to your scripts.

This entry assumes a good understanding of ActionScript and is aimed at advanced users.

Description

Native ActionScript objects (`MovieClip`, `Sound`, `TextField`, `XML`, etc) are hidden from the `for...in` loop, so you cannot search for their properties and methods, and neither can you overwrite them. These protect the user from the intricacies of the underlying language, or from breaking it by making mistakes in their code. That's fine when you are creating content and don't want any distractions from creating code that does the job, but if you want to delve into ActionScript and the Flash player itself for some tinkering and exploration, you may want to access this underlying structure occasionally.

The `ASSetPropFlags` **action** is an undocumented action that allows you to unlock the ActionScript objects so that you can view this structure. Most interestingly, it allows you to unhide *all* methods contained within ActionScript and fish for anything that Macromedia are not telling us about just yet...

You can also use it to hide *your* methods and actions from `for...in`, or protect them from being overwritten or deleted, something that may be useful for creating open source code, such as components (although *they will still be viewable via the debugger*).

The `AssetPropFlags` action has the following arguments:

`AssetPropFlags(object, properties, protection, permit)`

object is the object that you want to work with (or the level in the object tree you want to cycle through with `for...in`)

properties is the list of properties (expressed as strings) that you want to change the hide/overwrite settings for.

- If you want to change all of the properties, specify `null`.
- If you want to change a single property, specify it as a string such as `"myProp"`
- If you want to change a subset of the properties, specify it as a comma delimited array within a string, such as `"myProp1, myProp2, myProp3"`.

protection is a bit pattern that defines what the level of protection on the properties specified in the last argument will be. The last three bits are the active bits:

- bit 0 tells Flash whether the properties should be hidden from `for...in` (1=hidden)
- bit 1 tells Flash whether the properties should be protected from deletion (1=protected)
- bit 2 tells Flash whether the properties should be protected from being overwritten (1=protected)

permit is a flag that allows you to make changes to the default values (i.e. it allows you to set any of the Protection bits to zero for native ActionScript objects). Always set it to `true`.

For example, setting Protection to 4 gives bit2 =1, bit1=0, bit0=0.

B

gotoAndStop()
hitTest()
loadMovie()
loadVariables()
loadVariables()
nextFrame() play()
prevFrame()
removeMovieClip()
setMask() startDrag()
startDrag()
swapDepths()
unloadMovie()
attachMovie()
createEmptyMovieClip()
createTextField()
duplicateMovieClip()
gotoAndPlay()

Boolean

A Boolean can take one of two values, `true` or `false`. An expression will yield `true` if it is logically correct, and `false` if it is logically incorrect. For example:

```
x = 6>2;
y = "cat"=="dog"
```

Would give x as `true` (because 6 is indeed greater than 2), and y would be `false`, because the string cat is not equal to the string dog.

Using Booleans

Booleans are generally used in decision-making structures:

```
if (x){
    // code A
}
while (y<5){
    // code B
}
```

Code block A will only be run if x = `true` (and will therefore not run if x is equal to `false`) and code block B will continue to loop as long as y<5 is a `true` statement (as long as y is less than 5).

Creating Booleans

In general, you never need to define a Boolean object, because there is no difference in practice between a `Boolean` object and a Boolean variable. Flash will convert a Boolean variable into a `Boolean` object itself internally, so in most cases you don't have to worry about `Boolean` objects, and can usually get by simply assuming Boolean variables are `Boolean` objects. In particular, both a `Boolean` object and a Boolean variable can use the methods of the `Boolean` object.

Boolean (as a Constructor and Initializer)

```
a = new Boolean();
```

or

```
b = new Boolean(c);
```

Where a and b are new Boolean objects. c is an argument that may be used to set the new Booleans initial value. It should equate to either `true` or `false`. Note that the rules used to derive the value of c if it is an expression may produce unexpected results (if c = "true", b is false for example), so you are best advised to keep the argument to either `true` or `false` if you use it.

This constructor is compatible with **Flash 5 or later.** There are generally no advantages in creating Boolean objects over creating Boolean variables, and you are very unlikely to ever need to use this constructor.

Description

The Boolean **constructor** is used to construct (and optionally set the initial value of) a new Boolean object. There is, however no advantage of doing this over simply using Boolean variables, not least because all the methods of the Boolean object can be applied to a Boolean variable:

For example, to define a Boolean object called myBool and set it to true, you would use the following code:

```
myBool = new Boolean(true);
```

To create what is to all intents and purposes the same thing, you could simply treat myBool as a variable thus:

```
myBool = true;
```

Code	Notes

`x = new Boolean(true);`
`y = new Boolean();`
`trace(x);`
`trace(y);`
	x = true
	y = false
	
	NB – There is no point using new Boolean(false); because false is the default value.

`a = new Boolean("true");` `trace(a);`	a = false See the dictionary entry for **Boolean (as a function)** for an explanation of this.

Boolean (as a function)

```
a = Boolean(b);
```

Where b is an expression, property, variable, or value that you want to convert to a Boolean. a will be returned as the Boolean value true or false.

This global function is compatible with **Flash 5 and later.**

Description

The Boolean **function** will:

- Assume all strings are `false`, except those that can be converted to a non-zero number.
- Return `false` for `undefined` and zero length strings.
- Return `true` for all non-zero numbers (or expressions that evaluate to non-zero numbers).
- Return `false` for zero.

Code	Notes
`x = Boolean(0);`	`x = false`
`y = Boolean(1.2);`	`y = true`
`z = Boolean(-300);`	`z = true`
`a = Boolean("true");`	`a = false`
`b = Boolean(3<4);`	`b = true`
`c = Boolean("3<4");`	`c = false`
`d = Boolean("-300");`	`d = false`
`e = Boolean("300");`	`e = true`

Boolean.toString

```
a = myBool.toString()
```

Where `myBool` is a Boolean. `a` will be returned as a string containing the Boolean value (`true` or `false`) of `myBool`.

This method is compatible with **Flash 5 or later**.

Description

This is a simple and little used **method**. It is the only way to retrieve the internal value of a `Boolean` object directly as a string, but you will find that you never actually have to do this, assuming you only create Boolean variables (see the entry for **Boolean (as a constructor and initializer)** for an explanation of why this is the case).

Code	Notes
`a = new Boolean(true);` `b = a.toString();`	`b = "true"`
	If you debug this FLA, you will see the following output:

Name	Value
$	"WIN 6,0,21,0"
a	
b	"true"

Note that the value of the Boolean object a cannot be accessed directly, but the value of b can.

```
a = 3;
b = a.toString();
```

b = "3"

Because the String and Number objects also have a toString method, Boolean.toString will **not** automatically force the conversion to assume that a is a Boolean if it turns out to be anything else. **Boolean.toString** cannot therefore convert non-Booleans to the corresponding Boolean value as part of the conversion.

Boolean.valueOf

```
a = myBool.valueOf()
```

Where myBool is a Boolean. a will be returned as the literal Boolean value (true or false) of myBool.

This method is compatible with **Flash 5 or later**.

Description

This is a simple and little used **method**. It is the only way to retrieve the internal and current literal value of a Boolean object directly, but you will find that you never actually have to do this, assuming you only create Boolean variables (see the entry for **Boolean (as a constructor and initializer)** for an explanation of why this is the case).

Code	Notes
`a = New Boolean(true);` `b = a.valueOf();`	b = "true"

If you debug this FLA, you will see the following output:

Name	Value
$	"WIN 6,0,21,0"
a	
b	true

Note that the value of the Boolean object a cannot be accessed directly, but the value of b can.

```
a = 3;
b = a.valueOf();
```

b = "3"

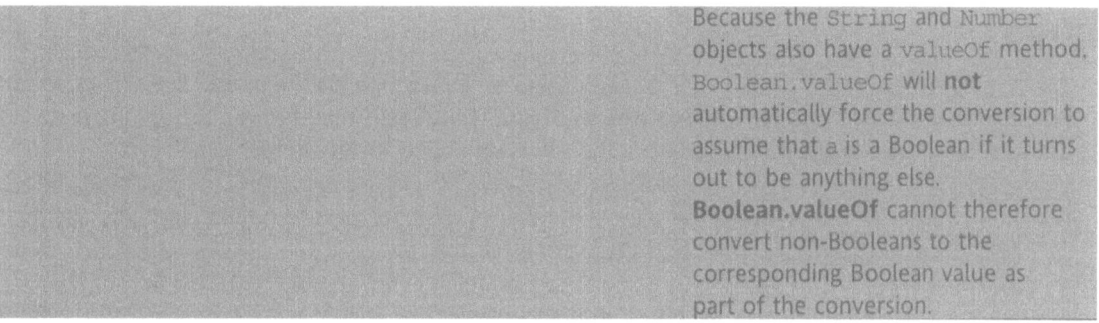

Because the String and Number objects also have a valueOf method, Boolean.valueOf will **not** automatically force the conversion to assume that a is a Boolean if it turns out to be anything else. **Boolean.valueOf** cannot therefore convert non-Booleans to the corresponding Boolean value as part of the conversion.

break

```
break;
```

On encountering a break action during a looping code block (such as a for or while), the rest of the code block (and any remaining loops) will be skipped, and execution will continue from the end of the block onwards.

This action is compatible with **Flash 4 or later**. It is associated with the **for, for... in, do... while**, and **while** loops, and **provides a means of exiting such loops prematurely**. It is usually combined with an **if** action that is used to define the premature exit conditions.

Description

The break **action** allows you to exit a loop at a specific point. See examples below;

Code	Notes
```for (i=0; i<100; i++) { if (i>50) { break; } trace(i) }```	The **for** loop is configured to loop 100 times (i = 0 to 99). It will however only make it to 50 because the **for** will execute the **break** action the first time i is greater than 50.
```x = 3; while (true) { x++; trace(x); if (x>9) { break; } }```	The **while** loop will never exit on its own because its while condition is always true. The break causes an exit when x>9. The loop will run for x = 4 to 10.

See also the example arguments.caller.fla and arguments.caller.swf on the CD.

Button

The Button object is the main means of capturing user interaction via the mouse in Flash. In versions of Flash before Flash MX, **the button was not an object**. This means that the way buttons are used in Flash MX is different (although you can still use the old Flash coding styles without problems).

For the ActionScript programmer, there are a number of basic features to remember if you use the Flash MX style of creating button scripts, and these are listed below.

In Flash MX, the button is now an object and this means that it has many properties and methods in common with the Movie Clip, including size (**Button._height, Button._width, Button._xscale, Button._yscale**), position (**Button._x, Button._y**), alpha (**Button._alpha**), rotation (**Button._rotation**), and visibility (**Button._visibility**).

The most important feature of the Flash MX Button object to the coder is that it now has an instance name. This means that you can now write event handlers (more commonly known as "button scripts") that are not attached to the button directly.

In Flash 5, a button script would typically look like this:

```
on(release){
    gotoAndPlay("myLabel");
}
```

The button that the script is associated with is the button it is attached to.

In Flash 6, if your button has an instance name myButton_btn, you can define the following script to achieve the same thing:

```
myButton_btn.onRelease = function(){
    gotoAndPlay("myLabel");
}
```

or

```
function buttonHandler() {
    gotoAndPlay("myLabel");
}
myButton_btn.onRelease = buttonHandler;
```

This effectively treats the event handler as a general variable (or object) that is linked to the event itself, rather than the Flash 5 version, which treats the event handler as a fixed entity.

The beauty of this form is that you can define this script without it having to be attached to the button directly. This means that you can define all your button scripts in one place (usually frame 1 of _root).

This makes for more readable and potentially modular code. To write scripts in this format you *must* make sure that the button exists on the timeline when you define the button script for it. You should also note that the scope of these scripts is the timeline they are on, and not the timeline the button is on (the scope of a function is always the scope of the timeline it is on unless you use **this**). This can actually make coding *easier* because the scope of your button scripts is the same place (_root) *unless you actively change it with* this. Simply converting Flash 5 scripts to the Flash MX style by changing Flash 5 onCipEvent (SomeEvent) events to Flash 6 MovieClip.onSomeEvent = function style events will not always work; you also have to change the scope by adding this in the Flash 6 event script where it was previously assumed in the Flash 5 script. So:

```
onClipEvent (enterFrame) {
    _x++;
}
```

becomes:

```
myClip.onEnterFrame = function() {
    this._x++;
};
```

In Flash MX, the **Movie Clip** object and components (**FCheckBox, FPushButton, FRadioButton**, along with **FStyleFormat**) can be used to replace or extend basic Button object functionality. In particular, the Movie Clip object can easily be modified to do anything that the Button object can, but it has the advantages of its own timeline and a *far* richer set of methods.

The Button object is also harder to debug when you are using advanced ActionScript, because although you can assign local variables to a button, they are not accessible *and* there is no **Button.valueOf** method to make such values accessible. This means that you can only see them in the debugger if you assign them to a variable on a movie clip timeline (which is a rather large work around if you have many buttons!).

The only other way to see the value of a variable local to a button is if you use **trace** to send the value to the Output window during testing. This issue can quickly become non-trivial with large ActionScript heavy sites, because the internal values held by a Button object are hidden from you unless you take the time to explicitly track them.

The button remains useful because of its simplicity and ease of implementation, particularly where basic website navigation or simple mouse detection is required.

Button._alpha

```
my_btn._alpha = a;
b = my_btn._alpha;
```

Where a is the value you want to assign to the button alpha value.

b is a variable that is equated to the current value of the buttons alpha value.
The alpha value range is from 0 to 100 (see below for a special exception).

This property is compatible with **Flash 6 or later**. When using previous versions of Flash, buttons are not objects and do not therefore have properties.

Description

The _alpha **property** of a button defines the button's alpha setting, and this can range between 0 (fully transparent) and 100% (fully solid) per pixel. The _alpha property is **read/write**.

Code	Button appearance	Notes
my_btn._alpha = 0;		Button is fully transparent
my_btn._alpha = 25;		Button is approximately 25% opaque.
my_btn._alpha = 50;		Button is approximately 50% opaque.
my_btn._alpha = 100;		Button is solid and fully opaque.
my_btn._alpha = 1000;		A little known trick; super high values of alpha setting provide a high contrast effect if your graphics are composed of gradient and radial fills that have varying alpha. This occurs because the alpha value is *per pixel*. See also the *Tips and precautions* section (on the CD)
my_btn._alpha = -50;		Negative values of _alpha are rendered as if they were 0%.

See the examples button._alpha.fla and button._alpha.swf on the CD.

Button._height

```
instanceName._height = a;
b = instanceName._height;
```

Where instanceName is the instance name of a button, and a is the value you want to assign to the button's height in pixels.

b is a variable that is equated to the current value of the button's `_height` property value.

This property is compatible with **Flash 6 or later**. When using previous versions of Flash, buttons are not objects and do not therefore have properties.

Description

The `_height` **property** of a button defines the buttons current height in pixels. The `_height` property is **read/write**.

In many cases, the **_xscale** and **_yscale** properties of the `Button` object are more useful to the Motion Graphics programmer, and the `_height` (and **_width**) property is less used.

Code	Button appearance	Notes
		Initial appearance of button `my_btn`.

`my_btn.onRollOver =`
`function() {`
   `this._height += 40;`
`};`
		If `my_btn` is rolled over with the mouse, the height of `my_btn` will increase by 40pixels, resulting in a stretched appearance.

See the examples `button._height.fla` and `button._height.swf` on the CD.

Button._highquality

```
instanceName._highquality = a;
b = instanceName._highquality;
```

Where `instanceName` is the instance name of a button, and a is the `_quality` value you want to apply to the whole FLA. b is a variable that is equated to the current value of the FLA's `_highquality`.

This global property is compatible with **Flash 6 or later**. It allows you to set the quality that the Flash render engine works to when drawing graphics. More specifically, it allows control of the pixel anti-aliasing (or pixel smoothing) applied. When using previous versions of Flash, buttons are not objects and do not therefore have properties.

The **MovieClip._highquality**, **Button._highquality**,and **TextField._highquality** properties are identical to the Flash 4 (and above) global property, **_highquality**, and you are recommended to use **_highquality** if compatibility is an issue.

The related action **toggleHighQuality** and properties **_quality** and **Button._highquality** also allow you to fine control the rendering quality that the Flash Player works to in drawing graphics to the stage during runtime. These properties should generally be used in preference to **Button._highquality** because of the greater levels of control they allow.

Description

The _highquality **property** of a running SWF can be accessed/set as a property of the Button object, and is also available as a property of the **Movie Clip** or **TextField** objects. In short, the _highquality property is available as a property of *all the graphic objects available in Flash*. It is important to realize that when applied to any such object, the _highquality property is applied to *everything on the stage, including Movie Clips, Buttons, TextFields, and any other graphics.*

A fuller description of aliasing and anti-aliasing is presented in the entry for **Button._quality**. Refer to that entry for further details.

Code	Rendered quality	Notes
`my_btn._highquality` `= 0;`		This is the lowest quality setting available via ActionScript. No anti-aliasing (pixel smoothing) will take place, and "jaggies" will result. This setting gives the fastest performance. This setting corresponds to the low quality setting in the Publish Settings window. This setting is best used when you are creating FLAs for low performance devices (which may include PDA devices). It is also useful when writing retro Flash games (or websites with the same design influences), where the chunky pixilated feel is a definite advantage!
`my_btn._highquality` `= 1;`		This is the middle available quality setting via _highquality. No anti-aliasing (pixel smoothing) will take place on moving bitmaps, but anti-aliasing is applied to everything else. This setting corresponds to the high quality setting in the Publish Settings window.
`my_btn._highquality` `= 2;`		This is the highest available quality setting via ActionScript. Anti-aliasing is applied to everything on the stage. This setting is exactly the same as the

last example, except that bitmaps are always smoothed.

This setting corresponds to the best quality setting in the Publish Settings window.

This setting is best used for largely static displays.

| ```
myFirst_btn._highquality
= 2;
mySecond_btn._highquality =
1;
myFirst_mc._highquality
= 0;
``` | This code is attempting to apply individual quality settings to individual graphic objects. The _highquality setting is a *global* property; everything will always use the last setting seen. |

Button._name

```
this._name = a;
```

Where this is the currently scoped button instance, a is returned as a string containing the instance name of the currently scoped button instance.

This property is compatible with **Flash 6 or later**. Previous versions of Flash do not treat buttons as objects, and buttons do not therefore have this property. This property can be read as well as written to, although there are no reasons you would ever want to change a button's name (and the syntax to do this is therefore not shown – although it is seen below).

Description

The _name **property** of a button defines the button's instance name. There is generally only one reason you would want to use this property: when you have applied the same button event handler to a number of buttons, and you are using the _name property to differentiate between them.

Code	Notes
| ```
function pressHandler() {
   message = "you pressed "+this._name;
   trace(message);
}
button1.onRelease = pressHandler;
button2.onRelease = pressHandler;
button3.onRelease = pressHandler;
``` | The same event handler is applied to three button instances. The event handler needs to differentiate between the three buttons it is attached to, and it does this by looking at the _name, which is the only thing that *must* be different even if every other property of the three buttons is identical. |

```
x = my_btn._name;
```

There is never any reason to do this, because you already know the _name of the button (my_btn) and you actually need to know the _name property to be able to access the _name property!

See the examples button._name.fla and button._name.swf on the CD.

Button._parent

```
instanceName._parent;
```

Where instanceName is the instance name of a button. The instanceName._parent combination forms a relative path to the parent object of instanceName.

This property is compatible with **Flash 6 or later**. Previous versions of Flash do not treat buttons as objects, and buttons do not therefore have this property. This property is **read only**. Because a button event script usually scopes the button's parent timeline if you use Flash MX style event scripts, and *always* scopes the button's parent timeline in Flash 5, you will rarely have to refer to this property.

Description

The _parent of a button instance returns the name of the timeline the button is embedded on (NB – although you *can* embed buttons into other buttons, the practice has no merits and you should not do this). The _parent timeline is usually a movie clip (in which case the _parent will be an instance name corresponding to this Movie Clip) or the **_root** timeline of the current level (in which case _parent will be _leveln where n is the level number). You can refer to the _parent property more than once to see the _parent._parent, and so on.

```
my_btn._parent
```

refers to the timeline the button my_btn is on.

```
my_btn._parent.parent
```

refers to the parent of the timeline the button is on

Code	Notes

`my_btn.onRelease = function() {`
`_x++;`
`};`
	The first script accesses the _parent timelines _x property, and will move it one pixel to the right every time you press the button my_btn.

`my_btn.onRelease = function() {` `this._x++;`	The second script is actually identical because of the implied scope of the

event script, it doesn't need to refer to the my_btn._parent path (because the event script is already scoping it). This is the normal situation, and there are therefore few reasons you ever need to use Button._parent.

Button._quality

```
instanceName._quality = a;
b = instanceName._quality;
```

Where instanceName is the instance name of a button, and a is the quality value you want to apply to the whole FLA. b is a variable that is equated to the current value of the FLA's _quality setting. The _quality setting is a measure of the anti-aliasing applied by Flash.

This global property is compatible with **Flash 6 or later**. When using previous versions of Flash, buttons are not objects and do not therefore have properties. The **MovieClip._quality**, **Button._quality**, and **TextField._quality** properties are identical to the Flash 4 (and above) global property, **_quality**, and you are recommended to use this form of the property if compatibility is an issue.

The related action **toggleHighQuality** allows an easy way to toggle smoothing. The related **Button._highquality** also allows some control, but you are advised to use _quality or Button.quality instead because these allow finer control.

Description

The _quality **property** of a running SWF can be accessed as a property of the Button object, and is also available as a property of the **MovieClip** or **TextField** objects. In short, the _quality property is available as a property of *all the graphic objects available in Flash*. It is important to realize that when applied to any such object, the _quality property is applied to everything on the stage, including Movie Clips, Buttons, TextFields, and any other graphics.

Aliasing is a form of noise seen in an electronic audio signal and the math that defines it comes from signal processing theories (particularly digital signal processing). Aliasing errors in graphics are the visual form of the audio noise that makes your voice sound more mechanical than it actually is when heard on a telephone line, and this process is generally known as *under-sampling*. It is caused by trying to replicate a signal with less data than is seen in the original. It is caused in graphics by trying to reproduce an image using less pixels than are needed to reproduce it adequately to fool the human eye. The process of reducing aliasing error (or hiding it) is called *anti-aliasing*.

The anti-aliasing used by Flash is based on an *averaging* algorithm. This tries to hide the fact that any image is built up of pixels by averaging the color of adjacent pixels. This hides the pixels due to blending (or to put it another way, "makes the image look like it consists of more data than it actually does"). The output becomes smoother the more pixels you use in the averaging process, but this can also reduce detail due to the smoothing.

Flash can be set up to use different levels of anti-aliasing:

- No anti-aliasing
- 2x2 grid
- 4x4 grid

No anti-aliasing

No anti-aliasing results in the blockiest image, but is also the one that gives maximum clarity and the sharpest image. When using small text fonts, no anti-aliasing results in the sharpest (and therefore most readable) text. The downside is that you can see the individual pixels that make up the screen, and this feature is referred to as "staircasing" or "jaggies".

2x2 grid

If you use all pixels adjacent to each target pixel, you are said to be using a 2x2 anti-aliasing pixel grid;

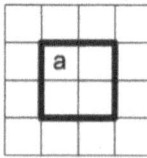

Each pixel position, a, is averaged with the three neighbors as shown, starting from the top left corner of the screen, top to bottom and left to right. Although the pixel a doesn't at first appear to be averaged with its neighbors above and to the left of it, remember that these pixel positions will already have been averaged when taking into account the pixel grids of other pixels to the left and above of a.

The cumulative effects of the averaging on each individual pixel a after all the pixels have been aliased, will actually add up so the effect statistically is as if you used a 3x3 grid, with pixel a at the center (or "anti-alias by one pixel in any direction from a"). The effects of anti-aliasing do in fact extend beyond the statistical 3x3 grid. This effect depends on how much you allow adjacent pixels to affect the color of your target pixel a, and this is something called the *weighting*, but the immediate neighbors to a in the 3x3 grid are the ones that will have the greatest effect.

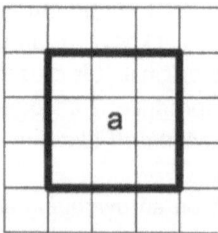

Using a 2x2 grid corresponds to the MEDIUM quality setting in Flash.

4x4 grid

The same principle occurs if you use a 4x4 grid. The effective statistical grid of neighboring pixels that have a strong effect on a is a 7x7 grid with a at its center (or "anti-alias by three pixels in any direction from a"). Although the math that proves this is beyond the scope of this book, you can see intuitively why this should be so:

- The top left corner of the 7x7 grid contains the farthest away pixel that uses a in it's own 4x4 pixel grid, so it is the farthest away pixel that is affected by pixel a.
- The bottom right corner of the 7x7 grid contains the farthest away pixel that a uses in its own 4x4 pixel grid, and so is the farthest away pixel that directly affects the anti-aliasing of pixel a.
- These two farthest away pixels form the diagonal of the effective statistical grid.

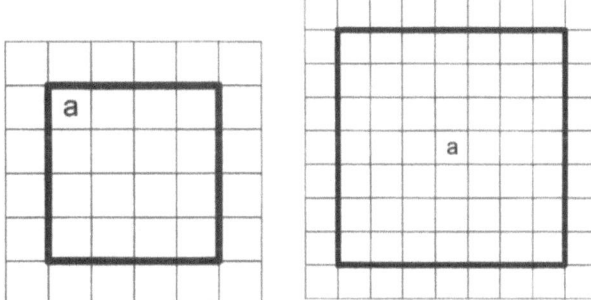

Using a 4x4 grid corresponds to the HIGH anti-aliasing quality setting in Flash.

You should note that **the anti-aliasing setting is not the only thing that affects the final appearance of the graphics seen in Flash**. There are three other issues that can affect appearance, and these are:

- **The user's screen resolution**. Although you cannot change this, you can find out what it is via the **Capabilites object**, and tailor your _quality setting accordingly.
- **The position of Flash's virtual screen co-ordinates** in relation to the true pixels used by your hardware. This relationship can be seen in the authoring environment as the **pixel snap grid**, and this has a very strong effect on anti-aliasing.
- The color scheme you use can affect the contrast between pixels. A low contrast color scheme makes "jaggies" less prominent before anti-aliasing, so you may be able to get away with a lower anti-aliasing setting.

See the *Tips and precautions* section (on the CD) for further discussion on these issues.

Code	Rendered quality	Notes
`my_btn._quality = "LOW";`		This is the lowest quality setting available via ActionScript. No anti-aliasing (pixel smoothing) will take

place, and "jaggies" will result. This setting gives the fastest performance.

This setting is the same as the Low quality setting in the Publish Settings window.

This setting is best used when you are creating FLAs for low performance devices (which may include PDA devices).

It is also useful when writing retro Flash games (or websites with the same design influences), where the chunky pixilated feel is a definite advantage!

```
my_btn._quality =
"MEDIUM;
```

This is the lowest available anti-aliased quality setting via ActionScript. No anti-aliasing (pixel smoothing) will take place on bitmaps, but anti-aliasing is applied to everything else.

This setting corresponds to the Medium quality setting in the Publish Settings window.

The difference between this setting and High quality is not normally apparent if your graphics are all moving constantly, even though this setting is actually of a lower quality.

```
my_btn._quality =
"HIGH";
```

This is the highest available quality setting via ActionScript. Anti-aliasing is applied to everything on the stage. This setting is exactly the same as the last example, except that bitmaps are always smoothed.

This setting corresponds to the High quality setting in the Publish Settings window. Because anti-aliasing is a smoothing effect, you may lose sharpness in the final image, particularly if your image has very small details.

```
my_btn._quality =
"BEST";
```

This is the highest available quality setting via ActionScript. Anti-aliasing is applied to everything on the stage. This setting is exactly the same as the last example, except that bitmaps are always smoothed.

This setting corresponds to the Best quality setting in the Publish Settings window. It is only different to the High setting in the way it deals with bitmaps. Bitmaps are *always* smoothed, and you may therefore prefer to use this setting if your presentation has large areas of static bitmaps (such as an online portfolio).

You should note however, that this setting is the most computationally expensive, and will slow down any animations considerably.

```
myFirst_btn._quality =
"LOW";
mySecond_btn._highquality
= "BEST";
myFirst_mc._highquality
= "LOW";
```

This code is attempting to apply individual quality settings to individual graphic objects. The _quality setting is a *global* property; everything will always use the last setting seen.

See the examples button._quality.fla and button._quality.swf on the CD.

Button._rotation

```
instanceName._rotation = a;
b = instanceName._rotation;
```

Where instanceName is the instance name of a button, and a is the value you want to assign to the button's rotation in pixels. b is a variable that is equated to the current value of the button's _rotation property value.

This property is compatible with **Flash 6 or later**. When using previous versions of Flash, buttons are not objects and do not therefore have properties. You should note that the _rotation value is expressed in **degree** measure, whereas the angles returned by the trigonometrical methods of the **Math** object are expressed in radian measure.

Description

The _rotation **property** of a button defines the button's current height in pixels. The _rotation property is **read/write**.

The rotation value range is from 0 to 360. A value of 0 is the same as 360, and additional multiples of 360 will result in the same rotation because of the nature of rotational measure. An equivalent measure can be specified in the opposite direction (0 to -360). A positive angle represents a clockwise turn, and a negative angle represents a counter-clockwise turn.

Code	Button appearance	Notes
		Initial appearance of button my_btn.
my_btn._rotation = 45;		The button is rotated by 45 degrees. This is a 45/360 or 1/8 turn in the clockwise direction.
my_btn._rotation = 180;		The button is rotated by 180 degrees. This is a 180/360 or a 1/2 turn in the clockwise direction.
my_btn._rotation = -45;		The button is rotated by -45 degrees. This is a 45/360 or 1/8 turn in the counter-clockwise direction. Compare the end result with the 45 degree turn above.
my_btn._rotation = 360;		The button is rotated by 360 degrees. This is a 360/360 turn or a full turn in the clockwise direction. The button will take up the rotational orientation that it was at 0 degrees. You would reach the same position if you rotated by -360 degrees.

See the examples button._rotation.fla and button._rotation.swf on the CD.

Button._soundbuftime

```
InstanceName._soundbuftime = a;
b = InstanceName._soundbuftime;
```

Where instanceName is the instance name of a button, and a is the _soundbuftime value you want to apply to the whole FLA. a has to be an integer. b is a variable that is equated to the current value of the

FLA's _soundbuftime setting. The _soundbuftime setting is the amount of a streaming sound that has to have been downloaded (in whole seconds) before a streaming sound will begin to play.

This global property is compatible with **Flash 6 or later**. When using previous versions of Flash, buttons are not objects and do not therefore have properties. The **MovieClip._soundbuftime**, **Button._soundbuftime**, and **TextField._soundbuftime** properties are identical to the Flash 4 (and above) global property, **_soundbuftime**, and you are recommended to use this form of the property if compatibility is an issue.

Description

The Button._soundbuftime **property** is the size of the global streaming sound buffer. The Flash Player will wait until the required amount of sound (in seconds) has been downloaded before the sound will begin to play. The default value of Button._soundbuftime is 5 seconds.

Code	Notes
`my_btn._soundbuftime = 10;`	Sets the streaming sound buffer to 10s.

`b1_btn._soundbuftime = 6;`
`b2_btn._soundbuftime = 8;`
`_root._soundbuftime = 12;`
	This code is attempting to apply individual sound buffer settings to individual graphic objects. The _soundbuftime setting is a *global* property; everything will always use the last setting seen.

Button._target

```
a = instanceName._target;
```

Where instanceName is the button instance name, a is returned as a string containing the target path (in Flash 4 "slash" notation).

This property is compatible with **Flash 6 or later**. Previous versions of Flash do not treat buttons as objects, and buttons do not therefore have this property. This property is **read only**.

Description

The _target **property** of a button defines the buttons absolute target path in the Flash 4 slash notation. The target path of a button is the absolute reference that differentiates each individual button. It includes two things:

- The *path* to the button.
- The *instance name* of the button.

You can find out the path to a button by using the **Insert Target Path** window (access is by clicking on the "crosshair" icon on the Actions window). Select the **Slashes** and **Absolute** radio buttons as shown below. The resulting reference shown in the **Target** window is the value that the _target property will be for any button instance (or any Movie Clip or TextField, given that they also have a _target property).

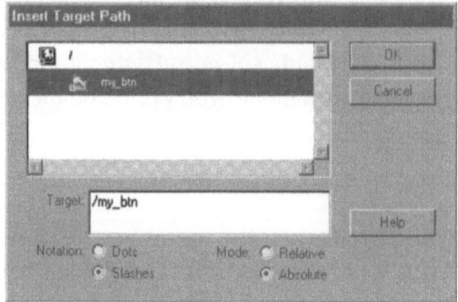

The only significant use of slash notation over dot notation is that the Flash Player will work slightly faster if you use it for simple tasks that do not require the additional features of dot notation, and this is probably because slash notation uses lower level code to work. Dot notation is more flexible and easier to use, and the extra features that give you this, result in a slight performance loss. As you shall see below, the effects of this performance increase, when considering other issues, may be negligible in most real life applications.

Code	Notes
```function disableMe(instance) { tellTarget (instance) { enabled = false; } } my_btn.onRelease = function() { disableMe(this._target); }; myOther_btn.onRelease = function() { disableMe(this._target); };```	Slash notation is associated with Flash 4, and this means that the only real way to use a slash notation target path (without introducing all sorts of shortcuts and fudges) is to use deprecated Flash 4 actions that recognize it.

The top script shows some code that causes two buttons to become disabled when they have been pressed once, and to do this it uses a general function disableMe().
This code not only uses deprecated and superceded actions (**tellTarget**) to recognize slash notation, it also ignores at least one major advantage the latest version of Flash (the ability to treat events and functions as variables (or objects) and equate them directly). |

of

```
function disableMe(instance) {
    this.enabled = false;
}
my_btn.onRelease = disableMe;
myOther_btn.onRelease = disableMe;
```

So, although slash notation is faster than dot notation, most recent and well written Flash code is usually faster overall because it requires less additional lines of code (as shown in the second block of code).

Button._url

```
a = instanceName._url;
```

Where `instanceName` is the instance name of a button. `a` will be returned as a string value holding the absolute path of the SWF that contains the button.

This global property is compatible with **Flash 6 or later**. When using previous versions of Flash, buttons are not objects and do not therefore have properties. This property is **read only**.

Description

The `_url` **property** returns the absolute address (including the name of the SWF file) of the SWF that contains the button. You can use this value to find out:

- The location the SWF is being run from.
- The name of the SWF.

A typical `_url` value for a SWF that was running from "my domain", www.mydomain.com, might be:

```
"http://www.mydomain.com/test.swf"
```

This would remain the same if I ran the same file from my browser cache (this would also occur quite normally if a visitor went back to my site soon after the initial visit, and the SWF was still in their browser cache).

If the visitor took it upon themselves to copy my SWF from their browser cache and placed it on their Windows machine's desktop folder, the `_url` would now be equal to:

```
"file://C:\WINDOWS\Desktop\test.swf"
```

And my SWF could quite legitimately assume it was about to be tampered with!

Code	Notes

`if (my_btn._url.slice(0, 4) != "http") {`
`    trace("oh no you dont!");`
`    // do something here to stop the swf`
	If the first four characters of the button `_url` property are not `http`, then your SWF has been moved from

```
}
```

the browser cache before being run. It may be wise to stop the SWF from running so that if it is being hacked by a SWF editing tool, at least you gave it your best shot at making life difficult for the hacker, and tried your best to protect your client's copyright.

Putting this sort of code somewhere that is not obvious (not on frame 1 of _root) and in a place where it is only run occasionally may make the hackers life more difficult still.

Consider unloading any loaded levels, going to the last frame and then sending program execution into a forever **while** loop as the "do something here to stop the SWF..." bit.

This would of course cause *you* problems if you added this functionality whilst still involved in development, so make sure you disable this protection when you are making legitimate modifications to the FLAs!

See also **String.slice**.

See the examples `button._url.fla` and `button._url.swf` on the CD.

Button._visible

```
instanceName._visible = a;
b = instanceName._visible;
```

Where `instanceName` is the instance name of a button, and `a` is the value you want to assign to the buttons viability (`true` for visible, and `false` for not visible). `b` is a variable that is equated to the current value of the button's visibility property value (`true` or `false`).

This property is compatible with **Flash 6 or later**. When using previous versions of Flash, buttons are not objects and do not therefore have properties.

Description

The `Button._visibility` **property** is somewhat misnamed since it does more than just decide whether a button can be seen or not. Setting `Button._visibility = false` is different to setting the `_alpha` property to `0`, because the `_visibility` property doesn't just draw the button at "zero visibility". Rather, it *doesn't draw the button at all!* See the *Tips and precautions* section (on the CD) to see the implications of this.

Code	Notes
`my_btn._visible = false;` `myOther_btn._visible = true;`	The button instance `my_btn` will no longer be drawn on stage. It will not be able to respond to most mouse-based events, and you can assume that it is effectively disabled as well as invisible. You can still make changes to it (such as changing its position via its `_x` and `_y` properties), and these will be remembered and reflected when you make the button visible again.
	The button instance `myOther_btn` has been made visible, and will operate as a normal button.

See the examples `button._visible.fla` and `button._visible.swf` on the CD.

Button._width

```
instanceName._width = a;
b = instanceName._width;
```

Where `instanceName` is the instance name of a button, and `a` is the value you want to assign to the buttons width in pixels. `b` is a variable that is equated to the current value of the button's `_width` property value.

This property is compatible with **Flash 6 or later**. When using previous versions of Flash, buttons are not objects and do not therefore have properties.

Description

The `_width` **property** of a button defines the buttons current width in pixels. The `_width` property is **read/write**.

In many cases, the **_xscale** and **_yscale** properties of the `Button` object are more useful to the Motion Graphics programmer, and the `_width` (and **_height**) property is less used.

Code	Button appearance	Notes
		Initial appearance of button my_btn.

`my_btn.onRollOver =`
`function() {`
`this._width += 40;`
`};`
		If my_btn is rolled over with the mouse, the width of my_btn will increase by 40 pixels, resulting in a stretched appearance.

See the examples `button._width.fla` and `button._width.swf` on the CD.

Button._x

```
instanceName._x = a;
b = instanceName._x;
```

Where `instanceName` is the instance name of a button, and a is the value you want to assign to the buttons _x value. b is a variable that is equated to the current value of the button's _x property value.

This property is compatible with **Flash 6 or later**. When using previous versions of Flash, buttons are not objects and do not therefore have properties. The `Button._x` property defines the button x co-ordinate on the stage.

Description
The `Button._x` **property** defines the x co-ordinate of the button. This property can be used to dynamically position a button on the stage.

Code	Button appearance	Notes
		Initial appearance of button my_btn.

`my_btn.onRelease =`
`function() {`
`    this._x += 40;`
`};`
		If my_btn is click-released, the button will move 40 pixels to the right.
		
		Normally however, you want to use the Button._x property to produce much smoother animation than sudden single frame movements. See the *Examples and practical uses* section (on the CD).

See the examples `button._x.fla` and `button._x.swf` on the CD.

Button._xmouse

```
a = instanceName._xmouse;
```

Where `instanceName` is the instance name of a button, and `a` is the value you want to assign to the button's `_xmouse` value.

This property is compatible with **Flash 6 or later**. When using previous versions of Flash, buttons are not objects and do not therefore have properties. The `Button._xmouse` property defines the x-axis co-ordinate of the mouse position, relative to the registration point of the `Button` object. You will rarely need to know this because you already know the mouse position implicitly when a `Button` event script runs; *it is over the button!*

Description

The `Button._xmouse` **property** defines the x-axis co-ordinate of the mouse position, relative to the registration point of the `Button` object. This measurement is shown in the following drawing. A point worth noting though, is that the button script will not become active *unless* the mouse position also happens to be in the mouse hit area so the effective area where you can detect the mouse position is actually very limited; it is the black hit area (an example of which for our button, is also shown below):

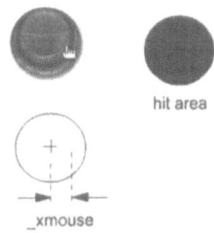

hit area

_xmouse

You will rarely need to know this because you already know the mouse position; it is over the button. Further, you can only run a button script on change of a button event *rather than every frame*. This means that you can typically only know the mouse position in a very limited number of cases:

- When the mouse first enters the hit area (for example, `onRollover`).
- When the mouse leaves the hit area (`onRollOut`).
- When the button is down (`onPress`).
- When the button is released (`onRelease`).

In particular, you cannot use the `Button._xmouse` property to:

- Know the mouse position every frame.
- Know the mouse position every frame when the mouse is in the button hit area.

This severely limits the usefulness of `Button._xmouse`. You are better off using the **MovieClip._xmouse** property instead, and/or using the movie clip as a button.

Code	Notes

```my_btn.onRelease = function() {```
```trace(this._xmouse);```
```};```
	If `my_btn` is click-released, the script will send the current `_xmouse` value to the Output window. As discussed above, this value is not normally useful.

```my_mc.onEnterFrame = function() {```
```trace(my_btn._xmouse);```
```};```
	This script uses an `onEnterFrame` script from a movie clip to constantly read the button `_xmouse` property.
	
	Although slightly more useful than the last example, there is really no need to use the `Button._xmouse` property here. You might as well stick with the `_xmouse` property of the movie clip `my_mc`, because you can then generalize to create better code. You can refer to `this._xmouse` instead, and this will return the `_xmouse` property of the currently scoped movie clip.

Button._xscale

```
instanceName._xscale = a;
b = instanceName._xscale;
```

Where `instanceName` is the instance name of a button, and a is the value you want to assign to the button's xscale in percent. b is a variable that is equated to the current value of the button's xscale property value

This property is compatible with **Flash 6 or later**. When using previous versions of Flash, buttons are not objects and do not therefore have properties.

Description

The `_xscale` **property** of a button defines the button's current width in percent. A value of 100% will result in a width measurement equal to the button instance in the library window. The `Button._width` property can be changed in two ways:

- By manual scaling of an instance on the stage.
- By changing the `Button._xscale` property via ActionScript.

Changing the width of the Button symbol in the library window will *not* change the _xscale property, which will remain at 100% (although it will change the **Button._width** property, which is an absolute measurement in pixels).

The _xscale property is **read/write**.

In many cases, the **_xscale** and **_yscale** properties of the Button object are more useful to the Motion Graphics programmer, and the **_width** and **_height** properties are less used.

Code	Button appearance	Notes
		Initial appearance of button my_btn.
`my_btn.onRollOver = function() { this._xscale += 40; };`		If my_btn is rolled over with the mouse, the xscale of my_btn will increase by 40, resulting in a stretched appearance.

See the examples button._x.fla and button._x.swf on the CD.

Button._y

```
instanceName._y = a;
b = instanceName._y;
```

Where instanceName is the instance name of a button, and a is the value you want to assign to the buttons _y value. b is a variable that is equated to the current value of the button's _y property value.

This property is compatible with **Flash 6 or later**. When using previous versions of Flash, buttons are not objects and do not therefore have properties. The Button._y property defines the button y co-ordinate on the stage.

Description
The Button._y **property** defines the y co-ordinate of the button. This property can be used to dynamically position a button on the stage.

Code	Button appearance	Notes
		Initial appearance of button my_btn.
`my_btn.onRelease = function() { this._y += 40;`		If my_btn is click-released, the button will move 40 pixels downwards

```
};
```

Normally however, you want to use the `Button._y` property to produce much smoother animation than sudden single frame movements. See the *Examples and practical uses* section (on the CD).

See the examples `button._y.fla` and `button._y.swf` on the CD.

Button._ymouse

```
a = instanceName._ymouse;
```

Where `instanceName` is the instance name of a button, and a is the value you want to assign to the button's _ymouse value.

This property is compatible with **Flash 6 or later**. When using previous versions of Flash, buttons are not objects and do not therefore have properties. The `Button._ymouse` property defines the y-axis co-ordinate of the mouse position, relative to the registration point of the `Button` object. You will rarely need to know this because you already know the mouse position implicitly when a `Button` event script runs: *it is over the button!*

Description

The `Button._ymouse` **property** defines the y-axis co-ordinate of the mouse position, relative to the registration point of the `Button` object. This measurement is shown in the following drawing. A point worth noting though, is that the button script will not become active *unless* the mouse position also happens to be in the mouse hit area so the effective area you can detect the mouse position is actually very limited; it is the black hit area (an example of which follows):

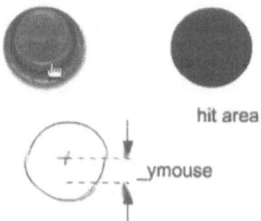

You will rarely need to know this because you already know the mouse position; it is over the button. Further, you can only run a button script on change of a button event *rather than every frame*. This means that you can typically only know the mouse position in a very limited number of cases:

- When the mouse first enters the hit area (for example, `onRollover`).
- When the mouse leaves the hit area (e.g. `onRollOut`).
- When the button is down (`onPress`).
- When the button is released (`onRelease`).

In particular, you cannot use the `Button._ymouse` property to:

- Know the mouse position every frame.
- Know the mouse position every frame when the mouse is in the button hit area.

This severely limits the usefulness of `Button._ymouse`. You are better off using the **MovieClip._ymouse** property instead, and/or using the movie clip as a button.

Code	Notes
```my_btn.onRelease = function() { trace(this._ymouse); };```	If my_btn is click-released, the script will send the current _ymouse value to the Output window. As discussed above, this value is not normally useful.
```my_mc.onEnterFrame = function() { trace(my_btn._ymouse); };```	This script uses an `onEnterFrame` script from a movie clip to constantly read the button _ymouse property. Although slightly more useful than the last example, there is really no need to use the `Button._ymouse` property here. You might as well stick with the _ymouse property of the movie clip my_mc, because you can then generalize to create better code. You can refer to `this._ymouse` instead, and this will return the _ymouse property of the currently scoped movie clip.

Button._yscale

```
instanceName._yscale = a;
b = instanceName._yscale;
```

Where `instanceName` is the instance name of a button, and a is the value you want to assign to the button's `yscale` in percent. b is a variable that is equated to the current value of the button's `yscale` property value.

This property is compatible with **Flash 6 or later**. When using previous versions of Flash, buttons are not objects and do not therefore have properties.

Description

The _yscale **property** of a button defines the buttons current height in percent. A value of 100% will result in a height measurement equal to the button instance in the library window. The `Button._yscale` property can be changed in two ways:

- By manual scaling of an instance on the stage.
- By changing the `Button._yscale` property via ActionScript.

Changing the height of the Button symbol in the library window will *not* change the _yscale property, which will remain at 100% (although it will change the **Button._height** property, which is an absolute measurement in pixels).

The _yscale property is **read/write**.

In many cases, the **_xscale** and **_yscale** properties of the `Button` object are more useful to the Motion Graphics programmer, and the **_width** and **_height** properties are less used.

Code	Button appearance	Notes
		Initial appearance of button my_btn.

`my_btn.onRollOver =`
`function() {`
`my_btn    this._yscale += 40;`
`};`
		If my_btn is rolled over with the mouse, the _yscale property of will increase by 40, resulting in a stretched appearance.

See the examples `button._yscale.fla` and `button._yscale.swf` on the CD.

Button.enabled

```
instanceName.enabled = a;
b = instanceName.enabled;
```

Where `instanceName` is the instance name of a button, and a is the value you want to assign to the button's enabled property (`true` for enabled, and `false` for not enabled). b is a variable that is equated to the current value of the button's enabled property value (`true` or `false`).

This property is compatible with **Flash 6 or later**. When using previous versions of Flash, buttons are not objects and do not therefore have properties.

Description

The `Button.enabled` **property** allows you to enable or disable a button. When enabled, the button will work as normal. When disabled, the button will:

- Stop responding to events, which means that any scripts you have attached to it will no longer execute.
- Cease to animate between its button states when you interact with it via the mouse.
- Not change the mouse pointer to a hand during roll overs.

The button will still allow you to access its properties, so you can still (for example) move the button about if you vary its _x and _y properties; the button doesn't simply "freeze" or start to act as if it is a graphic symbol. All that becomes disabled is the high level Button functions, and *not the low level property based functionality*. The button will continue to work as normal if you subsequently set the enabled property back to true.

Code	Notes
| ```
my_btn.onRelease = function() {
this.enabled = false;
};
myOther_btn.onRelease = function() {
my_btn.enabled = true;
};
``` | If click-released, the button instance my_btn will cease to respond.<br><br>If you click-release the button instance, this will:<br><br>- do nothing to my_btn if it is enabled.<br>- re-enable if it is currently disabled. |

See the examples button.enabled.fla and button.enabled.swf on the CD.

Button.onDragOut

```
instanceName.onDragOut = functionName;
```

Where instanceName is the instance name of a button, and functionName is a function containing the code you wish to execute every time the onDragOut button event occurs.

This **event handler** is compatible with **Flash 6 or later**. Previous versions of Flash did not support the use of function references as call-backs, so this form of event handler script was not supported. For adding button events to buttons in Flash 5 and previous versions, see the **on** action.

Description

Flash buttons generate *events* every time a mouse interaction occurs with respect to a button. For something to happen when an event occurs, you must define a script that you want to execute in response to the event, and this script is called the *event handler*. To understand the operation of Button.onDragOut requires two things: an understanding of the *event*, and how to set up the *event handler*.
```

The event

The onDragOut event will be invoked when the mouse is inside the button hit area and is then click-held and dragged outside the hit area.

If you leave the mouse down and then roll over and out of the button hit area, the onDragOut event will occur every subsequent time you drag out of the hit area until the mouse is released.

The onPress event will also occur during the process that causes the onDragOut. It will occur when you click on the button during the initial click in the "click-hold then drag out" sequence that causes onDragOut. If you also want to respond to this event, you should also attach a call-back to the Button.onPress event. See also **Button.onPress**.

The event handler

The Button.onDragOut event handler definition is used to identify the code that will act as the event handler when the onDragOut event occurs. This code is defined as a function. When a function is used as an event handler, it is known as a *call-back*, a term inherited from JavaScript.

- If no call-back is defined, the onDragOut event will do nothing.
- If a call-back is defined, the function will run once every time the onDragOut event occurs.

Code	Notes
```function myFunction() {` `trace("you dragged out");` `}` `my_btn.onDragOut = myFunction;```	This script defines myFunction as the call-back for the button my_btn.
```my_btn.onDragOut = function() {` `trace("you dragged out")` `};```	This script defines an anonymous call-back function for the button instance my_btn. The script doesn't define a function name, but actually defines the body of the function itself, linking it to the event.
```my_btn.onDragOut = undefined;```	This script un-defines a previously defined call-back. You can also set it to null to achieve the same effect.

See the examples button.ondragout.fla and button.ondragout.swf on the CD.

3utton.onDragOver

```
instanceName.onDragOver = functionName;
```

Where instanceName is the instance name of a button, and functionName is a function containing the code you wish to execute every time the onDragOver button event occurs.

This **event handler** is compatible with **Flash 6 or later**. Previous versions of Flash did not support the use of function references as call-backs, so this form of event handler script was not supported. For adding button events to buttons in Flash 5 and previous versions, see the **on** action.

Description

Flash buttons generate *events* every time a mouse interaction occurs with respect to a button. For something to happen when an event occurs, you must define a script that you want to execute in response to the event, and this script is called the event handler. To understand the operation of Button.onDragOver requires two things: an understanding of the *event*, and how to set up the *event handler*.

The event

The onDragOver event will be invoked when the mouse is inside the button hit area and is then click-held and dragged outside and then back into the button hit area.

If you leave the mouse down and then roll out and back in the button hit area, the onDragOver event will occur every subsequent time you drag back into the hit area until the mouse is released.

The onPress event will also occur during the process that causes the onDragOut. It will occur when you click on the button during the initial click in the "click-hold then drag out" sequence that causes onDragOut. See also **Button.onPress**.

The event handler

The Button.onDragOver event handler definition is used to identify the code that will act as the event handler when the onDragOver event occurs. This code is defined as a function. When a function is used as an event handler, it is known as a *call-back*, a term inherited from JavaScript.

- If no call-back is defined, the onDragOver event will do nothing.
- If a call-back is defined, the function will run once every time the onDragOver event occurs.

Code	Notes
```function myFunction() { trace("you dragged over"); } my_btn.onDragOver = myFunction;```	This script defines myFunction as the call-back for the button my_btn
```my_btn.onDragOver = function() { trace("you dragged over") };```	This script defines an anonymous call-back function for the button instance my_btn. The script doesn't define a function name, but actually defines the body of the function itself, linking it to the event.

`my_btn.onDragOver = undefined;`	This script un-defines a previously defined call-back. You can also set it to `null` to achieve the same effect.

See the examples `button.ondragover.fla` and `button.ondragover.swf`.

Button.onKeyDown

```
instanceName.onKeyDown = functionName;
```

Where `instanceName` is the instance name of a button, and `functionName` is a function containing the code you wish to execute every time the `onKeyDown` button event occurs.

This **event handler** is compatible with **Flash 6** or later. Previous versions of Flash did not support the use of function references as call-backs, so this form of event handler script was not supported. For adding button events to buttons in Flash 5 and previous versions, see the **on** action. This event requires the SWF to have browser focus and the button to have input focus before any keypresses will be seen.

Description

Flash buttons generate *events* every time a mouse interaction occurs with respect to a button. For something to happen when an event occurs, you must define a script that you want to execute in response to the event, and this script is called the *event handler*. To understand the operation of `Button.onKeyDown` requires two things an understanding of the *event*, and how to set up the *event handler*.

The event

The `onKeyDown` event will be invoked when a key is pressed down whilst the button has input focus. The normal way to give a button input focus is to press the TAB key until the button gets focus, and a yellow box is seen around the button (assuming normal Flash defaults).

This event will never occur if the button is the only thing on screen with the ability to take input focus (you would normally use input focus on a screen with a mixture of buttons and input `textFields`).

The event will occur every frame the key is held down. The event will not capture the name of the key(s) that is/are pressed, although you can retrieve this by using other methods (see following examples).

The `onKeyUp` event will also occur following the `onKeyDown`. It will occur when you release the key, and will occur once per key release. See also **Button.onKeyUp**.

The event handler

The `Button.onKeyDown` event handler definition is used to identify the code that will act as the event handler when the `onKeyDown` event occurs. This code is defined as a function. When a function is used as an event handler, it is known as a *call-back*, a term inherited from JavaScript.

■   If no call-back is defined, the `onKeyDown` event will do nothing.

■   If a call-back is defined, the function will run once every time the `onKeyDown` event occurs.

If you want to respond to specific keys, your call-back will have to recognize the last key pressed. See the following examples on how to do this.

Code	Notes
```function myFunction() { message = "you pressed "+String.fromCharCode(Key.getAscii()); trace(message); } my_btn.onKeyDown = myFunction;```	This script defines `myFunction` as the call-back for the button `my_Btn`.
```my_btn.onKeyDown = function() { message = "you pressed "+String.fromCharCode(Key.getAscii()); trace(message); };```	This script defines an anonymous call-back function for the button instance `my_btn`. The script doesn't define a function name, but actually defines the body of the function itself, linking it to the event.
`my_btn.onKeyDown = undefined;`	This script un-defines a previously defined call-back. You can also set it to `null` to achieve the same effect.

Button.onKeyUp

```
instanceName.onKeyUp = functionName;
```

Where `instanceName` is the instance name of a button, and `functionName` is a function containing the code you wish to execute every time the `onKeyUp` button event occurs.

This **event handler** is compatible with **Flash 6** or later. Previous versions of Flash did not support the use of function references as call-backs, so this form of event handler script was not supported. For adding button events to buttons in Flash 5 and previous versions, see the **on** action. This event requires the SWF to have browser focus and the button to have input focus before any key-presses will be seen.

Description

Flash buttons generate *events* every time a mouse interaction occurs with respect to a button. For something to happen when an event occurs, you must define a script that you want to execute in response to the event, and this script is called the *event handler*. To understand the operation of `Button.onKeyUp` requires two things: an understanding of the *event*, and how to set up the *event handler*.

The event

The onKeyUp event will be invoked when a key is released whilst the button has input focus. The normal way to give a button input focus is to press the TAB key until the button gets focus, and a yellow box is seen around the button (assuming normal Flash defaults).

This event will never occur if the button is the only thing on screen with the ability to take input focus (you would normally use input focus on a screen with a mixture of buttons and input textFields).

The onKeyDown event will also occur before the onKeyUp. See also **Button.onKeyUp**.

The event handler

The Button.onKeyUp event handler definition is used to identify the code that will act as the event handler when the onKeyDown event occurs. This code is defined as a function. When a function is used as an event handler, it is known as a *call-back*, a term inherited from JavaScript.

- If no call-back is defined, the onKeyUp event will do nothing.
- If a call-back is defined, the function will run once every time the onKeyUp event occurs.

The event will not tell you which key has been released if multiple keys were pressed at the same time. The only way you can do this is to poll specific keys using **Key.isDown** to see if they are still being pressed.

Code	Notes
```function myFunction() {trace("you released a key");}my_btn.onKeyUp = myFunction;```	This script defines myFunction as the call-back for the button my_btn.
```my_btn.onKeyUp = function() {trace("you released a key");};```	This script defines an anonymous call-back function for the button instance my_btn. The script doesn't define a function name, but actually defines the body of the function itself, linking it to the event.
```my_btn.onKeyUp = undefined;```	This script un-defines a previously defined call-back. You can also set it to null to achieve the same effect.

Button.onKillFocus

```
instanceName.onKillFocus = functionName;
```

Where instanceName is the instance name of a button, and functionName is a function containing the code you wish to execute every time the onKillFocus button event occurs. You can also capture the target path to the instance that now holds the input focus by defining a function that includes the argument `newFocus` as shown:

```
my_btn.onKillFocus = function(newFocus) {...};
```

This **event handler** is compatible with **Flash 6 or later**. Previous versions of Flash did not support the use of function references as call-backs, so this form of event handler script was not supported. For adding button events to buttons in Flash 5 and previous versions, see the **on** action. This event is only ever used when building forms.

Description

Flash buttons generate *events* every time a mouse interaction occurs with respect to a button. For something to happen when an event occurs, you must define a script that you want to execute in response to the event, and this script is called the *event handler*. To understand the operation of `Button.onKillFocus` requires two things: an understanding of the *event*, and how to set up the *event handler*.

The event

The `onKillFocus` event will be invoked when the button has lost input focus. This can occur for a number of reasons such as:

- You have cycled through the objects on screen that can have focus using the TAB key. Having given the button input focus (when this happens the button will gain a yellow bounding box, assuming you have not changed the defaults), then hit the TAB key again to force the button to lose focus.
- You have selected a text input field, having previously had the input focus on the button. This causes the button to lose focus.

If the button is the only thing on the stage that can get/lose focus, there will never be a change in input focus, and this event will never occur.

If the button is configured to exclude itself from input focus (**Button.tabEnabled** = `false`), this event will never occur.

The `onSetFocus` event will also occur during the process that causes the `onKillFocus`. It will occur when the button first gets focus, assuming it hasn't had focus all the time. See also **Button.onSetFocus**.

NB – Also worth noting is that once the button has got input focus, it will respond to two other events:

- If the ENTER key is pressed the button will see the `onPress` event. See also **Button.onPress**.
- Immediately after the `onPress`, the button will see the `onRelease` event. See also **Button.onRelease**. The `onRelease` is usually the event you will look at whilst the button has input focus.

The event handler

The `Button.onKillFocus` event handler definition is used to identify the code that will act as the event handler when the `onKillFocus` event occurs. This code is defined as a function. When a function is used as an event handler, it is known as a *call-back*, a term inherited from JavaScript.

- If no call-back is defined, the `onKillFocus` event will do nothing.
- If a call-back is defined, the function will run once every time the `onKillFocus` event occurs.

If you want to use the optional argument `newFocus` (which will be a string containing the target path of the instance that now has focus), you should use an anonymous call-back. An example of this is shown in the following examples.

Code	Notes

<pre>function myFunction() {
    trace("I have lost focus");
}
my_btn.onKillFocus = myFunction;</pre>
	This script defines a function `myFunction()` as the call-back.

<pre>my_btn.onKillFocus = function() {
    trace("I have lost focus");
};</pre>
	This script defines an anonymous function as the call-back.

<pre>my_btn.onKillFocus = function(newFocus) {
    message = "I have lost focus to "+newFocus;
    trace(message);
};</pre>
	This script defines an anonymous function as the call-back, and this function uses the `newFocus` argument to capture the name of the object that now has input focus.

<pre>my_btn.onKillFocus = undefined;</pre>	This script un-defines a previously defined call-back. You can also set it to `null` to achieve the same effect.

<pre>function myFunction() {
    trace("I have lost focus");
}
my_btn.onKillFocus = myFunction;
my_btn.tabEnabled = false;</pre>
	The call-back will never occur because `my_btn` is excluded from getting input focus via the last line in this script. See also **Button.tabEnabled**.

See the examples `button.onkillfocus.fla` and `button.onkillfocus.swf` on the CD.

Button.onPress

```
instanceName.onPress = functionName;
```

Where `instanceName` is the instance name of a button, and `functionName` is a function containing the code you wish to execute every time the `onPress` button event occurs.

This **event handler** is compatible with **Flash 6 or later**. Previous versions of Flash did not support the use of function references as call-backs, so this form of event handler script was not supported. For adding button events to buttons in Flash 5 and previous versions, see the **on** action. This event is not often used, in preference to **onRelease**, which has the advantage of allowing the user to see the button graphic change from the *up* state to the *down* state before the event is raised.

Description

Flash buttons generate *events* every time a mouse interaction occurs with respect to a button. For something to happen when an event occurs, you must define a script that you want to execute in response to the event, and this script is called the *event handler*. To understand the operation of `Button.onPress` requires two things: an understanding of the *event*, and how to set up the *event handler*.

The event

The `onPress` event will be invoked when the button is pressed. This can occur for one of two reasons:

- The button is clicked with the mouse.
- The button has input focus and the ENTER key has been pressed on the keyboard. See also **Button.onKillFocus**, **Button.onSetFocus**.

The event handler

The `Button.onPress` event handler definition is used to identify the code that will act as the event handler when the `onPress` event occurs. This code is defined as a function. When a function is used as an event handler, it is known as a *call-back*, a term inherited from JavaScript.

- If no call-back is defined, the `onPress` event will do nothing.
- If a call-back is defined, the function will run once every time the `onPress` event occurs.

Code	Notes
```function myFunction() { trace("I have been pressed"); } my_btn.onPress = myFunction;```	This script defines a function `myFunction()` as the call-back for this event.
```my_btn.onPress = function() { trace("I have been pressed"); };```	This script defines an anonymous function as the call-back.
```my_btn.onPress = undefined;```	This script un-defines a previously defined call-back. You can also set it to `null` to achieve the same effect.

See the examples `button.onpress.fla` and `button.onpress.swf` on the CD.

Button.onRelease

```
instanceName.onRelease = functionName;
```

Where `instanceName` is the instance name of a button, and `functionName` is a function containing the code you wish to execute every time the `onRelease` button event occurs.

This **event handler** is compatible with **Flash 6 or later**. Previous versions of Flash did not support the use of function references as call-backs, so this form of event handler script was not supported. For adding button events to buttons in Flash 5 and previous versions, see the **on** action. This event is the most common button event, and is used for almost all buttons.

Description

Flash buttons generate *events* every time a mouse interaction occurs with respect to a button. For something to happen when an event occurs, you must define a script that you want to execute in response to the event, and this script is called the *event handler*. To understand the operation of `Button.onRelease` requires two things: an understanding of the *event,* and how to set up the *event handler.*

The event

The `onRelease` event will be invoked when the button is click-released. This can occur for one of two reasons:

- The button is click-released with the mouse.
- The button has input focus and the ENTER key has been pressed on the keyboard. See also **Button.onKillFocus**, **Button.onSetFocus**.

The `onPress` event will also occur during the process that causes the `onRelease`. It will occur when the button is clicked. See also **Button.onPress**.

The event handler

The `Button.onRelease` event handler definition is used to identify the code that will act as the event handler when the `onRelease` event occurs. This code is defined as a function. When a function is used as an event handler, it is known as a *call-back*, a term inherited from JavaScript.

- If no call-back is defined, the `onRelease` event will do nothing.
- If a call-back is defined, the function will run once every time the `onRelease` event occurs.

Code	Notes
```function myFunction() { trace("I have been click-released"); } my_btn.onRelease = myFunction;```	This script defines a function `myFunction()` as the call-back for this event.

| ```
my_btn.onRelease = function() {
    trace("I have been click-released");
};
``` | This script defines an anonymous function as the call-back. |
| ```
my_btn.onRelease = undefined;
``` | This script un-defines a previously defined call-back. You can also set it to null to achieve the same effect. |

See the examples button.onrelease.fla and button.onrelease.swf on the CD.

Button.onReleaseOutside

```
instanceName.onReleaseOutside = functionName;
```

Where instanceName is the instance name of a button, and functionName is a function containing the code you wish to execute every time the onReleaseOutside button event occurs.

This **event handler** is compatible with **Flash 6 or later**. Previous versions of Flash did not support the use of function references as call-backs, so this form of event handler script was not supported. For adding button events to buttons in Flash 5 and previous versions, see the **on** action.

Description

Flash buttons generate *events* every time a mouse interaction occurs with respect to a button. For something to happen when an event occurs, you must define a script that you want to execute in response to the event, and this script is called the *event handler*. To understand the operation of Button.onReleaseOutside requires two things: an understanding of the *event*, and how to set up the *event handler*.

The event

The onReleaseOutside event will be invoked when the button is click-held and the mouse is then released outside the button-hit area.
The onPress event will also occur during the process that causes the onReleaseOutside. It will occur when the button is clicked. See also **Button.onPress**.

The event handler

The Button.onReleaseOutside event handler definition is used to identify the code that will act as the event handler when the onReleaseOutside event occurs. This code is defined as a function. When a function is used as an event handler, it is known as a *call-back*, a term inherited from JavaScript.

- ■ If no call-back is defined, the onReleaseOutside event will do nothing.
- ■ If a call-back is defined, the function will run once every time the onReleaseOutside event occurs.

Code	Notes
```function myFunction() { trace("I have been click-releasedOutside"); } my_btn.onReleaseOutside = myFunction;```	This script defines a function myFunction() as the call-back for this event.
```my_btn.onReleaseOutside = function() { trace("I have been click-releasedOutside"); };```	This script defines an anonymous function as the call-back.
```my_btn.onReleaseOutside = undefined;```	This script un-defines a previously defined call-back. You can also set it to null to achieve the same effect.

See the examples `button.onreleaseoutside.fla` and `button.onreleaseoutside.swf` on the CD.

Button.onRollOut

```
instanceName.onRollOut = functionName;
```

Where `instanceName` is the instance name of a button, and `functionName` is a function containing the code you wish to execute every time the `onRollOut` button event occurs.

This **event handler** is compatible with **Flash 6 or later**. Previous versions of Flash did not support the use of function references as call-backs, so this form of event handler script was not supported. For adding button events to buttons in Flash 5 and previous versions, see the **on** action.

Description

Flash buttons generate *events* every time a mouse interaction occurs with respect to a button. For something to happen when an event occurs, you must define a script that you want to execute in response to the event, and this script is called the *event handler*. To understand the operation of `Button.onRollOut` requires two things; an understanding of the *event,* and how to set up the *event handler.*

The event

The `onRollOut` event will be invoked when the mouse moves out of the button-hit area. The user does not have to have clicked on the button, although the SWF does have to have browser focus.

The `onRollOver` event will also occur during the process that causes the `onRollOut`. It will occur when the mouse enters the button hit area. See also **Button.onRollover**.

The event handler

The `Button.onRollOut` event handler definition is used to identify the code that will act as the event handler when the `onRollOut` event occurs. This code is defined as a function. When a function is used as an event handler, it is known as a *call-back*, a term inherited from JavaScript.

- If no call-back is defined, the `onRollOut` event will do nothing.
- If a call-back is defined, the function will run once every time the `onRollOut` event occurs.

Code	Notes
``` function myFunction() { trace("I have been rolled out "); this } my_btn.onRollOut = myFunction; ```	This script defines a function `myFunction()` as the call-back for this event.
``` my_btn.onRollOut = function() { trace("I have been rolled out"); }; ```	This script defines an anonymous function as the call-back.
``` my_btn.onRollOut = undefined; ```	This script un-defines a previously defined call-back. You can also set it to `null` to achieve the same effect.

See the examples `button.onrollout.fla` and `button.onrollout.swf` on the CD.

Button.onRollOver

```
instanceName.onRollOver = functionName;
```

Where `instanceName` is the instance name of a button, and `functionName` is a function containing the code you wish to execute every time the `onRollOver` button event occurs.

This **event handler** is compatible with **Flash 6 or later**. Previous versions of Flash did not support the use of function references as call-backs, so this form of event handler script was not supported. For adding button events to buttons in Flash 5 and previous versions, see the **on** action.

Description

Flash buttons generate *events* every time a mouse interaction occurs with respect to a button. For something to happen when an event occurs, you must define a script that you want to execute in response to the event, and this script is called the *event handler*. To understand the operation of `Button.onRollOver` requires two things: an understanding of the *event*, and how to set up the *event handler*.

The event

The onRollOver event will be invoked when the mouse moves into the button hit area. The user does not have to have clicked on the button, although the SWF does have to have browser focus.

The onRollOut event will also occur during the process that causes the onRollOver. It will occur when the mouse leaves the button-hit area. See also **Button.onRollOut**.

The event handler

The Button.onRollOver event handler definition is used to identify the code that will act as the event handler when the onRollOver event occurs. This code is defined as a function. When a function is used as an event handler, it is known as a *call-back*, a term inherited from JavaScript.

- If no call-back is defined, the onRollOver event will do nothing.
- If a call-back is defined, the function will run once every time the onRollOver event occurs.

Code	Notes
```function myFunction() { trace("I have been rolled over "); } my_btn.onRollOver = myFunction;```	This script defines a function myFunction() as the call-back for this event.
```my_btn.onRollOver = function() { trace("I have been rolled over"); };```	This script defines an anonymous function as the call-back.
```my_btn.onRollOVer = undefined;```	This script un-defines a previously defined call-back. You can also set it to null to achieve the same effect.

See the example button.onrollover.fla and button.onrollover.swf on the CD.

Button.tabEnabled

```
instanceName.tabEnabled = a;
b = instanceName.tabEnabled;
```

Where instanceName is the instance name of a button, and a is the value you want this property to take. a should be either true or false. b is a value that you want to equate to the current Button.tabEnabled value.

This **property** is compatible with **Flash 6 or later**. Previous versions of Flash did not support the button as an object, so the button has no properties in versions of Flash previous to Flash MX.

Description

The input focus of a SWF defines which object (button, movie clip, or text field) currently has input focus. The object with input focus can respond to key-presses from the keyboard, and will also be able to generate events from key-presses (for a button, these events are **Button.onKeyUp** and **Button.onKeyDown**. Refer to these entries for further information on input focus).

To make a `textField` the current input focus, you have to select it. To make a button or movie clip the current input focus, you have to hit the TAB key until it becomes highlighted. A button that has gained input focus via the TAB key will be highlighted as shown below right:

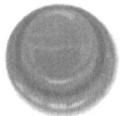

You can control whether the button is able to gain input focus in this way by setting the `tabEnabled` property. The button will be able to gain input focus only if its `tabEnabled` property is `true`. See also the **Button.tabIndex** property, which allows you to change the *order* of the button in the input focus list.

Code	Notes
`my_btn.tabEnabled = true;`	The button instance `my_btn` is able to take input focus.
`my_btn.tabEnabled = false;`	The button instance `my_btn` is **not** able to take input focus.

See the examples `button.tabenabled.fla` and `button.tabenabled.swf` on the CD.

Button.tabIndex

```
instanceName.tabIndex = a;
b = instanceName.tabIndex;
```

Where `instanceName` is the instance name of a button, and a is the value you want this property to take. a should be a positive integer. b is a value that you want to equate to the current `Button.tabIndex` value.

This **property** is compatible with **Flash 6 or later**. Previous versions of Flash did not support the button as an object, so the button has no properties in versions of Flash previous to Flash MX.

Description

The input focus of a SWF defines which object (button, movie clip, or text field) currently has input focus. The object with input focus can respond to key-presses from the keyboard, and will also be able to generate events from key-presses (for a button, these events are **Button.onKeyUp** and **Button.onKeyDown**. Refer to these entries for further information on input focus).

To select a textField as the current input focus, you have to select it. To make a button or movie clip the current input focus, you have to hit the TAB key until it becomes highlighted. A button that has gained input focus via the TAB key will be highlighted as shown below right.

By default, the place the button occupies in the TAB ordering is defined by the order in which it was placed on the stage. You can control the order of the button in the input focus list by assigning each object (button, movie clip, text field) that can accept input focus with a tabIndex value. You can also *exclude* a button from input focus with the **Button.tabEnabled** property.

Code	Notes
`my_btn.tabIndex = 5;` `myOther_btn.tabIndex = 6;`	The button instance my_btn will come before myOther_btn in the input focus order. When you hit the TAB key, my_btn will be selected first.

See the example button.tabindex.fla and button.tabindex.swf on the CD.

Button.trackAsMenu

```
instanceName.trackAsMenu = a;
b = instanceName.trackAsMenu;
```

Where instanceName is the instance name of a button, and a is the value you want this property to take. a should be a positive integer. b is a value that you want to equate to the current Button.trackAsMenu value.

This **property** is compatible with **Flash 6 or later**. Previous versions of Flash did not support the button as an object, so the button has no properties in versions of Flash previous to Flash MX.

Description

The `trackAsMenu` lets you decide what you want to do when a click-release event can start on one button and finish on another. It is useful for specifying to Flash what you want to happen when buttons are very close to each other. This typically happens on pulldown menus, or whenever buttons are so close to each other they overlap. The following example illustrates the concept, and the effect of the `Button.trackAsMenu` property:

Assume you have two buttons on the stage as shown:

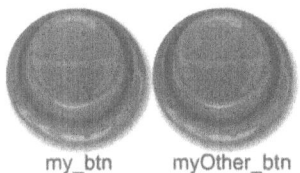

my_btn   myOther_btn

and you also have a script as shown:

```
my_btn.onRelease = function() {
    trace("you hit my_btn");
};
myOther_btn.onRelease = function() {
    trace("you hit myOther_btn");
};
```

If you click-release on the instance `my_btn`, you will see the message `you hit my_btn` in the Output window, and you will see the message `you hit myOther_btn` if you click-release `myOther_btn`.

Because the buttons are so close, it is possible to click-hold on one button, and with the mouse button still down, drag the mouse over to the other button. When you release on the other button *no onRelease event is detected*.

The same happens if you click outside either button and then drag-release over one of the two buttons.

For certain elements that you can make using buttons, this is undesirable.

The situation described above will occur if the `trackAsMenu` property of both buttons is set to `false`. It is set to this value by default.

NB – You can set this property to `true` manually via the Property inspector, as shown, so the property may be set outside ActionScript if you have changed the drop-down shown:

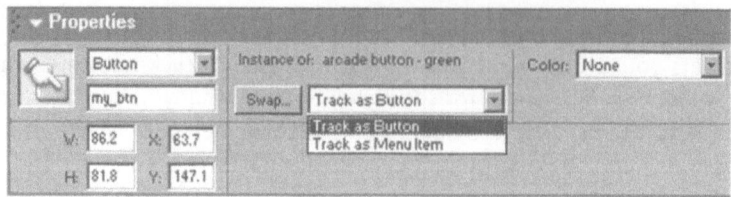

If you now add the last two lines to your script, you will see the effects of the trackAsMenu property:

```
my_btn.onRelease = function() {
    trace("you hit my_btn");
};
myOther_btn.onRelease = function() {
    trace("you hit myOther_btn");
};
my_btn.trackAsMenu = true;
myOther_btn.trackAsMenu = true;
```

The changes in operation caused by these new lines are:

- If you click-hold on one of the two buttons, and then drag-release onto the other button, the onRelease event will be detected by the second button. Previously, the onRelease was not being detected.
- If you click-hold outside both of the buttons, and then drag-release so that the release occurs over one of the buttons, the onRelease will be detected by that button. Previously, the onRelease was not being detected.

Code	Notes
my_btn.trackAsMenu = true;	The button instance my_btn has its trackAsMenu property set to true. This will cause onRelease events to be detected by this button, even if the initial click occurred over another button.

Button.useHandCursor

```
instanceName.useHandCursor = a;
b = instanceName.useHandCursor;
```

Where instanceName is the instance name of a button, and a is the value you want this property to take. a should be a positive integer. b is a value that you want to equate to the current Button.useHandCursor value.

This **property** is compatible with **Flash 6 or later**. Previous versions of Flash did not support the button as an object, so the button has no properties in versions of Flash previous to Flash MX.

Description

The useHandCursor lets you decide whether you want the mouse to change to a hand cursor when it is over a button hit area. This change is disabled if you set useHandCursor to false.

Code	Notes
`my_btn.useHandCursor = true;`	The hand cursor will be shown if the mouse goes over the hit area of the button instance my_btn. This is the default setting.
`my_btn.useHandCursor = false;`	The hand cursor will **not** be shown if the mouse goes over the hit area of the button instance my_btn.

gotoAndStop()
hitTest()
loadMovie()
loadVariables()
loadVariables play()
nextFrame()
prevFrame() removeMovieClip()
setMask() startDrag() startDrag()
swap Depths()
unloadMovie
attach Movie
createEmptyMovieClip
createTextField
duplicateMovie
getBounds

call

```
call(a);
```

or

```
call("mylabel");
```

Where a is a frame number. You can also use a frame label instead of a number.

This action is **compatible with Flash 4 or later**. This action is deprecated and not recommended if creating content for Flash 5 and above, where the **function** action can be used instead.

See this entry on the CD for a fuller explanation.

Capabilities

See the **System** entry.

case

```
case a :
   // do this
```

Where a is a condition or value.

This action is **compatible with Flash 5 or later**. Although the Flash 5 environment does not support it, content created in the Flash 6 environment and exported as Flash 5 does. This action forms part of the switch structure, and you should also refer to the entry for that action.

Description
The case **action** forms part of the **switch** structure, and other actions that are typically also used are **break** and **default**. See also the entries for these actions.

The case action is used to create the condition part of the switch structure.

Examples

```
input_btn.onRelease = function() {
   switch (Number(input_txt.text)) {
   case 1 :
      output_txt.text = "you selected 1";
      break;
   case 2 :
```

```
         output_txt.text = "you selected 2";
         break;
      case 3 :
         output_txt.text = "you selected 3";
         break;
      default :
         output_txt.text = "please enter 1, 2 or 3";
      }
};
```

This is a typical input scheme for the sort of setup shown below. Once the text is entered by the user, the button event handler is used as the input validation script.

input_txt		accept
output_txt		

If the user enters 1, 2, or 3, the input is accepted. If any other input is entered, a default script is run.

The following actions are also used here:

- **switch (expression)**:
  This defines the start of the whole switch construction, and also defines the expression or variable that is used as the case conditional. The case statements are used following this to say "if the result of *expression* is 1, do this, but if it is 2, do this, if it is 3, do this, and finally, if it is anything else, do this".
- **break**:
  The break action means "ignore anything else and "break out" of the current code block. It means that if expression turns out to be 1, after completing the script for case 1 :, Flash will not look at the other conditions. Although you usually want to have a break after each case script, there are some where you don't, as we shall see in a moment.

  Another way to look at break is to compare the script with the equivalent **if...** structure:

```
switch (Number(input_txt.text)) {
case 1 :
   output_txt.text = "you selected 1";
   break;
case 2 :
   output_txt.text = "you selected 2";
break;
   case 3 :
   output_txt.text = "you selected 3";
   break;
default :
```

```
      output_txt.text = "please enter 1, 2 or 3";
   }
```

The previous script is equivalent to the following script (and will actually be parsed to *become* this script, given that the Flash player doesn't actually understand `switch`, but only thinks in terms of **if...**):

```
expression = Number(input_txt.text);
if (expression == 1) {
   output_txt.text = "you selected 1";
} else if (expression== 2) {
   output_txt.text = "you selected 2";
} else if (expression== 3) {
   output_txt.text = "you selected 3";
} else {
   output_txt.text = "please enter 1, 2 or 3";
}
```

Without the `break` actions, the case is equivalent to the following less efficient script:

```
expression = Number(input_txt.text);
if (expression == 1) {
   output_txt.text = "you selected 1";
}
if (expression == 2) {
   output_txt.text = "you selected 2";
}
if (expression == 3) {
   output_txt.text = "you selected 3";
}
if ((expression != 1) && (expression != 2) && (expression != 3)) {
      output_txt.text = "please enter 1, 2 or 3";
}
```

- **default**:
  As can be seen from the previous scripts, default is the same as the **else** branch of the **if...** structure. It is the last branch and essentially means "otherwise do this".

This script is the classic "bouncing ball" animation script, except that it uses `switch/case` instead of `if...` structures. Note the use of `switch (true)`. An animation based on this script is included as the example `case.fla` and `case.swf` on the CD.

```
ball_mc.onEnterFrame = function() {
   // limits
   switch (true) {
   case (this._x<0) :
      this.speedX = -this.speedX;
```

```
      break;
   case (this._x>550) :
      this.speedX = -this.speedX;
      break;
   }
   switch (true) {
   case (this._y<0) :
      this.speedY = -this.speedY;
      break;
   case (this._y>400) :
      this.speedY = -this.speedY;
   }
   // animate
   this._x += this.speedX;
   this._y += this.speedY;
};
ball_mc.speedX = 10;
ball_mc.speedY = 10;
```

The following example is used to check whether three variables are not particular values. This illustrates one big advantage of switch/case over if... structures. An if... can only directly test for true (you get round this by checking for !true or "not something" = true, which is still fundamentally the same as checking for true), whereas a switch/case can check directly for the false condition. Although the difference is not important by the time the script is parsed for the Flash player (given that it is all converted to if... statements anyway), it can make the intent of your source code clearer.

Note also the way break is no longer used in this script. Because we want to check each of the three case branches, we omit it.

```
x = 3;
y = 3;
z = 5;
switch (false) {
case (x == 3) :
   trace("x is not equal to 3");
case (y == 4) :
   trace("y is not equal to 4");
case (z == 2) :
   trace("z is not equal to 2");
}
```

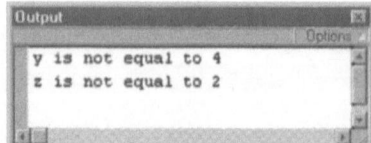

See the example `case.fla` and `case.swf` on the CD.

chr

```
a = chr(b);
```

Where b is a number. a will be returned as the corresponding string character.

This action is compatible with Flash 4 and above. It is deprecated in Flash 5 and above, and you are advised to use the equivalent Flash 5 String method shown below:

```
a = String.fromCharCode(b);
```

Description

The `chr` action is useful in accessing characters not normally found on a keyboard.

It is deprecated by the `String.fromCharCode()` method, and you are advised to use this alternative in all new Flash content. See also **String.fromCharCode**.

Code	Notes
`a = chr(169);`	a = "©"
`b = chr(174);`	b = "®"

clearInterval

```
clearInterval(a);
```

Where a is the identifier of the interval you want to clear (remove).

This action is compatible with Flash 6 or later. The `clearInterval` action is paired with **setInterval**, which sets (assigns) interval events.

Description

The `clearInterval` action clears an interval event associated with a previously defined named interval via `setInterval`. When using interval events for animation, you may also need to use the **updateOnEvent** action, particularly if your interval is greater than the frame rate of the main timeline (typically every 83.3ms for the default 12 fps timeline). See also the entry for **updateOnEvent**.

The interval event is a major advance in the abilities of ActionScript to control the motion graphics environment. In particular, if you use `setInterval/clearInterval` together, it can allow the advanced coder to emulate independent timelines with *variable frame rates*. This has implications in:

- Optimizing events so that they only run as often as needed, and not every frame.
- Creating animation based event code that updates faster/slower than the normal timeline based onEnterFrame event handler.

This issue is illustrated briefly in the following sections via additional FLA examples.

Code	Notes
`myInterval = setInterval(myFunction, 100);` `clearInterval(myInterval);`	Line 1 defines an interval event that will execute the function myFunction() every 100ms, or as close to this as Flash can achieve. Line 2 clears this event
`setInterval(myFunction, 100);`	Although the setInterval shown here will correctly create an interval event that executes myFunction every 100ms, this line does not assign this event with an identifier. Because the interval is *anonymous*, you cannot clear this interval using clearInterval. Do not use this syntax if you wish to later use clearInterval.

See the example `clearinterval.fla` and `clearinterval.swf` on the CD.

Color

This object is more fully addressed in *Chapter 6*.

The Color object is used to change the color of a graphic object. You can use the Color object with the following:

Object	Compatibility
movieClip	Flash 5
	Flash 6
Button	Flash 6
textField	Flash 6

If you wish to use the Color object with buttons or text fields in Flash 5, an easy workaround is to place the button/text inside a movie clip and then target the movie clip in your Color object. The programming term for this is called *"creating a wrapper"*; you control something that would be otherwise inaccessible to your code by wrapping it in something that is accessible, making the thing you want to control appear as if it were the wrapper object itself.

NB – A major new use of the Color object in Flash 6 is that if you embed a video object inside a movie clip, you can apply color effects to the video clip (effectively using the movie clip as a wrapper again). This feature can be used to great effect when you control the Color object with the Color.setTransform method to create color fades and tints. More usefully, the setTransform method also supports alpha variations, and this allows you to use it for true fades and cross fades. This feature is not discussed further, because the theory to use the Color object with video is the same as the theory you would use to apply it to a still or animating standard movie clip.

For more information on this object, see the full entry on the CD.

Color constructor

```
myColor = new Color(a);
```

Where myColor is the name of a new color object that will be applied to the graphic object identified by the target path a.

This constructor is **compatible with Flash 5 or later**. In Flash 5, the Color object can be applied to movie clips only. In Flash 6, it can be applied to movie clips, buttons, or dynamic/input text fields. See the entry for **Color** to see how you can work around this via a *wrapper*.

Description

The Color object **constructor** creates a new color object, and applies it to the specified targeted graphic object. Upon construction, the color object will be initialized with the RGB color value of the target.

Code	Notes
| ```
myColor = new Color(_root.my_txt);
myOtherColor = new Color(my_mc);
mySiteColor = new Color(_root);
``` | The color object myColor will control the color of the text field object _root.my_txt. This will only work in Flash 6.<br><br>The color object myOtherColor will control the color of the movie clip object my_mc. Because this is a relative path, my_mc must be on the same timeline as this code. |
```

The color object `mySiteColor` is
attached to the timeline `_root`. This
will work because `_root` is really only
a special case of the movie clip object.
You can use `mySiteColor` to alter the
overall color of your site (typically via
tinting).

See also the example `colorconstructor.fla` and `colorconstructor.swf` on the CD.

Color.getRGB

```
a = myColor.getRGB();
```

Where `a` is the variable that you want to equate to the current RGB value of the color object `myColor`.

This method is **compatible with Flash 5 or later**. In Flash 5, the `Color` object can be applied to movie clips only. In Flash 6, it can be applied to movie clips, buttons, or dynamic/input text fields. See the entry for **Color** to see how you can work around this via a *wrapper*.

NB – This method is rarely used, and can give confusing information when used. You are better advised to write code that tracks the changes it has made via the color object by storing changes you want to recall latter in variables specially set up for this task.

Description
This method will hold the value of the color object's current RGB value. This value will not always be equal to the current RGB color value of the target associated with the color object. See also **Color constructor** for a definition of the *target*.

Code	Notes

`my_color = new Color(my_mc);`
`my_color.setRGB(0x0000FF);`
`trace(my_color.getRGB().toString(16));`
	A new color object is created called `my_color`. A **Color.setRGB()** method is then used to set the target clip, my_mc to blue. The last line returns the value of this color change (0xFF).
	
	Note the use of **String.toString(16)** to convert the decimal value to Hex before displaying it. Without the ".`toString(16)`" part, the value returned would be 255.

`my_color = new Color(my_mc);` `trace(my_color.getRGB().toString(16));`	The getRGB value will be zero if the color object has not yet applied any method that makes color changes. In other words, the getRGB method

<table>
<tr><td>

```
my_color = new Color(my_mc);
myColorTrans = {ra:70, rb:77, ga:70, gb:77,
ba:70, bb:0, aa:100, ab:0};
my_color.setTransform(myColorTrans);
trace(my_color.getRGB().toString(16))
```

</td><td>

cannot be relied on as giving the current color of the target.

The getRGB value returns the last RGB value applied vie the last applied **Color.setTransform**, but because this transformation is one that will leave the target with more than one color, the getRGB value is all but useless. See also **Color.setTransform**.

</td></tr>
</table>

Color.getTransform

```
a = myColor.getTransform();
```

Where a is the variable that you want to equate to the color transform object that was used as the argument of the last color transformation using the color object myColor.

This method is **compatible with Flash 5 or later**. In Flash 5, the Color object can be applied to movie clips only. In Flash 6, it can be applied to movie clips, buttons, or dynamic/input text fields. See the entry for **Color** to see how you can work around this via a *wrapper*.

NB – This method is very rarely used.

Description

This **method** will hold the value of the color object's current color transform object. This value will be equal to the object that created the last color transformation, assuming that at least one color transformation has taken place. If the last color transformation was made manually (i.e. via the Color dropdown menu in the Property inspector, the corresponding color transform object for that transform will be returned.

See also **Color.setTransform**, which describes the color transform object.

Code	Notes

``
my_color = new Color(my_mc);
myColorTrans = {ra:70, rb:77, ga:70, gb:77,
ba:70, bb:0, aa:100, ab:0};
my_color.setTransform(myColorTrans);
//
// read last transform object...
a = my_color.getTransform();
for (prop in a) {
   message = prop+"= "+a[prop];
   trace(message);
``
	This will trace the values of myColorTrans, the color transform object that is used earlier in the script to transform the target my_mc.

```
}
```

```my_color = new Color(my_mc);```
 ```my_color.setRGB(0xFFFFFF);```
 ```// read last transform object...```
 ```// a = my_color.getTransform();```
 ```for (prop in a) {```
     ```message = prop+"= "+a[prop];```
     ```trace(message);```
 ```}```
	Because the **Color.setRGB** is really just a simplified form of **Color.setTransform**, the script will still return a color transform object. In this case it will have properties as shown:
	
	 ab= 0
	 aa= 100
	 bb= 0xFF
	 ba= 0
	 gb= 0xFF
	 ga= 0
	 rb= 0xFF
	 ra= 0

```my_color = new Color(my_mc);```
 ```// read last transform object...```
 ```// a = my_color.getTransform();```
 ```(prop in a) {```
     ```message = prop+"= "+a[prop];```
     ```trace(message);```
 ```}```
	This code makes no color transformations prior to requesting the object used to form the last for transformation. This will not raise an erroneous response, given that the object returned is one that would make no change to a target's default color, and this object will have properties as shown:
	
	 ab= 0
	 aa= 100
	 bb= 0
	 ba= 100
	 gb= 0
	 ga= 100
	 rb= 0
	 ra= 100

See also the example FLA, `color.gettransform.fla` and `color.gettransform.swf` on the CD.

Color.setRGB

```
myColor.setRGB(a);
```

Where `myColor` is a color object, and `a` is the color you want to use.

This method is **compatible with Flash 5 or later**. In Flash 5, the `Color` object can be applied to movie clips only. In Flash 6, it can be applied to movie clips, buttons, or dynamic/input text fields. See the entry for **Color** to see how you can work around this via a *wrapper*.

Description

This **method** allows you to *color* a movie clip, button, or text field. See the entry for **Color** for a fuller discussion on the terms *color*, *mix*, *filter*, and *tint*, which is the full set of available color transforms using the color object.

The argument for this method is best expressed in hexadecimal. See also the entry for **Color** for a fuller discussion and links that explain the use of hexadecimal with color representation.

You must construct a color object before using this (or any other) method. See also the entry for **Color constructor**. The examples below also show you haw to create a color object in the first line of each example listing.

Code	Original clip	Clip after transformation

`my_color =`
`new Color(my_mc);`
`my_color.setRGB`
`(0x000000);`
	The original clip is a filled gray circle.	The transformed clip is a filled black circle because 0x000000 = black.

`my_color = new`
`Color(my_mc);`
`my_color.setRGB`
`(0xAAAAAA);`
	The original clip is multi colored	The transformed clip is a mid gray, as defined by the RGB color value 0xAAAAAA.
		
		Note that the original color information is lost.

`my_color = new`
`Color(my_mc);`
`my_color.setRGB`
`(0xFF0000);`
	The original clip has a color gradient applied to it.	The transformed clip has lost the color gradient, and is now a solid color.

`my_color = new`
`Color(my_mc);`
`my_color.setRGB`
`(0xFF0000);`
	The original clip has a color gradient applied to it that uses alpha (the white area is "black with zero alpha".	The transformed clip is still solid, but retains the alpha. This allows the gradient to retain its appearance. Although using alpha can give more pleasing effects with setRGB, you are better off using *mix* or *tint* effects via **Color.setTransform** because this allows more control.

See the example `color.setrgb.fla` and `color.setrgb.swf` on the CD.

Color.setTransform

```
myColor.setTransform(a);
```

Where `myColor` is a color object, and a is the color transform object that represents the color changes you want to apply during the transform.

This method is **compatible with Flash 5 or later**. In Flash 5, the `Color` object can be applied to movie clips only. In Flash 6, it can be applied to movie clips, buttons, or dynamic/input text fields. See the entry for **Color** to see how you can work around this via a *wrapper*.

Description

This **method** allows you to apply *color*, *mix*, *filter*, and *tint* effects to a movie clip, button or text field. See the entry for **Color** for a fuller discussion on the terms *color*, *mix*, *filter*, and *tint*.

The argument for this method is best expressed in hexadecimal. See also the entry for **Color** for a fuller discussion and links that explain the use of hexadecimal with color representation.

You must construct a color object before using this (or any other) method. See also the entry for **Color constructor**. The examples in the table below also show you how to create a color object in the first line of each example listing.

You must construct a color transform object before using this method. See the full entry on the CD for a full set of examples.

The color transform object contains the same information as that entered in the **Advanced Effect** window. See the entry for **Color** for more information on how to use this window.

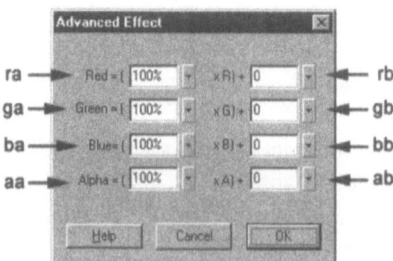

ra   The red RGB channel (in percent of the original symbol color value) to use in the final color transformed symbol.

ga   The green RGB channel (in percent of the original symbol color value) to use in the final color transformed symbol.

ba   The blue RGB channel (in percent of the original symbol color value) to use in the final color transformed symbol.

aa   The alpha value (in percent of the original symbol) to use in the final color transformed image.

rb   The red channel offset (-255 to +255) to add to the red channel of the original symbol.

gb   The green channel offset (-255 to +255) to add to the red channel of the original symbol.

bb   The blue channel offset (-255 to +255) to add to the red channel of the original symbol.

ab   The alpha offset (-255 to +255) to add to the red channel of the original symbol.

See also the example `color.settransform.fla` and `color.settransform.swf` on the CD.

continue

```
continue;
```

This action has no arguments.

This Action is compatible with Flash 4 and later.

Description

The `continue` **action** is used within loops. It allows you to skip the current iteration of the loop and go straight to the next loop. The `continue` is usually enclosed within an **if...** statement that checks for the condition that will invoke the need to continue out of the current loop iteration.

Code	Notes
```for (i=1; i<101; i++) { if (i%2 == 0) { continue } trace(i); }```	Assuming we want to only print out odd numbers between 1 and 100, the script shown is one way of doing it. If the number is divisible by 2 with no remainder then it must be even, so we skip to the next loop, otherwise we carry on to the part of the loop that traces the number to the output window.

```
Date.UTC(year, 0, 0, 0, 0, second);
```

This method is **compatible with Flash 5 or later**.

Description

This **method** allows you to specify a time in UTC time. This has advantages when you want to represent the same *instant* to an international audience. For example, if you created a Flash page that tells people to look, say, at the planet Venus at 3 O'clock today (EST time), folks in Germany will be looking at Venus at the wrong time, because they will look at Venus at 3 O'clock *their time*, and not at the same instant as you.

Code	Notes
```my_date = new Date(Date.UTC(2003, 0, 29, 9, 50)); trace(my_date.toString());```	This code allows the user to read the authors next birthday to the nearest minute, expressed as the equivalent time in their time zone, so all the readers of this book can light a candle at the same instant in time...or not!

gotoAndStop()
hitTest()
loadMovie()
loadVariables()
loadVariables()
nextFrame()   play()
prevFrame() removeMovieClip()
removeMovie   setMask()   startDrag()
Frame startDrag() startDrag()
Variable swap Depths()
rame swapMovie unloadMovie()
ame attach Movie()
Drag createTextField()
Drag DD createText
createEmptyMovieClip
createEmptyMovie
duplicateMo
Te

Date

This object is addressed more fully in *Chapter 13*.

Definitions

The Date object allows you to track the date and time. It uses two time measurement systems:

- **The local time as specified by your operating system**: this is the time held by the users computer, and this will differ between two users in different time zones.
- **UTC (coordinated universal time, also known as Universal time and World time)**: Greenwich mean time was based around astronomical measurements, but UTC supercedes it, and closely follows International Atomic Time (TAI), given that the standard measurement of 1 second is now defined in terms of the atomic frequencies of cesium.

NB – For anyone wondering why the abbreviations UTC/TAI don't seem to match the full terms, think French!

See the CD for the full entry with examples.

See also the examples date1.fla and date1.swf on the CD, which show the creation of a Flash clock and date2.fla and date2.swf, which show the creation of a calendar.

These examples are extended in date3.fla, date4.fla, date5.fla, and date3.swf, date4.swf, date5.swf.

Date constructor

```
my_date = new Date();
```

or

```
my_date = new Date(year, month, date, hour, minute, second, millisecond);
```

Where my_date is the name of a new Date object. The first form will initialize the new Date object, my_date to the current local time of the user's computer clock.

The second form allows you to specify some or all of the start time of the newly defined object. You can start specifying from left to right, and stop when you have reached the max accuracy for your application. For example, if you only want to set the year, month, and date, you can use the syntax:

```
my_date = new Date(year, month, date);
```

and if you want to specify up to the nearest minute you would do this:

```
my_date = new Date(year, month, date, hour, minute, second);
```

NB – If you do this, any omitted parameters in the date will be initialized as zero

This constructor is compatible with **Flash 5 or later**.

Description
The Date object **constructor** creates a new Date object. You need to construct a Date object before you can use its methods, and have to recreate it every time you want the time held by this object to update.

Code	Notes
| ```
my_date = new Date();
my_date = new Date(80, 0, 14, 13, 30);
trace(my_date.toString());
``` | Creates a Date object called my_date. Creates a Date object with the following initial start value:<br><br>Mon Jan 14 13:30:00 GMT+0000 1980<br><br>Note that on this particular computer, the daylight saving time has been correctly defined; January in the UK has no daylight saving to be added. |
| ```
my_date = new Date(80, 7, 14, 13, 30);
trace(my_date.toString());
``` | Creates a Date object with the following initial start value:<br><br>Thu Aug 14 13:30:00 GMT+0100 1980<br><br>Note that daylight saving time has been correctly noted with respect to GMT/UTC. |
| ```
_root.onEnterFrame = function() {
my_date = new Date();
    trace(my_date.toString());
};

_root.onEnterFrame = function() {
    trace(my_date.getSeconds());
};
my_date = new Date();
``` | The following code creates a new version of the Date instance my_date every frame. This causes the script to keep returning an updated value of the current date/time. Because the Date object is not refreshed by creating a new version every frame, the seconds value will continually return the same value. |

See the full entry on the CD for a more detailed explanation of the last two examples in the previous table.
```

Date.getDate

```
a = my_date.getDate();
```
a will be returned as an integer value corresponding to the day of the month. This value will be an integer between 1 and 31

This method is compatible with **Flash 5 or later**.

Description

This **method** will return the day of month (integer value, 1 to 31). The source of this data is the local clock in the user's computer, and the accuracy of this method is dependent on the accuracy (or otherwise) of this clock.

You must construct a Date object before you can use this method, as shown in the example below.

Code	Notes
`my_date = new Date();` `day = my_date.getDate();`	This script creates a new Date object and uses it to get the current day of the month.

`my_date = new Date();`
`day = my_date.getDate();`
`if (day<10) {`
`    day = "0"+day;`
`}`
	The date will be returned as 1 to 9 if the day of the month is less than 10. If you want to display the date, you may prefer 01 to 09. This code adds the leading zero as required.

See the example `date2.fla` and `date2.swf` on the CD.

Date.getDay

```
a = my_date.getDay();
```

a will be returned as an integer value corresponding to the day of the week. Sunday is taken as the first day and is equal to 0.

This method is compatible with **Flash 5 or later**.

Description

This **method** will return the day of week as the integer value, 0 to 6, with Sunday as 0. The source of this data is the local clock in the user's computer, and the accuracy of this method is dependent on the accuracy (or otherwise) of this clock.

You must construct a Date object before you can use this method, as shown in the examples:

Code	Notes
`my_date = new Date();` `day = my_date.getDay();`	This script creates a new `Date` object and uses it to get the current day of the week.

`days = ["sun", "mon", "tue", "wed", "thu",`
`"fri", "sat"]`
`my_date = new Date();`
`today = days[my_date.getDay()];`
`trace(today);`
	The day will be returned as the integer 0 to 6. A better representation would be a string value representing the day names. By using the array `days` and the `getDate` method as an offset into it, we can do this. This script will print the variable `today` as the string value `"sun"` through to `"sat"`.

See the examples `date2.fla` and `date2.swf` on the CD.

Date.getFullYear

```
a = my_date.getFullYear();
```

a will be returned as a four digit integer value corresponding to the year.

This method is compatible with **Flash 5 or later**.

Description

This **method** will return the day of week as the integer value, 0 to 6, with Sunday as 0. The source of this data is the local clock in the user's computer, and the accuracy of this method is dependent on the accuracy (or otherwise) of this clock.

You must construct a `Date` object before you can use this method, as shown in the example below:

Code	Notes
`my_date = new Date();` `year = my_date.getFullYear();`	This script creates a new `Date` object and uses it to get the current year

See the examples `date1.fla` and `date1.swf` on the CD.

Date.getHours

```
a = my_date.getHours();
```

a will be returned as an integer value corresponding to the hour of the day in 24-hour format.

This method is compatible with **Flash 5 or later**.

Description

This **method** will return the hour of the day as the integer value 0 to 23. The source of this data is the local clock in the users computer, and the accuracy of this method is dependent on the accuracy (or otherwise) of this clock.

You must construct a Date object before you can use this method, as shown in the examples below:

Code	Notes
```my_date = new Date();``` ```hours = my_date.getHours();```	This script creates a new Date object and uses it to get the current hour of the day.

```my_date = new Date();```
```hours = my_date.getHours();```
```if (hours>12) {```
```   hours -= 12;```
```   ampm = " pm";```
```} else {```
```   ampm = " am";```
```}```
```if (hours == 0) {```
```   hours = 12;```
```}```
```displayHours = hours+ampm;```
```trace(displayHours);```
	The hour of the day will be returned in 24-hour format. If you want it in 12 hour plus am/pm, this following code will do it.

See the examples date1.fla and date1.swf on the CD.

Date.getMilliseconds

```
a = my_date.getMilliseconds();
```

a will be returned as an integer value 0-999 corresponding to the number of milliseconds in the current second.

This method is compatible with **Flash 5 or later**.

Description

This **method** will return the number of milliseconds 0-999 in the current second. The source of this data is the local clock in the user's computer, and the accuracy of this method is dependent on the accuracy (or otherwise) of this clock.

You must construct a Date object before you can use this method, as shown in the examples below:

Code	Notes
`my_date = new Date();` `milli = my_date.getMilliseconds();`	This script creates a new Date object and uses it to get the current hour of the day.

`_root.onEnterFrame = function() {`
`    my_date = new Date();`
`    trace(my_date.getMilliseconds());`
`};`
	Because Flash is frame-based, and the frame rate is of the order of tenths of a second, Flash by definition does not have millisecond accuracy and this is shown by the output of the script shown. You cannot measure anything via the Date object to a greater accuracy than the frame rate.
	
	NB – There are a other methods available in Flash that have accuracies greater than this script. See also **setInterval** and **sound.onSoundComplete**.

Date.getMinutes

```
a = my_date.getMinutes();
```

a will be returned as an integer value corresponding to minutes in the current hour.

This method is compatible with **Flash 5 or later**.

Description

This **method** will return the minutes in the current hour. The source of this data is the local clock in the user's computer, and the accuracy of this method is dependent on the accuracy (or otherwise) of this clock.

You must construct a Date object before you can use this method, as shown in the example below:

Code	Notes
```my_date = new Date();``` ```hours = my_date.getMinutes();```	This script creates a new Date object and uses it to get the current minutes in the hour.

See the examples date1.fla and date1.swf on the CD.

Date.getMonth

```
a = my_date.getMonth();
```

a will be returned as an integer value corresponding to the month of the year. January is taken as month 0.

This method is compatible with **Flash 5 or later**.

Description

This **method** will return the month of the year as the integer value, 0 to 11, with January as 0. The source of this data is the local clock in the user's computer, and the accuracy of this method is dependent on the accuracy (or otherwise) of this clock.

You must construct a Date object before you can use this method, as shown in the examples below:

Code	Notes

```my_date = new Date();```
```month = my_date.getMonth();```
```trace(month);```
	This script creates a new Date object and uses it to get the current month of the year as the integer.

```months = ["jan", "feb", "mar", "apr",```
```"may", "jun", "jul", "aug", "sept","oct",```
```"nov", "dec"];```
```my_date = new Date();```
```thisMonth = months[my_date.getMonth()];```
```trace(thisMonth);```
	The month will be returned as the integer 0 to 11. A better representation would be a string value representing the month name. By using the array months and the getMonth method as an offset into it, we can do this. The following script will

print the variable `thisMonth` as the
string value `jan` through to `dec`.

See the examples `date2.fla` and `date2.swf` on the CD.

Date.getSeconds

```
a = my_date.getSeconds();
```

a will be returned as an integer value (0 to 59) corresponding to seconds in the current minute.

This method is compatible with **Flash 5 or later**.

Description

This **method** will return the seconds in the current minute. The source of this data is the local clock in the users computer, and the accuracy of this method is dependent on the accuracy (or otherwise) of this clock.

You must construct a `Date` object before you can use this method, as shown in the example below.

Code	Notes
`my_date = new Date();` `hours = my_date.getSeconds();`	This script creates a new `Date` object and uses it to get the seconds in the current minute.

See the examples `date1.fla` and `date1.swf` on the CD.

Date.getTime

```
a = my_date.getTime();
```

a will be returned as an integer value corresponding to the milliseconds since midnight of January 1st 1970. Dates before this will return negative values, and dates after it will be positive.

This method is compatible with **Flash 5 or later**.

Description

This **method** will return the base time variable that all the other methods of the `Date` object use. You can use this value to derive the time between two dates, or as a countdown timer.

Code	Notes
`my_date = new Date();`	This script calculates the age of a

```
timeNow = my_date.getTime();
//
// set date of birth...
my_date.setYear(1967, 0, 29);
my_date.setHours(9);
my_date.setMinutes(50, 0, 0);
//
// aprox how many years old is this person?
timeThen = my_date.getTime();
age = (timeNow-timeThen)/(1000*60*60*24*365);
trace(age);
```

person born at 9:50 on the morning of January 29th 1967 (which incidentally makes them Aquarius with Aries Rising; hardworking, idealistic, but extremely stubborn).

The time today is first stored in `timeNow`. The `set` methods are then used to set the raw millisecond time to January 29th 1967, 0950.

Finally, the age is calculated from the number of milliseconds between `timeThen` and `timeNow`, divided by `1000` (milliseconds) x `60` (seconds) x `60` (minutes) x `24` (hours) x `365` (days).

Fun for all the family; set your date of birth as `timeThen`, convert the script to run via an `onEnterFrame` event, and watch the `age` increase for a really depressing few minutes!

```
// what day was this date?
trace(my_date.getDay());
```

Carrying on from the example above, we can find the day of the week that the person above was born on, by looking at the `getDay()` method. This will return `0` (a Sunday).

In reviewing the above example, see also **Date.setYear**, **Date.setHours**, and **Date.setMinutes** methods, and **Date.setMilliseconds**.

Date.getTimezoneOffset

```
a = my_date.getTimeZoneOffset();
```

a will be returned as an integer value in minutes corresponding to the difference between the local time held in the user's computer clock, and UTC time.

This method is compatible with **Flash 5 or later**.

Description
This **method** will return the time difference between the internal clock of the user's computer, and UTC time. This difference will consist of two components:

- The difference due to time zones. UTC time zone offsets are the same as those specified for GMT (Greenwich Mean Time). See also the entry for **Date** for a fuller description of UTC time.
- The difference due to daylight saving hours. This will only occur of the user's operating system is set up to support daylight saving, and the user has enabled it.

You should note that although, in real life, UTC is the most accurate time, in Flash it can be *less* accurate than the user's local time. See also the *Tips and precautions* section (on the CD) for an explanation of this.

Code	Notes

`my_date = new Date();`
`offset = my_date.getTimeZoneOffset();`
`trace(offset);`
	At the time of writing the author is at a location within the GMT/UTC +0 time-zone during the summer.
	
	The result of this code will return -60.
	
	Although the local time is equal to GMT/UTC, the local clocks have also been put forward an hour for daylight saving (British Summer Time = GMT/UTC+ 1 hour). This means that UTC is one hour behind, hence -60.

Date.getUTCDate

```
a = my_date.getUTCDate();
```

a will be returned as an integer value corresponding to the day of the month in UTC time. This value will be an integer between 1 and 31.

This method is compatible with **Flash 5 or later**.

Description
This **method** will return a value expressed in UTC time, but is otherwise identical to the method **Date.getDate**. See the entry for that method for more details.

The difference between UTC time and local time is available via the **Date.getTimezoneOffset** method. See also the entry for **Date** for a fuller description of the difference between UTC and local time.

Date.getUTCDay

```
a = my_date.getUTCDay();
```

a will be returned as an integer value corresponding to the day of the week in UTC time. This value will be an integer between 0 and 6, with 0 = Sunday.

This method is compatible with **Flash 5 or later**.

Description

This **method** will return a value expressed in UTC time, but is otherwise identical to the method **Date.getDay**. See the entry for that method for more details.

The difference between UTC time and local time is available via the **Date.getTimezoneOffset** method. See also the entry for **Date** for a fuller description of the difference between UTC and local time.

Date.getUTCFullYear

```
a = my_date.getFullYear();
```

a will be returned as an integer value corresponding to the day of the month in UTC time. This value will be a four figure integer, such as 1984.

This method is compatible with **Flash 5 or later**.

Description

This **method** will return a value expressed in UTC time, but is otherwise identical to the method **Date.getFullYear**. See the entry for that method for more details.

The difference between UTC time and local time is available via the **Date.getTimezoneOffset** method. See also the entry for **Date** for a fuller description of the difference between UTC and local time.

Date.getUTCHours

```
a = my_date.getUTCHours();
```

a will be returned as an integer value corresponding to the hour in the day, expressed in UTC time (24-hour clock time). This value will be an integer between 0 and 23.

This method is compatible with **Flash 5 or later**.

Description

This **method** will return a value expressed in UTC time, but is otherwise identical to the method **Date.getHours**. See the entry for that method for more details.

The difference between UTC time and local time is available via the **Date.getTimezoneOffset** method. See also the entry for **Date** for a fuller description of the difference between UTC and local time.

Date.getUTCMilliseconds

```
a = my_date.getUTCMilliseconds();
```

a will be returned as an integer value 0-999 corresponding to the number of milliseconds in the current second, expressed in UTC time.

This method is compatible with **Flash 5 or later**.

Description

This **method** will return a value expressed in UTC time, but is otherwise identical to the method **Date.getMilliseconds**. See the entry for that method for more details.

The difference between UTC time and local time is available via the **Date.getTimezoneOffset** method. See also the entry for **Date** for a fuller description of the difference between UTC and local time.

Date.getUTCMinutes

```
a = my_date.getMinutes();
```

a will be returned as an integer value corresponding to minutes in the current hour, expressed in UTC time.

This method is compatible with **Flash 5 or later**.

Description

This **method** will return a value expressed in UTC time, but is otherwise identical to the method **Date.getMinutes**. See the entry for that method for more details.

The difference between UTC time and local time is available via the **Date.getTimezoneOffset** method. See also the entry for **Date** for a fuller description of the difference between UTC and local time.

Date.getUTCMonth

```
a = my_date.getMonth();
```

a will be returned as an integer value corresponding to the month of the year, expressed in UTC time. January is taken as month 0.

This method is compatible with **Flash 5 or later**.

Description

This **method** will return a value expressed in UTC time, but is otherwise identical to the method **Date.getMinutes**. See the entry for that method for more details.

The difference between UTC time and local time is available via the **Date.getTimezoneOffset** method. See also the entry for **Date** for a fuller description of the difference between UTC and local time.

Date.getYear

```
a = Date.getYear()
```

Returns the current year as the raw year value held by Flash, with 1900 expressed as year 0.

Description

You are much better off using the **Date.getFullYear** method, which returns a full four-digit value, such as 1984. See the entry for that method.

Date.setDate

```
Date.setDate(a);
```

Where a is the date you want to set the local time to, expressed in milliseconds since midnight January 1st 1970.

This method is compatible with **Flash 5 or later**.

Description

This **method** is not useful and very rarely (if ever) used, given that knowing a date in milliseconds from the date specified is not normally something that happens!

The method exists because the internal Flash clock is a raw value in milliseconds that takes zero as midnight Jan 1st 1970. You are better off specifying a date via the **Date.setYear**, **Date.setHours**, **Date.setMinutes**, and **Date.setMilliseconds** if you are really keen. See the entries for these methods.

Note that setting a Date object will not alter the internal clock on the user's computer, but will only change the values returned by a specific Date object instance.

Date.setFullYear

```
Date.setFullYear(YYYY);
```

or

```
Date.SetFullYear(YYYY, MM);
```

or

```
Date.setFullYear(YYYY, MM, DD);
```

Where YYYY is the year you want to set the local Flash Date object to. You can also specify a fuller date that includes the year (four digit number), month (one or two digit number), and date (one or two digit number).

This method is compatible with **Flash 5 or later**.

Description

This **method** allows you to set the year (and optionally, month, and day of month as well). The year should be specified as a four figure integer such as "1984", and not "84", which would result in the year 84AD! So strictly speaking 84 is better off being expressed as 0084.

Setting values outside range will result in the method setting the value modulo the max limit. For example, if you entered 32 as the day of month, the method would use 32%31 = 1.

The following example shows the use of the most commonly used set methods, setYear, setHours, and setMinutes.

Code	Notes
| ```
my_date = new Date();
timeNow = my_date.getTime();
//
// set date of birth...
my_date.setYear(1967, 0, 29);
my_date.setHours(9);
my_date.setMinutes(50, 0, 0);
//
// aprox how many years old is this person?
timeThen = my_date.getTime();
age = (timeNow-timeThen)/(1000*60*60*24*365);
trace(age);
``` | This script calculates the age of a person born at 9.50 on the morning of January 29th 1967 (which incidentally makes them Aquarius with Aries Rising; hardworking, idealistic, but extremely stubborn).<br><br>The time today is first stored in timeNow. The set methods are then used to set the raw millisecond time to January 29th 1967, 0950.<br><br>Finally, the age is calculated from the number of milliseconds between timeThen and timeNow, divided by 1000 (milliseconds) x 60 (seconds) x 60 (minutes) x 24 (hours) x 365 (days).<br><br>Fun for all the family: set your date of birth as timeThen, convert the script to run via an onEnterFrame event, and watch the age increase for a really depressing few minutes! |
```

Date.setHours

```
Date.setHours(a);
```

Where a is the hours in the day you want to set the Flash Date object to.

This method is compatible with **Flash 5 or later**.

Description

This **method** allows you to set the hour of the day, expressed in 24-hour time (an integer 0 to 23).

Setting an hour value outside range will result in changes to the day, month, or year, so you can specify values such as 900 and get the month to update correctly.

The following example shows the use of the most commonly used set methods, setYear, setHours, and setMinutes.

Code	Notes
``my_date = new Date();
timeNow = my_date.getTime();
//
// set date of birth...
my_date.setYear(1967, 0, 29);
my_date.setHours(9);
my_date.setMinutes(50, 0, 0);
//
// aprox how many years old is this person?
timeThen = my_date.getTime();
age = (timeNow-timeThen)/(1000*60*60*24*365);
trace(age);```	This script calculates the age of a person born at 9.50 on the morning of January 29th 1967 (which incidentally makes them Aquarius with Aries Rising; hardworking, idealistic, but extremely stubborn). The time today is first stored in timeNow. The set methods are then used to set the raw millisecond time to January 29th 1967, 0950. Finally, the age is calculated from the number of milliseconds between timeThen and timeNow, divided by 1000 (milliseconds) x 60 (seconds) x 60 (minutes) x 24 (hours) x 365 (days). Fun for all the family: set your date of birth as timeThen, convert the script to run via an onEnterFrame event, and watch the age increase for a really depressing few minutes!

Date.setMilliseconds

```
Date.setMilliseconds(a)
```

Where a is the integer value in milliseconds you want to update the Date object to.

This method is compatible with **Flash 5 or later**.

Description
This **method** allows you to set a Date object to a specified value in seconds.

You should note that this method does not specify a value for the Date to be advanced by, but rather an absolute value it is to be set to.

Code	Notes

```my_date = new Date();```
 ```// display current time...```
 ```myTime = my_date.getHours()+":"+my```
 ```➥_date.getMinutes()+":"+my_date.getSeconds();```
 ```trace(myTime);```
 ```// advance time by 1/2 a minute..```
 ```my_date.setMilliseconds(my_date.getSeconds()```
 ```➥+30000);```
 ```// display new time...```
 ```myTime = my_date.getHours()+":"+my```
 ```➥_date.getMinutes()+":"+my_date.getSeconds();```
 ```trace(myTime);```
	The script shown here advances the time by 30 seconds.

Date.setMinutes

```
Date.setMinutes(mm);
```

or

```
Date.setMinutes(mm, ss);
```

or

```
Date.setMinutes(mm, ss, ms);
```

Where mm is the integer value in minutes you want to update the Date object to. You can also specify seconds (ss) and milliseconds (ms).

This method is compatible with **Flash 5 or later**.

Description

This **method** allows you to advance a specified Date object in minutes and/or seconds and/or milliseconds.

Code	Notes
| ```
my_date = new Date();
timeNow = my_date.getTime();
//
// set date of birth...
my_date.setYear(1967, 0, 29);
my_date.setHours(9);
my_date.setMinutes(50, 0, 0);
//
// aprox how many years old is this person?
timeThen = my_date.getTime();
age = (timeNow-timeThen)/(1000*60*60*24*365);
trace(age);
``` | This script calculates the age of a person born at 9.50 on the morning of January 29th 1967 (which incidentally makes them Aquarius with Aries Rising; hardworking, idealistic, but extremely stubborn). The time today is first stored in timeNow. The set methods are then used to set the raw millisecond time to January 29th 1967, 0950. Finally, the age is calculated from the number of milliseconds between timeThen and timeNow, divided by 1000 (milliseconds) x 60 (seconds) x 60 (minutes) x 24 (hours) x 365 (days). Fun for all the family; set your date of birth as timeThen, convert the script to run via an onEnterFrame event, and watch the age increase for a really depressing few minutes! |

Date.setMonth

```
Date.setMonth(a);
```

Where a is the month in the year you want to set the Flash Date object to.

This method is compatible with **Flash 5 or later**.

Description

This **method** allows you to set the Date object to a specified value in months.
```

You should note that this method does not specify a value for the Date to be advanced by, but rather an absolute value it is to be set to.

Code	Notes

```my_date = new Date();```
```// advance date by 8 months...```
```my_date.setMonth(my_date.getMonth()+8);```
```// display new date...```
```myDateUSA = (my_date.getMonth()+1)+"/"+my```
```➥ _date.getDate()+"/"+my_date.getFullYear();```
```trace(myDateUSA);```
	This script advances the date by 8 months. The year will also change if a crossover to the next year occurs.

Date.setSeconds

```
Date.setSeconds(a);
```

Where a is the value in seconds you want to update the Date object to.

This method is compatible with **Flash 5 or later**.

Description

This **method** allows you to set the Date object in seconds.

You should note that this method does not specify a value for the Date to be advanced by, but rather an absolute value it is to be set to.

Code	Notes

```my_date = new Date();```
```// trace original time...```
```myTime = my_date.getHours()+":"+my```
```➥ _date.getMinutes()+":"+my_date.getSeconds();```
```trace(myTime);```
```// advance time by 30s...```
```my_date.setSeconds(my_date.getSeconds()+30);```
```// display updated time...```
```myTime = my_date.getHours()+":"+my```
```➥ _date.getMinutes()+":"+my_date.getSeconds();```
```trace(myTime);```
	The script shown here advances the time by 30s.

Date.setUTCDate

This method is exactly the same as **Date.setDate**, except that it uses UTC time. See the entry for **Date.setDate**. See also the entry for **Date** for a discussion on UTC time and local time.

Date.setUTCFullYear

This method is exactly the same as **Date.setFullYear**, except that it uses UTC time. See the entry for **Date.setFullYear**. See also the entry for **Date** for a discussion on UTC time and local time.

Date.setUTCHours

This method is exactly the same as **Date.setHours**, except that it uses UTC time. See the entry for **Date.setHours**. See also the entry for **Date** for a discussion on UTC time and local time.

Date.setUTCMilliseconds

This method is exactly the same as **Date.setMilliseconds**, except that it uses UTC time. See the entry for **Date.setMilliseconds**. See also the entry for **Date** for a discussion on UTC time and local time.

Date.setUTCMinutes

This method is exactly the same as **Date.setMinutes**, except that it uses UTC time. See the entry for **Date.setMinutes**. See also the entry for **Date** for a discussion on UTC time and local time.

Date.setUTCMonth

This method is exactly the same as **Date.setMonth**, except that it uses UTC time. See the entry for **Date.setMonth**. See also the entry for **Date** for a discussion on UTC time and local time.

Date.setUTCSeconds

This method is exactly the same as **Date.setSeconds**, except that it uses UTC time. See the entry for **Date.setSeconds**. See also the entry for **Date** for a discussion on UTC time and local time.

Date.setYear

This method is exactly the same as **Date.setYear**, except that it uses UTC time. See the entry for **Date.setYear**. See also the entry for **Date** for a discussion on UTC time and local time.

Date.toString

```
a = my_date.toString();
```

a will be returned as the value held by the Date object my_date in the default date format.

This method is compatible with **Flash 5 or later**.

Description

Returns the full value of the time and date held by the Date object to second accuracy, and this is returned via a string.

Code	Notes
`dateStamp = new Date().toString();`	If all you want is a quick and easy string to use as a date stamp, this line of code will do it. The returned value will be of the form: `Fri Jun 21 11:15:53 GMT+0100 2002`
`my_date = new Date();` `trace(my_date.toString());`	Long-hand version of the above example.

Date.UTC

```
Date.UTC(year, month, date, hour, minute, second, millisecond);
```

This method is a conversion function that allows you to specify a date in UTC format.

You can start specifying the date from left to right, and stop when you have reached the max accuracy for your application. For example, if you only want to set the year, month, and date, you can use the syntax:

```
Date.UTC(year, month, date);
```

and if you want to specify up to the nearest minute you would do this:

```
Date.UTC(year, month, date, hour, minute);
```

If you wanted to set the year and seconds, but leave everything as it was, you could do this:

```
Date.UTC(year, undefined, undefined, undefined, undefined, second);
```

The undefined values are ignored (and the current value as specified by the user's clock is retained).

Whereas the following would set the year and seconds, but everything else in between (month, date, hour, minute) would be zero.

```
Date.UTC(year, 0, 0, 0, 0, second);
```

This method is compatible with **Flash 5 or later**.

Description

This **method** allows you to specify a time in UTC time. This has advantages when you want to represent the same *instant* to an international audience. For example, if you created a Flash page that tells people to look, say, at the planet Venus at 3 O'clock today (EST time), folks in Germany will be looking at Venus at the wrong time, because they will look at Venus at 3 O'clock *their time*, and not at the same instant as you.

Code	Notes

`my_date = new Date(Date.UTC(2003, 0, 29,`
 `➥9, 50));`
 `trace(my_date.toString());`
	This code allows the user to read the authors next birthday to the nearest minute, expressed as the equivalent time in their time zone, so all the readers of this book can light a candle at the same instant in time...or not!

default

```
default :
    // do this
```

This action has no arguments.

This action is compatible with **Flash 5 or later**. Although the Flash 5 environment does not support it, content created in the Flash MX environment and exported as Flash 5 does. This action forms an optional part of the **switch** structure, and you should also refer to the entry for that action.

Description

The default **action** forms part of the **switch** structure, and other actions that are typically also used are **break** and **case**. Also see the entries for these actions.

The default action is used to create the default (condition-less) branch part of a switch decision tree, and this branch is executed if all the case conditions above it are false.

The default branch should be placed as the last branch of a switch decision tree.

Code	Notes
`input_btn.onRelease = function() {` `    switch (Number(input_txt.text)) {`	This is a typical input scheme for the sort of setup shown below. Once the

```
            case 1 :
                output_txt.text = "you selected 1";
                break;
            case 2 :
                output_txt.text = "you selected 2";
                break;
            case 3 :
                output_txt.text = "you selected 3";
                break;
            default :
                output_txt.text = "please enter 1, 2 or 3";
        }
};
```

text is entered by the user, the button event handler is used as the input validation script.

If the user enters 1, 2, or 3, the input is accepted. If any other input is entered, a default script is run, and this handles all other inputs.

As can be seen from the script, default is the same as the **else** branch of the **if** structure. It is the last branch and essentially means 'otherwise do this'.

See the example files case.fla and case.swf on the CD.

delete

```
b = delete a;
```

Where a is a variable, object, or property. b will be returned as true if a was successfully deleted, and false if it wasn't. It is more usual to use the following syntax:

```
delete a;
```

This operator is compatible with **Flash 5 and later**. It allows you to delete variables and objects that you have previously defined.

Description

This **operator** allows you to delete a variable or object. It also has an undocumented feature; it allows you to delete **functions**, and this has some useful implications for Flash MX. See the *Tips and Precautions* section on the CD for more details.

The usefulness of delete is that it removes variables or objects *completely*, and this means something different from simply equating the object or variable to undefined.

Supposing you have an array, x. Once you have finished with it, it is a good idea to clear it from memory for the sake of efficiency, and also performance if x is very large.

If you delete it as follows:

```
x = [20, 30, 50, 50];
x = undefined;
```

... you will find that the elements of x disappear, but x itself still exists, albeit undefined. To clear x **completely**, you need to do the following:

```
x = [20, 30, 50, 50];
delete x;
```

This will remove x completely, and you can confirm this by running this script in debug mode. x will no longer exist if you look on the _root timeline.

Code	Notes

`a = 10;`
`trace(a);`
`b = delete a;`
	If you debug this script, you will see that b = true and a no longer exists; a has been deleted.

`myObject = {p1:10, p2:30, p3:2.3, p4:6};` `delete myObject.p3;`	After line 1, the object myObject is equal to:

After line 1, the object myObject is equal to:

⊟	myObject	
	p1	10
	p2	30
	p3	2.3
	p4	6

After line 2 it becomes:

⊟	myObject	
	p1	10
	p2	30
	p4	6

Property p3 of myObject is deleted.

```
delete Math.abs;
delete my_mc;
```

You cannot delete variables, objects, or properties that you have not previously defined.

You cannot delete graphic objects (movie clips, buttons, or textfields).

See the example files delete.fla and delete.swf on the CD.

do while

```
do {
```

```
    //do this...
} while (a);
```

The do while will continue to loop until condition a is false.

This **action** is compatible with **Flash 4 or later**.

Description

The do while loop allows you to create a loop that will cycle while the loop condition remains true. The important difference between the do while loop and the **while** loop is that do while will always execute at least once, whereas the while loop may not execute at all. This is due to while checking for a true value at the start of the loop, whereas do while checks at the end of the loop.

Code	Notes

<pre>function factorial(y) {
    var y;
    var result = 1;
    do {
        result *= y;
        y--;
    } while (y>1);
    return result;
}
trace(factorial(56));
trace(factorial(3));
trace(factorial(0));</pre>
	This script shows one of the more efficient ways of working out the factorial of a number (and without using much less efficient recursive techniques). It will correctly give the results of 56!, 3!, and 0! as 7.10998587804863e+74, 6, and 0 respectively.

<pre>do {
    // do this...
} while (true);</pre>
	This script will result in a forever loop, something that is **Very Bad News**. Forever loops will cause the Flash Player to ignore further scripts, effectively crashing the ActionScript byte code interpreter.

<pre>do {
    this._x++
} while (this._x<300);</pre>
	You should not use a do loop to produce animation. All ActionScript loops complete in a single frame, and this makes them unsuitable for animating content in the way suggested by this script.

<pre>myClip_mc.onEnterFrame = function() {
    this._x++;
    if (this._x>300) {
        this.onEnterFrame = undefined;
    }
};</pre>
	This script illustrates one way of providing animation correctly. It is better suited to animation because it makes changes per frame.

duplicateMovieClip

```
duplicateMovieClip(target, instanceName, depth);
```

Where `target` is the target of the movie clip that you want to duplicate, `instanceName` is the name of the copy, and `depth` is the depth of the copy.

This action is compatible with **Flash 4 or later**. In Flash 5, you should use the **MovieClip.duplicateMovieClip** action when duplicating movie clips. The `duplicateMovieClip` action has some advantages over the method-based version, however, in that it has some useful undocumented features. See the *Tips and Precautions* section on the CD. See also Chapter 1.

Description

The `duplicateMovieClip` **action** is the Flash 4 version of the Flash 5 `MovieClip.duplicate MovieClip` method. The two are not identical in their operation however:

- They have different syntaxes. See also **MovieClip.duplicateMovieClip.**
- The `duplicatMovieClip` action can duplicate textfields and buttons as well as movie clips, whereas the method-based versions cannot (there is no `Button.duplicateMovieClip` or `TextField.duplicateMovieClip` methods, either documented or undocumented). See also the *Tips and Precautions* section on the CD.

The `duplicateMovieClip` action allows you to make copies of a movie clip instance already on the stage. The copy will have all the properties as the original **except**:

- **Current frame number**. The copies will always start at frame 1 irrespective of the current frame number of the original.
- **Timeline variables**. The copies will not inherit the variables/data objects on the timeline of the original, although they will inherit any embedded graphic objects (movie clips, buttons, textfields) on the timeline of the original.

Duplicated clips will also **not** have the events of the original attached.

The instance name of the copy should be unique. If you keep the instance name the same, Flash will not be able to differentiate between the copy and the original, and this will cause problems.

The ordering of symbols on the stage, per timeline, is done by looking at a property called **depth**. Flash looks at the depths of all symbols on the stage, and draws them in the order specified by it, lowest depth first (lowest down). This means that a symbol with a higher depth will be drawn over one with a lower depth. If any symbol has embedded symbols, Flash will look at the local depths of that timeline, and order them in that depth order within the symbol.

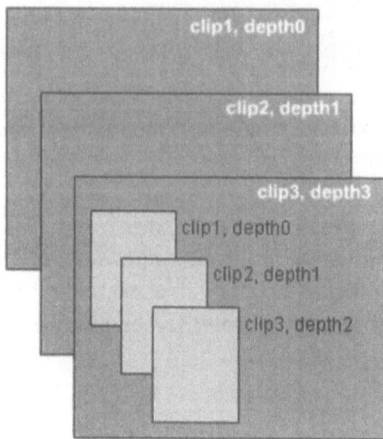

Symbols that are placed on stage manually during content creation have depths that are not accessible to ActionScript (or rather, they are accessible, just not documented, the depths of such symbols are *negative*).

The depths of symbols that are placed on stage via ActionScript have the following rules:

- They must be positive (assuming you are following the documented features).
- If you place a symbol on a timeline at an already occupied depth, the previous symbol at that depth will be overwritten and effectively deleted.

duplicateMovieClip is somewhat superceded by a number of newer methods. These include:

- **MovieClip.attachMovie**
- **MovieClip.createEmptyMovieClip**

Also, to remove a duplicated movie clip, see **removeMovieClip** and **MovieClip.removeMovieClip**.

Code	Notes
`duplicateMovieClip("my_mc", "myOther_mc", 1);`	Duplicates the existing movie clip my_mc and calls the copy myOther_mc.

`for (i=0; i<10; i++) {`
`    duplicateMovieClip("my_mc", "clip"+i, i);`
`}`
	Duplicates the existing movie clip my_mc ten times. The copied clips will be called clip0 to clip9 and will exist at a depth of 0 to 9.

gotoAndStop()
hitTest()
loadMovie()
loadVariables()
loadVariables()
nextFrame()   play()
prevFrame()
removeMovieClip()
setMask()   startDrag()
startDrag()
swap Depths()
unloadMovie()
attach Movie()
createEmptyMovie
createTextField
duplicateMovie
getBound

else

```
} else {
    // do this..
```

This action is compatible with **Flash 4 or later**. The else action is part of the **if... else if... else** branching structure, and you should read this description in conjunction with the entries for **if** and **else if**.

Description

The else is one of two optional **actions** (**else** and **else if**) that can be used with the **if** statement.

The **if** action will execute its associated script if its condition is true. The trace action below will only execute if x is equal to zero:

```
if (x == 0) {
    trace("x is equal to zero");
}
```

If x is not equal to zero, you may want to apply more conditions. For example, you may also want to check if x is 1 or 2. This is performed via the **else if**. This first else if will execute the associated trace if x is 1, and the second will execute if x=2. An important point to realize is that:

- x has to be *not* equal to 0 for the first else if to run.
- x has to be *not* equal to either 0 or 1 for the second else if to run.

This is because only one branch of an if will ever run, so if x is zero, no further parts of the if will be looked at.

```
x = 1;
if (x == 0) {
    trace("x is equal to zero");
} else if (x == 1) {
    trace("x is equal to one");
} else if (x == 2) {
    trace("x is equal to 2");
}
```

The else action is the 'catch all' that you can put at the end of the if structure. **It will run if none of the other if or else if branches run**:

```
x = 1;
if (x == 0) {
    trace("x is equal to zero");
} else if (x == 1) {
```

```
    trace("x is equal to one");
} else if (x == 2) {
    trace("x is equal to 2");
} else {
    trace("sorry, I don't know what x is");
}
```

The `else` branch will execute its associated `trace` action if x is not equal to 0, 1, or 2.

Code	Notes

```weather = "sunny";```
 ```if (weather == "sunny") {```
 ```   trace("time to go out and play!");```
 ```} else {```
 ```   trace("mmmm... time to stay in and do```
 ```➥ some writing.");```
 ```}```
	If the variable weather is sunny, then the time to go out and play message will appear.
	
	 If it is not sunny, then it is a good chance that sunbathing in the back yard is out for this author, so now is a good chance to catch up on some work.
	
	 Notice that the else branch can assume what the weather is *not* without having to test for it. If the weather was sunny, the else would not have executed, so by the time we get past the initial if, we can assume no-sunbathing-in-the-yard weather.

```if (sunny) {```
 ```} else {```
 ```   trace("no sun today!");```
 ```}```
	The else can be used to execute on the false condition. If sunny is true, then nothing will happen, but if it is false, the else branch will execute.

```x = 5;```
 ```if (x>5) {```
 ```   trace("x is greater than 5");```
 ```} else if (x<5) {```
 	
 ```   trace("x is less than 5");```
 ```} else {```
 ```   trace("x is equal to 5");```
 ```}```
	This is a good example of the fact that you can assume what the true condition will be by the time you reach the else.
	
	 If x is not greater than 5, nor is it less than 5, it *must* be equal to 5, and the else here assumes this.

```if (x == 0) {```
 ```   trace("x is equal to zero");```
 ```} else {```
 ```   trace("sorry, I don't know what x is");```
 ```} else if (x == 1) {```
	The else should always be the last branch of an if. Having other conditions after the else will raise a syntax error.

```
       trace("x is equal to one");
} else if (x == 2) {
      trace("x is equal to 2");
}
```

```
weather = "raining";
if (weather == "sunny") {
    trace("time to go out and play!");
} else {
    if (weather == "warm") {
        trace("hmm, might go out for a
➡while.");
    } else {
        trace("awful! I'm staying in
➡today.");
    }
}

weather = "raining";
if (weather == "sunny") {
    trace("time to go out and play!");
} else if (weather == "warm") {
    trace("hmm, might go out for a
➡while.");
} else {
    trace("awful! I'm staying in today.");
}
```

A common mistake for beginners is to use else where it is not actually needed.

The first example looks reasonable, but it can actually be written in the shorter script shown below it.

As a rule, if an else is immediately followed by an if, you can *always* replace the else and if by a single else if.

else if

```
} else if (condition){
    // do this..
```

This action is compatible with **Flash 4 or later**. The else if action is part of the **if... else if... else** branching structure, and you should read this description in conjunction with the entries for **if** and **else**.

Description

The else if is one of two optional **actions** (**else** and **else if**) that can be used with the **if** statement.

The else if action will execute its associated script if its condition is true *and* all previous conditions in the if statement so far have been false. In short, the else if action allows you to modify a basic if action by adding further alternative conditions. Consider the script below:

```
if (x == 0) {
    trace("x is equal to zero");
}
```

If x is not equal to zero, you may want to apply more conditions. For example, you may also want to check if x is 1 or 2. This is performed via the `else if`. This is because only one branch of an `if` will ever run, so if x is zero, no further parts of the `if` will be looked at.

```
x = 1;
if (x == 0) {
    trace("x is equal to zero");
} else if (x == 1) {
    trace("x is equal to one");
} else if (x == 2) {
    trace("x is equal to 2");
}
```

The first `else if` will execute the associated trace if x is 1, and the second will execute if x=2. An important point to realize is that **an if... else will only run one of the possible branches**, and this means that an `else if` branch will not run if a branch above it has already run:

- x has to be *not* equal to 0 for the first `else if` to run (because then the initial x==0 condition would be true, and `trace("x is equal to zero")` would run).
- x has to be *not* equal to either 0 or 1 for the second `else if` to run.

Code	Notes

```weather = "sunny";```
 ```if (weather == "sunny") {```
 ```   trace("time to go out and play!");```
 ```} else if (weather=="cold"){```
 ```   trace("mmmm... time to stay in and do```
 ```➥ some writing.");```
 ```}```
	If the variable weather is sunny, then the time to go out and play message will appear.
	
	 If weather is cold, then it is a good chance that sunbathing in the back yard is out for this author.
	
	 Notice that if weather is neither sunny nor cold, then no message will appear. If you want a message to appear whatever the weather variable is, then you probably need to add an **else** at the end of this code. See also the entry for **else**.

```if (x == 0) {```
 ```   trace("x is equal to zero");```
 ```} else if (x == 1) {```
 ```   trace("x is equal to one");```
 ```} else if (x == 2) {```
 ```   trace("x is equal to 2");```
 ```}```
	You can have multiple else ifs.

```
x = 5;
if (x>5) {
    trace("x is greater than 5");
} else if (x<5) {
    trace("x is less than 5");
} else if (x==5){
    trace("x is equal to 5");
}

x = 5;
if (x>5) {
    trace("x is greater than 5");
} else if (x<5) {
    trace("x is less than 5");
} else{
    trace("x is equal to 5");
}
```

A common mistake for beginners is to use else if when you could just as well use the more efficient else.

In the first example, the last check (x==5) is redundant. If x is neither greater than nor less than 5, then it *must* be equal to 5. It would be better therefore to use the else action, and this is shown in the second example.

Although this change may seem trivial, when you have complex conditions, or when you are applying the same decision trees many times, creating efficient **if... else if... else** structures is the key to writing code that runs quickly.

eq

```
a = b eq c;
```

Where a is a Boolean that will be true if:

- **Flash 4**: the two strings b and c are equal.
- **Flash 5 and above**: the value of the two objects, variables, or literal values b and c are equal.

This operator is compatible with **Flash 4 or later**. This operator is deprecated in Flash 5 and above, where you should use the == (equality) operator in preference.

This operator is the same as **== equality** except that when used in Flash 4, it can test for equality between two strings only. See also the entry for **== equality**.

escape (as a function)

```
a = escape(b);
```

Where a will be returned as the URL encoded version of the string b. If b is not a string, escape will attempt to use the value of b expressed as a string.

This global function is compatible with **Flash 5 and later**. See also Chapter 12. To convert URL encoded text back to standard text, you should use **unescape**.

Description

This global **function** is used to convert a string to URL encoded text. In URL encoded text, all non-alphanumeric characters (including space) are deleted and a '%' followed by the deleted character's character code (in hexadecimal) is inserted at the same position.

Code

```
a = String.fromCharCode(169)+" 2002";
trace(a);
b = escape(a);
trace(b);
```

Notes

This code will produce the following output:

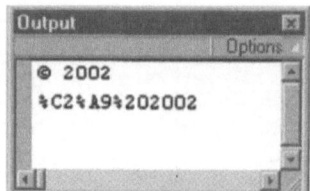

The original © character is converted to %C2 (0xC2=169), and " 2002" is converted to %202002 (% followed by 20 (hexadecimal for 32) followed by 2002).

---

eval

```
a = eval(b);
```

b is an expression that evaluates to a variable name, and a will be equated to the **value** of this variable.

This global function is compatible with **Flash 4 and later**. Although it is not deprecated in Flash 5 (and later), you will never have to use it in any other version other than Flash 4, given that there are better ways of achieving the same functionality in later versions of Flash.

Description

The eval global **function** allows you to simulate the ability to access dynamic variable names and target paths. For example, if you want to access the variable a and assign it to b you write:

```
b = a;
```

Suppose instead that you wanted to assign b to a variable whose identity you will only know at runtime. You can't do this in Flash 4 because variable names are literal references. The eval function allows you to get around this constraint by taking an expression as its argument so that it evaluates as a variable name.

So now you can make your name dynamic:
```
b = eval("my"+"Variable");
```

... will equate b to the variable myVariable.

Note that this will equate b to the value of myVariable rather than the string literal "myVariable".

In Flash 5 and later versions, you can use dot notation to do the same thing, and so therefore do not need to use eval:

```
b = _root["my" + "Variable"];
```

Code	
	Notes
`i = 5;` `x = eval("myVariable"+i);`	Variable x is equated to the value of variable myVariable5.

`for (i=0; i<10; i++) {`
`    tellTarget (eval("myClip"+i)) {`
`        gotoAndStop(2);`
`    }`
`}`
 	
`for (i=0; i<10; i++) {`
`    _root["myClip"+i].gotoAndStop(2);`
`}`
	The first script will make the ten movie clips myClip0 to myClip9 go to frame 2 on their respective timelines. This script is written in a Flash 4 style.
	
	The shorter second script will do the same thing, but is written in a much more up-to-date style (that doesn't need eval).

evaluate

evaluate is not a part of ActionScript, but is rather a way of direct typing a single line of code when in Normal mode. This allows you to enter lines of ActionScript that cannot be otherwise entered whilst in Normal mode.

In Expert mode, there is no need to use evaluate, given that all lines are typed directly by default.

F

gotoAndStop()
hitTest()
loadMovie()
loadVariables()
loadVariables()   play()
nextFrame()
prevFrame()   removeMovieClip()
setMask()   startDrag()   startDrag()
swapDepths()
unloadMovie()
attachMovie()
createEmptyMovieClip
createTextField
duplicateMovieClip
getBounds

false

```
false
```

This literal value is compatible with **Flash 5 or later**.

Description
The `false` **literal** value corresponds to the Boolean state 'false'.

Code	Notes
`a = 5==6;`	a will be returned as `false` because `5==6` is a false statement: 5 is not equal to 6.

`a = 6;`
`b = 6;`
`c = (a != b);`
	c will be returned as `false` because `a!=b` is a false statement: 6 is not unequal to 6.

`a = 6;`
`b = false;`
`c = a+b;`
`d = a*b;`
	`c = 6`
	`d = 0`
	
	If you treat `false` as a number, it will act as if it were the number zero.

FComponent

Covers **FcheckBox, FComboBox, FListBox, FPushButton, FRadioButton, FScrollbar, FscrollPane.**

Flash MX introduces the **Component**. This is a special type of modular movie clip that allows for content creation using general user interface building blocks.

Although the objects and methods that are introduced by components are not strictly part of the ActionScript language, any book that sets out to teach practical scripting needs to address them, so we will treat component-specific features as part of ActionScript within this reference.

We will cover the first component set released by Macromedia (and is the set that has come 'out of the box' with all releases of Flash MX). At the time of writing, there is a second component set available for download at the Macromedia site. We will not cover that (or subsequent issues of components from Macromedia or other major third parties), given that the methods and features available for other components will be based on the initial set, and an understanding of the first set is therefore the core skill to move forward.

To prevent repetition, we have grouped all the separate component objects **FCheckBox**, **FComboBox**, **FListBox**, **FPushButton**, **FRadioButton**, **FScrollBar**, **and FScrollPane** into one general object **FComponent**. If for example, you want to look up **FCheckBox.setEnabled**, you should instead look up **FComponent.setEnabled**.

You should also note that we have taken a tutorial-based approach to some of the entries rather than the more concise reference style. This is because most component-based techniques require you to use a number of methods, or to have set up some very specific initial conditions before the method under discussion can actually be used. This document is primarily a practical 'real world usage' guide rather than a language lexicon, so tutorial-based material is used where it will aid understanding faster than a large body of potentially unrelated facts.

Beginning components

For the reader hoping for a quick and easy entry into how to use components, the array of available methods can be a little daunting (to say the least!). However, it is actually possible to write scripts that interface with components using only **one** method, **FComponent.getValue**. You are advised to read the entry for this method first if you have not used components before. The reason that you can get away with only one method is that most methods are simply code-based versions of things you can set up manually using the Property inspector. If you use the Property inspector based route to set up your components, the only other thing you have to do is actually read the values of the component.

So the upshot of using components for the beginner is this: Components are easy to use once you know the identity of the magic method that opens up their power, and we have already told you that.

Advanced components

The only components that require more advanced techniques are:

- Scrollbars that are not controlling textfields. The standard use of a scrollbar is a simple process of drag and drop. You simply drag the scrollbar over a textfield and the scrollbar will simply snap to the edge nearest the textfield edge you dropped it on (you must have View > Snap to Objects enabled). After that, the scrollbar will take care of everything else. You can also use the scrollbar for other things, such as volume control sliders, and so on. If you want to use scrollbars in this way, you have to use some fairly specialized methods, because this is a non-standard use of the component (but still acceptable).

- Scroll panes are used to simply display content, and are therefore a little different from the other components. They are actually very versatile, and allow you to create all sorts of window based UI elements. You can get by with just manual configuring via the Property inspector, but using the **FComponent.loadScrollContent** method allows you to load content on demand, and this opens up many more possibilities for using the scroll pane in website design.

General

When using components, one thing to always be aware of is that **the bandwidth profiler does not take into account the effects of SWF compression**. When adding components to the stage, you will notice that certain components can increase the file size by up to 30k per component type. Components actually compress very well (given that they consist largely of code, and that compresses *very* well), so the bandwidth profiler can be very misleading. You should instead look at the file size of the final SWF files.

The methods available for each component are listed below. We have ordered them in a way that reflects workflow rather than ActionScript syntax, and have included all component methods as methods of a fictitious object **FComponent** (this way of ordering also removes the high level of duplication of methods between components, and therefore allows you to learn all the common methods much quicker because you see them in terms of all the components that they are applicable to).

We have listed the individual methods that work with each component below, so that you can quickly see which methods apply to which components. If you want to see how all the methods applicable to **FCheckBox** work, simply replace 'FCheckBox' in the list below with 'FComponent', and look up those methods in the dictionary. So for example, to look up FCheckBox.getEnabled, look up **FComponent.getEnabled**.

FCheckBox

```
FCheckBox.getEnabled
FCheckBox.getLabel
FCheckBox.getValue
FCheckBox.registerSkinElement
FCheckBox.setChangeHandler
FCheckBox.setEnabled
FCheckBox.setLabel
FCheckBox.setLabelPlacement
FCheckBox.setSize
FCheckBox.setStyleProperty
FCheckBox.setValue
```

FComboBox

```
FComboBox.addItem
FComboBox.addItemAt
FComboBox.getEnabled
FComboBox.getItemAt
FComboBox.getLength
FComboBox.getRowCount
FComboBox.getScrollPosition
FComboBox.getSelectedIndex
FComboBox.getSelectedItem
FComboBox.getValue
FComboBox.registerSkinElement
FComboBox.removeAll
FComboBox.removeItemAt
FComboBox.replaceItemAt
FComboBox.setChangeHandler
FComboBox.setDataProvider
FComboBox.setEditable
FComboBox.setEnabled
FComboBox.setItemSymbol
FComboBox.setRowCount
FComboBox.setSelectedIndex
FComboBox.setSize
FComboBox.setStyleProperty
FComboBox.setValue
FComboBox.sortItemsBy
```

FListBox

```
FListBox.addItem
FListBox.addItemAt
FListBox.getEnabled
FListBox.getItemAt
FListBox.getLength
FListBox.getRowCount
FListBox.getScrollPosition
FListBox.getSelectedIndex
FListBox.getSelectedIndices
FListBox.getSelectedItem
FListBox.getSelectedItems
FListBox.getSelectMultiple
FListBox.getValue
FListBox.registerSkinElement
FListBox.removeAll
```

FListBox.removeItemAt
FListBox.replaceItemAt
FListBox.setAutoHideScrollBar
FListBox.setChangeHandler
FListBox.setDataProvider
FListBox.setEnabled
FListBox.setItemSymbol
FListBox.setRowCount
FListBox.setScrollPosition
FListBox.setSelectedIndex
FListBox.setSelectedIndices
FListBox.setSelectMultiple
FListBox.setSize
FListBox.setStyleProperty
FListBox.setWidth
FListBox.sortItemsBy

FPushButton

FPushButton.getEnabled
FPushButton.getLabel
FPushButton.registerSkinElement
FPushButton.setClickHandler
FPushButton.setEnabled
FPushButton.setLabel
FPushButton.setSize
FPushButton.setStyleProperty

FRadioButton

FRadioButton.getData
FRadioButton.getEnabled
FRadioButton.getLabel
FRadioButton.getState
FRadioButton.getValue
FRadioButton.registerSkinElement
FRadioButton.setChangeHandler
FRadioButton.setData
FRadioButton.setEnabled
FRadioButton.setGroupName
FRadioButton.setLabel
FRadioButton.setLabelPlacement
FRadioButton.setSize
FRadioButton.setState
FRadioButton.setStyleProperty

FRadioButton.setValue

FScrollBar

FScrollBar.getEnabled
FScrollBar.getScrollPosition
FScrollBar.registerSkinElement
FScrollBar.setChangeHandler
FScrollBar.setEnabled
FScrollBar.setHorizontal
FScrollBar.setLargeScroll
FScrollBar.setScrollContent
FScrollBar.setScrollPosition
FScrollBar.setScrollProperties
FScrollBar.setScrollTarget
FScrollBar.setSize
FScrollBar.setSmallScroll
FScrollBar.setStyleProperty

FScrollPane

FScrollPane.getPaneHeight
FScrollPane.getPaneWidth
FScrollPane.getScrollContent
FScrollPane.getScrollPosition
FScrollPane.loadScrollContent
FScrollPane.refreshPane
FScrollPane.registerSkinElement
FScrollPane.setDragContent
FScrollPane.setHScroll
FScrollPane.setScrollContent
FScrollPane.setScrollPosition
FScrollPane.setSize
FScrollPane.setStyleProperty
FScrollPane.setVScroll

FComponent.addItem

(This method is applicable to **FComboBox.addItem** and **FListBox.addItem**.)

```
MyComponent.addItem(label, data);
```

Where label is an additional label that you want to add to the end of the existing list of labels for a combobox or listbox component. You can also add a data item. This second argument is optional.

This method is compatible with **Flash 6**.

Description

When adding listbox or combobox components, you have to populate the Labels and Data fields in the Property inspector (as shown below for the combobox).

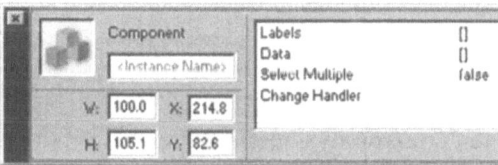

The Labels values define the selectable titles that will appear in the component at run time. For example, if you defined the labels to be horse, mouse, goat, cat, dog, aardvark, and moose, the combobox would look like this at runtime:

The Data field allows you to add a corresponding data (literal) value that will be made available to the changeHandler function whenever one of the labels is selected (see also **FComponent.setChangeHandler**). Adding data per label is optional – if you don't enter one for a label, a string corresponding to the label will be returned.

The addItem method allows you to do the same thing during runtime via ActionScript. You can add additional labels/data, and also define all the labels from scratch.

Code	Notes
`myUI.addItem("red");`	Adds a new label "red" to a combobox or listbox. If there are existing labels already defined, the new label will be added to the end of the list. When the user clicks on the new label, the value returned via the **Fcomponent.getValue** method will be the string value "red".
`myUI.addItem("red", 2);`	Adds a new label "red" to a combobox or listbox. If there are existing labels already defined, the new label

> will be added to the end of the list. When the user clicks on the new label, the value returned via the **Fcomponent.getValue** method will be the number value 2.

See the files fcomponentadditem.fla and fcomponentadditem.swf on the CD.

FComponent.addItemAt

(This method is applicable to **FComboBox.addItemAt** and **FListBox.addItemAt**.)

```
MyComponent.addItemAt(index label, data);
```

Where label is an additional label that you want to add at position index of the existing list of labels for a combobox or listbox component. You can also add a data item. This second argument is optional.

This method is compatible with **Flash 6**.

Description

This method is the same as **Fcomponent.addItem** except that labels are added at a specified position rather than the end of the list. See **Fcomponent.addItem** for more details on this method.

Code	Notes
`myUI.addItemAt(3, "red");`	Adds a new label "red" to a combobox or listbox at an index value of 3, which would make 'red' the fourth label down the list. When the user clicks on the new label, the value returned via the **Fcomponent.getValue** method will be the string value "red".
`myUI.addItemAt(3, "red", 2);`	Adds a new label "red" to a combobox or listbox at an index value of 3, which would make 'red' the fourth label down the list. When the user clicks on the new label, the value returned via the **Fcomponent.getValue** method will be the number 2.

See the files fcomponentadditemat.fla and fcomponentadditemat.swf on the CD.

FComponent.getData

(This method is applicable to **FRadioButton.getData**.)

```
a = myComponent.getData();
```

Where myComponent is a radio button instance. The data value of the last selected radio button in a radio button group will be returned and stored as the variable a.

This method is compatible with **Flash 6**.

Description

Before you can use this method, you need to have a properly set up radio button group. Radio buttons are usually set up as groups, and you can only have one button selected at any time. The following description briefly shows how to set up a group:

1. Place three radio buttons on the stage as shown:

    ○ Radio Button

    ○ Radio Button

    ○ Radio Button

2. Name the instances (from top to bottom) button1 to button3. For button1, fill out properties as shown (via the Property inspector):

    - Label = yes
    - Initial State = false
    - Data = 0
    - LabelPlacement = right
    - ChangeHandler = radioHandler

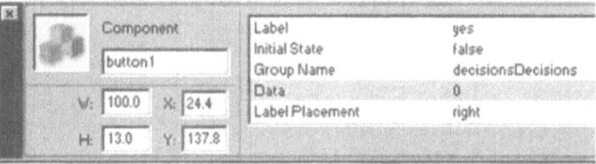

3. Do the same for button2 and button3 except:

    - Give them instance names button2 and button3.
    - Give them Data values of 1 and 2.

The buttons will now look like this:

> ○ yes
> ○ no
> ○ maybe

Finally, add the following code on the same frame as the buttons:

```
function radioHandler(component) {
    message = "you just selected "+component.getData();
    trace(message);
}
```

The function is the `radioHandler` we specified earlier, and this will run every time we change the currently selected radio button. Within this function you can see how the `getData` method is used – it retrieves the data associated with the newly selected radio button.

This example shows the standard use of `getData`; you use it in the `radioHandler` function to find out the currently selected button. Although you can use a frame based polling scheme (whereby you look at the `getData` value only when you need it), the event driven way of doing it has far less potential pitfalls, and you are strongly recommended to use it in preference.

See also fcomponentgetdata.fla and fcomponentgetdata.swf on the CD.

FComponent.getEnabled

(This method is applicable to **FCheckBox.getEnabled**, **FComboBox.getEnabled**, **FListBox.getEnabled**, **FPushButton.getEnabled**, **FRadioButton.getEnabled**, and **FScrollBar.getEnabled**.)

```
a = myComponent.getEnabled();
```

For all components except the radio button:

a is returned as either `true` or `false`, depending on whether the component instance is enabled or not.

For radio button instances (via `FRadioButton`):

a is returned as either `true`, `false`, or `undefined` as follows:

- `true` if the radio button instance `myComponent` is enabled.
- `true` if all radio buttons in the group `myComponent` are enabled.
- `false` if the radio button instance `myComponent` is disabled.
- `false` if all radio buttons in the group `myComponent` are disabled.
- `undefined` if there is a mixture of enabled/disabled buttons in the button group `myComponent`.

This method is compatible with **Flash 6**.

Description

The getEnabled method tells you whether a component is enabled or disabled. Radio buttons are a special case because you usually build up a group of radio buttons, and are more interested in this group rather than individual radio buttons.

Code	Notes
a = myScroller.getEnabled();	a will be true if the component myScroller is enabled, and false if it is not.
a = myGroup.getEnabled();	a will be true if all radio buttons in the group myGroup are enabled, false if they are all disabled, and undefined if a mixture of enabled/disabled radio buttons exists within the group.

See also the examples fcomponentgetenabled.fla and fcomponentgetenabled.swf on the CD.

FComponent.getGroupName

(This method is applicable to **FRadioButton.getGroupName**.)

```
a = myComponent.getGroupName();
```

Where myComponent is a radio button instance. Variable a stores the returned value, which is a string value that contains the name of the group that this instance is a member of.

This method is compatible with **Flash 6**.

Description

Radio buttons are usually configured as a group. To include a set of individual buttons within a group manually, you would set the Group Name property of each button to the same value (via the Property inspector):

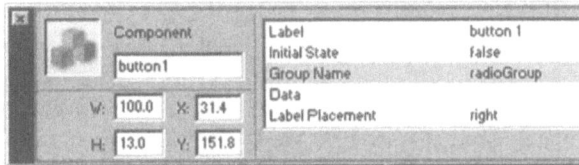

Setting such a group has a number of useful implications:

- Only one radio button within the group can be selected at any time.
- You can treat the group as a single component. For example, using **FComponent.SetEnabled** with the group name as the 'instance name' will disable all radio buttons in the group. This feature is particularly useful when you use the **FComponent.getData** and **FComponent.getValue** methods on a group.

Code	Notes
`a = button1.getGroupName();`	The value of a will be returned as the name (as a string) of the group that the radio button button1 is a member of. If button1 is not a member of a group, then a will be equate to "" (an empty string).

See also the examples fcomponentgetgroupname.fla and fcomponentgetgroupname.swf on the CD.

FComponent.getLabel

(This method is applicable to **FCheckBox.getLabel**, **FPushButton.getLabel**, and **FRadioButton.get Label**.)

```
a = myComponent.getLabel();
```

Where the variable a represents a string value corresponding to the label value of the component instance myComponent.

This method is compatible with **Flash 6**.

Description

The checkbox, push button, and radio button components have a single label associated with each of them, and you can set the value of this property manually via the Label field in the Property inspector:

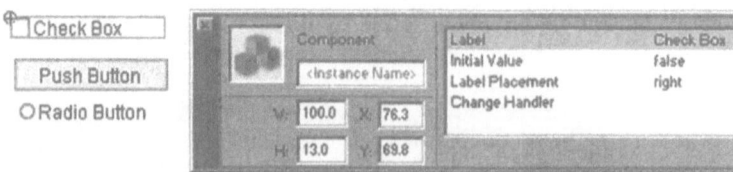

You can retrieve this value later though ActionScript via the getLabel method.

Code	Notes
`a = myComponent.getLabel();`	The value of a will be returned as the string value corresponding to the label

of myComponent. If the Property
inspector field Label is left blank, an
empty string will be returned rather
than undefined.

a = myRadioButtonGroup.gelLabel();	A radio button group does not have a label, so using this method with a radio button group is not supported.

F*Component*.getLength

(This method is applicable to **FComboBox.getLength** and **FListBox.getLength**.)

```
a = myComponent.getLength();
```

Where the value of variable a is returned as the number of labels displayed in the component instance
myComponent.

This method is compatible with **Flash 6**.

Description

Both the listbox and combobox allow you to select from a list of available options. The getLength
method allows you to retrieve the number of these options. Both the combobox and listbox shown below
have a length of 5 (labels 0 to 4).

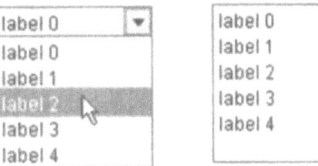

Code	Notes
a = myComponent.getLength();	a will equate to the length (number of labels) that exist in myComponent.

F*Component*.getPaneHeight

(This method is applicable to **FScrollPane.getPaneHeight**.)

```
a = myComponent.getPaneHeight();
```

Where the variable a equates to the value of the height of the display area for the scroll pane instance
myComponent.

This method is compatible with **Flash 6**

Description

This method allows you to retrieve the height of a scroll pane's display area. You would typically need the value returned by this method when you want to resize a pane.

Code	Notes
a = myScrollPane.getPaneHeight();	Variable a is equated to the height value of the scroll pane instance myScrollPane.

See the example files fcomponentgetpaneheight.fla and fcomponentgetpaneheight.swf on the CD.

FComponent.getPaneWidth

(This method is applicable to **FScrollPane.getPaneWidth.**)

a = myComponent.getPaneWidth();

Where the variable a equates to the value of the width of the display area for the scroll pane instance myComponent.

This method is compatible with **Flash 6**.

Description

This method allows you to retrieve the width of a scroll pane's display area. You would typically need the value returned by this method when you want to resize a pane.

Code	Notes
a = myScrollPane.getPaneWidth();	Variable a is equated to the width value of the scroll pane instance myScrollPane.

See the examples fcomponentgetpaneheight.fla and fcomponentgetpaneheight.swf on the CD.

FComponent.getRowCount

(This method is applicable to **FComboBox.getRowCount** and **FListBox.getRowCount.**)

a = myComponent.getRowCount();

Where the variable a equates to the number of labels that are visible at any one time for the instance myComponent.

This method is compatible with **Flash 6**.

Description

This method is applicable for those components that display a list of options, and this includes the combobox and listbox. For the combobox and listbox shown below, the getRowCount method will return 8 and 6 respectively.

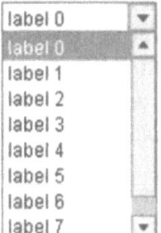 

Code	Notes
`a = myListBox.getRowCount();`	Variable a is equated to the row count value of the listbox instance myListBox.

See the example files fcomponentgetrowcount.fla and fcomponentgetrowcount.swf on the CD.

FComponent.getScrollPosition

(This method is applicable to **FComboBox.getScrollPosition**, **FListBox.getScrollPosition**, **FScrollBar.getScrollPosition** and **FScrollPane.getScrollPosition**.)

`a = myComponent.getScrollPosition();`

Where the variable a equates to the scroll position for the instance myComponent.

This method is compatible with **Flash 6**.

Description

This method is applicable for those components that include a scrollbar. These components include the combobox, listbox, scroll pane, and of course, the scrollbar itself. The value returned will vary between different types of component.

For the combobox and listbox, the position returned will be the index of the topmost visible label (noting that the label index starts at zero). For the combobox below, which has labels "label 0", "label 1"... "label 9", the getScrollPosition method would return 0 (left) and 3 (right).

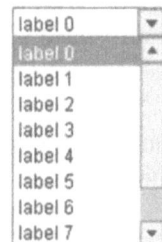

For the scrollbar the value returned will be one of two things:

- It will return a value between the maximum and minimum (maxPos and minPos) scroll positions if the scrollbar is not controlling the scroll position of a textfield, and these max/min values can be set via the **FComponent.setScrollProperties** method.
- It will return the line number of the top line in the textfield if the scrollbar is controlling the scroll position of a text field. The first line in a textfield is taken to be 1.

For the scroll pane there are two scrollbars (the horizontal one and the vertical one). The getScrollPosition() method will return two values via the properties x and y:

- getScrollPosition().x will return the number of pixels the left margin of the scroll pane is away from the left edge of the content.
- getScrollPosition().y will return the number of pixels the top margin of the scroll pane is away from the top edge of the content.

Code	Notes
a = scroller.getScrollPosition();	Variable a is equated as the scroll position of instance scroller. This value will vary depending on context, as discussed above, and illustrated in the examples below.

See the following files on the CD:

fcomponentgetscrollposition1.fla / fcomponentgetscrollposition1.swf
fcomponentgetscrollposition2.fla / fcomponentgetscrollposition2.swf
fcomponentgetscrollposition3.fla / fcomponentgetscrollposition3.swf
fcomponentgetscrollposition4.fla / fcomponentgetscrollposition4.swf

FComponent.getSelectedIndex

(This method is applicable to **FComboBox.getSelectedIndex** and **FListBox.getSelectedIndex**.)

```
a = myComponent.getSelectedIndex();
```

Where the variable a is equated to the selected index of the component instance myComponent.

This method is compatible with **Flash 6**.

Description

This method will return the currently selected index in a combobox or listbox, or undefined if no selection has yet been made. If the first label in the component is selected, then 0 is returned, 1 for the second, and so on.

It is standard practice to use the `getSelectedIndex` method within the change handler to retrieve the newly selected choice via the **onChange** event.

If you want the component to instead return the selected label or the data associated with it, you should use the **FComponent.getSelectedItem**.

Code	Notes
`a = myCombo.getSelectedIndex();`	a will be equated to the currently selected index of the component instance `myCombo`.

See the example files fcomponentgetselectedindex.fla and fcomponentgetselectedindex.swf on the CD.

FComponent.getSelectedIndices

(This method is applicable to **FListBox.getSelectedIndices**.)

`a = myComponent.getSelectedIndex();`

Where a is equated to the selected index(es) of the component instance `myComponent`.

This method is compatible with **Flash 6**.

Description

A listbox allows the user to make multiple selections if they make additional selections whilst pressing down the CONTROL or SHIFT keys.

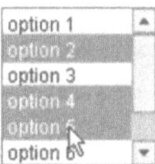

To enable this feature (it is disabled by default) you can either use the **FComponent.setSelectMultiple** method, or set the Select Multiple field of the listbox to `true`.

This method will then return an array containing the currently selected indices in the listbox instance, or `undefined` if no selection has yet been made. If the first label in the component is selected, then `0` is returned, `1` for the second, and so on.

It is standard practice to use the `getSelectedIndices` method within the change handler to retrieve the newly selected choice via the **onChange** event.

If you want the component to instead return the selected label or the data associated with it, you should use the **FComponent.getSelectedItems** method.

Code	Notes
`a = myCombo.getSelectedIndices();`	a will be equated to the currently selected index of the component instance `myCombo`. a will be in the form of an array. The elements will be arranged with most recently selected first (`a[0]` will be the most recently selected index).
`lastSelected = myCombo.getSelectedIndices()[1];`	`lastSelected` will be returned as the last selected index in the group selection (and the currently selected item will be available via `getSelectedIndices[0]`). If only one item has been selected so far, `lastSelected` will be `undefined`.

See the example files fcomponentgetselectedindices.fla and fcomponentgetselectedindices.swf on the CD.

FComponent.getSelectedItem

(This method is applicable to **FComboBox.getSelectedItem** and **FListBox.getSelectedItem**.)

```
a = myComponent.getSelectedItem();
```

Where a is returned as an object that contains:

1. the string value of the selected label
2. the data value of the selected label

... of the component instance `myComponent`. If no selections have yet been made, the method will return `undefined`.

This method is compatible with **Flash 6**.

Description

This method will return both the string value corresponding to the value of the selected label, and the data value (if defined).

It is standard practice to use the `getSelectedIndex` method within the change handler to retrieve the newly selected choice via the **onChange** event.

If you want the component to instead return the selected index, you should use the **FComponent.getSelectedIndex**.

Code	Notes
`a = myCombo.getSelectedItem().label;` `b = myCombo.getSelectedItem().data;`	For the component `myCombo`: ■ a will be equated to the string value of the currently selected label. ■ b will be equated to the data value defined for the currently selected label.
`mySelection = myCombo.getSelectedItem();`	For the component `myCombo`, `mySelection` will be equated to an object with the following properties: ■ `mySelection.label` will be returned as the string value of the currently selected label. ■ `mySelection.data` will be returned as the data value defined for the currently selected label.

See the examples file fcomponentgetselecteditem.fla and fcomponentgetselecteditem.swf on the CD.

FComponent.getSelectedItems

(This method is applicable to **FListBox.getSelectedItems**.)

```
a = myComponent.getSelectedItems();
```

Where the variable a is equated to an array, each element of which is an object that contains:

1. the string value of the selected label
2. the data value of the selected label

... of the listbox instance myComponent. If no selections have yet been made, the method will return undefined.

This method is compatible with **Flash 6**.

Description

A listbox allows the user to make multiple selections if they make additional selections whilst pressing down the CONTROL or SHIFT keys.

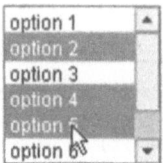

To enable this feature (it is disabled by default) you can either use the **FComponent.setSelectMultiple** method, or set the Select Multiple field of the Property inspector to true.

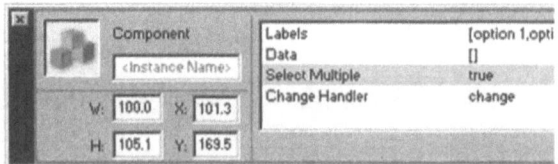

You also have to define a data value for each label, and you can do this by entering them in the Data field in the Property inspector. Although this is optional, you will gain no real advantage over using the simpler **FComponent.getSelectedIndexes** if you don't.

It is standard practice to use the getSelectedItems method within the change handler to retrieve the newly selected choices via the **onChange** event.

Code	Notes
mySelection = myListBox.getSelectedItems();	a will be equated to an array of objects each with properties label and data. **Note** that there is also an undocumented property called 0586-__ID__, and this is discussed in the *Tips and Precautions* section on the CD.
	A typical object structure is shown in the diagram. For simplicity, we have only selected 1 item (the label

option 3, which has a data value of 3).

See the examples fcomponentgetselecteditems.fla and fcomponentgetselecteditems.swf on the CD.

FComponent.getSelectMultiple

(This method is applicable to **FListBox.getSelectMultiple**.)

```
a = myComponent.getSelectMultiple();
```

Where a is equated to a Boolean value that signifies whether the ability for the user to make multiple selections is enabled (true) or not (false) for the listbox instance myComponent.

This method is compatible with **Flash 6**.

Description

This method will return whether or not a listbox instance will allow multiple selections to be made. A listbox that has this feature enabled is shown below:

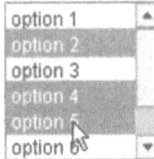

This feature is set to false (disabled) by default. There are two ways to change this:

1. You can change the Select Multiple value in the Property inspector during content creation.

2. You can change the value during runtime via **FComponent.setSelectMultiple**.

The ability to retrieve multiple selections (via **FComponent.getSelectedIndices** and **FComponent.getSelectedItems**) relies on the ability to make multiple selections being enabled.

Code	Notes
`a = myListBox.getSelectMultiple();`	a will be equated to true or false depending on whether the ability to

make multiple selections is enabled or
not on the instance myListBox.

FComponent.getState

(This method is applicable to **FRadioButton.getState**.)

```
a = myComponent.getState();
```

Where a is equated to a Boolean value that signifies whether the radio button instance myComponent is currently selected (true) or unselected (false).

This method is compatible with **Flash 6**.

Description

The radio button has two different types of output:

1. **The currently selected radio button in the radio button group**. This value tells you which of several related (or grouped) radio buttons is selected. This is usually the output you are interested in knowing. See also **FComponent.getValue()**, as applied to a radio button.
2. **The state of a particular radio button instance**. This value tells you whether a specific radio button within a group is currently selected or not. This value is returned via the getState method. This output is not usually needed because the getValue method is more relevant.

The reason why getValue is more relevant is as follows. If you have a single radio button, you can select it by clicking on it, *but you cannot unselect it*. If you have radio buttons within a group, then you select any radio button by clicking on it, and you can now unselect it by clicking on any other radio button within the same group. This means that radio buttons are usually grouped, and your code will treat the radio button group as if it were a single component; you do not need to consider individual radio buttons.

Code	Notes
a = myRadioButton.getState();	a will be equated to a Boolean that reflects the current state of the instance myRadioButton.

See these example files on the CD:

fcomponentgetstate1.fla / fcomponentgetstate1.swf
fcomponentgetstate2.fla / fcomponentgetstate2.swf

FComponent.getValue

(This method is applicable to **FCheckbox.getValue**, **FComboBox.getValue**, **FListBox.getValue** and **FRadioButton.getValue**.)

```
a = myComponent.getValue();
```
Where the variable a is equated to the value of the component instance myComponent. Depending on which component you are using, this value will be:

- **Checkbox**: either true or false depending on whether the check box instance is checked (true) or unchecked (false).
- **Combobox**: returns a string corresponding to the label of the currently selected item.
- **Listbox**: returns a string corresponding to the currently selected item.
- **Radio button**: returns a string or the data corresponding to the currently selected radio button in a radio button group.

This **method** is compatible with **Flash 6**. This method returns the value for all applicable components. It does not apply to the push button (which doesn't return a value, but instead generates an event when it is pressed, as do all buttons), and the scrollbar/scroll pane (which have their own specialized method to return their value, **FComponent.getScrollPosition**).

Description

This is one of the more important methods, because it is the method you will use the most. If you use the Property inspector to manually configure your components, it is the *only* method you need to get your code working with most of the components, as we shall see...

Checkbox

To set up a checkbox the procedure is as follows:

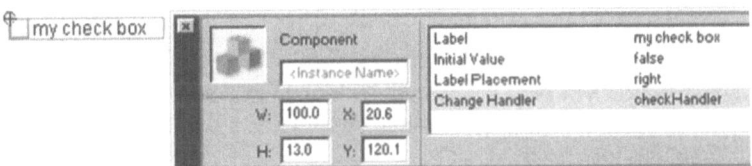

Drag a checkbox instance onto the stage. You can either configure the checkbox via scripting or manually via the Property inspector. Because the configurable values of the checkbox rarely change, there is no reason not to just use the Property inspector, and one big advantage is that once configured, the only method you have to use is getValue, so there's not really much else to remember by way of scripting!

Set the Label field of the checkbox to whatever text you want the textfield to be labeled with.

Set the Initial Value field to true if you want the checkbox to be initially checked, or false for

Set the Change Handler to the name of a function that you want to run every time the checkbox's state changes. This function will be executed every time the checkbox goes from checked to unchecked, or unchecked to checked.

Also, you have to define your change handler. We have called this function `checkHandler` in our version's Property inspector, and our function would look something like this:

```
function checkHandler(component) {
    if (component.getValue()) {
        //code you want to execute when
        //the checkbox is checked goes here
    } else {
        // code you want to execute when
        // the checkbox is unchecked goes here
    }
}
```

The `getValue` method for a checkbox will return either `true` (checkbox is checked) or `false` (checkbox is unchecked) and the **if** and **else** branches of the **if** structure are used to conditionally run two sections of code that look after each eventuality. Notice that the function has an argument `component`. This argument is passed to all change handlers, and refers to the instance name of the checkbox that has just called the function in this case.

There is only one other complication you need to consider, and that's what to do if you have more than one checkbox. There are two options:

1.   You can assign a different change handler to each checkbox. You would then have a separate function per checkbox.

2.   You can give each checkbox a unique instance name. Using this name, you can then configure the function to behave differently depending on which function called it. For example, supposing you had two checkbox instances `check1` and `check2`, you could have a single change handler that handles both of them that looks something like this:

```
function checkHandler(component) {
    switch (component) {
    case check1 :
        if (component.getValue()) {
            //code you want to execute when the checkbox
            //instance "check1" is checked goes here
        } else {
            //code you want to execute when the checkbox
            //instance "check1" is unchecked goes here
        }
```

```
            break;
        case check2 :
            if (component.getValue()) {
                //code you want to execute when the checkbox
                //instance "check2" is checked goes here
            } else {
                //code you want to execute when the checkbox
                //instance "check2" is unchecked goes here
            }
        }
    }
}
```

There are of course other, more complex options (such as using part of the instance name as an index of an array whose values specify what to do when each checkbox is checked/unchecked), but this shows you the basic schemes available. As you can see, if you configure the checkbox manually using the Property inspector, the `getValue` method is the only other thing you will need to interface your code with the checkbox.

See the example files fcomponentgetvalue1.fla and fcomponentgetvalue1.swf on the CD.

Combo box
To set up a combobox, the procedure is as follows:

Drag a combobox instance onto the stage. You can either configure the combobox via scripting or manually via the Property inspector. Unless you are driving your combobox via dynamic data (in which case you will also have to use the other methods of the combobox as well as `getValue`) you can get away with configuring the combobox manually via the Property inspector. If your application allows you to do this, then the only method you need to know about is `getValue`.

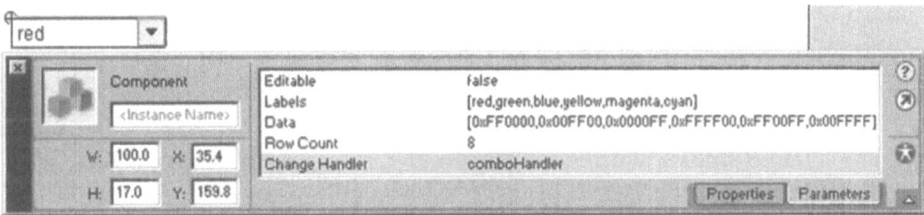

The Editable value defines whether the fields in the combobox will be editable or not. If you want the standard dropdown and uneditable menu, you will want to leave this as `false`.

The Labels define what will appear in the combobox dropdown. Assuming the values seen here (the colors red, green, blue, yellow, magenta, cyan), the final runtime combo would look like this:

The image to the left is the closed combo. The middle one is what you will see if you open it, and the final one is the closed combo with a selection made.

The Data field is optional. If you don't fill it in then the value returned when you select a label will be the default value, which is the label text itself as a string value. So if you selected 'yellow' (as we have done above), the getValue method would return `"yellow"`. If however, you enter a data value (in the Property inspector above, we have entered the corresponding hex values for the colors), you would see `"0xFFFF00"` as the returned value. The choice on whether to use a data field or not is usually down to your application, but the following tips might be useful:

- If you are going to use the returned values mathematically, you should populate the Data field, because that is the only way you will get a number.
- If you simply want the numbers 0 for red, 1 for green, and so on through to 5 for cyan, you would be better off just filling in the labels and using the **FComponent.getIndex** method, which will return the numbers you require, because they correspond to the index of the selected label.
- If you have made the combobox editable, you most likely want the edited Label strings to be returned, in which case you should not fill in the Data fields.

The Row Count is the maximum size of the dropdown. If the size is greater than the number of labels (as in the cases seen previously), you will simply see all the labels. If it is *less* than the number of labels, then that number of labels will be seen at any one time, and a scrollbar will appear to allow you to see the other options. For example, if you set this to 3 for our combo above, you would now see this:

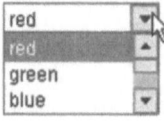

Finally, you need to enter the Change Handler. As before for the checkbox, this is the function that will run whenever you make a change to the combobox.

Typical examples of it would be:

```
function comboHandler(component) {
    x = component.getValue();
}
```

This would equate x to the last label that was selected (if no data has been defined for the label) or the **Data** value (if it has).

```
function comboHandler(component) {
    switch (component.getValue()) {
    case 1 :
        text_txt.text = "To create red, use the RGB value 0xFF0000.";
        break;
    case 2 :
        text_txt.text = "To create green, use the RGB value 0x00FF00.";
        break;
    case 3 :
        text_txt.text = "To create blue, use the RGB value 0x0000FF.";
        break;
    case 4 :
        text_txt.text = "Yellow is red plus green so you need to AND red and
➥green, giving 0xFFFF00.";
    }
}
```

If the next combo shown had a Data field of [1, 2, 3, 4], then this code would run a different branch of its switch statement for each option selected.

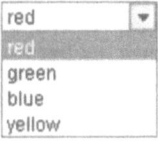

The strategy for creating event handlers that can deal with multiple comboboxes is the same as that one discussed for the checkbox discussed above.

List box

To set up a listbox the procedure is as follows.

Drag a listbox instance onto the stage. You can either configure the listbox via scripting or manually via the Property inspector. Unless you are driving your listbox via dynamic data (in which case you will also have to use the other methods of the listbox as well as getValue) you can get away with configuring the listbox manually via the Property inspector. If your application allows you to do this, then the only method you need to know about is getValue.

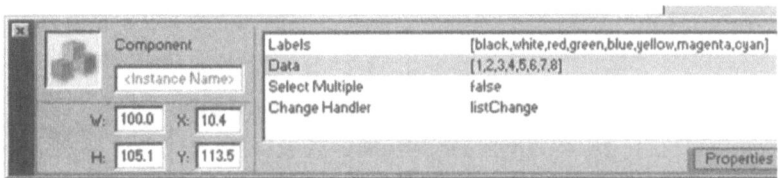

The Labels field defines what will appear in the listbox. Each string you enter will be used as a label for one of the available listbox options. In the listbox shown, we have configured the labels to be colors, the first one being black.

The Data field is optional. If you don't fill it in then the value returned, when you select a label, will be the default value, which is the label text itself as a string value. If however, you enter a data value (in the Property inspector above, we have entered the numbers 1 to 8), you would see 1 returned by getValue. The choice on whether to use a data field or not is usually down to your application, but the following tips might be useful:

- If you are going to use the returned values mathematically, you should populate the Data field, because that is the only way you will get a number.
- If you simply want the numbers 0 for black, 1 for white, and so on through to 7 for cyan, you would be better of just filling in the labels and using the **FComponent.getIndex** method, which will return the numbers you require, because they correspond to the index of the selected label.

The Select Multiple field allows you to specify whether or not the user can make a multiple selection or not. A combobox with this feature enabled is shown below. The user can make multiple selections by holding down the CONTROL or SHIFT keys. If you enable this property, be aware that the values returned by getValue will become non trivial, because the current item selected is not a single thing anymore, but a selection of variable length. To see how to handle listboxes with Select Multiple enabled, see the entry for **FComponent.getSelectedItems** and **FComponent.getSelectedIndices**.

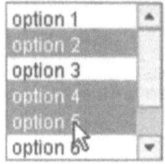

Finally, you need to enter the Change Handler. As before for the previous components, this is the function that will run whenever you make a change to the listbox. You can use exactly the same kind of functions discussed for the combobox. The combobox and listbox are actually identical in terms of programming, as long as you have not enabled Select Multiple in the listbox.

Radio button

The radio button will seem slightly non-standard when compared to the other components until you realize that the radio button **group** is equivalent to other components, not the individual radio button instances themselves. You need a group of radio buttons before they become useful.

The purpose of a radio button group is to allow the user to select from one or more groups of *mutually exclusive options*. That sounds a bit dense, but is actually quite simple. Coffee anyone?

I would like a   ○ strong   ● regular   ○ healthy option   cup of coffee with   ○ nothing   ○ milk, no sugar   ● milk, sugar   ○ sugar   thanks!

The first set of options for your coffee are strong, regular, and weak (or in these days of 'up-side' marketing, healthy option not weak). These strength options are mutually exclusive; you can only choose one out of the group. The second group is the same deal. Ignoring the variations of milk and sugar quantity, there are really only four different types of coffee: 'with nothing', with 'milk no sugar', 'with milk, sugar', and 'with sugar'. You can only have one of these four *with* options, so this group is also mutually exclusive.

This is the sort of selections that radio buttons are used for, and you can start to see that our two groups are really components in their own right rather than individual sets of radio buttons. In particular, the **getValue method looks at the group, and returns one value per group**. It doesn't return the value of one individual radio button, because that is very rarely relevant.

To set up a radio button group the procedure is as follows:

Drag the number of radio buttons you need in your group onto the stage. You can either configure the radio buttons via scripting or manually via the Property inspector. Unless you are driving your radio buttons via dynamic data (in which case you will also have to use the other methods of the radio button as well as getValue) you can get away with configuring manually via the Property inspector. If your application allows you to do this, then the only method you need to know about is getValue.

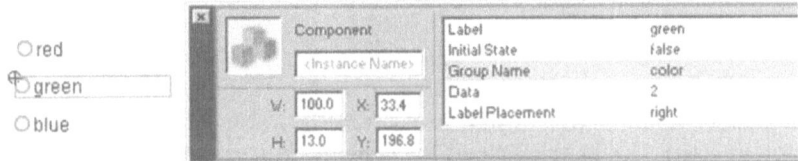

The Label field defines the label that will appear next to each radio button.

The Initial State defines whether this radio button will start as selected (true) or unselected (false). You should only have one button as true per group. If you have more than one set to true, Flash will still only set one during runtime.

The Group Name defines the radio button group, and this is synonymous with the instance name for other components; **the most important methods of the radio button will take the component name to be this group name**. During runtime, only one radio button in each group is allowed to be selected at any one time. You should have at least two radio buttons in each group name. If you have one radio button it is impossible to unselect it once selected!

The Data field is optional. If you don't fill it in then the value returned when you select a label will be the default value, which is the label text itself as a string value. If however, you enter a data value (2 in the example below), you would see that value returned by getValue. The choice on whether to use a data field or not is usually down to your application, but if you are going to use the returned values mathematically, you should populate the Data field, because that is the only way you will get a number.

The Label placement specifies the justification of the label. You can have either left or right justification.

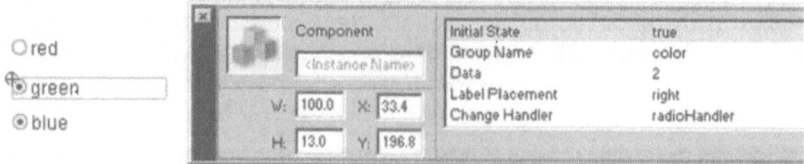

The Change Handler field *may* be hidden when you first open the Property inspector, and you will have to scroll down to see it. As before for the previous components, this is the function that will run whenever you make a change to the radio handler. It is slightly different to other components, because as mentioned above, the argument for this function is not the name of the radio button that has changed, *but the name of the radio button group that contains it*. This is reasonable, given that the radio button group is actually more important generally. The most basic radio handler is shown below. This simply traces the getValue value to the Output window. If we selected the green radio button, this function would return either "green" (if we had not defined the Data value of 2) or 2 (if we had, as seen in the pictures above).

```
function radioHandler(radioGroup) {
    trace(radioGroup.getValue());
}
```

A more useful handler would have a **switch** or **if... else if... else** that executed a different bit of code per radio button selected. This handler shows the general structure of such a handler:

```
function radioHandler(radioGroup) {
    switch (radioGroup.getValue()) {
    case 1 :
        trace("you have selected red");
        break;
    case 2 :
        trace("you have selected green");
        break;
    default :
        trace("you have selected blue");
    }
}
```

See also the example files fcomponentgetvalue4.fla and fcomponentgetvalue4.swf on the CD.

FComponent.loadScrollContent

(This method is applicable to **FscrollPane.loadScrollContent**.)

```
myComponent.loadScrollContent(URL);
```

Where URL is the URL or location of the external content you want to load into the scroll pane component myComponent. You can also specify a function that runs as soon as the content is loaded:

```
myComponent.loadScrollContent(URL, function);
```

This method is compatible with **Flash 6**.

Description

This **method** allows you to load content into a scroll pane from an external URL. You can also load content into a scroll pane from the library by using the related method **FComponent.setScrollContent**.

Preparing your content

To do this, simply create a new SWF, and place your content on the stage. If your content is smaller than the stage area, place it at the top left hand corner (because the top left corner of the stage will be placed at the top left hand corner (x=0, y=0) of the scroll pane when it is loaded in):

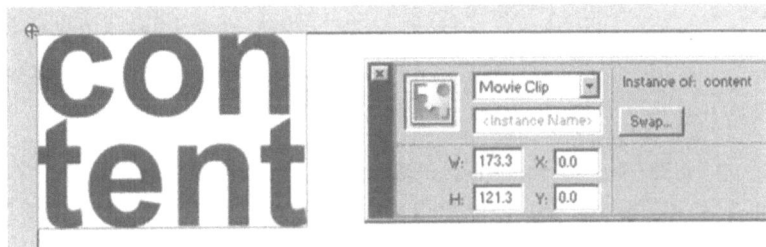

When loading this content, you have to specify the URL (if online) or directory path (if offline) to the SWF created by this FLA.

Setting up the scroll pane

Drag an instance of the scroll pane onto the stage. You can set the properties of the scroll pane via the Property inspector as follows:

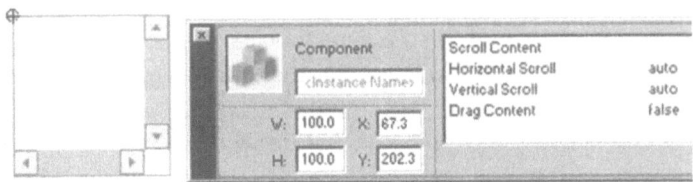

The Scroll Content property defines the content you want to be loaded into the scroll pane. In general, you would only define this manually if you were loading from the library. If you are using an external SWF, you will gain maximum benefit if you load the content when the user actually requests it, and this means using the loadScrollContent method.

The Horizontal Scroll and Vertical Scroll properties allow you to decide how you want the scroll pane scrollbars to work. You can either set them to `true` (always have scrollbars – if they are not needed, they will appear disabled), `false` (never show – if the content is too big to fit in the scroll pane, it will not be possible to see the portion of it outside the scroll pane borders) or `auto` (show scrollbars if they are required).

The Drag Content property is either `true` (can drag content within the window by click-hold-dragging within the pane) or `false` (cannot).

Note that the scroll pane usually will appear too small for most content when you first drag it onto the stage (100x100). To scale it you should do it manually on the stage, or via the methods of the scroll pane. You should not use the properties of the movie clip. See also **FComponent.setSize**.

Using scripting

Assuming you have prepared your external SWF as described above, called it `content.swf`, and saved it in the same place as your main SWF, the code to load it into a scroll pane called `myPane` will be:

```
myPane.loadScrollContent("content.swf");
```

See also fcomponentloadscrollcontent.fla and fcomponentloadscrollcontent.swf. You must run this SWF file from the same place as content.swf (see also content.fla).

You can also add a second parameter that identifies a function that will run once the content is fully loaded. Assuming you wanted to run a function `loaded` as soon as `content.swf` was loaded, you would do this:

```
function loaded(component) {
    message_txt.text = "Content in scroll pane "+component+" has loaded.";
}
myPane.loadScrollContent("content.swf", "loaded");
```

The function will write a message to the textfield `message_txt` upon completion of loading. See also example files fcomponentloadscrollcontent2.fla and fcomponentloadscrollcontent2.swf.

Finally, if the function `loading` is not on the same timeline as the current script, you can specify a path to the function. The following method will look for the function `loading` on the timeline `_root`:

```
myPane.loadScrollContent("content.swf", "loaded", _root);
```

See the examples fcomponentloadscrollcontent3.fla and fcomponentloadscrollcontent3.swf on the CD.

FComponent.registerSkinElement

(This method is applicable to **FCheckBox.registerSkinElement**, **FComboBox.registerSkinElement**, **FListBox.registerSkinElement**, **FPushButton.registerSkinElement**, **FRadioButton.registerSkin Element**, **FScrollBar.registerSkinElement** and **FScrollPane.registerSkinElement**.)

```
myComponent.registerSkinElement(symbol, styleMethod);
```

Where `myComponent` is a component instance, `symbol` is the name of a symbol (usually a movie clip) that makes up a part of the component graphics, and `styleMethod` is the method of the **FStyleFormat** object that you want to associate the symbol with.

This method is compatible with **Flash 6**.

Description

The default components allow you to change the graphics that define how they look, and this process is called **skinning**. It is during this process that you may have to use the `registerSkinElement` **method**. By registering your custom skin, you retain all the features of the **FStyleFormat** object. FStyleFormat allows the designer to make style changes to components, (such as color and text format changes). See also the entries for **FStyleFormat**.

Note that although you can skin any of the default components that ship with Flash as well as define the mapping between your new skins and FStyleFormat, other third party components may not support either skinning or FStyleFormat.

To skin a component you:

- Design the replacement component graphics.
- Once you have done this, separate your design into individual movie clips that correspond to the movie clips you will find in the Flash UI Components / Component Skins folder of the library. These individual clips are your **skins**. If you do not want to make your skins compliant with FStyleFormat, then you have finished. If you do, then the next two steps apply.
- Subdivide each skin into further sub-elements within each skin. These are your **skin elements**.
- Register the new skin elements. This is done via the `registerSkinElement` method. In many cases, you will be able to retain the original `registerSkinElement` methods defined by Macromedia.

You can see the process better by looking at the default Macromedia components. For example, drag the scrollbar component onto the stage. Looking in the library, you will see that a folder called Flash UI Components is created. This contains the scrollbar component and its assets. If you now open the Component / Skins / FScrollBar Skins sub-directory, you will see the individual default skins for the scrollbar. They will all be named with a 'fsb_' prefix.

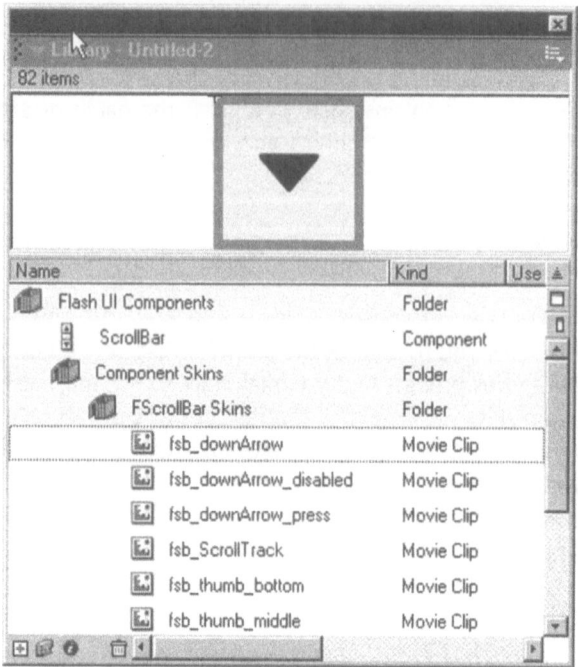

If you now look on the timeline of a particular skin (say `fsb_downArrow`), you will see the following:

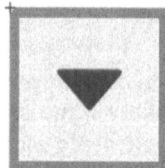

This skin is further subdivided into skin elements. You cannot see all of them immediately, and some of them are actually difficult to see, given that they are white. To combat this, you are recommended to temporarily change the movie background to a non-white color. The following diagram does this, and identifies all the separate skin elements that make up the skin `fsb_downArrow`.

(You know when you have found all of the skin elements when the number of elements is equal to the number of `registerSkinElement` definitions that you see in the README layer. See below.)

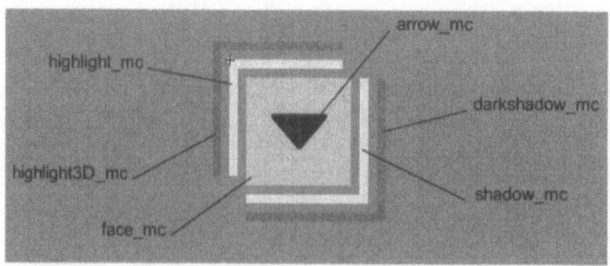

On the README layer of the `fsb_downArrow` clip, you will see the following code:

```
component.registerSkinElement(arrow_mc, "arrow");
component.registerSkinElement(face_mc, "face");
component.registerSkinElement(shadow_mc, "shadow");
component.registerSkinElement(darkshadow_mc, "darkshadow");
component.registerSkinElement(highlight_mc, "highlight");
component.registerSkinElement(highlight3D_mc, "highlight3D");
```

These are the default `registerSkinElement` definitions. The first one associates the `arrow_mc` skin element with the **FStyleFormat.arrow** method. This means that when ActionScript sees this method, it will apply all color changes specified by it onto the `arrow_mc` skin element. A similar connection is made for the other skin elements of `fsb_downArrow`.

If you have designed your new skin elements so that they have the same names as the default skin elements, then **you do not need to change any of the code**. You only need to change the default `registerSkinElement` definitions if:

- Your replacement skin elements do not have all the skin elements of the default skins. For example, the `fsb_downArrow` has elements `highlight_mc`, `highlight3D_mc`, `darkshadow_mc`, and `shadow_mc` that are to do with faux 3D. If your replacement is, for example, an organic style that doesn't need drop shadows and highlights, then your skins will not have the corresponding skin elements. You can therefore remove the 3D related `registerSkinElement` definitions. Practical experience suggests that it is better to comment unused definitions out rather than delete them. You may, at a later date, change some or all of your graphics, and may want to re-instate some definitions.
- Your replacement skin elements have differently named skin elements to the default elements. You will have to change the default `registerSkinElement` associations to reflect your new instance names.
- Your replacement skin elements are not compliant with `FStyleFormat`. You can safely delete the `registerSkinElement` definitions. Practical experience suggests that it is better to comment them out rather than delete them – you may, at a later date, want to make your skins `FStyleFormat` compliant.

FComponent.removeAll

(This method is applicable to **FComboBox.removeAll** and **FListBox.removeAll**.)

```
myComponent.removeAll();
```

Where `myComponent` is a combobox or listbox instance.

This method is compatible with **Flash 6**.

Description

This **method** removes all labels in a combobox or listbox, and redraws the component to reflect the fact that it is now empty.

Code	Before code is executed	After code is executed
`myListBox.removeAll();`	Foundation Flash Foundation ActionScript New Masters of Flash Flash Math Creativity Flash Studio Games Studio	

See the example files fcomponentremoveall.fla and fcomponentremoveall.swf on the CD.

FComponent.removeItemAt

(This method is applicable to **FComboBox.removeItemAt** and **FListBox.removeItemAt**.)

```
a = myComponent.removeItemAt(index);
```

Where `myComponent` is a combobox or listbox instance. The label at index `index` will be removed, and `a` will be equated to an object with properties `label` and `data`, which will contain the label and data associated with the deleted item (or `undefined` if they don't have a value).

This method is compatible with **Flash 6**.

Description

This **method** will delete the label at the specified index. The combobox or listbox will be redrawn to reflect this change.

Code	Notes
`myListBox.removeItemAt(4);`	Removes the label at index 4 of the list box `myListBox`. This will remove the fifth label from the top (because the indexes start at zero).
`component.removeItemAt` `(component.getSelectedIndex());`	Removes the last selected item of instance `component`. See also **FComponent.getSelectedIndex**. You would typically use this code within the component change handler.
`selected = component.removeItemAt`	Removes the last selected item and

<table>
<tr><td>

```
(component.getSelectedIndex());
    for (prop in selected) {
        message = prop+" = "+selected[prop]
        trace(message);
    }
```

</td><td>

assigns the label, data, and __ID__ properties to variable selected, making it an Object object. The for... in loop traces the values of these properties to the Output window.

You would typically use this code within the component change handler.

</td></tr>
</table>

See the examples fcomponentremoveitemat.fla and fcomponentremoveitemat.swf on the CD.

FComponent.replaceItemAt

(This method is applicable to **FComboBox.replaceItemAt** and **FListBox.replaceItemAt**.)

```
myComponent.replaceItemAt(index, label);
myComponent.replaceItemAt(index, label, data);
```

Where myComponent is a combobox or listbox instance. The label at index index will be removed, and replaced by a new label label. You can optionally also add a new data item associated with the new label.

This method is compatible with **Flash 6**.

Description

This **method** will delete the label at the specified index and replace it. The combobox or listbox will be redrawn to reflect this change.

Code	Notes
`myListBox.replaceItemAt(4, "blue");` `myListBox.replaceItemAt(5, "red", 45);`	The first line removes the label at index 4 of the listbox myListBox. This will remove the fifth label from the top and replace it with the label "blue". The second line will remove the label at index 5 (sixth label down) and replace it with the label "red" and associated data value 45.
`component.replaceItemAt` `(component.getSelectedIndex(), "selected");`	Replaces the last selected label with "selected". See also **FComponent.getSelectedIndex**. You would typically use this code within the component change handler.

See also the examples fcomponentreplaceitemat.fla and fcomponentreplaceitemat.swf on the CD.

FComponent.setRowCount

(This method is applicable to **FComboBox.setRowCount** and **FListBox.setRowCount**.)

```
myComponent.setRowCount(rowCount);
```

Where myComponent is a combobox or listbox instance. The integer rowCount specifies the maximum number of labels that can be shown at any one time.

This method is compatible with **Flash 6**.

Description

This **method** allows you to dynamically set the row count of a listbox or combobox. This allows you to grow or shrink the component so that all the available options can always be seen without having to use scrollbars. The effects of this are best seen by reviewing the example file described in the *Examples and practical uses* section on the CD.

Code	Notes
myListBox.setRowCount(10);	The row count for the listbox instance myListBox will be set to 10. This means that the listbox will grow to 10 labels in size. It will do this even if there are less than 10 labels to display.
myComboBox.setRowCount(10);	The combobox myComboBox's drop-down menu will grow to accommodate either the current number of labels (if it is less than 10) or 10 labels (if there are 10 or more labels). Note that the combobox behaves slightly differently to the listbox; the combobox does not grow to accommodate empty label positions, whereas the listbox does.

See also the example files fcomponentsetrowcount.fla and fcomponentsetrowcount.swf on the CD.

FComponent.setAutoHideScrollBar

(This method is applicable to **FListBox.setAutoHideScrollBar**.)

```
myListBox.setAutoHideScrollBar(Boolean);
```

Where `myListBox` is a listbox instance. `Boolean` should be set to `true` if you want to enable auto scrollbar hiding to `true`, and `false` if you don't. The default is `false`.

This **method** is compatible with **Flash 6**.

Description

The listbox will show a scrollbar at all times by default. If the scrollbar is needed, it will appear as active. If it is not required, then it will appear as disabled. Setting the `setAutoHideScrollBar` argument to `true` will modify this by making the scrollbar not appear at all when it is not needed.

A typical listbox will look as shown below during default operation. The left listbox has more labels than it can show, and therefore has an active scrollbar. The listbox on the right has fewer labels than it can display, and so the unneeded scrollbar becomes disabled. This is the default condition, and corresponds to `setAutoHideScrollBar(false)`.

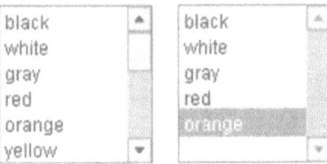

If you set the auto hide method to `true` instead, you will see the following when the scrollbar is no longer needed:

Code	Notes
`myListBox.setAutoHideScrollBar(false);`	The scrollbar on instance `myListBox` will appear disabled when it is not required. This is the default condition.
`myListBox.setAutoHideScrollBar(true);`	The scrollbar on instance `myListBox` will not appear when it is not required.

F*Component*.setChangeHandler

(This method is applicable to **FCheckBox.setChangehandler**, **FComboBox.setChangeHandler**, **FListBox.setChangeHandler**, **FRadioButton.setChangeHandler**, and **FScrollBar.setChangeHandler**.)

```
myComponent.setChangeHandler(functionName);
Component.setChangeHandler(functionName, location);
```

Where myComponent is a component instance. When a change is detected associated with the component, the function functionName is run. The function will be assumed to be defined on the current timeline. If it is not, you can add a second optional argument location, and this should point to the location of the function.

This **method** is compatible with **Flash 6**.

Description

When a checkbox, combobox, listbox, or scrollbar has its value changed, you can set up a function that will be run on every frame that a new change is detected. This function can be configured to accept a single argument that identifies the component that has invoked it. This function is called the **change Handler**, **onChangeHandler**, or **call back**.

The situation for a radio button is the same, except that the process works per radio button group rather than per radio button instance.

Code	Notes
myComponent.setChangeHandler("myFunction");	The function myFunction is assigned as the change handler for the component instance myComponent.
myComponent.setChangeHandler ("myFunction", _root);	The function myFunction is assigned as the change handler for the component instance myComponent. The function myFunction is on the timeline root.
myPushButton.setChangeHandler("myFunction");	The push button does not have a permanent change of state or value because its change is fleeting. It instead has a **click handler**, and you can set this via the **FComponent.setClickHandler** method.

F*Component*.setClickHandler

(This method is applicable to **FPushButton.setClickHandler**.)

```
myComponent.setClickHandler(functionName);
Component.setClickHandler(functionName, location);
```

Where myComponent is a push button instance. When a click is detected associated with the push button, the function functionName is run. The function will be assumed to be defined on the current timeline. If it is not, you can add a second optional argument location, and this should point to the location of the function.

This **method** is compatible with **Flash 6**.

Description

With the push button you can set up a function that will be run every time a click occurs. This function can be configured to accept a single argument that identifies the component that has invoked it. This function is called the **click handler** or **call back**.

The click handler will react in the same way to a click as the **Button.onRelease** or the **on(release)** events.

Code	Notes
myComponent.setClickHandler("myFunction");	The function myFunction is assigned as the click handler for the push button instance myComponent.
myComponent.setClickHandler("myFunction", _root);	The function myFunction is assigned as the click handler for the push button instance myComponent. The function myFunction is on the timeline _root.

F*Component*.setData

(This method is applicable to **FRadioButton.setData**.)

```
myRadio.setData(data);
```

Where myRadio is a radio button instance. When this radio button is selected, the value data will be returned. If no such entry is defined, a string value corresponding to the radio button's label will be returned.

This **method** is compatible with **Flash 6**.

Description

When a radio button is selected, the **FComponent.getValue** method will return one of two values:

- If no data value is defined for the radio button, the string value corresponding to the radio button's label will be returned.
- If a data value is defined, the data value will be returned.

You should use the setData method if you do not want the getValue method to return the label value.

Code	Notes
myRadio.setData(2);	The radio button data value is set to 2.

FComponent.setDataProvider

(This method is applicable to **FComboBox.setDataProvider** and **FListBox.setDataProvider**.)

```
myComponent.setDataProvider(object);
```

Where myComponent is a combobox or listbox component, and object is the external data object (or type Array or DataProviderClass) that defines its parameters.

This **method** is compatible with **Flash 6**. This method is intended for advanced coders, and requires a good understanding of the relationship between a component and its configuration data.

Description

When defining the label and data fields of a listbox or combobox, the values are usually either entered manually or via the methods of the combobox or listbox. If you elect to use an external object (and this will usually be an array of Object objects or the component specific data class DataProviderClass), then you can also use the methods of the external object. For example, if you choose to use an external Array object then:

- You can use features of the Array object's methods that are not available via the methods of the combobox or listbox, such as the ability to sort, concatenate, change case, and split an array.
- You can interface the external Array object to data coming from a remote server script better than you could with a combobox or listbox directly, because the Array is more flexible.

If you were creating dynamic combo or listboxes, you would have to create variables external to the component in any case. Creating a structured Array object and being able to associate it directly with a component allows a much more structured linkage between your dynamic data and the component.

Code	Notes
`myCombo.setDataProvider(myArray);`	Assigns the array `myArray` as the external data provider of the combo instance `myCombo`.

See the example files on the CD:

fcomponentsetdataprovider1.fla / fcomponentsetdataprovider1.swf
fcomponentsetdataprovider1b.fla / fcomponentsetdataprovider1b.swf
fcomponentsetdataprovider1c.fla / fcomponentsetdataprovider1c.swf
fcomponentsetdataprovider2.fla / fcomponentsetdataprovider2.swf

FComponent.setDragContent

(This method is applicable to **FScrollPane.setDragContent**.)

`myScrollPane.setDragContent(Boolean);`

Where `myScrollPane` is a scroll pane instance. When `Boolean` is set to `true`, the user is able to scroll around the scroll pane by click-dragging the content. When `Boolean` is set to `false`, this feature is disabled.

This **method** is compatible with **Flash 6**.

Description
To scroll around a scroll pane, you usually have to use the scrollbars. By using a `setDragContent(true)`, you can also scroll by click-dragging on the content. When draggable content is enabled, a hand cursor will appear whenever the mouse rolls over the scroll pane.

Code	Notes
`myPane.setDragContent(false);`	Disables draggable content. This is the default condition.
`myPane.setDragContent(true);`	Enables draggable content.

See the example files fcomponentsetdragcontent.fla and fcomponentsetdragcontent.swf on the CD.

FComponent.setEditable

(This method is applicable to **FComboBox.setEditable**.)

`myComboBox.setEditable(Boolean);`

Where `myComboBox` is a combobox instance. When `Boolean` is set to `true`, the user is able to edit the selected value. When `Boolean` is set to `false`, this feature is disabled.

This **method** is compatible with **Flash 6**.

Description

The combobox allows the user to edit their entry if the value they want to input does not appear on the dropdown. To retrieve the value entered, you need to use the **FComponent.getValue()** method.

Code	Notes
`myComboBox.setEditable(false);`	Disables the ability for the user to edit text. This is the default condition.
`myComboBox.setEditable(true);`	Enables the ability for the user to edit text.

See the example files fcomponentseteditable.fla and fcomponentseteditable.swf on the CD.

FComponent.setEnabled

(This method is applicable to **FCheckBox.setEnabled**, **FPushButton.setEnabled**, **FRadioButton.set Enabled**, **FScrollBar.setEnabled**, and **FListBox.setEnabled**.)

```
myComponent.setEnabled(Boolean);
```

Where `myComponent` is a component instance or radio button group. When `Boolean` is set to `true`, the component is enabled and will respond to user interaction. When it is set to `false`, the component will be displayed grayed out and will not respond to user inputs.

This **method** is compatible with **Flash 6**.

Description

This method allows you to enable or disable components. A disabled component will not respond to user interaction, but will respond to all relevant methods that do not rely on user interaction to work.

Enabled appearance	Disabled appearance	Notes
◉ button1 ○ button 2 ○ button 3	○ button1 ○ button 2 ◉ button 3	This shows the effect of disabling one radio button in a group. The remaining buttons are still active. The following code disables a radio button:

one.setEnabled(false);

Where one is the instance name of the top button in the group.

◉ **button1**	○ button1	This shows the effect of disabling a radio button group. All buttons in the group become disabled. The following code disables the group: group.setEnabled(false); Where group is the group name that all three buttons are members of.
○ **button 2**	○ button 2	
○ **button 3**	○ button 3	

This shows the effect of disabling a listbox. The list becomes grayed out and its scrollbar becomes disabled.

The following code disables the listbox:

myList.setEnabled(false);

Where myList is the name of the listbox.

FComponent.setHorizontal

(This method is applicable to **FScrollBar.setHorizontal**.)

myScrollBar.setHorizontal(Boolean);

Where myScrollBar is a scrollbar instance. When Boolean is set to true, the component will be vertical, and it will be horizontal if set to false.

This **method** is compatible with **Flash 6**.

Description

When you drop a scrollbar onto a text field, it will automatically align itself to the nearest edge of the text field (assuming View > Snap to objects is checked). If you drop a scrollbar onto the stage the scrollbar will appear vertical by default. You can change this automatic alignment during content creation via the Property inspector's Horizontal value. You can also set it dynamically during runtime via the setHorizontal method.

Code	Notes
`myScrollBar.setHorizontal(true);`	The scrollbar instance `myScrollBar` will appear horizontal.
`myScrollBar.setHorizontal(false);`	The scrollbar instance `myScrollBar` will appear vertical.

FComponent.setHScroll

(This method is applicable to **FScrollPane.setHScroll**.)

`myScrollPane.setHScroll(setting);`

Where `myScrollPane` is a scroll pane instance. When `setting` is set to `true`, the scroll pane's horizontal scrollbar will always be displayed. If `setting` is set to `false`, it will never be displayed. If `setting` is set to `"auto"`, the scrollbar will only appear when required.

This **method** is compatible with **Flash 6**.

Description

The scroll pane horizontal scrollbar functionality can be controlled by the Horizontal Scroll property of the Property inspector during content creation. It can also be controlled dynamically via the `setHScroll` method:

- If the argument to this method is set to `true`, the scrollbar will always be shown. If it is required, it will appear enabled. If it is not required it will appear but be disabled.
- If the argument is set to `false`, the scrollbar will never be shown.
- If the argument is set to `"auto"`, the scrollbar will be shown if the content requires it, but hidden otherwise

Code	Notes
`myScrollPane.setHScroll(true);`	The horizontal scrollbar of scroll pane instance `scrollPane` will always be shown. If it is required, it will appear enabled. If it is not required, it will still appear, but will be disabled.
`myScrollPane.setHScroll(false);`	The scrollbar will never be shown. If the content is bigger than the scroll pane, the user must have some other method of revealing the hidden portions, otherwise the user will not be able to see them.
`myScrollPane.setHScroll("auto");`	The scrollbar will appear/disappear as required. It will appear if the content

> width is larger than the width of the
> scroll pane.

See the examples fcomponentsethscroll.fla and fcomponentsethscroll.swf on the CD.

FComponent.setItemSymbol

(This method is applicable to **FComboBox.setItemSymbol** and **FListBox.setItemSymbol**.)

```
myComponent.setItemSymbol(linkageID);
```

Where `linkageID` is the linkage ID you want Flash to use when building up the textfields within the combobox or listbox instance `myComponent`.

This **method** is compatible with **Flash 6**.

Description

When building up the combobox or listbox, the symbol used to create the individual textfields is called `FComboBoxItem` (combobox) or `FListBoxItem` (listbox). These symbols have linkage identifiers of their name plus `symbol`. Although you can edit these symbols to create your own custom item graphics, the practice is not recommended, given that the default symbols also define some fairly advanced code as well as supply the basic graphic elements.

If you are set on experimenting with this method, then you are best advised to:

- Copy the default symbol (`FComboBoxItem` or `FListBoxItem`).
- Give it a new linkage identifier and use the `setItemSymbolID` to refer to the new linkage ID.
- Lock the existing layers and create a new one to add new content without affecting the existing elements.
- Play about with it!

Be warned though, the default symbol is not really designed to be modified. It is hard going for even accomplished programmers because the code is undocumented. You will get better results by using the supported and documented **FStyleFormat** object.

FComponent.setLabel

(This method is applicable to **FCheckBox.setLabel**, **FPushButton.setLabel**, and **FRadioButton.set Label.**)

```
myComponent.setLabel(label);
```

Where myComponent is a component instance. label is a string value that you want to assign to the label field of the instance.

This **method** is compatible with **Flash 6**.

Description
The checkbox, push button, and radio button have one label, and you can change this during content creation via the Label property in the Property inspector. You can change the label dynamically via the setLabel method.

Code	Appearance	Notes
radio.setLabel ("radio button");	○ radio button	The radio button instance radio has its label set to the string "radio button".
checkBtn.setLabel ("check this!");	☐ check this!	The checkbox instance checkBtn has its label set to the string "check this!".
pushBtn.setLabel ("push me!");	push me!	The push button instance pushBtn has its label set to the string "push this!".

FComponent.setLabelPlacement

(This method is applicable to **FCheckBox.setLabelPlacement** and **FRadioButton.setLabelPlacement**.)

```
myComponent.setLabelPlacement(placement);
```

Where `myComponent` is a component instance. `placement` is a string value that can be either `left` or right.

This **method** is compatible with **Flash 6**.

Description

The checkbox and radio button have one label, and you can change the position of this in relation to the graphic (so that it is placed either to the left or right of it) during content creation via the Label Placement property of the Property inspector. You can do the same thing dynamically with the `setLabelPlacement` method.

Code	Appearance	Notes
`radio.setLabel ("radio button"); radio.setLabelPlacement ("right");`	○ radio button	The radio button instance `radio` has its label set to the string `"radio button"`, and this is printed to the right of the radio button graphic.
`radio.setLabel ("radio button"); radio.setLabelPlacement ("left");`	radio button ○	The radio button instance `radio` has its label set to the string `"radio button"`, and this is printed to the left of the radio button graphic.

FComponent.selectMultiple

(This method is applicable to **FListBox.selectMultiple**.)

`myComponent.selectMultiple(boolean);`

Where `Boolean` is a Boolean value that signifies whether the ability for the user to make multiple selections is enabled (`true`) or not (`false`) for the listbox instance `myComponent`.

This **method** is compatible with **Flash 6**.

Description

This **method** will return whether or not a listbox instance will allow multiple selections to be made. A listbox that has this feature enabled is shown below:

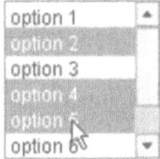

This feature is set to `false` (disabled) by default. There are two ways to change this:

- You can change the Select Multiple value in the Property inspector during content creation.

- You can change the value during runtime via `FComponent.setSelectMultiple`.

When the select multiple functionality is enabled, the user can make multiple selections by holding down the SHIFT or CONTROL keys whilst clicking.

Code	Notes
`myListBox.selectMultiple(true);`	The ability to make multiple selections is enabled for the list box instance `myListBox`.

FComponent.setLargeScroll

(This method is applicable to **FScrollBar.setLargeScroll**.)
`myScrollBar.setLargeScroll(integer);`

Where `integer` is an integer value that specifies how many units the scrollbar will move by when the user clicks on the scrollbar's scroll track.

This **method** is compatible with **Flash 6**.

Description
The 'large scroll' value is the amount that the scrollbar will move every time you click on the scroll track. A related value is the 'small scroll' and this is the amount the scrollbar will move every time the top and bottom arrows are clicked.

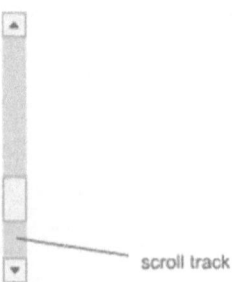

scroll track

The large scroll value is usually set to the height of the textfield it is controlling minus one line. This means that if you do a large scroll downwards, the line that was previously at the bottom line of the text field will end up at the top line. This setting occurs automatically as soon as you drop the scrollbar onto a textfield. You can also set the page size dynamically via the **FComponent.setScrollProperties** method. The FComponent.setLargeScroll allows you to modify the large scroll value.

Code	Notes
myScrollBar.setLargeScroll(20);	Sets the large scroll value of the scrollbar instance myScrollBar to 20.

See also the example files fcomponentsetlargescroll.fla and fcomponentsetlargescroll.swf on the CD.

FComponent.setSmallScroll

(This method is applicable to **FScrollbar.setSmallScroll**.)

```
myScrollBar.setSmallScroll(integer);
```

Where integer is an integer value that specifies how many units the scrollbar will move by when the user clicks on the scrollbar's up and down arrows.

This **method** is compatible with **Flash 6**.

Description
The small scroll value defines how far the scrollbar will move when you click on the up or down arrows of the scrollbar. When attached to a textfield, the default value is one line.

Code	Notes
myScrollBar.setSmallScroll(3);	Sets the small scroll value of the scrollbar instance myScrollBar to 3.

See the example files fcomponentsetsmallscroll.fla and fcomponentsetsmallscroll.swf on the CD.

FComponent.setScrollContent

(This method is applicable to **FScrollPane.setScrollContent**.)

```
myScrollPane.setScrollContent(identifier);
```

Loads the content specified by identifier (which should either be a linkage identifier to a symbol in the library or a target path reference to a movie clip on the stage) into the scroll pane instance myScrollPane.

This **method** is compatible with **Flash 6**.

Description

This **method** allows you to load content into a scroll pane from the library. To do this, you must define a linkage identifier for the content you wish to load.

Note that you should usually check Export for ActionScript and Export in first frame. Flash does not export library symbols that never appear on stage as part of its optimization when it creates the final SWF, but if you intend to use the clip via ActionScript, it may still be needed even though it never appears on a timeline. This is the function of the Export for ActionScript checkbox. Because you don't normally know when you will require your content by, the second checkbox covers all the bases by simply loading the clip in at frame 1.

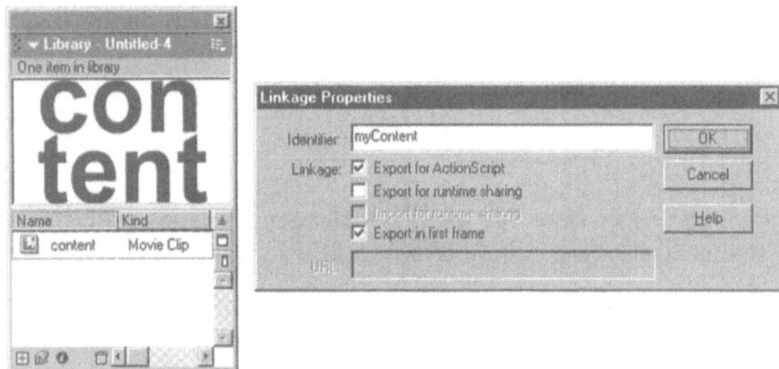

If your content is large enough to affect the downloading of your main site SWF, you should consider using the **FComponent.loadScrollContent** method instead. This loads the content on demand and not as part of your main SWF.

You can also load in a movie clip that is on the stage. This is an easier option than using linkage; all you have to do is refer to the clip by its target path. The target clip will be removed from its current position and placed inside the scroll pane. Using this technique allows you to retain the ability to stream your content, rather than having to load it in on frame 1 (you only have to make sure the clip is on the stage on the frame you load it into the scroll pane).

Code	Notes
`myPane.setScrollContent("content");`	Loads the symbol with linkage identifier `"content"` from the library and into instance `myPane`.
`myPane.setScrollContent(_root.content);`	Moves the movie clip currently on the stage with target path `_root.content` into the scroll pane instance `myPane`.

See the example files on the CD:

fcomponentsetscrollcontent.fla / fcomponentsetscrollcontent.swf
fcomponentsetscrollcontent2.fla / fcomponentsetscrollcontent2.swf

FComponent.setScrollPosition

(This method is applicable to **FListBox.setScrollPosition**, **FScrollBar.setScrollPosition** and **FScroll Pane.setScrollPosition**.)

```
myComponent.setScrollPosition(integer);
```

Applies to a listbox or scrollbar, and sets the scroll position of the component myComponent to the integer value integer.

```
myComponent.setScrollPosition(xPixel, yPixel);
```

Applies to a scroll pane, and sets the scroll to the right (xPixel) and down (yPixel) in pixels

This **method** is compatible with **Flash 6**.

Description

This **method** allows you to dynamically scroll to a position specified.

For a listbox, the scroll position is referred to in terms of the label index positions. A scroll position of 3 means 'scroll to the position where the label at index 3 is at the top of the listbox'. Note that the indexes start at zero; by default, the listbox appears scrolled to the start of the list, which is equivalent to setScroll(0).

For a scrollbar, the value specified must be between the minimum and maximum scroll values as specified by minPos and maxPos within the **FComponent.setScrollProperties method**.

For a scroll pane, the xPixel and yPixel values represent the horizontal and vertical scroll values in pixel measure.

See the examples fcomponentsetscrollposition.fla and fcomponentsetscrollposition.swf on the CD.

FComponent.setScrollProperties

(This method is applicable to **FScrollBar.setScrollProperties**.)

```
myScrollBar.setScrollProperties(pageSize, minPos, maxPos);
```

Where pageSize is the size of the scroll page, minPos is the value at the top of a vertical scrollbar (or left if horizontal), and maxPos is the value at the bottom (right) of the scrollbar.

This **method** is compatible with **Flash 6**. It is intended for use with scrollbars when you are using them as sliders or other similar controls.

Description

When used to control the scroll position of a textfield, the scroll properties are set automatically, and there is usually no reason to change them. If however, you are using the scrollbar as a slider, the scroll properties must be defined. In this case, the scroll properties represent the following:

The pageSize sets both the size of the scroll slider box and the default value of the 'large scroll' value (the amount that the scroll bar will change by if you click on the scroll track). See also **FComponent.setLargeScroll**.

Code	Notes
`scroller.setScrollProperties(10, 20, 100);`	Sets up a scrollbar with a maximum value of 100, minimum value of 20, and page size (and therefore 'large scroll' value) of 10.

See fcomponentsetscrollproperties.fla and fcomponentsetscrollproperties.swf on the CD for an example.

FComponent.setScrollTarget

(This method is applicable to **FScrollbar.setScrollTarget**.)

`myScrollbar.setScrollTarget(textField);`

Where textfield is the instance name of a textfield object that will be controlled by the scrollbar instance myScrollBar. The textfield must be on the same timeline as the scrollbar, as the textField argument does not allow you to specify a path.

This **method** is compatible with **Flash 6**.

Description

When you drop a scrollbar onto a textfield during content creation, the scrollbar will snap to the nearest edge of the textfield (assuming you have View > Snap to objects enabled), and the Target Text Field property of the Property inspector will automatically pick up the name of the textfield.

The `setScrollTarget` method allows you to set a textfield target dynamically.

Code	Notes
`myScroller.setScrollTarget(my_txt);`	The scrollbar `myScroller` is associated with the textfield `my_txt`.

See the examples fcomponentsetscrolltarget.fla and fcomponentsetscrolltarget.swf on the CD.

FComponent.setSize

(This method is applicable to **FCheckBox.setSize**, **FComboBox.setSize**, **FListBox.setSize**, **FPushButton** **.setSize**, **FRadioButton.setSize**, **FScrollBar.setSize**, and **FScrollPane.setSize**.)

`myComponent.setSize(width, height);`

Applies to push button, scroll pane, and listbox components.

`myComponent.setSize(width);`

Applies to radio button, checkbox, and combobox components.

`myComponent.setSize(length);`

Applies to the scrollbar component.

Where `myComponent` is a component instance. `width`, `height`, and `length` are the pixel measurements you want to resize the component to.

This **method** is compatible with **Flash 6**.

Description

You can resize your components during content creation using the standard Flash tools (Free Transform tool or Property inspector/Transform panel), and the `setSize` method allows you to do the same dynamically. There are three groups of components:

Components that let you set width and height

This includes the push button, scroll pane, and listbox.

In the example below, the listbox bands has some pop acts with single word names. There is one band, however, that is much longer than the rest, and cannot be seen:

Adding the following line of code fixes the problem:

```
bands.setSize(200, 105);
```

No longer obscured, but perhaps still a little obscure (in a cool kind of way).

Components that let you set width only

This includes the radio button, checkbox, and combobox components. You can only change the width of these components to make room for long label fields. Consider the radio button group artist below.

The parents of the last artist obviously couldn't come to an agreement about surnames, but we can fix this via the code below:

```
artist.setSize(150);
```

Tip - the default width for all components is 100, so you have a good idea of the original length. Alternatively, just read the original width of the W: value on the Property inspector.

The scrollbar

Irrespective of whether the scrollbar is horizontal or vertical, the length of the scrollbar is the pixel measure from the up arrow to the down arrow. To change the length of the scrollbar `scroll` to 200 pixels, you would do the following:

```
scroll.setSize(200);
```

FComponent.setState

(This method is applicable to **FRadioButton.setState**.)

```
myRadio.setState(Boolean);
```

Where `myRadio` is a radio button component and `Boolean` denotes whether it will start selected (`true`) or unselected (`false`).

This **method** is compatible with **Flash 6**.

Description

After dragging a radio button instance onto the stage, you can manually set the state of one of the radio buttons per group to selected via the Property inspector Initial State property. The `setState` method allows you to do this dynamically. The default state of a radio button is unselected.

You should note that a radio button group allows only one radio button within it to be selected. If you define more than one radio button in a group to be selected, only the last one to be defined as selected will actually become selected.

Code	Notes
`radio.setState(true);`	The radio button `radio` will become selected. Any other radio button within the same radio button group that are currently selected will become unselected.

FComponent.setStyleProperty

(This method is applicable to **FCheckBox.setStyleProperty**, **FComboBox.setStyleProperty**, **FListBox.setStyleProperty**, **FPushButton.setStyleProperty**, **FRadioButton.setStyleProperty**, and **FScrollPane.setStyleProperty**.)

```
myComponent.setStyleProperty(prop, val);
```

Where myComponent is a component that you want to apply a style change to. This style change will be a property prop of the **FStyleFormat** object, and will take on a value val.

This **method** is compatible with **Flash 6**.

Description
When using the **FStyleFormat** object the procedure is to:

- Create a FStyleFormat object.
- Register any components that you want to be affected by this FStyleFormat object as listeners to it.
- Change properties of the FStyleFormat object. These changes will be reflected in the appearance of all registered components when you apply the changes to the FStyleFormat object.

This provides an efficient way to change the style of a large number of components via a single centralized object (the FStyleFormat object), but can be cumbersome if you simply want to change the odd property of a single component instance.

Rather than have to go through the whole process of defining a FStyleFormat object and registering listeners just because you want to (say) change a push button's color to green, you can apply simple and localized changes via the setStyleProperty method.

See also the available properties of the FStyleFormat object by looking at the entry for **FStyleFormat**.

Code	Notes
`button1.setStyleProperty("face", 0x0000FF);` `button1.setStyleProperty("textColor", 0xFFFFFF);`	Changes the color ("face") of the push button instance button1 to blue and the text color of the same button to white.

See the following examples on the CD:

fcomponentsetstyleformat1.fla / fcomponentsetstyleformat1.swf
fcomponentsetstyleformat2.fla / fcomponentsetstyleformat2.swf

FComponent.setValue

(This method is applicable to **FCheckBox.setValue**, **FComboBox.setValue**, and **FRadioButton.set Value**.)

```
mycheck.setValue (Boolean);
```

Where `myCheck` is the component and `Boolean` denotes whether it will be set to `true` or unchecked `false`.

This **method** is compatible with **Flash 6**.

Description

Let's look at the checkbox component as an example. After dragging a checkbox instance onto the stage, you can manually set the state of one of it via the Property inspector's Initial Value property. The `setValue` method allows you to do this dynamically.

The default state of a checkbox is unchecked.

Code	Notes
`checkBox.setValue(true);`	The checkbox `checkBox` will become checked. Any change handler defined for the checkbox will execute on the change if the checkbox was previously unchecked.

FComponent.setVScroll

(This method is applicable to **FScollPane.setVScroll.**)

`myScrollPane.setVScroll(setting);`

Where `myScrollPane` is a scroll pane instance. When `setting` is set to `true`, the scroll pane's vertical scrollbar will always be displayed. If `setting` is set to `false` it will never be displayed. If `setting` is set to `"auto"`, the scrollbar will only appear when required.

This **method** is compatible with **Flash 6**.

Description

The scroll pane vertical scrollbar functionality can be controlled by the Vertical Scroll parameter of the Property inspector during content creation. It can also be controlled dynamically via the `setVScroll` method:

- If the argument to this method is set to `true`, the scrollbar will always be shown. If it is required, it will appear enabled. If it is not required it will appear but be disabled.
- If the argument is set to `false`, the scrollbar will never be shown.
- If the argument is set to `"auto"`, the scrollbar will be shown if the content requires it, but hidden otherwise.

Code	Notes
`myScrollPane.setVScroll(true);`	The vertical scrollbar of scroll pane instance `scrollPane` will always be shown. If it is required, it will appear enabled. If it is not required, it will still appear, but will be disabled.
`myScrollPane.setVScroll(false);`	The scrollbar will never be shown. If the content is bigger than the scroll pane, the user must have some other method of revealing the hidden portions, otherwise the user will not be able to see them.
`myScrollPane.setVScroll("auto");`	The scrollbar will appear/disappear as required. It will appear if the content width is larger than the width of the scroll pane.

FComponent.setWidth

(This method is applicable to **FListBox.setWidth**.)

`FListBox.setWidth(width)`

Where `FListBox` is a listbox component and `width` is the width in pixels that you want to set it to.

This **method** is compatible with **Flash 6**.

Description

You can resize your listbox width during content creation using the standard Flash tools (Free Transform tool or Property inspector/Transform panel), and the `setWidth` method allows you to do the same dynamically. You should also consider using the **FComponent.setSize** method, which lets you set both width and height together.

The default width of a listbox is 100 pixels.

Code	Notes
`list.setWidth(200);`	Sets the width of the listbox instance `list` to 200 pixels.

for

```
for (a; b; c){
statement
}
```

Where a is an initialization, b is a condition, and c is an increment or decrement used to update the value of the Loop Control Variable (LCV), which eventually causes the condition to fail, thus ending the loop.

for is compatible with **Flash 5 and above**. The for loop performs the same actions as the **while** loop, although **can be written in fewer lines of code**. You should be aware of a **known issue** with the for loop: if a parameter is missing from the for loop (for example, if you are missing a, b, or c), Flash MX will become **unresponsive or crash**. Related actions include the **++ increment** and **decrement** operators, and the **for...in** loop.

Description
This **action** is used to repeatedly loop through and execute a piece of code. A for loop will repeat the iterations until a value of false is returned.

Code	Returned value(s)	Notes

`for (i=1; i<=10; i++){`
`trace (i);`
`}`
	1 2 3 4 5 6 7 8 9 10	A var statement can also be used in a for loop. Additional values can be added and separated by a comma operator.

`var myStr = "this is a`
`string.";`
`trace(myStr.length);`
`for (i=0;`
`i<myStr.length; i++) {`
`    trace(i`
`+"="+myStr.substr(i,`
`1));`
`}`
	17
	0=t
	1=h
	2=i
	3=s
	4=
	5=i
	6=s
	7=
	8=a
	9=
	10=s
	11=t
	12=r
	13=i
	14=n
	15=g
	16=.
		Either numbers or strings can be returned from a for loop.

```
for (i=0; i<10; i—) {          See notes.
trace("i="+i+") will not
work");
}
```

This forms an infinite loop, where an end condition can never be achieved, so a long list of values will be returned until the processor is maxed out. At this time an error should display.

See the examples for.fla and for.swf on the CD.

for...in

```
for (a in b) {
statement
}
```

Where a is a property, and b is an object. The for...in loop will iterate through the properties of the object one time.

The for...in loop is compatible with **Flash 5 and above**. You should be aware that the returned values **are not returned in any particular order**. You therefore **cannot rely on a predictable stack order** in the array of returned properties. Related entries include **for** and **ASSetPropFlags**.

Description

This action **statement** returns each property of an object.

Code	Returned value(s)	Notes

`for (x in System) {`
`trace (x +"=="+`
`typeof(System[x]));`
`}`
	`Security==object`
	`ShowSettings==function`
	`Product==function`
	`Capabilities==object`
		Predefined objects are returned using a for...in loop.

`var cat = new Object();`
`cat.age = 5;`
`cat.fur = "black";`
`cat.size = "big";`
 	
`for (var prop in cat) {`
`trace("The cat is " +`
`cat[prop]);`
`}`
	`The cat is big`
	`The cat is black`
	`The cat is 5`
		The properties of an object are returned. The use of var is permitted.

```for (x in``` ```System.ShowSettings) {``` ```trace (x +"=="+``` ```typeof(System.ShowSettings``` ```[x]));``` ```}```	*N/A*	Do not try to loop over something which is not an object or array. For example, you cannot loop over a function.

See the example `for...in.fla` and `for...in.swf` on the CD.

fscommand()

```
fscommand ("a", "b");
```

Where a is a command which is passed to the host application or the stand-alone application. b consists of parameters made of a string or value, which is passed to the Flash Player or plug-in.

Compatible with **Flash 3 or later**. `fscommand` **does not work in several situations** noted below in the *Tips and precautions* section (in the full entry on the CD). It will work with programs that are compatible with Active X controls. The **commands passed back to the Flash player can only be predefined parameters** including `quit`, `fullscreen`, `allowscale`, `showmenu`, `exec`, and `trapallkeys`. Related actions include the **getURL** function.

Description

This **function** is used to communicate with external applications by sending commands to the other application, or send commands back to the Flash Player.

Code	HTML document	Notes
```fscommand``` ```("fullscreen","true");```	N/A	This will cause the stand-alone Flash Player to resize the window. You should make sure you have a button on the Stage for closing the Player window.
```on (release){``` ``` fscommand("myAlert",``` ```"Welcome to the site");``` ```}```	```if (command ==``` ```"myAlert") {``` ``` alert (args);``` ```}```	With this `fscommand`, a JavaScript "alert box" will pop up with an alert reading `Welcome to the site`.

```on (release) { fscommand ("panIt"); }```	```if (command == "panIt"){ fscommand01_test.Pan (25,25,1); }```	This `fscommand` will pan a zoomed in movie by 25% (horizontally and vertically) each time the button is clicked. The value of 1 measure pan in percentages, and a value of 0 measures pan in pixels.

FStyleFormat

```
a = new FStyleFormat([b,c,n])
```

Where a is the name of a new **formStyleFormat**, and b, c, n are optional properties assigned to the custom style format.

Compatible with **Flash MX**. This object is used to change the color and style of the text in Flash UI components, custom components, and third party components. **You cannot use this object to change the graphics of components themselves. You wouldn't use this object to change a single instance of a component.** Instead of using `FStyleFormat`, it is best to use the **setStyleProperty** method. Refer to related entries on the **FStyleProperty.addListener**, **FStyleProperty.applyChanges**, and **FComponent.setStyleProperty** methods.

Description
This **object** is used to create a custom style format for Flash UI components.

Code	Shortcut	Notes
```var myStyle = new FStyleFormat(); myStyle.textSize = 8; myStyle.textColor= 0xFF0000; myStyle.applyChanges(); myStyle.addListener (myListBox);```	```myStyle = new FStyleFormat ({textSize:8, textColor: 0xFF0000}); myStyle.applyChanges(); myStyle.addListener (myListBox);```	Using `var` in the `FStyleFormat` object is optional. There are two ways to use the constructor, as seen in the shortcut.
```myNewStyle = new FStyleFormat(); myNewStyle.textColor = #99CCFF; myNewStyle.applyChanges();```	```myNewStyle = new FStyleFormat({textColor: #99CCFF}); myNewStyle.applyChanges();```	Colors must be written using the 0xRRGGBB format. You must also add a listener using the myNewStyle.addListener(); method.

See the examples `fstyleformat.fla` and `fstyleformat.swf` on the CD.

FStyleFormat.addListener

```
a.addListener(c [d,e,f,n]);
```

Where a is the name of the custom style format, and c to n are the instance names of the components you are applying the style to.

Compatible with **Flash MX**. This method is used to **apply custom style formats to component instances**. You must provide at least one component instance to add a listener to. Refer to the related entry on **FStyleFormat.removeListener**.

Description
This **method** adds listeners to one or more component instances.

Code	Returned value(s)	Notes
myStyle.addListener (myButton);	*none*	This code adds a style format to a single component instance.
myStyle.addListener (myButton, myListBox, myScrollbar);	*none*	A comma operator can be used to separate several different component instances. Several instances can listen to the same custom style format.
myStyle.addListener();	*none*	You must provide the name of a component instance to add your listener to.
myComponent.addListener (myStyle);	*none*	You **cannot** construct the method in this way: component.addListener (FStyleFormat);

See the examples `fstyleformat.addlistener.fla` and `fstyleformat.addlistener.swf` on the CD.

FStyleFormat.applyChanges

```
a.applyChanges(["b","c","d",n]);
```

Where a is a custom style format, and b,c,d, and n are optional text strings of **FStyleFormat** property names.

Compatible with **Flash MX.** This method will apply the changes you make to a style format. You use this after you have made changes to a style format. Refer to the related entry on **FStyleFormat.addListener**.

Description
This **method** will update and apply the changes you make to a style format. If you make changes to an existing format and do not include this method, no changes will be made to the appearance of the component instance.

Code	Returned values	Notes
myStyle.applyChanges ("textColor", "highlight");	*none*	This will apply changes to the specified properties. Properties are written in quotations.
myStyle.applyChanges();	*none*	All of the changed properties will be applied to the style format.
myStyle.applyChanges ("myArrow", "myStyle");	*none*	Changes are made to the properties in the style format, and not the instances themselves. Listeners are used to apply style format changes to components.

See the examples fstyleformat.applychanges.fla and fstyleformat.applychanges.swf on the CD.

FStyleFormat.arrow

```
a.arrow = b;
```

Where a is the name of your style format, and b is a RGB color value being assigned to the arrow.

Compatible with **Flash MX.** This property will affect the color of arrows used in ScrollBar, ScrollPane, ListBox, and ComboBox Flash UI Components. It will not change the color of the arrow in disabled components. The RGB color value is written using the **0xRRGGBB format**. Use **FStyleFormat.foregroundDisabled** to change the value of disabled arrow.

Description
This **property** assigns a new color value to the scrollbar arrow used by several Flash UI components.

Code	Shortcut	Notes

myStyle =
 new FStyleFormat();
 myStyle.arrow = 0x99CCFF;
 myStyle.applyChanges();
 myStyle.addListener
 (myListBox);
	myStyle =
	 new FStyleFormat
	 ({arrow:0x99CCFF});
	 myStyle.applyChanges();
	 myStyle.addListener
	 (myListBox);
		This assigns a light blue color to the arrow instances in the custom myStyle style format.

myStyle.arrow = #99CCFF;	N/A	The color is not written in the correct RGB format.

See the example `fstyleformat.arrow.fla` and `fstyleformat.arrow.swf` on the CD.

FStyleFormat.background

```
a.background = b;
```

Where a is the name of your style format, and b is a RGB value being assigned to the background region.

Compatible with **Flash MX.** This property only affects the background region of components supporting this property. The RGB color value assigned to this property is written using the **0xRRGGBB format**. Refer to **FStyleFormat.face** and **FStyleFormat.backgroundDisabled** entries for information on how to change these elements.

Description
This **property** changes the color of the background area of the RadioButton, ListBox, and ComboBox components. It will affect the color of the background of the text area, and the background of the radio button and check box components.

Code	Shortcut	Notes
`myStyle = new FStyleFormat(); myStyle.background = 0xFF99CC; myStyle.applyChanges(); myStyle.addListener (myComponent);`	`myStyle = new FStyleFormat({background: 0xFF99CC}); myStyle.applyChanges(); myStyle.addListener (myComponent);`	This code will change the background color of `myComponent` by assigning a listener to the component instance and applying the changes using `applyChanges();`

See the examples `fstyleformat.background.fla` and `fstyleformat.background.swf` on the CD.

FStyleFormat.backgroundDisabled

```
a.backgroundDisabled = b;
```

Where a is the name of your style format, and b is a RGB value being assigned to the background regions of disabled component instances.

Compatible with **Flash MX.** You should be aware that this will affect the color of the background of disabled `list box`, `combo box`, `check box`, and `radio button` components. It will affect any other disabled custom or third party components supporting this property. The RGB color value is expressed using the **0xRRGGBB format**. Also see the entries on **FStyleFormat.foregroundDisabled** and **FStyleFormat.textDisabled**.

Description

This **property** assigns a new RGB color value to the background property when you create a new custom style format.

Code	Shortcut	Notes
`myStyle = new FStyleFormat(); myStyle.background Disabled = 0x99CCFF; myStyle.applyChanges(); myStyle.addListener (myComponent);`	`myStyle = new FStyleFormat ({backgroundDisabled: 0x99CCFF}); myStyle.applyChanges(); myStyle.addListener (myComponent);`	This code will change the background region of `myComponent` when it is in a disabled state.

See the example `fstyleformat.backgroundDisabled.fla` and `fstyleformat.backgroundDisabled.swf` on the CD.

FStyleFormat.check

```
a.check = b;
```

Where a is the name of your style format, and b is a new RGB value being assigned to the check graphic.

Compatible with **Flash MX.** This will change the color value of the check used in the check box component, and any custom and/or third party components using this particular property. The RGB color value is assigned to the property using the **0xRRGGBB format**. Related entries include those for the **FCheckBox component**.

Description

This **property** sets the check mark of a component instance to the specified RGB value.

Code	Shortcut	Notes
`myCheckmark = new FStyleFormat(); myCheckmark.check = 0xFF0000; myCheckmark.applyChanges(); myCheckmark.addListener (myCheckBox);`	`myCheckmark = new FStyleFormat ({check:0xFF0000}); myCheckmark.applyChanges(); myCheckmark.addListener (myCheckBox);`	This code applies a new color value to the check in the check box component.

See the examples `fstyleformat.check.fla` and `fstyleformat.check.swf` on the CD.

FStyleFormat.darkshadow

```
a.darkshadow = b;
```

Where a is the name of your custom style format, and b is a RGB value being assigned to the darkshadow regions of Flash UI components.

Compatible with **Flash MX.** You should be aware that this will affect the color of the darkshadow region in components containing this specified area. The RGB color value is assigned to the property using the **0xRRGGBB format**. Related entries include those for **FStyleFormat.highlight**, **FStyleFormat.highlight3D**, and **FStyleFormat.shadow**.

Description

This **property** assigns a color value to the darkshadow region of the component instances.

Code	Shortcut	Notes
```myStyle = new FStyleFormat(); myStyle.darkshadow = 0xFF0000; myStyle.applyChanges(); myStyle.addListener (myComponent);```	```myStyle = new FStyleFormat ({darkshadow:0xFF0000}); myStyle.applyChanges(); myStyle.addListener (myComponent);```	This code applies a red colored darkshadow region to the instance of myComponent.

See the examples `fstyleformat.darkshadow.fla` and `fstyleformat.darkshadow.swf` on the CD.

FStyleFormat.face

```
a.face = b;
```

Where a is the name of your custom style format, and b is the RGB value assigned to the face property of this format.

Compatible with **Flash MX.** Using this property will change the color value of the face region used in scrollbar buttons, and push buttons. It will also modify any other developed components supporting this property. The RGB color value is assigned to the property using the **0xRRGGBB format**. Related properties include **FStyleFormat.textColor** and **FStyleFormat.arrow**.

Description

This **property** of a style format sets the face region of "listening" component instances to the specified RGB value.

Code	Shortcut	Notes
```myStyle = new FStyleFormat(); myStyle.face = 0x99CCFF; myStyle.applyChanges(); myStyle.addListener (myButton);```	```myStyle = new FStyleFormat ({face:0x99CCFF}); myStyle.applyChanges(); myStyle.addListener (myButton);```	These will change the color of the face region in the component instance myButton.

See in the example `fstyleformat.face.fla` and `fstyleformat.face.swf` on the CD.

FStyleFormat.foregroundDisabled

```
a.foregroundDisabled = b;
```

Where a is the name of your custom style format, and b is the RGB value assigned to the foreground area of a disabled component instance.

Compatible with **Flash MX.** You should be aware that this will affect the color of the arrows used in disabled component instance scrollbars. It will also modify any other installed components supporting this property. The RGB color value is written using the **0xRRGGBB format**. Related entries include **FStyleFormat.backgroundDisabled** and **FStyleFormat.selectionDisabled**.

Description
This **property** sets the foreground regions of the disabled component instance(s) to a specified RGB value.

Code	Shortcut	Notes
myStyle = new FStyleFormat(); myStyle.foreground Disabled = 0x99CCFF; myStyle.applyChanges(); myStyle.addListener (myBG);	myStyle = new FStyleFormat ({foregroundDisabled: 0x99CCFF}); myStyle.applyChanges(); myStyle.addListener (myBG);	This code changes the background color of myBG to a light blue shade when it is in a disabled state.

See the example fstyleformat.foregroundDisabled.fla and fstyleformat.foregroundDisabled.swf on the CD.

FStyleFormat.highlight

```
a.highlight = b;
```

Where a is the name of your custom style format, and b is a RGB value assigned the highlight regions of components.

Compatible with **Flash MX.** This property changes the color value for the highlight regions specified in several components. The RGB color value is assigned to the highlight property using the **0xRRGGBB format**. Related entries include those for **FStyleFormat.shadow**, **FStyleFormat.highlight3D**, and **FStyleFormat.darkshadow**.

Description
This **property** sets the highlight regions of components to the specified RGB value.

Code	Shortcut	Notes
myHighlight = new FStyleFormat(); myHighlight.highlight = 0x99CCFF; myHighlight.applyChanges(); myHighlight.addListener (myComponent);	myHighlight = new FStyleFormat ({highlight:0x99CCFF}); myHighlight.applyChanges(); myHighlight.addListener (myComponent);	This code will change the highlight color of the myComponent instance to light blue.

See the example `fstyleformat.highlight.fla` and `fstyleformat.highlight.swf` on the CD.

FStyleFormat.radioDot

```
a.radioDot = b;
```

Where a is the name of your custom style format, and b is a RGB color value given to a radio dot.

Compatible with **Flash MX.** This component is used to change the color value of a radioDot graphic. The RGB color value is assigned to the radioDot property using the **0xRRGGBB format**. Related entries include the methods within the **FRadioButton** component.

Description
This **property**, within a custom style format, changes the RGB value of a radio dot listening to the custom style.

Code	Shortcut	Notes
myStyle = new FStyleFormat(); myStyle.radioDot = 0xFF0000; myStyle.applyChanges(); myStyle.addListener (myRadio);	myStyle = new FStyleFormat ({radioDot:0xFF0000}); myStyle.applyChanges(); myStyle.addListener (myRadio);	This code will change the color of the radio dot in component instance myRadio to red.

See the examples `fstyleformat.radiodot.fla` and `fstyleformat.radiodot.swf` on the CD.

FStyleFormat.removeListener

```
a.removeListener(b);
```

Where a is the name of your style format, and b is an instance of a component to remove from the style format.

Compatible with **Flash MX.** This method is used to a **remove a listener from a component instance**. This is typically used when you need a component instance to **listen to a different style format**, or return to the **globalStyleFormat**. Related entries include **FStyleFormat**, **FStyleFormat.addListener**, and **FStyleFormat.applyChanges**.

Description
This **method** removes an instance of a component from listening to a custom or global style format.

Code	Returns	Notes
myStyle.removeListener (myComponent);	*none*	This method does not require the FStyleFormat constructor. Here a component myComponent is removed from its assignment to the myStyle custom format.
var removeStyle = [button1, button2]; for (i in removeStyle) { myStyle.removeListener (removeStyle[i]); }	*none*	To remove a large number of component instances from a custom style format, you can use an array to loop through to remove listeners. This is to avoid listing each one separately.
myComponent.removeListener (myStyle);	*none*	The action **cannot** be expressed as **component**.removeListener (FStyleFormat);
myStyle.removeListener (myComponent1, myComponent2);	*none*	You cannot list more than one component to be removed simultaneously.

See the examples fstyleformat.removelistener.fla and fstyleformat.removelistener.swf on the CD.

FStyleFormat.scrollTrack

```
a.scrollTrack = b
```

Where a is the name of a custom style format, and b is a color expressed in RGB values.

Compatible with **Flash MX.** The scroll track is used in several components, including the ListBox and ComboBox components. The RGB color value is assigned to the scrollTrack property, and uses the **0xRRGGBB format.** Related entries include **FStyleFormat.face**, and those for the **FScrollBar** component.

Description
This **property** is used to change the color of the scroll track contained within the scrollbar.

Code	Shortcut	Notes
var myStyle = new FStyleFormat(); myStyle.scrollTrack = 0xFF0000; myStyle.applyChanges(); myStyle.addListener (myListbox);	var myStyle = new FStyleFormat ({scrollTrack:0xFF0000}); myStyle.applyChanges(); myStyle.addListener (myListbox);	This code changes the scroll track of the scroll bar in myListbox to red.

See the examples fstyleformat.scrolltrack.fla and fstyleformat.scrolltrack.swf on the CD.

FStyleFormat.selection

```
a.selection = b
```

Where a is the name of the custom style format, and b is the RGB value being applied to the text selection area.

Compatible with **Flash MX.** The text selection is used to represent which item in a listbox or combo box is currently selected. The RGB color value is assigned to the selection property by using the **0xRRGGBB format.** Related entries include **FStyleFormat.selectionDisabled**, **FStyleFormat.selectionUnfocused**, and **FStyleFormat.textSelected**.

Description
This **property** assigns a new color value for **selection** to a custom style format.

Code	Shortcut	Notes
var myStyle = new FStyleFormat(); myStyle.selection = 0xFF0000; myStyle.applyChanges(); myStyle.addListener (myListBox);	var myStyle = new FStyleFormat ({selection:0xFF0000}); myStyle.applyChanges(); myStyle.addListener (myListBox);	This code applies a new RGB value for the selection property by creating a new style format. Changes are applied, and the myScrollBar listener is added.

See the examples fstyleformat.selection.fla and fstyleformat.selection.swf on the CD.

FStyleFormat.selectionDisabled

```
a.selectionDisabled = b;
```

Where a is the name of the custom style format and b is a RGB value being applied to the disabled selection area.

Compatible with **Flash MX.** This color region is active only if a selection is made, and then the component is disabled in the movie. Related entries include those for **FStyleFormat.selection**, **FStyleFormat.backgroundDisabled**, and **FStyleFormat.selectionUnfocused**.

Description
This **property** assigns a new color value to a disabled selection.

Code	Returned values	Notes
var myStyle = new FStyleFormat(); myStyle.selectionDisabled = 0x99CCFF; myStyle.applyChanges(); myStyle.addListener (myListBox);	var myStyle = new FStyleFormat(); myStyle.selectionDisabled = 0x99CCFF; myStyle.applyChanges(); myStyle.addListener (myListBox);	This code assigns a light blue color to the selectionDisabled property. If a selection is made and the component myListBox becomes disabled, this color will highlight the text.

See the examples fstyleformat.selectiondisabled.fla and fstyleformat.selectiondisabled.swf on the CD.

FStyleFormat.selectionUnfocused

```
a.selectionUnfocused = b;
```

Where a is the name of your style custom format, and b is a RGB color value being assigned to the unfocused selection area.

Compatible with **Flash MX.** This property is used to set the color of the selection area when a component has a selection made, but focus is on another component. The RGB color value is written using the **0xRRGGBB format**. Related entries include **FStyleFormat.selection**.

Description
This **property** assigns a new color value to an unfocused text selection.

Code	Shortcut	Notes
myStyle = new FStyleFormat(); myStyle.selectionUnfocused = 0x99CCFF; myStyle.applyChanges(); myStyle.addListener (myListBox);	myStyle = new FStyleFormat ({selectionUnfocused: 0x99CCFF}); myStyle.applyChanges(); myStyle.addListener (myListBox);	This assigns a light blue color to a selecton area when the component on the stage is unfocused.

See the example `fstyleformat.selectionunfocused.fla` and `fstyleformat.selectionunfocused.swf` on the CD.

FStyleFormat.shadow

```
a.shadow = b;
```

Where a is the name of your style format, and b is a RGB value being assigned to the shadow region of component instances.

Compatible with **Flash MX.** This color value is given to the shadow regions, which help make up the edges of various components. The RGB color value assigned to this property is written using the **0xRRGGBB format**. Related entries include those for **FStyleFormat.highlight**, **FStyleFormat.highlight3D**, and **FStyleFormat.darkshadow**.

Description
This **property** changes the RGB color value of the shadow property.

Code	Shortcut	Notes
myStyle = new FStyleFormat(); myStyle.shadow = 0xFF99CC; myStyle.applyChanges(); myStyle.addListener (myComponent);	myStyle = new FStyleFormat ({shadow: 0xFF99CC}); myStyle.applyChanges(); myStyle.addListener (myComponent);	This code will change the shadow region of the instance myComponent to a light blue color.

See the examples fstyleformat.shadow.fla and fstyleformat.shadow.swf on the CD.

FStyleFormat.textAlign

    a.textAlign = "b";

Where a is the name of your style format, and b is a text string of left, center, or right.

Compatible with **Flash MX**. The value assigned to the global style format for this property is **left**. Related entries include those on **FStyleFormat.textIndent**, **FStyleFormat.textLeftMargin**, and **FStyleFormat.textRightMargin**.

Description

This **property** justifies the text in a component by specifying center, left, or right alignment.

Code	Shortcut	Notes
myStyle = new FStyleFormat(); myStyle.textAlign = "center"; myStyle.applyChanges(); myStyle.addListener (myComponent);	myStyle = new FStyleFormat ({textAlign:"center"}); myStyle.applyChanges(); myStyle.addListener (myComponent);	This code centers the text in myComponent, which is listening to the myStyle custom style format.
myStyle = new FStyleFormat(); myStyle.textAlign = center; myStyle.applyChanges(); myStyle.addListener (myComponent);	myStyle = new FStyleFormat ({textAlign:center}); myStyle.applyChanges(); myStyle.addListener (myComponent);	This property value is expressed as a string, so you must have double quotations around right, center, or left alignment.

See the examples `fstyleformat.textalign.fla` and `fstyleformat.textalign.swf` on the CD.

FStyleFormat.textBold

```
a.textBold = b;
```

Where a is the name of your custom style format, and b is a Boolean value of `true` or `false`.

Compatible with **Flash MX.** Component instance text is made bold by setting this property to `true`. The default setting in the global style format is `false` (not bold.) Also refer to the entry for the **FStyleFormat.textItalic** and **FStyleFormat.textUnderline** properties.

Description

This **property** is used to apply or remove boldface to all text within the component instances listening to the style format.

Code	Shortcut	Notes
myBold = new FStyleFormat(); myBold.textBold = true; myBold.applyChanges(); myBold.addListener (radio1);	myBold = new FStyleFormat ({textBold:true}); myBold.applyChanges(); myBold.addListener (radio1);	This code make the text label of the radio button instance, radio1, a boldfaced font. It is listening to the myBold style format.
myBold = new FStyleFormat(); myBold.textBold = "true"; myBold.applyChanges(); myBold.addListener (radio1);	myBold = new FStyleFormat ({textBold:"true"}); myBold.applyChanges(); myBold.addListener (radio1);	true and false are expressed as a value and not a string. Therefore, double quotation marks are not required.

See the examples `fstyleformat.textbold.fla` and `fstyleformat.textbold.swf` on the CD.

FStyleFormat.textColor

```
a.textColor = b;
```

Where a is the name of your custom style format, and b is a RGB value being assigned to the text within the component instance(s).

Compatible with **Flash MX.** This will be the primary color of all text within the component instances assigned to this style format. The RGB color value is assigned to the property using the **0xRRGGBB format**. Related entries include those for **FStyleFormat.textSelected**, and **FStyleFormat.textDisabled**.

Description
This **property** assigns a new color value to text within components listening to the custom style format.

Code	Shortcut	Notes

myStyle = new FStyleFormat();
myStyle.textColor = 0xFF0000;
myStyle.applyChanges();
myStyle.addListener (myComponent);
	myStyle = new FStyleFormat ({textColor:0xFF0000});
	myStyle.applyChanges();
	myStyle.addListener (myComponent);
		This code changes the text color in the instance myComponent to red.

See the examples `fstyleformat.textcolor.fla` and `fstyleformat.textcolor.swf` on the CD.

FStyleFormat.textDisabled

```
a.textDisabled = b;
```

Where a is the name of your custom style format, and b is the RGB value assigned to text in a disabled component.

Compatible with **Flash MX.** When a component is disabled, the text will change to the color value you assign for this property. The RGB color value is assigned using the **0xRRGGBB format**. Related entries include **FStyleFormat.backgroundDisabled** and **FStyleFormat.selectionDisabled**.

Description
This **property** changes the color value of the text in a disabled component instance.

Code	Shortcut	Notes

myStyle = new FStyleFormat();
myStyle.textDisabled = 0x99CCFF;
myStyle.applyChanges();
myStyle.addListener (myListBox);
	myStyle = new FStyleFormat ({textDisabled:0x99CCFF});
	myStyle.applyChanges();
	myStyle.addListener (myListBox);
		These will change the color of text when the component instance myListBox is in a disabled state.

See the examples `fstyleformat.textDisabled.fla` and `fstyleformat.textDisabled.swf` on the CD.

FStyleFormat.textFont

```
a.textFont = "b";
```

Where a is the name of your custom style format, and b is the name of a system font or the Linkage identifier of a Font embedded into your movie.

Compatible with **Flash MX.** You should be aware that if you use a system font, it will only be used by the component if the computer you are playing your movie on contains the font face. If you use an embedded font, the same text font will be seen by all users, but your movie will have a higher file size.

Description
This **property** sets the foreground regions of the disabled component instance(s) to a specified RGB value.

Code	Shortcut	Notes
myStyle = new FStyleFormat(); myStyle.textFont = "Arial"; myStyle.applyChanges(); myStyle.addListener (myButton);	myStyle = new FStyleFormat ({textFont:"Arial"}); myStyle.applyChanges(); myStyle.addListener (myButton);	This code changes the font face of the text in myButton to appear in Arial. This will only occur if the end user has Arial on their computer system.
myEmbedStyle = new FStyleFormat(); myEmbedStyle.textFont = "myFont"; myEmbedStyle.embedFonts = true; myEmbedStyle.apply Changes(); myEmbedStyle.addListener (myButton);	myEmbedStyle = new FStyleFormat ({textFont:"myFont", embedFonts:true}); myEmbedStyle.apply Changes(); myEmbedStyle.addListener (myButton);	In order to make sure your font is visible on all machines, you can embed a font in the library, set a Linkage name (myFont), and set embedFonts to true.

See the examples `fstyleformat.textfont.fla` and `fstyleformat.textfont.swf` on the CD.

FStyleFormat.textIndent

```
a.textIndent = b;
```

Where a is the name of your custom style format, and b is the number of pixels you want your text to be indented by.

Compatible with **Flash MX.** This property is used to indent all text in component instances listening to the custom style format. Related entries include **FStyleFormat.textAlign**, **FStyleFormat.textRightMargin**, and **FStyleFormat.textLeftMargin**.

Description

This **property**, within a custom style format, changes the RGB value of a radio dot listening to the custom style.

Code	Shortcut	Notes
myStyle = new FStyleFormat(); myStyle.textIndent = 8; myStyle.applyChanges(); myStyle.addListener (myButton);	myStyle = new FStyleFormat ({textIndent:8}); myStyle.applyChanges(); myStyle.addListener (myButton);	This code is used to indent the text on an instance called myButton by 8 pixels.

See the examples `fstyleformat.textindent.fla` and `fstyleformat.textindent.swf` on the CD.

FStyleFormat.textItalic

```
a.textItalic = b;
```

Where a is the name of your custom style format, and b is a Boolean value of `true` or `false`.

Compatible with **Flash MX.** You will want to use this property to change all text in assigned components to appear italic. Related entries include **FStyleFormat.textBold** and **FStyleFormat.textUnderline**.

Description

This **property** will make all text italic within the component instances listening to the style format.

Code	Shortcut	Notes
myStyle = new FStyleFormat(); myStyle.textItalic = true; myStyle.applyChanges(); myStyle.addListener (myListbox);	myStyle = new FStyleFormat ({textItalic:true}); myStyle.applyChanges(); myStyle.addListener (myListbox);	This code makes the text within the myListbox instance italic.

See the examples fstyleformat.textitalic.fla and fstyleformat.textitalic.swf on the CD.

FStyleFormat.textLeftMargin

```
a.textLeftMargin = b;
```

Where a is the name of your custom style format, and b is a number measured in pixels to specify a margin.

Compatible with **Flash MX.** You should use this property to create a left margin width. The integer is measured in pixels. Related entries include **FStyleFormat.textRightMargin** and **FStyleFormat.textIndent**.

Description

This **property** specifies a left margin for text in all component instances listening to the custom style format.

Code	Shortcut	Notes
myStyle = new FStyleFormat(); myStyle.textLeftMargin = 7; myStyle.applyChanges(); myStyle.addListener (myComponent);	myStyle = new FStyleFormat ({textLeftMargin:7}); myStyle.applyChanges(); myStyle.addListener (myComponent);	This code will specify a left margin for myComponent of 7 pixels width.

See the examples fstyleformat.textleftmargin.fla and fstyleformat.textleftmargin.swf on the CD.

FStyleFormat.textRightMargin

```
a.textRightMargin = b;
```

Where a is the name of your custom style format, and b is an integer specifying the width of the right margin.

Compatible with **Flash MX.** The number measuring the width of the right margin is measured in pixels. Related entries include **FStyleFormat.textLeftMargin** and **FStyleFormat.textIndent**.

Description
This **property**, within a custom style format, changes the pixel width of the right margin.

Code	Shortcut	Notes
```myStyle = new FStyleFormat(); myStyle.textRightMargin = 12; myStyle.applyChanges(); myStyle.addListener (myButton);```	```myStyle = new FStyleFormat ({textRightMargin:12}); myStyle.applyChanges(); myStyle.addListener (myButton);```	This code adjusts the right margin of the myButton instance by 12 pixels.

See the examples fstyleformat.textrightmargin.fla and fstyleformat.textrightmargin.swf on the CD.

FStyleFormat.textSelected

```
a.textSelected = b;
```

Where a is the name of your custom style format, and b is a RGB color assigned to the text.

Compatible with **Flash MX.** The RGB color value assigned to this property must use the **0xRRGGBB format**. Related entries include **FStyleFormat.selection**, **FStyleFormat.selectionUnfocused**, and **FStyleformat.textDisabled**.

Description
This **property** changes the RGB value of selected text within a component listening to the style format.

Code	Shortcut	Notes
```myStyle = new FStyleFormat(); myStyle.textSelected = 0xFF0000; myStyle.applyChanges(); myStyle.addListener (myListbox);```	```myStyle = new FStyleFormat ({textSelected:0xFF0000}); myStyle.applyChanges(); myStyle.addListener (myListbox);```	This code creates a style format, myStyle, changes the textSelected value to red and applies changes to the format. The myListbox component is listening to the style.

See the example `fstyleformat.textselected.fla` and `fstyleformat.textselected.swf` on the CD.

FStyleFormat.textSize

```
a.textSize = b;
```

Where a is the name of your custom style format, and b is an integer specifying the point-size of the text.

Compatible with **Flash MX.** This property should be considered when setting the textFont property, and the size of your component. Related entries include **FStyleFormat.textFont**, and **FComponent.setSize**.

Description

This **property**, within a custom style format, changes the size of the text in a component listening to the custom style.

Code	Shortcut	Notes
```myStyle = new FStyleFormat(); myStyle.textSize = 8; myStyle.applyChanges(); myStyle.addListener (myButton);```	```myStyle = new FStyleFormat ({textSize:8}); myStyle.applyChanges(); myStyle.addListener (myButton);```	This code will change the point size of the text face in the instance myButton to 8.

See the example `fstyleformat.textsize.fla` and `fstyleformat.textsize.swf` on the CD.

FStyleFormat.textUnderline

```
a.textUnderline = b;
```

Where a is the name of your custom style format, and b is a Boolean value of true or false.

Compatible with **Flash MX.** A Boolean value of true will underline all text in component instances listening to the style format. Related entries include **FStyleFormat.textBold** and **FStyleFormat.textItalic**.

Description

This **property**, within a custom style format, changes all of the text within components listening to the style to an underlined font face.

Code	Shortcut	Notes
myStyle = new FStyleFormat(); myStyle.textUnderline = true; myStyle.applyChanges(); myStyle.addListener (myRadio);	myStyle = new FStyleFormat ({textUnderline:true}); myStyle.applyChanges(); myStyle.addListener (myRadio);	This code will change all of the text in the myRadio instance to be underlined.

See the example fstyleformat.textunderline.fla and fstyleformat.textunderline.swf on the CD.

function/Function

```
function [a]([b,c,n]){
    statements
}
```

Where a is the optional name of the function, and b through n are optional parameters.

The Function **object** is compatible with **Flash MX.** The function **action** is compatible with **Flash 5 and above**. Functions should be used when you are repeatedly performing the same task. Also refer to the **return** action.

Description

The Function **object** contains the methods **Function.apply, Function.call,** and property **Function.prototype**. The Function object is exclusive to Flash MX, and its methods and properties are used to call or invoke functions. See the following entries: **Function.apply** and **Function.call,** for more information on this object. The function **action** is used in programming when the same block of code is needed many times during the application. A function is used for centralizing and reusing code, and functions can be found in other languages such as JavaScript and other Object Oriented programming languages. These kind of functions contain a series of statements, which define a task to perform.

Code	Returned values	Notes
``var thisDate = new Date();
trace(dayAsString
(thisDate.getDay()));
function dayAsString(thisDay) {
var dayNames = new Array("Sun.",
"Mon.", "Tue.", "Wed.", "Thu.",
"Fri.", "Sat.");
return dayNames[thisDay];
}```	*current day*	This function returns the day of the week as a string. Note that the day of the week is zero based in Flash, so Sunday is 0, and Saturday is 6.
``var x = 5;
var y = 6;

function addIt(x,y){
return x + y;
}``` | 11 | This function adds two numbers together, and returns the value. |
| ```function nextF(){
nextFrame();
}``` | goes to the next frame | This simple function will make a movie step one frame forward. |
| ```function isWrong(){
return;
_root.gotoAndPlay(5);
}``` | *none* | Anything after return will not be processed by the function. |
| ```var x = 5;
var y = 6;

function addMe(x,y){
var z = x + y;
}``` | *none* | The calculation is not returned to the caller since no return was specified. |

See the examples `function.fla` and `function.swf` on the CD.

Function.apply

```
a.apply(b,c)
```

Where a is the name of the function, b is the object a is being applied to, and c is an array of elements being passed to a as parameters.

Compatible with **Flash MX**. This method is used when you want to attach a function to an object. Also refer to the related entry on **Function.call.**

Description

This **method** allows ActionScript to call a function. It returns the value specified by the function.

Code	Returned values	Notes

`function moveTo(x) {`
`    this._x = x;`
`}`
 	
`moveTo.apply(_root.myMC,`
`[35]);`
	none	This will attach the moveTo function to the _root.myMC movie clip.

`function moveTo(x,y) {`
`    this._x = x;`
`    this._y = y;`
`}`
 	
`moveTo.apply(_root.myMC,`
`[35,20]);`
	none	This will attach the moveTo function to the _root.myMC movie clip and passes a new _x and _y position.

`myFunction.apply(_root.` `myMC, 35,20,12,12);`	*none*	This won't work because the parameters are not being passed as an array.

See the examples `function.apply.fla` and `function.apply.swf` on the CD.

Function.call

```
a.call(b, [c,d,n])
```

Where a is the name of the function, b is an object specifying a value of this, and c to n are optional parameters.

Compatible with **Flash MX**. This method is similar to the call action in earlier versions of Flash. **Functions are called and executed when using this method.** Also refer to entries on **Function.apply** and **Function**.

Description
This **method** is used to invoke a function being represented by a Function object.

Code	Returned values	Notes
`myFunction.call(null, "john");`	*none*	This code executes the function myFunction and passes in john as a variable.
```function myFunction(myArray) { var total = 0; for (i=0;i<myArray.length;i++) { total += myArray[i]; } return total; } trace(myFunction.call(null, [1,2,4]));```	the sum of the array	In this example, an array of strings are passed to our function.

See the examples function.call.fla and function.call.swf on the CD.

ge

    a ge b

Where a and b are expressions, which can be numbers, strings, or variables.

Compatible with **Flash 4**. This operator was **deprecated in Flash 5 and does not work in either Flash 5 or Flash MX**. Related entries include **gt** and the **>=** operator.

Description

This **comparison operator** is used to compare two expressions. If the first expression is greater than or equal to the second expression, a Boolean value of true is returned. Otherwise, a false value is returned.

Code	Returned values	Notes
var1 ge var2	true or false	This operator is deprecated and does not return accurate results. Instead, write var1 >= var2.

getTimer

    getTimer()

Compatible with **Flash 4 and later**. This function returns the elapsed time that your movie has been running in milliseconds. Related entries include those for the **getSeconds** and **getTime** methods of the **Date** object.

Description

This **function** will return, in milliseconds, the elapsed time since your Flash movie started playing.

Code	Returned values	Notes
if (getTimer()>5000){ gotoAndStop("tooSlow") }	*milliseconds of movie duration*	When the timer reaches 5000 milliseconds, the movie will go to and stop on the frame tooSlow.
setInterval(function (){ _level0.mytext.text = getTimer();	*none*	Time cannot be expressed on the _root of movies loaded onto other levels.

```
}, 500);
```

See the samples `gettimer.fla` and `gettimer.swf` on the CD.

getVersion

```
getVersion()
```

Compatible with **Flash 5 and later**. This function is used to check for the version of the Flash Player, 5 or later, installed on a users system. It cannot be used to check for the presence of a Flash Player. Related entries include System.capabilities.version.

Description

This **function** returns a string indicating the installed Flash Player version, and platform of the host computer.

Code	Returned values	Notes
`_root.playerversion.text = getVersion();`	*displays current version player and operating system.*	Displays the current player in a text field. An example of a returned string for the Flash Player 6r29 on a Windows system is WIN 6,0,29,0

See the examples `getversion.fla` and `getversion.swf` on the CD.

gotoAndPlay

```
gotoAndPlay(a)
```

or

```
gotoAndPlay("a"[,b])
```

Where a is the name or number of a frame or the name of a scene. Scene and frame names are put in double quotation marks. b is an optional frame number.

Compatible with **Flash 2.and later**. This is one of the many actions used to control the playhead in your Flash movies. The playhead is sent to a frame, and it plays the movie from this location forward. Also refer to the related entries on **Movieclip.gotoAndPlay**, **play**, **nextFrame**, **Movieclip.play**, and **gotoAndStop**.

Description

This **action** is used to send the playhead to a frame, and from that location it will continue to play.

Code	Notes	Notes
```on (release){ gotoAndPlay("page2"); }```		This action placed on a button causes the playhead to move to the frame labeled with page2, and play.
`this.myMC.gotoAndPlay(45);`		On the main timeline, this action moves the playhead within a movie clip, myMC, to move to 45 and play.
`myMC.gotoAndPlay(1);`	Frame 1 of myMC has a stop action.	It is probable that the movie will play past the stop action. In this situation, make sure you use gotoAndStop instead.

See the examples gotoandplay.fla and gotoandplay.swf on the CD.

gotoAndStop

gotoAndStop(a)

or

gotoAndStop("a"[,b])

Where a is the name or number of a frame or the name of a scene. Scene and frame names are put in double quotation marks. b is an optional frame number.

Compatible with **Flash 2 and later**. This action is used to send the playhead to a specified frame location, where the playhead will stop. Also refer to the related entries on **Movieclip.gotoAndStop**, **stop**, **Movieclip.stop**, and **gotoAndPlay**.

Description

This **action** is used to control the playhead in a Flash movie. The playhead is sent to a designated frame, where it will stop.

Code	Notes	Notes
`gotoAndStop("scene4", "myLabel")`		This action placed on the main timeline causes the playhead to be sent to a scene called scene4, and stop on the frame labelled myLabel.
`on(release){ _level2.gotoAndStop(10); }`		A button action on the main timeline moves the playhead within a movie loaded onto level 2, to frame 10. The playhead then stops.
`_root.myMC.gotoAndStop (myNewFrame);`		Frame names and scene names must be written within double quotation marks. Be careful with scoping when using _root, particularly if you are loading a movie with myMC into another SWF file.

See the examples `gotoandstop.fla` and `gotoandstop.swf` on the CD.

gt

`a gt b`

Where a and b are expressions, which can be numbers, strings, or variables.

Compatible with **Flash 4**. This operator is **deprecated in Flash 5, and does not work reliably in Flash MX**. Related entries include **ge** and the **>** operator.

Description
This **comparison operator** is used to compare two expressions. If the first expression is greater than the second expression, a Boolean value of `true` is returned. Otherwise, a `false` value is returned.

Code	Returned values	Notes
`var1 gt var2`	`true` or `false`	Since this operator is deprecated and not working in Flash MX, returned results are unpredictable. It is recommended to instead use `var1 > var2`.

.

if

```
if (a){
    statement(s);
}
```

Where a is a condition, and statement(s) are executed if a returns a value of true.
or

```
(a) ? b : c;
```

Where a is a condition, b is the value to return if the condition is true, and c is the value to return if the condition is false. b and c can also be **functions** or statements to execute. This also may be referred to as a **ternary** operator.

Compatible with **Flash 4 and later.** This action is used when several possible conditions may be encountered. Related actions include **else**, and **else...if**, and **switch**.

Description
This **action** tests to see if a condition is true. If the condition is true, the block of code will be executed. If the condition evaluates to false, then the code block is skipped. Flash then tests all subsequent else...if blocks until a true condition is met or an else block is encountered.

Code	Shortcut	Notes
`if (passwd == "password"){ gotoAndStop ("secretpage"); }else{ gotoAndStop("tryagain"); }`	`gotoAndStop(passwd == "password" ? "secretpage" : "tryagain");`	This code is a basic example of an if...else statement where we check to see if the supplied password matches our predefined value. If it matches then the condition is true and we go to the secretpage. Otherwise the condition evaluates to false and the user tries again.

Code	Shortcut	Notes
```if (name == "john") {trace("hello john");} else if (name == "jane") {trace("hello jane.");} else {trace("howdy, stranger");}```	```switch (name) {case "john":trace ("hello john.");break;case "jane":trace ("hello jane.");break;default:trace("howdy, stranger");}```	This code demonstrates the else...if and else syntax. If the name equals john then our output window would trace hello john. and then skip the else...if and else code blocks. If the name equals jane then the code would check the first if condition and evaluate to false. Then it tries the else...if statement, where it would evaluate to true, and skip the final else statement. You should note that switch cannot *always* be used as a shortcut for an if... statement, though in many cases it can.

```
if (name == "john") {
trace ("hello john.");
}
if (name == "jane") {
trace ("hello jane.");
}
if (name == "billy") {
trace ("hello billy");
}
```

Since the value of name can only evaluate to a single value, three separate if statements should not be executed. It would be better form to use else... if statements instead of three if statements because once a match is found, Flash will skip the rest of the code block and proceed. In this case, the movie would instead run through the entire code block.

```
if (name == "john") {
trace ("hello john.");
}
if (name == "jane") {
trace ("hello jane.");
}
else {
trace ("hello stranger");
}
```

In this example we have forgotten to put an else statement after the first if code block. Therefore, if the supplied name is john, then our Output window will show hello john.. Since we don't have an else after that if, it will evaluate the next if...else code block, failing on the if condition. The code would execute the else code block and display hello stranger in the Output window.

Code	Shortcut	Notes

`if (x < 0)`
`    x = 0;`
`    _root.message =`
`"Please recheck your`
`value";`
`    gotoAndPlay(1);`
		In this example, curly brackets are forgotten after the condition. In this case only the first line of code after the `if` statement would be executed if our statement were `true`. The following two lines of code would be executed regardless of how the `if` statement executed. To correct this problem we would need to enclose the statements between a pair of curly brackets.

See the examples `if.fla` and `if.swf` on the CD.

ifFrameLoaded

```
ifFrameLoaded(a){
    statement;
}
```

or

```
ifFrameLoaded("a",b){
    statement;
}
```

Where a is the name or number of a frame or scene, and b is a number of a frame.

Compatible with **Flash 3**. This property is **deprecated in Flash 5** in favor of the **MovieClip._framesloaded action**. **This action currently works in Flash MX**. Related entries include the **getBytesLoaded** and **getBytesTotal** methods, and **MovieClip._framesloaded**.

Description
This **action** checks to see if a specified frame has loaded. When this frame has loaded, the statement executes.

Code	Returned value	Notes

```ifFrameLoaded("mymovie",15)```
 ```{```
 ```gotoAndStop("mymovie ", 1);```
 ```}```
		This action will go to frame 1 of the scene `mymovie` after frame 15 of `mymovie` has loaded.

See the example `ifframeloaded.fla` and `ifframeloaded.swf` on the CD.

Infinity

```
Infinity
```

```
-Infinity
```

Compatible with **Flash 5 and later**. This global property works in the same way as **Number.POSITIVE_INFINITY** and **Number.NEGATIVE_INFINITY**. This is an undocumented property in Flash MX. Refer to entries on these related properties for further information on how to use this constant, as well as the entry for **isFinite**.

Description

This **constant** is a **global property.** It represents a positive infinite or negative infinite number.

Code	Returned value	Notes
`Math.Infinity-` `Math.Infinity`	0	This equation returns an accurate value.
`Math.Infinity/` `Math.Infinity`	NaN	An inaccurate value is returned in this equation. The returned value should be 1.
`Infinity-Infinity`	NaN	Returns an inaccurate result, as above. This should be 0.
`trace(Infinity);`	Infinity	Since infinity is a state rather than representative of an integer, this trace will return `Infinity`.

Code	Returned value	Notes
Number.NEGATIVE_INFINITY/ Number.NEGATIVE_INFINITY	NaN	This result should be 1. Infinity/Infinity instead returns a broken result.

instanceof

```
a instanceof b
```

Where a is an object, and b is a class.

Compatible with **Flash MX**. The class referred to in this operator is a **reference to a constructor function in ActionScript**, such as **MovieClip**. Also refer to the related entry of **typeof**.

Description

This **operator** returns a true or false Boolean value when determining if an instance or object is part of a class.

Code	Returned value	Notes
myObject instanceof Button	false	In this example, the object is not an instance of the Button class.
for (i in _level0) { trace(_level0[i]+" is "+(_root[i] instanceof MovieClip)); }	All movie clip instance names in root, and returns true for all movie clip instances on the stage.	This will trace the names of all movie clip objects into the output window, and a value of true for the instances which are movie clips.
function newCat(whiskers) { this.whiskers = whiskers; } var myCat = new newCat("Buddy"); trace (myCat instanceof newCat);	true	This code will trace to see if myCat is an instance of the new newCat class. myCat therefore is an instance of newCat and Buddy is a parameter to the function.

See the examples instanceof fla and instanceof swf on the CD

int

```
int(a)
```

Where a is a numeric value which is rounded to an integer.

Compatible with **Flash 4**. This function is **deprecated in Flash 5**, and it is suggested you use the **Math.round** method instead. However, the function **int still works in Flash MX**. Refer to the entries for **Math.round** and **Math.floor**.

Description

This global **function** is used to round values to the nearest whole integer. int removes anything beyond the decimal point, so it does not round up or down to the closest whole integer.

Code	Returned value	Notes
int(7.9)	7	7.9 is rounded to an even integer of 7.
int(-7.9)	-7	-7.9 is rounded to an even integer of -7.
int(true)	1	Boolean values return 1 for true, and 0 for false.

isFinite

```
isFinite(a)
```

Where a is an expression. This expression may include a variable or Boolean value that returns a numeric value.

Compatible with **Flash 5 and later**. This function is typically used to evaluate mathematical errors, which may include division by 0. Related entries include **Infinity**, **isNaN**, **Number.POSITIVE_INFINITY**, and **Number.NEGATIVE_INFINITY**.

Description

This **function** evaluates the expression, and will return a Boolean value of true or false depending on whether or not it is positive infinity or negative infinity.

Code	Returned value	Notes
isFinite(56);	true	This code checks if 56 is a finite integer. The returned value is true.
isFinite(Number.MAX_VALUE * 6);	false	This code returns false, as it is a multiple of the max number, which returns Infinity.
isFinite(Math.infinity/ Math.infinity);	false	NaN is returned by the expression, so a false value is returned. Refer to the entry on Infinity.

isNaN

isNaN(a)

Where a is an expression which may include a variable or a Boolean value.

Compatible with **Flash 5**. You would use this function to check if a value returned is a number or a string, which would indicate a mathematical error. You would not use this function to check for the validity of the value. Related entries include **isFinite**.

Description
This **function** will return true if the value returned is not a number, and false if the value is a number.

Code	Returned value	Notes
isNaN(13);	false	This returns a Boolean value of false since 13 is a number.
isNaN("string");	true	This returns a Boolean value of true since string is a not a number.
trace (isNaN(33r));	none	An error is thrown if you attempt to trace a value beginning with a number and ending with a string. However, if you trace isNaN(r33) a value of false is returned.

See the examples isnan.fla and isnan.swf on the CD.

Key

```
new Key()
```

Compatible with **Flash Player 6 and later.**

The Key object is used to provide properties with specific keyboard key values, as well as methods to determine key codes of pressed keys on the keyboard.

Description

The Key **object** contains several methods, properties, and event handler for working with keyboard keys and their values.

There are several methods contained in the Key object (all covered in their own reference later). These methods and their purposes are:

- Key.getASCII – returns the ASCII value of the last key that changed state (was either pressed or released). If no key has been pressed, it will return zero.
- Key.getCode – returns the key code of the last key pressed, which in most cases gives the same value as the getASCII method.
- Key.isDown – returns true if a specified key is pressed or continues to be pressed.
- Key.isToggled – returns true if the NUM LOCK or CAPS LOCK key is on.

There are many properties in the Key object (which are also examined in their own reference sections), which you can use instead of the less programmer friendly raw ASCII values:

- Key.BACKSPACE – the BACKSPACE key (ASCII 9)
- Key.CAPSLOCK – the CAPS LOCK key (ASCII 20)
- Key.CONTROL – the CTRL key (ASCII 27)
- Key.DELETEKEY — the DELETE key (ASCII 46)
- Key.DOWN – the down arrow (ASCII 40)
- Key.END – the END key (ASCII 35)
- Key.ENTER – the ENTER or "return" key (ASCII 13)
- Key.HOME – the HOME key (ASCII 36)
- Key.INSERT – the INSERT key (ASCII 45)
- Key.LEFT – the "eft arrow (ASCII 37)
- Key.PGDN – the PAGE DOWN or PGDN key (ASCII 34)
- Key.PGUP – the PAGE UP or PGUP key (ASCII 33)
- Key.RIGHT – the right arrow (ASCII 39)
- Key.SHIFT – The SHIFT key (ASCII 16)
- Key.SPACE – the SPACEBAR (ASCII 32)
- Key.TAB – the TAB key (ASCII 9)
- Key.UP – the up arrow (ASCII 38)

Key.addListener

```
Key.addListener (listener_name)
```

Where `listener_name` is the `Key` object to be watched for key presses and releases; `listener_` name has two methods called `onKeyDown` and `onKeyUp`. If `listener_name` is already registered, the `Key.addListener` command is ignored.

Compatible with **Flash Player 6 and later**. There are no known issues with any versions of Flash that support this method.

When a `Key` object has been registered using the `Key.addListener` method it **responds to all key presses and key releases**. Any number of objects can be registered. Whenever a key press or release is detected, all registered `Key` objects have their `onKeyDown` or `onKeyUp` methods invoked.

Description

`Key` **objects** have `onKeyDown` and `onKeyUp` methods associated with them. For these methods to be invoked the `Key` object has to be registered using the `Key.addListener` method. After registering, all key presses and releases are relayed to the registered objects and the `onKeyUp` and `onKeyDown` methods, respectively, are triggered. (See also **Key.onKeyDown** and **Key.onKeyUp**.)

Code	Additional explanation	Notes
`Key.addListener` `(myKeyobject)`	Registers `myKeyobject` so the `onKeyDown` and `onKeyUp` methods are invoked on key activity.	If `myKeyobject` is already registered nothing happens.

Key.BACKSPACE

```
Key.BACKSPACE
```

Compatible with **Flash Player 5 and later**. There are no known issues with any versions of Flash that support this method.

`Key.BACKSPACE` is a data constant assigned the ASCII value for the BACKSPACE key (ASCII 9).

Description

`Key.BACKSPACE` holds the ASCII value (ASCII 9) for the BACKSPACE key. It cannot be reassigned.

Code	Notes
```_root.onEnterFrame = function() { if (Key.isDown(Key.BACKSPACE)) { trace("backspace key is down"); } };```	The "do something" code will be executed for every frame the BACKSPACE key is down.

Key.CAPSLOCK

Key.CAPSLOCK

Compatible with **Flash Player 5 and later**. There are no known issues with any versions of Flash that support this method.

Key.CAPSLOCK is a data constant assigned the ASCII value for the CAPS LOCK key (ASCII 20).

Description
Key.CAPSLOCK holds the ASCII value (ASCII 20) for the CAPS LOCK key. It cannot be reassigned.

Code	Notes
```_root.onEnterFrame = function() { if (Key.isDown(Key.CAPSLOCK)) { trace("Caps Lock key is down"); } };```	The "do something" code will be executed for every frame the CAPS LOCK key is down.

Key.CONTROL

Key.CONTROL

Compatible with **Flash Player 5 and later**. There are no known issues with any versions of Flash that support this method.

Key.CONTROL is a data constant assigned the ASCII value for the Control (CTRL) key (ASCII 17).

Description
Key.CONTROL holds the ASCII value (ASCII 17) for the Control (CTRL) key. It cannot be reassigned.

code	Notes
| ```
_root.onEnterFrame = function() {
   if (Key.isDown(Key.CONTROL)) {
      trace("control key is down");
   }
};
``` | The "do something" code will be executed for every frame the Control key is down. |

Key.DELETEKEY

Key.DELETEKEY

Compatible with **Flash Player 5 and later**. There are no known issues with any versions of Flash that support this method.

Key.DELETEKEY is a data constant assigned the ASCII value for the DELETE key (ASCII 46).

Description

Key.DELETEKEY holds the ASCII value (ASCII 46) for the DELETE key. It cannot be reassigned.

code	Notes
| ```
_root.onEnterFrame = function() {
   if (Key.isDown(Key.DELETKEY)) {
      trace("delete key is down");
   }
};
``` | The "do something" code will be executed for every frame the DELETE key is down. |

Key.DOWN

Key.DOWN

Compatible with **Flash Player 5 and later**. There are no known issues with any versions of Flash that support this method.

Key.DOWN is a data constant assigned the ASCII value for the "down arrow" key (ASCII 40).

Description

Key.DOWN holds the ASCII value (ASCII 40) for the "down arrow" key. It cannot be reassigned. See also **Key.UP**, **Key.RIGHT**, and **Key.LEFT** for the other arrow keys.

Code	Notes
| ```
_root.onEnterFrame = function() {
   if (Key.isDown(Key.DOWN)) {
      trace("down arrow key is down");
   }
};
``` | The "do something" code will be executed for every frame the "down arrow" key is down. |

Key.END

Key.END

Compatible with **Flash Player 5 and later**. There are no known issues with any versions of Flash that support this method.

Key.END is a data constant assigned the ASCII value for the END key (ASCII 35).

Description

Key.END holds the ASCII value (ASCII 35) for the END key. It cannot be reassigned.

Code	Notes
| ```
_root.onEnterFrame = function() {
   if (Key.isDown(Key.END)) {
      trace("end key is down");
   }
};
``` | The "do something" code will be executed for every frame the END key is down. |

Key.ENTER

Key.ENTER

Compatible with **Flash Player 5 and later**. There are no known issues with any versions of Flash that support this method.

Key.ENTER is a data constant assigned the ASCII value for the Enter key (ASCII 13).

Description

Key.ENTER holds the ASCII value (ASCII 13) for the ENTER key. It cannot be reassigned.

code	Notes
| ```
_root.onEnterFrame = function() {
   if (Key.isDown(Key.ENTER)) {
      trace("enter key is down");
   }
};
``` | The "do something" code will be executed for every frame the ENTER key is down. |

Key.ESCAPE

Key.ESCAPE

Compatible with **Flash Player 5 and later**. There are no known issues with any versions of Flash that support this method.

Key.ESCAPE is a data constant assigned the ASCII value for the Escape (Esc) key (ASCII 27).

Description

Key.ESCAPE holds the ASCII value (ASCII 27) for the Escape (Esc) key. It cannot be reassigned.

code	Notes
| ```
_root.onEnterFrame = function() {
   if (Key.isDown(Key.ESCAPE)) {
      trace("escape key is down");
   }
};
``` | The "do something" code will be executed for every frame the Escape key is down. |

Key.getASCII

Key.getASCII();

Compatible with **Flash Player 5 and later**. There are no known issues with any versions of Flash that support this method.

Key.getASCII returns the ASCII code of the last key pressed or released. No parameters are allowed.

Description

Key.getASCII returns the ASCII value of the last key press or key release.

Code	Additional explanation	Notes
Key.getASCII();	Holds the ASCII value of the last key pressed or released.	Holds an ASCII value. Does not take parameters.

The following is a list of the ASCII codes and the characters they refer to:

8	Backspace	47	Help	74	J	99	Num-pad 3	119	F8
9	Tab	48	0	75	K	100	Num-pad 4	120	F9
12	Clear	49	1	76	L	101	Num-pad 5	121	F10
13	Enter	50	2	77	M	102	Num-pad 6	122	F11
16	Shift	51	3	78	N	103	Num-pad 7	123	F12
17	Control	52	4	79	O	104	Num-pad 8	124	F13
18	Alt	53	5	80	P	105	Num-pad 9	125	F14
20	Caps Lock	54	6	81	Q	106	Multiply *	126	F15
27	Escape	55	7	82	R	107	Add +	144	Num Lock
32	Spacebar	56	8	83	S	108	Enter	186	; :
33	Page Up	57	9	84	T	109	Subtract -	187	= +
34	Page Down	65	A	85	U	110	Decimal .	189	- _
35	End	66	B	86	V	111	Divide /	191	/ ?
36	Home	67	C	87	W	112	F1	192	\Q ~
37	Left Arrow	68	D	88	X	113	F2	219	[{
38	Up Arrow	69	E	89	Y	114	F3	220	\ |
39	Right Arrow	70	F	90	Z	115	F4	221	] }
40	Down Arrow	71	G	96	Num-pad 0	116	F5	222	" '
45	Insert	72	H	97	Num-pad1	117	F6		
46	Delete	73	I	98	Num-pad 2	118	F7		

Key.getCode

```
Key.getCode();
```

Compatible with **Flash Player 5 and later**. There are no known issues with any versions of Flash that support this method.

Key.getCode returns the virtual key code of the last key pressed or released. No parameters are allowed.

Description

Key.getCode returns the virtual key code of the last key press or key release. Virtual key codes are assigned to every key on a keyboard, regardless of operating system and platform, for which there is a Flash Player.

Code	Additional explanation	Notes
Key.getCode();	Returns the virtual key code of the last key pressed or released.	Holds a virtual key code. Does not take parameters.

Key.HOME

```
Key.HOME
```

Compatible with **Flash Player 5 and later**. There are no known issues with any versions of Flash that support this method.

`Key.HOME` is a data constant assigned the ASCII value for the HOME key (ASCII 36).

Description

`Key.HOME` holds the ASCII value (ASCII 36) for the HOME key. It cannot be reassigned.

Code	Notes
```_root.onEnterFrame = function() { if (Key.isDown(Key.HOME)) { trace("home key is down"); } };```	The "do something" code will be executed for every frame the HOME key is down.

Key.INSERT

```
Key.INSERT
```

Compatible with **Flash Player 5 and later**. There are no known issues with any versions of Flash that support this method.

`Key.INSERT` is a data constant assigned the ASCII value for the INSERT key (ASCII 45).

Description

`Key.INSERT` holds the ASCII value (ASCII 45) for the INSERT key. It cannot be reassigned.

Code	Notes
```_root.onEnterFrame = function() { if (Key.isDown(Key.INSERT)) { trace("insert key is down"); } };```	The "do something" code will be executed for every frame the INSERT key is down.

Key.isDOWN

```
Key.isDOWN(code);
```

Where `code` is the key code value or a `key` object property of a particular key.

Compatible with **Flash Player 5 and later**. There are no known issues with any versions of Flash that support this method.

`Key.isDOWN` returns `true` if the specified key code is pressed (and held down).

Description

`Key.isDOWN` returns `true` if the key code value parameter matches the key code of a pressed key.

Code	Additional explanation	Notes
`Key.isDOWN(key);`	If key is pressed, returns true.	Matches key code values as well as `key` object properties assigned to specific keys.
		Macintosh Caps Lock and Num Lock keys have identical key codes.

Key.isToggled

```
Key.isToggled(code);
```

Where `code` is the key code value for either the Num Lock (144) or Caps Lock (20) keys.

Compatible with **Flash Player 5 and later**. There are no known issues with any versions of Flash that support this method.

`Key.isToggled` returns `true` if the specified key code is toggled on.

Description

`Key.isDOWN` returns `true` if the key code value parameter is toggled on. This method is used only for the Caps Lock and Num Lock key values.

Code	Additional explanation	Notes
`Key.isToggled(144);`	If the Num Lock key is pressed, returns `true`.	Macintosh Caps Lock and Num Lock keys have identical key codes.

Key.LEFT

`Key.LEFT`

Compatible with **Flash Player 5 and later**. There are no known issues with any versions of Flash that support this method.

`Key.LEFT` is a data constant assigned the ASCII value for the left arrow key (ASCII 37).

Description

`Key.LEFT` holds the ASCII value (ASCII 37) for the left arrow key. It cannot be reassigned. See also **Key.DOWN**, **Key.UP**, and **Key.RIGHT** for the other arrow keys.

Code	Notes

<pre>_root.onEnterFrame = function() {
    if (Key.isDown(Key.LEFT)) {
        trace("left arrow key is down");
    }
};</pre>
	The "do something" code will be executed for every frame the left arrow key is down.

Key.onKeyDown

`Key.onKeyDown;`

Compatible with **Flash Player 6 and later**. The movie clip key events don't work so you have to use this method if you want to detect key presses via an event driven route.

The `Key.onKeyDown` method is used with a listener object registered using `Key.addListener`. This method is triggered when a key is pressed.

Description

`Key.onKeyDown` is a **method** invoked when a key is pressed. It will be triggered only on a registered object (see **Key.addListener**).

Code	Additional explanation	Notes

`Key.onKeyDown() =`
`function { // do`
`something`
`};`
	When a key is pressed the
	onKeyDown method is
	invoked.
		Works only on registered
		listening objects.

Key.onKeyUp

```
Key.onKeyUp;
```

Compatible with **Flash Player 6 and later**. The movie clip key events don't work so you have to use this method if you want to detect key presses via an event driven route.

The `Key.onKeyUp` method is used with a listener object registered using `Key.addListener`. This method is triggered when a key is released.

Description

`Key.onKeyUp` is a **method** invoked when a key is released. It will be triggered only on a registered object (see **Key.addListener**).

Code	Additional explanation	Notes

`Key.onKeyUp() =`
`function { // do`
`something`
`};`
	When a key is released the
	onKeyUp method is invoked.
		Works only on registered
		listening objects.

Key.PGDN

```
Key.PGDN
```

Compatible with **Flash Player 5 and later**. There are no known issues with any versions of Flash that support this method.

`Key.PGDN` is a data constant assigned the ASCII value for the PAGE DOWN key (ASCII 34).

Description

`Key.PGDN` holds the ASCII value (ASCII 34) for the PAGE DOWN key. It cannot be reassigned.

Code	Notes
```_root.onEnterFrame = function() { if (Key.isDown(Key.PGDN)) { trace("Page Down key is down"); } }; ```	The "do something" code will be executed for every frame the PAGE DOWN key is down.

Key.PGUP

```
Key.PGUP
```

Compatible with **Flash Player 5 and later**. There are no known issues with any versions of Flash that support this method.

`Key.PGUP` is a data constant assigned the ASCII value for the PAGE UP key (ASCII 33).

Description

`Key.PGUP` holds the ASCII value (ASCII 35) for the PAGE UP key. It cannot be reassigned.

Code	Notes
```_root.onEnterFrame = function() { if (Key.isDown(Key.PGUP)) { trace("Page Up key is down"); } }; ```	The "do something" code will be executed for every frame the PAGE UP key is down.

Key.removeListener

```
Key.removeListener (listener_name)
```

Where `listener_name` is the Key object to be removed from watching for key presses and releases.

Compatible with **Flash Player 6 and later**. There are no known issues with any versions of Flash that support this method.

When a Key object has been registered using the `Key.addListener` method and you want to remove it from the listener list, use `Key.removeListener`. If the listener is successfully removed, the method returns `true`.

Description

Key objects that have been registered to listen for key pressed and releases using `Key.addListener` can be removed from the listener list using `Key.removeListener`. If the listener is successfully removed, `true` is returned. If the listener did not exist on the list of listener objects, `false` is returned.

Code	Additional explanation	Notes
`Key.removeListener(myKeyobject)`	Removes `myKeyobject` from the listener.	If `myKeyobject` is registered and removed successfully, `true` is returned.
		If `myKeyobject` is either not removed or not registered as a listener, `false` is returned.

Key.RIGHT

`Key.RIGHT`

Compatible with **Flash Player 5 and later**. There are no known issues with any versions of Flash that support this method.

`Key.RIGHT` is a data constant assigned the ASCII value for the "right arrow" key (ASCII 39).

Description

`Key.RIGHT` holds the ASCII value (ASCII 39) for the "right arrow" key. It cannot be reassigned. See also **Key.DOWN**, **Key.UP**, and **Key.LEFT** for the other arrow keys.

Code	Notes
| ```
_root.onEnterFrame = function() {
    if (Key.isDown(Key.RIGHT)) {
        trace("right arrow key is down");
    }
};
``` | The "do something" code will be executed for every frame the "right arrow" key is down. |

Key.SHIFT

`Key.SHIFT`

Compatible with **Flash Player 5 and later**. There are no known issues with any versions of Flash that support this method.
```

Key.SHIFT is a data constant assigned the ASCII value for the SHIFT key (ASCII 16).

Description

Key.SHIFT holds the ASCII value (ASCII 16) for the SHIFT key. It cannot be reassigned.

Code	Notes
```_root.onEnterFrame = function() { if (Key.isDown(Key.SHIFT)) { trace("shift key is down"); } };```	The "do something" code will be executed for every frame the SHIFT key is down.

Key.SPACE

Key.SPACE

Compatible with **Flash Player 5 and later**. There are no known issues with any versions of Flash that support this method.

Key.SPACE is a data constant assigned the ASCII value for the SPACEBAR key (ASCII 32).

Description

Key.SPACE holds the ASCII value (ASCII 32) for the SPACEBAR key. It cannot be reassigned.

Code	Notes
```_root.onEnterFrame = function() { if (Key.isDown(Key. SPACE)) { trace("space key is down"); } };```	The "do something" code will be executed for every frame the SPACEBAR key is down.

Key.TAB

Key.TAB

Compatible with **Flash Player 5 and later**. There are no known issues with any versions of Flash that support this method.

Key.TAB is a data constant assigned the ASCII value for the TAB key (ASCII 9).

`Key.SHIFT` is a data constant assigned the ASCII value for the SHIFT key (ASCII 16).

Description

`Key.SHIFT` holds the ASCII value (ASCII 16) for the SHIFT key. It cannot be reassigned.

Code	Notes
| ```
_root.onEnterFrame = function() {
   if (Key.isDown(Key.SHIFT)) {
      trace("shift key is down");
   }
};
``` | The "do something" code will be executed for every frame the SHIFT key is down. |

Key.SPACE

`Key.SPACE`

Compatible with **Flash Player 5 and later**. There are no known issues with any versions of Flash that support this method.

`Key.SPACE` is a data constant assigned the ASCII value for the SPACEBAR key (ASCII 32).

Description

`Key.SPACE` holds the ASCII value (ASCII 32) for the SPACEBAR key. It cannot be reassigned.

Code	Notes
| ```
_root.onEnterFrame = function() {
   if (Key.isDown(Key. SPACE)) {
      trace("space key is down");
   }
};
``` | The "do something" code will be executed for every frame the SPACEBAR key is down. |

Key.TAB

`Key.TAB`

Compatible with **Flash Player 5 and later**. There are no known issues with any versions of Flash that support this method.

`Key.TAB` is a data constant assigned the ASCII value for the TAB key (ASCII 9).

gotoAndStop()
hitTest()
loadMovie()
loadVariables()
loadVariables()
nextFrame() play()
prevFrame()
removeMovieClip()
setMask() startDrag()
startDrag() startDrag()
swapDepths()
unloadMovie()
attachMovie()
createEmptyMovie()
createTextField()
duplicate

le

```
string1 le string2
```

Where `string1` and `string2` are two strings.

Compatible with **Flash Player 4 and later**. Deprecated with **<=** in Flash 5 and later.

The `le` operator is used for string "less than or equal to" comparisons. Flash 5 and later emphasizes the use of the more common `<=` comparison operator instead, but `le` is still supported.

Description

The `le` **operator** is used for "less than or equal to" comparisons between **strings only** (whereas `<=` will work for all data types). It can be used instead of the `<=` operator in Flash 5 and higher, although the latter is the preferred format because of consistency with non-string operations. String comparisons are left to right, using ASCII values.

Code	Additional explanation	Notes
`string1 le string2`	If `string1` is less than or equal to `string2` in an ASCII comparison from left to right, `true` is returned.	Deprecated for `<=` in Flash 5 and later.

loadMovie

```
loadMovie (URL [, target] [, GET|POST]);
```

Where `URL` is the absolute or relative URL for a movie or JPEG file to be loaded, `target` specifies a target movie clip to be replaced, and `GET|POST` indicates the method used to send variables to the movie.

Compatible with **Flash Player 3 and later**.

The `loadMovie()` **action** is used to load a new movie into a Flash Player, without terminating the existing Flash Player process and starting another.

Description

Normally a Flash Player will play through a movie and then close. The `loadMovie()` action allows you to play additional movies in an existing player without terminating the current player. Using `loadMovie()` you can play several movies in sequence, or play several movies simultaneously. The `loadMovie()` action requires the URL for the movie or JPEG file to be loaded into the Player. The URL can be specified with an absolute or relative address. The URL must point to the same folder that the current movie is being played from and cannot include drive specifications. The `loadMovie()` action is similar in purpose, but not the same action as, the `MovieClip.loadMovie` method.

Arguments for `loadMovie()` include the name of the movie to be replaced (with the new movie inheriting the level, rotation, scale, and position of the existing movie) as well as whether to use GET or POST methods for passing variables to the movie. If you specify a level instead of a movie name, the action `loadMovieNum()` is invoked instead of `loadMovie()`. If you load a movie into level 0, all existing movies and their variables are unloaded and replaced with the specified file. See also **loadMovieNum**, **unloadMovie**, and **loadVariables**.

The GET and POST methods indicate how the movie will communicate variable values. The GET method uses a URL to send variables and their values, while the POST method uses an HTTP header. If there are a lot of variables to be sent, POST is the better method. If there are no variables involved, leave off this option.

Code	Additional explanation	Notes
`loadMovie ("sample.swf",` `"oldstuff.swf");`	Replaces the movie `oldstuff.swf` with `sample.swf` in the existing Flash Player, inheriting all the characteristics of the window.	Assumes the file is in the same directory as the current movie. You can specify a JPEG file to be loaded, instead of movie.
`loadMovie ("sample.swf",` `"oldstuff.swf", GET)`	Will use the GET method to transfer variables to the movie.	The GET or POST methods can be used for variable transfer. GET is suitable for a few values, while POST is better for many variables.
`loadMovie ("newmovie.swf",` `"_root.oldmovie")`	Replaces "oldmovie.swf" in the _root level with "newmovie.swf"	
`loadMovie ("c:/wwwroot/sample.swf");`	URLs cannot include drive or folder specifications; all SWF files must be in the same folder.	
`loadMovie ("sample.swf");`	No target movie is specified	This would be valid if referring to the MovieClip.loadMovie method.
`loadMovie ("sample.swf", 0);`	Loads and plays the movie sample.swf in the existing Flash Player. The new movie is loaded into level 0.	This action actually invokes loadMovieNum instead of loadMovie.

replacing all existing movies
and variables at all levels.

loadMovieNum

```
loadMovieNum (URL, level] [, GET|POST]);
```

Where URL is the absolute or relative URL for the movie (SWF) file to be loaded, level is the level into which the movie is loaded, and GET|POST indicates the method used to send variables to the movie.

Compatible with **Flash Player 4 and later**.

The loadMovieNum() **action** is used to load a new movie into a Flash Player at a specific level, without terminating the existing Flash Player process and starting another.

Description

Normally a Flash Player will play through a movie and then close. The loadMovieNum() action allows you to play additional movies in an existing player without terminating the current player. The loadMovieNum() action is a variation on loadMovie(), but loadMovieNum() always specifies a level, while loadMovie() specifies a name.

Using loadMovieNum() you can play several movies in sequence, or play several movies simultaneously. The loadMovieNum() action requires the URL for the movie or JPEG file to be loaded into the Player. The URL can be specified using absolute or relative addressing. The URL must be in the same folder as the current movie being played and cannot include drive specifications.

Arguments for loadMovieNum() include the level at which to place the loaded movie as well as whether to use GET or POST methods for passing variables to the movie. If you load a movie into level 0, all existing movies and their variables are unloaded and replaced with the specified file. See also **loadMovie**, **unloadMovie**, and **loadVariables**.

The GET and POST methods indicate how the movie will communicate variable values. The GET method uses a URL to send variables and their values, while the POST method uses an HTTP header. If there are a lot of variables to be sent, POST is the better method. If there are no variables involved, leave off this option.

Code	Additional explanation	Notes
loadMovie ("sample.swf", 0);	Loads and plays the movie sample.swf in the existing Flash Player. The new movie is loaded into level 0, replacing all existing movies and variables at all levels.	Assumes the file is in the same directory as the current movie.

| loadMovieNum
("c:/wwwroot/sample.swf",2
); | URLs cannot include drive or
folder specifications; all SWF
files must be in the same folder. |
| loadMovieNum
("sample.swf"); | No target level is specified |

LoadVariables

```
loadVariables (URL, target [,GET|POST]);
```

Where URL is the absolute or relative URL where the variables are located, target is the movie clip into which the variables are to be loaded, and GET|POST indicates the method used to send the variables.

Compatible with **Flash Player 4 and later**. Flash 5 and later will automatically convert Flash 4 files to the proper format.

The loadVariables() action is used to load variables for a movie, either to set initial values or to update them.

Description

The loadVariables() **action** allows you to transfer variables and their values to a movie or movie clip already loaded with loadMovie or loadMovieNum. The variables can come from a file (either static or created by a server-side script). The loadVariables() action can be used to update existing values as a movie plays.

The loadVariables() action requires a URL for the location of the variable file. This file and the movie itself must be in the same sub-domain.

The optional GET and **POST** methods indicate how the variables and their values will be sent to the movie. The GET method uses a URL descriptor while the POST method uses an HTTP header. If there are a lot of variables to be sent, POST is the better method.

The loadVariables() action is similar in purpose to the method MovieClip.loadVariables, but the syntax is different. The LoadVars object has methods that can accomplish the same task.

Code	Additional explanation	Notes
LoadVariables "varvalues.dat", newMovie.swf");	Loads the variables and values defined in the file varvalues.dat into the movie newMovie. The	Assumes the file is in the same directory as the current movie. The target movie should be already loaded.

variables and values may be
new or replace existing values.

Code	Additional explanation	Notes
LoadVariables("data.dat");	No level or target is specified into which to load the variables.	

loadVariablesNum

```
loadVariablesNum (URL, level [,GET|POST]);
```

Where URL is the absolute or relative URL where the variables are located, level is the level into which the variables are to be loaded, and GET|POST indicates the method used to send the variables.

Compatible with **Flash Player 4 and later**. Flash 5 and later will automatically convert Flash 4 files to the proper format.

The loadVariablesNum() action is used to load variables for a movie, either to set initial values or to update them, by specifying the movie level.

Description

The loadVariablesNum() **action** allows you to transfer variables and their values to a movie in a level already loaded with loadMovie or loadMovieNum. The variables can come from a file (either static or created by a server-side script). The loadVariablesNum() action can be used to update existing values as a movie plays. (The loadVariablesNum() action is similar to loadVariables, except a level number is specified instead of a movie name.)

The loadVariablesNum() action requires a URL for the location of the variable file. This file and the movie itself must be in the same sub-domain.

The optional GET and POST methods indicate how the variables and their values will be sent to the movie. The GET method uses a URL descriptor while the POST method uses an HTTP header. If there are a lot of variables to be sent, POST is the better method.

The LoadVars object has methods that can accomplish the same task.

Code	Additional explanation	Notes
loadVariablesNum ("varvalues.dat", 0);	Loads the variables and values defined in the file varvalues.dat into the movie loaded in level 0. The variables and values may be new or replace existing values.	Assumes the file is in the same directory as the current movie.

```
LoadVariables("data.dat");  No level is specified into
                            which to load the variables.
```

LoadVars

```
new LoadVars()
```

Compatible with **Flash Player 6 and later**.

The `LoadVars` object is used to transfer variables. The `LoadVars` object is an alternative to the `loadVariables` and `loadVariablesNum` actions.

Description

The `LoadVars` **object** contains several methods, properties, and event handlers for transferring variables and their values between a movie and a URL.

There are several methods contained in the `LoadVars` object (all covered in their own reference later). These methods and their purposes are:

- `LoadVars.load` – loads variables from a URL.
- `LoadVars.getBytesLoaded` – the total number of bytes downloaded.
- `LoadVars.getBytesTotal` – the number of total bytes downloaded.
- `LoadVars.send` – sends variables to a URL.
- `LoadVars.sendAndLoad` – sends variables to a URL and downloads the response.
- `LoadVars.toString` – returns a string containing all variables.

`LoadVars.load` and `LoadVars.send` perform opposite actions, reading or writing data from a URL to an instance, or vice versa. `LoadVars.sendAndLoad` does both actions with one command. `LoadVars.getBytesLoaded` and `LoadVars.getBytesTotal` are used to determine the number of bytes sent.

There are two properties in the `LoadVars` object (which are also examined in their own reference sections):

- `LoadVars.contentType` – the MIME type used to transfer data.
- `LoadVars.load` – a Boolean showing whether a load operation is complete

There is one event handler for the `LoadVars` object called `LoadVars.onLoad`, which is invoked when a load or `sendAndLoad` method is completed.

LoadVars.contentType

```
instancename.contentType
```

Where `instancename` is an instance of the `LoadVars` object.

Compatible with **Flash Player 6 and later**.

The `LoadVars.contentType` property is used to specify a MIME content type used by an instance's `LoadVars.send()` and `LoadVars.sendAndLoad()` methods.

Description

`LoadVars.contentType` is a **property** of a `LoadVars` instance that is used to set the MIME type for the `Loadvars.send()` and `Loadvars.sendAndLoad()` methods. If the MIME type is set incorrectly, the data may not be properly understood. The default MIME type is `application/s-www-urlform`.

Code	Additional explanation	Notes
`myMovieVars.contentType = "application/s-www-urlform";`	Sets the MIME content type for the `myMovieVars` instance.	The default MIME type of `application/s-www-urlform` is widely used but can be overridden.

LoadVars.getBytesLoaded

`instancename.getBytesLoaded()`

Where `instancename` is an instance of the `LoadVars` object.

Compatible with **Flash Player 6 and later**.

The `LoadVars.getBytesLoaded()` method returns the number of bytes transferred.

Description

The `LoadVars.getBytesLoaded()` **method** returns an integer specifying the number of bytes transferred with a `.send()` or `.sendAndLoad()` method. If no `.send()` or `.sendAndLoad()` method has been invoked, or the operation is still underway, a value of `undefined` is returned. The `LoadVars.getBytesTotal` method can be used to determine the number of bytes that has been sent by a data transfer using one of the `LoadVars` methods.

Code	Additional explanation	Notes
`transferred= myMovieVars.getBytesLoaded ();`	Determines the number of bytes sent with the last `.send()` or `.sendAndLoad()` method and returns that value as an integer, storing it in the variable transferred.	If no operation has been conducted or the operation is underway, `undefined` is returned.

LoadVars.getBytesTotal

```
instancename.getBytesTotal()
```

where `instancename` is an instance of the `LoadVars` object.

Compatible with **Flash Player 6 and later**.

The `LoadVars.getBytesTotal` method returns the number of bytes that are being transferred.

Description

The `LoadVars.getBytesTotal` **method** returns an integer specifying the number of bytes that are transferred with a `.send()` or `.sendAndLoad()` method while the send is underway. If no `.send()` or `.sendAndLoad()` method has been invoked, a value of `undefined` is returned. If the number of bytes cannot be determined because no HTTP content-length message was sent, the value of `undefined` is also returned. The `LoadVars.getBytesTotal()` method indicates the total number of bytes to be sent by an operation, while the method `LoadVars.getBytesLoaded()` indicates the number of bytes that were sent.

Code	Additional explanation	Notes
`totalsize=` `myMovieVars.getBytesTotal` `()`	Determines the number of bytes to be sent with the last `.send()` or `.sendAndLoad()` method and returns that value as an integer, storing it in the variable `totalsize`.	If no operation is underway or the number of bytes cannot be determined, `undefined` is returned.

LoadVars.load

```
instancename.load(url)
```

Where `instancename` is an instance of the `LoadVars` object and `url` is the location of the variables to be transferred.

Compatible with **Flash Player 6 and later**.

The `LoadVars.load()` method loads variables into a `LoadVars` instance.

Description

The `LoadVars.load()` **method** is used to retrieve variables and their values from a URL and place them in an instance of the `LoadVars` object. The downloaded variables are sent in `application/x-www-urlform-encoded` MIME format only. If existing variables with the same name are present in the instance, they are overwritten.

Code	Additional explanation	Notes
myMovieVars.load("data.txt");	Opens the MIME format data in data.txt, parses it, and places the resulting variable names and values in the myMovieVars instance.	Existing variables of the same name are overwritten.

LoadVars.loaded

    instancename.loaded

Where instancename is an instance of the LoadVars object.

Compatible with **Flash Player 6 and later**.

The LoadVars.loaded property indicates if a load operation is underway or completed.

Description

The LoadVars.loaded **property** normally has a value of undefined. When a .load() or a .sendAndLoad() operation has begun, the property has the value set to false. After the operation has completed, the property is set to true.

Code	Additional explanation	Notes
Xferflag=myMovieVars.loaded;	If a load or sendAndLoad has begun, Xferflag is false. If the load or sendAndLoad is complete, Xferflag is true. If no transfer is underway, Xferflag is undefined.	If a transfer has begun but fails without success, the property is still set to false.

LoadVars.onLoad

    instancename.onLoad(flag)

Where instancename is an instance of the LoadVars object and flag is a Boolean with a value of true or false.

Compatible with **Flash Player 6 and later**.

The LoadVars.onLoad event handler indicates whether a load operation has ended successfully or not.

Description

The LoadVars.onLoad() **method** is an event handler that returns a Boolean which indicates whether a .load() or a .sendAndLoad() operation has been successful or failed. If it was successful, the event handler returns true; a false indicates failure. If no .load() or .sendAndLoad() operation is being performed, the Boolean is undefined.

Code	Additional explanation	Notes
DidIt=myMovieVars.onLoad( );	If a load operation completed successfully, DidIt (a Boolean) is true; otherwise it is false.	By default a value of undefined will be returned unless a load operation has been performed.

LoadVars.send

```
instancename.send(url [,target [,method]])
```

Where instancename is an instance of the LoadVars object, url is the location of the variables to be transferred, target is the frame window into which responses are to be displayed, and method is a GET or POST method

Compatible with **Flash Player 6 and later**.

The LoadVars.send() method sends instance variables into a specified URL.

Description

The LoadVars.send() **method** sends variables from the instance as a string to a URL (the opposite action of the .load() method). By default, all the variables in the instance are concatenated into an application/x-www-urlform-encoded MIME format and sent using the POST method unless the GET method is specified. If LoadVars.contentType was used to specify a new MIME format prior to calling this method, that format is used instead of application/x-www-urlform-encoded.

If there is a response from the server where the URL is located, it is discarded unless a target frame window has been specified.

Code	Additional explanation	Notes
`myMovieVars.send("data.txt");`	Creates a MIME format string from the variable names and values in the `myMovieVars` instance and writes them into a file called `data.txt` using the HTTP `POST` method.	
`myMovieVars.send("data.txt", GET);`	Uses the `GET` method to transfer the variable names and values from the `myMovieVars` instance to the file `data.txt`.	

LoadVars.sendAndLoad

```
instancename.sendAndLoad(url, target [,method])
```

Where `instancename` is an instance of the `LoadVars` object, `url` is the location of the variables to be transferred, `target` is the `LoadVars` object to receive the data, and `method` is a `GET` or `POST` method.

Compatible with **Flash Player 6 and later**.

The `LoadVars.send()` method loads variables into a specified URL, waits for a response, parses it, and places the response in a second `LoadVars` object.

Description

The `LoadVars.sendAndLoad()` **method** sends variables from one `LoadVars` instance as a string to a URL, waits for the response, then places the result in another `LoadVars` instance. This method is the same as using `LoadVars.send()` to place variables in a URL, then a `LoadVars.load()` to place the URL contents in a `LoadVars` instance. By default, all the variables in the instance are concatenated into an `application/x-www-urlform-encoded` MIME format and sent using the `POST` method unless the `GET` method is specified. If `LoadVars.contentType` was used to specify a new MIME format previous to issuing this method, that format is used instead of `application/x-www-urlform-encoded`.

Code	Additional explanation	Notes
`myMovieVars.sendAndLoad ("data.txt", myMovie2);`	Creates a MIME format string from the variable names and values in the `myMovieVars` instance and writes them into a file called `data.txt` using the HTTP POST method, then reads the file (which may contain a response from a CGI script), and sends that data to the `myMovie2` instance.	The same instance of LoadVars can send and receive using this method.

LoadVars.toString

```
instancename.toString()
```

Where `instancename` is an instance of the `LoadVars` object.

Compatible with **Flash Player 6 and later**.

The `LoadVars.toString()` method returns a string of all variables in the instance.

Description

The `LoadVars.toString()` **method** returns a string of all the variables and their values in an instance of the `LoadVars` object, using the `application/x-www-urlform-encoded` MIME format. This string can be assigned to a variable.

Code	Additional explanation	Notes
`myVars=myMovieVars.to String();`	Creates a MIME format string from the variable names and values in the `myMovieVars` instance and stores them in the variable `myVars` (which will be a string).	

lt

```
string1 lt string2
```

Where `string1` and `string2` are two strings.

Compatible with **Flash Player 4 and later**. Deprecated for < in Flash 5 and later.

The lt **operator** is used for string "less than" comparisons. Flash 5 and later emphasizes the use of the more common < comparison operator (which can compare all data types) instead, but lt is still supported.

Description

The lt operator is used for "less than" comparisons between **strings only**. It can be used instead of the < operator in Flash 5 and higher, although the latter is the preferred format because of consistency with non-string operations. String comparisons are left to right, using ASCII values.

Code	Additional explanation	Notes
string1 lt string2	If string1 is less than string2 in an ASCII comparison from left to right, true is returned.	Deprecated for < in Flash 5 and later.

M

gotoAndStop()
hitTest()
loadMovie()
loadVariables()
loadVariables()
nextFrame()   play()
prevFrame()   removeMovieClip
removeMovie() setMask() startDrag()
startDrag()   swapDepth
unloadMovie
attachMovie
createEmptyMovie
createTextFiel
duplicate

Math

Compatible with **Flash Player 4 and later**.

The `Math` object's methods and properties are used to perform basic mathematical operations.

Description

The `Math` **object** can be used without a constructor. You can simply call the object and the method or property using the standard dot notation (such as `Math.round()`, `Math.log()`, or `Math.PI`) without creating an instance of the `Math` object.

The `Math` object contains several methods and properties used to perform basic mathematical operations. The `Math` methods and their purposes are:

- `abs()` – computes absolute value
- `acos()` – computes the arc cosine
- `asin()` – computes the arc sine
- `atan()` – computes the arc tangent
- `atan2()` – computes the angle from the x-axis to a point
- `ceil()` – rounds up to the next integer
- `cos()` – computes the cosine
- `exp()` – computes an exponential value
- `floor()` – rounds down to the next integer
- `log()` – computes the natural logarithm
- `max()` – determines the larger of two numbers
- `min()` – determines the smaller of two numbers
- `pow()` – raises a number to a power
- `random()` – returns a pseudo-random number
- `round()` – rounds to the nearest integer
- `sin()` – computes the sine
- `sqrt()` – computes the square root
- `tan()` – computes the tangent

Each of these methods is examined separately in the following entries.

The `Math` object properties (which are also examined in their own reference sections) are:

- `E` – Euler's constant
- `LN2` – base 2 logarithm
- `LOG2E` – base 2 logarithm of e
- `LN10` – base 10 logarithm
- `LOG10E` – base 10 logarithm of e
- `PI` – Value of pi
- `SQRT1_2` – reciprocal of square root of 0.5
- `SQRT2` – square root of 2

All the Math methods and properties are static. All properties are defined using double-precision floating-point numbers.

Math.abs

```
a = Math.abs(b);
```

Where a is the variable that you want to equate to the absolute value of b (with absolute value being the number b without the positive or negative sign).

This method is compatible with **Flash 5 or later**.

Description

This **method** will return any number passed to it, without the positive or negative sign. This is the absolute value of the number. In maths, this is written as:

```
a = | b |
```

Code	Notes
`a = Math.abs(5);` `b = Math.abs(-5);`	In the first line, a will be set to 5. In the second line, b will be set to 5, because the negative sign was stripped off.
`c = -9;` `d = Math.abs(c);`	In the third example, c is being set to the number -9, and therefore d will be set to 9.
`e = "-15";` `f = Math.abs(e);`	In the final example, e is being set to the string -15. Flash will convert this from a string to a number before it then applies the Math.abs function, and returns 15.
`c = Math.abs ("text");`	If anything other than a number is passed into the function, then Flash will return NaN, which stands for "Not a Number".

See the examples math.abs.fla and math.abs.swf on the CD.

Math.acos

```
a = Math.acos(b);
```

Where a is the variable that you want to equate to the arc cosine of b.

This method is compatible with **Flash 5 or later**.

Description
This **method** will return the arc cosine value of the number passed to it. The number passed in must be from -1.0 to 1.0. Generally, Math.acos returns an angle that you already have the cosine value of, and the angle is returned in radians.

Code	Notes
a = Math.acos(0);	In the first line, a will be set to 1.5707963267949, which is one half of the mathematical constant, PI.
b = Math.acos(-1);	In the second line, b will be set to 3.14159265358979, which is the mathematical constant, PI.
c = Math.acos(1);	In the third example, c will be set to 0, because the arc cosine of 1 is 0.
d = Math.acos(2);	In the first example, d will be set to NaN, because 2 is not within the range of -1.0 to 1.0
e = Math.acos ("text");	If anything other than a number is passed into the function, then Flash will return NaN, which stands for "Not a Number".

See the examples math.acosplot.fla and math.acosplot.swf on the CD.

Math.asin

```
a = Math.asin(b);
```

Where a is the variable that you want to equate to the arc sine of b.

This method is compatible with **Flash 5 or later**.

Description
This **method** will return the arc sine value of the number passed to it. The number passed in must be from -1.0 to 1.0. Generally, Math.asin returns an angle that you already have the sine value of, and the angle is returned in radians.

Code	Notes
a = Math.asin(0);	In the first line, a will be set to 0, because the arc sine of 0, is 0.
b = Math.asin(-1);	In the second line, b will be set to -1.5707963267949, which is negative one half of the mathematical constant, PI.
c = Math.asin(1);	In the third example, c will be set to 1.5707963267949, which is one half of the mathematical constant, PI.
d = Math.asin(2);	In the first example, d will be set to NaN, because 2 is not within the range of -1.0 to 1.0.
e = Math.asin ("text");	If anything other than a number is passed into the function, then Flash will return NaN, which stands for "Not a Number".

See the examples math.asinplot.fla and math.asinplot.swf on the CD.

Math.atan

```
a = Math.atan(b);
```

Where a is the variable that you want to equate to the arc tangent of b.

This method is compatible with **Flash 5 or later**.

Description
This **method** will return the arc tangent value of the number passed to it. Generally, Math.atan returns an angle that you already have the tangent value of.

Code	Notes
a = Math.atan(0);	In the first line, a will be set to 0, because the arc tangent of 0, is 0.

`b = Math.atan(-1);`	In the second line, b will be set to -0.785398163397448.
`c = Math.atan(1);`	In the third example, c will be set to 0.785398163397448.
`d = Math.atan(-Infinity);`	In the fourth example, d will be set to -1.5707963267949, which is negative one half of the mathematical constant, PI.
`e = Math.atan(Infinity);`	In the fifth example, e will be set to 1.5707963267949, which is one half of the mathematical constant, PI.
`f = Math.atan ("text");`	If anything other than a number is passed into the function, then Flash will return NaN, which stands for "Not a Number".

See the examples `math.atanplot.fla` and `math.atanplot.swf` on the CD.

Math.atan2

```
a = Math.atan2(y, x);
```

Where a is the variable that you want to equate to the arc tangent of the ratio between y and x. The ratio is computed as y/x by the function, and then a simple atan is applied to that ratio.

This method is compatible with **Flash 5 or later**.

Description
This **method** will return the arc tangent value of the two numbers passed to it. Usually, these two numbers will be distances along the x-axis and the y-axis. It is these two distances, which are required in order to compute the desired angle.

Code	Notes
`a = Math.atan2(0, 0);`	In the first line, a will be set to 0.
`b = Math.atan2(-1, -1);`	In the second line, b will be set to -2.35619449019234 radians, which is -135 degrees (a 45 degree angle down and to the left).

Code	Notes
`c = Math.atan2(1, 1);`	In the third example, c will be set to 0.785398163397448 radians, which is 45 degrees.
`d = Math.atan2(1, 0);`	In the fourth example, d will be set to 1.5707963267949, which is one half of the mathematical constant, PI. This is 90 degrees straight down.
`e = Math.atan2(0, 1);`	In the fifth example, e will be set to 0 degrees because it's a horizontal line.
`f = Math.atan2 ("text", "text");`	If anything other than two numbers are passed into the function, then Flash will return NaN, which stands for "Not a Number".

See the examples `math.atan2.fla` and `math.atan2.swf` on the CD.

Math.ceil

```
a = Math.ceil(b);
```

Where a is the variable that you want to equate to the ceiling of b.

This method is compatible with **Flash 5 or later**.

Description

This **method** will return the value of b rounded up to the nearest whole number that is greater than, or equal to b.

Code	Notes
`a = Math.ceil(0);`	In the first line, a will be set to 0.
`b = Math.ceil(1.1);`	In the second line, b will be set to 2, because the next whole integer greater than 1.1 is 2.
`c = Math.ceil(-1.1);`	In the third example, c will be set to −1, because the next whole integer greater than −1.1 is −1.
`d = Math.ceil(9.0000001);`	In the fourth example, d is set to 10, because even though the fractional portion is very small, Math.ceil will

still round up to the next *greatest* whole number.

```
e = Math.ceil ("text");
```
If anything other than a number is passed into the function, then Flash will return NaN; which stands for "Not a Number".

See the examples `math.ceilplot.fla` and `math.ceilplot.swf` on the CD.

Math.cos

```
a = Math.cos(b);
```

Where a is the variable that you want to equate to the cosine of b.

This method is compatible with **Flash 5 or later**.

Description

This **method** will return the cosine of the angle b. This angle must be in radians, and the method will return a number from -1.0 to 1.0.

Code	Notes
`a = Math.cos(0);`	In the first line, a will be set to 1; the starting position of the cosine wave.
`b = Math.cos(Math.PI);`	In the second line, b will be set to -1, which is exactly halfway through the cycle.
`c = Math.cos(-Math.PI);`	In the third example, c will also be set to -1, because the wave is identical in the negative direction.
`d = Math.cos ("text");`	If anything other than a number is passed into the function, then Flash will return NaN, which stands for "Not a Number".

To see `Math.cos` plotted on a graph, see the examples `math.cosplot.fla` and `math.cosplot.swf` on the CD. See also the examples `math.cos.fla` and `math.cos.swf` on the CD.

Math.E

```
a = Math.E;
```

Where a is the variable that you want to equate to the mathematical constant e.

This method is compatible with **Flash 5 or later**.

Description

This **constant** is the base of all natural logarithms, and is expressed as e in mathematics. It is approximately equal to 2.71828182845905.

Code	Notes
a = Math.E;	In the first line, a will be set to approximately 2.718.
b = Math.log(Math.E);	In the second line, b will be set to 1, which is the result of taking the natural logarithm of e. See **Math.log**

Math.exp

```
a = Math.exp(b);
```

Where a is the variable that you want to equate to the value of e to the power of b, where e is the natural logarithm constant in Math.E.

This **method** is compatible with **Flash 5 or later**.

Description

Returns the result of the formula:

$$a = e^b$$

where e is 2.71828182845905, and b is the parameter passed to the method.

Code	Notes
a = Math.exp(0);	In the first line, a will be set to 1, because anything to the power of 0 is simply 1.
b = Math.exp(1);	In the second line, b will be set to the value of Math.E.

c = Math.exp(2);
 	
d = Math.E * Math.E;
	The third and fourth lines are both equal. That is, c and d are equal, with both approximately 7.389, since the top line is like

$$c = e^2$$

and the bottom line is like

$$d = e * e$$

which are both identical.

See the examples `math.expplot.fla` and `math.expplot.swf` on the CD.

Math.floor

```
a = Math.floor(b);
```

Where a is the variable that you want to equate to the floor of b.

This method is compatible with **Flash 5 or later**.

Description

This **method** will return the value of b rounded down to the nearest whole number that is less than, or equal to b.

Code	Notes
`a = Math.floor(0);`	In the first line, a will be set to 0.
`b = Math.floor(1.1);`	In the second line, b will be set to 1, because the next whole integer less than 1.1 is 1.
`c = Math.floor(-1.1);`	In the third example, c will be set to −2, because the next whole integer less than −1.1 is −2.
`d = Math.floor(8.999999);`	In the fourth example, d is set to 8, because even though the fractional portion is very close to 9, Math.floor will still round down to the next *lesser* whole number.
`e = Math.floor ("text");`	If anything other than a number is passed into the function, then Flash will return NaN, which stands for "Not a Number".

See the examples `math.floor.fla` and `math.floor.swf` on the CD.

To see `Math.floor` plotted on a graph see also the examples `math.floorplot.fla` and `math.floorplot.swf` on the CD.

Math.log

```
a = Math.log(b);
```

Where a is the variable that you want to equate to the natural logarithm of b.

This **method** is compatible with **Flash 5 or later**.

Description
Computes the natural logarithm (logarithm based on e). The parameter, b, must be a value greater than 0.

Code	Notes
`a = Math.log(1);`	In the first line, a will be set to 0, because the natural logarithm of 1, is 0.
`o = Math.log(Math.E);`	In the second line, b will be set to the 1, because the natural logarithm of e is 1.
`c = Math.log(0);`	In the third line, c will be set to −Infinity.

See the examples `math.logplot.fla` and `math.logplot.swf` on the CD.

Math.LOG2E

```
a = Math.LOG2E;
```

Where a is the variable that you want to equate to the base-2 logarithm of the constant e, or `Math.E`. This is a constant.

This method is compatible with **Flash 5 or later**.

Description

This **constant** is approximately equal to 1.442695040888963387. A base-2 logarithm is taken as "2 to the power of". We can use this constant to convert a natural logarithm into a base-2 logarithm.

Code	Notes
a = Math.LOG2E;	In the first line, a will be set to approximately 1.442695.
b = Math.log(64) * Math.LOG2E;	In the second line, b will be set to 6, because 2 to the power of 6 is 64. We're using the natural logarithm Math.log, and converting it into a base-2 logarithm using the Math.LOG2E constant.

Math.LOG10E

```
a = Math.LOG10E;
```
Where a is the variable that you want to equate to the base-10 logarithm of the constant e, or Math.E. This is a constant.

This method is compatible with **Flash 5 or later**.

Description

This **constant** is approximately equal to 0.434294481903252. A base-10 logarithm is taken as "10 to the power of". We can use this constant to convert a natural logarithm into a base-10 logarithm.

Code	Notes
a = Math.LOG10E;	In the first line, a will be set to approximately 0.43429.
b = Math.log(10000) * Math.LOG10E;	In the second line, b will be set to 4, because 10 to the power of 4 is 10,000. We're using the natural logarithm Math.log, and converting it into a base-10 logarithm using the Math.LOG10E constant.

Math.LN2

```
a = Math.LN2;
```

Where a is the variable that you want to equate to this constant; the natural logarithm of 2.

This method is compatible with **Flash 5 or later**.

Description

This **constant** is approximately equal to 0.693147180559945. This is simply the natural logarithm of the number 2.

Code	Notes
a = Math.LN2;	In the first line, a will be set to approximately 0.693147.
b = Math.log(2);	In the second line, b will be equal to the same number, approximately 0.693147.

Math.LN10

```
a = Math.LN10;
```

Where a is the variable that you want to equate to this constant; the natural logarithm of 10.

This method is compatible with **Flash 5 or later**.

Description

This **constant** is approximately equal to 2.30258509299405. This is simply the natural logarithm of the number 10.

Code	Notes
a = Math.LN10;	In the first line, a will be set to approximately 2.302585.
b = Math.log(10);	In the second line, b will be equal to the same number, approximately 2.302585.

Math.max

```
a = Math.max(b, c);
```

Where a is the variable that you want to equate to the larger value of b or c.

This method is compatible with **Flash 5 or later**.

Description
This **method** will compare both b and c, and will return the larger of the two numbers. The method expects two numbers.

Code	Notes
a = Math.max(0, 5);	In the first line, a will be set to 5, because 5 is the larger of 5 or 0.
b = Math.max(3, 3);	In the second line, b will be set to 3, because both numbers are equal to 3.
c = Math.max(-1, -2);	In the third example, c will be set to −1, because −1 is the larger of −1 or −2.
d = Math.max ("h", 3);	If anything other than a number is passed into the function, then Flash will return NaN; which stands for "Not a Number".

See the examples math.max.fla and math.max.swf on the CD.

Math.min

```
a = Math.min(b, c);
```

Where a is the variable that you want to equate to the smaller value of b or c.

This method is compatible with **Flash 5 or later**.

Description
This **method** will compare both b and c, and will return the smaller of the two numbers. The method expects two numbers.

Code	Notes
`a = Math.min(0, 5);`	In the first line, a will be set to 0, because 0 is the smaller of 5 or 0.
`b = Math.min(3, 3);`	In the second line, b will be set to 3, because both numbers are equal to 3.
`c = Math.min(-1, -2);`	In the third example, c will be set to −2, because −2 is the smaller of −1 or −2.
`d = Math.min ("p", 3);`	If anything other than a number is passed into the function, then Flash will return NaN, which stands for "Not a Number".

See the examples `math.min.fla` and `math.min.swf` on the CD.

Math.PI

```
a = Math.PI;
```
Where a is the variable that you want to equate to the mathematical constant PI.

This method is compatible with **Flash 5 or later**.

Description

This is a **constant** used extensively in the trigonometry methods. It represents the number of radians in half of a circle. Were we measuring in degrees, PI would be 180 degrees. The value of PI is approximately 3.14159265358979, meaning that there are 6.28318530717959 radians in one full circle. In mathematics, PI is drawn with the symbol Π.

Code	Notes
`a = Math.PI;`	In the first line, a will be set to approximately 3.14159.
`b = Math.cos(Math.PI);`	In the second line, b will be set to −1, because the cosine of PI is −1.

Math.pow

```
a = Math.pow(b, c);
```

Where a is the variable that you want to equate to b to the power of c.

This method is compatible with **Flash 5 or later**.

Description
This **method** takes b, and raises it to the power of c, and returns the result. In a mathematical formula, it looks like this:

$$a = b^c$$

Code	Notes
`a = Math.pow(2, 2);`	In the first line, a will be set to 4, because 2 to the power of 2 is 4.
`b = Math.pow(2, 8);`	In the second line, b will be set to 256, because 2 to the power of 8 is 256.
`c = Math.pow(10, 5);`	In the third example, c will be set to 100000, because 10 to the power of 5, is 100,000.
`d = Math.pow(25, 0.5);`	In the fourth example, d will be set to 5, because 25 to the power of 0.5 means square root of 25, which is 5. **Anything to the power of 0.5 is the square root.**
`e = Math.pow(27, 1/3);`	In the fifth example, e will be 3, because anything to the power of 0.333333 (or 1/3) is the cubed root.
`f = Math.pow ("r", 3);`	If anything other than a number is passed into the function, then Flash will return NaN, which stands for "Not a Number".

See the examples `math.powplot.fla` and `math.powplot.swf` on the CD.

Math.random

```
a = Math.random();
```

Where a is the variable that you want to equate to a random number between 0 and 1.

This **method** is compatible with **Flash 5 or later**.

Description

Computes a completely random, non-repeating number from 0, up to (but not including) 1. Between 0 and 0.99999, one might say.

Code	Notes
`a = Math.random();`	In the first line, a will be set to a random number, such as: 0.956732779275626 or 0.106070402078331 or 0.761447730474174, etc.
`b = Math.random() * 10;`	In the second line, b will be set to a random number between 0 and 9.9999999.
`c = (Math.random() * 10) - 5;`	In the third line, c will be set to a random number between –5 and 4.9999999.

To see `Math.random` plotted on a graph see the examples `math.randomplot.fla` and `math.randomplot.swf` on the CD.

See also the examples `math.random.fla` and `math.random.swf` on the CD.

Math.round

```
a = Math.round(b);
```

Where a is the variable that you want to equate to the value of b rounded to the nearest whole number.

This method is compatible with **Flash 5 or later**.

Description

This **method** will return the value of b rounded up or down to the nearest whole. Any number with a fraction lower than 0.5 will be rounded down, and any number with a fraction greater than or equal to 0.5 will be rounded up.

Code	Notes
a = Math.round(0);	In the first line, a will be set to 0.
b = Math.round(1.1);	In the second line, b will be set to 1, because the closest whole integer to 1.1 is 1.
c = Math.round(1.9);	In the third example, c will be set to 2, because the closest whole integer to 1.9 is 2.
d = Math.round(6.5);	In the fourth example, d is set to 7, because 6.5 rounded to the nearest whole number is 7.
e = Math.round(8.4999);	In the fifth example, e is set to 8, because the fractional portion is less than 0.5, so Math.round rounds down.
f = Math.round ("text");	If anything other than a number is passed into the function, then Flash will return NaN; which stands for "Not a Number".

See the example math.roundplot.fla and math.roundplot.swf on the CD.

Math.sin

```
a = Math.sin(b);
```

Where a is the variable that you want to equate to the sine of b.

This method is compatible with **Flash 5 or later**.

Description

This **method** will return the sine of the angle b. This angle must be in radians, and the method will return a number from -1.0 to 1.0.

Code	Notes
`a = Math.sin(0);`	In the first line, a will be set to 0, the starting position of the sine wave.
`b = Math.sin(Math.PI);`	In the second line, b will be set to 0, which is exactly halfway through the cycle.
`c = Math.sin(-Math.PI);`	In the third example, c will also be set to 0, because the wave is identical in the negative direction.
`d = Math.sin ("text");`	If anything other than a number is passed into the function, then Flash will return NaN, which stands for "Not a Number".

See the examples `math.sinplot.fla` and `math.sinplot.swf` on the CD.

See also the examples `math.sin.fla` and `math.sin.swf` on the CD.

Math.sqrt

```
a = Math.sqrt(b);
```

Where a is the variable that you want to equate to the square root of b.

This **method** is compatible with **Flash 5 or later**.

Description

Computes the square root of b. The parameter, b, must be a value greater than or equal to 0.

Code	Notes
`a = Math.sqrt(1)`	In the first line, a will be set to 1, because the square root of 1 is 1.
`b = Math.sqrt(16);`	In the second line, b will be set to the 4, because the square root of 16 is 4.
`c = Math.sqrt(46);`	In the third line, c will be set to 6.78233.

See the examples `math.sqrtPlot.fla` and `math.sqrtPlot.swf` on the CD.

See the examples `math.sqrt.fla` and `math.sqrt.swf` on the CD.

Math.SQRT1_2

```
a = Math.SQRT1_2;
```

Where `a` is the variable that you want to equate to this constant; the square root of one half (`0.5`).

This method is compatible with **Flash 5 or later**.

Description
This **constant** is approximately equal to `0.707106781186`. This is simply the square root of the number 0.5.

Code	Notes
`a = Math.SQRT1_2;`	In the first line, a will be set to approximately `0.7071`.
`b = Math.sqrt(0.5);`	In the second line, b will be equal to the same number, approximately `0.7071`.

Math.SQRT2

```
a = Math.SQRT2;
```

Where `a` is the variable that you want to equate to this constant; the square root of 2.

This method is compatible with **Flash 5 or later**.

Description
This **constant** is approximately equal to `1.4142135623731`. This is simply the square root of the number 2.

Code	Notes
`a = Math.SQRT2;`	In the first line, a will be set to approximately `1.41421`.
`b = Math.sqrt(2);`	In the second line, b will be equal to

the same number, approximately
1.41421.

Math.tan

```
a = Math.tan(b);
```

Where a is the variable that you want to equate to the tangent of b.

This method is compatible with **Flash 5 or later**.

Description

This **method** will return the tangent of the angle b. This angle must be in radians, and the method will return a number from $-\text{Infinity}$ to Infinity.

Code	Notes
`a = Math.tan(0);`	In the first line, a will be set to 0; the starting position of the tangent wave.
`b = Math.tan(Math.PI);`	In the second line, b will be set to 0, which is the next point that the tangent wave crosses 0.
`c = Math.tan(Math.PI / 2);`	In the third example, c will essentially be undefined, because at PI/2, tangent technically returns Infinity. See the graph in the *Examples and practical uses section* on the CD.
`c = Math.tan ("text");`	If anything other than a number is passed into the function, then Flash will return NaN, which stands for "Not a Number".

To see Math.tan plotted on a graph see the examples math.tanplot.fla and math.tanplot.swf on the CD.

maxscroll

```
num = varname.maxscroll;
```

Where `varname` is a textfield variable name and `num` is the maximum value to be used for the `scroll` property.

This property is compatible with **Flash 4 and later**. It is deprecated in Flash MX and should not be used except for legacy Flash 4/5 applications.

The `maxscroll` property is a read-only property that signifies the maximum number of lines you can scroll down a text field.

Description

When using textfields in Flash 5, it was normal to read/write a textfield's contents by reading and writing to the variable associated with it. This variable is defined in the Var: field of the Property Inspector. **You are not recommended to use this feature in Flash MX**, because changing textfield contents using the `textfield` variable is not supported by components; a scrollbar component will ignore all changes to this value, and this is because components (and much of everything else) respond to *methods*. In Flash MX you are advised to use **TextField.text** instead of the `textfield` variable.

The `textfield` variable has `scroll` and `maxscroll` properties:

- `scroll` is the current scroll position of a text field, with 1 being the first line (rather than zero)
- `maxscroll` is the maximum value of that `scroll` can take.

Assuming we have a textfield displaying the following text:

```
line 1
line 2
line 3
line 4
line 5
line 6
line 7
line 8
line 9
line 10
```

... and the maximum number of lines that the textfield can display at any time is 5, then the `maxscroll` property will be 6. Why?

Well, the diagrams below should make it clear (you can also have a look at `maxscrollex01.fla` and `maxscrollex01.swf` if you get confused). If we start with the scrollbar at the top position (below left), then we have to move the scrollbar down 6 lines (including the line the textfield is on when we start) to get to the lowest position:

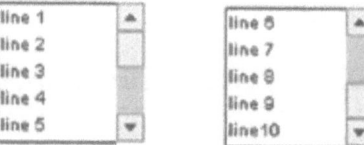

Put another way, `maxscroll` is the line at the top of the text field when you are at the maximum scroll position.

The `maxscroll` property is important because it gives us the step range that a scrollbar will move through between the top and bottom of the scroll. It was therefore used in Flash 4/5 to create scrollbars, something that is no longer necessary in Flash MX.

See also `maxscroll.fla` and `maxscroll.swf` on the CD.

mbchr

```
mbchr(num);
```

Where `num` is an ASCII value to convert to a multibyte character

Compatible with **Flash 4 and later**. Deprecated **by String.fromCharCode** in Flash 5 and later.

The `mbchr()` string function converts an ASCII value to a multibyte character.

Description

The `mbchr()` **function** is a string function for converting an ASCII numeric value to a multibyte character, especially useful for non-QWERTY characters (such as those with accents or non-English character sets).

code	Additional explanation	Notes
myVar=mbchr(56)	Converts ASCII value 56 to a multibyte character, assigning it to myVar.	MyVar = "8"
myVar=mbchr()	An argument must be supplied.	
myVar=mbchr("A")	The argument must be an ASCII numeric value, not a character.	
myVar=mbchr(435)	The parameter is not a valid ASCII value.	

mblength

```
mblength(string)
```

Where `string` is a string.

Compatible with **Flash 4 and later**. Deprecated **by String methods** in Flash 5 and later.

The `mblength()` string function returns the length of a string.

Description
The `mblength()` **function** is a string function for returning the number of characters in a string.

code	Notes
myVar=mblength("test")	Returns the length of the string and stores it in myVar.
myVar=mblength()	An argument must be supplied.

mbord

```
mbord(char);
```

Where `char` is a character to convert to an ASCII value

Compatible with **Flash 4 and later**. Deprecated **by String.fromCharAt** in Flash 5 and later.

The `mbord()` string function converts a character to an ASCII value.

Description
The `mbord()` **function** is a string function for converting a character to an ASCII numeric value.

code	Notes
myVar=mbord("A")	Converts the "A" character to its ASCII value, assigning it to myVar.
myVar=mbord()	An argument must be supplied.
myVar=mbord ("ABCDE")	The argument must be a single character, not a string.

mbsubstring

```
mbsubstring(string, num, count);
```

Where `string` is a string, `num` is the number of the first character to extract, and `count` is the number of bytes to extract.

Compatible with **Flash 4 and later**. Deprecated **by String.substr** in Flash 5 and later.

The mbsubstring() string function extracts a substring from a longer string, starting at a particular position and extending for a specified number of characters. The first character in the string is taken to be position 1.

Description

The mbsubstring() **function** is a string function extracting a substring from a longer string. You have to provide the string (either directly or through the use of a variable), as well as the starting position of the substring within the string, and the length of the substring to extract.

Code	Additional explanation
myVar=mbsubstring ("This is a test", 6, 2)	Extracts a substring from "This is a test" starting at the sixth character and extending two characters. The string value "is" is returned.
myVar=mbsubstring()	An argument must be supplied.
myVar=mbsubstring ("This is a test", 6)	There are not enough arguments supplied.

method

```
object.method = function {...};
```

Where object is an object name, method is a method name, and function is a function name

Compatible with **Flash 6 .**

The method action (method is not a reserved work but a placeholder for a method name) allows you to define methods for objects when developing code in normal mode.

Description

The method **action** is used in Flash's Normal mode to allow you to define a method for an object. The keyword method is not used; instead you use the method's name and define it with a function. Any number of methods can be defined for an object.

Mouse

Compatible with **Flash 6 .**

The Mouse object contains several methods and events.

Description

The Mouse **object** contains four methods:

- `Mouse.addListener` – registers a mouse object to receive event notification.
- `Mouse.hide` – hides the mouse pointer.
- `Mouse.removeListener` – removes a mouse object from the list of listeners.
- `Mouse.show` – displays the mouse pointer in a movie.

There are three events that are available to objects registered as listeners to the Mouse object:

- `myListener.onMouseDown` – triggered when a mouse button is pressed.
- `myListener.onMouseMove` – triggered when a mouse is moved.
- `myListener.onMouseUp` – triggered when a mouse button is released.

Note that these events are also available to all movie clips via **MovieClip.onMouseDown, MovieClip.onMouseMove,** and **MovieClip.onMouseUp**.

Mouse.addListener

```
Mouse.addListener (listener_name);
```

Where `listener_name` is the name of an Object object that you want to register as a listener.

Compatible with **Flash 6 .**

`Mouse.addListener()` registers an Object object as a listener to the Mouse object. The listener object gains a number of methods that allow it to respond to mouse events.

Description
A Mouse listener gains **onMouseDown(), onMouseMove(),** and **onMouseUp()** events.
The procedure for registering a Mouse listener object is as follows:

- Create an Object object that you want to use as a listener (all listeners have to be Object objects so that they can inherit the appropriate listener methods; if you try to use normal variables, the listener will not gain any methods). If we wanted to register an object myListener, we would do this:

```
myListener = new Object();
```

- Next, you register the Object as a listener to the Mouse object:

```
Mouse.addListener(myListener);
```

All the methods are now available through the object myListener. The following code sets up a function to respond to the onMouseMove event:

```
myListener.onMouseMove = function() {
    trace("I heard you move!");
};
```

Mouse.hide

    Mouse.hide()

Compatible with **Flash 5 and later.**

The `Mouse.hide()` method hides the mouse cursor.

Description

By default the mouse cursor is visible in a movie. To hide the cursor the `Mouse.hide()` **method** can be used. When hidden, the cursor still exists but is not visible to the user. The mouse can be made visible again using the `Mouse.show()` method.

Code	Additional explanation	Notes
Mouse.hide()	Hides the mouse cursor	Nothing is returned from the Mouse.hide() method.

See the files `mousehide.fla` and `mousehilde.swf` on the CD.

Mouse.onMouseDown

    MouseObject.onMouseDown

Where `MouseObject` is the name of a mouse object.

Compatible with **Flash 6 .**

When a `Mouse` object has been registered using the `Mouse.addListener()` method, the `onMouseDown()` event handler is invoked whenever a mouse button is pressed down.

Description

When a mouse button is pressed, the `onMouseDown()` **event handler,** associated with each `Mouse` listener, is invoked. `Mouse` listeners are registered to listen for these events using `Mouse.addListener()`. When a mouse button press is detected, all registered mouse listeners are informed of the event, and the `onMouseDown()` call back function in each event (if defined) is invoked. There can be an unlimited number of registered `mouse` listeners, all with these methods associated with them.

The procedure to set up a `Mouse` listener that responds to this event is as follows:

■ Create an `Object` object that you want to use as a listener (all listeners have to be `Object` objects so that they can inherit the appropriate listener methods; if you try to use normal variables, the listener will not gain any methods). This occurs on line 1 of the listing.

- Next, you register the `Object` as a listener to the `Mouse` object (line 2).

All the methods of `Mouse` listeners (onMouseUp, onMouseDown, onMouseMove) are now available through the object `myListener`. The code sets up a function to respond to the `onMouseDown` event via a callback function.

```
myListener = new Object();
Mouse.addListener(myListener);
myListener.onMouseDown = function() {
    trace("I heard you press the mouse!");
};
```

You will see the message appear every time you press the mouse.

If you want to respond to mouse events to control some feature of a movie clip, you are better off simply using the **MovieClip.onMouseUp**, **MovieClip.onMousedown,** and **MovieClip,onMouseMove** events, and you can do this without having to set up a listener. See also the entries for these events.

Mouse.onMouseMove

`MouseObject.onMouseMove`

Where `MouseObject` is the name of a `mouse` object.

Compatible with **Flash 6 .**

When a `Mouse` object has been registered using the `Mouse.addListener()` method, the `onMouseMove()` event handler is invoked whenever a mouse movement is detected.

Description

When the mouse is moved, the `onMouseMove()` **event handler** associated with each mouse listener is invoked. `Mouse` listeners are registered to listen for these events using `Mouse.addListener()`. When a mouse move is detected, all registered `mouse` listeners are informed of the event, and the `onMouseMove()` callback function in each listener (if defined) is invoked. There can be an unlimited number of registered `mouse` listeners, all with these methods associated with them.

The procedure to set up a Mouse listener that responds to this event is as follows:

- Create an `Object` object that you want to use as a listener (all listeners have to be `Object` objects so that they can inherit the appropriate listener methods; if you try to use normal variables, the listener will not gain any methods). This occurs on line 1 of the listing

- Next, you register the `Object` as a listener to the `Mouse` object (line 2).

All the methods of Mouse listeners (onMouseUp, onMouseDown, onMouseMove) are now available through the object myListener. The code sets up a function to respond to the onMouseMove event via a callback function.

```
myListener = new Object();
Mouse.addListener(myListener);
myListener.onMouseMove = function() {
    trace("I heard you move!");
};
```

You will see the message appear every time you move the mouse. Note that this event occurs very often!

Although there are no limits to the number of Mouse objects that can respond to movement activity after being registered, registering too many objects can cause slow response from Flash. The code inside the onMouseMove() method will be executed line by line for each registered mouse event, so some delay may be caused when long methods or many registered objects are involved, particularly because this is a very frequent event.

If you want to respond to mouse events to control some feature of a movie clip, you are better off simply using the **MovieClip.onMouseUp**, **MovieClip.onMousedown,** and **MovieClip.onMouseMove** events, and you can do this without having to set up a listener. See also the entries for these events.

Mouse.onMouseUp

MouseObject.onMouseUp

Where MouseObject is the name of a mouse object.

Compatible with **Flash 6 .**

When a Mouse object has been registered using the Mouse.addListener() method, the onMouseUp() **event handler** is invoked whenever a pressed mouse button is released.

Description

When a mouse button is pressed, the onMouseDown() event handler associated with each Mouse listener is invoked. When that button is released, the onMouseUp() event is invoked. Mouse listeners are registered to listen for these events using Mouse.addListener(). When a mouse button release is detected, all registered mouse events are informed of the event, and the onMouseUp() callback in each event (if defined) is invoked. There can be an unlimited number of registered mouse listeners, all with these methods associated with them.

Mouse.removeListener

Mouse.removeListener (listener_name)

Where `listener_name` is the name of a `mouse` object.

Compatible **with Flash 6.**

When a listener object has been registered using the `Mouse.addListener()` method, it listens to all mouse movement, button presses and button release events and is capable of responding to these events via if the corresponding call back functions (if defined). The `Mouse.removeListener()` method removes a `mouse` object from the list of listeners for these events. The event call-backs will still be defined, but the events needed to trigger them will no longer propagate to the object.

Description

A registered mouse object has `onMouseMove()`, `onMouseDown()` and `onMouseUp()` callbacks invoked when mouse movements, button presses, or button releases are relayed to the registered objects. To remove a mouse object from the list of listening objects, and hence stop receiving the event notifications, use the `Mouse.removeListener()` **method**.

Code	Additional explanation	Notes
`Mouse.removeListener` `(myMouseobject)`	Removes `myMouseobject` from the list of registered listeners.	Nothing happens when a mouse event occurs because the listener object is no longer sent any mouse events to listen to.

Mouse.show

`Mouse.show()`

Compatible with **Flash Player 6.**

The `Mouse.show()` method makes the mouse cursor visible in a movie.

Description

By default the mouse cursor is visible in a movie. It can be hidden using the `Mouse.hide()` method. To display the mouse cursor again, use the `Mouse.show()` **method**.

Code	Additional explanation	Notes
`Mouse.show()`	Displays the mouse cursor.	Nothing is returned from the `Mouse.show()` method.

See also `mouseshow.fla` and `mouseshow.swf` on the CD.

MovieClip

Compatible with **Flash 5 and later**.

The MovieClip object is the most important object for the motion graphics programmer because it is the building block used to create much of any Flash presentation. It includes *all* timelines; as well as movie clips that the user creates. The following are also movie clips:

- _root
- All loaded levels such as _level0, _level1, etc.

Because of its position as one of the most important building blocks, the MovieClip has a very large set of properties and methods.

Learning how to use them to control your animations and site UIs, instead of using traditional timeline-based animation (keyframes, tweens) is the most important use of ActionScript for the designer who wants to get into scripting. In many ways, the MovieClip methods and properties represent the link between the scripting environment and the animation environment, because they are the part of the language that actually allows ActionScript to access graphics for the purpose of animation.

A simple way to see this would be to assume that the MovieClip object represents the animation commands of ActionScript. This is not strictly true (the Button, TextField, Stage and Color objects also play a part), but knowing the MovieClip object will give you approximately 75% of everything you need to programmatically control animation.

The properties of _level0 are particularly significant because some of them define the appearance of the whole Flash Player, and they are:

- MovieClip.getBytesLoaded / MovieClip._framesloaded – can be used to tell you how much of your site has streamed into the users machine in bytes/frames respectively.
- MovieClip.getBytesTotal / MovieClip._totalframes – can be used to tell you the size of your swf in bytes/frames respectively, and when used with the previous entry, can be used to tell you how much of the site has streamed in.
- MovieClip._highquality – This property defines the level of anti-aliasing applied by the Flash πlayer on all graphics. Although this property is actually available for both the Button and TextField, it is always applied as level0.highQuality, and is therefore really only applicable to the movie clip.

The Flash MX implementation of the MovieClip gives it many of the events and features of the Button, and this makes the Button largely redundant for advanced scripters. A description of how to create movie clip buttons is included in the entry **MovieClip.hitArea**.

Description

The `MovieClip` **object** has many methods attached to it that can be invoked to control the actions of a movie clip. The `MovieClip` object does not need a constructor to call these methods for a `MovieClip` object.

The `MovieClip` object contains these methods:

- `MovieClip.attachMovie` – attaches a movie currently in the Library.
- `MovieClip.createEmptyMovieClip` – creates an empty movie clip.
- `MovieClip.createTextField` – creates an empty text field.
- `MovieClip.duplicateMovieClip` – creates a duplicate of the movie clip.
- `MovieClip.getBounds` – returns the x and y coordinates of a movie clip.
- `MovieClip.getBytesLoaded` – returns the number of bytes of a movie clip that have loaded.
- `MovieClip.getBytesTotal` – returns the total size of a movie clip in bytes.
- `MovieClip.getDepth` – returns the level (depth) of the movie.
- `MovieClip.getURL` – returns contents from a URL.
- `MovieClip.globalToLocal` – converts stage coordinates to local movie clip coordinates.
- `MovieClip.gotoAndPlay` – move the playhead to a particular location and start playback.
- `MovieClip.gotoAndStop` – move the playhead to a particular location and stop playback.
- `MovieClip.hitTest` – checks for intersection between bounding boxes.
- `MovieClip.loadMovie` – loads a movie clip.
- `MovieClip.loadVariables` – loads variables from a URL into a movie clip.
- `MovieClip.localToGlobal` – converts from local coordinates to stage coordinates.
- `MovieClip.nextFrame` – moves the playhead to the next frame.
- `MovieClip.play` – plays the movie clip.
- `MovieClip.prevFrame` – moves the playhead to the previous frame.
- `MovieClip.removeMovieClip` – removes the movie clip from the timeline.
- `MovieClip.setMask` – uses one movie clip as a mask for another.
- `MovieClip.startDrag` – lets a movie clip be dragged.
- `MovieClip.stop` – stops playing the current movie.
- `MovieClip.stopDrag` – stops the dragging of the movie clip.
- `MovieClip.swapDepths` – swaps the depths (levels) of two movies.
- `MovieClip.unloadMovie` – removes a loaded movie.

The `MovieClip` object also has several properties associated with it:

- `MovieClip._alpha` – the transparency of the movie clip.
- `MovieClip._currentframe` – frame number the playhead is over.
- `MovieClip._droptarget` – absolute path of the movie clip.
- `MovieClip.enabled` – shows whether a button movie clip is enabled.
- `MovieClip.focusEnabled` – lets a movie clip receive focus.
- `MovieClip._focusrect` – shows whether a movie clip has a yellow rectangle around it.
- `MovieClip._framesloaded` – number of frames loaded from a streaming movie.
- `MovieClip._height` – height of the movie clip.
- `MovieClip.hitArea` – sets another movie clip to be a hit area for a button.

- `MovieClip._highquality` – sets the rendering quality.
- `MovieClip._name` – name of the movie clip instance.
- `MovieClip._parent` – movie clip name that contains the current movie clip.
- `MovieClip._rotation` – degrees of rotation of the movie clip.
- `MovieClip._soundbuftime` – number of seconds of sound to buffer before streaming.
- `MovieClip.tabChildren` – sets whether the children of the movie clip are included in tab ordering.
- `MovieClip.tabEnabled` – sets whether the movie clip is enabled in tab ordering.
- `MovieClip.tabIndex` – the tab order of the movie clip.
- `MovieClip._target` – target path of the movie clip.
- `MovieClip._totalframes` – number of frames in the movie clip.
- `MovieClip.trackAsMenu` – sets whether buttons can receive mouse release events.
- `MovieClip._url` – URL of the movie clip.
- `MovieClip.useHandCursor` – displays a hand icon when the cursor rolls over a button movie clip.
- `MovieClip._visible` – sets whether the movie clip is hidden or visible.
- `MovieClip._width` – the width of the movie clip in pixels.
- `MovieClip._x` – x coordinate of the movie clip.
- `MovieClip._xmouse` – x coordinate of the cursor within a movie clip.
- `MovieClip._xscale` – percentage of horizontal scaling within a movie clip.
- `MovieClip._y` – y coordinate of the movie clip.
- `MovieClip._ymouse` – y coordinate of the cursor within a movie clip.
- `MovieClip._yscale` – percentage of vertical scaling within a movie clip.

The `MovieClip` object also has several event handlers associated with it:

- `MovieClip.onData` – invoked when all data is loaded.
- `MovieClip.onDragOut` – invoked when the pointer is pressed inside a button then rolls outside.
- `MovieClip.onDragOver` – invoked when the pointer is over a button, pressed, rolled outside the button, then moved back over the button.
- `MovieClip.onEnterFrame` – invoked when a frame is entered.
- `MovieClip.onKeyDown` – invoked when a key is pressed.
- `MovieClip.onKeyUp` – invoked when a key is released.
- `MovieClip.onKillFocus` – invoked when focus is removed from a button.
- `MovieClip.onLoad` – invoked when a movie is loaded on the timeline.
- `MovieClip.onMouseDown` – invoked when a mouse button is pressed.
- `MovieClip.onMouseMove` – invoked when the mouse is moved.
- `MovieClip.onMouseUp` – invoked when a mouse button is released.
- `MovieClip.onPress` – invoked when the mouse button is pressed while over a button.
- `MovieClip.onRelease` – invoked when the mouse button is released over a button.
- `MovieClip.onReleaseOutside` – invoked when a mouse button is pressed over a button, then released when the pointer is outside a button.
- `MovieClip.onRollOut` – invoked when the mouse rolls outside a button area.
- `MovieClip.onRollOver` – invoked when the mouse rolls over a button area.
- `MovieClip.onSetFocus` – invoked when a button has focus and a key is released.
- `MovieClip.onUnload` – invoked when the movie clip is removed from the timeline.

Note that the MovieClip object contains methods to create TextField Objects!

The movie clip has all the events of the Button object. For advanced scripters, the movie clip supercedes the button. The standard button is still useful for creating simple buttons, although the movie clip has a structure that makes it more useful for advanced ActionScript (particularly the facts that it has a timeline and a richer set of properties).

Some properties have a '_' preceding them. This is purely a historic convention in keeping with Flash 4, and is retained in subsequent versions for backward compatibility. The only relevance of properties without the '_' is that they were introduced in Flash MX, and the '_' is not therefore needed for backwards compatibility.

MovieClip._alpha

```
instanceName._alpha = a;
b = my_mc._alpha;
```

Where `instanceName` is the instance name of a movie clip, and a is the value you want to assign to the clip alpha value. b is a variable that is equated to the current value of the movie clip alpha value. The alpha value range is from 0 to 100.

This property is compatible with **Flash 5 and later**.

Description
The _alpha **property** of a movie clip defines the clip's alpha setting, and this can range between 0 (fully transparent) and 100% (fully solid) per pixel. The _alpha property is read/write.

Code	Movie clip	Notes
`my_mc._alpha = 0;`		Movie clip is fully transparent.
`my_mc._alpha = 25;`	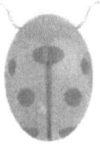	Movie clip is approximately 25% opaque.
`my_mc._alpha = 50;`	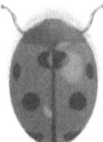	Movie clip is approximately 50% opaque.

`my_mc._alpha = 100;`		Movie clip is solid and fully opaque.
`my_mc._alpha = 1000;`		A little known trick; super high values of alpha setting provide a high contrast effect if your graphics are composed of gradient and radial fills that have varying alpha. This occurs because the alpha value is *per pixel*. See also *Tips and precautions* section.on the CD
`my_mc._alpha = -50;`		Negative values of _alpha are rendered as if they were 0%.

MovieClip.attachMovie

`myMovieClip.attachMovie (linkage, instancename, depth [,propertyobject])`

Where `myMovieClip` is a movie clip instance upon whose timeline you want to attach (or 'copy from the Library') your movie clips, `linkage` is the linkage name of the movie clip in the Library that you want to attach, `instancename` is the instance name you want to give the attached movie clip, `depth` is the level at which the movie is to be copied into, and `propertyObject` is the name of an object that contains properties to be given to the attached instance.

Compatible with **Flash 5 and later.**

The `MovieClip.attachMovie()` method takes a symbol from the Library and attaches it to a timeline on the stage.

Description

The `MovieClip.attachMovie()` **method** is used to attach a movie clip from the Library and place a copy of it onto a movie timeline currently on the stage (noting that _root is also a movie clip!).

Although this method may seem very similar to `MovieClip.duplicateMovieClip` (and the examples we are using are almost identical to the ones seen in that entry) there is one fundamental difference: duplicateMovieClip copies from a *timeline* whereas attachMovie copies from the *Library*. See the *Tips and precautions section* of **MovieClip.duplicateMovieClip** to see the implications of this.

To set up a movie clip to be attached onto the stage, you must define a **linkage identifier**. A linkage identifier (sometimes shortened to 'linkageID' or 'identifier') is a string value that ActionScript will use to refer to the movie clip whilst it is in the Library. There are several ways to enter this value:

- By selecting Export for ActionScript in the Convert to Symbol window. The string in the Identifier field is your linkage identifier. Note that you may need to hit the Advanced button to show these options **(this is replaced by Basic when the options are expanded)**. This allows you to define the linkage identifier during movie clip creation.

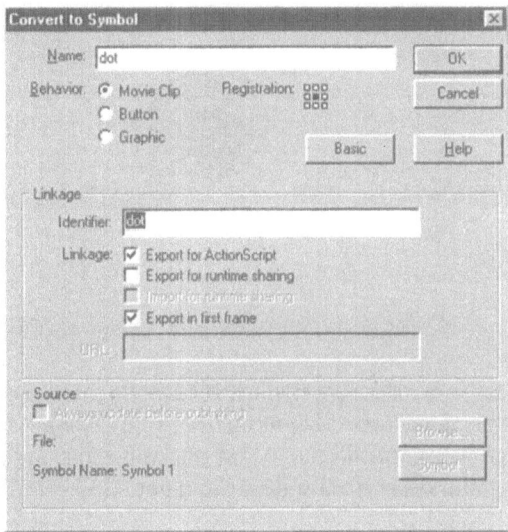

- By selecting: the Linkage... option in the Library right-click menu or Library window drop-down menu. This will open the Linkage Properties window, which contains a subset of the Convert To Symbol window shown above.

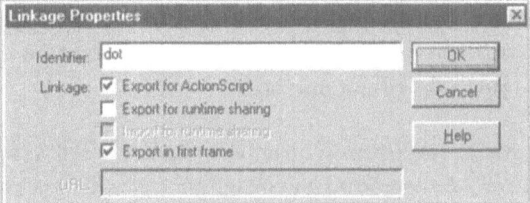

- By selecting the **Properties...** icon on the Library window (the little blue circle with a white 'i' in it at the bottom of the Library window).

- By selecting the **Properties...** option in the Library right click menu or Library window dropdown menu.

The last two options will bring up the Symbol Properties window, which is actually identical to the Convert to Symbol window seen above, except that it lets you modify components after you have created the movie clip.

Once you have defined the linkage identifier successfully (or if you forget what you defined as the linkage name three minutes later!), you will be able to see it in the Linkage column of the Library (something that is normally hidden unless you resize the Library to 'Narrow Library view', so you might have never noticed it!).

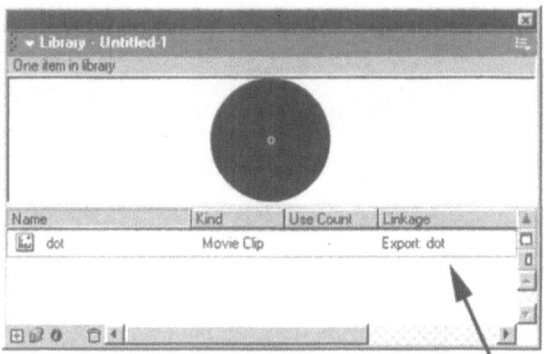

The linkage identifier you use in your scripting must be *exactly* the same as the linkage identifier, and if you get it wrong **Flash will raise no error** (silent failure), so be wary! As a general rule, it is a good idea to accept the default linkage name specified by Flash (make it the same as the Library movie clip name, unless you have used a long and descriptive movie clip name).

The following will attach the above movie clip dot to the _root timeline, and give it an instance name of dot01:

```
_root.attachMovie("dot", "dot01", 0);
```

You should also be aware that the depth of each movie clip on a given timeline should be unique. You are only allowed to have one symbol in each depth, and if you try to do otherwise, the movie clip already at that depth will be replaced by the new clip.

When you use attachMovie as shown above, the movie clip will be placed at a position 0,0 because its _x and _y properties will be zero. You can change this by adding an additional propertyObject. These objects properties will be added to the timeline of the newly attached movie clip if they are not movie clip properties, or will be used as initial values for the movie clip properties if they are. This sounds more complicated than it actually is, so lets see it in action.

If we define an object initObject as shown and then add it to your attachMovie method as a new parameter:

```
dotInit = { _x:200, _y:200, myVariable:10};
_root.attachMovie("dot", "dot01", 0, dotInit);
```

⊟	dotInit	
	_x	200
	_y	200
	myVariable	10

... the properties of _x and _y will be used to define the initial position properties dot01._x and dot01._y. The myVariable property of dotInit does not correspond to a movie clip property, and will instead appear as a variable on the timeline of dot01 (it will of course appear as _root.dot01.myVariable).

Assuming that we have the movie clip defined above (a movie clip that is a small black dot graphic with linkage identifier dot), then the following examples show the results of various uses of attachMovie:

Examples

```
attachMovie("dot", "dot01", 0);
```

If you use attachMovie without a movie clip instance, the timeline of the current script is assumed. This script will attach an instance dot01 to _root if the timeline is on _root, as shown in the included file mcattachmovieex01.fla and mcattachmovieex01.swf.

```
_root.attachMovie("dot", "dot01", 0);
```

This line will do exactly the same as the last example, but is the preferred syntax as it explicitly specifies the timeline to attach dot01.

This code shows how attachMovie can be used to create multiple clips. The code attaches 500 instances of dot, called dot0 to dot499. See also the files mcattachmovieex02.fla and mcattachmovieex02.swf.

```
initDot = new Object();
for (i=0; i<500; i++) {
    initDot._x = Math.random()*550;
    initDot._y = Math.random()*400;
    attachMovie("dot", "dot"+i, i, initDot);
}
```

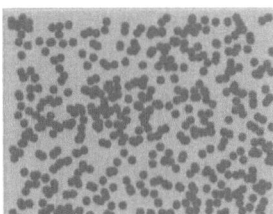

Try doing this manually!

Notice the following features of this code:

- The use of initdot to give each dot clip a random position on the stage.

- The use of the **for** loop variable and the way it is used to give each dot instance a unique name via string concatenation ("dot"+i) and the way it is also used to give each instance a unique depth.

In this final example, the dots are not only created dynamically, but also animated dynamically to create a magnetism particle effect. Hitting the mouse button will toggle the nature of the attractions from magnetic to repulsive... you will have to run this effect to realize why the file is called tapeworm.fla (tapeworm.swf).

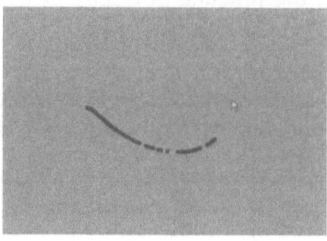

```
function animateDot() {
    this._x -= this.magnetism*(this._x-_root._xmouse)/this.inertia;
    this._y -= this.magnetism*(this._y-_root._ymouse)/this.inertia;
}
function reversePolarity() {
    this.magnetism = -this.magnetism;
}
initDot = new Object();
initDot.magnetism = 1;
for (i=0; i<200; i++) {
    initDot._x = Math.random()*550;
    initDot._y = Math.random()*400;
    initDot.inertia = Math.random()*30+2;
    _root.attachMovie("dot", "dot"+i, i, initDot);
    _root["dot"+i].onEnterFrame = animateDot;
    _root["dot"+i].onMouseDown = reversePolarity;
}
```

Notice the way that the dot instances are referenced *after* they have been created with root["dot"+i].

See also the example file movieclipattachmovie.fla and movieclipattachmovie.swf on the CD.

MovieClip.beginFill

```
myMovieClip.beginFill(hexColor, alpha);
```

Where myMovieClip is a movie clip instance, hexcolor is the hexadecimal RGB value of the fill color, and alpha is the alpha (transparency) level of this fill. You can omit the alpha value:

```
myMovieClip.beginFill(hexColor);
```

If no alpha value is specified then 100 is assumed.

Finally, you can use the method with no arguments:

```
myMovieClip.beginFill();
```

Generally, this will do the same as **MovieClip.endFill.**

IMPORTANT NOTE – This last form of the syntax has some unfortunate results if used out of context (it has been known to lock up the Flash authoring environment). You are advised to *never* use this method with no arguments, even though the documentation says it is permissible.

Compatible with **Flash 6.**

The `MovieClip.beginFill()` method specifies the start of a path that will be filled, or completes an existing path and fills it with a fill color (if specified) set at a particular alpha level (if specified).

Description

The `MovieClip.beginFill()` **method** is used to create fills on the stage. It must be used in conjunction with other Drawing API actions to produce a result; you need to define something called a 'fill path' before the area you want to fill is defined. The diagrams below show the fill path being created.

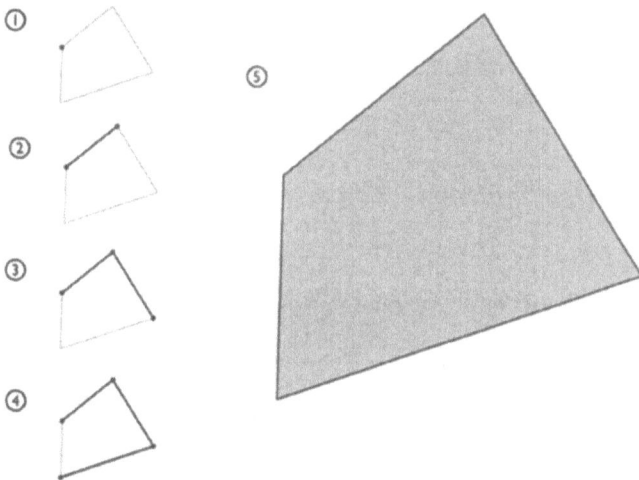

These steps are defined in greater detail below. You can also see a working version of the figure above by opening `fillexample01.fla` and `fillexample01.swf` on the CD.

Before starting, it is a good idea to define your colors as variables, something that gives you the ability to tweak the final colors easily once you have seen the fully drawn shape (Time wasting warning): tweaking code created by the drawing API to uncover better effects and animations is a very addictive waste of time!!). We have therefore defined our two colors as shown below:

```
black = 0x000000;
lightGrey = 0xCCCCCC;
```

Step 1

The first step is to set up your line style and fill color. Line 1 below sets a line thickness of 1 and the color black (which is of course our variable black defined previously). The beginFill method is then used to define the start of our fill path. Finally, we move to the start point of our fill with line 3. At this point we have not drawn anything on screen, but have simply moved the drawing position to the start of our fill path.

```
_root.lineStyle(1, black, 100);
_root.beginFill(lightGrey, 100);
_root.moveTo(320, 110);
```

There are a number of variations you can use here:

- To create fills with no borders, set the lineStyle thickness to undefined:

  ```
  _root.lineStyle(1, black, 100);
  ```

- To create a hairline line style, set the lineStyle thickness to 0 (you can also use null):

  ```
  _root.lineStyle(0, black, 100);
  ```

Steps 2, 3 and 4

We then move around the perimeter of our shape, drawing lines as we go:

```
// step 2
_root.lineTo(420, 20);

// step 3
_root.lineTo(510, 150);

// step 4
_root.lineTo(320, 220);
```

Some similar graphics languages allow you to move around the fill area rather than have to draw around it, something that can be done faster if you do not want a line around your shape. Flash *does not* allow you to do this, and the following code would not work because of this:

```
_root.lineStyle(undefined, black, 100);
_root.beginFill(lightGrey, 100);
_root.moveTo(320, 110);
_root.moveTo(420, 20);
_root.moveTo(510, 150);
_root.moveTo(320, 220);
_root.endFill();
```

You should use a lineStyle of undefined instead, as discussed in **step 1**.

Step 5

Finally, we need to define the end of our fill path. On seeing this method, Flash will draw to the first point in the fill path, and fill the area created with light gray (color 0xCCCCCC).

```
_root.endFill();
```

You can also use the following line, but it has been seen to crash the Flash authoring environment on some operating systems (particularly Windows) if there are errors in your code (if the previous fill path was not closed properly, then the beginFill will be taken as the start of the next fill path, and this can crash the authoring application).

```
root.beginFill();
```

The example files on the CD:

```
movieclipbeginfill.fla / movieclipbeginfill.swf
fillexample02.fla / fillexample02.swf
```

MovieClip.beginGradientFill

myMovieClip.beginGradientFill(gradientFillType, colors, alphaValues, ratioValues,
➡ matrix);

Where:

- gradientFillType is either the string linear or radial.#
- colors is an array of colors that are used to define the gradient (you can have as many as you want to define your gradient).
- alphaValues is an array that has a corresponding alpha setting for each of the colors entries (you must have as many entries for alphas as you do for colors and ratios or the method will fail).

- ratioValues is an array that specifies where each color is on the gradient (you must have as many entries for ratios as you do colors and alphas or the method will fail).
- matrix is a 3x3 matrix that is used as a transformation matrix or a parameter list for a simplified box transform.

This method also requires a very good understanding of **MovieClip.lineTo**, **movieClip.moveTo**, **MovieClip.endFill**, and **MovieClip.beginFill**. You are advised to learn about those methods before attempting this one.

See the CD for in-depth coverage of this action.

MovieClip.clear

```
myMovieClip.clear()
```

Where myMovieClip is a movie clip instance.

Compatible with **Flash 6.**

The MovieClip.clear() method removes all graphics within a movie clip.

Description

The MovieClip.clear() **method** removes any and all drawing commands associated with the movie clip instance calling the method. Any established settings for the current line style are also cleared.

Code	Notes
myClip.clear()	Clears all graphics that were created in the movie clip myClip via the drawing API methods.

See the example files movieclipclear.fla and movieclipclear.swf on the CD.

MovieClip.createEmptyMovieClip

```
myMovieClip.createEmptyMovieClip (instance, depth);
```

Where myMovieClip is a movie clip instance, instance is a string identifying the new empty movie clip, and depth is the level at which to place the new clip.

Compatible with **Flash 6.**

The MovieClip.createEmptyMovieClip() method creates a new, empty movie clip and places it at a specified level. The new clip is a child of the existing clip.

Description

The `MovieClip.createEmptyMovieClip()` **method** creates a new movie clip which has no contents, and assigns it as a child of the calling movie clip instance.

The following line will create an empty movie clip on the `_root` timeline:

`_root.createEmptyMovieClip` called `bob` on the timeline `_root`;

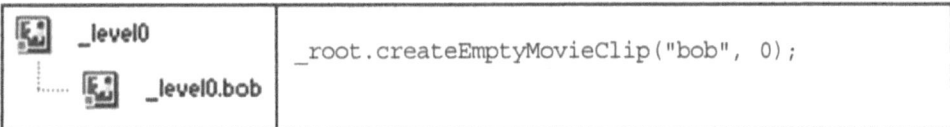

The following lines will create both `bob` and `bill`. Note that the depth has been made unique so that `bill` doesn't overwrite `bob`:

 _level0 ├─ _level0.bill └─ _level0.bob	`_root.createEmptyMovieClip("bob", 0);` `_root.createEmptyMovieClip("bill", 1);`

The following code will create two movie clips `bob` and `bill`, and also create two new movie clips `bob` and `bill` inside `bob`. Notice that the depth numbers start at zero again – the depth levels are unique per timeline:

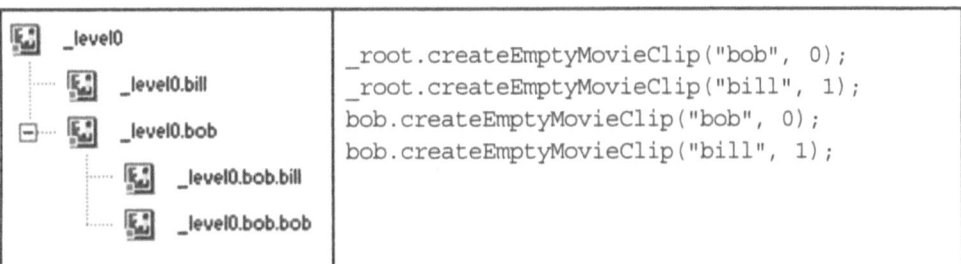

Finally, the following code wlll create all of the above, but also adds a new clip `sue` at depth 0 of `_root`. This will have the effect of not only overwriting `bob`, but also the embedded clips `bob` and `bill` inside it:

 _level0
├─ _level0.bill
└─ _level0.sue
	`_root.createEmptyMovieClip("bob", 0);`
	`_root.createEmptyMovieClip("bill", 1);`
	`bob.createEmptyMovieClip("bob", 0);`
	`bob.createEmptyMovieClip("bill", 1);`
	`_root.createEmptyMovieClip("sue", 0);`

MovieClip.createTextField

```
myMovieClip.createTextField (instance, depth, x, y, width, height);
```

Where myMovieClip is a movie clip instance, instance is a string identifying the new empty movie clip, depth is the level at which to place the new clip, x and y are the coordinates at which to position the text field, width is the width of the field, and height is the height of the field.

Compatible with **Flash 6.**

The MovieClip.createTextField() **method** creates a new text field inside the current clip.

Description

The MovieClip.createTextField() creates a new text field within the current clip:

```
myMovieClip.createtextField("myField", 3, 200, 200, 500, 100);
```

This will create a new text field called myField which is a child of myMovieClip. It is placed at a depth 2 and has coordinates of 200, 200 within myMovieClip, a width of 500 pixels and a height of 100 pixels.

By default, the MovieClip.createTextField() method uses these default text and TextFormat object properties (see the **TextFormat** object reference for more information on these properties):

- align = "left"
- background = false
- bold = false
- border = false
- bullet = false
- embedFont = false
- font = "Times New Roman"
- html = false
- indent = 0
- italic = false
- leading = 0
- leftMargin = 0
- maxChar = null
- multiline = false
- rightMargin = 0
- size = 12
- tabstops = []
- target = ""
- textColor = 0x000000
- type = "dynamic"
- underline = false
- url = ""
- variable = null

Some properties can be overridden prior to the text field being created, like this:

```
_root.createTextField("myTextField", 3, 200, 200, 500, 100);
// set default properties
myTextField.multiline = true;
// set TextFormat object properties
myTextFormat = new TextFormat();
myTextFormat.color = 0x0000FF;
myTextFormat.italic = true;
myTextFormat.align = "right";
// set text and call with new format settings
myTextField.text = "This is a test. This is only a test. Do not panic.";
myTextField.setTextFormat(myTextFormat);
```

See the files `movieclipcreatetextfield.fla` and `movieclipcreatetextfield.swf` on the CD.

MovieClip._currentframe

```
myMovieClip._currentframe;
```

Where `myMovieClip` is a movie clip instance.

Compatible with **Flash 4.**

The `MovieClip._currentframe` **property** shows the number of the current frame (the frame where the playhead is located).

Description

The `MovieClip._currentframe` property returns the frame number of the frame the playhead is currently positioned over in the timeline, whether the frame is being played or not.

code	Additional explanation	Notes
myCurrentFrame = myMovieClip._currentframe;	Stores the frame number the playhead is over to the variable myCurrentFrame	The playhead position in a frame is not dependent on the playback state of the movie.
myMovieClip.gotoAndPlay(_currentframe + 2);	Moves the playhead two frames and begins playback.	
myMovieClip._currentFrame+=5	The _currentframe property is read-only.	To advance the timeline relative to the current position, use methods such as MovieClip.gotoAndPlay().

MovieClip.curveTo

`myMovieClip.curveTo( x1, y1, x2, y2 );`

Where `myMovieClip` is a movie clip instance, x1 and y1 are the _x and _y coordinates of the control point, and x2 and y2 are the _x and _y coordinates of the anchor point.

Compatible with **Flash 6.**

The `MovieClip.curveTo()` **method** draws a curve from the current draw position, to the anchor point. The curvature of the point is defined by the position of the control point.

Description

The `MovieClip.curveTo()` method is used to draw a curve using the current line style from the current draw position to a second point called the **anchor point**. The curvature is defined by the third point, which is called the **control point**.

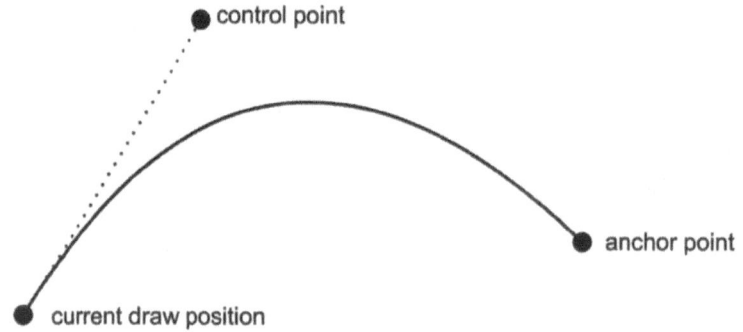

You may need to perform a `MovieClip.moveTo` if the draw position is not where you want it (it is at (0,0) if you have not changed it with other drawing methods). The control point acts rather like a 'bow tie':

- The direction of the curve is defined by the line from the current draw position to the control point. From the diagram you can see that the control point forms a line (dotted) that is the tangent that goes through the current draw position.
- The length of the dotted line is a measure of the curvature.

Although this sounds a bit mathematical, it becomes immediately obvious as soon as you use it interactively. See the example files `mccurvetoexample01.fla` and `mccurvetoexample01.swf`.

The starting point for the curve is always the current drawing point. If there is no current drawing point, the 0,0 coordinates are used. If there is already a line being drawn on the movie (with a `lineto` method, for example), the `MovieClip.curveTo()` method continues from that point.

All coordinates are relative to the registration point of the movie clip you are drawing into .

For example, the command:

```
myMovieClip.curveTo(200, 200, 300, 400);
```

... creates a curved line from the current drawing point (usually set by moveto) to the anchor point 300,400. The point 200,200 is used to control the amount of curve. All points are relative to the registration point of the movie clip.

Many MovieClip.curveTo() methods can be called in sequence:

```
moveto(100,100);
curveto(150, 150, 200, 200);
curveto(150, 150, 300, 400);
```

Code	Notes
myMovieClip.curveTo(300, 100, 300, 400);	Draws a curve from the current position to 300,400 relative to the registration point of myMovieClip, using a control point of 300,100.
	Note If any parameters are missing or illegal, the command fails.

See also the files on the CD:

```
(arrayaccessindex).fla / (arrayaccessindex).swf
movieclipcurveto.fla / movieclipcurveto.swf
```

MovieClip._droptarget

```
myMovieClip._droptarget;
```

Where myMovieClip is a movie clip instance.

Compatible with **Flash 4.**

The MovieClip._droptarget property returns the absolute path of the movie clip instance.

Description

The MovieClip._droptarget **property** returns the absolute path (using slash notation) of the movie clip instance on which the clip was dropped. Although most Flash designers have stopped using slash notation, slash notation is still used on those methods that are likely to break Flash 4 SWFs still on the web if the Flash Player were to be updated to return dot notation.

This is not a problem, because you can simply use **eval** to convert to dot notation.

code	Notes
myPath = myMovieClip._droptarget;	If myClip is on _root, then myPath will be returned as: /myMovieClip
myPath = eval(myMovieClip._droptarget);	This time eval is used to convert the path into dot notation, and myPath will be returned as: _level0.myMovieClip

See also the example files on the CD:

```
movieclipdroptarget.fla / movieclipdroptarget.swf
mcdroptargetsmooth.fla / mcdroptargetsmooth.swf
```

MovieClip.duplicateMovieClip

```
myMovieClip.duplicateMovieClip (copyName, depth [,propertyobject]);
```

Where myMovieClip is a movie clip. copyName is the copy that this method will create on the timeline of myMovieClip. The copy will be created at a depth of depth, and you can use the optional parameter propertyObject (which is an Object object) to initialize the copy.

Compatible with **Flash 5 and later.**

The MovieClip.duplicatemovieClip() **method** takes an existing movie clip on the stage and copies it.

Description

The MovieClip.duplicateMovieClip() method is used to duplicate a movie clip (that is already somewhere on the stage) to the current timeline.

Although this method may seem very similar to MovieClip.attachMovie (and the examples we are using are almost identical to the ones seen in that entry) there is one fundamental difference: duplicateMovieClip copies from a *timeline* whereas attachMovie copies from the *Library*. See the *Tips and precautions section* to see the implications of this, and when to use each version.

To create a movie clip that can be duplicated, you must make sure that it has streamed in by the frame you first use attempt to copy it. The easiest way to do this is to place it on a keyframe on (or before) the MovieClip.duplicateMovieClip that attempts to use it. If you do not want the movie clip you intend to duplicate to be seen, you can simply make it invisible to the user by placing it either offscreen or making its MovieClip._visible property false.

The examples in this heading are backed up by the files mcduplicatemovieclipex01.fla and mcduplicatemovieclipex01.swf. These show the various ways to duplicate a movie clip called dot. Before (left) and after (right) results from this file are shown below, and you should refer to it if any of the written examples cause you grief.

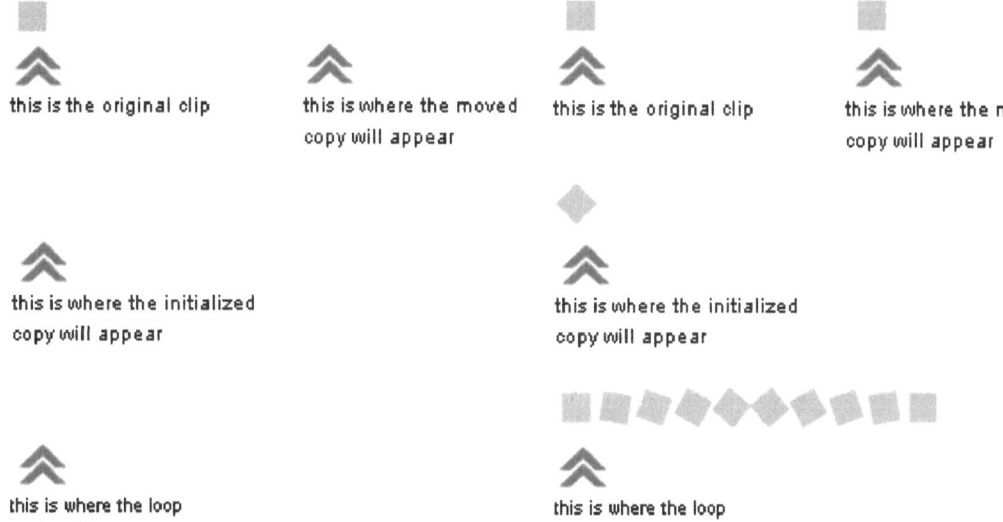

this is the original clip

this is where the moved copy will appear

this is the original clip

this is where the moved copy will appear

this is where the initialized copy will appear

this is where the initialized copy will appear

this is where the loop copies will appear

this is where the loop copies will appear

The following code will duplicate an existing movie clip dot as dot01, and the copy will have a depth of 0.

```
_root.dot.duplicateMovieClip("dot01", 0);
```

Since the duplicated movie clip occupies the same place as the original, you may have trouble seeing it (although you will see that there actually is now two versions of the movie clip if you look in the Debugger). The best way round this is to move the copy after creating it:

```
_root.dot.duplicateMovieClip("dot01", 0);
_root.dot01._x += 150;
```

You should also be aware that the depth of each movie clip on a given timeline should be unique. You are only allowed to have one symbol in each depth, and if you try to do otherwise, the new clip will replace the symbol already at that depth. Assuming that you have placed dot on a timeline manually (recommended), then it will have a **negative depth** (as does all content placed on the stage during authoring time) and you don't have to worry about overwriting it with an attachMovie or duplicateMovieClip because you use positive depths with these methods.

Note: Some advanced scripters have used undocumented negative values with MovieClip.duplicateMovieClip and MovieClip.attachMovie with some success, although there seems little merit in doing this.

You can move the copy in a more structured way by adding the additional `propertyObject` argument. This object's properties will be added to the timeline of the newly attached movie clip if they are not movie clip properties, or will be used as initial values for the movie clip properties if they are. This sounds more complicated than it actually is, so let's see it in action.

If we define an object `initObject` as shown and then add it to your `duplicatemovieClip` method as a new parameter:

```
initObject = {_x:200, _y:200, myVariable:10};
_root.dot.duplicateMovieClip("dot01", 0, initObject);
```

⊟	initObject	
	_x	200
	_y	200
	myVariable	10

... the properties `initObject._x` and `initObject._y` will be used to define the initial position properties `dot01._x` and `dot01._y`. The `myVariable` property of `initObject` does not correspond to a movie clip property, and will instead appear as a variable on the timeline of `dot01` (it will of course appear as `_root.dot01.myVariable`).

Assuming that we have the movie clip defined as above (a movie clip with instance name `dot` that is a small dot graphic), then the following examples show the results of various uses of `duplicateMovieClip` (the same examples are also used in `MovieClip.attachMovie`, so you can look at those as well to compare and contrast):

Examples

```
_root.dot.duplicateMovieClip("dot01", 0);
```

This will copy the existing movie clip `dot` as `dot01`. You will not see any change to the screen because both the original and the duplicate occupy the same position. You can however see that the duplicate exists by looking in the Debugger.

See also `mcduplicatemovieclipex02.fla` and `mcduplicatemovieclipex02.swf`.

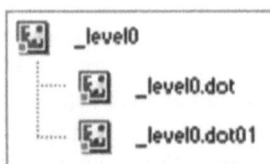

This code shows how `MovieClip.duplicateMovieClip` can be used to create multiple clips. The code attaches 500 instances of `dot`, called `dot0` to `dot499`. See also the mcduplicatemovieclipex03.fla / mcduplicatemovieclipex03.fla.swf.

```
dot._visible = false;
initDot = new Object();
initDot._visible = true;
for (i=0; i<500; i++) {
 initDot._x = Math.random()*550;
 initDot._y = Math.random()*400;
 _root.dot.duplicateMovieClip("dot"+i, i, initDot);
}
```

Try doing this manually!

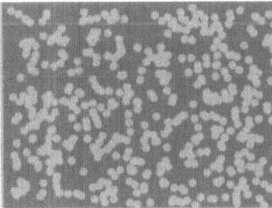

Notice the following features of this code:

- The way we have made the original clip disappear by setting its _visible property to false, and set the _visible of each duplicate to true via initDot.
- The use of initDot to give each dot clip a random position on the stage.
- The use of the for loop variable i to give each dot instance a unique name via string concatenation ("dot"+i) and the way it is also used to give each instance a unique depth.

In this final example, the dots are not only created dynamically, but also animated dynamically to create a magnetism particle effect. Hitting the mouse button will toggle the nature of the attractions from magnetic to repulsive. (The same effect can be seen using the attachMovieClip method in tapeworm.fla and tapeworm.swf – see also the entry for **MovieClip.attachMovieClip.**)

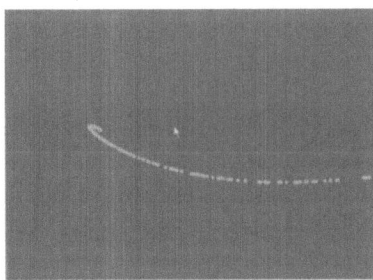

```
function animateDot() {
 this._x -= this.magnetism*(this._x-_root._xmouse)/this.inertia;
 this._y -= this.magnetism*(this._y-_root._ymouse)/this.inertia;
}
function reversePolarity() {
this.magnetism = -this.magnetism;
}
dot._visible = false;
```

```
initDot = new Object();
initDot._visible = true;
initDot.magnetism = 1;
for (i=0; i<200; i++) {
initDot._x = Math.random()*550;
initDot._y = Math.random()*400;
initDot.inertia = Math.random()*30+2;
_root.dot.duplicateMovieClip("dot"+i, i, initDot);
_root["dot"+i].onEnterFrame = animateDot;
_root["dot"+i].onMouseDown = reversePolarity;
}
```

Notice the way that the dot instances are referenced *after* they have been created with root["dot"+i].

See also the example files mcduplicatemovieclip.fla and mcduplicatemovieclip.swf on the CD.

MovieClip.enabled

```
myMovieClip.enabled;
```

Where myMovieClip is a movie clip instance.

Compatible with **Flash 6.**

The MovieClip.enabled property indicates whether a button movie clip is enabled.

Description

The MovieClip.enabled property returns a Boolean that indicates whether a button movie clip is enabled or not. If they are not enabled, the button's methods are unavailable and the event handlers do not receive Mouse events.

The MovieClip.enabled **property** has been inherited from the Button object. See also **Button.enabled**.

Code	Notes
myEnabled = myMovieClip.enabled;	Stores the current setting of the button movie clip to the variable myEnabled. myEnabled must be a Boolean.
myMovieClip.enabled = false;	Disables the button movie clip.

See also the example files on the CD:

movieclipenabled.fla / movieclipenabled.swf

MovieClip.endFill

```
myMovieClip.endFill();
```

Where `myMovieClip` is a movie clip instance.

Compatible with **Flash 6.**

The `MovieClip.endFill()` denotes the end of the current fill path. If the path has been properly defined, the fill path is filled as soon as the `endFill` method is seen.

The `MovieClip.endFill` method is always used in conjunction with `MovieClip.beginFill`, and the pair of methods are really part of the same thing; they define the start and end of the fill path definition. The main description for these methods is included in the entry for **MovieClip.beginFill**. also see that entry.

Description

The `MovieClip.endFill()` **method** causes the current fill path to be closed and filled. To understand how `endFill` works, an understanding of fill paths is required.

The diagram below shows the steps in creating a typical fill path, and they are:

- **Step 1:**. Use `MovieClip.beginFill` to denote the start of the fill path and then move to the start of the path (if you are not there already) using `MovieClip.moveTo`.
- **Steps 2-4:**. Draw the fill path using either `MovieClip.lineTo` or `MovieClip.curveTo`.
- **Step5:**. Use `MovieClip.endFill` to denote the end of the fill path. This will cause the closing of the fill path (by drawing to the start position) and the resulting outline will be filled.

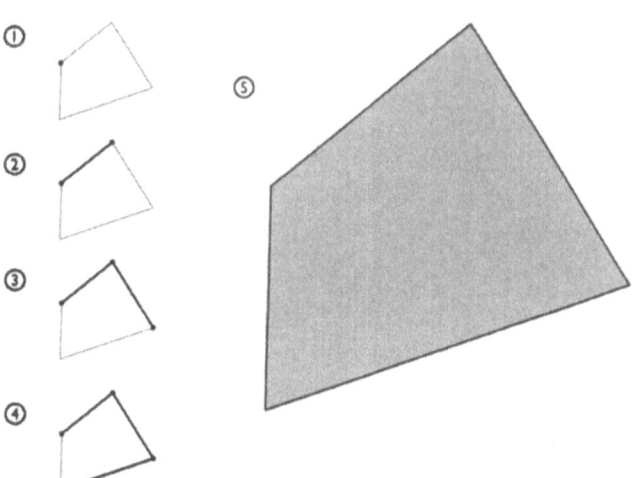

These steps are defined in greater detail in the entry **MovieClip.beginFill**. See that entry and the examples that go with it for more details.

MovieClip.focusEnabled

`myMovieClip.focusEnabled`

Where `myMovieClip` is a movie clip instance.

Compatible with **Flash 6.**

The `MovieClip.focusEnabled` **property** indicates whether a movie clip can have input focus.

Description

A movie clip that has input focus will be able to see `MovieClip.onKeyDown` and `MovieClip.onKeyUp` events.

The `MovieClip.focusEnabled` property returns a Boolean that indicates whether a movie clip can receive input focus or not. If a movie clip has this property set to `true`, it can receive input focus even if the clip is not a 'button movie clip' (a movie clip that has button events). The `MovieClip.focusEnabled` property sets the ability to receive focus.

Code	Notes
`myFocusEnabled = myMovieClip.focusEnabled;`	Stores the current setting of the movie clip focus enable status to the variable `myEnabled`.
`myMovieClip.focusEnabled = false;`	`myFocusEnabled` must be a Boolean. Prevents the movie clip from receiving input focus.

MovieClip._focusrect

`myMovieClip._focusrect;`

Where `myMovieClip` is a movie clip instance.

Compatible with **Flash 6.**

The `MovieClip._focusrect` property indicates whether a movie clip that has keyboard focus has a yellow rectangle around it.

Description

The `MovieClip._focusrect` **property** returns a Boolean that indicates whether a movie has a yellow rectangle around it when keyboard focus is active. If set to `true`, the yellow rectangle appears; if set to `false`, no yellow rectangle is shown. The movie clip below on the left is shown with input focus and the rectangle enabled.

Code	Notes
`myMovieClip._focusrect= false;`	Prevents the movie clip from having a yellow rectangle around it when it has keyboard focus.

MovieClip._framesloaded

`myMovieClip._framesloaded`

Where `myMovieClip` is a movie clip instance.

Compatible with **Flash 4 and later.**

The `MovieClip._framesloaded` **property** returns a number indicating how many frames have been loaded in a streaming movie

Description

The `MovieClip._framesloaded` property is used to determine the number of frames that have been loaded in a streaming movie. The `MovieClip._framesloaded` property can be checked at intervals to allow you to gauge the progress of a clip's loading process.

You can compare this with the **MovieClip._totalframes** method to see what fraction of the movie clip has loaded in:

```
loaded = _100*(root.framesloaded/_root.totalframes);
```

... will give you the percentage of the SWF loaded (in terms of frames loaded).

MovieClip.getBounds

`myMovieClip.getBounds( referenceClip)`

Where myMovieClip is the movie clip you want to get the bounding box size for, and these values will be with respect to the movie clip referenceClip.

Compatible with **Flash 5 and later.**

The MovieClip.getBounds() **method** returns the corner points of the bounding box that would enclose the movie clip.

Description

When you select any symbol in Flash, a bounding box will appear around it:

The movieClip.getBounds() method gives you the two corner points of a similar box shape that would completely enclose the original movie clip. Assuming our clip above was called bug then:

bugBoundingBox = bug.getBounds(_root);

... will return the corner points of the bounding box as properties of bugBoundingBox (relative to _root) as shown:

(xMin, yMin)

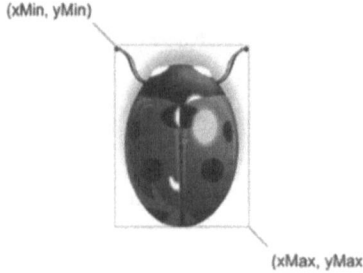

(xMax, yMax)

	bugBoundingBox	
	xMax	323.5
	xMin	275
	yMax	263
	yMin	200

These values can be used to draw the bounding box using values for the found corner points as shown:

(xMin, yMin)   (xMax, yMin)

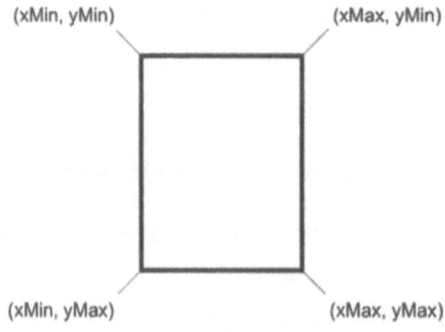

(xMin, yMax)   (xMax, yMax)

(Remember that the positive y direction in Flash is the print-based version (downwards) not the Cartesian one (upwards).)

The significance of the properties returned by clipA.getBounds(clipB) is not immediately obvious. They give you enough information to draw a bounding box in clipB that will enclose clipA.

Code	Notes
myBounds = myMovieClip.getBounds(_root);	myBounds will be returned with properties: myBounds.xMax myBounds.xMin myBounds.yMax myBounds.yMin
myXMax = clip1_mc.getBounds(clip2_mc).xMax;	only the xMax property is returned.

See the example files movieclipgetbounds.fla and movieclipgetbounds.swf on the CD.

MovieClip.getBytesLoaded

```
myMovieClip.getBytesLoaded();
```

Where myMovieClip is a movie clip instance.

Compatible with Flash 6 and later.

The MovieClip.getBytesLoaded() method returns the number of bytes that have been loaded.

Description

The MovieClip.getBytesLoaded() method returns an integer indicating the number of bytes that have been loaded from a streaming clip. If you apply it to _root, it can be used to tell you the total bytes loaded in the current SWF.

Code	Notes
myBytes = myMovieClip.getBytesLoaded();	Returns the number of bytes loaded in the myMovieClip clip and stores the result in myBytes. An integer is returned from the method.

MovieClip.getBytesTotal

```
myMovieClip.getBytesTotal();
```

Where myMovieClip is a movie clip instance.

Compatible with **Flash 6.**

The MovieClip.getBytesTotal() method returns the total number of bytes in a movie clip.

Description

The `MovieClip.getBytesTotal()` **method** returns an integer indicating the total number of bytes that are in a movie clip. If the clip is external, the returned integer is the size of the SWF file.

Code	Notes
`myTotal = myMovieClip.getBytesTotal();`	Returns the total number of bytes in the `myMovieClip` clip. An integer is returned from the method.
`myTotal = .getBytesTotal(myMovieClip);`	No parameters are expected by the method, and no target movie clip instance is indicated.

MovieClip.getDepth

`myMovieClip.getDepth()`

Where `myMovieClip` is a movie clip instance.

Compatible with **Flash 6.**

The `MovieClip.getDepth()` **method** returns the level of the movie clip instance.

Description

The `MovieClip.getDepth()` method returns an integer indicating the level (depth) of the movie clip. integer is returned.

Code	Notes
`myDepth = myMovieClip.getDepth();`	Returns the depth of `myMovieClip`. An integer is returned from the method

MovieClip.getURL

`myMovieClip.getURL( URL [, target, varmethod]);`

Where `myMovieClip` is a movie clip instance, `URL` is the URL from which to get content, `target` is the window or frame in which the content is loaded, and `varmethod` is the method of transferring variables (`GET` or `POST`).

Compatible with **Flash 5 and later.**

The `MovieClip.getURL()` method loads a document from a URL into a particular location.

Description

The `MovieClip.getURL()` **method** loads a document (such as a data file) into a location that may be explicitly specified as an argument. The optional `GET` and `POST` methods indicate how the variables and their values will be sent to the movie.

Code	Additional explanation	Notes
`myMovieClip.getURL("datafile.txt");`	Loads the contents of `datafile.txt` into the current movie.	If no target is specified, the current movie is assumed.
`myMovieClip.getURL("datafile.txt",` ➥ `_self, POST);`	Loads the contents of `datafile.txt` into the current window using a `POST` method.	`GET` or `POST` only needs to be specified if variables are to be transferred
`myMovieClip.getURL();`	No parameters are specified.	

MovieClip.globalToLocal

```
myMovieClip.globalToLocal(coords);
```

Where `myMovieClip` is a movie clip instance and `coords` is an object that represents an `(x, y)` point. `coords` should be an `Object` object with properties `x` and `y`.

Compatible with **Flash 5 and later.**

The `MovieClip.globalToLocal()` **method** converts global (stage) coordinates to local (movie clip) coordinates. It is useful when using the drawing API, or when creating animations in embedded timelines. In both cases, it is sometimes useful to know what a point's coordinates are with respect to the stage.

Description

```
myClip.globaltoLocal(point);
```

... converts a point on the stage to the same point with respect to the registration point of `myClip`. That sounds like gobbledygook in words, but it's much simpler to understand in pictures.

Suppose that you create a movie clip as follows:

```
_root.createEmptyMovieClip("myClip", 0);
```

This movie clip is created at position 0,0 on the stage, so the global (stage) coordinates are the same as the local (myClip) coordinates. If you placed a dot at point (50, 50) on._root, and did the same thing on the timeline of `myClip`, they would be in the same position when you looked at the final SWF (bellow, left).

If you now moved myClip:

```
myClip._x+=25;
myClip._y+=25;
```

... this would have the effect of also moving the registration point of myClip, and with it the local coordinate system of myClip. If you placed a dot at (60, 60) on myClip, it would be at (60+25, 60+25) = (85, 85) relative to _root.

The two dots would no longer be in the same position; they are at the same position relative to their timeline coordinates, but because the two timelines _root and myClip, now have different coordinate systems, the two points will be at different **absolute** positions.

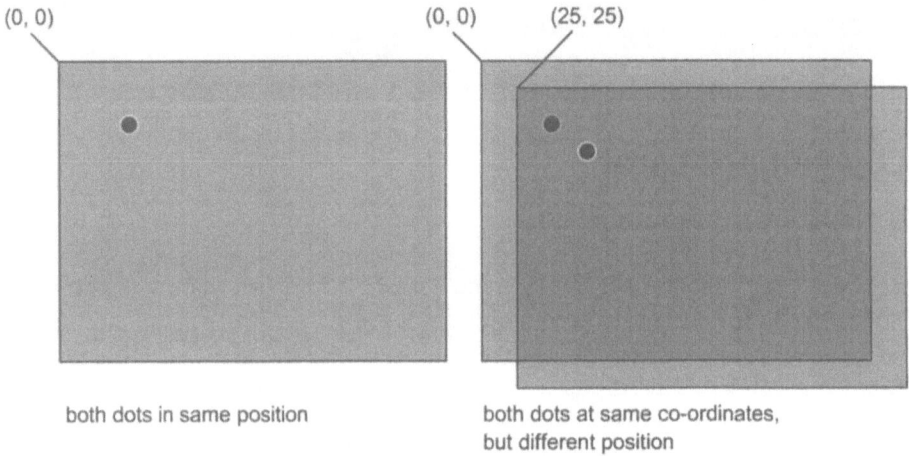

both dots in same position   both dots at same co-ordinates,
                                     but different position

The MovieClip.localToGlobal() method can be used in two ways:

1.   Use MovieClip.localToGlobal directly

If we create our point (50,50) as an Object object and then transform it to the corresponding global coordinate object, we will be able to find out where on myClip we need to place the dot so that it is back over the dot in _root:

```
_root.createEmptyMovieClip("myClip", 0);
myClip._x += 25;
myClip._y += 25;
point = {x:60, y:60};
myClip.localToGlobal(point);
trace(point.x);
trace(point.y);
```

This converts the local coordinates of the point on myClip to global coordinates (or coordinates of the point on _root).

Having all the point data in one coordinate system allows us to see the difference between the point on _root and the point on myClip without having to know where the two timelines are in relation to each other in coordinate space.

2. Find out the 'offset zero' for MyClip

You can fins out the difference in position between _root and myClip, and use that in all your subsequent animations:

```
_root.createEmptyMovieClip("myClip", 0);
myClip._x += 25;
myClip._y += 25;
registration = {x:0, y:0};
myClip.localToGlobal(registration);
trace(registration.x);
trace(registration.y);
```

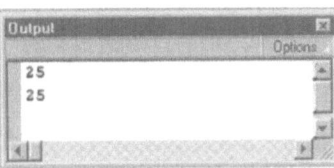

The localToGlobal method takes our object registration and returns the difference between the point (0,0) on _root (*global zero*) and (0,0) on myClip (*local zero*).

The x,y properties of registration once they have been transformed by localToGlobal represent the **offset zero**. By subtracting this value from any coordinates on myClip, you get the corresponding absolute coordinates.

So to move our point back so that it is in the same position as the point on _root we *subtract* the offset zero:

```
(50-registration.x, 50-registration.y) = (25, 25)
```

Using an offset zero has two advantages:

■ We can do the reverse transform ('globalTolocal') without having to use MovieCliplocalToGlobal().
■ We don't have to keep using either method once we know the offset value, something that will speed up any 2D or 3D vector/fill engine you are creating within Flash.

Although this method is relatively easy, it's one of those things that still has the capability to make your head hurt, and you lose track of it all if you look up for more than ten seconds (yeah, we know, it even happens to us!), so there is a full animated example in the next section! Don't worry if you're starting to get a little uptight!

See the CD example files:

```
mcglobaltolocala.fla / mcgloballocala.swf
mcglobaltolocalb.fla / mcglobaltolocalb.swf
mcglobaltolocalc.fla / mcglobaltolocalc.swf.
```

MovieClip.gotoAndPlay

myMovieClip.gotoAndPlay(frame)

Where myMovieClip is a movie clip instance and frame is the frame number to go to.

Compatible with **Flash 5 and later.**

The MovieClip.gotoAndPlay() **method** positions the playhead at a specific frame number and begins playback from that point.

Description
The MovieClip.gotoAndPlay() method is used to move the playhead to a frame number and begin playback from that frame on.

Code	Additional explanation	Notes
myMovieClip.gotoAndPlay(6);	Goes to frame 6 and starts playback there.	The framenumber must be valid or the command fails.
myMovieClip.gotoAndPlay();	No frame number is specified.	

MovieClip.gotoAndStop

myMovieClip.gotoAndStop(frame);

Where myMovieClip is a movie clip instance and frame is the frame number to go to.

Compatible with **Flash 5 and later.**

The MovieClip.gotoAndStop() method positions the playhead at a specific frame number but does not start playback.

Description
The MovieClip.gotoAndStop() **method** is used to move the playhead to a frame number and wait for a play command to be issued. Playback does not start automatically with the MovieClip.gotoAndStop() method.

Code	Additional explanation	Notes
`myMovieClip.gotoAndStop(6);`	Goes to frame 6 and stops there.	The frame number must be valid or the command fails.
`myMovieClip.gotoAndStop();`	No frame number is specified.	

MovieClip._height

```
instanceName._height = a;
b = instanceName._height;
```

Where `instanceName` is the instance name of a movie clip, and `a` is the value you want to assign to the movie clip height in pixels. `b` is a variable that is equated to the current value of the movie clip `_height` property value.

This property is compatible with **Flash 4 and later**.

Description

The `_height` **property** of a movie defines the buttons current height in pixels. The `_height` property is read/write. In many cases, the **_xscale** and **_yscale** properties of the `MovieClip` object are more useful to the Motion Graphics programmer, and the `_height` (and **_width**) property is less used.

Code	MovieClip appearance	Notes
	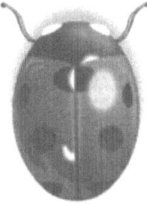	Initial appearance of movie clip `my_mc`.
`my_mc._height += 40;`	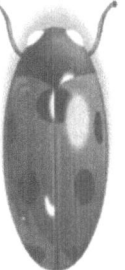	The height of `my_mc` increases by 40 pixels, resulting in a stretched appearance.

See the example files `movieclipheight.fla` and `movieclipheight.swf` on the CD

MovieClip._highquality

```
instanceName._highquality = a;
b = instanceName._highquality;
```

Where `instanceName` is the instance name of a movie clip, and a is the `_quality` value you want to apply to the whole FLA. b is a variable that is equated to the current value of the FLA's `_highquality`.

This global property is compatible with **Flash 4 or later**. It allows you to set the quality that the Flash render engine works to when drawing graphics. More specifically, it allows control of the pixel anti-aliasing (or pixel smoothing) applied.

The **MovieClip._highquality, Button._highquality,** and **TextField._highquality** properties are identical to the Flash 4 (and above) global property **_highquality**, and you are recommended to use this form of the property if compatibility is an issue. The related action **toggleHighQuality** and property **_quality** also allow you to fine control the rendering quality that the Flash Player works to in drawing graphics to the stage during runtime. These properties should generally be used in preference to `MovieClip._highquality` because of the greater levels of control they allow.

Description

The `_highquality` **property** of a running SWF can be accessed/set as a property of the `MovieClip` object, and is also available as a property of the `Button` or `TextField` objects. In short, the `_highquality` property is **available as a property of all the graphic objects available in Flash**. It is important to realize that when applied to any such object, **the _highquality property is applied to everything on the stage, including movie clips, buttons, text fields, and any other graphics**.

A fuller description of aliasing and anti-aliasing is presented in the entry for **MovieClip._quality**. Refer to that entry for further details.

Code	Rendered quality	Notes
`my_mc._highquality = 0;`		This is the lowest quality setting available via ActionScript. No anti-aliasing (pixel smoothing) will take place, and 'jaggies' will result. This setting gives the fastest performance. This setting corresponds to the Low quality setting in the Publish Settings window. This setting is best used when you are creating FLAs for low

performance devices (which may include PDA devices).

It is also useful when writing retro Flash games (or web sites with the same design influences), where the chunky pixilated feel is a definite advantage!

```
my_mc._highquality = 1;
```

This is the middle available quality setting via _highquality. No anti-aliasing (pixel smoothing) will take place on moving bitmaps, but anti-aliasing is applied to everything else.

This setting corresponds to the High quality setting in the Publish Settings window.

```
my_mc._highquality = 2;
```

This is the highest available quality setting via ActionScript. Anti-aliasing is applied to everything on the stage. This setting is exactly the same as the last example, except that bitmaps are always smoothed.

This setting corresponds to the Best quality setting in the Publish Settings window.

This setting is best used for largely static displays.

```
myFirst_mc._highquality = 2;
mySecond_mc._highquality = 1;
```

This code is attempting to apply individual quality settings to individual graphic objects. The _highquality setting is a global property; everything will always use the last seen setting.

MovieClip.hitArea

```
myClip.hitArea = hitClip;
```

Where `myClip` is a movie clip button and `hitClip` is the movie clip you want to act as its hit area.

Compatible with **Flash 6.**

The `MovieClip.hitArea` **property** designates a movie clip as a hit area for a button movie clip.

Description

Flash MX allows you to use button events with movie clips. A 'button event' is a historic term for the events that only buttons were allowed to use in Flash 5. In Flash MX you can recognize them because they are those events that the movie clip has in common with the button.

As soon as you add a button event to a movie clip it will start acting like a button. Although Macromedia use the term 'movie clip button' it is important to realize that a movie clip button is *not* a new object; it is still a `MovieClip`. The movie clip button is, however, different in the way you use and set it up.

Movie clip buttons are very useful for the advanced scripter, and they effectively supercede buttons because they are so versatile. Buttons are still useful with regard to workflow though; they are easier to set up and maintain, plus there is no real advantage in using movie clip buttons if all you want is simple button features.

Code	Notes

`clip1.hitArea = clip2;`
`clip1.onRelease = function() {`
`  trace("hello!")`
`};`
	Movie clip `clip2` is defined as the hit area for `clip1`.
	
	The `onRelease` callback for `clip1` will run every time `clip2` is click-released.

`clip1.hitArea = clip2;`	A movie clip doesn not start behaving as a button until you give it at least one button event. Although `clip1` has a hit area defined for it, it will not start acting as a button until a button event is defined for it. In particular, the cursor will *not* change to a hand cursor when you roll over `clip2`.

See the files `movieclipenabled.fla` and `movieclipenabled.swf` on the CD.

MovieClip.hitTest

```
myMovieClip._hitTest( target );
myMovieClip._hitTest( x, y, shape );
```

Where `myMovieClip` is a movie clip instance, `target` is the target path of the hit area, `x` and `y` are the coordinates of the hit area, and `shape` is a Boolean signifying whether to evaluate the entire shape of the clip (`true`) or just the bounding box (`false`). `shape` can only be specified if the `x` and `y` are.

Compatible with **Flash 5 and later.**

The `MovieClip.hitTest()` **method** checks a movie clip to see if it overlaps a hit area and returns a Boolean indicating the result.

Description

`MovieClip.hitTest()` provides the ability to perform collision detection between either two movie clips or between a point and a movie clip. The method returns a Boolean value that is `true` for a collision, and `false` otherwise.

Collision detection between two movie clips

Movie clip collision detection between two movie clips is calculated based on movie clip bounding boxes. Two movie clips are in collision if the bounding boxes overlap.

The usual code to use this form is:

```
if (movieClip1.hitTest(movieClip2)) {
    // code to handle collision
    // goes here
}
```

If a collision is detected, the method will give `true`, causing the 'code to handle collision' script to be executed.

You can see this effect interactively via the example files `mchittestex01.fla` and `mchittestex01.swf`.

click-drag either clip to see the results of
MovieClip.hitTest(*target*)

The collision detection code for this animation looks like this:

```
star1.onEnterFrame = function() {
    if (this.hitTest(star2)) {
        message.text = "hit";
    } else {
        message.text = "";
    }
};
```

The code checks for a collision between star1 and star2. Both star clips are draggable. If the bounding boxes overlap you will see the message 'hit'.

As you will see, this code gives very rough collision detection accuracy. The condition illustrated is a valid collision for example, because the bounding boxes overlap, although the two graphics obviously do not!

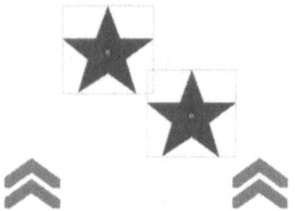

This is not actually as useless as it might initially seem. Most of the old 8-bit gaming classics (*Space Invaders*, *Defender*, et all) got round this issue by either:

- Making the graphics fast so that you could not see that the collisions were based around bounding boxes rather than the actual shapes.
- Making the graphics fill their bounding boxes. If you look at some of the old retro artwork that went into early motion graphics, you will see that they are designed within the limitations of the time. Fast sprite collision detection was only possible with bounding boxes, so the graphics were designed to fill their bounding boxes (so that it is impossible to hit the bounding box and miss the graphic) *in the direction they were most likely to be hit*. The space invaders seen here were most likely to be hit from below by a bullet moving upwards from the player. Notice how the pixels fill the bounding box in this direction so that *it looks like shape collision rather than bounding box collision is taking place*.

Collision detection between a point and a movie clip

Collision detection between a point and a movie clip has two forms. The first one detects collisions between a point and a movie clip bounding box. The general code used is very similar to the last one:

```
if (clip1.hitTest(x, y, false)) {
    // code to handle collision
    // goes here
}
```

The shape argument is false, and this tells Flash to use the bounding box of the movie clip clip1. You can see this in the interactive example files mchittestex03.fla and mchittestex03.swf.

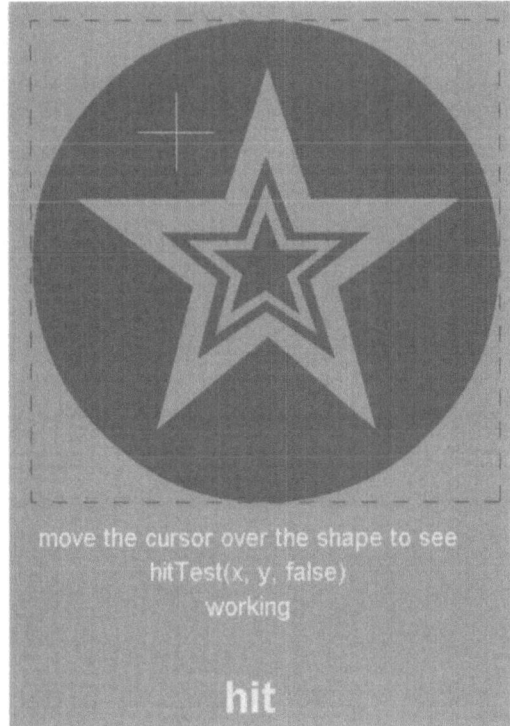

clip1 is the black areas, and the point (x, y) is represented by the crosshair cursor. You will see that clip1 is taken to be the much simpler bounding box shape.

This form of hitTest is not often used.

The real gem is the final form:

```
if (clip1.hitTest(x, y, true)) {
    // code to handle collision
    // goes here
}
```

As soon as you set the shape parameter to true, Flash now checks for collisions between the point (x,y) *and non zero pixels in the movie clip* clip1. There is no other way to test for collisions to pixel accuracy than using this form of hitTest. You can see this method in operation in the files mchittestex02.fla and mchittestex02.swf.

This time, the test gives `true` only when the cursor is actually over the pixels of the movie clip:

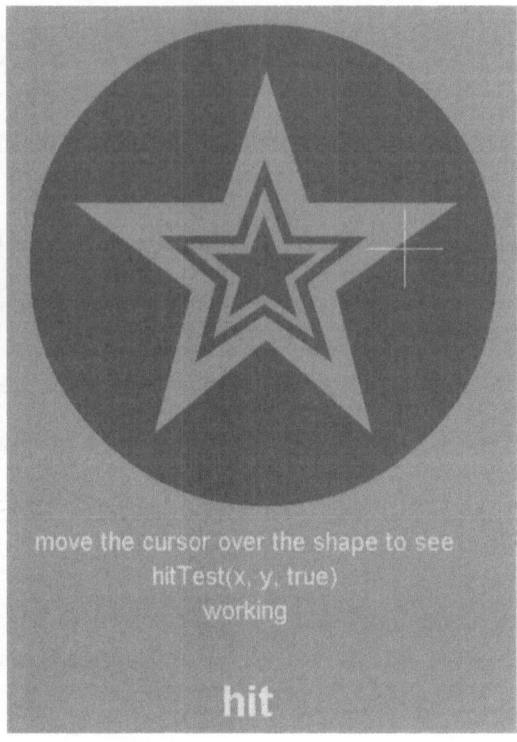

The issue that confuses most users is that you cannot perform pixel perfect collision detection between two movie clips; you can only do it between a point and a movie clip.

This is not actually an abnormal situation; in most other motion graphics fields you cannot detect a collision between two objects accurately; you have to test for a collision between a point and an edge:

- Most objects are most likely to collide with any other object in the line they are currently traveling in. You do not have to test for a speeding car getting hit from behind, and even when you do, the car that hits it will usually do so with its front bumper.
- Most games actually check for collisions between a number of points and an edge. Even in the latest third person shooters such as *Quake III*, collision detection occurs between the *points* that make up a player character and the surroundings, and not the player *outline* (shape) and the surroundings.

Generally, the art of good collision detection involves:

- Choosing the collision points so that it looks like the collision detection is occurring between two shapes rather than a point and a shape.
- Making the collision detections look accurate (even if they are not) by modifying the graphics.

MovieClip.lineStyle

```
myMovieClip.lineStyle( [thickness [, color [ ,alpha]]])
```

Where myMovieClip is a movie clip instance, thickness is the width of the line in points, color is the hexadecimal code of the color, and alpha sets the transparency.

Compatible with **Flash 6.**

The MovieClip.lineStyle() method sets the line style that will be used by drawing methods.

Description

The MovieClip.lineStyle() method is used to set the default line style for any future drawing methods. The line style set with the MovieClip.lineStyle() method remains in effect until reset with another lineStyle() method or a **MovieClip.clear()** method is seen.

Code	Notes
myMovieClip.lineStyle(10);	Sets the line style to a 10 point black line.
myMovieClip.lineStyle(10, 0xFF0000, 100);	Sets the line style to a 10 point red solid line. **Note:**Point sizes for lines range from 0 (hairline) to 255 points.

See the example files moviecliplinestyle.fla and moviecliplinestyle.swf on the CD.

MovieClip.lineTo

```
myMovieClip.lineTo( x, y )
```

Where myMovieClip is a movie clip instance and x and y are the coordinates of the end point.

Compatible with **Flash 6.**

The MovieClip.lineTo() method draws a line from the current drawing position to the specified end point.

Description

The MovieClip.lineTo() **method** is used to draw a straight line between two points within the specified movie clip. The starting point is the current drawing position, and the end point is provided as parameters to the MovieClip.lineTo() method. All coordinates are relative to the registration point of the movie. The line is drawn with the current line style.

Code	Additional explanation	Notes
myMovieClip.lineTo(100,300);	Draws a line from the current drawing location to 100, 300.	The current line style is used.

See the example files `moviecliplineto.fla` and `moviecliplineto.swf` on the CD.

MovieClip.loadMovie

    myMovieClip.loadMovie(URL [, method])

Where `myMovieClip` is a movie clip instance, `URL` is the path to the movie SWF file, and `method` is the means of transferring variables (if any) to the method (`GET` or `POST`).

Compatible with **Flash 5 and later.**

The `MovieClip.loadMovie()` method plays a movie without closing the Flash Player.

Description

The `MovieClip.loadMovie()` **method** is used to load a new movie into an existing Flash Player and play that movie, without closing and reloading the player. The `MovieClip.loadMovie()` method can load SWF and JPEG files while a movie is still playing, allowing multiple movies to play one after another. (Usually, the Flash Player loads a single movie and closes after that movie has played.)

Code	Additional explanation	Notes
myMovieClip.loadMovie("aMovie.swf");	Loads the SWF file into the existing Flash Player.	The URLfor the movie file must be inthe same subdomain as the existing movie.
myMovieClip.loadMovie("aMovie.swf", ➥ GET);	Loads the SWF file into the existing Flash Player and loads variables using the GET method.	The GET or POST parameter must be passed as a string.
myMovieClip.loadMovie("aMovie.mpg");	Only SWF and JPEG files can be loaded with this method.	

MovieClip.loadVariables

    myMovieClip.loadVariables(URL [, method]);

Where `myMovieClip` is a movie clip instance, `URL` is the absolute or relative URL where the variables are located, and `GET/POST` indicates the `method` used to send the variables.

Compatible with **Flash 5 and later.**

The `MovieClip.loadVariables()` **method** is used to load variables into a movie from an external file.

Description

The `MovieClip.loadVariables()` action allows you to transfer variables and their values to a movie or movie clip already loaded. The variables can come from a file (either static or created by a server-side script). The `MovieClip.loadVariables()` action can be used to update existing values as a movie plays. The file to be read must be maintained in `application/x-www-urlform-encoded` MIME format.

The `MovieClip.loadVariables()` action requires a URL for the location of the variable file. This file and the movie itself must be in the same subdomain.

The optional GET and POST methods indicate how the variables and their values will be sent to the movie. The GET method uses a URL descriptor while the POST method uses an HTTP header. If there are a lot of variables to be sent, POST is the better method.

The `MovieClip.loadVariables()` action is similar in purpose to the method **loadVariables()**, but the syntax is slightly different.

Code	Additional explanation	Notes
`myMovieClip.loadVariables("timdata.txt");`	Loads the variables and values defined in the file `timdata.txt` into the movie myMovieClip. The variables and values may be new or replace existing values.	Assumes the file is in the same directory as the current movie. The target movie should be already loaded.
`LoadVariables("data.dat");`	No movie clip is specified.	

MovieClip.localToGlobal

`myMovieClip.localToGlobal(coords)`

Where myMovieClip is a movie clip instance and coords is the identifier of an object specifying the x and y coordinates.

Compatible with **Flash 5 and later.**

The `MovieClip.localToGlobal()` **method** converts local (movie clip) coordinates into global (stage) coordinates. The method is the reverse of the MovieClip.globalToLocal method. See this entry for more details of how the method functions and for examples.

MovieClip.moveTo

```
myMovieClip.moveTo( x, y )
```

Where `myMovieClip` is a movie clip instance and `x` and `y` are the coordinates of the point to move to.

Compatible with **Flash 6 and later.**

The `MovieClip.moveTo()` method moves the current drawing position to the specified point.

Description
The `MovieClip.moveTo()` **method** is used to move the drawing position to a new point. All coordinates are relative to the registration point of the movie. The line is drawn with the current line style.

Code	Additional explanation	Notes
`myMovieClip.moveTo(100,300);`	Moves the current drawing location to `100`, `300`.	Coordinates are relative to the registration point of the clip.

MovieClip._name

```
myMovieClip._name
```

Where `myMovieClip` is a movie clip instance.

Compatible with **Flash 4 and later.**

The `MovieClip._name` property returns the name of the movie clip instance.

Description
The `MovieClip._name` **property** simply returns the name of the movie clip instance. This is often used in generic scripts to store the clip name in a variable.

Code	Notes
`myName = myMovieClip._name;`	Assigns the name of the movie clip instance to `MyName`.
`myName = myMovieClip._name(_parent);`	No parameters are specified.

MovieClip.nextFrame

```
myMovieClip.nextFrame()
```

Where `myMovieClip` is a movie clip instance.

Compatible with **Flash 5 and later.**

The `MovieClip.nextFrame()` method places the playhead on the next frame and stops playback at that point.

Description

The `MovieClip.nextFrame()` **method** moves the playhead to the next frame in the timeline and stops playback at that point.

Code	Additional explanation	Notes
`myMovieClip.nextFrame();`	Moves the playhead to the next frame of `myMovieClip` and pauses there.	Playback is always paused when going to the next frame.
`myMovieClip.nextFrame(5);`	No parameter is specified	If parameters are not provided the for this method.command fails.

MovieClip.onData

`myMovieClip.onData`

Where `myMovieClip` is a movie clip instance.

Compatible with **Flash 5 and later.**

The `MovieClip.onData` event handler is invoked when a movie receives data, usually from a **loadVariables()** or **loadMovie()** method. To use the `MovieClip.onData` event handler a function must be written.

Description

The `MovieClip.onData` **event handler** is invoked any time new data is received by a movie, whether that data is a set of variables or a new movie load. When the `MovieClip.onData` event handler is invoked, the function associated with the event handler is launched.

MovieClip.onDragOut

`myMovieClip.onDragOut`

Where `myMovieClip` is a movie clip instance.

Compatible with **Flash 6.**

The `MovieClip.onDragOut` **event handler** is invoked when the cursor is pressed and dragged outside and then over the movie clip's area.

This event is the same as the corresponding Button event **Button.onDragOut.** See the entry for **Button.onDragOut.**

MovieClip.onDragOver

`myMovieClip.onDragOver`

Where `myMovieClip` is a movie clip instance.

Compatible with **Flash 6.**

The `MovieClip.onDragOver` **event handler** is invoked when the cursor is pressed while over a movie, dragged outside the movie, and then dragged back over the movie clip's area.

This event is the same as the corresponding Button event **Button.onDragOver.** See the entry for **Button.onDragOver.**

MovieClip.onEnterFrame

`myMovieClip.onEnterFrame`

Where `myMovieClip` is a movie clip instance.

Compatible with **Flash 6.**

The `MovieClip.onEnterFrame` **event handler** is invoked continually as each frame in a movie is entered.

Description

The `MovieClip.onEnterFrame` event handler is invoked as the playback head enters each frame in a movie. Any actions associated with the event handler are invoked as each frame is entered.

MovieClip.onKeyDown

`myMovieClip.onKeyDown`

Where `myMovieClip` is a movie clip instance.

Compatible with **Flash 6.**

The `MovieClip.onKeyDown` **event handler** is invoked when a key is pressed and the movie has input focus.

This event is the same as the corresponding Button event **Button.onKeyDown.** See the entry for **Button.onKeyDown.**

MovieClip.onKeyUp

`myMovieClip.onKeyUp`

Where `myMovieClip` is a movie clip instance.

Compatible with **Flash 6.**

The `MovieClip.onKeyUp` **event handler** is invoked when a key is released and the movie has input focus.

This event is the same as the corresponding Button event **Button.onKeyUp.** See the entry for **Button.onKeyUp.**

MovieClip.onKillFocus

`myMovieClip.onKillFocus(newobject)`

Where `myMovieClip` is a movie clip instance and `newobject` is the object to receive focus.

Compatible with **Flash 6.**

The `MovieClip.onKillFocus` event handler is invoked when a movie loses keyboard input focus. A new object to receive the focus is specified inside the event handler function.

This event is the same as the corresponding Button event **Button.onKillFocus.** See the entry for **Button.onKillFocus.**

MovieClip.onLoad

`myMovieClip.onLoad`

Where `myMovieClip` is a movie clip instance.

Compatible with **Flash 6.**

The `MovieClip.onLoad` event handler is invoked when the movie clip is instantiated.

Description

The `MovieClip.onLoad` **event handler** is invoked when the movie clip is first loaded and appears on the timeline. The function associated with the `MovieClip.onLoad` event handler is executed when this happens.

The Flash MX `MovieClip.onLoad` event is different to the Flash 5 `onClipEvent (load)` event because of the order Flash processes the event model and associated scripts (events are generated first and then the scripts on frames are executed). This means that the `MovieClip.onLoad` event has already occurred by the time the `onLoad` event is actually defined, and the event handler will not run. In most cases, you don't need this event handler in any case.

This script will not initialize `myVariable`, and the `onEnterFrame` script will continually display `undefined`:

```
myClip.onLoad = function() {
    this.myVariable = 10;
};
myClip.onEnterFrame = function() {
    trace(myVariable);
};
```

That's not actually a problem once you understand how Flash MX works, because you can just as well do this:

```
myClip.myVariable = 10;
    myClip.onEnterFrame = function() {
        trace(myVariable);
};
```

This time you will get your `10`.

The real application for `MovieClip.onLoad` is when creating prototypes. The prototype definition occurs *before* the movie clip is placed on the stage, so the `MovieClip.onLoad` will work.

```
myProto = function () {
    this.onLoad = function() {
        trace("I am onLoad");
    };
    this.onEnterFrame = function() {
        trace("I am onEnterFrame");
    };
};
myProto.prototype = new MovieClip();
Object.registerClass("myClip", myProto);
//
```

```
_root.attachMovie("myClip", "myNewClip", 0);
```

The onLoad event now occurs as expected:

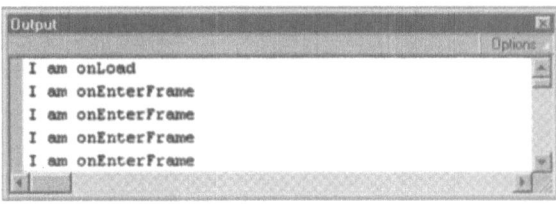

There is a known ' feature' of MovieClip.onLoad though. If you attach *any* code to a movie clip in the Flash 5 style (click on the movie clip itself and add an onClipEvent(event) handler directly to the instance), the Flash MX MovieClip.onLoad event now starts to work, and it does this even if you just add a single space (no code) to the movie clip. **This is undocumented at the time of writing, and you are recommended to not rely on it for the future.**

As we said earlier, Flash MX doesn't really need onLoad outside a prototype definition anyway!

MovieClip.onMouseDown

myMovieClip.onMouseDown

Where myMovieClip is a movie clip instance.

Compatible with **Flash 6.**

The MovieClip.onMouseDown **event handler** is invoked when a mouse button is pressed.

Description

The MovieClip.onMouseDown event handler is invoked any time a mouse button is pressed. The function associated with the MovieClip.onMouseDown event handler is launched when this happens.

MovieClip.onMouseMove

myMovieClip.onMouseMove

Where myMovieClip is a movie clip instance.

Compatible with **Flash 6.**

The MovieClip.onMouseMove event handler is invoked when the mouse moves.

Description

The MovieClip.onMouseMove **event handler** is invoked any time a mouse is moved. The function associated with the MovieClip.onMouseMove event handler is launched when this happens.

MovieClip.onMouseUp

`myMovieClip.onMouseUp`

Where `myMovieClip` is a movie clip instance.

Compatible with **Flash 6.**

The `MovieClip.onMouseUp` event handler is invoked when a mouse button is released.

Description

The `MovieClip.onMouseUp` **event handler** is invoked any time a mouse button is released. The function associated with the `MovieClip.onMouseUp` event handler is launched when this happens.

MovieClip.onPress

`myMovieClip.onPress`

Where `myMovieClip` is a movie clip instance.

Compatible with **Flash 6.**

The `MovieClip.onMousePress` **event handler** is invoked when a mouse button is pressed on a movie clip.

This event is the same as the corresponding Button event **Button.onPress.** See the entry for **Button.onPress.**

MovieClip.onRelease

`myMovieClip.onRelease`

Where `myMovieClip` is a movie clip instance.

Compatible with **Flash 6.**

The `MovieClip.onRelease` **event handler** is invoked when a mouse button is released on a button movie clip.

This event is the same as the corresponding Button event **Button.onRelease.** See the entry for **Button.onRelease.**

MovieClip.onReleaseOutside

`myMovieClip.onReleaseOutside`

Where `myMovieClip` is a movie clip instance.

Compatible with **Flash 6.**

The `MovieClip.onReleaseOutside` **event handler** is invoked when a mouse button has been pressed over a button movie clip then is released outside that clip.

This event is the same as the corresponding Button event Button.**onReleaseOutside.** See the entry for **Button.onReleaseOutside.**

MovieClip.onRollOut

`myMovieClip.onRollOut`

Where `myMovieClip` is a movie clip instance.

Compatible with **Flash 6.**

The `MovieClip.onRollOut` **event handler** is invoked when the mouse moves outside a movie clip area.

This event is the same as the corresponding Button event **Button.onRollOut.** See the entry for **Button.onRollOut.**

MovieClip.onRollOver

`myMovieClip.onRollOver`

Where `myMovieClip` is a movie clip instance.

Compatible with **Flash 6.**

The `MovieClip.onRollOver` **event handle**r is invoked when the mouse moves over a movie clip area.

This event is the same as the corresponding Button event **Button.onRollOver.** See the entry for **Button.onRollOver.**

MovieClip.onSetFocus

`myMovieClip.onSetFocus(oldobject)`

Where `myMovieClip` is a movie clip instance and `oldobject` is the object that lost focus.

Compatible with **Flash 6.**

The `MovieClip.onSetFocus` event handler is invoked when a movie gets keyboard input focus. The object that loses the focus is specified inside the event handler function.

Description

The `MovieClip.onSetFocus` **event handler** is invoked when a movie is given input focus. The function associated with the `MovieClip.onSetFocus` event handler is launched when this happens and that function specifies a new object to receive the focus.

MovieClip.onUnload

`myMovieClip.onUnload`

Where `myMovieClip` is a movie clip instance.

Compatible with **Flash 6.**

The `MovieClip.onUnload` event handler is invoked when the movie clip is removed from the timeline.

Description

The `MovieClip.onUnload` **event handler** is invoked when the movie clip is removed from the timeline. The function associated with the `MovieClip.onUnload` event handler is launched when this happens. The event handler resides in the first frame of the movie.

MovieClip._parent

`myMovieClip._parent`

Where `myMovieClip` is a movie clip instance.

Compatible with **Flash 6.**

The `MovieClip._parent` property is a reference to the movie clip that contains the current movie clip instance.

Description

The `MovieClip._parent` **property** is a reference to the name of the movie clip instance's parent – the movie that contains the clip. This is often used in generic scripts to store the clip name in a variable.

Code	Notes
`myName = myMovieClip._parent;`	Assigns the path of the movie clip instance's parent to `MyName`. If the movie clip is not a child, nothing is returned.

```
myName = myMovieClip._parent(_parent);                    No parameters can be specified.
```

MovieClip.play

```
myMovieClip.play();
```

Where `myMovieClip` is a movie clip instance.

Compatible with **Flash 5 and later.**

The `MovieClip.play()` method begins playback of the movie.

Description
The `MovieClip.play()` **method** begins playback of the movie at the current playhead location.

Code	Additional explanation	Notes
myMovieClip.play();	Starts playing myMovieClip.	Playback continues until stopped by some event or action.
myMovieClip.play(5);	No parameter can be specified for this method.	If parameters are provided, the command fails.

MovieClip.prevFrame

```
myMovieClip.prevFrame()
```

Where `myMovieClip` is a movie clip instance.

Compatible with **Flash 5 and later.**

The `MovieClip.prevFrame()` method places the playhead on the previous frame and stops playback at that point.

Description
The `MovieClip.prevFrame()` **method** moves the playhead to the previous frame in the timeline and stops playback at that point.

Code	Additional explanation	Notes
`myMovieClip.prevFrame();`	Moves the playhead to the previous frame of `myMovieClip` and pauses there.	Playback is always paused when going to the previous frame.
`myMovieClip.prevFrame(5);`	No parameter can be specified for this method.	If parameters are provided, the command fails.

MovieClip.removeMovieClip

`myMovieClip.duplicateMovieClip()`

Where `myMovieClip` is a movie clip instance.

Compatible with **Flash 5 and later.**

The `MovieClip.removeMovieClip()` method removes a movie clip instance and frees the previously occupied depth.

Description

The `MovieClip.removeMovieClip()` **method** is used to remove an instance of a movie clip.

Code	Notes
`myMovieClip.removeMovieClip()`	Removes `myMovieClip`.
`myMovieClip.removeMovieClip("myNewCopy");`	No target name can be specified; the instance calling the method is removed.

MovieClip._rotation

`myMovieClip._rotation`

Where `myMovieClip` is a movie clip instance.

Compatible with **Flash 4 and later.**

This property represents the number of degrees the movie clip is rotated.

Description

The MovieClip._rotation **property** is the number of degrees the movie clip is rotated. The property can be set and queried.

Code	Notes
myName = myMovieClip._parent;	Assigns the path of the movie clip instance's parent to myName. If the movie clip is not a child, nothing is returned.
myName = myMovieClip._parent(_parent);	No parameters are specified.

MovieClip.setMask

MyMovieClip.setMask(maskclip)

Where myMovieClip is a movie clip instance and maskclip is the name of the movie clip to be used as a mask.

Compatible with **Flash 4 and later.**

The MovieClip.setMask() method is used to set one movie clip as a mask for the movie clip instance.

Description

The MovieClip.setMask() method allows you to designate another movie clip that will be used as a mask for the current movie clip, showing only specific areas depending on the content of the mask clip. The MovieClip.setMask() method is used for multi-layer complex movies where you want to block off (mask) parts of a clip. Changes to MovieClip.setMask() method take effect immediately.

Code	Additional explanation	Notes
myMovieClip.setMask(myMaskMovie);	myMaskMovie masks myMovieClip.	Only another setmask() method can change a mask condition.
myMovieClip.setMask(null);	Removes any mask layer for myMovieClip.	
myMovieClip.setMask();	No parameters are specified.	

MovieClip._soundbuftime

```
myMovieClip._soundbuftime
```

Where myMovieClip is a movie clip instance.

Compatible with **Flash 6.**

The MovieClip._soundbuftime property specifies the number of seconds of sound to load before starting to play the movie.

Description

The MovieClip._soundbuftime **property** is used to set the number of seconds of time to preload a movie (buffer it) prior to starting playback of the movie.

Code	Notes
myTotalFrames = myMovieClip._framesloaded;	Stores the number of frames loaded so far into myTotalFrames.The result is always an integer and counts frames.
myMovieClip._framesloaded();	No method of this name exists.

MovieClip.startDrag

```
MyMovieClip.startDrag( [ lock [, left, top, right, bottom]] );
```

Where myMovieClip is a movie clip instance, lock is a Boolean indicating whether the clip is locked in the center of the mouse pointer, and left, top, right, and bottom are a coordinates of a constraining rectangle for the clip.

Compatible with **Flash 5 and later.**

The MovieClip.startDrag() method is used to indicate whether a movie clip is draggable, and if it is, whether there are bounds on the areas that can be dragged.

Description

The MovieClip.startDrag() **method** allows you to designate whether a movie clip is draggable or not. Only one movie clip can be draggable at a time. If you do set a movie clip to be draggable, you can enter coordinates for a rectangle that restrain the coordinates of the drag operation.

Code	Additional explanation	Notes
myMovieClip.startDrag(true);	Lets a user drag myMovieClip.	Only one movie clip can be draggable at a time.
myMovieClip.startDrag(false); myMovieClip.startDrag(true, ➡100, 600, 700, 50);	Locks myMovieClip in place. Places boundaries on the draggable area of myMovieClip.	
myMovieClip.startDrag();	No parameters are specified.	

MovieClip.stop

myMovieClip.stop()

Where myMovieClip is a movie clip instance.

Compatible with **Flash 5 and later.**

The MovieClip.stop() method stops playback of the movie.

Description
The MovieClip.stop() **method** halts playback of the movie at the current playhead location.

Code	Additional explanation	Notes
myMovieClip.stop();	Stops playing myMovieClip.	Playback halts until started again by some event or action.
myMovieClip.stop(5);	No parameter can be specified for this method	If parameters are provided, the command fails.

MovieClip.stopDrag

MyMovieClip.stopDrag();

Where myMovieClip is a movie clip instance.

Compatible with **Flash 5 and later.**

The MovieClip.stopDrag() method is used to stop a movie clip from being draggable.

Description

The `MovieClip.stopDrag()` **method** turns off the draggability of a movie clip that was made draggable by a **MovieClip.startDrag()** method.

Code	Additional explanation	Notes
`myMovieClip.stopDrag();`	Stops `myMovieClip` from being draggable.	Only one movie clip is draggable at a time.
`stopDrag(myMovieClip);`	No parameters are allowed.	

MovieClip.swapDepths

```
myMovieClip.swapDepths(depth);
myMovieClip.swapDepths(target);
```

Where `myMovieClip` is a movie clip instance, `depth` is a level to be swapped with, and `target` is a movie to swap levels with.

Compatible with **Flash 5 and later.**

The `MovieClip.swapDepth()` method is used to swap depths with another movie.

Description

The `MovieClip.swapDepth()` **method** lets two movies swap depths.

Code	Additional explanation	Notes
`myMovieClip.swapDepth(2);`	Swaps `myMovieClip` with the movie in level 2.	Both movies must have the same parent.
`myMovieClip.swapDepth ("oldMovie");`	Swaps depths of `myMovieClip` and `oldMovie`.	
`myMovieClip.swapDepth();`	No parameters are specified.	

MovieClip.tabChildren

```
myMovieClip.tabChildren
```

Where `myMovieClip` is a movie clip instance.

Compatible with **Flash 6.**

The MovieClip.tabChildren property controls whether the movie clip's children are included in automatic tab ordering.

Description

The MovieClip.tabChildren **property** lets you control what is included in automatic tab ordering. If the MovieClip.tabChildren property is set to true or undefined (the default value), all children of the movie clip are included in automatic tab ordering. If the value of the MovieClip.tabChildren property is set to false, the children are not included in automatic tab ordering.

Code	Additional explanation	Notes
myMovieClip.tabChildren = false;	Children of myMovieClip are not included in automatic tab ordering.	By default, the value is undefined, which indicates inclusion in automatic tab ordering (as does setting the property to true).
myMovieClip.tabChildren = "true";	Only Boolean values are allowed (this is a string).	

MovieClip.tabEnabled

myMovieClip.tabEnabled

Where myMovieClip is a movie clip instance.

Compatible with **Flash 6.**

The MovieClip.tabEnabled **property** controls whether the object instance is included in automatic tab ordering.

Description

The MovieClip.tabEnabled property lets you control whether the object is included in automatic tab ordering. If the MovieClip.tabEnabled property is set to true or undefined (the default value), the object is included in automatic tab ordering. If the value of the MovieClip.tabEnabled property is set to false, the object is not included in automatic tab ordering.

Code	Additional explanation	Notes
myMovieClip.tabEnabled = false;	myMovieClip is not included in automatic tab ordering	By default the value is undefined, which indicates inclusion in automatic tab

ordering (as does setting the property to `true`).
This property has no effect on children of the object.

```
myMovieClip.tabEnabled = "true";        Only Boolean values are allowed
                                         (this is a string).
```

MovieClip.tabIndex

`myMovieClip.tabIndex`

Where `myMovieClip` is a movie clip instance.

Compatible with **Flash 6.**

The `MovieClip.tabIndex` property controls automatic tab ordering of objects in a movie.

Description

The `MovieClip.tabIndex` **property** lets you control how all objects in a movie are handled by tab ordering. If an object in a movie has the `MovieClip.tabIndex` property, automatic tab ordering is disabled and the values specified in the `MovieClip.tabIndex` property are used for ordering instead. If the `MovieClip.tabIndex` property is set to a positive integer then all integers are sorted into increasing order when tab ordering is performed. Only objects with the `MovieClip.tabIndex` property are included in the sort.

Code	Additional explanation	Notes
`myMenu.tabIndex = 6;`	Sets the `tabIndex` property of `myMenu` to 6.	By default all objects have the `MovieClip.tabIndex` property value `undefined`.
`myMenu.tabIndex();`	There is no method with this name, only a property.	

MovieClip._target

`myMovieClip._target`

Where `myMovieClip` is a movie clip instance.

Compatible with **Flash 4 and later.**

Description
The MovieClip._target **property** returns the target path of the movie clip instance.

Code	Notes
myPath = myMovieClip._target;	Stores the path of myMovieClip in myPath.
myPath = myMovieClip._target();	There is no method with this name.

MovieClip._totalframes

myMovieClip._totalframes

Where myMovieClip is a movie clip instance.

Compatible with **Flash 4 and later.**

See also the **MovieClip._framesloaded** entry.

Description
The MovieClip._totalframes **property** returns the total number of frames in the movie clip instance.

Code	Notes
myFrames = myMovieClip._totalframes;	Stores the total number of frames in myMovieClip in myFrames.
myFrames = myMovieClip._totalframes();	There is no method with this name.

MovieClip.trackAsMenu

myMovieClip.trackAsMenu

Where myMovieClip is a movie clip instance.

Compatible with **Flash 4 and later.**

The MovieClip.trackAsMenu **property** is a Boolean indicating whether buttons and movie clips can receive mouse events.

This event is the same as the corresponding Button event **Button.trackAsMenu.** See the entry for **Button.trackAsMenu.**

MovieClip.unloadMovie

```
myMovieClip.unloadMovie()
```

Where `myMovieClip` is a movie clip instance.

Compatible with Flash 5 and later.

The `MovieClip.unloadMovie()` method unloads a movie clip.

Description

The `MovieClip.unloadMovie()` method is used to unload a movie that was loaded with a **MovieClip.loadMovie()** or **MovieClip.attachMovie()** method.

Code	Notes
`myMovieClip.unloadMovie();`	Unloads the movie `myMovieClip`.
`loadMovie("myMovieClip");`	This method does not take parameters.

MovieClip._url

```
myMovieClip._url
```

Where `myMovieClip` is a movie clip instance.

Compatible with **Flash 4 and later.**

The `MovieClip._url` property returns the URL of the SWF file for the current movie.

Description

The `MovieClip._url` **property** returns the full URL of the location of the SWF file that was downloaded for the current movie clip instance.

Code	Notes
`myFile = myMovieClip._url;`	Stores the URL of `myMovieClip` in `myFile`.
`myFile = myMovieClip._url();`	There is no method with this name.

MovieClip.useHandCursor

`myMovieClip._useHandCursor`

Where `myMovieClip` is a movie clip instance.

Compatible with **Flash 6.**

The `MovieClip._useHandCursor` **property** indicates whether to use a hand cursor when over a button movie clip.

This event is the same as the corresponding Button event **Button.useHandCursor.** See the entry for **Button.useHandCursor.**

MovieClip._visible

`myMovieClip._visible`

Where `myMovieClip` is a movie clip instance.

Compatible with **Flash 4 and later.**

The `MovieClip._visible` property determines whether the movie clip is visible or not.

Description

The `MovieClip._visible` **property** is a Boolean that indicates whether the movie clip instance is visible or not. If not visible, the clip is disabled.

Code	Additional explanation	Notes
`myMovieClip._visible = true;`	The `myMovieClip` object is visible and can be clicked.	Non-visible objects cannot be clicked.
`myMovieClip._visible = "true";`	Only Booleans can be used for this property (this is a string).	

MovieClip._width

`myMovieClip._width`

Where `myMovieClip` is a movie clip instance.

Compatible with **Flash 4 and later.**

The `MovieClip._width` **property** sets or retrieves the width of the movie clip in pixels. This property is exactly the same as `MovieClip._height` except that it affects width instead of height. See the entry for **MovieClip._height**.

MovieClip._x

`myMovieClip._x`

Where `myMovieClip` is a movie clip instance.

Compatible with **Flash 3 and later.**

The `MovieClip._x` property sets or retrieves the horizontal coordinate of a movie clip.

Description

The `MovieClip._x` **property** is used to both set and display the horizontal (x) coordinate of a movie clip instance's registration point. If a movie clip is in the main timeline, the value returned by the `MovieClip._x` property is relative to the upper left corner (0,0) of the stage. If there is a parent movie clip, the `MovieClip._x` property is relative to the parent's. If the movie clip is inside another clip, the `MovieClip._x` property is relative to the enclosing movie clip's coordinates.

Code	Additional explanation	Notes
`myMovieClip._x = 100;`	Stores the x coordinate of `myMovieClip` to 100 pixels.	x coordinates are relative to the parent or timeline.
`myMovieClip._x(100);`	No method of this name exists.	

MovieClip._xmouse

`myMovieClip._xmouse`

Where `myMovieClip` is a movie clip instance.

Compatible with **Flash 5 and later.**

This property retrieves the horizontal coordinate of the mouse.

Description

The `MovieClip._xmouse` **property** displays the horizontal (x) coordinate of the mouse cursor.

Code	Notes
`myMouse = myMovieClip._xmouse;`	Stores the x coordinate of the mouse to `myMouse.x` coordinates are relative to the parent or timeline.
`myMovieClip._xmouse(100);`	No method of this name exists.

MovieClip._xscale

`myMovieClip._xscale`

Where `myMovieClip` is a movie clip instance.

Compatible with **Flash 4 and later.**

The `MovieClip._xscale` property sets or retrieves the horizontal scale of a movie clip.

Description

The `MovieClip._xscale` **property** is used to determine the horizontal scale of a movie clip's registration point, relative to the (0,0) default registration point. This lets you calculate positions of objects based on scaling effects.

Code	Additional explanation	Notes
`myMovieClip._xscale = 0.5;`	Sets the horizontal scaling to 0.5.	x coordinates are relative to the (0,0) registration point.
`myMovieClip._xscale(0.5);`	No method of this name exists.	

MovieClip._y

`myMovieClip._y`

Where `myMovieClip` is a movie clip instance.

Compatible with **Flash 3 and later.**

The `MovieClip._y` **property** sets or retrieves the vertical coordinate of a movie clip. This property is exactly the same as `MovieClip._x` except that it affects the vertical instead of horizontal value. See the entry for **MovieClip._x**.

MovieClip._ymouse

```
myMovieClip._ymouse
```

Where myMovieClip is a movie clip instance.

Compatible with **Flash 5 and later.**

The MovieClip._ymouse **property** retrieves the vertical coordinate of the mouse. This property is exactly the same as MovieClip._xmouse except that it affects the vertical instead of horizontal value. See the entry for **MovieClip._xmouse.**

MovieClip._yscale

```
myMovieClip._yscale
```

Where myMovieClip is a movie clip instance.

Compatible with **Flash 4 and later.**

The MovieClip._yscale **property** sets or retrieves the vertical scale of a movie clip. This property is exactly the same as MovieClip._xscale except that it affects the vertical scaling instead of horizontal scaling. See the entry for **MovieClip._xscale.**

gotoAndStop()
hitTest()
loadMovie()
loadVariables()
loadVariables()
loadVariable()
nextFrame()   play()
prevFrame()
removeMovieClip()
setMask() startDrag()
startDrag()
swapDepths()
unloadMovie()
attachMovie()
createEmptyMovie()
createTextField()
duplicateMovie()

NaN

NaN

The NaN variable is a predefined value for "Not a Number".

This variable is compatible with **Flash Player 5 and later**. Flash 4 will return a value of undefined instead of NaN.

See also **Number.NaN** and **isNaN()**..

Description

The NaN **variable** is the IEEE-754 standard value for **Not a Number**. The value Not a Number can occur when a non-numeric value is used instead of a numeric value or when a result that should be a number is returned as anything other than a number from a function. For example, if you try to convert the string "Flash" to a number, the result will be NaN. Converting an empty string to a number will likewise cause NaN. However, you could convert the string "345" properly to a number. This conversion from string to number occurs most often with the Flash 5 and later **Number()** function. Also, a value of NaN will arise when obtaining input from a user, expecting a number but obtaining a string instead. For example, if the user types "ten" instead of "10", a value of NaN will result. The NaN variable can be used in tests using the **if** statement to ensure you are working with numeric values. NaN has the same value as **Number.NaN**.

Code	Additional explanation	Notes
`Math.round("foo");` `trace(Number("Fifteen"));` `trace(Number(1+"ten"));` `trace(Number(""));`	These actions will return NaN as these strings cannot be converted to a number.	Any numeric operation that is performed on a string will result in NaN if the string cannot be converted to a number.
`if (myNum == NaN){...`	If myNum has the value NaN, returns true otherwise returns false.	You can explicitly test for the value NaN using a comparison.
`if (num1 == num2) {...`	If either variable is a NaN, the result is false.	Comparison operations with NaN will always be false except for **not equal (!=)**.
`Num1=Math.round("string");` `Num2=Num1+5;`	Num2 will result in a value of 5. Any operation performed with a NaN value will not cause another NaN. Instead, the NaN value is treated as a number in the calculation, even though it has no real value.	Performing operations on a value that was set to NaN for any reason will not cause execution errors in the script, but will most likely cause errors in results. The only way to discover these errors is careful analysis of the code and the use of breakpoints

and `trace()` actions to examine variable values.

See the example files `nan.fla` and `nan.swf` on the CD.

ne

```
expression1 ne expression2
```

Where `expression1` and `expression 2` are Flash expressions (strings, variables, or values) to be checked for equality.

This action is compatible with **Flash 4 and later.** With Flash 5 and later the `ne` operator was deprecated for the **!=** operator so should be used only when creating legacy applications.

The `ne` operator checks for non-equality between two expressions.

Description

The `ne` operator is used inside an **if** condition to check for non-equality between the two expressions on either side of the operator. The `ne` **operator** returns `true` if the first expression is not equal to the second, based on a character-by-character comparison from left to right. If the two expressions are equal, the `ne` operator returns `false`. This is the opposite of the **equality (==) operator** and the same as the **inequality (!=) operator**. The `ne` operator was deprecated in Flash 5 and later releases for the more common `!=` operator. See the **!= operator** entry for more details and examples.

Code	Additional explanation	Notes
`if (expression1 ne expression2) {...`	If expression1 is not equal to expression 2, returns `true`.	Deprecated with `!=` in Flash 5 and later

`if (myVar ne 10){`
`    // do this`
`}`
	The `do this` code will execute if variable `myVar` is not equal to `10`.	The second listing uses the preferred syntax for Flash 5 and later. Use the `ne` operator only for Flash 4 legacy code.

`if (myVar != 10){`
`    // do this`
`}`		

new

```
new objectconstructor([parms])
```

Where objectconstructor() is a constructor of a Flash object for which a new object is to be created, and parms are any values to be passed to the constructor's functions.

This action is compatible with **Flash 5 and later.**

The new operator calls a constructor to create a new object.

Description
The new **operator** creates a new object (usually of one of the Flash object types such as Object, Number, and so on) and calls any functions identified in the constructor. If any parameters are included in the call to the new operator, they are passed to the constructor's functions. The prototype's properties and methods of the constructor are copied into the new object. (See **Object._proto** for more information on constructor prototypes.)

Code	Additional explanation	Notes
myString = new String();	Creates a new object based on the constructor of the parent object.	
myArray = new Array();		
myNumber = new Number();		
myMath = new Math();	The Math object does not have a constructor function and new objects cannot be created from it.	Some objects are predefined and you cannot create new instances of them.

newline

newline

This action is compatible with **Flash 4 and later.**

The newline constant is a predefined value for a carriage return.

Description
The newline **constant** inserts a carriage return and is used to move down a line. It is usually used in string variables to insert a line break.

Code	Additional explanation	Notes
Str1="Hello"; Str2="Goodbye"; trace(Str1 + newline + Str2); Hello Goodbye	Displays the contents of Str1 followed by a carriage return, followed by the contents of Str2 on the next line so the output looks like this: Hello Goodbye	New lines can be inserted anywhere in strings to force a line break.
Str1="Hello"; Str2="Goodbye"; trace(Str1 + newline + newline + Str2);	Displays the contents of Str1 followed by a blank line, followed by the contents of Str2 on the next line so the output looks like this: Hello Goodbye	

nextFrame

```
nextFrame()
```

This method is compatible with **Flash 2 and later.**

The nextFrame() method moves the playhead to the next frame and stops there. See also **prevFrame()**, **MovieClip.nextFrame()**, and **MovieClip.prevFrame()**.

Description

The nextFrame() **method** moves the playhead to the next frame in the timeline, and stops playback at that point. See also **MovieClip.nextFrame()** for an explanation and examples.

Code	Additional explanation	Notes
nextFrame();	Moves the playhead to the next frame.	Playback is stopped when the nextFrame() method is called.
nextFrame(3);	No frame number can be specified; see **gotoAndStop()**.	A frame number could be specified with this method in Flash 2 through Flash 4, but is not supported with Flash 5 and later.

nextScene

```
nextScene()
```

This method is compatible with **Flash 2 and later.**

The nextScene() method moves the playhead to the first frame of the next scene and stops there.

Description
The nextScene() **method** moves the playhead to the first frame of the next scene in the timeline, and stops playback at that point.

Code	Additional explanation	Notes
nextScene();	Moves the playhead to the first frame in the next scene of a movie and stops the playback at that point.	Playback is stopped when the nextScene() method is called.
nextScene(2);	No frame number can be specified; see gotoAndStop() for the ability to specify frames.	

not

```
not expression
```

Where expression is a Flash expression (strings, variables, or values).

This action is compatible with **Flash 4 and later.** With Flash 5 and later the not operator is **deprecated** for the more common **!** operator. Unless you are writing legacy Flash 4 code, use the ! operator instead.

The not operator performs a logical NOT operation.

Description
The not **operator** negates the expression, reversing the logic. It is usually used with an if statement to reverse the condition's true and false conditions.

Code	Additional explanation	Notes

myNum = 5;
if (myNum == 5) {
    trace("five");
}
	The first code will display the trace() message if the condition is true (which it is). The second code will not display the trace() message	Flash 5 and above should use the ! operator instead of not. The if statement shown on the left should be written as:

`myNum = 5;`
`if (not(myNum == 5)) {`
`    trace("not five");`
`}`
	because the condition is negated. This is not the same as saying `myNum` `!= 5`. Instead, the condition is true, but the `not` negates it to `false` (see next example).	`if (!(myNum == 5)) {`
		`    trace("not five");`
		`}`

`myNum = not false;` `    myNum = not true;`	The `not` negates the value, so `not false` is `true`, and `not true` is `false`.	

null

```
null
```

This keyword is compatible with **Flash 5 and later.**

The `null` keyword indicates values that are missing or `undefined`.

Description

The `null` **keyword** is a special value usually assigned to variables when a value is missing or there is no defined type. Numerically, it evaluates to zero. This is not the same as **NaN** (Not a Number).

Code	Additional explanation	Notes
`if (myVar == null) {...}`	The condition is `true` if `myVar` does not have a value assigned or is an invalid data type (both result in a `null`).	`null` values should be tested for if there is a critical step in a movie depending on a variable's value.
`if (myVar != null) {...}`	The condition is `false` if `myVar` does not have a value assigned or is an invalid data type.	

Number (used as a function)

```
Number(expression)
```

Where `expression` is an expression to be converted to a number.

This function is compatible with **Flash 4 and later.**

The `Number()` function converts an expression into a number. It is used primarily for deprecating Flash 4 operators in movies played on Player 5 or above.

Description

The Number() **function** converts the expression provided as an argument into a number, and returns a value based on these values for the expression:

- **Boolean** – returns 1 if true, 0 if false.
- **Number** – returns the number.
- **String** – attempts to parse the string as a number (returns a number if successful, NaN if not; see NaN for more information on this value).
- **Undefined** – returns 0 if the expression is an undefined variable or a method with an undefined result.

The Number() function should not be confused with the Number object, which is a wrapper for the Number data type.

Code	Additional explanation	Notes
`MyBool = true;` `myVal = Number(myBool);`	Returns a 1 as the argument if a Boolean and is true.	Booleans values are either 0 (false) or 1 (true).
`MyNum = 45;` `myVal = Number(myNum);`	Returns the value 45.	Numbers are returned as numbers.
`MyNum = "3.4E5";` `myVal = Number(myNum);`	Returns the value 340000.	Strings are parsed as exponential numbers.
`MyNum = null;` `myVal = Number(myNum);`	Returns a value of 0.	undefined and null values are returned as 0.

Number (used as an object)

```
myNum = new Number();
myNum = new Number(val);
```

Where myNum is an instance of the Number object, and val is an argument used to set the new Number instance's initial value.

This object is compatible with **Flash 5 and later.**

Description

The Number object is a wrapper for the number data type and allows you to create new Number instances using the constructor function. It has several methods and properties associated with it that allow you to perform basic manipulations on numeric data types. Number instances must be instantiated with a constructor when calling the methods or properties. Having said all that, there is no advantage in Flash to using the Number constructor to create a new Number object over performing the same tasks using variables of the Number data type. Both methods that are associated with the Number object are available for `Number` variables, and the constants associated with the object can be achieved through other means. In other words, instead of defining a new `Number` object with a value of 10 like this:

```
myNumber = new Number(10);
```

... you could simply write:

```
myNumber = 10;
```

... and accomplish exactly the same task. So, **there is no practical advantage whatsoever in using the Number object over Number variables**. For the record, though, the `Number` object contains two methods used to return strings and values:

- `Number.toString` – returns the object value as a string.
- `Number.valueOf` – returns the object value.

The `Number` object also has several properties associated with it:

- `Number.MAX_VALUE` – the largest number representable.
- `Number.MIN_VALUE` – the smallest (negative) number representable.
- `Number.NaN` – constant for Not a Number.
- `Number.NEGATIVE_INFINITY` – constant representing negative infinity.
- `Number.POSITIVE_INFINITY` – constant representing infinity.

Code	Additional explanation	Notes
`myNum1 = new Number(5);` `trace(myNum1);`	Returns a value for `myNum1` of 5.	
`myNum2 = new Number();` `trace(myNum2);`	Returns a value for `myNum2` of 0.	Since undefined number data types default to a value of zero, there is no advantage to using the `Number` object.

Number.MAX_VALUE

`Number.MAX_VALUE`

Where `Number` is the `Number` object.

This property is compatible with **Flash 5 and later.**

The `Number.MAX_VALUE` property is the largest number that can be represented.

Description

The Number.MAX_VALUE **property** is a value representing the largest number that can be stored in a Flash number data type. This is a double precision number equal to approximately 1.79 * 10^308 (1.79E+308). The Number.MAX_VALUE property is still a real number and can have values subtracted or divided from it, but cannot be added to or multiplied by. The Number.MAX_VALUE property is accessed by reference to the Number object itself, not an instance of that object.

Code	Additional explanation	Notes
myNum = Number.MAX_VALUE;	Assigns the largest possible number to myNum (based on the data type used for double-precision numbers).	While the maximum value possible for MAX_VALUE would be different for platforms that have different double-precision representation, Flash uses the IEEE-754 standard to determine the maximum value.
myNum = Number.MAX_VALUE+1;	Since Number.MAX_VALUE is the maximum number possible, you can't add to it without exceeding the capabilities of the double-precision number type.	

Number.MIN_VALUE

Number.MIN_VALUE

Where Number is the Number object.

This property is compatible with **Flash 5 and later.**

The Number.MIN_VALUE property is the smallest number that can be represented.

Description

The Number.MIN_VALUE property is a value representing the smallest number that can be stored in a Flash number data type. This is a double-precision number adhering to the IEEE-754 standards and is equal to approximately 5.0 * 10^-324 or 5.0E-324. The Number.MIN_VALUE property is a real number and can have values added and multiplied by it, but cannot be subtracted from or divided by, as those results would exceed the double-precision representation.

Code	Additional explanation	Notes
myNum = Number.MIN_VALUE;	Assigns the smallest possible number to myNum (based on the data type used for double-precision numbers).	Flash uses the IEEE-754 standard to determine the minimum value.
myNum = Number.MIN_VALUE-10;	Since Number.MAX_VALUE is the smallest number possible, you can't subtract from it without exceeding the capabilities of the double-precision number type.	

Number.NaN

Number.NaN

Where Number is the Number object.

This property is compatible with **Flash 5 and later.**

The Number.NaN property represents the value "Not a Number".

Description

The Number.NaN **property** represents the value "Not a Number", which arises when a number is expected but is not present. For example, if a string is used instead of a number, the value NaN is returned.

Number.NEGATIVE_INFINITY

Number.NEGATIVE_INFINITY

Where Number is the Number object.

This property is compatible with **Flash 5 and later.**

The Number.NEGATIVE_INFINITY property represents negative infinity. See also **Number.POSITIVE_INFINITY** and **Infinity.**

Description

The Number.NEGATIVE_INFINITY **property** is a value representing negative infinity. A number which has a value of Number.NEGATIVE_INFINITY is so small that nothing can be added to it, or no value multiplied by it, to get it out of negative infinity and into the realm of numbers handled by Flash.

Code	Additional explanation	Notes
`myNum = Number.NEGATIVE_INFINITY;`	Assigns the value of negative infinity to `myNum`. You cannot perform mathematical operations on this value to get into the range specified by `Number.MIN VALUE`.	The value `NEGATIVE_INFINITY` can be used for comparison. It is the smallest number imaginable.
`myNum = Number.NEGATIVE_INFINITY * 10000;`	Any mathematical operation on `NEGATIVE_INFINITY` still results in the value of `NEGATIVE_INFINITY`.	

Number.POSITIVE_INFINITY

```
Number.POSITIVE_INFINITY
```

Where `Number` is the `Number` object.

This property is compatible with **Flash 5 and later.**

The `Number.POSITIVE_INFINITY` property represents infinity. See the **Infinity** entry for more information.

Description

The `Number.POSITIVE_INFINITY` **property** is a value representing infinity. You cannot perform mathematical operations on `Number.POSITIVE_INFINITY` into numbers representable by Flash (those below **Number.MAX_VALUE**). Flash does not perform all manipulations with infinity properly. For example, infinity/infinity should result in 1, and infinity-infinity should result in 0, but Flash does not do this correctly.

Code	Additional explanation	Notes
`myNum = Number.POSITIVE_INFINITY;`	Assigns the value of infinity to `myNum`. You cannot perform mathematical operations on this value to get into the range specified by **Number.MAX VALUE**.	The value `POSITIVE_INFINITY` can be used for comparison. It is the largest number imaginable.
`myNum = Number.POSITIVE_INFINITY / 10000;`	Any mathematical operation on `POSITIVE _INFINITY` still results in the value of `POSITIVE _INFINITY`.	

Number.toString

`myNumber.toString(num)`

Where `myNumber` is an instance of the `Number` object or a variable, and `num` is the numeric base to use for conversion.

This property is compatible with **Flash 5 and later.**

The `Number.toString()` method converts a number to a string.

Description
The `Number.toString()` **method** converts a number to a string. By default, a base-10 radix is used for converting the number, but you can specify another radix in the range from 2 to 36. The use of a radix allows you to handle binary, octal, hexadecimal, and other number base systems.

Code	Additional explanation	Notes

`myNumber = 15`
`myString =`
`myNumber.toString();`
	Converts `myNumber`'s value to a string, which will be 15.	If no radix is specified, base 10 is assumed.

`myNumber = 12`
`myString =`
`myNumber.toString(16);`
	Converts `myNumber`'s value to a hexadecimal (base 16) string, resulting in C.	

`myNumber = 183`
`myString =`
`myNumber.toString(2);`
	Converts `myNumber`'s value to a binary (base 2) string, resulting in 10110111.	

See the `numbertostring.fla` and `numbertostring.swf` examples on the CD.

Number.valueOf

`Number.valueOf()`

Where `Number` is the `Number` object.

This property is compatible with **Flash 5 and later.**

The `Number.valueOf()` method returns the value type of the `Number` object.

Description
The `Number.valueOf()` **method** returns the primitive value type of the number object.

Code	Notes
`myType = myNumber.valueOf();`	Returns the value type of `myNumber`, storing it in `myType`.

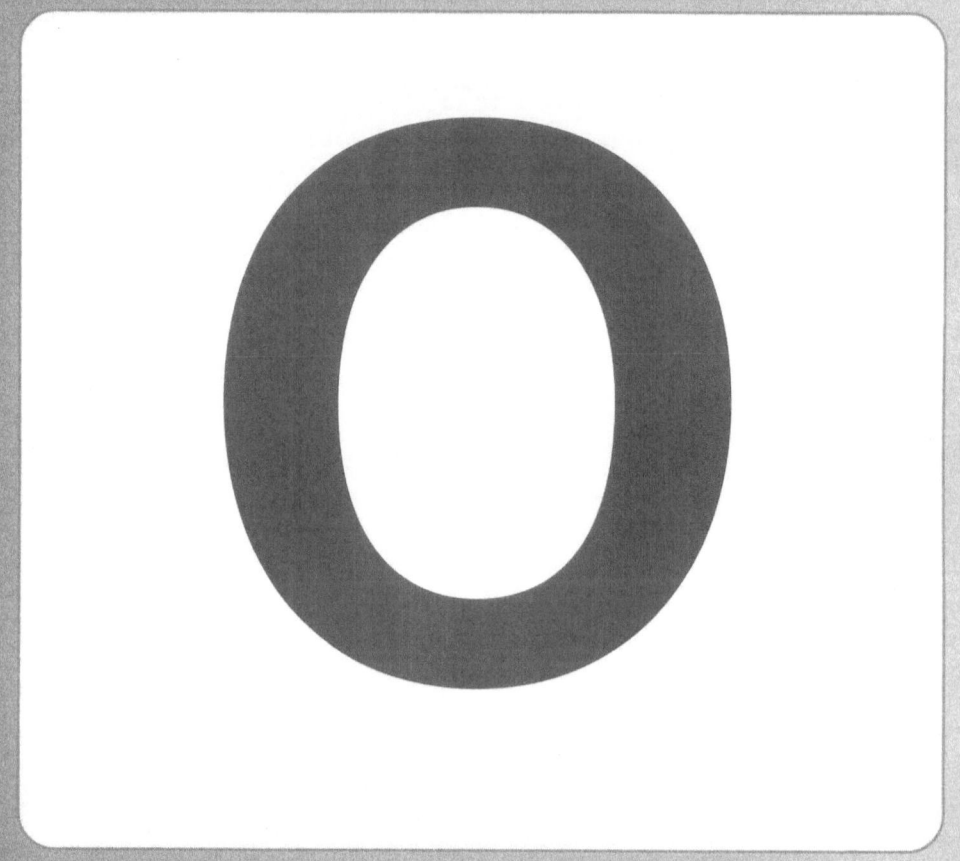

Object

This action is compatible with **Flash 5 and later.** With Flash MX and later releases, the Object object is the basic object type used to build other objects in Flash.

The Object object is a generic Object data type.

Description

Using the term "object" can get confusing because Flash uses the term in two ways. The first refers to anything on the stage that can be selected and which has a line and fill style associated with it. For example, a shape you draw on the stage is an object that can be selected. The second use of the term "object" is in the object-oriented programming sense (the same usage employed by ActionScript). Here, an object is a specific symbol or data type that has methods and properties that are unique. For example, a movie clip is an object because it has properties and methods, but a graphic is not an object (it doesn't have movies or methods unless you explicitly create a new object type for the graphic).

There are several predefined objects in Flash (and you can always create your own objects). The well-known predefined objects Flash provides are **Key**, **Math**, **Mouse**, **MovieClip**, and **Selection**. In addition there are other objects that are created from predefined classes. These use a constructor function. These objects are **Array**, **Boolean**, **Color**, **Date**, **Number**, **Object**, **Sound**, **String**, **XML**, and **XMLSocket**.

The Object object is a generic object class used as the root class for ActionScript. This means that all the other objects are built from the Object object, adding more methods and properties to provide specific functionality. The Object object itself contains several methods, all of which are inherited by other objects created from the Object object:

- Object.addProperty – adds a property to the object.
- Object.registerClass – assigns a class to a movie clip.
- Object.toString – returns the object value as a string.
- Object.unwatch – removes the registration created by the watch() method.
- Object.valueOf – returns the object value.
- Object.watch – registers a call-back function invoked when a property changes.

The Object object also has one property associated with it:

Object._proto_ – the prototype property of the constructor.

Object.addProperty

```
myObject.addProperty( name, getfunction, setfunction )
```

Where myObject is an Object instance, name is the name of the property to create, getfunction is a function invoked to retrieve the value of the property, and setfunction is a function invoked to set the value of the property.

This method is compatible with **Flash 6 and later.**

The `Object.addProperty()` method adds a new property and a value to an object.

Description

The `Object.addProperty()` **method** is used to add a new property to an object. When using the `Object.addProperty()` method you specify three parameters: the property name that will be added; a `get` function (used to retrieve a new value for the property); and a `set` function (which assigns a value to the property). If the value for the `set` function is `null`, the property is set to read-only.

The `get` function is a `function` object and has no parameters. When run, the function can return a value of any type and the type may change each time the function is executed. When a value is returned from the function, the returned value is the value assigned to the property.

The `set` function is a function that accepts one (and only one) parameter. That parameter is the new value of the property. If there is no `set` function (it is set to `null`) a new value cannot be assigned to the property.

Code	Additional explanation	Notes
`myObject.addProperty (` `"myProp",` `myObject.getProp,` `myObject.setProp);`	Creates a property called `myProp` in the object `myObject` which invokes the `getProp` method when a value is requested, and the `setProp` method when an attempt is made to set the value.	Set the `setProp` to `null` to create a read-only property.
`myObject.addProperty (` `"myProp",` `myObject.getProp);`	Incorrect number of parameters. The command will fail and return `false`.	

Object._ _proto_ _

    myObject._ _proto_ _

Where `myObject` is an `Object` instance.

This property is compatible with **Flash 5 and later.**

Description

The `Object._ _proto_ _` **property** is a reference to the prototype property in the object's constructor function. A prototype is present for each class in Flash. It can be empty, or contain methods and properties. Whenever an object's method or properties is requested by some ActionScript code, Flash checks the defined methods and properties, and if it can't find them, then checks the prototype of the class that the object was created from. This is the process of inheritance, as the class prototype methods and properties are available to the objects of that class.

The same applies when subclasses are created from classes. Each subclass inherits the parent's prototype properties and methods. Each subclass can have additional properties and methods in their prototype. Anything created from those subclasses will inherit the parent's prototype properties and methods, as well as the parent's parent's properties and methods (unless they have been overridden by the parent).

Object.registerClass

```
Object.registerClass( link, constructor )
```

Where `link` is a reference to the movie clip symbol and `constructor` is a reference to the class that contains the new constructor function to use.

This method is compatible with **Flash 6 and later.**

The `Object.registerClass()` method associates a movie clip with a class other than `MovieClip`.

Description

The `Object.registerClass()` **method** is used to associate a movie clip with an `object` class other than the `MovieClip` class so a different constructor function can be used. When an instance of the movie clip is placed on the timeline or created using a method like `attachMovie()`, it is registered to the class specified in the `Object.registerClass()` method rather than with the `MovieClip` class. If the `Object.registerClass()` method is used for a reference that already exists, the existing reference is overwritten with the new values.

If the constructor reference in the `Object.registerClass()` method parameters is `null`, the association is removed instead of being created. Any existing instances remain unchanged but all new instances will reference the `MovieClip` class instead.

If the class registration is completed successfully, the `Object.registerClass()` method returns `true`, otherwise `false` is returned.

Code	Additional explanation	Notes
`Object.registerClass ("myMovieClip", myUIStuff);`	Associates `myMovieClip` with the class `myUIStuff`. Any new instances of `myMovieClip` will invoke the `myUIStuff` constructor instead of the `MovieClip` constructor.	The `Object.registerClass` method associates a different constructor to instances of a movie clip (instead of the `MovieClip` object constructor).
`Object.registerClass ("myMovieClip", null);`	Removes any existing constructor reference from `myMovieClip`. Any new instances will refer to the `MovieClip` class instead.	Any existing instances of `myMovieClip` will still have references to the previous constructor, but new instances will not

Object.registerClass ("myMovieClip");	Incorrect number of parameters. The command will fail and return false.	A false will be returned to indicate failure of the registration attempt.

Object.toString

```
myObject.toString()
```

Where myObject is an Object instance.

This method is compatible with **Flash 5 and later.**

The Object.toString() method converts the object to a string.

Description

The Object.toString() **method** converts the object to a string and then returns the string.

Code	Notes
myString = myObject.toString();	Converts myObject to a string and stores the result in myString. In most cases, this will result in a description of the data type used by myObject.
myObject.toString("test");	No parameters are allowed.

Object.unwatch

```
myObject.unwatch ( property )
```

Where myObject is an Object instance and property is the object property to stop watching, specified as a string.

This method is compatible with **Flash 6 and later.** See the **Object.watch()** method for more details on watching properties.

Description

The Object.watch() **method** is used to monitor a property (so that when the value of that property changes, a call-back function is executed). **The Object.unwatch() method stops the watching of the object**. If the removal of the watchpoint is successfully, the Object.unwatch() method returns true; otherwise a false value is returned.

Code	Additional Explanation	Notes
myObject.unwatch ("myProp");	Stops watching the myProp property of myObject.	Returns true if the watch point is removed successfully.

Object.valueOf

```
myObject.valueOf()
```

Where myObject is an Object instance.

This method is compatible with **Flash 5 and later.**

The Object.valueOf() method returns the value of the object.

Description

The Object.valueOf() **method** returns the primitive value of the object. If the object does not have a value, the object itself is returned.

Code	Notes
myType = myObject.valueOf();	Returns the value type of myObject, storing it in myType.

Object.watch

```
myObject.watch( property, changefunction [, data])
```

Where myObject is an Object instance, property is the object property to watch, changefunction is the call-back function to call when the value of the property changes, and data is any data to be passed to the call-back function.

This method is compatible with **Flash 6 and later.**

The Object.watch() method lets you watch a property and execute a function when the value of the property changes.

Description

The Object.watch() **method** is used to monitor a property. When the value of that property changes, a call-back function is executed. If the watchpoint is successfully created, the Object.watch() method returns true; if the watchpoint could not be created a false value is returned. See the *Examples and practical uses* section on the CD for information on call-backs.

Code	Additional Explanation	Notes
myObject.watch ("myProp", myCallback);	Defines a watchpoint for the myProp property of myObject, and calls myCallback when the value changes.	Returns true if watchpoint created successfully.
myObject.watch (myCallback);	No property to be watched is specified.	

onClipEvent

```
onClipEvent(event){
  code;
}
```

Where event is one of several events and code is the statement(s) to be executed when the event is detected.

This method is compatible with **Flash 5 and later.**

The onClipEvent() method runs an event-triggered set of statements. Flash MX and later allow you to assign functions as an **event handler** instead of using the onClipEvent() method. The newer coding approach is advisable for an event handler. **With Flash MX and later, there is a move away from using the onClipEvent() method in favor of the MovieClip, Mouse, and Key methods of the same names.**

Description

The onClipEvent() **method is** an event handler used to monitor a movie clip for a particular event. The onClipEvent() method is always attached to a movie clip instance. If an event is detected, the statements inside the code block are executed. The events that can be monitored and the triggering conditions are:

- data – triggered when data is received in a loadVariable or loadMovie action.
- enterFrame – triggered when the playhead enters a new frame.
- keyDown – triggered when a keyboard key is depressed.
- keyUp – triggered when a keyboard key is released.
- load – triggered when a movie clip is instantiated and appears on the timeline.
- mouseDown – triggered when a mouse button is depressed.
- mouseMove – triggered when the mouse is moved.
- mouseUp – triggered when a mouse button is released.
- unload – triggered when a movie clip is removed from the timeline.

Whenever one of these events is detected, if an onClipEvent() method has been defined for that event the code inside that code block is executed.

on

```
on (event) {
  code;
}
```

Where event is one of several mouse events and code is the statement(s) to be executed when the event is detected

This method is compatible with **Flash 2 and later.** Not all events are supported with Flash 2.

The on() method runs a mouse event triggered set of statements.

Description

The on() **method** deals with mouse specific events. The on() method is an event handler used to monitor the mouse for a particular event. If that event is detected, the statements inside the code block are executed. The events that can be monitored and the triggering conditions are:

- dragOut – triggered when the cursor is over a button, pressed, then dragged outside the button area.
- dragOver – triggered when the cursor is over the button, pressed, rolled outside the button area, then rolled back over the button area.
- keyPress (key) – triggered when the specific key is pressed.
- press – triggered when a mouse button is pressed while the cursor is over a button.
- release – triggered when a mouse button is released while over a button.
- releaseOutside – triggered when a mouse button is released while the cursor is outside the button, after the button was pressed.
- rollOut – triggered when the pointer rolls outside the button area.
- rollOver – triggered when the pointer rolls over a button.

Whenever one of these events is detected, if an on() method has been defined for that event, the code inside that code block is executed.

or

```
condition1 or condition2
```

Where condition1 and condition2 are conditions to be evaluated to true or false.
This operator is compatible with **Flash 4 and later.** With Flash 5 and later the or operator was deprecated for the more common **|| operator.**

The or operator checks for one of two conditions being true.

Description

The or **operator** returns true if either of the two conditions specified are true. This is a **Logical OR** event. If either of the two conditions are true, the or operator returns true.

Code	Additional explanation	Notes
condition1 or condition2	If condition1 or condition2, are true, returns true.	Deprecated to be replaced by || in Flash 5 and later.

ord

```
ord(char)
```

Where char is the character to convert to an ASCII value.

This function is compatible with **Flash 4 and later.** With Flash 5 and later the **ord** function was deprecated for the **String.charCodeAt() method.** See also **String.charCodeAt().**

Description

The ord **function** returns the ASCII value of a character.

Code	Additional explanation	Notes
myNum = ord("Z");	Returns the ASCII value of the string "Z".	Deprecated and replaced with the String.charCodeAt() method in Flash 5 and later.

_parent

```
_parent.property
_parent._parent.property
```

Where `property` is the property referred to.

This property is compatible with **Flash 4 and later.**

Description

The _parent **property** refers to the parent of the current movie clip or object. You can use the _parent property to specify relative paths to movie clips or objects that are above the current movie clip or object.

Code	Notes
_parent.prop	Refers to the prop property of the parent of the current object of movie clip.

parseFloat

```
parseFloat(string)
```

Where `string` is the string to convert to a floating point number.

This method is compatible with **Flash 5 and later.** See also the entry for **parseInt**.

Description

The parseFloat() **method** is used to convert a string into a floating point number and return the result. The numbers in the string are parsed prior to conversion. If the parse operation reaches a non-numeric value; parsing stops at that point. If no numbers are in the string, NaN is returned. Whitespace is ignored in the string.

Code	Notes
myNum = parseFloat("23h8");	Returns the value 23.
myNum = parseFloat("2.6325Z");	Returns the value 2.6325.
myNum = parseFloat("a23h8");	Returns 63 (it stops parsing at the first non-numeric value).
myNum = parseFloat("63a764");	Returns NaN.
myNum = parseFloat("2+2");	Returns the value 2.

The parseFloat() method cannot be used to evaluate expressions, since the operators are treated as non-numeric characters.

See `parse.fla` and `parse.swf` on the CD for examples of the results of `parseInt()` and `parseFloat()` operations.

parseInt

```
parseInt(string [, radix])
```

Where `string` is the string to convert to an integer number and `radix` is the base for number conversion.

This method is compatible with **Flash 5 and later**. See also the entry for **parseFloat**.

The `parseInt()` method converts a string to an integer number.

Description

The `parseInt()` **method** is used to convert a string into an integer and return the result. The numbers in the string are parsed prior to conversion. If the parse operation reaches a non-numeric value parsing stops at that point. If no numbers are in the string, NaN is returned. Whitespace is ignored in the string. If the string begins with "0x" it is assumed the numbers are hexadecimal (base 16). If the string begins with a "0" (or the radix is specified as 8) the numbers are treated as octal. To use any other radix, specify the value as a parameter. See also the **parseFloat()** method for converting strings to floating point numbers.

Code	Additional explanation	Notes
myNum = parseInt("23h8");	Returns the value 23.	Only numbers up to the first non-numeric character are converted to an integer.
myNum = parseInt("2.6325Z");	Returns the value 2.	The decimal point is treated as a non-numeric character by ().
myNum = parseInt("a23h8");	Returns NaN as the first character is non-numeric so no numbers can be extracted.	
myNum = parseInt("78", 16);	Returns the value of 78 using base 16 (hexadecimal).	
myNum = parseInt("34+23")	Returns the value 34.	The parseInt() method cannot be used to evaluate

expressions, since the
operators are treated as
non-numeric characters

See `parse.fla` and `parse.swf` on the CD for examples of the results of `parseInt()` and `parseFloat()` operations.

play

```
play()
```

This action is compatible with **Flash 2 and later.**

The `play()` action starts the playback of a movie on the timeline.

Description

The `play()` **action** is used to start playback of a movie loaded in the timeline. The playhead will move across the timeline as the playback progresses. If the movie is already being played, issuing another `play()` action will have no effect. For a complete discussion on the use of this action, see the **MovieClip.play()** entry.

Code	Additional explanation	Notes
`play();`	Starts playback of the movie.	By itself, the `play()` action starts playing the timeline This that this action resides . on action is usually encountered in an event handler for a button, in which case it will start playing the timeline the button is on.

`with(root.myMovieClip(){`
   `play();`
`}`
		The `play()` action starts playing the timeline of the movie clip `_root.myMovieClip`.

prevFrame

```
prevFrame()
```

This method is compatible with **Flash 2 and later.**

This moves the playhead to the previous frame and stops there.

Description

The prevFrame() **method** moves the playhead to the previous frame in the timeline, and stops playback at that point. If the current frame is Frame 1, the playhead does not move. See also **nextFrame()**, **MovieClip.nextFrame()**, and **MovieClip.prevFrame()**.

Code	Additional explanation	Notes
prevFrame();	Moves the playhead to the previous frame.	Playback is stopped when the prevFrame() method is called.
prevFrame(5);	No frame number can be specified; see gotoAndStop().	

prevScene

prevScene()

This method is compatible with **Flash 2 and later.**

Description

The prevScene() **method** moves the playhead to the first frame of the previous scene in the timeline, and stops playback at that point. **If there is no previous scene, the playhead does not move.**

Code	Additional explanation	Notes
prevScene();	Moves the playhead to the first frame in the previous scene of a movie and stops the playback at that point.	Playback is stopped when the prevScene() method is called.
prevScene(2);	No frame number can be specified; see gotoAndStop().	

print

print ("target" [, "bounding box"])

Where target is the name of the movie clip to print, and bounding box sets the area of the movie to print.

This method is compatible with **Flash 4 and later.** When using a level, the **printNum()** method is called instead. See also the entry for **printNum**.

The print() method lets you print some or all of a movie.

Description

The print() **method** is used to print some or all of a movie based on boundaries that can be set within the movie.

Code	Additional explanation	Notes
`print("myMovie");`	Prints myMovie.	The movie must be completely loaded before print begins.
`print("myMovie", "bframe");`	Prints myMovie using each frame's bounding box area.	
`myMovie.print("bframe");`	This is not a valid format for the parameters.	

printAsBitmap

```
printAsBitmap ("target" [, "bounding box"])
```

Where target is the name of the movie clip to print and bounding box sets the area of the movie to print.

This method is compatible with **Flash 4 and later.**

The printAsBitmap() method lets you print some or all of a movie.

Description

The printAsBitmap() **method** is used to print some or all of a movie based on boundaries that can be set within the movie, treating the movie clip as a bitmap. The printAsBitmap() method will always print at the highest possible resolution the printer will support.

Code	Additional Explanation	Notes
`printAsBitmap ("myMovie");`	Prints myMovie	The movie must be completely loaded before print begins.
`printAsBitmap ("myMovie", "bframe");`	Prints myMovie using each frame's bounding box area.	
`myMovie.printAsBitmap ("bframe");`	This is not a valid format for the parameters.	

printAsBitmapNum

```
printAsBitmapNum (level [, "bounding box"])
```

Where `level` is the level in the movie to print and `bounding box` sets the area of the movie to print.

This method is compatible with **Flash 4 and later.**

The `printAsBitmapNum()` method lets you print some or all of a movie.

Description

The `printAsBitmapNum()` **method** is used to print some or all of a movie based on boundaries that can be set within the movie, treating the movie clip as a bitmap. The `printAsBitmapNum()` method will always print at the highest possible resolution the printer will support.

Code	Additional explanation	Notes
`printAsBitmapNum(6);`	Prints the movie in level 6.	The movie must be completely loaded before printing begins.
`printAsBitmapNum (6, "bframe");`	Prints level 6 using each frame's bounding box area.	
`myMovie.printAsBitmapNum ("bframe");`	This is not a valid format for the parameters.	

printNum

`printNum (level [, "bounding box"])`

Where `level` is the level in the movie to print and `bounding box` sets the area of the movie to print.

This method is compatible with **Flash 4 and later.** When using a target movie name, the `print()` method is called instead.

The `printNum()` method lets you print some or all of a movie.

Description

The `printNum()` **method** is used to print some or all of a movie based on boundaries that can be set within the movie.

Code	Additional explanation	Notes
`printNum(5);`	Prints the movie in level 5.	The movie must be completely loaded before print begins.
`myMovie.printNum("5");`	This is not a valid format for the parameters.	

Q/R

_quality

```
_quality
```

This property is compatible with **Flash 5 and later.**

The `_quality` property sets or retrieves the amount of anti-aliasing applied to a movie.

Description

The `_quality` **property** sets or retrieves the amount of anti-aliasing applied to a movie clip. The amount of anti-aliasing directly affects the quality of the clip. The possible values of the `_quality` property are:

- LOW – no anti-aliasing on graphics and no smoothing on bitmaps.
- MEDIUM – graphics are anti-aliased with a 2x2 grid and no smoothing on bitmaps.
- HIGH – graphics are anti-aliased with a 4x4 grid and smoothing is applied on static bitmaps.
- BEST – graphics are anti-aliased with a 4x4 grid and smoothing is applied to all bitmaps.

The default value is "HIGH". For a more complete description and examples of using the `_quality` property see the entries for **Button._quality** and **MovieClip._highquality**.

Code	Additional explanation	Notes
`_quality = LOW;`	Never applies anti-aliasing, producing the lowest quality clips.	Anti-aliasing can involve considerable processing overhead.

random

```
random(num)
```

Where num is one more than the maximum random number to generate.

This method is compatible with **Flash 4 and later**. This function was deprecated in Flash 5 in favor of the **Math.random() method**. Unless you are writing legacy Flash 4 code, use the **Math.random()** method instead. See the entry for **Math.Random**.

The `random()` method produces a random number.

Description

The `random()` **method** can be used without a constructor. The method generates a pseudo-random integer number between 0 and one less than the number provided as a parameter. This function was deprecated in Flash 5 in favor of the `Math.random()` method. See the `Math.random()` method for more examples and a description of random numbers.

Code	Additional explanation	Notes
`myNum = random(10);`	Chooses a random number between 0 and 9 and stores that number in Num1.	Generated numbers are only pseudo-random and can be predicted with several runs of random number generation.
`myNum = random();`	No parameters are specified for the range.	This syntax is more in line with that used by `Math.random()`, but is not allowed with the `random()` function, which requires a parameter.

removeMovieClip

```
removeMovieClip(movie)
```

Where `movie` is the name of the movie clip to remove.

This method is compatible with **Flash 4 and later.**

The `removeMovieClip()` method deletes a movie clip instance. For a more detailed description of this method as well as examples, see the **MovieClip.removeMovieClip()** method.

Description

The `removeMovieClip()` **method** is used to delete a movie clip instance that was created with either the **duplicateMovieClip()** or **attachMovie()** methods. See the `MovieClip.removeMovieClip()` method for more information.

Code	Notes
`removeMovieClip("myMovieClip");`	Deletes the movie clip instance `myMovieClip`.
`removeMovieClip();`	No movie clip instance was specified.

return

```
return [expression]
```

Where `expression` is the expression to evaluate and return as a value to the function.

This action is compatible with **Flash 5 and later.**

Description

The return **action** is used to return a value from a function. We can specify an expression to be returned, or the return action can be used with a parameter to signify the completion of the function called.

Code	Additional explanation	Notes
`return;`	Returns execution to the calling code.	If the return action is used without any expression, it returns a null.
`return expression;`	Returns the value of the expression to the calling code.	

_root

```
_root.action
_root.method
_root.MovieClip
_root.property
```

Where action, method, MovieClip, or property is the item referred to. The _root property refers to the root movie clip or object.

This property is compatible with **Flash 4 and later.**

Description

The _root **property** refers to the root of the current movie clip or object. If the currently executing movie has multiple levels, the current level is the _root reference. The _root property is the same as specifying an absolute path (as opposed to _parent which uses relative paths).

Code	Additional explanation	Notes
`_root.prop;`	Refers to the prop property of the root of the current object of movieclip.	Root are determined for multiple levels based on the current level.

scroll

```
textfieldname.scroll = val;
```

Where `textfieldname` is the text field and `val` is the value to scroll.

This property is compatible with **Flash 4 and later**. Note that in Flash 4 and 5 the `textfieldname` refers to the variable name of the text field – this is depreciated in Flash MX. In Flash MX, textfieldname refers to the instance name of the text field.

The `scroll` property defines where in the text field content display starts for the user.

Description

The `scroll` **property** is used to control how much of a text field's content is shown to the user in a text field. The property defines the starting point in the content that is shown on-screen.

Code	Notes
`myText.scroll += 5;`	Moves down 5 lines in the content of `myText`.

Selection

This object is compatible with **Flash 6 and later.**

The `Selection` object is used to control which objects (usually text fields) can be activated by the cursor. When an object has the cursor active in it, it has input focus (as opposed to browser focus).

Description

The `Selection` **object** has many methods attached to it that can be invoked to control the use of an object such as a text field. There is no constructor for the `Selection` object (only one field can have focus at a time).

The `Selection` object deals with selection spans (such as moving through many text fields or buttons). Selection spans indicate which fields are to receive focus in turn. Selection span indexes are zero based (so the first field is 0, the second is 1, and so on). Whenever you are using one of the `Selection` methods, keep in mind that they only work on text fields that have input focus. Only one text field can have input focus at a time.

The `Selection` object contains these methods:

- `Selection.addListener` – registers the text field instance to receive `onSetFocus` events.
- `Selection.getBeginIndex` – returns the index at the beginning of the selection span.
- `Selection.getCaretIndex` – returns the current caret position.

- `Selection.getEndIndex` – returns the index at the end of the selection span.
- `Selection.getFocus` – returns the name of the variable for the current focus.
- `Selection.removeListener` – stops a text field instance from receiving `onSetFocus` events.
- `Selection.setFocus` – sets the text format to have focus.
- `Selection.setSelection` – sets the beginning and end indexes of the selection span.

The `Selection` object has one event handler associated with it:

- `Selection.onSetFocus` – invoked when a field receives focus.

See the subsequent **Selection.*name*** entries for more details on the event handler and individual methods.

Selection.addListener

    Selection.addListener (listener_name)

Where `listener_name` is an object with an `onSetFocus` method.

This method is compatible with **Flash 6 and later.**

The `Selection.addListener()` method registers an object to receive keyboard focus changes.

Description

The `Selection.addListener()` **method** registers the object to allow it to receive keyboard focus change notifications. Whenever a focus change is detected, all registered objects have their `onSetFocus()` method invoked.

Code	Additional explanation	Notes
`Selection.addListener (myObject);`	Registers `myObject` so the `onSetFocus()` method is invoked on focus.	If `myObject` is already registered nothing happens.

Selection.getBeginIndex

    Selection.getBeginIndex()

This method is compatible with **Flash 6 and later.**

The `Selection.getBeginIndex()` method returns the number of the index at the start of the selection span.

Description

The `Selection.getBeginIndex()` **method** returns the index number at the start of the selection span. If no text field has focus, or there is no selection –1 is returned. Finally, if a text field does have focus but there are no characters in that text field, the current value of `Selection.getCaretIndex()` is returned.

Code	Additional explanation	Notes
`selspan1 = Selection.getBeginIndex ();`	Stores the starting index of the selection span in `selspan1`.	If no field has focus a value of –1 is returned.
`selspan1 = Selection.getBeginIndex. () - 1;`	Stores one place to the left of the current position in `selspan1`.	

See `getbeginindex.fla` and `getbeginindex.swf` on the CD for an example of using both methods.

Selection.getCaretIndex

```
Selection.getCaretIndex()
```

This method is compatible with **Flash 6 and later.**

The `Selection.getCaretIndex()` method returns the position of the cursor in the selected text.

Description

The `Selection.getCaretIndex()` method returns the index number where the blinking cursor is currently positioned. If there is no blinking cursor (in other words, the text field does not have input focus) –1 is returned. If the text field has focus but is empty, the value of zero is returned.

Code	Additional explanation	Notes
`selcur = Selection.getCaretIndex ();`	Stores the index of the blinking cursor's object in `selcur`.	If no cursor is present a value of –1 is returned.

See getcaretindex.fla / getcaretindex.swf on the CD for an example of using the `Selection. getCaretIndex()` method.

Selection.getEndIndex

```
Selection.getEndIndex()
```

This method is compatible with **Flash 6 and later.**

The `Selection.getEndIndex()` method returns the index of the character at the end of the selection span.

Description

The `Selection.getEndIndex()` **method** returns the index of the character at the end of the current selection. If no text field has focus, or there is no index –1 is returned. If a text field does have focus but there are no characters in that text field, the current value of `Selection.getCaretIndex()` is returned.

Code	Additional explanation	Notes
`selspan1 = Selection.getEndIndex();`	Stores the ending index number of the selection span in `selspan1`.	If no index is present a value of –1 is returned.

See `getbeginindex.fla` and `getbeginindex.swf` on the CD for an example of using both methods.

Selection.getFocus

`Selection.getFocus()`

This method is compatible with **Flash 6 and later.**

The `Selection.getFocus()` method returns the variable name of the field that has focus.

Description

The `Selection.getFocus()` **method** returns variable name assigned to the text field that has focus. If no text field has focus `null` is returned. The `Selection.getFocus()` method returns the target path as a string if a button or text field instance has focus.

Code	Additional explanation	Notes
`curr = Selection.getFocus();`	Stores the variable name of the field with focus in `curr`.	If no field has focus a `null` is returned.

Selection.onSetFocus

```
Selection.onSetFocus = function (oldfocus, newfocus) {
  Code
}
```

Where `oldfocus` and `newfocus` are the objects, which had and have focus, respectively.

This event handler is compatible with **Flash 6 and later.**

The `Selection.onSetFocus()` event handler is invoked whenever focus changes.

Description

The `Selection.onSetFocus()` **event handler** is invoked whenever focus changes. To have this method invoked the object should be listening (see **Selection.addListener()** to register an object).

Selection.removeListener

`Selection.removeListener (listener_name)`

Where `listener_name` is the `Selection` object to be removed from watching for focus changes.

This object is compatible with **Flash 6 and later.**

When a `Selection` object has been registered using the `Selection.addListener()` method and you want to remove it from the listener list, use `Selection.removeListener()`. See also the entry for **Selection.addListener**.

Description

`Selection` objects that have been registered to listen for focus using `Selection.addListener()` can be removed from the listener list using `Selection.removeListener()` **method**. If the listener is successfully removed, `true` is returned. If the listener did not exist on the list of listener objects, `false` is returned.

Code	Additional explanation	Notes
`Selection.removeListener (myTextobject);`	Removes `myTextobject` from the listener.	If `myTextobject` is either not removed or not registered as a listener, `false` is returned.
		If `myTextobject` is registered and removed successfully, `true` is returned.

Selection.setFocus

`Selection.setFocus("variable")`

Where `variable` is a string indicating the path to the variable associated with the field.

This method is compatible with **Flash 6 and later.**

The `Selection.setFocus()` method applies focus to a field.

Description

The `Selection.setFocus()` **method** is used to apply focus to an editable text field specified as a parameter. The parameter is a string indicating the path to the variable (relative and absolute paths, as well as dot and slash notation are allowed). When a text field or button instance path is specified with the `Selection.setFocus()` method, that button or text field has focus. If a parameter of `null` is provided, current focus is removed. If the focus is set correctly using the `Selection.setFocus()` method, a `true` Boolean is returned; if the focus fails, a `false` value is returned.

Code	Additional explanation	Notes
`Selection.setFocus ("_root.myName");`	Sets focus on `_root.myName`.	If a `null` is specified, focus is removed.

Selection.setSelection

```
Selection.setSelection (begin, end)
```

Where `begin` and `end` are the beginning and ending indices of the selection span and both are non-negative integers.

This method is compatible with **Flash 6 and later.**

The `Selection.setSelection()` method sets the selection span of the current object.

Description

The `Selection.setSelection()` **method** sets the selection span of the current object usually by highlighting the selection range. The new selection span applied to that object will begin at the first parameter and end at the second. If no text field has focus, the `Selection.setSelection()` method has no effect.

The `setSelection()` method selects (highlights) the characters from `beginIndex` to `endIndex-1` in the text field with focus. If no field has focus, `setSelection()` has no effect. It is commonly used to highlight problematic user input.

Code	Additional explanation	Notes
`Selection.setSelection ( 3, 9);`	Sets the selection span to start at 3 and end at 9.	If no text field has current focus the command is ignored.

set variable

```
set(variable, expression);
```

Where a new variable will be created with the name of `variable` and its value will be `expression`.

This function is compatible with **Flash 4 and later**. There are **no known issues** with any version of Flash that supports this object.

The `set` function is used to assign a value, `expression`, to a variable, `variable`. You can use the `set` function regardless of `expression`'s data type (`String`, `Number`, `Boolean`, etc.). The data type of the new variable will be established at runtime (when the code is executed, not compiled) and can be modified. See also the **var** operator.

Description
Use this **function** to assign a value to a variable.

Code	Additional Explanation	Notes
`set("myVariable", "foobar");`	Returns a variable, `myVariable`, with a value of `"foobar"`.	
`set("myObject", new Object());`	Returns an object named `myObject`.	
`set("person", {name: "foobar", age: 21});`	Returns an object named `person`.	The `person` object will contain two properties, `name` and `age`, with the values `foobar` and `21`.

`extension = "bar";`
`set("foo"+extension,`
➥ `"string");`
	Returns a variable, `foobar`, with a value of `string`.	This example uses the **+ (addition operator)** to concatenate two strings to form the name of a variable.

`set(myVariable, "string");`	Returns nothing.	The first parameter of the `set` function must be a String.

See the examples `set.fla` and `set.swf` on the CD.

setInterval

```
setInterval(functionName, interval [, arg1, ...., argN]);
setInterval(object, methodName, interval [, arg1, ...., argN]);
intID = setInterval(functionName, interval [, arg1, ...., argN]);
```

Syntax 1

Where `functionName` is a named function, `interval` is the desired length of time, in milliseconds, in which the function will be repeatedly called, and `arg1` through `argN` are optional parameters that will be passed to `functionName`.

Syntax 2

Where `object` is a reference to an object (or class), `methodName` is the name of a method of `object` which will be executed, and `interval` is the length of time, in milliseconds, in which the method will be executed, continually. `arg1` through `argN` are optional parameters.

Syntax 3

Where everything is identical to Syntax 1 but `intID` will contain a number representing that particular interval's ID.

This object is compatible with **Flash 6**. There are **no known issues** with the version of Flash that supports this object.

The `setInterval` function is used to create an event that repeats continuously until the Flash movie is closed or the **clearInterval** function is passed the interval's ID.

A method of an object, a named function, or an anonymous function can be supplied to the `setInterval` function and it will always return a number (a reference for the interval). The `interval` parameter should be a number representing the number of milliseconds in which to repeat the event. See also **clearInterval**.

Description

This **function** is used to set up a repeat event in which the user defines how often the event will occur.

Code	Additional Explanation	Notes
`setInterval( function () {` `trace("repeat event"); },` `1000);`	The following code will send the string `repeat event` to the Output window.	This code uses an anonymous function. Therefore the only way to manipulate this repeat event is to remove the interval using `clearInterval`, the interval's ID, and redefine it referencing a named function or new anonymous function.

Code	Additional Explanation	Notes

```myObject = new Object();```
 ```myObject.myMethod =```
 ```function () {```
 ```   trace("my trace");```
 ``` }```
 	
 ```setInterval(myObject,```
 ```➥ "myMethod", 1000);```
	The following code sets a repeat event to call the myMethod method of the myObject object every second.	This example uses the object version of the setInterval function.

```function intCallback(arg1,```
 ```arg2) {```
 ```   trace(arg1);```
 ```   trace(arg2);```
 ```}```
 	
 ```setInterval(intCallback,```
 ```➥1000, "argument 1",```
 ```➥ "argument 2");```
	The following code passes two arguments to the intCallback function.	

```function```
 ```intCallback(argument```
 ```String) {```
 ```   trace(argumentString[0]);```
 ```   trace(argumentString[1]);```
 	
 ```}```
 	
 ```setInterval(intCallback,```
 ```➥1000, ["argument 1",```
 ```➥"argument 2"]);```
	The following code passes two arguments to the intCallback function.	The arguments are supplied in the array argumentString with each argument in a different key.

```function traceValue() {```
 ```   // code here```
 ```}```
 	
 ```setInterval("traceValue",```
 ```➥1000);```
	This code will not create an interval.	If you're using the function method of the setInterval function (rather than the object method), don't pass the function name as a string. You need to pass a reference to the function.

This code will not create an interval.	If you're using the function method	of the setInterval function (rather than the object method), you need to reference the function, not name it.

``
myObject = new Object();
myObject.myMethod =
function () {
 	
    trace("my trace");
 	
}
 	
setInterval(myObject,
myMethod, 1000);
``
	This code will not create an interval.	The methodName parameter of the setInterval function (when using it in object mode) needs to be a String. However, the actual reference to the object cannot be a String value.

See the examples setinterval.fla and setinterval.swf on the CD.

SharedObject

This object is addressed in Chapter 11.

SharedObject is a top level object that doesn't need to be invoked by the new constructor. It is used to store information on the client's hard drive, much like a cookie stored by web browsers. Shared objects are useful for storing information that you want to retrieve the next time the SWF file is accessed, such as a user's name and details, game high scores, notes, etc. See also **SharedObject.getLocal**, **SharedOject.data**, and Chapter 12.

This object is compatible with **Flash 6**. There is one known issue with the flush method of this object, see **SharedObject.flush** for more information.

Description

This **object** is used to store data on a client's machine that can be retrieved, altered, and re-saved as needed.

SharedObject.data

```
mySO.data.username = "foobar";
```

Where an attribute, username, of the data property from the shared object referenced by mySO will be created with a string value of foobar.

The property is compatible with **Flash 6 and above**. There are **no known issues** with any version of Flash that supports this object.

The data property of the SharedObject object is used to hold all the information that is to be saved to the disk. The attributes of this property will be written to a local file when the SharedObject.flush method is executed or the Flash movie is ended. Shared objects can store any of the following data types: Array, Boolean, Date, Object, Number, String, and XML object. See also **SharedObject.flush** and **SharedObject.getSize**.

The data property is an object of the type Object object of the SharedObject object, hence the dot notation used to access its attributes. The data type of the data property cannot be changed and will remain an object. All attempts to modify its data type will be ignored.

Description
This **property** holds all the information that will be written to a local file when the SharedObject.flush method is executed.

Code	Additional Explanation	Notes
mySO.data.username = ➡"foobar";	Using a String data type.	
mySO.data.allowAccess = true;	Using a Boolean data type.	
mySO.data.count = 1;	Using a Number data type.	
mySO.data.information = new Array({name: "John", age:45}, {name: "Dan", age:43}, {name: "Joe", age:14});	Returns the information property containing an array with three keys. Each key is an object containing two properties, name and age.	An example of using one attribute of the data property to store both Array data types and Object data types.

mySO.data = "String	Returns nothing.	The data property has a data type
⇒data type";		of Object object. This cannot be
		changed, all attempts to alter this,
		such as this example, are ignored.

See the examples `sharedobjectflush.fla` and `sharedobjectflush.swf` on the CD.

SharedObject.flush

```
mySO.flush();
mySO.flush(bytes);
soflush = mySO.flush(bytes);
```

Where the shared object referenced by mySO is saved to a local file on the client's hard drive. The optional parameter, bytes, is the amount of disk space that is required for the shared object.

This method is compatible with **Flash 6**. There are **no known issues** with the version of Flash that supports this method. See also **SharedObject.getSize**.

A shared object has the same format and structure as an object of the type Object object. However you need to use the supplied methods and properties of the SharedObject object to access and manipulate a shared object. See also **SharedObject.getSize**.

The flush method can return three possible values: the Boolean values of true and false or a string value of pending. If a true value is returned, the shared object has been successfully saved to the client's hard disk. This means the client has permitted local information storage for shared objects from your domain and the amount of allotted disk space is sufficient for the size of the shared object.

If the Boolean false is returned by the flush method, it means the client has explicitly denied local information storage from the current domain, or the user has denied the amount of information required to store the local shared object. The Boolean false may also be returned if the shared object failed to write the information to disk.

If a string with the value of pending is returned, the amount of disk space allotted for this domain is insufficient to write the shared object to disk. In this case, a dialog box is presented to the user asking to increase the amount of disk space allotted for this domain. If the user denies this request **SharedObject.onStatus** is invoked with a code property of SharedObject.flush.failed.

Description
This **method** is used to immediately write shared objects to a local file.

Code	Additional Explanation	Notes
`mySO.flush();`		Saves the locally persistent shared object to the client's hard drive.
`mySO.flush(1000);`	The `1000` parameter represents bytes.	Use the optional `bytes` parameter to acquire the minimum amount of disk space you'll need. You should work out the minimum amount of disk space (in bytes) that your shared object will require. Pass that amount when using `flush` for the first time. This will allow your shared object to enlarge in size over time without requiring the user to accept or modify settings continuously.

See the examples `sharedobjectflush.fla` and `sharedobjectflush.swf` on the CD.

SharedObject.getLocal

```
mySO = SharedObject.getLocal("objectName");
mySO = SharedObject.getLocal("objectName", "path");
```

Where a local shared object with the name of `objectName` is retrieved or created and assigned to the `mySO` variable. The optional `path` parameter defines a specific path to the shared object file.

This method is compatible with **Flash 6**. There are **no known issues** with the version of Flash that supports this object.

This method is used to both retrieve and create a local shared object. The shared object, retrieved or created, is locally persistent and available only to the current client. `getLocal` should be the first method called when working with shared objects. Once you have retrieved the shared object, you can check for the existence of attributes of the `data` property that have been saved in previous sessions. See also **SharedObject.flush**.

The `objectName` parameter can include a forward slash, for example `globalsharedobjects/userinformation` or `globalsharedobjects/historyinformation`. However, the name cannot include any of the following characters: ~ % & \ ; : " ' , < > ? #. It should be noted that the name you choose for a shared object will alter the path and filename of the SOL file associated with your shared object. If you include a forward slash in the name, for example `mySO = SharedObject.get`

`Local("so/myso");` (from a SWF file named `mySoTest.swf`) the file will be stored in the follow directory:

`{pathToSharedObject}/{domain}/mySoTest.swf/#so/myso.sol.`

The `path` parameter is optional; if you don't pass a value for this parameter the Flash Player automatically use the default value. The default value is the full path to the SWF file that created shared object. For example, you may have visited a page on `macromedia.com` that loaded a SWF file created a shared object named `flashcookie` at:

`http://www.macromedia.com/software/flash/mx/information.swf.`

The shared object would reside in the following location on your hard drive:

`{pathToSharedObject}/macromedia.com/software/flash/mx/information.swf/flashcoo` `.sol`

Using the full path as the default value avoids shared object name collisions between domains and wit the same domain. This will enable two different domains to have the same name for a shared ob without any conflicts.

The `path` parameter is optional and will define the path to the local shared object (on the hard dri however, all shared objects will be stored in the current `{domain}` folder. The following table show range of different settings and results when using the `path` parameter.

Location of SWF file	Shared object name and path	Resulting .sol file location
`http://www.macromedia.com` `/software/flashplayer/ve` `rsion6/mymovie.swf`	`SharedObject.getLocal` `("flashcookie", "/");`	`{pathToSharedObject}` `/macromedia.com/fla` `shcookie.sol`
`http://www.macromedia.com` `/software/flashplayer/ve` `rsion6/mymovie.swf`	`SharedObject.getLocal` `("flashcookie",` `"/generalinfo/");`	`{pathToSharedObject}` `/macromedia.com/gen` `eralinfo/flashcookie.sol`
`http://www.macromedia.com` `/software/flashplayer/ve` `rsion6/mymovie.swf`	`SharedObject.getLocal` `("flashcookie/mySo",` `"/software/flashplayer");`	`{pathToSharedObject}` `/macromedia.com/sof` `tware/flashplayer/#` `flashcookie/mySo.sol`

Description

This **method** is used to retrieve or create a locally persistent shared object.

Code	Additional Explanation	Notes

`mySO = Shared`
`Object.getLocal("foo");`
 	
`if (mySO.data.username ==`
`undefined) promptFor`
`Username();`
		A common use for shared objects is to store information about a user such as a username, real name, and an age. This code retrieves a shared object, checks for the username attribute, and if it doesn't exist, executes a custom function to retrieve a username.

`mySO = Shared`
`Object.getLocal("foo");`
 	
`t = new Date();`
`currentDate = t.getDate();`
 	
`if (mySO.data.last`
`Accessed < currentDate`
`- 5) updateNews();`
		This is an example of using shared objects to create a session. It subtracts 5 days from the `currentDate` variable and checks that value against the date the movie was last accessed (store in the `lastAccessed` attribute). If the movie hasn't been accessed in five days, the movie calls the custom `updateNews` function, which could be used to pull information from a server.

`mySO = new SharedObject();` Incorrect usage. `mySO.getLocal("foo");`		The `SharedObject` object is a top level object and doesn't need to be initiated via the `new` constructor. This object exists as soon as the Flash Player starts executing your file, much like the `Stage` object.

See the following examples on the CD:

```
SharedObject.getLocal.fla / SharedObject.getLocal.swf
SharedObject.getLocal2.fla / SharedObject.getLocal2.swf
SharedObject.getLocal3.fla / SharedObject.getLocal3.swf
```

SharedObject.getSize

```
var sizeOfSO = mySO.getSize();
```

Where the variable `sizeOfSO` is defined and its value is the size, in bytes, of the shared object referenced as `mySO`.

This method is compatible with **Flash 6**. There are **no known issues** with the version of Flash that supports this object.

This method is used to evaluate the size of a shared object. This method can be used before the `flush` method to determine if an increase in the allocated disk space for the current domain is needed. If so, you could warn the user with an explanation of what may happen and why, before you execute the `flush` method. See also **SharedObject.flush**.

Description
This **method** is used to retrieve the size of a locally persistent shared object, in bytes.

Code	Notes

`var sizeOfSO = mySO.getSize();`
 	
`if (sizeOfSO > 100) warnUser();`	

`if (mySO.getSize() > 100) warnUser();`	This example uses the method within an `if` statement, without the prior assignment of its value to a variable.

See the examples `sharedobjectgetsize.fla` (`sharedobjectgetsize.swf`)on the CD.

SharedObject.onStatus

```
mySO.onStatus = function(obj) { //code in here };

statusCheck = function (obj) { //code here};
mySo.onStatus = statusCheck;
```

Syntax 1
Where the `onStatus` event is being assigned to an anonymous function (the event handler). `obj` is an `information` object that has two properties, `code` and `level`.

Syntax 2
Where the `onStatus` event is being assigned to the named `statusCheck` function (the event handler). `obj` is an `information` object that has two properties, `code` and `level`.

This method is compatible with **Flash 6 and above**. There is **one known issue** with Flash 6 and this method. When testing your movie in the Flash MX authoring mode, using Control > Test Movie, the Macromedia Flash Player Settings dialog will not always display if needed (to request for more allocated space) and the request for more allocated disk space is automatically denied. However, if you test the same code in a browser or the stand-alone Flash Player, the Macromedia Flash Player Settings dialog will display as normal. (Note that this error is intermittent and will not always occur.) There are no other known issues. See also **SharedObject.flush**.

The onStatus event is the only event of the SharedObject object. It is invoked on error, warning, or for any piece of information regarding the status of a shared object. The error, warning, or information messages within the onStatus event are passed to the parameter object (also known as the information object), obj. Access the information object and its properties to retrieve the error, warning, or information messages. There are two properties of the information object, level and code. The level property contains the level or class of the status event with three possible string values (error, status, warning). The code property details why the onStatus event was invoked. The following table details what the code property will be depending on the level property.

level of status event	The string value of the code property	Explanation
error	`"SharedObject.Flush.Failed"`	This means the SharedObject.flush command that returned the string "pending" failed to write the shared object. This could be because of an error, or the user rejected the request for more allocated disk space.
status	`"SharedObject.Flush.Success"`	This means the SharedObject.flush command that returned the string "pending" has successfully written the shared object to disk. This means that either the user already had the required amount of disk space allotted to the current domain, or that the user accepted the request for more allocated disk space.
warning		This means that the flush was successful but returned some minor issues.

Description
This **event** is used to provide error, warning, or information messages about the status of a shared object.

Code	Notes
```mySO.onStatus = function(obj) {` ` //code in here` `}```	Assigning an anonymous function to the event.
```statusCheck = function (obj) {` ` //code here` `}``` `mySo.onStatus = statusCheck;`	Assigning a named function to the event.
`mySO.onStatus = "functonName";`	Will result in no onStatus event handler. You need to reference a function or assign an anonymous function. You can't use a string literal.

See the example `sharedobjectonstatus.fla` and `sharedobjectonstatus.swf` **on the CD.**

Sound

This object is addressed in Chapter 5.

This object is used when you want to dynamically add sound to your Flash movie at runtime. With this object you can add sound, load sounds from files on a server, and among others alter the volume of the sound. You should use this method to retain ultimate control over your sound, rather than applying a sound to a frame, which gives you limited options at runtime for dynamically controlling the sound. See also **Sound Constructor** and Chapter 5.

The object is compatible with **Flash 5 and later**. There are **no known issues** with any version of Flash that supports this object.

Description

The Sound **object** is used to add and control sound elements in a Flash movie via ActionScript, at runtime.

Sound Constructor

```
mySound = new Sound();
mySound = new Sound(targetMovieClip);
```

Syntax 1

Where an instance of the Sound object is being defined as mySound.

Syntax 2

Where an instance of the Sound object is being defined as mySound. The optional parameter targetMovieClip defines the target object of the sound.

The object is compatible with **Flash 5 and later**. There are **no known issues** with any version of Flash that supports this object.

The Sound constructor is used to create a new instance of the Sound object. Using the Sound object gives you ultimate control over a particular sound in your Flash movie. If you were to simply place a sound on a timeline in authoring mode, your options are very limited if you want to modify or control the sound. Therefore this object should be used to add sound to your movie if you want to manipulate it at runtime. It will ensure you have flexibility and customization options available when working with sounds.

The optional parameter targetMovieClip can be used to specify a movie clip in which to wrap the Sound object. If you don't specify a target movie clip the sound will become a global sound. See below for more information.

Description

This **constructor** will create a new instance of the Sound object.

Code	Notes
mySound = new Sound();	Creating an instance of the Sound object without a target. It is a global sound.
mySound = new Sound(mySoundTarget);	A target is specified this time, so you can control this sound independently of the global sounds.

See the example files sound.fla and sound.swf on the CD.

Sound.attachSound

```
mySound.attachSound("myButtonSound")
```

Where the sound from the Library with a linkage identifier of myButtonSound will be attached to the mySound instance of the Sound object.

This method is compatible with **Flash 5 and later**. There are **no known issues** with any version of Flash that supports this object.

The attachSound method is used to attach a sound from the Library at runtime. If you want to use this method you need to import a sound into your Library while in authoring mode. Any sounds that you wish to use via the attachSound method need to have unique linkage identifier names. See also **Sound.start** and **Sound.loadSound**.

Description
This **method** attaches a sound from the library to the specified Sound object using a linkage identifier.

Code	Notes
mySound.attachSound("buttonSound");	Basic use of the attachSound method.
mySound.attachSound(userDefinedSound);	Using a variable for the identifier parameter. The value of userDefinedSound should be a string that matches the linkage identifier from one of the sounds in the Library.

See the example soundattachsound.fla and soundattachsound.swf on the CD.

Sound.duration

```
var totalLength = mySound.duration;
```

Where totalLength will have a value equal to that of the length of the mySound Sound object.

This method is compatible with **Flash 6**. There are **no known issues** with the version of Flash that supports this object.

The duration read-only property references the length of a particular sound. This property is internally defined when the sound loads and the value is expressed in milliseconds. This property can be used for programming purposes or to inform users of how long a sound will play or has left to play. See also **Sound.position**.

Description

This **method** returns the length of the specified Sound object in milliseconds.

Code	Notes
`var totalLength = mySound.duration;`	Typical use of the duration property.

`var milliseconds = mySound.duration;`
 	
`var seconds = milliseconds/100;`
	Will return the length of a particular sound in seconds.

`mySound.duration = 100;`	Incorrect usage. The duration property is read-only and therefore cannot be defined.

See the examples soundduration.fla and soundduration.swf on the CD.

Sound.getBytesLoaded

```
var bytesLoaded = mySound.getBytesLoaded();
```

Where the variable bytesLoaded will be defined with a value equal to the number of bytes progressively loaded in the specified Sound object.

This method is compatible with **Flash 6**. There are **no known issues** with the version of Flash that supports this object.

The bytesLoaded method retrieves the number of bytes of a sound file that is loading into the Flash Player at the time the method is executed. This information can be used to determine the percentage of the sound that has loaded. This method only works in conjunction with a sound that is being loaded via the loadSound method. See all **Sound.loadSound** and **Sound.getBytesTotal**.

Description

This **method** retrieves the number of bytes of a sound file that is loading into the Flash Player.

Code	Notes
```onClipEvent(enterFrame) { var bytesLoaded = mySound.getBytesLoaded(); trace("The sound has loaded " + bytesLoaded + "sound"); }```	On every new frame, information about how many bytes have loaded will be sent to the Output window.
```onClipEvent(enterFrame) { percentage = mySound.getBytesLoaded() / mySound.getBytesTotal() * 100; }```	This code finds the percentage of the sound which has loaded on every new frame and sets the percentage variable accordingly.

See the examples soundgetbytesloaded.fla and soundgetbytesloaded.swf on the CD.

Sound.getBytesTotal

```
var totalSize = mySound.getBytesTotal();
```

Where the variable totalSize is being defined with a value equal to that of the total bytes of the specified Sound object.

The object is compatible with **Flash 6**. There are **no known issues** with the version of Flash that supports this object.

This method is used to retrieve the total size, in bytes, of a sound file that is being loaded from a remote location. Used in conjunction with the getBytesLoaded method you can use the values to determine the percentage of the sound that has loaded. See also **Sound.getBytesLoaded.**

Description
This **method** returns the total size, in bytes, of a remote sound file.

Code	Notes

`mySound = new Sound();`
`mySound.loadSound("mySound.mp3");`
 	
`var totalSize = mySound.getBytesTotal();`
	`totalSize` will be a number representing the size of the sound file, in bytes.

`mySound = new Sound();`
`mySound.attachSound("mySound");`
 	
`var totalSize = mySound.getBytesTotal();`
	`totalSize` will be equal to `undefined`.
	
	You can only use the `getBytesTotal` method on a `Sound` object which uses `loadSound` to load in a sound file.

See the examples `soundgetbytestotal.fla` and `soundgetbytestotal.swf` on the CD.

Sound.getPan

```
var soundPan = mySound.getPan ()
```

Where the variable `soundPan` will have a value equaling that of the pan setting of the `mySound` Sound object.

This method is compatible with **Flash 5 and later**. There are **no known issues** with any version of Flash that supports this object.

The `getPan` method is used to retrieve the pan setting of the specified sound. The pan of a sound is the left-right balance in which the sound will play through the speakers. The `getPan` method will return an integer between the values -100 and 100, with -100 being the left channel (left speaker) and 100 being the right channel (right speaker). 0 is the equivalent of the sound being played equally through the left and right channels. This method could be used to reset the panning of a sound if it has been changed by the user. See also **Sound.setPan**, **Sound.setVolume**, and **Sound.setTransform**.

Description
This **method** will return an integer between -100 and 100 representing the left-right balance of a Sound object.

Code	Notes
`var soundPan = mySound.getPan();`	Standard format of this method.

`if (mySound.getPan() != "0") mySound.setPan(0);`	This `if` statement will check if the sound is evenly balanced between the left and right speakers. If it isn't, it will balance the sound equally

See the examples `soundgetpan.fla` and `soundgetpan.swf` on the CD.

Sound.getTransform

```
var soundTransform = mySound.getTransform();
```

Where the variable `soundTransform` is being defined with a value equal to that set by the last `setTransform` method call.

This method is compatible with **Flash 5 and later**. There are **no known issues** with any version of Flash that supports this object.

The `getTransform` method will return the settings established with the last known `getTransform` call. This method should be used to query the current transform settings and then perform an action based on the results. See also **Sound.setTransform**. The return data type is an object with the following properties: `rl`, `rr`, `lr`, `ll`. Even if you haven't applied transform settings using the `setTransform` method, an object with those properties will still be returned.

Description
This **method** returns an object containing properties representing settings applied with the last `getTransform` method call.

Code	Notes
`var soundTransform = mySound.getTransform();`	The standard format for this method.

`var soundTransform = mySound.getTransform();`
 	
`if (soundTransform.rr == 100) {`
 	
`    mySound.setTransform({rr: 50, lr: 50});`
 	
`}`
	This code checks the `rr` property to see if it is the default, which is `rr`. If it is, it modifies the `rr` and `lr` properties, causing the sound to be played primarily through the left speaker.

See the examples `soundgettransform.fla` and `soundgettransform.swf` on the CD.

Sound.getVolume

```
var soundVolume = mySound.getVolume();
```

Where the variable soundVolume is being defined representing the volume of the mySound Sound object.

This method is compatible with **Flash 5 and later**. There are **no known issues** with any version of Flash that supports this object.

This method is used to evaluate the volume level of a particular sound. It will return an integer from 0 (sound off) to 100 where the volume is at full level. From there you can do a wide range of things to manipulate the sound. You could use it to apply a percentage level on the current volume. For example, if the current volume was at 50 and you wanted to decrease the volume by 50%, the new volume would be 25.

Description
This **method** will retrieve the volume level of the specified sound.

Code	Notes
`var soundVolume = mySound.getVolume();`	The standard format for this method.

`var soundVolume = mySound.getVolume();`
 	
`if (soundVolume > 80 && userSettings.soundLevel`
`➥ == "soft") warningAlert("Volume is too high for`
`➥ the users current settings.");`
	This code evaluates the current volume level against predefined settings chosen by the user. This user has chosen to have a soft sound volume and the example code states that sound volume of 80 or higher is too loud so the custom warningAlert function has been called.

`getVolume(mySound);`	Incorrect usage. getVolume is a property of the Sound object, not a global function. Therefore an instance of the sound object must be used to call this method.

See the examples soundgetvolume.fla and soundgetvolume.swf on the CD.

Sound.loadSound

```
mySound.loadSound("soundFile", streaming);
```

Where the sound file soundFile is being dynamically loaded into the mySound instance of the Sound object. The optional streaming parameter denotes if the sound is an event sound or a streaming sound.

This method is compatible with **Flash 6**. There are **no known issues** with the version of Flash that supports this object.

The loadSound method dynamically loads the specified sound file into the Flash movie. The first parameter references the path, from the current Flash movie to the sound file, and the second parameter streaming, denotes if the file should be streamed or not. Only the Boolean values true or false will be accepted for the streaming parameter. If it is set to true, the file will start playing as soon as enough data has been loaded. If the streaming parameter is set to false, the sound will load but won't start playing. You will need to call the Sound.start method to start the sound playing once it has finished loading. An mp3 file is the only sound type that can be loaded. See also **Sound.start** and **Sound.onLoad**.

Description

This **method** loads a sound file into the Flash movie at runtime.

Code	Notes
`mySound.loadSound("sounds/mySound.mp3", true);`	This will load in the mySound.mp3 file from the sounds directory. The sound is set to streaming so the sound will begin playback as soon as enough data has loaded.

`mySound.loadSound("sounds/mySound.mp3", false);`
`mySound.onLoad = function () {`
 	
`    mySound.start();`
`}`
	This sound file will load in full before it can start playback. The start method will need to be executed to start the sound playing.

`mySound.loadSound(sounds/mySound.mp3, true);`	Incorrect usage. The first parameter needs to be a string literal, or a variable of a String data type containing the path to sound file.

```
mySound.loadSound("sounds/mySound.mp3");
```

Incorrect usage. loadSound requires
two parameters to load a sound file.

See the examples `soundloadsound.fla` and `soundloadsound.swf` on the CD.

Sound.onLoad

```
mySound.onLoad = function () { //code here }
mySound.onLoad = onLoadCallback;
```

Where the onLoad event is, firstly, receiving an anonymous function and, secondly, referencing a named function, onLoadCallback, used as an onLoad event handler.

This method is compatible with **Flash 6**. There are **no known issues** with the version of Flash that supports this object.

The onLoad event is invoked when a sound which has been loaded via the loadSound method has completely loaded. You could incorporate methods to start the sound playing or notify the user that the sound is ready for use. See also **Sound.loadSound**, **Sound.start** and **Sound.onSoundComplete**.

Description
This **event** is invoked when a sound file has completely loaded into an instance of the Sound object.

Code	Notes

`mySound.onLoad = function () {`
 	
    `notifyUser({sound: "loaded"});`
 	
`}`
	Using an anonymous function as an event handler for the mySound Sound object.

`onLoadCallback = function () {`
 	
    `notifyUser();`
 	
`}`
 	
`mySound.onLoad = onLoadCallback;`
	Using a named function to handle the onLoad event.

See the examples `soundonload.fla` and `soundonload.swf` on the CD.

Sound.onSoundComplete

```
mySound.onSoundComplete = function () { // code here }
mySound.onSoundComplete = myCallbackFunction;
```

Where the onSoundComplete event is being assigned to an anonymous function, and secondly, assigning a named function to the onSoundComplete event.

The object is compatible with **Flash 6**. There are **no known issues** with the version of Flash that supports this object.

The onSoundComplete event will give notification to a callback function when the particular sound has finished playing. To receive notification from the onSoundComplete event, you need to reference an anonymous function or a named function. The following example is using an anonymous function:

```
mySound.onSoundComplete = function () {
  trace("mySound onSoundComplete");
}
```

... and the following code uses a named function:

```
myCallbackFunction = function () {

  trace("mySound onSoundComplete");

}
mySound.onSoundComplete = myCallbackFunction;
```

Description

This **event** is invoked when a particular sound is finished playing.

Code	Notes

`mySound.SoundComplete = function () {`
`    mySound.start();`
`}`
	A sound loop. When the sound finishes playing it will be automatically started again.

See the examples soundattachsound.fla and soundattachsound.swf on the CD.

Sound.position

```
var soundPosition = mySound.position;
```

Where the variable `soundPosition` will have a value equal to that of the number of milliseconds that the `mySound` Sound object has been playing for.

This property is compatible with **Flash 6 and later**. There are **no known issues** with the version of Flash that supports this object.

This read-only property will return a number, expressed in milliseconds, representing how long the sound has been playing. The `position` property will be reset to 0 each time the sound loops. The `position` property is useful for indicating to the user where the sound is currently at, compared with the length of the sound. The `position` property can be used with the `duration` property to determine the current position of the song in a percentage of the total and elapsed times.

Description

This **property** represents how long the sound has been playing, expressed in milliseconds.

Code	Notes

`var soundPosition = mySound.position;`
 	
`trace("the song has been playing for " +`
`soundPosition/1000 + " seconds.");`
	A number, expressed in seconds, will be sent to the Output window representing how long the sound has been playing.

`mySound.position = 200;`	Incorrect usage. The position property is read-only and can therefore not be defined by the user.

See the examples `soundposition.fla` and `soundposition.swf` on the CD.

Sound.setPan

```
mySound.setPan(pan);
```

Where the `setPan` method is executed specifying the panning of the `mySound` Sound object.

This method is compatible with **Flash 6**. There are **no known issues** with the version of Flash that supports this object.

The `setPan` method is used to define the left-right balance of the sound. The parameter pan, will accept an integer in the range of -100 to 100, where -100 is left and 100 is right. Therefore a pan value of 0 is centered, with the sound being played equally through both the left and right speakers.

Description
This **method** is used to specify the left-right balance of which the sound will play through the speakers.

Code	Additional Explanation	Notes
`mySound.setPan(-100);`	This will result in all of the sounds for the mySound Sound object playing through the left speaker.	
`mySound.setPan(mySound.getPan()+20);`		Modifying the pan of a sound using the current value of the pan.
`mySound.setPan("left");`	Incorrect usage.	The setPan method only accepts an integer, not a string or any other data type.

See the examples `soundsetpan.fla` and `soundsetpan.swf` on the CD.

Sound.setTransform

```
mySound.setTransform(transformObject);
```

Where the `transformObject` object is being supplied to the `mySound` instance of the `Sound` object.

This method is compatible with **Flash 5 and later**. There are **no known issues** with any version of Flash that supports this object.

The `setTransform` method is used to alter the left-right balance of a sound. Using this method you can simulate a stereo sound as a mono sound, and a mono sound as a stereo sound. You can create sound effects that you commonly can't with the `setPan` and `setVolume` methods, even when they're combined.

To apply these settings you need to pass an object with pre-determined properties to the `setTransform` method. The following table has list of the properties of a transform object and what they represent.

Property	Represents
"ll"	Represents how much of the left input to the play in the left speaker and should be an integer between 0 and 100.
"lr"	Represents how much of the right input to play in the left speaker and should be an integer between 0 and 100.
"rr"	Represents how much of the right input to play in the right speaker and should be an integer between 0 and 100.
"rl"	Represents how much of the left input to play in the right speaker and should be an integer between 0 and 100.

Based on the values of those properties, a result for both the left and right output is determined using the following formula:

```
leftOutput = left_input * ll + right_input * lr
rightOutput = right_input * rr + left_input * rl
```

In the formula, the values for left_input and right_input are determined by which type of sound you are using (either stereo or mono). Mono sounds play all sound output in the left speaker.

The following is the default transform setting for stereo sounds:

```
ll = 100
lr = 0
rr = 100
rl = 0
```

The following is the default transform setting for mono sounds:

```
ll = 100
lr = 100
rr = 0
rl = 0
```

Description
This **method** supplies a transform object to the Sound object, which modifies the left-right balance of a sound.

Code	Additional Explanation	Notes

`transformObject = new Object();`
 	
`transformObject.ll = 50;`
`transformObject.lr = 50;`
`transformObject.rr = 50;`
`transformObject.rl = 50;`
 	
`mySound.setTransform (transformObject);`
	The sound will play half of the left input through the left speaker and half of the left input through the right speaker; half of the right input through the right speaker and half of the right input through the left speaker.	This will take each channel of a stereo sound, split them up, and distribute evenly between all channels (speakers).

`mySound.setTransform ("transformObject");`	Incorrect data type.	The parameter must reference a transform object, therefore it can't be a string data type.

See the example soundgettransform.fla / soundgettransform.swf on the CD.

Sound.setVolume

```
mySound.setVolume(volume);
```

Where the volume level of mySound will be set to the value of volume.

The object is compatible with **Flash 5 and later**. There are **no known issues** with any version of Flash that supports this object.

The setVolume method is used to modify the volume of the sound. The method will accept an integer between 0 and 100, where 0 is silent and 100 is full volume. The integer you pass actually represents a percentage of the total volume. See also **Sound.getVolume** and **Sound.setTransform**.

Description
This **method** defines the loudness of a Sound object, using an integer representing a percentage of the full volume.

Code	Notes
`mySound.setVolume(50);`	Setting the volume to 50% of full Volume.

`on(release) {`
`    mySound.setVolume(mySound.getVolume()+10);`
`}`
	This is an example of controlling the sound through the `onRelease` event of a button. When the button is released, after being pressed, the sound will increase by 10%.

`mySound.setVolume("100");`	This code will fail. Only an integer will be accepted by `setVolume`.

See the examples `soundsetvolume.fla` and `soundsetvolume.swf` on the CD.

Sound.start

```
mySound.start();
mySound.start(offset);
mySound.start(offset, loop);
```

Where `mySound` will start playing. There are two optional parameters, `offset` and `loop`. `offset` specifies how far into the sound to start playing, in seconds. For example if you have a 30 second sound and you want to start playing in the middle, you would use the following code:

```
mySound.start(15);
```

The `loop` parameter defines how many times to loop the sound. The loop will play consecutively as soon as the last loop has finished. As the `loop` parameter is a second parameter you must define a value for `offset`, even if you don't want to offset the sound. The following code presents a quick work-around:

```
mySound.start(0, 10);
```

The object is compatible with **Flash 5 and later**. There are **no known issues** with any version of Flash that supports this object.

Description
This **method** will start the specified sound playing.

Code	Additional Explanation	Notes
`mySound.start();`	The result of this code will start the sound playing through once at the beginning of the sound.	
`mySound.start(10);`	This will result in the code being started 10 seconds into the sound.	
`mySound.start(10, 10);`	This will result in the sound being started 10 seconds into the sound and looping the sound 10 times.	Every time the sound loops, it will start playing from 10 seconds into the sound.

See the examples `soundstart.fla` and `soundstart.swf` on the CD.

Sound.stop

```
mySound.stop(idName);
```

Where the `mySound` instance of the `Sound` object will stop playing.

This method is compatible with **Flash 5 and later**. There are **no known issues** with any version of Flash that supports this object.

The `stop` method performs a very simple task, that is to stop the sound from playing. Which sounds will stop depends on how the sound is loaded and which value you pass as the `idName` parameter. See the *Tips and precautions section* on the CD for more information on which sound will stop. See also **Sound.start**.

Description
This **method** will stop the specified sound from playing.

Code	Notes
`mySound.stop();`	Stop all sounds that were attached using the `attachSound` method.

`mySound.stop("yourSound");`	Will stop only the sound `yourSound` that was attached using the `attachSound` method.

See the examples `soundstop.fla` and `soundstop.swf` on the CD.

Stage

The `Stage` object is a top level object and doesn't need to be initialized with a constructor. The `Stage` object defines all information about the stage of the Flash movie, and using its methods and properties you can alter the stage of a Flash movie. See also **Stage.onResize**.

This object is compatible with **Flash 6**. There are **no known issues** with the version of Flash that supports this object.

With the `Stage` object you can catch certain events, such as when the Flash movie is resized. With all but one of the properties of the `Stage` object being read-only, this object is primarily used to gather information. This information can be used when using ActionScript to format or design elements of your Flash movie at runtime. For example, the information can be used to alter the look of your movie. You may want to have a particular movie clip right-aligned to your stage regardless of the width of the stage being altered. To do this use the following code:

```
Stage.align = "TL";
Stage.scaleMode = "noScale";
// Enter the name of the movie clip instance here
clip = instanceName;
listener = new Object();
listener.onResize = function () {
    clip._x = Stage.width - _root.clip._width;
}
Stage.addListener(listener);
```

Description
The `Stage` **object** is used to both provide information and alter various aspects of the stage in a Flash movie.

Stage.addListener

```
Stage.addListener(myListener);
```

Where `myListener` is an object containing an `onResize` method which the `Stage` object will send information to when the `onResize` method is invoked.

This method is compatible with **Flash 6**. There are **no known issues** with the version of Flash that supports this object.

This method is used to assign a `listener` object to respond to the `onResize` event. If a `listener` object is defined, every time a user resizes the Flash player the `onResize` event is invoked and the `onResize` method of the `listener` object is executed. You can add multiple listeners for the purpose of generating different responses to the same event. See also **Stage.removeListener** and **Stage.onResize**.

`Stage.addListener` returns a Boolean value, `true` or `false`.

Description

This **method** adds a reference to an object containing an `onResize` method, which is used to handle the `onResize` event.

Code	Notes
| ```
myListener = new Object();
myListener.onResize = function () {
    // response code here
}

Stage.addListener(myListener);
``` | Example of a basic object listener and `addListener` code snippet. |
| ```
onResizeResponse = function () {
    // response code here
}
myListener2 = new Object();
myListener2.onResize = onResizeResponse;

Stage.addListener(myListener2);
``` | Using a named function and assigning it to handle the `onResize` event. |

```
myListener = new Object();
myListener.onResize = function () {
    // code here
}

Stage.addListener("myListener");
```

Incorrect usage.

You must pass a reference to the listener object, so it can't be a string literal.

See the example `stageaddlistener.fla` and `stageaddlistener.swf` on the CD.

Stage.align

```
Stage.align = "TR"
```

Where the Flash movie will align to the top-right of the stage.

This method is compatible with **Flash 6**. There are **no known issues** with the version of Flash that supports this object. See also **Stage.scaleMode**.

The `align` property is accessed and altered to effect the position of the Flash movie within the stage. There are some legal string values that must be used; all other values will center the movie to the stage, both horizontally and vertically. Note that the string value for this property is *not* case sensitive. The following is a list of legal properties:

Align Mode	Vertical Setting	Horizontal Setting
"T"	top	center
"B"	bottom	center
"L"	center	left
"R"	center	right
"TL"	top	left
"TR"	top	right
"BL"	bottom	left
"BR"	bottom	right

Description

This **property** defines the alignment of the Flash movie on the stage.

Code	Additional Explanation	Notes
Stage.align = "BR";		A typical example of using the align method.
Stage.align("BR");	Incorrect usage.	As align is a property of the object, you need to explicitly define its value just like any other variable or property.

See the example files stagealign.fla and stagealign.swf on the CD.

Stage.height

```
var stageHeight = Stage.height;
```

Where the variable stageHeight will have a value of the property Stage.height (the height of the stage in the Flash Player).

This method is compatible with **Flash 6**. There are **no known issues** with the version of Flash that supports this object.

This read-only property of the Stage object is the exact height of the stage. This however is determined by a few factors discussed below. See also **Stage.width**.

Description
This property represents the height of the stage, in pixels.

Code	Additional Explanation	Notes
var stageHeight = ➥ Stage.height;		Equates the value of the stage height to a variable so that this fixed value can be used.
Stage.height = 400;	Incorrect usage.	You cannot define the value of the height property. It is a read-only property and therefore cannot be altered through ActionScript. If you want to alter the size of the stage you must drag the borders of the Flash Player.

```
Stage.height(400);          Incorrect usage.           height is a property of the Stage
                                                       object, not a method, and secondly
                                                       it is a read-only property, so it cannot
                                                       be defined through ActionScript.
```

See the example file `stageheight.fla` and `stageheight.swf` on the CD.

Stage.onResize

```
myListenerObject = new Object();
myListenerObject.onResize = function () { //code }
Stage.addListener(myListenerObject);

var success = Stage.addListener(myListenerObject);
```

Where `myListenerObject` is assigned as a `listener` object of the `Stage` object. The `onResize` method of `myListenerObject` will be executed when the `onResize` event of the `Stage` object is invoked.

This event is compatible with **Flash 6 and above**. There are **no known issues** with the version of Flash that supports this object.

Being the only event of the `Stage` object, the `onResize` event will execute the `onResize` method of any listening objects. Your `onResize` event handler code should reside within the `listener` object's `onResize` method. To register the object as a listener of the `Stage` object, use the `Stage.addListener` method. See also **Stage.addListener** and **Stage.removeListener**.

Description
This **event** is invoked when the size of the stage is modified.

Code	Additional Explanation	Notes

`myListener = new Object();`
`myListener.onResize =`
`function () {`
`    // code here`
`}`
`Stage.addListener`
`➡ (myListener);`
		Typical code for creating a `listener` object and assigning the object as a listener to the `Stage` object.

Code	Additional Explanation	Notes

`Stage.onResize =`
`function () {`
`    // code here`
`}`
 	
`Stage.onResize =`
`➡functionName;`
	Incorrect usage.	You cannot directly define a named or anonymous function to the onResize event. You should instead create a listener object of the Stage object, which is used as callback function to handle the onResize event.

See the examples `stageonresize.fla` and `stageonresize.swf` on the CD.

Stage.removeListener

```
Stage.removeListener(myListenerObject);
var success = Stage.removeListener(myListenerObject);
```

Where `myListenerObject` will be removed as a listener from the Stage object and will no longer receive callback notification from the onResize event.

This method is compatible with **Flash 6**. There are **no known issues** with the version of Flash that supports this object.

This method is used to remove a listener object from receiving callback notification from the onResize event of the Stage object. Once you have removed a listener object, you can re-add it using the addListener method. See also **Stage.addListener**, **Stage.onResize**.

The removeListener method returns a Boolean value, true or false. true will be returned if the listener was successfully removed and false if it failed. This method will return false if the specified listener object has already been removed.

Description
This **method** removes a listener object from the Stage object.

Code	Notes
`Stage.removeListener(myListenerObject);`	This is the most common form of using the method.

`clearListener =` `➥Stage.removeListener(myListenerObject);`	The `removeListener` method will return `true` on success and `false` on failure. Assign the returned information to a variable to determine its success.

See the examples `stageremovelistener.fla` and `stageremovelistener.swf` on the CD.

Stage.scaleMode

```
Stage.scaleMode = "exactFit";
```

Where the `scaleMode` property of the `Stage` object is being set to the string `exactFit`, a legal setting for the `scaleMode` property.

This property is compatible with **Flash 6**. There are **no known issues** with the version of Flash that supports this object.

The `scaleMode` property defines the way your movie scales when the stage size is altered. You can adjust the scaling mode to one of the following settings: "exactFit", "showAll", "noBorder", and "noScale". Each of these legal string values will cause a different effect. If you try to set the `scaleMode` property to an illegal string value (or un-recognized string value), the `scaleMode` property will return to the default value, "showAll". See also **Stage.align**.

Description
This **method** will alter the way your Flash movie scales.

Code	Additional Explanation	Notes
`Stage.scaleMode =` `➥ "noScale";`		Setting the `scaleMode` property to a legal string value. The `noScale` value will stop the movie scaling within the size of the stage. If the movie is larger than the size of the stage, the movie will be cropped as needed.

Code	Additional Explanation	Notes
Stage.scaleMode = ➡"wrong";	Incorrect string value.	This will result in the scaleMode property equaling the default setting showAll because the defined string value, wrong, is not recognized (an illegal value).

See the examples stagescalemode.fla and stagescalemode.swf on the CD.

Stage.showMenu

```
Stage.showMenu = true;
```

Where the showMenu property of the Stage object is being set to true.

This property is compatible with **Flash 6**. There are **no known issues** with the version of Flash that supports this object.

The showMenu property is used to hide the Zoom In, Zoom Out, 100%, and Show All options from the right-click (Windows) or CTRL-click (Mac) context menu. This setting controls both the Flash Player plug-in and the Flash Player stand-alone (or projector). You can use this property to define if you would like users to the see these items in the context menu. You may want to curb access to items on the menu such as Zoom In and Zoom out.

Description
This **method** determines if various options on the Flash Player context menu are visible.

Code	Notes
Stage.showMenu = true;	Standard usage of this property.
Stage.showMenu = "true";	Incorrect usage. The showMenu will only accept a Boolean value of true or false. Any incorrect string value will result in the property being equal to false; therefore the context menu will hide the items.

See the examples stageshowmenu.fla and stageshowmenu.swf on the CD.

Stage.width

```
var stageWidth = Stage.width
```

Where the variable `stageWidth` will have a value of the property `Stage.width` (the width of the stage).

This property is compatible with **Flash 6**. There are **no known issues** with the version of Flash that supports this object.

The `width` property of the `Stage` object references the size of the stage, in pixels. See also **Stage.height** and **Stage.scaleMode**. Depending on the `scaleMode` of the movie, the width can represent different things. Look under the *Tips and precautions section* of this property on the CD for more information.

Description
This **property** represents the width of the stage, in pixels.

Code	Additional Explanation	Notes
`var stageWidth = Stage.width;`		

`if (Stage.width < 100) {`
`    // code here`
`}`
		Usage of the `Stage.width` property within a conditional. Use this conditional code as a basis for performing a function based on the width of the stage.

`myListener = new Object();`
`myListener.onResize =`
`function () {`
`    rePositionNav(Stage.width);`
`    // code here`
`}`
`Stage.addListener`
`(myListener);`
	Event handling.	This is an example of using the `width` property in an `onResize` event handler. The new width of the stage is passed to the custom `rePositionNav` function, which will reposition the navigation buttons based on the size of the stage.

`Stage.width = 100;`	Incorrect usage.	`width` is a read-only property of the `Stage` object and can therefore not be altered through ActionScript. You must drag the border of the Flash Player with your mouse to increase the size of the stage.

See the examples `stagewidth.fla` and `stagewidth.swf` on the CD.

startDrag

```
startDrag(targetMovieClip);
startDrag(targetMovieClip, [lock, left, top, right, bottom]);
```

Where the movie clip `targetMovieClip` in which the code is written will attach to the mouse and follow it around.

This **function** is compatible with **Flash 4 and later**. There are **no known issues** with any version of Flash that supports this object.

The `startDrag` function will cause a movie clip to follow the mouse around the stage. This function is very similar to the `MovieClip.startDrag` method, which gives you more control over the dragging movie clip. The mandatory parameter, `targetMovieClip` is a reference to the movie clip that you want to drag. The following table details the five other parameters and what they'll do:

Parameter	Represents
`"lock"`	Set this to `true`, if you want center of the movie clip to lock the mouse.
`"left"`	Specifies the left boundary. The movie clip won't be able to go to the left of this value.
`"top"`	Specifies the top boundary. The movie clip won't be able to go to go higher than this value.
`"right"`	Specifies the right boundary. The movie clip won't be able to go farther right than this value.
`"bottom"`	Specifies the bottom boundary. The movie clip won't be able to go below this value.

See also **MovieClip.startDrag** and **stopDrag**.

Description
Makes the target movie clip follow the mouse.

Code	Notes

`onClipEvent(load) {`
 	
`    startDrag(this, true);`
 	
`}`
	Makes the movie clip, containing the onLoad event, follow the mouse around the stage and locks the center of the clip to the mouse.

`on(release) {`
 	
`    startDrag(this, true, 0, 0, 100, 100);`
 	
`}`
	When the button containing this code is released, the parent movie clip (containing the button) will follow the mouse around the stage within the defined boundaries, which are a 100-pixel wide rectangle.

See the examples `startdrag.fla` and `startdrag.swf` on the CD.

stop

```
stop();
```

This action is used to stop a timeline at the current frame (the frame in which the stop action is executed).

Compatible with **Flash 2 and later**. There are **no known issues** with any version of Flash that supports this action.

It can be used to **stop a timeline from playing** (therefore it only relates to halting movie clips and the _root timeline) in which the action is executed on.

Related actions include **MovieClip.stop** (which is the same as `stop`, except it references a particular movie clip) and **Sound.stop** (which is similar to `stop` in that it causes a particular sound to stop playing), **play** and **MovieClip.play**, as they are the opposite of `stop` (causing a timeline to play).

Description
This **action** is used only to stop an untargeted timeline playing.

Code	Notes
`stop();`	Will stop the timeline of the movie clip in which the action resides, being either on a frame or a button.

```
targetClip.onEnterFrame = function () {

    if (_root.stopMotion == true) {

    stop();

    }

}
```

Incorrect usage.

This code will not stop `targetClip`'s timeline (the intended usage), but will instead stop the timeline where this code resides.

See the following examples on the CD:

```
stoproottimeline.fla / stoproottimeline.swf
stopbutton.fla / stopbutton.swf
stoponenterframe.fla / stoponenterframe.swf
```

stopAllSounds

```
stopAllSounds();
```

Where all sounds currently playing will be stopped.

Compatible with **Flash 3 and later**. There are **no known issues** with any version of Flash that supports this action.

This function will stop all sounds that are currently playing from playing. There is an exception however. If a sound has been added to a frame in authoring mode and set to stream, the sounds will continue to play as the playhead moves over the frames they are in, for the first time only. If the frames were to loop the sound would stop playing.

Description
This **function** will stop all sounds that are currently playing from playing.

Code	Additional Explanation	Notes
stopAllSounds ();		Standard usage.
movieClipTarget. ➥stopAllSounds();	Incorrect usage.	The stopAllSounds function is not a method of the MovieClip object.

See the stopallsounds.fla and stopallsounds.swf examples on the CD.

stopDrag

stopDrag();

Where a movie clip that is being dragged, will cease following the mouse.

Compatible with **Flash 3 and later**. There are **no known issues** with any version of Flash that supports this action.

The stopDrag function is used to stop a movie clip from being dragged, which started being dragged using the startDrag function. This function is deprecated in Flash MX in preference of MovieClip.stopDrag. See also **MovieClip.stopDrag**.

Description
This **function** will cease the movie clip that is currently being dragged around from being dragged around.

Code	Notes

on(release) {
 	
    stopDrag();
 	
}
	When the mouse button is released, the movie clip will stop being dragged around.

String

This object is addressed in Chapter 12.

The String object is used to manipulate and manage strings. It is a wrapper for the string primitive data type, therefore allowing you to use the String object's properties and methods directly on primitive string data types.

In Flash MX, the String object has been converted to a native object. That means the String object has been converted to C++ code and compiled with the Flash Player whereas in previous versions it was interpreted in ActionScript. This means you'll see a huge increase in performance from the String object. Incidentally, the XML and Array objects were also converted to native objects. See also **String (function)** and **"" (String delimiter)**.

Description
This **object** is used to manipulate and manage strings.

String (function)

```
var myString = String(expression);
```

Where expression will be converted into a string and will be the value of the variable myString.

Compatible with **Flash 4 and later**. There are **no known issues** with any version of Flash that supports this action.

The String **function** will convert the value of expression into a string. Based on the data type of expression different strings will be returned. This function is deprecated in favor of the **String object.**

Description
Will convert expression into a string.

Code	Notes

myString = String(10);
myString = String("12");
myString = String("str");
	// returns "10"
	// returns "12"
	// returns "str"

myObject = new Object();
myString = String(myObject);
 	
mySound = new Sound();
myString = String(mySound);
	// returns "[object Object]"
	
	// returns "[object Object]"

String.charAt

```
newString = myString.charAt(index);
```

Where the variable newString will equal the character found at position index of myString.

The method is compatible with **Flash 5 and later**. There are **no known issues** with any version of Flash that supports this object.

The charAt **method** is used to return the character found at the specified index of the specified string. This method is excellent for quickly checking that a string confirms to specified rules. For example, you may issue passwords to all of your users with the mandatory string "p@" at the start of the passwords and "$" at the end of the password. You could use a chartAt check to make sure the user's password contains the "@" character at index 1, if it doesn't you know the password is wrong even before you've queried the server.

Description

Returns the character found at the specified index of the specified string.

Code	Notes
```myString = new String("http://www.macromedia.com"); if (myString.charAt(myString.length-4)) { // code here }```	The if statement will evaluate to true. A system that quickly checks if there is a "." in the position four from the end of the specified string. This example is running a simple check for a website string using a top level domain such as .net, .com or, .org.

See the examples stringcharat.fla and stringcharat.swf on the CD.

String.charCodeAt

```
newString = myString.charCodeAt(index);
```

Where variable newString will equal the code for the character found at index of myString.

The object is compatible with **Flash 5 and later**. There are **no known issues** with any version of Flash that supports this object.

The charCodeAt operator will return the decimal value of the character from the ASCII table, actually, a 16-bit integer from 0 to 65535. You could use this method for many reasons. For example, if you have a username and password to enter your site, you could retrieve the username and password from the user, create a string based on the codes returned by charCodeAt, and check this against the username and passwords on the server. The following code is an example:

```
// You would however, in your movie, retrieve these values from the user.
password = new String(passwordInput.text);

passString = new Array();
for (i = 0; i < password.length; i++) passString.push(password.charCodeAt(i));
passwordStr = passString.join("");
```

Then, you would send the passwordStr string to the server. Extract the password based on the supplied username from the database. Encode the password into the same format and then check the two against each other. If there's a match, you've got a correct password but if it fails, then the password is incorrect. This is a more secure way to check a password against the server, because you don't have to send the actual password over.

Description
This **method** retrieves the ASCII code of the character at the specified index from the specified string.

Code	Notes

`myString = new String("Joe John Bloggs");`
 	
`myCharCode = myString.charCodeAt(10);`
	Returns "108", the l in "Bloggs".

`myString = new String( "Joe John Bloggs");`
 	
`myCharCode =`
`myString.charCodeAt(myString.length-1);`
	Returns "115", the s in "Bloggs".

`myCharCode = myString.charCodeAt[i];`	Returns undefined. A common syntax mistake is to try and access the method using the array access operator. This usually occurs when programmers are tired and less careful.

String.concat

```
newString = myString.concat(value1, ...., valueN);
```

Where the variable `newString` will have a string value of all of the supplied arguments joined together along with the value of the specified string.

The object is compatible with **Flash 5 and later**. There are **no known issues** with any version of Flash that supports this object.

This method is used to join two or more strings together. A new string will be created, the variable that you are defining and the original string will remain unchanged. The parameters can be any data type and will be converted to a `String` data type before concatenated.

Description
This **method** will join the string value of the passed parameters with the value of the specified string object to create a new string.

Code	Notes
`myString = new String("Your name is: ");` `newString = myString.concact("Foobar");`	Returns the string: `Your name is: Foobar`.
`myString = new String("Your age is: ");` `newString = myString.concat(21);`	Returns the string: `Your age is 21`.

`age = 21;`
 	
`myString = new String("The data type is: ");`
`newString = myString.concat(typeof age, ".");`
	Returns the string: `The data type is: number`.

See the examples `stringconcat.fla` and `stringconcat.swf` on the CD.

String.indexOf

```
newString = myString.indexOf(substring [,startIndex]);
```

Where the variable `newString` will have a number value representing the first position of `substring` in `myString`.

The method is compatible with **Flash 5 and later**. There are **no known issues** with any version of Flash that supports this method.

This **method** will search through a specified string for the first occurrence of the second specified string, the parameter substring. If the word is found in the specified string, the method will return the index where the string starts. If the string isn't found the method will return -1.

Description

Returns an integer representing the starting point of the string to search for in the string to search in, and if it can't be found a value of -1 will be returned.

Code	Notes

```myString = new String(userMessage.text);```
 	
```if (myString.indexOf("badWord") != -1) {```
 	
```   // alert user this is a bad word```
 	
```}```
	This code checks a string to find any bad words that you may not want to be used, such as swear words, etc. This application of the indexOf method would be great for use in a message board or contact board where you may want to stop swearing.

```searchFor = "word";```
 	
```found = myString.indexOf(searchFor, 30);```
 	
```if (found != -1) {```
```   // string was found, code here```
```} else {```
```   // string was found```
```}```
	This code will search for the value of searchFor in the string myString. However, it will start searching from the 29th character in, not the start of the string.

See the examples stringindexof.fla and stringindexof.swf on the CD.

String.lastIndexOf

```
newString = myString.lastIndexOf(substring [, startIndex]);
```

Where newString will have a number value representing the index of the last occurrence of substring found in myString.

The method is compatible with **Flash 5 and later**. There are **no known issues** with any version of Flash that supports this object.

The `lastIndexOf` **method** will search through a string and return the index number of the last occurrence of the specified string. If the string wasn't found, a number value of -1 will be returned. Unlike the `indexOf` method, this method searches the string from right to left. See also **String.indexOf**.

Description

Searches a string, from left to right, for a specified string. If the string is found it will return the index number of the last occurrence of the string and if the string isn't found, the method will return the number value -1.

Code	Notes
| ```
searchIn = new String("try to find seachWord
➥in this string, but that last instance of
➥searchWord, not the first");
found = searchIn.lastIndexOf("searchWord");
``` | Will return 64, the index of the last occurrence of searchWord in the string. |

String.length

```
length = myString.length();
```

Where `length` will have a number value representing the number of characters in the specified string.

The property is compatible with **Flash 5 and above**. There are **no known issues** with any version of Flash that supports this property.

The read-only `length` property of the `String` object returns the number of characters in the specified string. If there are no characters, the property will return 0. This property applies not only to `String` object strings but to string literal values also. For example, the following code is an example using the `length` property on a `String` object:

```
str = new String("foobar");
trace(str.length); // sends 6 to the Output window
```

... whereas this code will have the same result as above, eventhough it is being used on a string literal:

```
str = "foobar";
trace(str.length); // sends 6 to the Output window
```

This is because the `length` property is generic. If you specify a string literal on any generic method or property of the `String` object, the ActionScript interpreter will automatically convert it to a temporary `String` object. Once it has finished it will discard the temporary `String` object and return the result.
```

Description

This **property** returns the number of characters in the specified string.

Code	Notes
```if (userMessage.text.length > 250) { // alert user, the message is too long }```	This code evaluates if the userMessage instance of a text field has more than 250 characters. If it does the user should be alerted and asked to cull some characters until the message fits within the limits. Notice the length property is being used directly on a text field.

String.slice

```
newString = myString.slice(start [, end]);
```

Where newString will have a value of myString from the start index to the end index.

The method is compatible with **Flash 5 and later**. There are **no known issues** with any version of Flash that supports this method

The slice method will create a new string from the calling string. The start parameter defines the index in which to start the new string from. The optional end parameter defines the index in which to end the new string from. If the end parameter is not supplied, the slice method will include all characters from the start index to the end of the calling string. It should be noted that the slice method creates a new string – it won't modify the calling string.

Description

The slice **method** will create a new string containing the characters from the start index of the calling string, to the end index of the calling string.

Code	Additional Explanation	Notes
```myString = new String ("This is a string with ➡ some words in it"); ➡ newString = ➡ myString.slice(5); trace(newString);```	Results in the string is a string with some words in it being sent to the Output window.	This example uses a String object. Also, an end parameter is not being passed, so the slice will end at the end of the string.

myString = "This is a ⟶string with some words ⟶in it"; newString = ⟶myString.slice(8, 16); trace(newString);	Result in the string a string being sent to the Output window.	This is an example of the slice method working with a string literal.
myString = "This is a ⟶string with some words ⟶in it "; newString = ⟶myString.slice(22, -1); trace(newString);	Result in the string some words in it being sent to the Output window.	If you set the end value to -1, it will end the slice at the last character in the string.

See the examples `stringslice.fla` and `stringslice.swf` on the CD.

String.split

```
newString = myString.split(delimiter [, limit]);
```

Where `newString` will be an array with each key containing the substrings of `myString` by breaking it wherever the `delimiter` parameter occurs.

The method is compatible with **Flash 5 and later**. There are **no known issues** with any version of Flash that supports this method.

The `split` **method** is used to split up a string into individual substrings based on the passed `delimiter`. The individual substrings are stored in an array. The `limit` parameter can be used to limit the number of substrings the calling string is split up into. If you do supply a `limit` value, as soon the number of substrings created has reach the `limit` value, the `split` method will stop searching the rest of the string. The `split` method is useful for many things, one of which is coding and de-coding information in a custom format. For example, the following code takes the string and enters the information into an array. Each array contains an object with name and age properties used to store the information from the string:

```
// The array used to hold the objects
stringData = new Array();

// The string to parse
codeString = "Tom:21|John:28|Joe:24|Adam:22";
```

```
// Split the string into arrays at every "|"
// which is used to seperate different people
nameArray = codeString.split("|");

// loop through the nameArray
for (var i in nameArray) {

  // split each key at every ":"
  // which is used to seperate the name from the age
  str = nameArray[i].split(":");

  // create an object and add it to the stringData array
  stringData.push({name: str[0], age: str[1]});
}
```

Description

Splits the calling string in substrings at every occurrence of the delimiter. The strings are stored in an array.

Code	Additional Explanation	Notes
`fullName = "John Doe";` `splitStr =` `fullName.split(" ");` `firstName = splitStr[0];` `lastName = splitStr[1];`	Returns two variables. `firstName` will equal John and `lastName` will equal Doe.	A simple piece of code to take a full name and get both the first and last names as separate variables. This code assumes the person only has two names, no middle name.

See `stringsplit.fla` and `stringsplit.swf` on the CD for examples.

String.substr

```
newString = myString.substr(start [, length]);
```

Where `newString` will have a string value equal to a portion of `myString` from start to start + length.

The method is compatible with **Flash 5 and later**. There are **no known issues** with any version of Flash that supports this method.

The `substr` method is used to extract a portion of characters from the specified string. This method could be used in a search and replace system, a bad words system where predefined words are removed from a users message, or to add and remove special characters.

You can pass a negative number for the start parameter. If you do, the starting position of the new string is determined from the end of the string, where -1 represents the last character. For example, the following code will start from eight characters to the right (not the left – which is what happens with a positive start parameter):

```
myString = "Number: 12345, Name: John Doe.";
memberNumber = myString.substr(-9, 4); // returns "John"
```

Because the J is the ninth character from the end, the string starts there and has a length of four characters.

Description

This **method** will create a new string from a portion of the specified string from the index start to the index at start + length.

Code	Additional Explanation	Notes

`myString = new String("Number: 12345,`
➡`Name: John Doe.");`
`memberNumber =`
➡`myString.substr(8, 5);`
	Returns the string "12345".	A basic piece of code used to extract a member number. This code assumes the member number will start at index 8 and contain five characters.

`myString = "Number:`
➡`12345, Name: John Doe.";`
`memberNumber =`
➡`myString.substr(8, 5);`
	Returns the string "12345".	An example of using the substr method with a string literal.

`myString = "Number:`
➡`12345, Name: John Doe.";`
`memberNumber =`
➡`myString.substr(-9, 10);`
	Returns the string "John Doe".	Using a negative number to start.

See the examples stringsubstr.fla and stringsubstr.swf on the CD.

String.substring

```
newString = myString.substring(start [, to]);
```

Where newString will contain a portion of myString from start to to.

The method is compatible with **Flash 5 and later**. There are **no known issues** with any version of Flash that supports this method.

The `substring` method is used to extract a portion of the specified string. A new string is created and the original string is not modified. If the `to` parameter is omitted, the length of the string is used (`myString.length`). See also **String.slice** and **String.substr**.

If the value of `to` is greater than the value of `from`, the parameters are swapped before the function executes. This code demonstrates this:

```
myString = "Number: 12345, Name: John Doe.";
memberNumber = myString.substring(5, 0); // returns Numbe
memberNumber = myString.substring(0, 5); // returns Numbe
```

The following code illustrates that if the value of start is negative, the value 0 is used, unlike `String.slice` and `String.substr`:

```
myString = "Number: 12345, Name: John Doe.";
memberNumber = myString.substring(-5, 10);
```

Description

This **method** is used to extract a portion.

Code	Notes
`myString = new String("Hello John");` `newString = myString.substring(6,10);`	Returns John. Using the substring method with the string object.
`myString = "Hello John";` `newString = myString.substring(6,10);`	Returns John. Using the substring method with a string literal.
`myString = new String("Hello John");` `newString = myString.substring(-2,5);`	Returns Hello. Uses 0 instead of the negative value to start the string from.
`myString = new String("Hello John");` `newString = myString.substring(6);`	Returns John. Omits the to parameter so the string.length is used in its place.

See the examples `stringsubstring.fla` and `stringsubstring.swf` on the CD.

String.toLowerCase

```
newString = myString.toLowerCase();
```

Where `newString` will be the same string as `myString`, only any uppercase characters appearing in `myString` will become lowercase.

The method is compatible with **Flash 5 and later**. There are **no known issues** with any version of Flash that supports this method.

The `toLowerCase` method will take a string and create a new string that equals the original string, only all characters will be lowercase. So all uppercase characters in the original string will be forced to lowercase. See also **String.toUpperCase** and **===**.

Description
This **method** will duplicate the specified string, only all characters will be lowercase.

Code	Notes
`origStr = new String("My String");` `lc = origStr.toLowerCase();`	Returns the string `my string`.
`myString = toLowerCase("My String");`	Returns undefined. `toLowerCase` is a method, so it must be invoked like a method.

See the examples `stringtolowercase.fla` and `stringtolowercase.swf` on the CD.

String.toUpperCase

```
newString = myString.toUpperCase();
```

Where `newString` will be equal to `myString` except all characters will be uppercase.

The method is compatible with **Flash 5 and later**. There are **no known issues** with any version of Flash that supports this method.

This **method** will create new string that is a duplicate of the calling string and convert all characters to uppercase. This method will not alter the calling string and instead creates a new string.

Description
Returns a duplicate string of the called string in which all characters are converted to uppercase.

Code	Notes
`myString = "myString".toUpperCase();`	Returns MYSTRING. The toUpperCase method working with string literals rather than a string object.
`myString = new String("John Doe");` `uppercaseName = myString.toUpperCase();`	Returns JOHN DOE. The toUpperCase method working with a string object.
`myString = toUpperCase("My String");`	Returns undefined. toUpperCase is a method of the String object and needs to be called as any other method does.

See the examples `stringtouppercase.fla` and `stringtouppercase.swf` on the CD.

substring

```
newString = substring("string", index, count);
```

Where the variable `newString` is defined with a value of that equal to `string` starting at `index` and being of length equal to `count`.

Compatible with **Flash 4 and later**. This function is depreciated in Flash 5 and above in favor of `String.substr`. See also **String.substr** and **String.substring**.

Description

This **function** will create a new string based on the specified string and mandatory parameters. The use of this function is deprecated; you should use the `String.substring` method instead.

Code	Notes
`newString = substring("foobar", 3, 3);`	`// will return the string "bar"`
`newString = substring("foobar", 0, 3);`	`// will return the string "foo"`

super

```
super([arg1, ...., argn]);
super.method([arg1, ...., argn]);
```

Where the super method of the method currently being executed will be executed with the arguments arg1 through argn being passed.

Compatible with **Flash 6**. There are **no known issues** with the version of Flash that supports this operator.

The subclass method is used to execute the method of the superclass function. The following code presents the superclass apples and the subclass oranges:

```
// define the superclass
function apples(typeOfApple) {
 this.appleType = typeOfApple;
}

// define the whichType method
apples.prototype.whichType = function () {
 trace(this.appleType);
}

// define the oranges class
function oranges(typeOfOrange) {
 this.orangeType = typeOfOrange;
}

// make oranges extend apples (the superclass)
oranges.prototype = new apples("nonApple");

// create an instance of the orange class (subclass)
orange = new oranges("sunOrange");

// what type of fruit and apple are we?
orange.whichType();

apple = new apples("red");
apple.whichType();
```

In the code above, the apples class is defined with a method named whichType. When the oranges class is defined, it also extends the apples class with the line oranges.prototype = new apples("nonApple");. The oranges class automatically inherits the whichType method from the apples class. However, add the following code to the code above and you'll see that the oranges class now extends the whichType method of the apples class. Test the movie with the new code and you'll see the extra trace call. See **prototype**.

```
oranges.prototype.whichType = function () {

  // trace(this.orangeType);
  super.whichType();

}
```

Description

Calls the method with the same name, if it exists, of the superclass.

Code	Notes

`function superClass() {`
`}`
`superClass.prototype.method = function () {`
`  trace("superClass.method");`
`}`
 	
`function subClass() {`
`}`
`subClass.prototype = new superClass();`
`subClass.prototype.method = function () {`
`  trace("subClass.method");`
`  super.method();`
`}`
 	
`instance = new subClass();`
`instance.method();`
	Will send the following code to the Output window:
	
	`subClass.method`
	`superClass.method`
	
	The superClass is created with a method named method. The subClass then extends the superClass class and extends the method method of the superClass.

See the examples super.fla and super.swf on the CD.

System

Previous to Flash MX, the only way to take a peek at the set-up of the machine the user was seeing your content on, was via JavaScript objects (such as window.screen, window.navigator, etc), which you would have to access via the **fsCommand** action and a JavaScript function embedded within the HTML of your web page. Although workable, experience shows that as soon as you start using more than one language to build your application, you become more prone to errors. In particular:

■ Most errors in well-written software occur at interfaces.

- Using more than one language (ActionScript and JavaScript) makes you more vulnerable to change; you are now counting on both languages staying the same in their next release for your application to continue working. In the fast moving world of the web, it is wiser not to have to make such assumptions!
- Although the difference between JavaScript and ActionScript is not that much, it would be nicer to be able to stay in one environment, and the graphic authoring environment of Flash looks more inviting than JavaScript for all but the hardcore scripter!
- Most mobile devices do not support JavaScript because they use proprietary or cut down browsers, so it becomes impossible to write truly cross-platform SWFs if you rely on it.

NB – It can be seen from the above discussion that one of the main uses of the `System.capabilities` object in the near future will be with dealing with non-standard configurations, such as wireless / mobile / pocket devices.

The `System` object fixes the need to have to look to external scripting and interrogating the browser directly to get attributes of the target machine by either:

1. Doing this itself.
2. Holding a set of generic constants within the Flash Player itself, which can be used to find out information about the typical platform that the version of the Flash Player you are accessing, would be expected to be running on.

NB – It is important to note that the two bullet points above mean that the `System.capabilities` properties fall into two types of value; those that are *specific to the current user,* and those that are *specific to the current Flash Player version and the platform it would run on.* The latter relates to non-standard systems only, and trying to derive information via this type of property for a standard PC / Mac user may give you inaccurate information. This is discussed further in the entries.

The **System.capabilities** object can be used to gain important information about the user, and if used properly, can be used to dynamically alter your content to suit a wide audience, rather than having to create a separate SWF for each of them. In particular:

- You can identify users with special needs by whether or not the machine has accessibility applications installed.
- You can detect the users screen resolution and other attributes, and from this infer whether the user's machine is a desktop or mobile device. You can further fine-tune the identification of mobile devices by looking at their media support facilities. You can still do this if the users machine does not support JavaScript.
- You can send the string value in the **System.capabilities.serverString** property to a server. This allows the server to dynamically decide which Flash content to send to the client machine. This is an important feature in the building of Flash-based dynamic content with universal device compatibility (PC, Mac, wireless device).
- You can find out the language used by the computer. This may also give you some idea about the location of the user.

- Although you cannot directly find the performance attributes of the user's machine, if the machine has particularly high screen attributes, you can infer a high performance processor.

The **System.security** object is used for assigning file security. It defines whether other domains are allowed access to your content. It has only one method. Refer to the entry for **System.allowDomain** for further details.

Related objects include:

- The **Screen** object (which tells you the size of the browser window).
- The **Accessibility** object (which tells you whether the machine has accessibility options).

The **System.capabilities** object has a very simple structure. It is an object with only properties. You can treat it as an object containing a set of values that are effectively constant per execution, since each time your SWF runs, the system capabilities of the machine it will be running on will remain constant.

You can quickly find out what the values are for the full set of `System.capabilities` properties on your machine by running the examples `system.capabilities.fla` and `system.capabilities.swf` on the CD.

The output will be something like this (models author's Windows laptop):

```
LANGUAGE on this machine is a string value equal to:  en
OS on this machine is a string value equal to:  Windows 98/ME
INPUT on this machine is a string value equal to:  point
MANUFACTURER on this machine is a string value equal to:  Macromedia Windows
SERVERSTRING     on     this     machine     is     a     string     value     equal     to:
A=t&MP3=t&AE=t&VE=t&ACC=f&DEB=t&V=WIN%206%2C0%2C21%2C0&M=Macromedia
Windows&R=1024x768&DP=72&COL=color&AR=1.0&I=point&OS=Windows 98/ME&L=en-UK
ISDEBUGGER on this machine is a boolean value equal to:  true
VERSION on this machine is a string value equal to:  WIN 6,0,21,0
HASAUDIO on this machine is a boolean value equal to:  true
HASMP3 on this machine is a boolean value equal to:  true
HASAUDIOENCODER on this machine is a boolean value equal to:  true
HASVIDEOENCODER on this machine is a boolean value equal to:  true
SCREENRESOLUTIONX on this machine is a number value equal to:  1024
SCREENRESOLUTIONY on this machine is a number value equal to:  768
SCREENDPI on this machine is a number value equal to:  72
SCREENCOLOR on this machine is a string value equal to:  color
PIXELASPECTRATIO on this machine is a number value equal to:  1
HASACCESSIBILITY on this machine is a boolean value equal to:  false
```

It also gives something very similar on a Mac.

This FLA consists of the simple `for...in` loop shown below:

```
for (prop in System.capabilities) {
    message = prop.toUpperCase()+" on this machine is a "+typeof
    (System.capabilities[prop])+" value equal to:
    "+System.capabilities[prop]+"\n\n";
  output_txt.text += message;
}
```

Some of the properties shown by this code are undocumented. They are **isDebugger** and **Input**. Refer to the next section for more details.

See this entry on the CD for the undocumented features.

System.capabilities.hasAccessibility

```
a = System.capabilities.hasAccessibility;
```

a will be returned as a Boolean value.

This property is compatible with **Flash 6 or later**. This property is **read only**.

Description

This **property** is used to find out whether the user has an accessibility application installed that is compatible with the current version of the Flash Player. It is a Boolean, and will be true if an accessibility application exists.

Code	Notes

`if (System.capabilities.hasAccessibility){`
`  // do this`
`}`
	If the users machine has accessibility options, you can check for this and act accordingly via simple **if...** logic.

See the examples `system.capabilities.fla` and `system.capabilities.swf` on the CD.

System.capabilities.hasAudio

```
a = System.capabilities.hasAudio;
```

a will be returned as a Boolean value.

This property is compatible with **Flash 6 or later**. This property is **read only**.

Description

This **property** is used to find out whether the user has a Flash Player installed that can handle audio. It is a Boolean, and will be `true` if an audio capability exists. For the Flash Player designed for a traditional laptop or desktop, this is true, but may vary for versions designed for other devices.

Code	Notes

`if (System.capabilities.hasAudio){`
`    // do this`
`}`
	If the user's machine has audio options, you can check for this and act accordingly via simple **if...** logic.

See the examples `system.capabilities.fla` and `system.capabilities.swf` on the CD.

System.capabilities.hasAudioEncoder

```
a = System.capabilities.hasAudioEncoder;
```

a will be returned as a Boolean value (PC/Mac) or an array containing the supported sound capabilities (wireless or pocket/portable device).

This property is compatible with **Flash 6 or later**. This property is **read only**.

Description

This **property** is used to find out the audio streams supported by the Flash Player. This is Boolean `true` for the standard Flash Player on a typical desktop, but will return an array containing the particular capabilities of the Flash Player for wireless or portable devices such as PDAs and pocket PCs.

System.capabilities.hasMP3

```
a = System.capabilities.hasMP3;
```

a will be returned as a Boolean value.

This property is compatible with **Flash 6 or later**. This property is **read only**.

Description

This **property** is used to find out whether the user has a Flash player installed that can handle MP3 audio. It is a Boolean, and will be `true` if the capability exists. For the Flash player designed for a traditional laptop or desktop, this is `true`, but may vary for versions designed for other devices.

Code	Notes

`if (System.capabilities.hasMP3){`
`    // do this`
`}`
	If the user's machine has audio options, you can check for this and act accordingly via simple **if...** logic.

See the examples `system.capabilities.fla` and `system.capabilities.swf` on the CD.

System.capabilities.hasVideoEncoder

    a = System.capabilities.hasVideoEncoder;

a will be returned as a Boolean value (PC/Mac) or an array containing the supported video capabilities (wireless or pocket/portable device).

This property is compatible with **Flash 6 or later**. This property is **read only**.

Description

This **property** is used to find out the video streams supported by the Flash Player. This is Boolean `true` for the standard Flash Player on a typical desktop, but will return an array containing the particular capabilities of the Flash Player for wireless or portable devices such as PDAs and pocket PCs.

See the examples `system.capabilities.fla` and `system.capabilities.swf` on the CD.

System.capabilities.Input

See the **System** entry.

System.capabilities.isDebugger

See the **System** entry.

System.capabilities.language

    a = System.capabilities.language;

a will be returned as a string value that returns an identifier for the language used by the operating system.

This property is compatible with **Flash 6 or later**. This property is **read only**.

Description

This **property** is used to find out the current user operating system, and will return a string value containing one of the following:

▪	English	"en", "en-US", or "en-UK" (depending on operating system and dialect selected)
▪	French	"fr"
▪	Korean	"ko"
▪	Japanese	"ja"

- Swedish   "sv"
- German   "de"
- Spanish   "es"
- Italian   "it"
- Chinese   "zh", "zh-CN", or "zh-TW" (depending on operating system and dialect selected)
- Portuguese   "pt"
- Polish   "pl"
- Hungarian   "hu"
- Czech   "cs"
- Turkish   "tr"
- Finnish   "fi"
- Danish   "da"
- Norwegian   "no"
- Dutch   "nl"
- Russian   "ru"
- Other   "xu"

See also the *Tips and precautions* section (on the CD) for the entry **System.capabilities.serverString**. Related properties include:

- **System.capabilities.os**
- **System.capabilities.language**
- **System.capabilities.manufacturer**
- The Flash player version variable **$Version**

See the examples `system.capabilities.fla` and `system.capabilities.swf` on the CD.

System.capabilities.manufacturer

```
a = System.capabilities.manufacturer
```

a will be returned as a string value that returns an identifier for the current Flash Player type.

This property is compatible with **Flash 6 or later**. This property is **read only**.

Description
This **property** is used to find out the current Flash Player type. There is a different Flash Player type for each family of the Flash Player:

- The Windows Flash Player will return "Macromedia Windows".
- The Mac Flash Player will return "Macromedia Macintosh".
- Other pocket/mobile/wireless devices will return a specific string identifying the Flash Player that runs on this product family.

Related properties include:

- **System.capabilities.os**
- **System.capabilities.language**
- The Flash Player version variable **$Version**

See the examples `system.capabilities.fla` and `system.capabilities.swf` on the CD.

System.capabilities.os

```
a = System.capabilities.os
```

a will be returned as a string value that returns an identifier for the users operating system.

This property is compatible with **Flash 6 or later**. This property is **read only**.

Description

This **property** is used to find out the current user operating system, and will return a string value containing one of the following:

- `"Windows XP"`
- `"Windows 2000"`
- `"Windows NT"`
- `"Windows 98/ME"`
- `"Windows 95"`
- `"MacOS"`
- An empty string

Related properties include:

- **System.capabilities.os**
- **System.capabilities.language**
- **System.capabilities.manufacturer**
- The Flash Player version variable **$Version**.

See the examples `system.capabilities.fla` and `system.capabilities.swf` on the CD.

System.capabilities.pixelAspectRatio

```
a = System.capabilities.pixelAspectRatio;
```

a will be returned as an integer value.

This property is compatible with **Flash 6 or later**. This property is **read only**.

Description

This **property** is used to find out the aspect ratio of the screen pixels. Pixels on a standard PC are square, giving an aspect ratio of 1.

See thes example `system.capabilities.fla` and `system.capabilities.swf` on the CD.

System.capabilities.screenColor

```
a = System.capabilities.screenColor;
```

a will be returned as a string value.

This property is compatible with **Flash 6 or later**. This property is **read only**.

Description

This **property** is used to find out the color capabilities of the users screen. For a standard desktop, it will be `color`. For other devices, it may be `color`, `gray`, or `bw`.

See the examples `system.capabilities.fla` and `system.capabilities.swf` on the CD.

System.capabilities.screenDPI

```
a = System.capabilities.screenDPI;
```

a will be returned as a number.

This property is **compatible with Flash 6 or later**. This property is **read only**.

Description

This **property** is used to find out the dots per inch of the users screen. For a standard desktop, or laptop screen, it is 72dpi. For other screens, the DPI setting may vary.

See the examples `system.capabilities.fla` and `system.capabilities.swf` on the CD.

System.capabilities.screenResolutionX

```
a = System.capabilities.screenResolutionX;
```

a will be returned as the resolution of the users screen in the x direction in absolute pixels.

This **property** is compatible with **Flash 6 or later**. This property is **read only**.

Description

The resolution of a users screen is a measure of how many pixels can be displayed. The screen resolution in the x (width) direction is held in the property **screenResolutionX**.

You should note that this *is not* an indication of the number of pixels available to the Flash Player, because the browser window will usually occupy only a proportion of the screen. This property is therefore best used in conjunction with a number of other properties and objects to build up a true picture of how the user is viewing your site. See the *Examples and practical uses* section (on the CD) for more details.

See the examples `system.capabilities.fla` and `system.capabilities.swf` on the CD.

System.capabilities.screenResolutionY

```
a = System.capabilities.screenResolutionY;
```

a will be returned as the resolution of the users screen in the y direction in absolute pixels.

This **property** is compatible with **Flash 6 or later**. This property is **read only**.

Description

The resolution of a users screen is a measure of how many pixels can be displayed. The screen resolution in the y (height) direction is held in the property **screenResolutionY**.

You should note that this *is not* an indication of the number of pixels available to the Flash Player, because the browser window will usually occupy only a proportion of the screen. This property is therefore best used in conjunction with a number of other properties and objects to build up a true picture of how the user is viewing your site. See the *Examples and practical uses* section (on the CD) for more details.

See the example `system.capabilities.fla` and `system.capabilities.swf` on the CD.

System.capabilities.serverString

```
a = System.capabilities.serverString
```

a will be returned as a string value encoded for server-side applications.

This **property** is compatible with **Flash 6 or later**. This property is **read only**.

Description

This **property** will return a long string containing all available `System.capabilities` information regarding the user environment. A typical server string is shown below. This is for the same machine, "models author's Windows laptop " as used in all the `System.capabilities` examples so far.

```
A = t & MP3 = t & AE = t & VE = t & ACC = f & DEB = t & V = WIN % 2 0 6 % 2 C 0 % 2 C 21 % 2 C 0 & M = Macromedia
Windows&R=1024x768&DP=72&COL=color&AR=1.0&I=point&OS=Windows 98/ME&L=en-UK
```

Server string	Description	Value	Notes
A	hasAudio	"t" or "f"	See **System.capabilities.hasAudio**
MP3	hasMP3	"t" or "f"	See **System.capabilities.hasMP3**
AE	hasAudioEncoder	"t" or "f"	See **System.capabilities.hasAudioEncoder**
VE	hasVideoEncoder	"t" or "f"	See **System.capabilities.hasVideoEncoder**
ACC	hasAccessibility	"t" or "f"	See **System.capabilities.hasAccessibility**
DEB	hasDebugger	"t" or "f"	Undocumented. Refers to debugging capability. See **System**
V	version	string descriptor	See **System.capabilities.version**
M	manufacturer	string descriptor	See **System.capabilities.manufacturer**
R	resolution	string descriptor	Returns a string of the form: **screenResolution.xxscreenResolution.y** This is related to the two properties below: **System.capabilities.screenResolution.x** **System.capabilities.screenResolution.y**
DP	screenDPI	value	See **System.capabilities.screenDPI**
COL	screenColor	string descriptor	See **System.capabilities.screenColor**
AR	pixelAspectRatio	value	See **System.capabilities.pixelAspectRatio**
I	input	string descriptor	Undocumented. Refers to input device. See **System**
OS	os	string descriptor	See **System.capabilities.os**
L	language	string descriptor	See **System.capabilities.language**

See the examples `system.capabilities.fla` and `system.capabilities.swf` on the CD.

System.capabilities.version

See the **System** entry.

System.product

See the **System** entry.

System.security.allowDomain

```
System.security.allowDomain(domain1, domain2,... domainN);
```

Where `domain1` to `domainN` are domain names that you to want to permit to share assets with the current SWF.

This method is compatible with **Flash 6 or later**.

Description

This **method** allows you to share assets between SWFs even if the SWFs originated from different domains.

System.showsettings

See the **System** entry.

targetPath

```
var tp = targetPath(movieClipReference);
```

Where the variable `tp` will be defined with the value of the target path of `movieClipReference`.

This function is **compatible with Flash 5 and above**. There are no known issues with any version of Flash that supports this operator.

The `targetPath` function is used to retrieve the path to the specified movie clip. **This function is depreciated in favor of the this operator**. For example these two lines of code, which reside in `_root.clip1.nested1.childChild` produce the same result:

```
onClipEvent(load) {
 trace(targetPath(this)); // returns _level0.clip1.nested1.childChild
}

onClipEvent(load) {
 trace(this); // returns _level0.clip1.nested1.childChild
}
```

Description

This function will return the path to the target object.

tellTarget

```
tellTarget("targetClip") {
 // code in here
}
```

Where the `targetClip` movie clip will be modified from the code within the braces.

Compatible with Flash 3 and above. This function is depreciated in Flash MX in favor of dot notation and the **with** action.

Description

The `tellTarget` function provides a method to control a movie clip from another timeline.

Code	Notes

`tellTarget(_root.myClip) {`
`    _xscale = 50;`
`    _yscale = 50;`
`}`
	This will control the MovieClip `_root.myClip` and set the `_xscale` and `_yscale` properties.

TextField

Compatible with **Flash Player 6 and later**.

The `TextField` object handles text fields appearance and behavior. All dynamic and input text fields in a Flash text field are instances of the `TextField` object.

Description

The `TextField` **object** has many methods attached to it that can be invoked to control the actions and appearances of a text field. The `TextField` object inherits from the `Object` object, so all methods and properties of the `Object` object are available to the `TextField` object. Text fields can be created statically, or dynamically using the `TextField.createTextField()` method.

The `TextField` object contains these methods:

- `TextField.addListener` – registers an object that will receive notification broadcasts from the text field events, `onChanged` and `onScroller`.
- `TextField.getDepth` – returns the level of the text field.
- `TextField.getNewTextFormat` – gets a `textformat` object, a copy of the text fields current text object.
- `TextField.removeListener` – removes a listener object from receiving event notification broadcasts from the text field.
- `TextField.setNewTextFormat` – sets a new text format for the text field.
- `TextField.replaceSel` – replaces the current selection.
- `TextField.setTextFormat` – sets the default text format.

The `TextField` object also has several properties associated with it:

- `TextField._alpha` – the transparency value.
- `TextField.autoSize` – controls sizing and alignment.
- `TextField.background` – a flag to define if the text field has a background.
- `TextField.backgroundColor` – the background color.
- `TextField.border` – a flag to define if the text field has a border.
- `TextField.borderColor` – the color of the border.
- `TextField.bottomScroll` – an integer representing the bottom-most line in a text field (read-only).
- `TextField.embedFonts` – a flag defining if the text field uses embedded fonts.
- `TextField._highquality` – an integer value used to determine the rendering quality.
- `TextField._height` – the height of the text field.
- `TextField.hscroll` – the horizontal scroll value.
- `TextField.html` – a flag to define if the text field's content contains HTML.
- `TextField.htmlText` – the HTML content of the text field.
- `TextField.length` – represents number of characters in the text field (read-only).
- `TextField.maxChars` – indicates the maximum number of characters.

- TextField.maxhscroll – represents maximum value of the TextField.hscroll property (read-only).
- TextField.maxscroll – represents the maximum value of TextField.scroll.
- TextField.multiline – defines if the text field is a multiline text field.
- TextField._name – the instance name of the text field.
- TextField._parent – a reference to the text field's parent movie clip (or level).
- TextField.password – a flag defining if the text field's contents should be hidden.
- TextField._quality – defines the rendering quality.
- TextField.restrict – indicates the set of characters that can be used.
- TextField._rotation – indicates the rotation of the instance.
- TextField.scroll – the current scroll position.
- TextField.selectable – a flag that indicates if the field can be selected.
- TextField._soundbuftime – indicates the amount of seconds of sound to buffer.
- TextField.tabEnabled – a flag indicating if the field is included in automatic tab ordering.
- TextField.tabIndex – indicates the index value of the text field in tab ordering.
- TextField.text – represents the string in the text field (non-HTML text).
- TextField.textColor – represents the color of the text (a hexadecimal color value, for example 0xFFFFFF).
- TextField.textHeight – indicates the height of the text (not the text field's bounding box).
- TextField.textWidth – indicates the width of the text (not the text field's bounding box).
- TextField.type – defines if the text field is a dynamic or an input text field.
- TextField._url – represents the URL of the SWF file in which the text field exists (read-only).
- TextField.variable – the name of the variable associated with the text field.
- TextField._visible – a flag that defines if the text field is visible.
- TextField._width – represents the width of the text field.
- TextField._x – represents the position (in pixels) of the text field on the x-axis.
- TextField._xmouse – the x coordinate of the mouse relative to the text field.
- TextField._xscale – indicates the scaling of the text field on the x-axis.
- TextField._y – represents the position of the text field on the y-axis.
- TextField._ymouse – the y coordinate of the mouse relative to the text field.
- TextField._yscale – represents the scaling of the text field on the y-axis.

The TextField object also has the following events:

- TextField.onChanged – invoked when the contents are changed.
- TextField.onKillFocus – invoked when focus is removed.
- TextField.onScroller – invoked when the scroll properties change.
- TextField.onSetFocus – invoked when a field receives focus.

The Movie clip object has one method that relates to text field creation:

- MovieClip.createTextField – creates a new text field.

TextField._alpha

```
myTextField._alpha
```

Where `myTextField` is an instance of a text field instance.

Compatible with **Flash Player 6 and later**.

The `TextField._alpha` property represents the alpha value (transparency) of a text field. Note: this property will only work if you use embedded fonts with the text field, see `TextField.embedFonts`.

Description

The `TextField._alpha` **property** represents the alpha transparency of a text field. Legal values are any integer ranging from 0 (totally transparent) to 100 (fully opaque).

Code	Additional Explanation	Notes
`myField._alpha = 10;`	Sets the transparency (alpha) level to 10.	Valid values range from 0 to 100.
`_alpha = 10;`	No object name is specified.	

See the examples `textfield._alpha.fla` and `textfield._alpha.swf` on the CD.

TextField._focusrect

```
myTextField._focusrect
```

Where `myTextField` is a `TextField` instance.

Compatible with **Flash Player 6 and later**.

The `TextField._focusrect` property indicates whether a text field that has a yellow rectangle around it has focus.

Description

The `TextField._focusrect` **property** returns a Boolean that indicates whether a text field has a yellow rectangle around it when focus is active. If set to `true`, the yellow rectangle appears; if set to `false`, no yellow rectangle is shown.

Code	Additional Explanation	Notes
myFocus = myTextField._focusrect;	Stores the current setting of the yellow rectangle status to the variable myFocus.	myFocus must be a Boolean.
myTextField._focusrect= false	Prevents the text field from having a yellow rectangle around it when it has focus.	

TextField._height

    myTextField._height

Where myTextField is a TextField instance.

Compatible with **Flash Player 6 and later**.

The TextField._height property sets or retrieves the height of the text field in pixels.

Description
The TextField._height **property** is used to both set and display the height of a text field. The height is reported in pixels.

Code	Additional Explanation	Notes
myHeight = myTextField._height;	Stores the height of myTextField in myHeight	Heights are measured in pixels.
myTextField._height = 400;	Sets the height of myTextField to 400 pixels.	
myHeight = myTextField._height();	No method of this name exists.	

TextField._highquality

myTextField._highquality

Where myTextField is a TextField instance.

Compatible with **Flash Player 6 and later**.

The TextField._highquality property sets the amount of anti-aliasing applied to a movie.

Description

The TextField._highquality **property** sets the amount of anti-aliasing applied globally throughout the SWF.

The textField._highquality value is *not* applied to the current text field.

Code	Additional Explanation	Notes
myTextField._highquality = 2;	Always applies anti-aliasing, producing the highest quality clips.	Anti-aliasing can involve considerable processing overhead.
myTextField._highquality = 5;	No method of this name exists.	Settings are 0, 1, or 2. Any other setting has no effect.

TextField._name

myTextField._name

Where myTextField is a TextField instance.

Compatible with **Flash Player 6 and later**.

The TextField._name property returns the name of the text field instance.

Description

The TextField._name **property** simply returns the name of the text field instance. This is often used in generic scripts to store the clip name in a variable.

Code	Additional Explanation	Notes
`myName = myTextField._name;`	Assigns the name of the text field instance to `myName`.	
`myName = myTextField._name(_parent);`	No parameters are specified.	

See the examples `textfield._name.fla` and `textfield._name.swf` on the CD.

TextField._parent

```
myTextField._parent
```

Where `myTextField` is a `TextField` instance.

Compatible with **Flash Player 6 and later**.

The `TextField._parent` property is a reference to the object that the text field resides in. In other words, the parent object of the text field. This object can be a button, graphic, or movie clip. The `TextField._parent` property is often used in testing of generic scripts to store the name of the text field's parent in the text field, which is excellent for debugging purposes. See the following code:

```
myTextField.text = myTextField._parent._name;
```

Description

The `TextField._parent` **property** is a reference to the object that the text field resides in.

Code	Additional Explanation	Notes
`myName = myTextField._parent;`	Assigns the path of the text field instance's parent to `myName`.	If the text field resides on the `_root` timeline, `_level0` will be returned.
`myName = myTextField._parent(_parent);`	No parameters are specified.	

See the examples `textfield._parent.fla` and `textfield._parent.swf` on the CD.

TextField._quality

    myTextField._quality

Where myTextField is a TextField instance.

Compatible with **Flash Player 6 and later**.

The TextField._quality property sets or retrieves the rendering quality used by a movie.

Description
The TextField._quality **property** lets you set the rendering quality used by a movie clip. This is a global property. The possible values of the TextField._quality property are:

- LOW – no anti-aliasing on graphics and no smoothing on bitmaps.
- MEDIUM – graphics are anti-aliased with a 2x2 grid and no smoothing on bitmaps.
- HIGH – graphics are anti-aliased with a 4x4 grid and smoothing is applied on static bitmaps.
- BEST – graphics are anti-aliased with a 4x4 grid and smoothing is applied to all bitmaps.

The **default value** is HIGH.

Code	Additional Explanation	Notes
myTextField._quality = "LOW";	Turns off anti-aliasing and smoothing to allow faster streaming.	This is a global setting.
myTextField._quality = true;	The argument must be one of four possible values.	If illegal parameters are provided, the command fails.

TextField._rotation

    myTextField._rotation

Where myTextField is a TextField instance.

Compatible with **Flash Player 6 and later**.

The TextField._rotation property is the number of degrees the text field is rotated.

Description

The `TextField._rotation` **property** is the number of degrees the text field is rotated. The property can be set and queried.

Code	Additional Explanation	Notes
`myTextField._rotation = 10;`	Rotates the text field 10 degrees.	

See the examples `textfield._rotation.fla` and `textfield._rotation.swf` on the CD.

TextField._soundbuftime

`myTextField._soundbuftime`

Where `myTextField` is a `TextField` instance.

Compatible with **Flash Player 6 and later**.

The `TextField._soundbuftime` property specifies the number of seconds of sound to load before starting to play the sound.

Description

The `TextField._soundbuftime` **property** is used to set the number of seconds of time to buffer before a sound starts playing. If you define 10 seconds, the sound will load in 10 seconds worth of sound before it starts playing. It is useful over slow or unreliable connections.

Code	Additional Explanation	Notes
`myTotalFrames = myTextField._soundbuftime`	Stores the number of frames buffered into `myTotalFrames`.	The result is always an integer and counts frames.
`myTextField._soundbuftime = 10;`	Sets the number of seconds to buffer to 10.	
`myTextField._frames loaded()`	No method of this name exists.	

TextField._target

```
myTextField._target
```

Where myTextField is a TextField instance.

Compatible with **Flash Player 6 and later**.

The TextField._target property returns the target path of the text field.

Description

The TextField._target **property** returns the target path of the text field instance.

Code	Additional Explanation	Notes
myPath = myTextField._target;	Stores the path of myTextField in myPath.	
myPath = myTextField._target();	There is no method with this name.	

See the examples textfield._target.fla and textfield._target.swf on the CD.

TextField._url

```
myTextField._url
```

Where myTextField is a TextField instance.

Compatible with **Flash Player 6 and later**.

The TextField._url property returns the URL of the SWF file that created the text field.

Description

The TextField._url **property** returns the full URL of the location of the SWF file that was downloaded for the current text field instance.

Code	Additional Explanation	Notes
myFile = myTextField._url;	Stores the URL of myTextField in myFile.	
myFile = myTextField._url();	There is no method with this name.	

See the examples textfield._url.fla and textfield._url.swf on the CD.

TextField._visible

myTextField._visible

Where myTextField is a TextField instance.

Compatible with **Flash Player 6 and later**.

The TextField._visible property determines whether the text field is visible or not.

Description

The TextField._visible **property** is a Boolean that indicates whether the text field instance is visible or not. If not visible, the text field is disabled and cannot be selected.

Code	Additional Explanation	Notes
myTextField._visible = true;	The myTextField object is visible and can be clicked.	Non-visible objects cannot be clicked.
myTextField._visible = "true";	Only Booleans can be used for this property.	

See the examples textfield._visible.fla and textfield._visible.swf on the CD.

TextField._width

```
myTextField._width
```

Where `myTextField` is a `TextField` instance.

Compatible with **Flash Player 6 and later**.

The `TextField._width` property sets or retrieves the width of the text field in pixels.

Description

The `TextField._width` **property** is used to both set and display the width of a text field. The width is reported in pixels.

Code	Additional Explanation	Notes
`myHeight = myTextField._height;`	Stores the height of `myTextField` in `myHeight`.	Heights are measured in pixels.
`myTextField._height = 400;`	Sets the height of `myTextField` to 400 pixels.	
`myHeight = myTextField._height();`	No method of this name exists.	

See the examples `textfield._width.fla` and `textfield._width.swf` on the CD.

TextField._x

```
myTextField._x
```

Where `myTextField` is a `TextField` instance.

Compatible with **Flash Player 6 and later**.

The `TextField._x` property sets or retrieves the horizontal coordinate of a text field.

Description

The `TextField._x` **property** is used to both set and display the horizontal (x) coordinate of a text field. If a text field is in the main timeline, the value returned by the `TextField._x` property is relative to the upper left corner (0,0) of the stage. If there is a parent text field, the TextField._x property is relative to the parent's.

Code	Additional Explanation	Notes
myTextField._x = 100;	Moves the text field from where it currently is to x = 100.	x coordinates are relative to the parent object, even if that is the _root timeline.
myTextField._x += 10;	Moves the text field 10 pixels to the right.	
myTextField._x -= 10;	Moves the text field 10 pixels to the left.	
myTextField._x(100);	No method of this name exists.	

See the examples textfield._x.fla and textfield._x.swf on the CD.

TextField._xmouse

myTextField._xmouse

Where myTextField is a TextField instance.

Compatible with **Flash Player 6 and later**.

The TextField._xmouse property retrieves the horizontal coordinate of the mouse relative to the text field.

Description
The TextField._xmouse **property** equals the horizontal (x) coordinate of the mouse cursor relative to the text field.

Code	Additional Explanation	Notes
myMouse = myTextField._xmouse;	Stores the x coordinate of the mouse to myMouse relative to myTextField.	x coordinates are relative to the text field.
myTextField._xmouse(100);	No method of this name exists.	

See the examples textfield._xmouse.fla and textfield._xmouse.swf on the CD.

TextField._xscale

    myTextField._xscale

Where myTextField is a TextField instance.

Compatible with **Flash Player 6 and later**.

The TextField._xscale property sets or retrieves the horizontal scaling of a text field as a percent. 100% is taken as the original scaling of the text field (the size it was when you first placed it on the stage).

Description

The TextField._xscale **property** is a read/write property that determines the width (x-axis) scaling of the text field instance. The registration point of a text field is taken to be the top left corner, so all scaling (and for that matter, rotation) is done relative to that point.

You can only use this property if you force Flash to treat the text field as a vector graphic, and you do this by embedding font outlines. See also the *Tips and precautions* section in the **TextField** entry (on the CD) for a discussion of this.

Assume the text field below is called my_txt. At 100% scaling (the default when you place it on the stage) it will look like the image below left, and when you test the FLA it will look like the image below right:

If you add the following line, the results will be as shown below (original on the left for this and all subsequent images):

```
my_txt._xscale = 50;
```

As you can see, the new text is 50% the size of the original. If you set the _xscale to 200, it will be twice the width of the original:

```
my_txt._xscale = 200;
```

Note that performing _xscale changes after rotations will still use the local x-axis of the text field:

```
my_txt._rotation = 45;
my_txt._xscale = 200;
```

This ensures that the text never becomes distorted. If that's what you actually *want* to do, you will have to break the text apart so that it becomes a raw graphic and then use the standard drawing tools and the **Transform** panel. You *cannot* create this effect using scripting (unless you opt for the much more complex route of actually drawing the text via the drawing API of the MovieClip object):

Also of note is the use of negative values. In this case, we have scaled by -200%. The resulting text is scaled by 200% "backwards":

```
my_txt._xscale = -200;
```

You can use the _xscale value, along with the **TextField._yscale**, **TextField._x**, **TextField._y**, and **TextField._rotation** properties to create animated effects. You should note that the text field does not have a frame based onEnterFrame event, so you would typically either have to embed the text in a movie clip, or attach the animation event on another movie clip (either _root or a dummy empty clip created via **MovieClip.createEmptyMovieClip**). Such animated text effects were quite popular in Flash 5, as used by designers such as Erik Natzke.

See the examples textfield._xscale.fla and textfield._xscale.swf on the CD.

TextField._y

myTextField._y

Where myTextField is a TextField instance.

Compatible with **Flash Player 6 and later**.

The TextField._y property sets or retrieves the vertical coordinate of a text field.

Description
The TextField._y **property** is used to both set and display the vertical (y) coordinate of a text field. If a text field is in the main timeline, the value returned by the TextField._y property is relative to the upper left corner (0,0) of the stage. If there is a parent text field, the TextField._y property is relative to the parent's.

Code	Additional Explanation	Notes
myTextField._y = 100;	Stores the y coordinate of myTextField to 100 pixels.	y coordinates are relative to the parent object, even if that is the _root timeline.
myTextField._y(100);	No method of this name exists.	

TextField._ymouse

myTextField._ymouse

Where myTextField is a TextField instance.

Compatible with **Flash Player 6 and later**.

The `TextField._ymouse` property retrieves the vertical coordinate of the mouse relative to the text field.

Description

The `TextField._ymouse` **property** displays the vertical (y) coordinate of the mouse cursor relative to the text field.

Code	Additional Explanation	Notes
`myMouse = myTextField._ymouse;`	Stores the y coordinate of the mouse to `myMouse` relative to `myTextField`.	y coordinates are relative to the text field.
`myTextField._ymouse(100);`	No method of this name exists.	

See the examples `textfield._ymouse.fla` and `textfield._ymouse.swf` on the CD.

TextField._yscale

`myTextField._yscale`

Where `myTextField` is a `TextField` instance.

Compatible with **Flash Player 6 and later**.

The `TextField._yscale` property sets or retrieves the vertical scale of a text field.

Description

The `TextField._yscale` **property** is used to determine the vertical scale of a text field's registration point, relative to the (0,0) default registration point. This lets you calculate positions of objects based on scaling effects.

Code	Additional Explanation	Notes
`myTextField._yscale = 0.5;`	Sets the vertical scaling to 0.5.	y coordinates are relative to the (0,0) registration point.
`myTextField._yscale(0.5);`	No method of this name exists.	

See the examples `textfield._yscale.fla` and `textfield._yscale.swf` on the CD.

TextField.addListener

```
myTextField.addListener (listenerObjectName)
```

Where `myTextField`, an instance of a text field, will broadcast event notification to `listenerObjectName` which is an `Object` object. To receive notification from the text field, the `listener object` (`listenerObjectName`) should contain two methods: `onChanged` and `onScroller`. These methods will be executed when the `onScroller` and `onChanged` events of the text field, `myTextField`, are invoked.

Compatible with **Flash Player 6 and later**.

Description

The Flash event model allows you to set up event handlers, but there are certain situations where this model doesn't allow you to write *totally* event driven code. Major failings include:

- Only the object that causes the event can respond to the event.
- Only one "event signal" is produced per event.

In short, it is not easy to *propagate events to other objects not involved with the initial event*. For example, you might want multiple scripts to automatically run on the occurrence of a single event. The listener model allows you to do this directly. The following example shows this in action; a single text field event is propagated to two listeners, so that in the final SWF, a change in the text field will generate *three* `onChanged` events:

- One in the text field `my_txt` (but we don't use it).
- One in the listener object `textListener`.
- One in the second listener object `textListener2`.

Code	Notes

```// set up listeners...```
```textListener = new Object();```
```textListener2 = new Object();```
```my_txt.addListener(textListener);```
```my_txt.addListener(textListener2);```
```//```
```textListener.onChanged = function() {```
```   trace("one heard you!");```
```};```
```textListener2.onChanged = function() {```
```   trace("two heard you!");```
```};```
	This code sets up two listeners, both of which will respond to the `onChanged` event of `my_txt`. To become a listener, an object has to be:
	- Initialized as an `Object` object via the new `Object()` constructor.
	- Added as a listener via `addListener`.
	Once you have done these two things, you can start adding events to the listener that will be generated by the text field being lisened to (in this case we have used the `onChanged` events).
	Remember, you need to create a text field with instance name of "my_text", set to `InputText`

See also the examples `textfield.addlistener01.fla` and `textfield.addlistener01.swf` on the CD.

TextField.autoSize

`myTextField.autoSize`

Where `myTextField` is a text field instance.

Compatible with **Flash MX and later**.

The `TextField.autoSize` property controls automatic alignment and sizing of a text field when text is entered, either manually through the keyboard or through ActionScript using the `TextField.text` or `TextField.htmlText` properties.

The `TextField.autoSize` property has four legal values, all of which should have a data type of String. They are `none`, `left`, `center`, and `right`. You can also set the `autoSize` property to `true` and `false`. The `true` value is an alias for `left` and `false` is an alias for `none`.

When the `autoSize` property is set to `none` the text field doesn't automatically resize or adjust when new or more text is added to the text field. When the `autoSize` property is set to `left`, the right and bottom sides of the text field are adjusted to fit the text. When the `autoSize` property is set to `right`, the text field adjusts the left and bottom sides of the text field. When the `autoSize` property is set to `center`, each side of the text field is adjusted to compensate for the new text.

Description

This **property** indicates the usage and method for automatic sizing and alignment of a text field.

Code	Additional Explanation	Notes
`myTextField.autoSize = "none"`	No automatic resizing of the field is performed.	The values of `true` and `false` are allowed, but are strings not Booleans.
`myTextField.autoSize = "left"`	The field's right and bottom sides expand to fit the contents.	
`myTextField.autoSize()`	The `TextField` object doesn't have an `autoSize` method.	

TextField.background

myTextField.background

Where myTextField is a text field instance.

Compatible with **Flash MX and later**.

The TextField.background property is used to define if a background is applied to a text field. This property has to be applied as a Boolean value, either true or false. A true value indicates the text field has a background and false indicates the text field doesn't have a background. If you set the property to true, you must then define the background color or the default value of 0xFFFFFF (white) will be used. See also **TextField.backgroundColor**.

Description

The TextField.background **property** defines whether a text field has a background.

Code	Additional Explanation	Notes
myTextField.background = true;	Applies a background to the text field.	Only Booleans are allowed.
myTextField.background = true; myTextField.background Color = 0xFF0099;	Applies a background to the text field and sets it to a pink color.	The default background color is white (0xFFFFFF).
myTextField.background (true);	The TextField object doesn't have a background method.	

See the examples textfield.backgroundcolor.fla and textfield.backgroundcolor.swf on the CD.

TextField.backgroundColor

myTextField.backgroundColor

Where myTextField is a text field instance.

Compatible with **Flash MX and later**.

The TextField.backgroundColor property defines the color of the background fill of a text field. In order for this property to take place, the TextField.background property must be set to true, if it isn't a background on the text field is not used. A hexadecimal value should be used, for example 0x000000 (black) or 0xFF0099 (hot pink).

Description

The TextField.backgroundColor **property** is used set the color of a text field's background.

Code	Additional Explanation	Notes
myColorFill = myTextField.background Color;	Assigns the color of the background from the text field, myTextField, to the myColorFill variable.	The default color of all text fields' backgrounds is white (0xFFFFFF).
myTextField.background Color = 0xFF0000;	Sets the background fill color to red.	
myTextField.background Color (0xFF0000);	The TextField object doesn't contain a backgroundColor method.	

See the examples textfield.backgroundcolor.fla and textfield.backgroundcolor.swf on the CD.

TextField.border

myTextField.border

Where myTextField is a text field instance.

Compatible with **Flash MX and later**.

The TextField.border defines if the border of the text field can be seen. The border property can be set to either true or false. This property can be used to differentiate between text fields used to accept input and text fields used only to display a string. See also **TextField.borderColor**.

Description

The TextField.border **property** defines if the border of the text field can be seen.

Code	Additional Explanation	Notes
myTextField.border = true	Makes borders visible for the text field.	Only Booleans are allowed.
myTextField.border (true)	The TextField object doesn't have a border method.	

See the examples textfield.border.fla and textfield.border.swf on the CD.

TextField.borderColor

myTextField.borderColor

Where myTextField is a text field instance.

Compatible with **Flash Player 6 and later**.

The TextField.borderColor property controls the color of a text field's border.

Description

The TextField.borderColor **property** is used set the color of a text field border. Hexadecimal values are provided to set the color.

Code	Additional Explanation	Notes

myColorBorder = myTextField.borderColor;
 	
 myTextField.borderColor = 0xFF0000;
	Assigns the current border color to the variable myColorBorder and then sets the border color of the myTextField text field to red.	The default color of text field borders is black (0x000000).

myTextField.borderColor (0xFF0000);	The TextField object doesn't have a borderColor method.	

TextField.bottomScroll

`myTextField.bottomScroll`

Where `myTextField` is a text field instance.

Compatible with **Flash MX and later**.

The `TextField.bottomScroll` **property** represents the bottom-most line of a text field. This property is commonly used when creating scrollbars and other elements that interact with text fields. The value of this property is a 1-based integer, meaning the first line of the text field is 1.

Description
The `TextField.bottomScroll` represents the bottom-most line of a text field.

Code	Additional Explanation	Notes
`myTextField.bottomScroll = 5;`	The bottom line visible in a text window is the fifth line.	The value specified is an integer.
`myTextField.bottomScroll (10);`	No method of this name exists.	

TextField.embedFonts

`myTextField.embedFonts`

Where `myTextField` is a text field instance.

Compatible with **Flash Player 6 and later**.

The `TextField.embedFonts` indicates whether embedded fonts are allowed.

Description
The `TextField.embedFonts` **property** is a Boolean that indicates whether embedded font outlines are to be rendered. If `true`, embedded fonts are allowed; if `false`, embedded fonts are not allowed.

Code	Additional Explanation	Notes
myTextField.embedFonts = true;	Embedded fonts can be used to render characters in the text field.	If set to false, device fonts must be used.
myTextField.embedFonts = "true";	Only Booleans are allowed.	

TextField.getDepth

myTextField.getDepth()

where myTextField is a TextField instance.

Compatible with **Flash Player 6 and later**.

The TextField.getDepth() method returns the level of the text field instance.

Description
The TextField.getDepth() **method** returns an integer indicating the level (depth) of the text field.

Code	Additional Explanation	Notes
myDepth = myTextField.getDepth();	Returns the depth of myTextField.	The return from the method is an integer.
myDepth = .getDepth(myTextField);	No parameters are expected by the method, and no target text field instance is indicated.	

TextField.getFontList

myTextField.getFontList()

Where myTextField is a TextField instance.

Compatible with **Flash Player 6 and later**.

The `TextField.getFontList()` method returns an array of all fonts on the Flash Player host system.

Description

The `TextField.getFontList()` **method** examines all the fonts on the host machine of a Flash Player and returns the list of fonts as an array. All fonts included in SWF files are included in the list. The array is returned using strings.

Code	Additional Explanation	Notes
`myFonts = myTextField.getFontList();`	Returns the list of fonts on the player's system.	The return from the method is an array of strings.
`myFonts = .getFontList(myTextField);`	No parameters are expected by the method.	

See the examples `textfield.getfontlist.fla` and `textfield.getfontlist.swf` on the CD.

TextField.getNewTextFormat

`myTextField.getNewTextFormat()`

Where `myTextField` is a `TextField` instance.

Compatible with **Flash Player 6 and later**.

The `TextField.getNewTextFormat()` method returns a `TextFormat` object containing a copy of a text field's text format. A `TextFormat` object defines how the text will be rendered, such as its style (bold, normal, italics, etc.), color, and so on.

Description

The `TextField.getNewTextFormat()` **method** returns a copy of a text field instance's text format. The return is as a `TextFormat` object. This text format is used for all new text inserted into the field.

Code	Additional Explanation	Notes
`myTextFormat = TextField.getNewText Format();`	Places the list of text formats in the `myTextFormat` variable.	The return from the method is in `TextFormat` layout.

Code	Additional Explanation	Notes
myTextFormat = .getNewTextFormat(myText Field);	No parameters are expected by the method.	

TextField.getTextFormat

```
myTextField.getTextFormat()
myTextField.getTextFormat(index)
myTextField.getTextFormat(firstIndex, lastIndex)
```

Where myTextField is a TextField instance, index is an integer that specifies a character inside a text field string, and firstIndex and lastIndex specify a range of characters inside a text field string.

Compatible with **Flash Player 6 and later**.

The TextField.getTextFormat() method returns a TextFormat object that contains all the text formatting information about a text field.

Description

The TextField.getTextFormat() **method** returns all information about a text field instance's text format. The return is as a TextFormat object. This text format is used for all new text inserted into the field. If there are different properties for text inside a text field, only common properties are returned. Any property that is not in common has null returned as a value. Instead of specifying an entire text field's content, you can select the text format at any one character in the text field, or a range of characters in that field. The same rules for properties not in common apply when specifying a range of characters.

Code	Additional Explanation	Notes
myTextFormat = Text Field.getTextFormat();	Places the list of text formats for the entire field in the myTextFormat variable.	The return from the method is in TextFormat layout.
myTextFormat = Text Field.getTextFormat(10);	Examines only the tenth character in the string and places the text format properties in the variable.	
myTextFormat = TextField. getTextFormat(10, 20);	Examines the substring of the tenth through twentieth character's properties.	

Code	Additional Explanation	Notes
myTextFormat = .getText Format (myTextField);	No parameters are expected by the method.	

TextField.hscroll

myTextField.hscroll

Where myTextField is a TextField instance.

Compatible with **Flash Player 6 and later**.

The TextField.hscroll property sets or retrieves the current horizontal scrolling position.

Description

The TextField.hscroll **property** is used to both set and display the current horizontal scrolling position. If the value is set to zero, there is no horizontal scrolling.

Code	Additional Explanation	Notes
myXPos = myTextField.hscroll;	Stores the horizontal scroll position of myTextField in myXPos.	A value of zero means no scrolling has occurred.
myTextField.hscroll += 10;	Scrolls the text in myTextField by ten characters.	
mypos = myTextField.hscroll ();	No method of this name exists.	

TextField.html

myTextField.html

Where myTextField is a TextField instance.

Compatible with **Flash Player 6 and later**.

The TextField.html property is a Boolean that indicates whether the text field contains an HTML representation.

Description

The TextField.html **property** indicates whether the context of a text field is an HTML representation. If true, an HTML text field is used; if false, the text field is non-HTML.

Code	Additional Explanation	Notes
TextField.html = true;	The text field is an HTML representation.	Only Booleans can be used.
TextField.html = "true";	The argument must be a Boolean.	

See the examples textfield.html.fla and textfield.html.swf on the CD.

TextField.htmlText

myTextField.htmlText

Where myTextField is a TextField instance.

Compatible with **Flash Player 6 and later**.

The TextField.htmlText property contains the HTML representation of a text field's contents.

Description

The TextField.htmlText **property** gives the HTML representation of a text field's contents. The TextField.html property must be true to allow HTML representations to be used. If the TextField.html property is false, any text in the field is interpreted literally (which means the HTML tags are treated as straight strings).

Code	Additional Explanation	Notes
myTextField.htmlText = "A string";	The text field is an HTML representation.	The TextField.html property must be true to allow HTML interpretation.
myTextField.htmlText = true;	The argument cannot be a Boolean.	

See the examples `textfield.htmltext.fla` and `textfield.htmltext.swf` on the CD.

TextField.length

`myTextField.length`

Were `myTextField` is a `TextField` instance.

Compatible with **Flash Player6 or later**.

The `TextField.length` property indicates the number of characters in a text field.

Description

The `TextField.length` **property** provides a count of the number of characters in a text field, including any special characters such as ENTER and TAB.

Code	Additional Explanation	Notes
`myStrLength = myTextField.length;`	Counts the number of characters in the `myTextField` text field and stores the result in `myStrLength`.	An integer is returned.
`myStrLength = length(myTextField);`	The `TextField.length` property is similar to the length property but is not a method when called as a `TextField` instance.	

See the examples `textfield.length.fla` and `textfield.length.swf` on the CD.

TextField.maxChars

`myTextField.maxChars`

Were `myTextField` is a `TextField` instance.

Compatible with **Flash Player 6 or later**.

The `TextField.maxChars` property indicates the maximum number of characters allowed in a text field.

Description

The TextField.maxChars **property** sets the maximum number of characters that can be entered in a text field, including any special characters such as ENTER and TAB.

Code	Additional Explanation	Notes
myTextField.maxChars = 10;	Sets the maximum number of characters allowed in myTextField to 10.	An integer must be specified.
myStrLength = myTextField.maxChars;	Stores the maximum number of characters allowed in myTextField to a variable.	

See the examples textfield.maxchars.fla and textfield.maxchars.swf on the CD.

TextField.maxhscroll

myTextField.maxhscroll

Where myTextField is a TextField instance.

Compatible with **Flash Player 6 and later**.

The TextField.maxhscroll property sets the maximum value of the TextField.hscroll property.

Description

The TextField.maxhscroll **property** is used to set the maximum TextField.hscroll value.

Code	Additional Explanation	Notes
myTextField.maxhscroll = 50;	Sets the maximum horizontal scroll position of myTextField to 50 characters.	Sets the maximum value that can be used by TextField.hscroll.
myTextField.maxhscroll();	No method of this name exists.	

TextField.maxscroll

myTextField.maxscroll

Where myTextField is a TextField instance.

Compatible with **Flash Player 6 and later**.

The TextField.maxscroll property sets the maximum value of the TextField.scroll property.

Description
The TextField.maxscroll **property** is used to set the maximum TextField.scroll value.

Code	Additional Explanation	Notes
myTextField.maxscroll = 5;	Sets the maximum scroll position of myTextField to 5 lines.	Sets the maximum value that can be used by TextField.scroll.
myTextField.maxscroll();	No method of this name exists.	

TextField.multiline

myTextField.multiline

Where myTextField is a TextField instance.

Compatible with **Flash Player 6 and later**.

The TextField.multiline property indicates whether multiple lines can be entered into a text field.

Description
The TextField.multiline **property** is a Boolean used to indicate whether the text field is multiline or not. If true, the text field is multiline; if false, it is a single line.

Code	Additional Explanation	Notes
myTextField.multiline = true;	Sets myTextField to allow multiple lines.	Only Booleans can be used.

Code	Additional Explanation	Notes
myTextField.multiline();	No method of this name exists.	

TextField.onChanged

myTextField.onChanged

Where myTextField is a TextField instance.

Compatible with **Flash Player 6 and later**.

The TextField.onChanged event handler is invoked whenever a change is made to the contents of a text field.

Description

The TextField.onChanged **event handler** is invoked when a change is made to a text field including adding or deleting a character of text. Moving a scrollbar associated with a text field does *not* count as a change. Any actions associated with the event handler are invoked as each change is entered. By default, the method is undefined.

TextField.onKillFocus

myTextField.onKillFocus(newobject)

Where myTextField is a TextField instance and newobject is the object (movie clip, button, or text field) to receive input focus.

Compatible with **Flash Player 6 and later**.

The TextField.onKillFocus event handler is invoked when a text field loses keyboard input focus.

Description

The TextField.onKillFocus **event handler** is invoked when a text field loses keyboard input focus. This will most commonly occur when the user unselects the current text field by selecting another one, or does the same thing by hitting the TAB key. When hitting the TAB key, it is possible for the user to give a button or a movie clip input focus. The optional argument newFocus will give the name of the text field, movie clip, or button that now has focus.

See the examples textfield.onkillfocus.fla and textfield.onkillfocus.swf on the CD.

TextField.onScroller

`myTextField.onScroller`

Where `myTextField` is a `TextField` instance.

Compatible with **Flash Player 6 and later**.

The `TextField.onScroller` event handler is invoked when a text field's scroll properties change.

Description

The `TextField.onScroller` **event handler** is invoked whenever the text field's scroll properties are changed. The function associated with the `TextField.onScroller` event handler is launched when this happens.

See the examples `text fieldAddListener.fla` and `text fieldAddListener.swf` on the CD, for an example of the `onScroller` event in use.

TextField.onSetFocus

`myTextField.onSetFocus(oldFocus)`

Where `myTextField` is a `TextField` instance and `oldFocus` is the object that lost focus.

Compatible with **Flash Player 6 and later**.

The `TextField.onSetFocus` event handler is invoked when a text field gets keyboard input focus. The object that loses the focus is specified inside the event handler function.

Description

The `TextField.onSetFocus` **event handler** is invoked when a text field is given input focus. The function associated with the `TextField.onSetFocus` event handler is launched when this happens and that function specifies a new object to receive the focus.

See the examples `textfield.onsetfocus.fla` and `textfield.onsetfocus.swf` on the CD.

TextField.password

`myTextField.password`

Where `myTextField` is a `TextField` instance.

Compatible with **Flash Player 6 and later**.

The `TextField.password` property indicates the text field is to be treated as a password field.

Description

The `TextField.password` **property** is a Boolean that indicates the text field is to be treated as a password field and have the characters that are entered into that field hidden. If `true`, the field is a password field; if `false`, the field is not a password field.

When the password property is set to `true`, the text is displayed using asterisks only.

See the examples `textfield.password.fla` and `textfield.password.swf` on the CD.

TextField._quality

`myTextField._quality`

Where `myTextField` is a `TextField` instance.

Compatible with **Flash Player 6 and later**.

The `TextField._quality` property sets or retrieves the rendering quality used by a movie.

Description

The `TextField._quality` **property** lets you set the rendering quality used by a movie clip. This is a global property. The possible values of the `TextField._quality` property are:

- `LOW` – no anti-aliasing on graphics and no smoothing on bitmaps.
- `MEDIUM` – graphics are anti-aliased with a 2x2 grid and no smoothing on bitmaps.
- `HIGH` – graphics are anti-aliased with a 4x4 grid and smoothing is applied on static bitmaps.
- `BEST` – graphics are anti-aliased with a 4x4 grid and smoothing is applied to all bitmaps.

The **default value** is `HIGH`.

Code	Additional Explanation	Notes
`myTextField._quality = "LOW";`	Turns off anti-aliasing and smoothing to allow faster streaming.	This is a global setting.
`myTextField._quality = true;`	The argument must be one of four possible values.	If illegal parameters are provided, the command fails.

See the examples `textfield._quality.fla` and `textfield._quality.swf` on the CD.

TextField.removeListener

`myTextField.removeListener(listenerObject_name)`

Where `listenerObject_name` is the `listener` object to stop receiving event notification broadcasts from `myTextField`.

Compatible with **Flash Player 6 and later**.

The `TextField.removeListener` method is used to remove a `listener` object, which was assigned to the text field using the `TextField.addListener` method. Apart from this, the method has no other function, and a `listener` object needs to be assigned to the text field (using the `TextField.addListener` method) prior to using this method. The Boolean `true` is returned if the listener object is successfully removed and `false`, if unsuccessful.

Description

This **method** removes a `listener` object from receiving call-back notification broadcasts from the `TextField` events..

Code	Additional Explanation	Notes
`myTextobject.remove Listener(mylistening Object);`	Removes `mylisteningObject` from the listener.	If `mylisteningObject` is registered and removed successfully, `true` is returned.
		If `mylisteningObject` is either not removed or not registered as a listener, `false` is returned.

See the examples `textfield.removelistener.fla` and `textfield.removelistener.swf` on the CD.

TextField.removeTextField

`myTextField.removeTextField()`

Where `myTextField` is a `TextField` instance.

Compatible with **Flash Player 6 and later**.

The `TextField.removeTextField()` method removes a text field instance.

Description

The `TextField.removeTextField()` **method** is used to remove an instance of a text field that was created with the `MovieClip.createTextField()` method.

Code	Additional Explanation	Notes
`myTextField.remove` `TextField()`	Removes `myTextField`.	
`myTextField.remove` `TextField("myNewCopy");`	No target name can be specified; the instance calling the method is removed.	

See the examples `textfield.removetextfield.fla` and `textfield.removetextfield.swf` on the CD.

TextField.replaceSel

`myTextField.replaceSel(text)`

Where `myTextField` is a `TextField` instance and `text` is the text to insert.

Compatible with **Flash Player 6 and later**.

The `TextField.replaceSel()` method is supposed to replace the current selection with new text, but is bugged, so you are unlikely to use it.

Description

The `TextField.replaceSel()` **method** is designed used to replace a text selection with another text string. It is bugged however, so you are unlikely to use it. The example files in the *Examples and practical uses* section (on the CD) shows the error and a workaround.

The examples `textfield.replacesel01.fla` and `textfield.replacesel01.swf` on the CD, documents the bug, and the additional files `textfield.replacesel02.fla` and `textfield.replacesel02.swf` document a possible workaround.

TextField.restrict

`myTextField.restrict`

Where `myTextField` is a `TextField` instance.

Compatible with **Flash Player 6 and later**.

The TextField.restrict property limits the characters that can be entered.

Description

The TextField.restrict **property** is used to limit the characters a user can enter into a text field. If the TextField.restrict property is set to null, any characters can be entered. If the TextField.restrict property is set to an empty string, no characters can be entered. Otherwise, you can specify a string that contains the characters or ranges of characters that are allowable.

Code	Additional Explanation	Notes
myTextField.restrict = "AEIOU";	The string contains all the allowable characters.	The ^ is used to negate (forbid) characters.
myTextField.restrict = "A-Z";	Ranges are specified with a hyphen.	
myTextField.restrict = "032-064";	ASCII codes cannot be entered in this manner. They must be converted to hex and preceded by \u.	

TextField.scroll

myTextField.scroll

Where myTextField is a TextField instance.

Compatible with **Flash Player 6 and later**.

The TextField.scroll property shows the vertical position of text in a text field.

Description

The TextField.scroll **property** shows the position of the current text in a text field vertically. The property can be set and queried.

Code	Additional Explanation	Notes
myTextField.scroll = 10;	Scrolls the text field 10 lines.	

See the examples `textfield.scroll.fla` and `textfield.scroll.swf` on the CD.

TextField.selectable

`myTextField.selectable`

Where `myTextField` is a `TextField` instance.

Compatible with **Flash Player 6 and later**.

The `TextField.selectable` property indicates whether the text field is selectable or not.

Description

The `TextField.selectable` **property** is a Boolean that indicates whether the text field is selectable or not. If `true` the field can be selected; if `false`, the field cannot be selected. The property can be set and queried.

Code	Additional Explanation	Notes
`myTextField.selectable = true;`	Lets the text field be selected by the user.	Only Boolean values are allowed.

See the examples `textfield.selectable.fla` and `textfield.selectable.swf` on the CD.

TextField.setNewTextFormat

`myTextField.setNewTextFormat(object)`

Where `myTextField` is a `TextField` instance and `object` is the `TextFormat` object that contains the text properties.

Compatible with **Flash Player 6 and later**.

The `TextField.setNewTextFormat()` method sets a `TextFormat` object for new text.

Description

The `TextField.setNewTextFormat()` **method** sets a `TextFormat` object for all new text inserted into the field. This applies to text typed by a user or inserted by a script with a `TextField.replaceSel()` method, for example. All assigned `TextFormat` properties are assigned to the new text entered into a text field.

Code	Additional Explanation	Notes
myTextFormat.setNewText Format(myObject);	Sets the properties of the myTextFormat text field to those defined in myObject.	The object is in an instance of the TextFormat object.
myTextFormat.setNewText Format();	No parameters are specified so the command fails.	

TextField.setTextFormat

```
myTextField.setTextFormat(TextFieldObject)
myTextField.setTextFormat(index, TextFieldObject)
myTextField.setTextFormat(firstIndex, lastIndex, object)
```

Where myTextField is a TextField instance, object is a TextFormat object, index is an integer that specifies a character position inside a text field string, and firstIndex and lastIndex specify a range of characters inside a text field string, starting (and including) position firstIndex, and ending at (but not including) lastIndex. The first character in a text field is taken to be index 0.

Compatible with **Flash Player 6 and later**.

The TextField.setTextFormat() method uses a TextFormat object that contains text formatting information and applies that format to a text field.

Description

The TextField.setTextFormat() **method** sets a text field instance's text format. This text format is used for all text in the field unless a specific character or range of characters is added as a parameter. Instead of specifying an entire text field's content, you can set the text format at any one character in the text field, or a range of characters in that field.

Code	Notes
myTextField.setTextFormat(myObject);	Uses the list of text formats in myObject for the all characters in the myTextFormat text field.
myTextField.setTextFormat(10, myObject);	Sets only the eleventh character in the string to have myObject's properties.

Code	Notes
`myTextFormat.setTextFormat(10, 20, myObject);`	Sets characters between character position 10 to 20 to the formatting properties defined by `myObject`.
`myTextFormat.setTextFormat();`	No parameters are given to the method so the command fails.

TextField.tabEnabled

`myTextField.tabEnabled`

Where `myTextField` is an input `TextField` instance.

Compatible with **Flash Player 6 and later**.

The `TextField.tabEnabled` property controls whether the object instance is included in automatic tab ordering.

Description

The `TextField.tabEnabled` **property** lets you control whether an input text field is included in automatic tab ordering. Dynamic text fields are not included in TAB ordering irrespective of this property. If the `TextField.tabEnabled` property is set to `true` or `undefined` (the default value), the text field is included in automatic tab ordering. If the value of the `TextField.tabEnabled` property is set to `false`, the text field is not included in automatic tab ordering.

Code	Additional Explanation	Notes
`myTextField.tabEnabled = false;`	`myTextField` is not included in automatic tab ordering.	By default the value is `undefined`, which indicates inclusion in automatic tab ordering (as does setting the property to `true`). This property has no effect on children of the object.
`myTextField.tabEnabled = "true";`	Only Boolean values are allowed.	

See the examples `textfield.tabenabled.fla` and `textfield.tabenabled.swf` on the CD.

TextField.tabIndex

    myTextField.tabIndex

Where myTextField is a TextField instance.

Compatible with **Flash Player 6 and later**.

The TextField.tabIndex property controls automatic tab ordering of objects in a movie.

Description

The TextField.tabIndex **property** lets you control how all objects are handled by tab ordering. If a text field has the TextField.tabEnabled property set to false, it will not be included in TAB ordering.

If the TextField.tabEnabled property is set to true, then the ordering is defined by the TextField.tabIndex property. Buttons and movie clips can also be included in the tab index (they also have the tabEnabled and tabIndex properties).

Code	Additional Explanation	Notes
myMenu.tabIndex = 6;	Sets the tabIndex property of myMenu to 6.	By default all objects have the TextField.tabIndex property value undefined.
myMenu.tabIndex();	There is no method with this name, only a property.	

See the examples textfield.tabindex.fla and textfield.tabindex.swf on the CD.

TextField.text

    myTextField.text

Where myTextField is a TextField instance.

Compatible with **Flash Player 6 and later**.

The TextField.text property is the text content of the text field.

Description

The `TextField.text` **property** is the text content, as a string, in the text field. Any lines are separated by carriage returns. If the text field is HTML, the HTML tags are stripped and the string contains only unformatted text. This is one of the most used properties of the text field. It allows you to read and write values of the string the text field is currently displaying.

Code	Additional Explanation	Notes
`myText = myTextField.text;`	Stores the text of `myTextField` in `myText`.	
`myTextField.text = "Test";`	Assigns the field's text to `Test`.	
`myPath = myTextField.text();`	There is no method with this name.	

TextField.textColor

`myTextField.textColor`

Where `myTextField` is a `TextField` instance.

Compatible with **Flash Player 6 and later**.

The `TextField.textColor` property sets or reads the color of the text of the text field.

Description

The `TextField.textColor` **property** is the color of any text content in a text field. Colors are defined using hexadecimal values.

Code	Additional Explanation	Notes
`myPath = myTextField.textColor;`	Stores the color property of `myTextField` in `myPath`.	
`myTextField.textColor = 0x000000`	Sets the text color to black.	
`myPath = myTextField.textColor();`	There is no method with this name.	

See the examples `textfield.textcolor.fla` and `textfield.textcolor.swf` on the CD.

TextField.textHeight

`myTextField.textHeight`

Where `myTextField` is a `TextField` instance.

Compatible with **Flash Player 6 and later**.

The `TextField.textHeight` property sets the height of the text in the text field.

Description
The `TextField.textHeight` **property** is the height of any text content in a text field.

Code	Additional Explanation	Notes
`myPath = myTextField.textHeight;`	Stores the height property of `myTextField` in `myPath`.	
`myTextField.textHeight = 10`	Sets the text height to 10.	
`myPath = myTextField.textHeight ();`	There is no method with this name.	

See the examples `textfield.textheight.fla` and `textfield.textheight.swf` on the CD.

TextField.textWidth

`myTextField.textWidth`

Where `myTextField` is a `TextField` instance.

Compatible with **Flash Player 6 and later**.

The `TextField.textWidth` property sets the width of the individual characters of the text field.

Description
The `TextField.textWidth` **property** sets the width of any text content in a text field.

Code	Additional Explanation	Notes
myPath = myTextField.textWidth;	Stores the width property of myTextField in myPath.	
myTextField.textWidth = 10	Sets the text width to 10.	
myPath = myTextField.textWidth();	There is no method with this name.	

See the examples `textfield.textwidth.fla` and `textfield.textwidth.swf` on the CD.

TextField.type

myTextField.type

Where myTextField is a TextField instance.

Compatible with **Flash Player 6 and later**.

The TextField.type property sets or retrieves the type of text field.

Description

The TextField.type **property** sets or retrieves the type of text field. There are two types: dynamic is a dynamic text field and cannot be selected by a user; and input is a non-dynamic input text field.

Code	Additional Explanation	Notes
myTextField.type = "dynamic";	Sets the text field type to be dynamic.	Only dynamic and input are allowed values.
myPath = myTextField.type();	There is no method with this name.	

See the examples `textfield.type.fla` and `textfield.type.swf` on the CD.

TextField.variable

```
myTextField.variable
```

Where `myTextField` is a `TextField` instance.

Compatible with **Flash Player 6 and later**.

The `TextField.variable` property returns the name of the variable associated with the text field.

Description

The `TextField.variable` **property** returns the name of the variable that is associated with the current text field instance, returning the result as a string.

Code	Additional Explanation	Notes
myFile = myTextField.variable;	Stores the name of myTextField in myFile.	
myFile = myTextField.variablel();	There is no method with this name.	

See the examples `textfield.variable.fla` and `textfield.variable.swf` on the CD.

TextField.wordWrap

```
myTextField.wordWrap
```

Where `myTextField` is a `TextField` instance.

Compatible with **Flash Player 6 and later**.

The `TextField.wordWrap` property determines whether the text field will wrap text or not.

Description

The `TextField.wordWrap` **property** is a Boolean that indicates whether the text field instance has word wrap capabilities or not. If set to `false`, word wrap is disabled; otherwise word wrap is active.

Code	Additional Explanation	Notes
myTextField.wordWrap = true;	The myTextField object allows text to be wrapped.	
myTextField.wordWrap = "true";	Only Booleans can be used for this property.	

See the examples textfield.wordwrap.fla and textfield.wordwrap.swf on the CD.

TextFormat

Compatible with **Flash Player 6 and later.**

The TextFormat object handles character appearance of one or more TextField objects. You apply a TextFormat object to a TextField using the TextField.setTextFormat method.

Description

The TextFormat **object** has many properties attached to it to control the appearances of text. A constructor must be used to create a new TextFormat instance.

The TextFormat object contains a single method:

- TextFormat.getTextExtent – gets the width and height of a text field.

The TextFormat object has several properties associated with it:

- TextFormat.align– sets the alignment of a paragraph.
- TextFormat.blockIndent – controls block indenting.
- TextFormat.bold – sets whether a text field is boldface.
- TextFormat.bullet – sets whether the text field has bulleted lists.
- TextFormat.color – sets the color of the text.
- TextFormat.font – sets the font used in text.
- TextFormat.indent – sets the indentation value.
- TextFormat.italic – sets whether the text is italicized.
- TextFormat.leading – sets the leading vertical space between lines.
- TextFormat.leftMargin – the left margin in points.
- TextFormat.rightMargin – the right margin in points.
- TextFormat.tabStops – sets the tab stops.
- TextFormat.target – returns the window in a browser where a hyperlink is displayed.
- TextFormat.size – sets the point size of text.
- TextFormat.underline – sets whether text is underlined.

■   `TextFormat.url` – sets the URL to which the text links.

See the examples `textformat.fla` and `textformat.swf` on the CD.

TextFormat.align

`myTextFormat.align`

Where `myTextFormat` is a `TextFormat` instance.

Compatible with **Flash Player 6 and later**.

The `TextFormat.align` property sets or retrieves the alignment of a paragraph.

Description
The `TextFormat.align` **property** is used to set or retrieve the alignment characteristics of text. The alignment is specified as a string. If the `TextFormat.align` property is set to `left`, text is left-aligned. Similarly, if set to `right`, text is right aligned. A setting of `center` means the text is centered in the field.

Code	Additional Explanation	Notes
`myTextFormat.align = "left";`	Sets the alignment of the text to left-align.	Only `left`, `right`, and `center` are allowed.
`myTextFormat.align = left;`	The alignment must be specified as a string.	

See the examples `textformat.align.fla` and `textformat.align.swf` on the CD.

TextFormat.blockIndent

`myTextFormat.blockIndent`

Where `myTextFormat` is a `TextFormat` instance.

Compatible with **Flash Player 6 and later**.

The `TextFormat.blockIndent` property sets or retrieves the block indentation of text in a field.

Description

The `TextFormat.blockIndent` **property** is used to set or retrieve the block indentation characteristics of all the text in a field. The value is specified as a number of points. If set to `null`, there is no block indentation.

Code	Additional Explanation	Notes
`myTextFormat.blockIndent = "10";`	Indents all text 10 points.	A `null` value means no indentation. Block indentation applies to all line in the field.
`myTextFormat.blockIndent = 10;`	The indentation must be specified as a number.	

See the examples `textformat.blockindent.fla` and `textformat.blockindent.swf` on the CD.

TextFormat.bold

`myTextFormat.bold`

Where `myTextFormat` is a `TextFormat` instance.

Compatible with **Flash Player 6 and later**.

The `TextFormat.bold` property indicates if the text is bold or not.

Description

The `TextFormat.bold` **property** is a Boolean used to indicate if the text is bolded. If `true`, the text is bolded; if `false`, text is not bolded. The default is `null`.

Code	Additional Explanation	Notes
`myTextFormat.bold = true;`	Text is bolded.	A `null` value means no bolding.

See the examples `textformat.bold.fla` and `textformat.bold.swf` on the CD.

TextFormat.bullet

```
myTextFormat.bullet
```

where `myTextFormat` is a `TextFormat` instance.

Compatible with **Flash Player 6 and later**.

The `TextFormat.bullet` property indicates whether the text is part of a bulleted list.

Description

The `TextFormat.bullet` **property** is a Boolean used to indicate if the text is bulleted. If `true`, the text is bulleted; if `false`, text is not bulleted. The default is `null`, which means no bullets. If bulleted, the text is indented to the right and a bullet appears to the left of the text.

Assuming we had a text field called `my_txt` as shown:

> option 1
> option 2
> option 3 with line over-running to the
> next line
> option 4

The following lines would result in a change as shown:

```
myTextFormat = new TextFormat();
myTextFormat.bullet = true;
my_txt.setTextFormat(myTextFormat);
```

> • option 1
> • option 2
> • option 3 with line over-running
>   to the next line
> • option 4

Code	Additional Explanation	Notes
`myTextFormat.bullet = true;`	Text is bulleted.	A `null` value means the value of the text field is unchanged.

See the examples `textformat.bullet.fla` and `textformat.bullet.swf` on the CD.

TextFormat.color

```
myTextFormat.color
```

Where myTextFormat is a TextFormat instance.

Compatible with **Flash Player 6 and later**.

The TextFormat.color property indicates the color of text.

Description

The TextFormat.color **property** is a hexadecimal value used to indicate the color of text.

Code	Additional Explanation	Notes
myTextFormat.color = 0x000000;	Text is black.	

See the examples textformat.color.fla and textformat.color.swf on the CD.

TextFormat.font

```
myTextFormat.font
```

Where myTextFormat is a TextFormat instance.

Compatible with **Flash Player 6 and later**.

The TextFormat.font property indicates the font-face being used with the TextFormat.

Description

The TextFormat.font **property** is a string value used to indicate the font of text.

Code	Additional Explanation	Notes
myTextFormat.font = "Arial";	Sets the text font to Arial.	Only strings should be used.

TextFormat.getTextExtent

`myTextFormat.getTextExtent (text)`

Where `myTextFormat` is a `TextFormat` instance and `text` is a string.

Compatible with **Flash Player 6 and later**.

The `TextFormat.getTextExtent` method returns the size of the text field that would display all of the string *text*, given that the text formatting specified by `myTextFormat` is applied to it. Unfortunately, the method is inaccurate and cannot be relied upon.

Description

The `TextFormat.getTextExtent` **method** returns the size of the specified text string as an `Object` object with properties of width and height. This object defines the size (in pixels) that a single line text field would have to be to display the string (as plain text with HTML and control code formatting ignored), when the string is formatted via the `TextFormat` object.

This would allow you to resize a text field after the `TextFormat` object is applied, such that all the text is still visible. Unfortunately, the method returns inaccurate values, and in tests was found to resize the text field too small in many cases. It cannot therefore be relied upon, and should not be used.

TextFormat.indent

`myTextFormat.indent`

Where `myTextFormat` is a `TextFormat` instance.

Compatible with **Flash Player 6 and later**.

The `TextFormat.indent` property sets or retrieves the amount of indentation of the first line of text in a paragraph.

Description

The `TextFormat.indent` **property** is used to set or retrieve the indentation characteristics of the first line of text in a paragraph. The value is specified as a number of points. If set to `null`, the value already set in the text field is preserved.

Code	Additional Explanation	Notes
`myTextFormat.indent = 10;`	Indents the first line of text 10 points.	

See the examples `textformat.indent.fla` and `textformat.indent.swf` on the CD.

TextFormat.italic

`myTextFormat.italic`

Where `myTextFormat` is a `TextFormat` instance.

Compatible with **Flash Player 6 and later**.

The `TextFormat.italic` property indicates whether the text is italicized.

Description
The `TextFormat.italic` **property** is a Boolean used to indicate if the text is italicized. If `true`, the text is in italics; if `false`, text is not italicized. The default is `null`, which means that the italic setting in the text field is retained.

Code	Additional Explanation	Notes
`myTextFormat.italic = true;`	Text is shown in italics.	

See the examples `textformat.italic.fla` and `textformat.italic.swf` on the CD.

TextFormat.leading

`myTextFormat.leading`

Where `myTextFormat` is a `TextFormat` instance.

Compatible with **Flash Player 6 and later**.

The `TextFormat.leading` property indicates the leading vertical space between lines.

Description
The `TextFormat.leading` **property** is a number indicating the amount of leading vertical space that is to be applied between lines of text in a text field. The default is `null` which means that the leading setting in the text field is retained.

Code	Additional Explanation	Notes
myTextFormat.leading = 5;	5 points is used between lines of text as a leading vertical space.	

See the examples `textformat.leading.fla` and `textformat.leading.swf` on the CD.

TextFormat.leftMargin

`myTextFormat.leftMargin`

Where `myTextFormat` is a `TextFormat` instance.

Compatible with **Flash Player 6 and later**.

The `TextFormat.leftMargin` property indicates the left margin.

Description
The `TextFormat.leftMargin` **property** is a number indicating the number of points of space applied to the left of all text in a text field. The default is `null` which means that the `leftMargin` setting in the text field is retained.

Code	Additional Explanation	Notes
myTextFormat.leftMargin = 5;	5 points is used as a left margin.	

See the examples `textformat.leftmargin.fla` and `textformat.leftmargin.swf` on the CD.

TextFormat.rightMargin

`myTextFormat.rightMargin`

Where `myTextFormat` is a `TextFormat` instance.

Compatible with **Flash Player 6 and later**.

The `TextFormat.rightMargin` property specifies the right margin.

Description

The `TextFormat.rightMargin` **property** is a number indicating the number of points of space applied to the right of all text in a text field. The default is `null` which means that the `rightMargin` setting in the text field is retained.

Code	Additional Explanation	Notes
`myTextFormat.rightMargin = 5;`	5 points is used as a right margin.	A `null` value means undefined.

See the examples `textformat.rightmargin.fla` and `textformat.rightmargin.swf` on the CD.

TextFormat.size

`myTextFormat.size`

Where `myTextFormat` is a `TextFormat` instance.

Compatible with **Flash Player 6 and later**.

The `TextFormat.size` property indicates the point size of the font.

Description

The `TextFormat.size` **property** is a number indicating the point size of all text in a text field. The default is `null` which means that the size setting in the text field is retained.

Code	Additional Explanation	Notes
`myTextFormat.size = 5;`	5 point fonts are used.	

See the examples `textformat.size.fla` and `textformat.size.swf` on the CD.

TextFormat.tabStops

`myTextFormat.tabStops`

Where `myTextFormat` is a `TextFormat` instance.

Compatible with **Flash Player 6 and later**.

The `TextFormat.tabStops` property sets custom tab stops.

Description

The `TextFormat.tabStops` **property** is an array of non-negative integers indicating tab stops, specified in points. The default is `null` meaning that the `tabStops` setting in the text field is retained.

Code	Additional Explanation	Notes
`myTextFormat.tabStops = [5, 10, 15];`	Tabs are placed at 5, 10, and 15 points.	Non-negative integers must be specified.

See the examples `textformat.tabstops.fla` and `textformat.tabstops.swf` on the CD.

TextFormat.target

`myTextFormat.target`

Where `myTextFormat` is a `TextFormat` instance.

Compatible with **Flash Player 6 and later**.

The `TextFormat.target` property indicates the target window that a dynamic text field will link to when it is being used as a hyperlink.

Description

The `target` **property** is relevant only to a text field that has all the following attributes:

- A dynamic text field.
- Rendered as HTML.
- Has a valid URL field.

In short, the text field is acting as a *hyperlink to another web page*.

As in JavaScript and HTML, any link should specify two things:

- The HTML document that you want to display. This is specified by the URL, which points to the document you want to open (OK, obvious!).
- The window you want to open the document in. This is specified by the **target** property.

The `target` property allows you to dynamically define the target browser window. The values of target are _blank, _parent, _self, and _top. If we call `thisSWF` the SWF containing the hyperlink, then:

- _blank means open the document in a new browser window.
- _parent means open the document in the _parent to the current browser frame that thisSWF is in. You would typically only use this target if thisSWF is embedded in a HTML document containing nested HTML frames. _parent means exactly the same as the parent property of the JavaScript Window object.
- _self signifies the current browser window. It is the same browser window that the SWF containing the hyperlink is in. _self means exactly the same as the self property of the JavaScript Window object.
- _top means the top-level browser window. _top means exactly the same as the top property of the JavaScript Window object.

If you don't specify a target (or one that Flash cannot recognize) _self is assumed.

Code	Additional Explanation	Notes
myTextFormat.target = "_parent";	The web page linked to by this text field will be opened in the parent browser window. If the URL associated with a text field this TextFormat was applied to, was index2.html, then the web page index2.html would be opened in the parent browser window (or frame).	

TextFormat.underline

    myTextFormat.underline

Where myTextFormat is a TextFormat instance.

Compatible with **Flash Player 6 and later**.

The TextFormat.underline property indicates whether the text is underlined.

Description
The TextFormat.underline **property** is a Boolean used to indicate if the text is underlined. If true, the text is underlined, if false text is not underlined. The default is null.

Code	Additional Explanation	Notes
`myTextFormat.underline =` `true;`	Text is shown underlined.	

See the examples `textformat.underline.fla` and `textformat.underline.swf` on the CD.

TextFormat.url

`myTextFormat.url`

Where `myTextFormat` is a `TextFormat` instance.

Compatible with **Flash Player 6 and later**.

The `TextFormat.url` property indicates the URL this text hyperlinks to.

Description

The `TextFormat.url` **property** is a string value indicating the URL the text hyperlinks to. If an empty string is used, there is no hyperlink. The default is `null`, which means an undefined value

Code	Additional Explanation	Notes
`myTextFormat.url =` `"testpage.htm";`	The string specifies the URL of the hyperlink text.	A `null` value means no link.

this

`this`

Compatible with **Flash 5 Player and later**.

The `this` keyword refers to the object containing the method or script.

Description

The `this` **keyword** is used to indicate which object or movie clip you are referring to when referencing methods, properties, or event handlers. When inside a movie clip using the `this` keyword in the script, it references the movie clip. When called from an object or instance, the `this` keyword refers to the calling entity. When called inside an event handler, the `this` keyword refers to the timeline, or the movie clip in which the event handler is targeted. In all cases, `this` refers to the *scope* of the current script.

Code	Additional Explanation	Notes
`this.size = 10;`	Refers to the object that is the current scope of the script.	When called inside an event handler or attached to a frame, `this` refers to the timeline. When called from an object, `this` refers to the object.

`person = new Object();`
`person.init =`
`function () {`
    `this.firstName =`
`"John";`
    `this.lastName =`
`"Doe";`
    `this.age = 21;`
 	
`}`
`person.init();`
	This piece of code, defines an object. The init method of the person object is also defined. When the init function is called, the object will contain the following properties, firstName, lastName, and age.	In this example, `this` refers to the object, person.

`onClipEvent (enterFrame) {`
    `this._x++;`
`}`
	This code will increment the x position of the movie clip by 1.	In this example, `this` refers to the movie clip in which this code resides.

See the examples `this.fla` and `this.swf` on the CD.

toggleHighQuality

```
toggleHighQuality()
```

Compatible with **Flash 2 Player and later**.

The `toggleHighQuality` property turns anti-aliasing on or off. See also **MovieClip._quality**.

Description

The `toggleHighQuality` **property** toggles anti-aliasing on or off to change the quality of a movie. When toggled on, anti-aliasing is applied and edges of objects are smoother. When off, no anti-aliasing is applied. There are a number of other issues that can affect the quality, and these include:

- Whether the graphics being anti-aliased are pixel snapped or not. Pixel snapped graphics are not aliased.
- The resolution of the users screen. Higher resolutions are less susceptible to "jaggies", and the need for aliasing is reduced.

A fuller description of aliasing and its effects is included in the entries **Button._highQuality**, **Button._quality** and the corresponding entries for the movie clip and text field objects.

Code	Additional Explanation	Notes
`toggleHighQuality();`	Toggles anti-aliasing on or off.	
`toggleHighQuality() = true;`	No values can be specified for the setting.	

trace

`trace(expression)`

Where `expression` is an expression to evaluate, such as a string.

Compatible with **Flash 4 Player and later**.

The `trace()` method evaluates an expression and displays the result in the Output window. This feature should only be used in the authoring environment as a debugging tool.

Description

The `trace()` **method** is used to perform an evaluation on an expression and display the result via the Output window. This window should only be used during authoring, and will not appear in the final SWF. Usually, the `trace()` method is used to display strings or variable values as required during the debugging process during content creation.

Code	Additional Explanation	Notes
`trace("string");`	Displays "`string`" on the output.	Any valid expression can be placed inside the `trace()` method; any returns from the expression are displayed.
`trace(var1);`	Displays the value of `var1`.	
`trace(Math.min(6, 4));`	Displays the minimum of the two numbers,	
`trace() = "string";`	No values can be specified for the `trace()` method in this manner.	
`trace (var1, var2);`	You can only specify one item for display.	

See the examples `trace.fla` and `trace.swf` on the CD.

true

`true`

Flash MX and later. Compatible with **Flash 6 Player and later.**

The `true` keyword indicates a positive Boolean result.

Description

The `true` **keyword** is a Boolean value to indicate a positive result. It is the opposite of `false`.

Code	Additional Explanation	Notes
`myTextFormat.italic = true;`	Sets the property to a positive Boolean value	`true` and `false` are the only Boolean values.

`a = 5;`
`b = 5;`
 	
`c = a == b;`
	`c = true`	c will return `true` as 5 is equal to 5.

`a = new Object();`
`b = new Object();`
 	
`c = (typeof a == typeof b);`
	`c = true`	c will return `true` as both a and b are objects of the type `Object` object.

`a = 10;`
`b = new String();`
 	
`c = (typeof a != typeof b);`
	`c = true`	c will return `true`, as a is of the type `Number` object and b is of the type `String` object, which aren't equal.

See the examples `trace.fla` and `trace.swf`, on the CD.

typeof

`typeof item`

Where `item` is a button, function, movie clip, string, or object.

Compatible with **Flash 5 Player and later.**

The `typeof` operator forces Flash to interpret the argument and return its type.

Description

The `typeof` **operator** is used to tell Flash to examine the argument as a specific type of entity and return the result of the examination. The result of the `typeof` operator is a string indicating whether the item is a button, function, movie clip, string, or object. Valid Flash items and the returns from the `typeof` operator are:

- Boolean – `boolean`
- Button – `object`
- Function – `function`
- Movie Clip – `movieclip`
- Number – `number`
- Object – `object`
- String – `string`
- Text Field – `object`
- Undefined – `undefined`

Code	Additional Explanation	Notes
`typeof myString;`	Returns `string` as `myString` is a string.	Objects, buttons, and text fields are all treated as `object`.

`a = new Object();`
`b = new Object();`
 	
`c = (typeof a == typeof b);`
	`c true`	`c` returns `true` as the equation in the brackets evaluates the `typeof` object that a is against b. Because they're both of the type `Object` object, it returns `true`.

`doSomething(10);`
 	
`function doSomething`
`(num) {`
`    // check 'num' is a`
`Number`
`    if (typeof num !=`
`"number") return false;`
 	
`    // code here as num`
`is a number`
`    trace("your code here");`
`}`
	Simple function, which requires the `num` parameter to be a Number.	The `if...` statement checks the `typeof` value of the passed parameter to make sure it is equal to the string `number`. If it isn't, it returns a `false` value. However, continues on if it is of the type `number`. This is a common practice when protecting users against improper use of your function.

See the examples `typeof.fla` and `typeof.swf` on the CD.

U/V/W

gotoAndStop()
hitTest()
loadMovie()
loadVariables()
loadVariables()
nextFrame()   play()
prevFrame()
removeMovieClip()
setMask() startDrag()
StartDrag() startDrag()
swap Depth s a c
un loadMovie()
attachMovie()
createEmptyMovi
createTextFielo
duplicate
gatRo

undefined

`undefined`

Compatible with **Flash Player 5 and later**.

The `undefined` keyword indicates an unassigned value.

Description

The `undefined` **keyword** is result of a query that has no value. For example, a variable that has not been assigned a value has a value of undefined.

See the examples `undefined.fla` and `undefined.swf` on the CD.

unescape

`unescape(string)`
Where string is an URL-encoded string.

Compatible with **Flash 5 and later**.

The `unescape` **function** is a top-level function used to decode strings which are in an URL-encoded format. An URL-encoded format is used to pass information through a web browser or on the end of an URL. URL-encoded strings are safe to use in a web browser's address bar as certain characters from the ASCII table need to be encoded before they can be used in an URL. All of these special characters in a string are converted to ASCII sequences upon being encoded to the URL-encoded format. The special characters are all non alpha-numeric characters in the ASCII table and some examples of hexadecimal characters are {}, [] , and a space.

You probably see URL-encoded strings quite regularly while surfing the web, it is common to see them after the name of a HTML page you're visiting along with the ? character. For example this is the URL-encoded URL from a Google search, http://www.google.com/search?hl=en&ie=UTF-8&oe=UTF-8&q=%7BFlash+MX+information%7D&btnG=Google+Search.

Description

The `unescape` is a top-level function used to decode an URL-encoded string.

Code	Additional Explanation	Notes
unescape ("hello%7B%7D")	Returns "hello{}" as an un-encoded URL string.	The parameter must be a string.

See the example unescape.fla and unescape.swf on the CD.

unloadMovie

```
unloadMovie (target);
```

Where `target` specifies the instance name of the target movie clip.

Compatible with **Flash Player 3 and later**.

The `unloadMovie()` action is used to unload a movie from a Flash player. See also **unloadMovieNum**, **MovieClip.unloadMovie**, and **MovieClip.loadMovie**.

Description

The `unloadMovie()` **action** is used to unload a movie that was loaded with a `loadMovie()` or `loadMovieNum()` action. You can unload a movie using the name of the movie clip or the level that the movie clip is loaded into if you use the `unloadMovieNum()` action instead.

Code	Additional explanation	Notes
`unloadMovie ("introMovie");`	Removes the movie with a instance name of `introMovie`.	
`unloadMovie(5);`	Although the target parameter is a number, rather than a string, which is expected, this still works as the `unloadMovie` function is automatically replaced with the `unloadMovieNum` function.	
`unloadMovie ("movieFilename.swf");`	Error	The instance name of the movie clip should be passed to the `unloadMovie` function, not the SWF's filename.

See the examples `unloadmovie.fla` and `unloadmovie.swf` on the CD.

unloadMovieNum

```
unloadMovieNum (level);
```

Where `level` is the level number of the movie.

Compatible with **Flash Player 3 and later**. See also, **unloadMovie**, **MovieClip.unloadMovie**, and **loadMovie**.

The `unloadMovieNum()` action is used to unload a movie from the Flash player. The `level` parameter passed will determine on which level the movie clip is unloaded from, and is usually determined by the parameter passed when the movie was loaded using `loadMovieNum`. Once the new movie clip has been loaded you can target it via the following, `_levelN`, where N is the passed level parameter.

Description

The `unloadMovieNum()` **action** is used to unload a movie from a specific level.

Code	Additional explanation	Notes
`unloadMovieNum(5)`	Unloads the movie in level 5, `_level5`.	
`unloadMovie(5);`	Although the `unload` function is used, rather than the `unloadMovieNum` function, the `unloadMovieNum` function is actually used as the parsed parameter was a number rather than a string.	
`unloadMovieNum();`	No target movie level is specified	

updateAfterEvent

`updateAfterEvent()`

Compatible with **Flash 5 and later**.

The `updateAfterEvent` action forces the Flash Player to redraw the stage. This function is useful in situations when the global `onEnterFrame` timeline event isn't updated frequently enough. For example, when using the `setInterval/clearInterval` commands the `updateAfterEvent` function is very important, as the intervals defined using `setInterval` may not necessarily coincide with the global `onEnterFrame` event, causing a visible lag in the Flash file when the frame is re-drawn.

Calling the `updateAfterEvent` command invokes the same process as the global `onEnterframeEvent`, only it is independent of the movie's frame-per-second rate, which usually controls the frame re-draw. See also **clearInterval** and **setInterval**.

Description

The `updateAfterEvent` **action** forces a frame redraw.

See the examples `updateafterevent.fla` and `updateafterevent.swf` on the CD.

Video

Compatible with **Flash 6 Player and above**. This object allows you to display video on the stage without embedding it in your SWF movie.

Description

The Video **object** will allow you to display video content in your movie without actually embedding it in your SWF file. For example, you can use the Video object to stream a live broadcast video, TV content, and FLV files.

video.attachVideo

```
myvideo.attachVideo(a)
```

Where myvideo is an instance of the video object, a is a camera object, or video source. To drop a connection or source, pass null for the value of a.

Compatible with **Flash 6 Player and above**. This method allows you to attach a source to an instance of the video object. Related entries include **Camera.get**.

Description

This **method** can be used to specify and display a live or streamed video (such as an FLV) on the stage. To display a streamed FLV or project a live Webcam stream to the masses, you will require the Flashcom server.

Code	Notes
```myCamera = Camera.get(); videoInstance.attachVideo(myCamera);```	Attaches the camera myCamera to the video instance aptly called videoInstance.

video.clear

```
myvideo.clear();
```

Where myvideo is an instance of the Video object.

Compatible with **Flash 6 Player and above**. This method allows you to clear the image in the designated video instance, in this case, myvideo. Refer to the related entry on **video.attachVideo**.

Description

This **method** is used to clear the current image which is in the video object instance.

Code	Notes
| ```
function clik(){
   myVideo.clear();
   _root.stop();
}
``` | Clears the video object instance. |

See the examples `video.clear.fla` and `video.clear.swf` on the CD.

Video

Compatible with **Flash 6 Player and above**. This object allows you to display video on the stage without embedding it in your SWF movie.

Description

The Video **object** will allow you to display video content in your movie without actually embedding it in your SWF file. For example, you can use the Video object to stream a live broadcast video, TV content, and FLV files.

video.attachVideo

`myvideo.attachVideo(a)`

Where `myvideo` is an instance of the video object, `a` is a camera object, or video source. To drop a connection or source, pass `null` for the value of `a`.

Compatible with **Flash 6 Player and above**. This method allows you to attach a source to an instance of the video object. Related entries include **Camera.get**.

Description

This **method** can be used to specify and display a live or streamed video (such as an FLV) on the stage. To display a streamed FLV or project a live Webcam stream to the masses, you will require the Flashcom server.

Code	Notes
| ```
myCamera = Camera.get();
videoInstance.attachVideo(myCamera);
``` | Attaches the camera `myCamera` to the video instance aptly called `videoInstance`. |

video.clear

```
myvideo.clear();
```

Where myvideo is an instance of the Video object.

Compatible with **Flash 6 Player and above**. This method allows you to clear the image in the designated video instance, in this case, myvideo. Refer to the related entry on **video.attachVideo**.

Description
This **method** is used to clear the current image which is in the video object instance.

Code	Notes

`function clik(){`
`    myVideo.clear();`
`    _root.stop();`
`}`
	Clears the video object instance.

See the examples `video.clear.fla` and `video.clear.swf` on the CD.

void

```
void a
```

Where a is an expression to evaluate.

Compatible with the **Flash 5 Player and above**. This operator is used to evaluate a given expression without returning a value to Flash.

Description
This **unary operator** is used to evaluate an expression, discard this value and then proceeds to return an undefined value.

Code	Notes

`if (init == void(0)) {`
`trace("your code is undefined");`
`}`
	This will return "your code is undefined" to the Output window if code is undefined.

`if (init == `**`void()`**`) {`	ActionScript syntax error.

```
trace("your code is undefined");
}
```

See the examples void.fla and void.swf from the CD.

while

```
while(a) {
    b;
}
```
Where a is a condition, and b is one or more statements.

Compatible with the **Flash 4 Player and above**. This action is used to execute statements until a condition is true. The expression is continually re-evaluated until a false value is returned. Related entries include **for, for..in**, **do while**, and **continue**.

Description
The while **action** is used to continually execute a statement or series of statements until an end condition of false is met. It starts by evaluating the condition. If this condition evaluates to true, it will execute the block of statements. Then it will return the beginning of the action, and loop through the steps again until the condition evaluates to false.

Code	Notes

```var i = 0;```
```while (i < 10) {```
    ```_root.createTextField("quote"+i, i, 10,```
➡ ```i*20, 100, 200);```
    ```_root["quote"+i].text = "hello,```
➡ ```i am quote "+ i;```
    ```i++;```
```}```
	This code creates text fields and numbers them from 0 to 9.

See the examples while.fla and while.swf on the CD.

with

```
with (a) {
    b;
}
```

Where a is an instance of a movie clip or an object, and b is a statement or group of statements.

Compatible with **Flash 5 Player and above**. This action is used to evaluate properties, variables or functions within a given object. Related entries include **tellTarget**.

Description

The with **statement** can be used as a shorthand method, so you do not have to continually reference properties of an object using a full scope. The with action is used to set properties, variables, or actions for any specified object in ActionScript.

Code	Notes
``with (_root.mytext) {
html = true;
_alpha = 45;
_x = 100;
_y = 400;
htmlText = "<i>hello</i> world";
}```	This block of code is shorthand for the following code: ```_root.mytext.html = true;
_root.mytext._alpha = 45;
_root.mytext._x = 100;
_root.mytext._y = 400;
_root.mytext.htmlText = "<i>hello</i> world";```

See the examples with.fla and with.swf on the CD.

while

```
while(a) {
    b;
}
```
Where a is a condition, and b is one or more statements.

Compatible with the **Flash 4 Player and above**. This action is used to execute statements until a condition is true. The expression is continually re-evaluated until a false value is returned. Related entries include **for, for..in, do while**, and **continue**.

Description

The while **action** is used to continually execute a statement or series of statements until an end condition of false is met. It starts by evaluating the condition. If this condition evaluates to true, it will execute the block of statements. Then it will return the beginning of the action, and loop through the steps again until the condition evaluates to false.

Code	Notes

``
var i = 0;
while (i < 10) {
    _root.createTextField("quote"+i, i, 10,
➡ i*20, 100, 200);
    _root["quote"+i].text = "hello,
➡ i am quote "+ i;
    i++;
}
``
	This code creates text fields and numbers them from 0 to 9.

See the examples `while.fla` and `while.swf` on the CD.

with

```
with (a) {
    b;
}
```

Where a is an instance of a movie clip or an object, and b is a statement or group of statements.

Compatible with **Flash 5 Player and above**. This action is used to evaluate properties, variables or functions within a given object. Related entries include **tellTarget**.

Description

The with **statement** can be used as a shorthand method, so you do not have to continually reference properties of an object using a full scope. The with action is used to set properties, variables, or actions for any specified object in ActionScript.

Code	Notes

``
with (_root.mytext) {
    html = true;
    _alpha = 45;
    _x = 100;
    _y = 400;
    htmlText = "<i>hello</i> world";
}
``
	This block of code is shorthand for the following code:
	
	``
	_root.mytext.html = true;
	_root.mytext._alpha = 45;
	_root.mytext._x = 100;
	_root.mytext._y = 400;
	_root.mytext.htmlText =
	"<i>hello</i> world";
	``

See the examples `with.fla` and `with.swf` on the CD.

gotoAndStop()
hitTest()
loadMovie()
loadVariables()
loadVariables() play()
nextFrame()
prevFrame() removeMovieClip()
setMask() startDrag()
startDrag() swap Depths
unloadMov
attachMov
createEmpty
create
dupli

XML

```
new XML([source]);
```

Compatible with **Flash Player 5 and above**. This constructor is used **to create a new XML object, instance**, into which XML data structures are loaded or created and then processed into usable information for a Flash movie. The source argument refers to an optional string of well-formed XML data.

See the extended entry on the CD for more details.

Description

The XML **object** has many methods attached to it that can be used to control the actions and appearances of XML documents and document trees. XML object instances must be instantiated with a constructor. To construct a new XML object instance myXML_xml, you would use the following format:

```
myXML_xml = new XML();
```

Then you load or create XML in this new myXML_xml object instance. You can either add XML within the brackets, such as:

```
myXML_xml = new XML("<laundry><shirts>3</shirts><socks>none</socks></laundry>");
```

Or you can load XML into a document using the XML.load method:

```
myXML_xml = new XML();
myXML_xml.load("laundry.xml");
```

This will load the laundry.xml document into the myXML object in Flash. Note that _xml is added to the instance name so Flash recognizes the name for code hinting purposes.

The XML object contains these methods:

- XML.appendChild – appends a node to the end of the child list
- XML.cloneNode – clones the specified node and children
- XML.createElement – creates an XML element
- XML.createTextNode – creates an XML text node
- XML.getBytesLoaded – returns the number of bytes of an XML document that have loaded
- XML.getBytesTotal – returns the total size of an XML document in bytes
- XML.hasChildNodes – indicates whether the node has child nodes
- XML.insertBefore – inserts a node in front of an existing node
- XML.load – loads an XML document from a URL
- XML.parseXML – parses an XML document into a tree
- XML.removeNode – removes a node
- XML.send – sends an XML document to a URL

- XML.sendAndLoad – sends an XML document to a URL and loads the server response
- XML.toString – converts the node to a string

The XML object also has several properties associated with it:

- XML.contentType – the MIME type sent by the server
- XML.docTypeDecl – a document's DOCTYPE declaration
- XML.firstChild – references the first child in the list
- XML.ignoreWhite – discards white-space only nodes
- XML.lastChild – references the last child in the list
- XML.loaded – checks if an XML document has loaded
- XML.nextSibling – references the next sibling in a node
- XML.nodeName – the tag name of the XML element
- XML.nodeType – the type of the XML element
- XML.nodevalue – the text of the XML element
- XML.parentNode – references the parent of the node
- XML.previousSibling – references the previous sibling in a node
- XML.status – the numeric status code of a parsing operation
- XML.xmlDecl – the XML document's declaration

The XML object has two collection summaries associated with it, and both are used to return node arrays:

- XML.attributes – all the attributes of the node
- XML.childNodes – all the child nodes of the node

The XML object also has two event handlers that are used to perform error checking when XML data is loaded into a movie:

- XML.onData – invoked when the document has been downloaded
- XML.onLoad – invoked for the XML.load and XML.sendAndLoad methods

See the examples xml.fla and xml.swf, which uses the xmldoc.xml, on the CD.

XML.appendChild

myXML_xml.appendChild(a)

Where myXML_xml is an XML instance and a is a child node to be added to the instance.

Compatible with **Flash 5 Player and above**. This method is used to **add a new child node** to a specified XML object. It is used in conjunction with the createElement and createText node methods, and is used to create new XML data in a Flash movie. Related entries include **XML.createElement** and **XML.createTextNode**.

Description

The XML.appendChild() **method** lets you append a new child node to an XML object's child list. If the node is already attached to a parent node, it is removed from the parent and attached to the XML instance.

Code	Returned values	Notes
myXML_xml = ➥ new XML(); myNode = myXML_xml. ➥createElement ➥("myname"); myXML_xml.appendChild ➥(myNode); trace(myXML_xml);	<myname />	Attaches myNode to myXML_xml

See the examples xml.appendchild.fla and xml.appendchild.swf on the CD.

XML.attributes

myXML.attributes

Where myXML is an XML instance, and attributes refers to the attributes of a specified node.

This property is compatible with the **Flash 5 Player and above**. It is used to extract attribute names and values, which can then be used in a Flash movie. **You are able to extract either the name, value or both name and value as an array**. See related entries on **for**, **for...in**, and the **XML** object.

Description

The XML.attributes **collection** can provide a complete list, or selected value or name of any attribute attached to an XML instance. The list of attributes can be returned as an associative array.

Code	Returned values	Notes
myXML_xml = new XML ➥ ("<cat catname= ➥'whiskers' ➥age='5'>"); trace(myXML_xml. ➥firstChild. ➥attributes.	whiskers	Displays the designated attribute value.

➥catname);

myXML_xml = new XML
➥("<cat catname=
➥'whiskers'
➥age='5'>");
for (i in myXML_xml.
➥firstChild.
➥attributes);
trace(i);
	catname
	age
		Loops through the attribute names and displays them in the Output window.

myXML_xml = new XML ➥("<cat catname= ➥'whiskers' ➥age='5'>"); for (i in myXML_xml. ➥firstChild. ➥attributes); trace(myXML_xml. ➥firstChild. ➥attributes[i]);	whiskers 5	Loops through the attribute values and displays them in the Output window.
myXML_xml = new XML ➥("<cat catname= ➥'whiskers' ➥age='5'>"); trace(myXML_xml. ➥firstChild. ➥attributes);	[type Object]	You need to specify an attribute, or loop through existing attributes.

See the examples xml.attributes.fla and xml.attributes.swf on the CD.

XML.childNodes

myXML.childNodes

Where myXML is an instance of the XML object.

This **method** is compatible with **Flash 5 Player and above**. The XML.childNodes collection is an array of the nodes' children. This method can be used in conjunction with other methods in the XML object to navigate to a particular node, and then return a part of it as usable data to the Flash movie. Related entries include **XML.nodeName**, **XML.nodeValue**, and **XML.nodeType**.

Description

The XML.childNodes **collection** provides a complete list of all the node's children attached to an XML instance. The list of children is returned as an array. You can return a portion of the array by indicating which node you want returned.

code	Returned values	Notes
myXML_xml = new XML ➥("<cat><catname> ➥Whiskers</catname> ➥<age>5</age></ ➥cat>"); trace(myXML_xml. ➥firstChild. ➥childNodes[0]);	<catname>Whiskers </catname>	Returns the specified childNode of the new XML object instance.
myXML_xml = new XML ➥("<cat><catname> ➥Whiskers</catname> ➥<age>5</age></ <age>5</age>cat>"); trace(myXML_xml. ➥firstChild. ➥childNodes[1]);	<age>5</age>	Returns the specified childNode of the new XML object instance.
myXML_xml = new XML ➥("<cat><catname> ➥Whiskers</catname> ➥<age>5</age></ ➥cat>"); trace(myXML_xml. ➥firstChild. ➥childNodes. ➥nodeName);	undefined	Need to specify which child node you want to output the nodeName of using a 0 based array.

See the examples xml.childnodes.fla and xml.childnodes.swf on the CD.

XML.cloneNode

myXML.cloneNode(a)

Where myXML is an XML instance and a is a Boolean value of true or false.

Compatible with **Flash Player 5 and later**. This method is used to return a new node of the same type as a specified node. Refer to the related entries **XML.appendChild**, **XML.createTextNode**, **XML.createElement**, and **XML.insertBefore**.

Description

The XML.cloneNode() **method** lets you clone a node, identical to an existing node, retaining the node types and all attributes. If the parameter is true, all the children of the node are recursively cloned as well. If the parameter is false, the children nodes of the specified node are not cloned.

Code	Returned Values	Notes
myXML_xml = new XML ➡("<cat>Whiskers ➡</cat>"); newXML = ➡ myXML_xml. ➡ firstChild. ➡ cloneNode(true); newXML.firstChild. ➡nodeValue = ➡ "Spooky"; myXML_xml.appendChild ➡ (newXML); trace(myXML_xml);	<cat>Whiskers</cat> <cat>Spooky</cat>	The first node is cloned, and then the values of the element and text node are change to reflect a second cat.

See also the examples xml.clonenode.fla and xml.clonenode.swf on the CD.

XML.contentType

myXML.contentType

Where myXML is an instance of the XML object.
XML.contentType is **compatible with Flash 5 Player (release 41) and above**. You would use this property to **set the MIME type** used by XML objects to send to a server. Refer to related entries on **XML.sendAndLoad** and **XML.send**.

Description

The XML.contentType **property** sets and retrieves the MIME type used when sending data to a server by the XML.send() and XML.sendAndLoad() methods. By default the value is set to application/x-www-form-urlencoded MIME format.

Code	Returned Values	Notes
myXML_xml = new ➡ XML(); myMime = myXML_xml. ➡ contentType; trace (myMime);	application/x-www-form-urlencoded	The default value is application/x-www-form-urlencoded.
myXML_xml = new	NaN	The content type must be

```
XML();
myXML_xml.contentType                              expressed as a string.
= application/xml;
myMime = myXML_xml.
contentType;
myXML_xml.send
("myserver.cfm",
"_blank");
trace (myMime);
```

See the examples xml.contenttype.fla and xml.contenttype.swf on the CD.

XML.createElement

    myXML.createElement("a")

Where myXML is an XML instance, and a is a string which represents the nodeName of the new element.

This method is compatible with **the Flash 5 Player and above**. Only **nontext XML nodes** are created using this method. See **XML.createTextNode** and **XML.appendChild** for related entries.

Description
The XML.createElement() **method** creates a new XML element, which can be added to an XML object instance using the appendChild method.

Code	Returned values	Notes
myXML_xml = new XML(); **myElement = myXML_xml. createElement ("socks");** myXML_xml. appendChild(myElement); trace (myXML_xml);	\<socks /\>.	Creates a new element with a nodeName of socks. Socks is stored in myElement, which is then appended to the myXML_xml object instance.

See the examples xml.createelement.fla and xml.createelement.swf on the CD.

XML.createTextNode

    myXML.createTextNode("a")

This is where myXML is an XML instance, and a is a text string of the newly created text node .

This method is compatible with **Flash 5 Player and above**. It is used to create text node data, but cannot be used for attributes or element nodes. See related entries on **XML.appendChild**, **XML.createElement**, and **XML.attributes** .

Description

The XML.createTextNode() **method** creates a new XML text node. The method returns a reference to the newly created text node. You must use the appendChild method in order to add the text node to the XML object instance.

Code	Returned Value	Notes
myXML_xml = new XML ➥("<laundry><shirts ➥/></laundry>"); myText = myXML_xml. ➥createTextNode("3"); myXML_xml.firstChild. ➥firstChild. appendChild(myText); trace(myXML_xml);	<laundry><shirts>3< /shirts></laundry>	A new text node of 3 was created for the <shirts> element in the myXML_xml object.
myXML_xml = new XML ➥("<laundry><shirts ➥/></laundry>"); myText = myXML_xml. ➥createTextNode("3"); myXML_xml.appendChild ➥(myText); trace(myXML_xml);	<laundry><shirts /></laundry>3	The child is not appended to the correct element, so it is not a well-formed structure!

See the examples xml.createtextnode.fla and xml.createtextnode.swf on the CD.

XML.docTypeDecl

myXML.docTypeDecl

Where myXML is an instance of the XML object.

Compatible with **Flash 5 Player and above**. The XML.docTypeDecl property can be used to **set and retrieve the DOCTYPE declaration**, although it is not used for XML validation of any sort. Also see the related entry on **XML.xmlDecl**.

Description

The `XML.docTypeDecl` **property** is used to set and retrieve information about an XML document's DOCTYPE declaration. If no declaration was found, the `XML.docTypeDecl` property has a value of `undefined` and no output is returned to the Flash movie.

Code	Returned value	Notes
myXML_xml = new XML ➡("<?xml version = ➡'1.0'?><!DOCTYPE ➡cats SYSTEM 'meow. ➡dtd'><catname> ➡Whiskers</catname>"); trace(myXML_xml. ➡docTypeDecl);	<!DOCTYPE cats SYSTEM 'meow.dtd'>	The DOCTYPE is returned, although no validation is performed in Flash.
myXML_xml = new XML ➡("<?xml version = ➡'1.0'?><catname> Whiskers</catname>"); trace(myXML_xml. ➡docTypeDecl);""""	undefined	If there is no DOCTYPE declaration, the property returns nothing (undefined).

See the examples `xml.doctypedecl.fla` and `xml.doctypedecl.swf` on the CD.

XML.firstChild

`myXMLNode.firstChild`

Where `myXMLNode` is an instance of a `XML` object or `XMLnodes` object.

The `XML.firstChild` property is **compatible with Flash Player 5 and above**. This property references the first child of a given instance of an `XML` or `XMLnodes` object. It is **exactly the same as any reference to XML.childNodes[0].** Refer to related entries **XML.appendChild()**, **XML.insertBefore()**, and **XML.removeNode()** for more information on manipulating children.

Description

The `XML.firstChild` **property** examines the XML object instance parent's child list and returns the name of the first child. If there is no first child, `null` is returned. If the first child is a text node, the value is set to `undefined`. This is a read-only property.

Code	Returned value	Notes
myXML_xml = new XML ➡("<cat><name>	<cat><name>Whiskers </name></cat>	Examines the parent of myXMLObject and returns

Code	Returned values	Notes
⇒Whiskers</name> </cat>"); trace(myXML_xml. ⇒firstChild);		the first child of the myXML_xml instance. This returns the entire node of firstChild, which is in this case, the XML document.
myXML_xml = new XML ⇒("<cat><name> ⇒Whiskers</name> </cat>"); trace(myXML_xml. ⇒firstChild.nodeName);	cat	Examines the parent of myXML_xml object and returns the nodeName of the <cat> node (which is the firstChild).
myXML_xml = new XML ⇒("<cat><name> ⇒Whiskers</name> ⇒</cat>"); trace(myXML_xml. ⇒firstChild.childNodes ⇒[0].childNodes[0]. ⇒firstChild);	null	A text node where no first child is present, returns null.

See the examples `xml.firstchild.fla` and `xml.firstchild.swf` on the CD.

XML.getBytesLoaded

```
myXML.getBytesLoaded()
```
Where `myXML` is an instance of the `XML` object.

This method is compatible with **Flash Player 6 and above**. `XML.getBytesLoaded()` is used to return the number of bytes that have been loaded. Refer to the related entry **XML.getBytesTotal().**

Description
The `XML.getBytesLoaded()` **method** returns an integer indicating the number of bytes that have been loaded from a streaming XML document.

Code	Returned values	Notes

myXML_xml = new
⇒XML();
myXML_xml.
⇒load("mydoc.xml");
_root.onEnterFrame
⇒= function(){
⇒trace(myXML_xml.
⇒getBytesLoaded());
}
	Returns the number of bytes loaded in the myXML document.	The output window returns 0 bytes then total bytes.

| ```
myXML_xml = new
⮕XML();
myXML_xml.load
⮕ ("mydoc.xml");
trace(myXML_xml.
⮕getBytesLoaded();
``` | 0 | This will trace the initial bytes loaded, which is nothing. |

See the examples xml.getbytesloaded.fla and xml.getbytesloaded.swf, which uses bigxmldoc.xml, on the CD.

XML.getBytesTotal

myXML.getBytesTotal()

Where myXML is an instance of the XML object.

Compatible with **Flash Player 6 and above**. The XML.getBytesTotal() method returns total number of bytes in a document, and is commonly used for **preloading** situations. Refer to the related entry **XML.getBytesLoaded()**.

Description

The XML.getBytesTotal() **method** returns an integer indicating the total number of bytes that are in an XML document.

Code	Returned values	Notes
| ```
myXML_xml = new
⮕ XML();
myXML_xml.load
⮕ ("mydoc.xml");
_root.onEnterFrame
⮕ = function(){
trace(myXML_xml.
⮕ getBytesTotal());
}
``` | Returns the total number of bytes in the myXML document once it has loaded. | The return from the method is an integer. When tracing this block of code, you will receive undefined, then the total amount of bytes in the document. |
| ```
myXML_xml = new
⮕XML();
myXML_xml.load
⮕ ("mydoc.xml");
trace(myXML_xml.
⮕getBytesTotal();
``` | undefined | Returning the initial value of undefined since it is not put on an enterFrame handler. |

See the examples xml.getbytestotal.fla and xml.getbytestotal.swf, which uses bigxmldoc.xml, on the CD.
```

XML.hasChildNodes

`myXMLNode.hasChildNodes()`

Where `myXMLnode` is a reference to the node of an `XML` object instance.

This property is compatible with the **Flash 5 Player and above**. The `XML.hasChildNodes` property is **used to check whether or not a specified node has any child nodes**. Refer to the related entry **XML.childNodes**.

Description

The `XML.hasChildNodes` **property** returns a Boolean value that indicates whether or not the specified node has child nodes. If it does, then `true` is returned. If there are no child nodes, `false` is returned. This is a **read-only** property.

Code	Returned values	Notes

`myXML_xml = new`
➥`XML("<cat><catname>`
➥`Whiskers</catname>`
➥`<age>5</age><fur>`
➥`black`
➥`</fur></cat>");`
`myNode = myXML_xml.`
➥`firstChild;`
`trace(myNode.`
➥`hasChildNodes());`
	true	This code checks whether or not the firstChild (<cat>) has any child nodes. It does, so `true` is returned.

`myXML_xml = new`
➥`XML("<cat>`
➥`<catname>`
➥`Whiskers`
`</catname><age>`
➥`5</age><fur>black`
`</fur></cat>");`
`myNode2 = myXML_xml.`
➥`firstChild.`
`childNodes[0].`
`firstChild;`
`trace(myNode2.`
➥`hasChildNodes());`
	false	This code checks whether or not a different node (the text node Whiskers) has any children (sub) nodes. It does not, so `false` is returned.

`myXML_xml = new`
➥`XML("<cat><catname>`
➥`Whiskers</catname>`
➥`<age>5</age><fur>`
`black</fur></cat>");`
	undefined	Incorrect syntax.

```
myNode = myXML_xml.
➥firstChild;
trace(myNode.
➥childNodes
➥(myXML_xml));
```

See the examples `xml.haschildnodes.fla` and `xml.haschildnodes.swf` on the CD.

XML.ignoreWhite

```
myXML.ignoreWhite = a;
```

Where `myXML` is an instance of the XML object, and `a` is either `true` or `false`.

Compatible with **Flash 5 Player (build 41) and above**. This property is **used to store a Boolean value**. You set the property to either `true` or `false`: **true will remove white spaces from your XML document**, and **false will leave them in**. It is important to note that you will have to manually strip whitespace (or use established AS #include files from the Flash community!) from earlier versions of the Flash 5 player. Refer to related content in **Chapters 18 and 19** about whitespace.

Description

The `XML.ignoreWhite` **property** is a Boolean indicating whether nodes that only contain white space are discarded during parsing. The default setting is `false`, which will leave the white-space text nodes in the document. When set to `true` only text nodes that contain only white space are discarded.

Code	Returned values	Notes

`myXML_xml = new`
➥`XML();`
`myXML_xml.`
➥`load("xmldoc.xml");`
`myXML_xml.`
➥`ignoreWhite = true;`
`trace(myXML_xml);`
	Contents of `xmldoc.xml` in one continuous string.	If you compare the original document with the Output window, you will notice the original appears in a structure, and the traced data does not. This is because all white spaces have been removed using the `ignoreWhite` property.

`myXML_xml.ignoreWhite` ➥`= false;`	none	If you set `ignoreWhite` to false, and then try to process your XML data structure, you will encounter some serious difficulty. All spaces will be treated as nodes, so it will be difficult to navigate.
`myXML_xml = new XML`	undefined	This property does not return

```
( "<cat><catname>                                          a Boolean value.
Whiskers</catname>
</cat>");
myWhite = myXML_xml.
ignoreWhite;
trace(myWhite);
```

See the examples `xml.ignorewhite.fla` and `xml.ignorewhite.swf` and the corresponding XML file `xmldoc.xml` on the CD.

XML.insertBefore

```
myNode.insertBefore(a, b);
```

Where `myNode` is a specified node of an XML object instance, a is **an existing node** in the XML object instance, and b is a child of `myNode`. **a will be inserted before b.**

Compatible with **Flash 5 Player and later**. This method is used to insert a new node into a specified location of an XML object's child list. Refer to the related entries **XML.appendChild** and **XML.cloneNode**.

Description

The `XML.insertBefore()` **method** inserts a new node in an XML object's child list. It positions the new node before the second parameter calls in the method.

Code	Returned value	Notes

`myXML_xml = new XML`
`("<cat>Whiskers`
`</cat>");`
`newXML = myXML_xml.`
`firstChild.cloneNode`
`(true);`
`newXML.firstChild.`
`nodeValue =`
`"Spooky";`
`myXML_xml.`
`insertBefore`
`(newXML,myXML_xml.`
`firstChild);`
`trace(myXML_xml);`
	`<cat>Spooky</cat><cat>`
	`Whiskers</cat>`
		The cloneNode method is used to clone a node, and then insert the cloned node before the original one.

`myXML_xml = new XML`
`("<cat>Whiskers`
`</cat>");`
`newXML = myXML_xml.`
	`<cat>Whiskers</cat><cat>`
	`Spooky</cat>`
		This XML is not in the correct order because appendChild has been used.

firstChild. cloneNode(true); newXML.firstChild. nodeValue = "Spooky"; myXML_xml. appendChild (newXML); myXML_xml. insertBefore (newXML,myXML_xml. firstChild); trace(myXML_xml);		
myXML_xml = new XML ("<cat><catname> Whiskers </catname><age>5 </age></cat>"); newElement = myXML_xml. createElement ("fur"); newText = myXML_xml. createTextNode ("black"); newElement. appendChild (newText); var thenode = myXML_xml. firstChild. firstChild. nextSibling; myXML_xml. insertBefore (newElement, thenode); trace(myXML_xml);	<cat><catname>Whiskers </catname><age>5</age></cat>	You need to specify myXML_xml.firstChild. insertBefore in order to get correct scoping.

See the example `xml.insertbefore.fla` and `xml.insertbefore.swf` on the CD.

XML.lastChild

```
myXMLNode.lastChild
```

Where myXML is an instance of the XML object.

Compatible with **Flash Player 5 and later**. The XML.lastChild property references the last child of the object, and is one of the properties **used to traverse the XML data hierarchy**. Refer to related entries on **XML.firstChild**, **XML.childNodes**, **XML.parentNode**, **XMLpreviousSibling**, and **XML.nextSibling**.

Description

The XML.lastChild **property** examines the XML object's parent's child list and returns the name of the last child in the list. It is used in practically the same way as the related properties listed above, such as XML.firstChild and XML.nextSibling. If the specified node does not have children, null is returned. This is a **read-only** property.

Code	Returned value	Notes
myXML_xml = new XML ➥("<cat><name>whiskers ➥</name><age>5</age> ➥</cat>"); trace(myXML_xml. ➥firstChild.lastChild);	<age>5</age>	The <age>5</age> node is the last in the XML structure.
myXML_xml = new XML ➥("<cat><name> ➥whiskers ➥</name><age>5</age> ➥</cat>"); trace(myXML_xml. ➥lastChild);	<cat><name>whiskers</name> <age>5</age></cat>	The entire XML structure is traced, because the <cat> node is both the first and last node.
myXML_xml = new XML ➥("<cat/>"); trace(myXML_xml. ➥firstChild. ➥lastChild);	null	There is no node to return.

XML.load

myXML.load(a)

Where myXML is an instance of the XML object, and a is a string specifying the location from which the XML document is being loaded from.

Compatible with **Flash Player 5 and later**. You can load the XML document from a location on your hard drive, or from a Web server, and the path can be absolute or relative. Refer to related entries **XML.loaded**, **XML.onLoad**, **XML.sendAndLoad**, **XML.getBytesLoaded**, **XML.getBytesTotal**, and **XML.status**.

Description

The `XML.load()` **method** is used to load an XML document from a specified location. The `XML` object instance has its content replaced with the newly loaded data. Whether or not the loading process is complete is monitored using the `XML.loaded` property.

Code	Returned values	Notes

`myXML_xml = new`
➡`XML();`
`myXML_xml.`
➡`load("xmldoc.xml");`
	none	This code loads `xmldoc.xml` into the `myXML_xml` object instance. The loading location can either be on your hard drive or on a web server. Relative or absolute paths are permitted.

`myXML_xml = new`
➡`XML();`
`myXML_xml.load`
➡`("http://`
➡`www.flash-mx.com`
➡`/xmldoc.xml");`
	none	The URL must be in the same subdomain as the current movie. For example, you could load the document from `www.flash-xm.com` addresses or `xml.flash-mx.com`, and so on.

`myXML_xml = new`
➡`XML();`
`myXML_xml.`
`load();`
	There is no location specified so the command fails	See the examples `xml.load.fla` and `xml.load.swf`, using the `xmldoc.xml` file, on the CD.

XML.loaded

`myXML.loaded`

Where `myXML` is an instance of the `XML` object.

This property is compatible with **Flash Player 5 and later**. It is used to determine whether or not the XML data has **completed loading into the XML instance** in Flash using **XML.load**. The **onLoad** handler is more commonly used for this procedure. See related entries on **XML.load**, **XML.onLoad**, and **XML.sendAndLoad**.

Description

The `XML.loaded` **property** indicates the progress of an `XML.load()` method. When the load begins the `XML.loaded` property is set to `false`. When the load is complete, the `XML.loaded` property is set to `true`. If there is an error during the load, the `XML.loaded` property remains set to `false`.

Code	Additional Explanation	Notes
`myXML_xml = new XML();`	`not loaded yet...`	In this code, we use
`myXML_xml.`		`onEnterFrame` to continually
`➥ignoreWhite = true;`	`it has loaded`	check if the document has
`myXML_xml.load`	`it has loaded`	loaded.
`➥("xmldoc.xml");`	`it has loaded`	
`_root.onEnterFrame`	`it has loaded`	
`➥= function() {`	`it has loaded`	
`  if (myXML_xml.`	`it has loaded`	
`➥loaded) {`	`it has loaded`	
`    trace("it`		
`➥has loaded");`	`(and so on)...`	
`  } else {`		
`    trace("not`		
`➥loaded yet...");`		
`  }`		
`};`		
`myXML_xml = new XML();`	`not loaded yet...`	This code will not return that
`➥myXML_xml.`		the document has loaded
`ignoreWhite = true;`		because it only checks once,
`myXML_xml.load`		instead of looping like
`➥("xmldoc.xml");`		`onEnterFrame`.
`if (myXML_xml.`		
`➥loaded) {`		
`    trace("it`		
`➥has loaded");`		
`➥} else {`		
`    trace("not`		
`➥loaded yet...");`		
`}`		

See the examples `xml.loaded.fla` and `xml.loaded.swf`, using `bigxmldoc.xml`, on the CD.

XML.nextSibling

`myXMLNode.nextSibling`

Where `myXMLNode` is a node within an instance of the `XML` object.

This property is compatible with **Flash 5 Player and above**. The `XML.nextSibling` property references the next child of the object's child list of a given node, and **is used to navigate XML document structures**. Refer to related entries on **XML.childNodes**, **XML.nodeName**, **XML.nodeValue**,

XML.previousSibling, **XML.firstChild**, and **XML.lastChild**. These entries are all used to traverse XML structure hierarchies.

Description

The `XML.nextSibling` **property** examines the XML object node's parent's child list. It returns the name of the next sibling in this list. If there is no next sibling, a `null` is returned. This is a read-only property.

Code	Returned values	Notes
myXML_xml = new XML to ➥("<cat><name> ➥whiskers ➥</name><age>5</age> ➥</cat>"); trace(myXML_xml. ➥firstChild. ➥firstChild. ➥nextSibling);	<age>5</age>	This is the next sibling node the <name> node specified.
myXML_xml = new XML ➥("<cat><name> ➥whiskers </name><age>5</age> ➥</cat>"); trace(myXML_xml. ➥firstChild. ➥nextSibling);	null	There is no nextSibling for the <cat> node because it is the root node.

See the example `xml.nextsibling.fla` and `xml.nextsibling.swf` on the CD.

XML.nodeName

myXMLNode.nodeName

Where `myXMLNode` is an instance of the `XML` object.

It is compatible with **Flash 5 Player and later**. The `XML.nodeName` property **returns the node name** of the specified node in an XML object instance. Refer to related entries on **XML.childNodes**, **XML.nodeType**, and **XML.nodeValue**.

Description

The `XML.nodeName` **property** is used to return the node name of a node, which you specify in the `XML` object instance hierarchy. If the object is an XML element the name of the tag representing the node is returned. If the object is a text node, `null` is returned.

Code	Returned values	Notes
myXML_xml = new XML ➡ ("<cat><name> ➡ whiskers ➡ </name><age>5</age> ➡ </cat>"); trace(myXML_xml. ➡ firstChild. ➡ nodeName);	cat	cat is returned because the first child is the <cat> element, and it is an element node, not a text node.
myXML_xml = new XML ("<cat><name> whiskers >/name><age>5</age> </cat>"); trace(myXML_xml. firstChild.childNodes [0].childNodes[0]); trace(myXML_xml. firstChild.childNodes [0].childNodes[0] .nodeName);	whiskers null	Since we are trying to access a text node (whiskers), we are returned a null for the second trace because it is a type 3 node.

See the examples `xml.nodename.fla` and `xml.nodename.swf` on the CD.

XML.nodeType

myXMLNode.nodeType

Where myXMLNode is an instance of the XML object.

Compatible with **Flash Player 5 and later**. This property **returns an integer of 1 or 3** based on the type of a specified node in an XML object instance. See related entries **XML.nodeName** and **XML.nodeValue**.

Description

The XML.nodeType **property** is used to return the node type of the XML object calling the property. If the object is an XML **element** the node type is 1. If the object is a **text node**, the node type is 3.

Code	Returned values	Notes
myXML_xml = new XML ➡ ("<cat/>"); trace(myXML_xml.	1	Returns a value based on the type of node it is. In this case, <cat> is an element node.

```
➡firstChild.nodeType);
```

Code	Returned values	Notes

`myXML_xml = new XML`
`➡("<cat>whiskers`
`➡</cat>");`
`trace(myXML_xml.`
`➡firstChild.`
`➡childNodes[0].`
`➡nodeType);`
	3	Returns a value based on the type of node it is. In this case, whiskers is a text node.

`myXML_xml = new XML`
`➡("<cat fur='black'`
`➡>whiskers</cat>");`
`trace(myXML_xml.`
`➡firstChild.`
`➡attributes.fur.`
`nodeType);`
	undefined	Cannot return the value of an attribute.

`myXML_xml = new XML`
`➡("<cat/>");`
`trace(myXML_xml.`
`➡firstChild.`
`➡firstChild.`
`nodeType);`
	undefined	There is no node at this location.

See the examples `xml.nodetype.fla` and `xml.nodetype.swf` on the CD.

XML.nodeValue

`myXMLNode.nodeValue`

Where `myXMLNode` is an instance of the `XML` object.

This property is compatible with the **Flash 5 Player and above**. `XML.nodeValue` returns the node value of an XML object. This is only applicable to type 3 text nodes. Refer to related entries on **XML.nodeType** and **XML.nodeName**.

Description

The `XML.nodeValue` **property** is used to retrieve the node value of a given type 3 node of an XML object instance. If the object is an XML element the node type is 1, the node value is `null`. If the object is a type 3 text node, the property returns the value of this node.

Code	Returned values	Notes

`myXML_xml = new XML`
`➡("<cat>whiskers`
`➡</cat>");`
`myNode = myXML_xml.`
	whiskers	whiskers is the node value of the first child node of `<cat>`.

```
➥firstChild.
➥childNodes[0];
trace(myNode.
➥nodeValue);
```

```
myXML_xml = new XML        undefined                          Invalid ActionScript syntax.
➥("<cat>whiskers
➥</cat>");
myNode = myXML_xml.
➥firstChild.
➥childNodes[0];
trace(myXML_xml.
➥nodeValue(myNode));
```

See the examples `xml.nodevalue.fla` and `xml.nodevalue.swf` on the CD.

XML.onData

```
myXML.onData([a])
```

Where `myXML` is an instance of the XML object, and `a` is an optional string of XML data that is unparsed.

Compatible with the **Flash 5 Player and above**. The `XML.onData()` event handler is **invoked when the Flash movie has received some new data**. See the related entry on **XML.onXML**.

Description
The `XML.onData()` **event handler** is invoked either when an XML document has been completed downloading new data from a server, or when an error has occurred during an attempted download. The `XML.onData()` event handler is called immediately, prior to any parsing of the XML content. The `XML.onData()` event handler returns the text in the document, or if the download was unsuccessful returns `undefined`.

Code	Returned values	Notes
`myXML_xml = new XML();` `myXML_xml.` ➥`load("xmldoc.` ➥`xml");` `myXML_xml.onData` ➥`= function` ➥`(thedata){` ➥`trace(thedata);` `};`	Contents of `xmldoc.xml`	This loads the contents of `xmldoc.xml` into the Flash movie, and calls the `onData` when it has finished the loading process.

See the examples `xml.ondata.fla` and `xml.ondata.swf` on the CD.

XML.onLoad

myXML.onLoad(a)

Where myXML is an instance of the XML object, and a is a Boolean value indicating whether or not the load was successful. A successful load returns true, and a failed load returns false.

Compatible with the **Flash 5 Player and above**. This handler is used to **indicate the success of a load**, and is usually used with **callback handlers** to intitiate processing or to stop the movie (with a failed load). This event handler is invoked automatically when a document has ceased downloading. See the related entries on **XML.load**, **XML.loaded**, **XML.sendAndLoad**, **XML.status**, and **XML.onData**.

Description

The XML.onLoad() **event handler** is invoked after an XML document has completed downloading from a server, and is called by XML.onData() event handler. The XML.onLoad() event handler has a Boolean argument indicating the success of the download process: if false, the download failed; if true the download was successful.

Code	Returned values	Notes
myXML_xml = new ➡ XML(); myXML_xml.load ➡ ("xmldoc.xml"); myXML_xml.onLoad ➡ = function ➡ (success) { trace(success); };	true	This code loads xmldoc.xml into the Flash document, and returns a value of true when loading is complete.

See the examples xml.onload.fla and xml.onload.swf on the CD.

XML.parentNode

myXMLNode.parentNode

Where myXMLNode is an instance of the XML object.

Compatible with the **Flash 5 Player and above**. The XML.parentNode property **references the parent node** of a given node in an XML object instance. This property is used in the same way as the related entires: **XML.childNodes**, **XML.nextSibling**, **XML.previousSibling**, **XML.lastChild** and **XML.firstChild**.

Description

The XML.nodeValue **property** is used to reference the parent node of an XML object. If there is no parent node, null is returned.

Code	Returned values	Notes
myXML_xml = new XML ⮕("<cat><catname> ⮕whiskers</catname> ⮕<age>5</age> </cat>"); whiskers = ⮕myXML_xml. ⮕firstChild. ⮕childNodes[0]. childNodes[0]; trace(whiskers. ⮕parentNode. nodeName);	catname	Returns catname because it is the node name of the parent node of the whiskers text node.
myXML_xml = new XML ⮕("<cat><catname> ⮕whiskers</catname> ⮕<age>5</age> </cat>"); trace(myXML_xml. ⮕parentNode);	null	A root node cannot have a parent node.

See the examples xml.parentnode.fla and xml.parentnode.swf, which use xmldoc.xml, on the CD.

XML.parseXML

myXML.parseXML([a])

Where myXML is an XML instance, and a is an optional XML data string to be parsed.

This method is compatible with the **Flash 5 Player and above**. XML.parseXML() is **used to parse an internal (in the Flash movie, not loaded) string XML document text**. See related entries on **XML.load**, **XML.sendAndLoad**, and **XML.status**.

Description

The XML.parseXML() **method** parses an XML structure and returns the result to the XML object instance, populating that object with the XML tree resulting from the parse operation. If there are any existing trees attached to the XML object, they are discarded.

Code	Returned values	Notes
myXML_xml = ➥ new XML(); **myXML_xml.parseXML** ➥ ("<drinks> ➥ <juice>iced ➥ tea</juice> ➥ <slurpee>grabe ➥ </slurpee> ➥ </drinks>"); **trace(myXML_xml);**	<drinks><juice>iced tea</juice><slurpee>grabe </slurpee></drinks>	
myXML_xml = new ➥XML(); myXML_xml. ➥parseXML();		There is no data source specified so the command fails

See the examples xml.parsexml.fla and xml.parsexml.swf on the CD.

XML.previousSibling

myXMLNode.previousSibling

Where myXMLNode is an instance of an XML object.

Compatible with **Flash 5 Player and above**. The XML.previousSibling property references the previous child of the object's child list. Refer to related entries **XML.firstChild**, **XML.lastChild**, **XML.childNodes**, **XML.nextSibling**, and **XML.parentNode**.

Description
The XML.previousSibling **property** examines the child list of an XML object instance's parent node and returns the name of the previous sibling in the list. If there is no previous sibling to the node indicated, a null is returned. This is a **read-only** property.

Code	Returned values	Notes
myXML_xml = new XML ➥("<drinks> ➥<juice>iced ➥tea</juice> ➥<slurpee>grape ➥</slurpee> </drinks>"); thenode =	<juice>iced tea</juice>	The node is <slurpee>grape</ slurpee>, so the previous sibling to that is what is returned.

```
➥myXML xml.
➥firstChild.
lastChild;
trace(thenode.
➥previousSibling);
```

myXML_xml = new XML null ➥("<drinks> ➥<juice>iced ➥tea</juice> ➥<slurpee>grape ➥</slurpee> ➥</drinks>"); thenode = myXML_xml. ➥firstChild; trace(thenode. ➥previousSibling);		The first child node does not have any previous siblings to trace. Therefore, null is returned.

See the examples `xml.previoussibling.fla` and `xml.previoussibling.swf` on the CD.

XML.removeNode

myXMLNode.removeNode()

Where myXMLNode is an instance of the XML object.

This method is compatible with **Flash Player 5 and later**. It is used to remove a node from part of the XML instances data structure. See related entries on **XML.childNodes** and **XML.appendChild**.

Description

The XML.removeNode() **method** removes the specified XML node object and all of the children and descendents from the specified node. Following this deletion, all of the properties of remaining parent nodes will be updated.

Code	Returned values	Notes
myXML_xml = new ➥XML("<cat><cat1> ➥<catname>whiskers ➥</catname><age>5 ➥</age></cat1><cat2> ➥<catname>Spooky ➥</catname></cat2> </cat>"); myXML_xml. ➥firstChild.	<cat><cat2><catname>Spooky </catname></cat2></cat>	Removes the indicated <cat1> node.

➥ childNodes[0].
removeNode();
trace(myXML xml);

myXML_xml = new ➥XML("<cat><cat1> ➥<catname>whiskers ➥</catname><age>5 ➥</age></cat1> ➥<cat2><catname> ➥Spooky</catname> </cat2></cat>"); myXML_xml. ➥removeNode(); trace(myXML xml);	<cat><cat1><catname> whiskers</catname><age>5 </age></cat1><cat2> <catname>Spooky</catname> </cat2></cat>	Does not indicate a node to remove, so none are removed and the entire string is returned.

See the examples `xml.removenode.fla` and `xml.removenode.swf` file on the CD.

XML.send

    myXML.send (a , b)

Where `myXML` is an instance of the `XML` object, `a` is the location (URL) to which the data is sent (generally a server script or middleware application), and `b` is the browser window or frame in which the returned data is displayed.

Compatible with **Flash Player 5 and later**. This method is used to send `XML` data to a location, but it is not returned to the Flash movie. Refer to related entries **XML.sendAndLoad**, **XML.loaded**, **XML.getBytesLoaded**, **XML.getBytesTotal**, and **XML.onLoad**.

Description
The `XML.send()` **method** encodes the specified `XML` object into an XML document and sends the instance to a specific location specified in the arguments. All documents are sent using HTTP transfer protocols. If a second parameter is specified, it refers to the window that will contain any data returned from the server. The default value for this window is `_self`.

Code	Returned values	Notes
myXML_xml = new XML ➥("<username>bob ➥</username>"); myXML_xml.send ➥("myserver.cfm", ➥"_blank");	none	The ColdFusion server is expecting XML formatted data. We are sending this myXML_xml instance to the server at the location myserver.cfm. The server processes this information,

<table>
<tr><td></td><td>and returns it to a new HTML window.</td></tr>
</table>

```
myXML_xml = new XML
➥ ("<username>bob
➥ </username>");
myXML_xml.send();
```

There is no target URL specified so the command fails.

See the examples `xml.send.fla` and `xml.send.swf`, which uses `redirect.cfm`, on the CD.

XML.sendAndLoad

```
myXML.sendAndLoad (a, b);
```

Where `myXML` is an instance of the XML object, `a` is the location (URL) to send the XML object instance to, and `b` is the name XML object instance which will receive returned data.

Compatible with **Flash 5 Player and above**. This method is **used to send data to a server, and then receive data back to the Flash movie**. It uses HTTP for transfer, and then stores the new data in a new instance of the XML object. Refer to related entries on **XML.send, XML.load, XML.loaded, XML.onLoad, XML.getBytesLoaded**, and **XML.getBytesTotal**.

Description

The `XML.sendAndLoad()` **method** encodes the specified XML object instance into an XML document. This document is then sent to a specified URL for further processing. This URL is usually of a server-side script or middleware application which can handle XML data. Any returned data from the server is placed in the second XML object instance specified as an argument.

Code	Returned values	Notes
| ```text
target_xml = new
➥ XML();
myXML_xml =
➥ new XML("<client>
➥ <username ID=
➥ '201'>bill
➥ </username>
</client>");
myXML_xml.
➥ sendAndLoad
➥ ("getclients.
➥ cfm",
➥ target_XML);
target_XML.onLoad
➥ = function () {
    trace
``` | n/a | This sends the `myXML_xml` instance to the ColdFusion server. XML data is sent back to the `target_xml` instance, and when it arrives, a trace is sent. |
```

```
➥ ("yay!");
 };
target_xml = new              n/a                          You will want to use a server-
➥XML();                                                   side script to handle your
myXML_xml =                                               XML documents
➥new XML("<client>
➥<username ID=                                            You should also specify your
➥'201'>bill                                              new container XML instance
➥</username>                                             to load the new data into.
➥</client>");
myXML_xml.
➥sendAndLoad
➥("getclients.
➥html");
target_XML.onLoad
➥= function () {
     trace("yay!");
};
```

See the examples `xml.sendandload.fla` and `xml.sendandload.swf`, which uses the `redirect.cfm` file, on the CD.

XML.status

myXML.status

Where myXML is an instance of the XML object.

Compatible with **Flash Player 5 and later**. The XML.status property indicates whether or not an XML document has been successfully parsed. Values returned are integers which specifiy what error occurred during parsing. Related entries include **XML.load**, **XML.sendAndLoad**, **XML.onLoad**, **XML.loaded**, and **XML.parseXML**.

Description
The XML.status **property** returns a numeric value indicating whether an XML document was successfully parsed into an instance of the XML object, or if there were any errors during parsing. The numeric values returned by the XML.status property are given below.

Code	Returned Value	Notes
myXML_xml = new ➥XML(); myXML_xml. ignoreWhite = true; myXML_xml.load	0	A return value of zero indicates success of a load, so our xmldoc.xml is well formed and parsed without error.

```
➥("xmldoc.xml");
myXML_xml.onLoad
➥= function() {
    trace(myXML_xml
.status);
};
```

See the examples `xml.status.fla` and `xml.status.swf` on the CD.

XML.toString

`myXMLNode.toString()`

Where `myXMLNode` is an instance of the `XML` object.

Compatible with **Flash Player 5 and later**. The `XML.toString()` method returns a string representing everything in the specified node. See the related entry on **XML.nodeValue**.

Description

The `XML.toString()` **method** returns a string of all the nodes, children, and attributes in specified node of the `XML` object instance, which is then returned as a string.

Code	Returned values	Notes

`myXML_xml = new XML`
`➥("<cat><catname>`
`➥whiskers</catname>`
`➥<age>5</age>`
`➥</cat>");`
`myNode = myXML_xml.`
`➥firstChild.`
`➥childNodes[0];`
`trace(myNode.`
`➥toString());`
	`<catname>whiskers</catname>`	Creates a string based on the specified node stored in `myNode`.

See the examples `xml.tostring.fla` and `xml.tostring.swf` on the CD.

XML.xmlDecl

`myXML.xmlDecl`

Where `myXML` is an instance of the `XML` object.

Compatible with **Flash Player 5 and later**. The XML.xmlDecl property sets and retrieves the XML declaration.

Description

The XML.xmlDecl **property** is used to retrieve information about an XML document's XML declaration. If no declaration was found, the XML.xmlDecl property has a value of undefined.

Code	Returned values	Notes
newXML = new XML ➥("<cat>whiskers ➥</cat>"); newXML.xmlDecl = ➥"<?xml version= ➥\"1.0\" ?>"; trace(newXML. ➥xmlDecl); trace(newXML);	<?xml version="1.0" ?> <?xml version="1.0" ?><cat> whiskers</cat>	Adds an XML declaration to an exisiting document.

See the examples xml.xmldecl.fla and xml.xmldecl.swf on the CD.

XMLSocket

```
mySocket = new XMLSocket();
```

The XMLSocket object is compatible with **Flash Player 5 and above**. The XMLSocket object instance works in conjunction with a socket server, which are installed on a server. They are used for fast and continuous communication between a Flash movie and an end user, as they can quickly transfer small amounts of data. The data does not need to be formatted as XML. Sockets facilitate the communication, and those using this socket connection listen to a designated port dedicated to the socket server. For detailed information on socket servers and Flash, refer to **Chapter 20**.

Description

The XMLSocket **object** is responsible for setting up socket server communication between a client and a server. A socket is a combination of an IP address, and a TCP port number that is used for two-way communications. A socket server is a collection of files (sometimes as an executable) which are installed on a server – essentially, software. It can be written in a number of languages (Java, ASP, Python, C++, and Perl among others), although Java seems to be a commonly used language in the community for Flash Socket servers. Any language can be used, as long as it has support for sockets and transmissions terminated by 0. Many socket servers have customized commands or objects sent between the movie and the server, which you can use to enhance your applications. Socket servers are complicated applications, and are often built by developers already well versed in one of these programming languages. Most Flash designers and developers do not build socket servers, but instead use free or commercial ones available for download already.

The XMLSocket object has methods and event handlers attached to it that are used to manage communications between multiple clients and the server. XMLSocket instances must be instantiated with a constructor.

The XMLSocket object contains three methods used to create and close a socket connection, as well as to send an XML document:

- XMLSocket.close – closes an open socket connection
- XMLSocket.connect – creates a new socket connection
- XMLSocket.send – sends XML data or other data to the server

The XMLSocket object also has four event handlers associated with it:

- XMLSocket.onClose – invoked when a socket is closed
- XMLSocket.onConnect – invoked when a socket is opened
- XMLSocket.onData – invoked when data arrives from the server
- XMLSocket.onXML – invoked when an XML object arrives from the server

XMLSocket.close

```
myXMLSocket.close()
```

Where myXMLSocket is an instance of the XMLSocket object.

Compatible with **Flash Player 5 and later**. The XMLSocket.close() method closes a connection made between the Flash movie and the socket server. Refer to the related entries on **XMLSocket.connect()** and **XMLSocket.onClose**.

Description

The XMLSocket.close() **method** closes a socket connection specified by the calling instance and terminating the persistent connection.

CodeReturned values	Returned values	Notes
mysocket = new ➥XMLSocket(); ➥("localhost", mysocket.connect ➥12345); _root.myButton. ➥onRelease = ➥function() { _root.mysocket.	n/a	When a button instance is pressed, the connection is terminated. However, if the connection never existed in the first place, the command will fail.

```
➥close();
};
```

See the examples `xmlsocket.close.fla` and `xmlsocket.close.swf` on the CD.

XMLSocket.connect

```
myXMLSocket.connect("a", b)
```

Where `myXMLSocket` is an `XMLSocket` instance, a is the IP address or domain name of the server you are connecting to, and b is the TCP port number to be listened to. You can also use `localhost` in place of a.

Compatible with **Flash Player 5 and later**. The `XMLSocket.connect()` method is used to **create a socket connection**. Refer to related entries on **XMLSocket.onConnect**, and **XMLSocket.close**.

Description

The `XMLSocket.connect()` **method** creates a socket connection to a specified server. A return of `true` indicates the socket was properly created, while a `false` indicates the connection attempt failed. The server can be identified by an IP address, a domain name, or the word `null` in order to indicate the same server that the movie resides on. The TCP port number must also be specified, and must be 1024 or higher for security reasons.

Code	Returned values	Notes
`mySocket = new` ➥`XMLSocket();` **`mySocket.connect`** ➥**`("http://www.mydomain`** ➥**`.com",12345);`**	`true` or `false`	Tries to create a socket connection between the socket server and SWF using TCP port 12345.
`mySocket = new` `XMLSocket();` **`mySocket.connect`** **`("localhost",`** **`12345);`**	`true` or `false`	When you are testing your movie locally, you can use `localhost` or `127.0.0.1` as your web server. You must have a socket server running locally.

See the examples `xmlsocket.connect.fla` and `xmlsocket.connect.swf` on the CD.

XMLSocket.onClose

```
myXMLSocket.onClose()
```

Where `myXMLSocket` is an instance of the `XMLSocket`.

Compatible with **Flash Player 5 and later**. The XMLSocket.onClose() event handler is **invoked when a connection is closed for any number of means by the server**. See the related entries: **XMLSocket.close** and **XMLSocket.connect**.

Description

The XMLSocket.onClose() **event handler** is used with a custom "callback" function that is invoked when a server closes a socket connection. By default there are no actions performed inside the XMLSocket.onClose() event handler.

Code	Returned values	Notes
mySocket = new ➡XMLSocket(); **mySocket.connect** ➡ **("http://www.mydomain** ➡ **.com",12345); mySocket.onClose** ➡ **= function(){** ➡ **_ _root.error.text** ➡ **= "connection** ➡ **lost";** }	connection lost	If the server drops the connection mySocket, the text field called error will display the text "connection lost".

See the examples xmlsocket.onclose.fla and xmlsocket.onclose.swf on the CD.

XMLSocket.onConnect

myXMLSocket.onConnect(a)

Where myXMLSocket is an instance of the XMLSocket object, and a is a Boolean indicating a successful or failed connection attempt.

Compatible with the **Flash 5 Player and above**. The XMLSocket.onConnect() event handler is **invoked when a connection request is completed**. See related entries: **XMLSocket.connect** and **XMLSocket.onClose**.

Description

The XMLSocket.onConnect() **event handler** is used with a "callback" function. The handler is invoked when a connection request is completed, and a true (success) or false (fail) result is sent back to the movie. Your "callback" function can execute custom tasks based on whether or not the connection is successful.

Code	Returned values	Notes

Code	Returned values	Notes
| ```
thesocket = new
➥XMLSocket();
thesocket.connect
➥("localhost",
➥12345);
thesocket.onConnect
➥= function(success) {
   if (success) {
      trace
➥("connection
➥made");
   } else {
      trace
➥("no connection");
   }
};
``` | connection made | If the server makes a connection, the output window will trace "connection made", and if not, "no connection". |

See the examples xmlsocket.onconnect.fla and xmlsocket.onconnect.swf on the CD.

XMLSocket.onData

```
myXMLSocket.onData()
```

Where myXMLSocket is an instance of the XMLSocket object.

Compatible with the **Flash 5 Player and above**. The XMLSocket.onData() event handler is **invoked when an XML message has been downloaded from a server**. Refer to the closely related entry on **XMLSocket.onXML()**.

Description
The XMLSocket.onData() **event handler** is a "callback" function that is invoked when a message has been downloaded. Each data transmission is terminated with a zero byte, and this is what causes the onData handler to execute.

Code	Returned values	Notes
| ```
thesocket = new
➥XMLSocket();
thesocket.connect
➥("localhost",
➥12345);
thesocket.send
➥("<myname>jepo
➥</myname>");
thesocket.onData
``` | | When data arrives to the movie, the content is traced, as well as an alert that it has arrived.

This data is not parsed by Flash. To parse this information, you would enter functions within the inline |

```
➥ = function
➥ (thedata) {
    trace("data
➥ arrived");
    trace
➥ (thedata);
};
```

function.

See the examples `xmlsocket.ondata.fla` and `xmlsocket.ondata.swf` on the CD.

XMLSocket.onXML

`myXMLSocket.onXML(a)`

Where `myXMLSocket` is an `XMLSocket` instance and a is an XML object instance that will contain the new parsed XML data.

Compatible with **Flash 5 Player and above**. The `XMLSocket.onXML()` **method is invoked when XML data is received**. The new XML data will be contained within the a argument. Refer to the related entry: **XMLSocket.onData().**

Description
The `XMLSocket.onXML()` **event handler** is used with a "callback" function. The handler is invoked by the Flash Player when an XML document has been received over an open socket connection. All XML messages are terminated with a zero byte, and when one is received, the handler is invoked.

Code	Returned values	Notes

`thesocket = new`
`➥XMLSocket();`
`thesocket.connect`
`➥("localhost",`
`➥12345);`
`thesocket.send`
`➥("<myname>jepo`
`➥</myname>");`
`thesocket.onXML =`
`➥function(xmldata) {`
`    trace("xml data`
`➥arrived");`
`    trace (xmldata);`
`};`
		When XML arrives to the movie, the content is traced, as well as an alert that it has arrived.
		
		This XML is not parsed by Flash. To parse this information, you would enter functions within the inline function.

See the examples `xmlsocket.onxml.fla` and `xmlsocket.onxml.swf` on the CD.

XMLSocket.send

```
myXMLSocket.send(a)
```

Where myXMLSocket is an instance of the XMLSocket object, and a is an XML object instance which is transmitted to the socket server.

Compatible with **Flash Player 5 and later**. The XMLSocket.send() method is **used to send data to the server as a string**. Refer to related entries, including **XMLSocket.onXML** and **XMLSocket.onData**.

Description
The XMLSocket.send() **method** is used to send information from the Flash movie to a socket server. This message sent to the server can be XML formatted data, or a string. The transmission terminates with a zero byte. This transmission, regardless of what happens at the server or if it is properly configured, will result in onXML being triggered.

Code	Returned values	Notes
thesocket = new ➥ XMLSocket(); thesocket.connect ➥ ("localhost", ➥ 12345); thesocket.send ➥ ("<myname>jepo ➥ </myname>");		This will send the data `<myname>jepo</myname>` to the localhost server.

See the examples xmlsocket.send.fla and xmlsocket.send.swf on the CD.

Index

The index is arranged hierarchically, in alphabetical order, with symbols preceding the letter A. Many second-level entries also occur as first-level entries. This is to ensure that users will find the information they require however they choose to search for it. Files used in the book are listed are listed under 'files'. A separate index has been provided for the bonus chapters which appear on the cd.

ActionScript Dictionary Cross Reference

The following reference lists all the ActionScript properties, methods, and events described in this book, and which entries to refer to, to find out more information about them. It is followed by a list of all the deprecated ActionScript terms covered in this book, which also points to their replacements.

_entries

_alpha **See** Button._alpha, MovieClip._alpha, TextField._alpha
_currentframe **See** MovieClip._currentframe
_droptarget **See** MovieClip._droptarget
_focusrect **See** MovieClip._focusrect, TextField._focusrect
_framesloaded **See** MovieClip._framesloaded
_height **See** Button._height, MovieClip._height, TextField._height
_highquality **See** Button._highquality, MovieClip._highquality, TextField._highquality
_name **See** Button._name, MovieClip._name, TextField._name
_parent **See** Button._parent, MovieClip._parent, TextField._parent
__proto__ **See** Object.__proto__
_quality **See** Button._quality, TextField._quality
_rotation **See** Button._rotation, MovieClip._rotation, TextField._rotation
_soundbuftime **See** Button._soundbuftime, MovieClip._soundbuftime, TextField._soundbuftime
_target **See** Button._target, MovieClip._target, TextField._target
_totalframes **See** MovieClip._totalframes
_url **See** Button._url, MovieClip._url, TextField._url
_visible **See** Button._visible, MovieClip._visible, TextField._visible
_width **See** Button._width, MovieClip._width, TextField._width
_x **See** Button._x, MovieClip._x, TextField._x
_xmouse **See** Button._xmouse, MovieClip._xmouse, TextField._xmouse
_xscale **See** MovieClip._xscale, TextField._xscale
_y **See** MovieClip._y, TextField._y
_ymouse **See** MovieClip._ymouse, TextField._ymouse
_yscale **See** MovieClip._yscale, TextField._yscale

A

abs **See** Math.abs
acos **See** Math.acos
addItemAt **See** FComponent.addItemAt
addition operator **See** Symbols section
addition assignment operator **See** Symbols section
addListener **See** FStyleFormat.addListener, Key.addListener, Mouse.addListener,

Selection.addListener, Stage.addListener, TextField.addListener
addProperty **See** Object.addProperty
align **See** Stage.align, TextFormat.align
allowDomain **See** System.security.allowDomain
_alpha **See** Button._alpha, MovieClip._alpha, TextField._alpha
appendChild **See** XML.appendChild
apply **See** Function.apply
applyChanges **See** FStyleFormat.applyChanges
Array access index **See** Symbols section
arrow **See** FStyleFormat.arrow
asin **See** Math.asin
assignment operator **See** Symbols section
atan **See** Math.atan
atan2 **See** Math.atan2
attachMovie **See** MovieClip.attachMovie
attachSound **See** Sound.attachSound
attachVideo **See** video.attachVideo
attributes **See** XML.attributes
autoSize **See** TextField.autoSize

B

background **See** FStyleFormat.background, TextField.background
backgroundColor **See** TextField.backgroundColor
backgroundDisabled **See** FStyleFormat.backgroundDisabled
BACKSPACE **See** Key.BACKSPACE
beginFill **See** MovieClip.beginFill
beginGradientFill **See** MovieClip.beginGradientFill
bitwise (binary) operator **See** Symbols section
Bitwise (binary) AND assignment operator **See** Symbols section
Bitwise (binary) XOR operator **See** Symbols section
Bitwise (binary) XOR assignment operator **See** Symbols section
Bitwise OR operator **See** Symbols section
Bitwise OR assignment operator **See** Symbols section
blockIndent **See** TextFormat.blockIndent
bold **See** TextFormat.bold
Boolean AND operator **See** Symbols section
border **See** TextField.border
borderColor **See** TextField.borderColor
bottomScroll **See** TextField.bottomScroll
braces **See** Symbols section
break **See** Boolean.break
bullet **See** TextFormat.bullet

C

call **See** Function.call
callee **See** arguments.callee
caller **See** arguments.caller
CAPSLOCK **See** Key.CAPSLOCK
ceil **See** Math.ceil
charAt **See** String.charAt
charCodeAt **See** String.charCodeAt
check **See** FStyleFormat.check
childNodes **See** XML.childNodes
clear **See** MovieClip.clear, video.clear
cloneNode **See** XML.cloneNode
color **See** TextFormat.color
Comment delimiter **See** Symbols section
components **See** FComponents
concat **See** Array.concat, String.concat
Conditional operator **See** Symbols section
connect **See** XMLSocket.connect
contentType **See** LoadVars.contentType, XML.contentType
CONTROL **See** Key.CONTROL
cos **See** Math.cos
createElement **See** XML.createElement
createEmptyMovieClip **See** MovieClip.createEmptyMovieClip
createTextField **See** MovieClip.createTextField
createTextNode **See** XML.createTextNode
_currentframe **See** MovieClip._currentframe
curveTo **See** MovieClip.curveTo

D

darkshadow **See** FStyleFormat.darkshadow
data **See** SharedObject.data
Decrement operator **See** − − operator
DELETEKEY **See** Key.DELETEKEY
Division operator **See** Symbols section
Division assignment operator **See** Symbols section
docTypeDecl **See** XML.docTypeDecl
Dot operator **See** Symbols section
DOWN **See** Key.DOWN
_droptarget **See** MovieClip._droptarget
duplicateMovieClip **See** MovieClip.duplicateMovieClip
duration **See** Sound.duration

E

E **See** Math.E
embedFonts **See** TextField.embedFonts
enabled **See** MovieClip.enabled
END **See** Key.END
endFill **See** MovieClip.endFill
ENTER **See** Key.ENTER
ESCAPE **See** Key.ESCAPE
exp **See** Math.exp

F

face **See** FStyleFormat.face
firstChild **See** XML.firstChild
floor **See** Math.floor
flush **See** SharedObject.flush
focusEnabled **See** MovieClip.focusEnabled
_focusrect **See** MovieClip._focusrect, TextField._focusrect
font **See** TextFormat.font
foregroundDisabled **See** FStyleFormat.foregroundDisabled
_framesloaded **See** MovieClip._framesloaded

G

getASCII **See** Key.getASCII
getBeginIndex **See** Selection.getBeginIndex
getBounds **See** MovieClip.getBounds
getBytesLoaded **See** LoadVars.getBytesLoaded, MovieClip.getBytesLoaded,
    Sound.getBytesLoaded, XML.getBytesLoaded
getBytesTotal **See** LoadVars.getBytesTotal, MovieClip.getBytesTotal, Sound.getBytesTotal,
    XML.getBytesTotal
getCaretIndex **See** Selection.getCaretIndex
getCode **See** Key.getCode
getData **See** FComponent.getData
getDate **See** Date.getDate
getDay **See** Date.getDay
getDepth **See** MovieClip.getDepth, TextField.getDepth
getEnabled **See** FComponent.getEnabled
getEndIndex **See** Selection.getEndIndex
getFocus **See** Selection.getFocus
getFontList **See** TextField.getFontList
getFullYear **See** Date.getFullYear
getGroupName **See** FComponent.getGroupName

H

hasAccessibility **See** System.capabilities.hasAccessibility
hasAudio **See** System.capabilities.hasAudio
hasAudioEncoder **See** System.capabilities.hasAudioEncoder
hasChildNodes **See** XML.hasChildNodes
hasMP3 **See** System.capabilities.hasMP3
hasVideoEncoder **See** System.capabilities.hasVideoEncoder
_height **See** Button._height, MovieClip._height, TextField._height
height **See** Stage.height
hide **See** Mouse.hide
highlight **See** FStyleFormat.highlight
_highquality **See** Button._highquality, MovieClip._highquality, TextField._highquality
hitArea **See** MovieClip.hitArea
hitTest **See** MovieClip.hitTest
HOME **See** Key.HOME
hscroll **See** TextField.hscroll
html **See** TextField.html
htmlText **See** TextField.htmlText

I

ignoreWhite **See** XML.ignoreWhite
indent **See** TextFormat.indent
indexOf **See** String.indexOf
inequality operator **See** Symbols section
Input **See** System
INSERT **See** Key.INSERT
insertBefore **See** XML.insertBefore
isDebugger **See** System
isDOWN **See** Key.isDOWN
isToggled **See** Key.isToggled
italic **See** TextFormat.italic

J

join **See** Array.join

L

language **See** System.capabilities.language
lastChild **See** XML.lastChild
lastIndexOf **See** String.lastIndexOf
leading **See** TextFormat.leading
LEFT **See** Key.LEFT

leftMargin **See** TextFormat.leftMargin

length **See** arguments.length, Array.length, String.length, TextField.length

lineStyle **See** MovieClip.lineStyle

lineTo **See** MovieClip.lineTo

load **See** LoadVars.load, XML.load

loaded **See** LoadVars.loaded

loaded **See** XML.loaded

loadMovie **See** MovieClip.loadMovie

loadScrollContent **See** FComponent.loadScrollContent

loadSound **See** Sound.loadSound

loadVariables **See** MovieClip.loadVariables

localToGlobal **See** MovieClip.localToGlobal

log **See** Math.log

LOG10E **See** Math.LOG10E

Logical NOT operator **See** Symbols section

Logical OR operator **See** Symbols section

LN2 **See** Math.LN2

LN10 **See** Math.LN10

M

manufacturer **See** System.capabilities.manufacturer

max **See** math.max

maxChars **See** TextField.maxChars

maxhscroll **See** TextField.maxhscroll

maxscroll **See** TextField.maxscroll

MAX_VALUE **See** Number.MAX_VALUE

min **See** Math.min

MIN_VALUE **See** Number.MAX_VALUE

modulo operator **See** Symbols section

Modulo assignment operator

moveTo **See** MovieClip.moveTo

multiline **See** TextField.multiline

Multiplication operator **See** Symbols section

Multiplication assignment operator **See** Symbols section

N

_name **See** Button._name, MovieClip._name, TextField._name

NaN **See** Number.NaN

NEGATIVE_INFINITY **See** Number.NEGATIVE_INFINITY

nextFrame **See** MovieClip.nextFrame

nextSibling **See** XML.nextSibling

nodeName **See** XML.nodeName
nodeType **See** XML.nodeType
nodeValue **See** XML.nodeValue

O

object initializer **See** Symbols section
onChanged **See** TextField.onChanged
onClose **See** XMLSocket.onClose
onConnect **See** XMLSocket.onConnect
onData **See** MovieClip.onData, XML.onData, XMLSocket.onData
onDragOut **See** MovieClip.onDragOut
onDragOver **See** MovieClip.onDragOver
onEnterFrame **See** MovieClip.onEnterFrame
onKeyDown **See** Key.onKeyDown, MovieClip.onKeyDown
onKeyUp **See** Key.onKeyUp, MovieClip.onKeyUp
onKillFocus **See** MovieClip.onKillFocus, TextField.onKillFocus
onLoad **See** LoadVars.onLoad, MovieClip.onLoad, Sound.onLoad, XML.onLoad
onMouseDown **See** Mouse.onMouseDown, MovieClip.onMouseDown
onMouseMove **See** Mouse.onMouseMove, MovieClip.onMouseMove
onMouseUp **See** Mouse.onMouseUp, MovieClip.onMouseUp
onPress **See** MovieClip.onPress
onRelease **See** MovieClip.onRelease
onReleaseOutside **See** MovieClip.onReleaseOutside
onResize **See** Stage.onResize
onRollOut **See** MovieClip.onRollOut
onRollOver **See** MovieClip.onRollOver
onScroller **See** TextField.onScroller
onSetFocus **See** MovieClip.onSetFocus, Selection.onSetFocus, TextField.onSetFocus
onSoundComplete **See** Sound.onSoundComplete
onStatus **See** SharedObject.onStatus
onUnload **See** MovieClip.onUnload
onXML **See** XMLSocket.onXML
operators **See** Symbols section
os **See** System.capabilities.os

P

_parent **See** Button._parent, MovieClip._parent, TextField._parent
parentNode **See** XML.parentNode
parseXML **See** XML.parseXML
password **See** TextField.password
PGDN **See** Key.PGDN
PGUP **See** Key.PGUP

PI **See** Math.PI
pixelAspectRatio **See** System.capabilities.pixelAspectRatio
Play **See** MovieClip.play
pop **See** Array.pop
position **See** Sound.position
POSITIVE_INFINITY **See** Number.POSITIVE_INFINITY
pow **See** Math.pow
prevFrame **See** MovieClip.prevFrame
previousSibling **See** XML.previousSibling
product **See** System
__proto__ **See** Object.__proto__
push **See** Array.push

Q

_quality **See** Button._quality, TextField._quality

R

radioDot **See** FStyleFormat.radioDot
random **See** Math.random
registerClass **See** Object.registerClass
registerSkinElement **See** FComponent.registerSkinElement
removeAll **See** FComponent.removeAll
removeItemAt **See** FComponent.removeItemAt
removeListener **See** FStyleFormat.removeListener, Key.removeListener, Mouse.removeListener,
    Selection.removeListener, Stage.removeListener, TextField.removeListener
removeMovieClip **See** MovieClip.removeMovieClip
removeNode **See** XML.removeNode
removeTextField **See**TextField.removeTextField
replaceItemAt **See** FComponent.replaceItemAt
replaceSel **See** TextField.replaceSel
restrict **See** TextField.restrict
reverse **See** Array.reverse
RIGHT **See** Key.RIGHT
rightMargin **See** TextFormat.rightMargin
_rotation **See** Button._rotation, MovieClip._rotation, TextField._rotation
round **See** Math.round

S

scaleMode **See** Stage.scaleMode
screenColor **See** System.capabilities.screenColor
screenDPI **See** System.capabilities.screenDPI

setState **See** FComponent.setState
setStyleProperty **See** FComponent.setStyleProperty
setTextFormat **See** TextField.setTextFormat
setTransform **See** Color.setTransform
setTransform **See** Sound.setTransform
setUTCDate **See** Date.setUTCDate
setUTCFullYear **See** Date.setUTCFullYear
setUTCHours **See** Date.setUTCHours
setUTCMilliseconds **See** Date.setUTCMilliseconds
setUTCMinutes **See** Date.UTCMinutes
setUTCMonth **See** Date.setUTCMonth
setUTCSeconds **See** Date.setUTCSeconds
setValue **See** FComponent.setValue
setVolume **See** Sound.setVolume
setVScroll **See** FComponent.setVScroll
setWidth **See** FComponent.setWidth
setYear **See** Date.setYear
shadow **See** FStyleFormat.shadow
shift **See** Array.shift
SHIFT **See** Key.SHIFT
show **See** Mouse.show
showMenu **See** Stage.showMenu
showsettings **See** System
sin **See** Math.sin
size **See** TextFormat.size
slice **See** Array.slice
slice **See** String.slice
sort **See** Array.sort
_soundbuftime **See** Button._soundbuftime, MovieClip._soundbuftime, TextField._soundbuftime
SPACE **See** Key.SPACE
splice **See** Array.splice
split **See** String.split
sqrt **See** Math.sqrt
SQRT1_2 **See** Math.SQRT1_2
SQRT2 **See** Math.SQRT2
start **See** Sound.start
startDrag **See** MovieClip.startDrag
status **See** XML.status
stop **See** MovieClip.stop, Sound.stop
stopDrag **See** MovieClip.stopDrag
strict inequality operator **See** Symbols section
style formats **See** FStyleFormat
substr **See** String.substr
substring **See** String.substring
subtraction operator **See** - operator

swapDepths **See** MovieClip.swapDepths

T

U

V

valueOf **See** Boolean.valueOf, Number.valueOf, Object.valueOf
variable **See** TextField.variable
version **See** System
_visible **See** Button._visible, MovieClip._visible, TextField._visible

W

watch **See** Object.watch
_width **See** Button._width, MovieClip._width, TextField._width
width **See** Stage.width
wordWrap **See** TextField.wordWrap

X

_x **See** Button._x, MovieClip_x, TextField._x
xmlDecl **See** XML.xmlDecl
_xmouse **See** Button._xmouse, MovieClip._xmouse, TextField._xmouse
_xscale **See** MovieClip._xscale, TextField._xscale

Y

_y **See** MovieClip._y, TextField._y
_ymouse **See** MovieClip._ymouse, TextField._ymouse
_yscale **See** MovieClip._yscale, TextField._yscale

DEPRECATED ENTRIES

chr **See also** String.fromCharCode
eq **See also** ==equality operator
ge **See also** gt and >=operator
gt **See also** > operator
mbchr **See also** byString.fromCharCode
ne **See also** !=inequality operator
not **See also** ! operator
or **See also** || operator
ord **See also** String.charCodeAt
random **See also** Math.random
targetPath **See also** this operator
tellTarget **See also** with action